Praise for *Head First Des*

"I received the book yesterday and started
gym and I expect people saw me smiling
fun but they cover a lot of ground and tl

— **Erich Gamma, IBM Distinguished Engineer,**
and co-author of Design Patterns

"'Head First Design Patterns' manages to mix fun, b
advice in one entertaining and thought provoking r
been using them for years, you are sure to get some

— **Richard Helm, coauthor of "De**
Gang of Four - Erich Gamma, I

"I feel like a thousand pounds of books have just be

— **Ward Cunningham, inventor of**
and founder of the Hillside Gro

"This book is close to perfect, because of the way it
authority and it reads beautifully. It's one of the ve
indispensable. (I'd put maybe 10 books in this categ

— **David Gelernter, Professor of C**
Yale University and author of "

"A Nose Dive into the realm of patterns, a land whe
things can also become complex. I can think of no

— **Miko Matsumura, Industry Ana**
Former Chief Java Evangelist, S

"I laughed, I cried, it moved me."

— **Daniel Steinberg, Editor-in-Chief, java.net**

"My first reaction was to roll on the floor laughing. After I picked myself up, I realized that not only is the
book technically accurate, it is the easiest to understand introduction to design patterns that I have seen.

— **Dr. Timothy A. Budd, Associate Professor of Computer Science at**
Oregon State University and author of more than a dozen books,
including "C++ for Java Programmers"

"Jerry Rice runs patterns better than any receiver in the NFL, but the Freemans have out run him.
Seriously...this is one of the funniest and smartest books on software design I've ever read."

— **Aaron LaBerge, VP Technology, ESPN.com**

More Praise for *Head First Design Patterns*

"Great code design is, first and foremost, great information design. A code designer is teaching a computer how to do something, and it is no surprise that a great teacher of computers should turn out to be a great teacher of programmers. This book's admirable clarity, humor and substantial doses of clever make it the sort of book that helps even non-programmers think well about problem-solving."

> — **Cory Doctorow, co-editor of Boing Boing**
> **and author of "Down and Out in the Magic Kingdom"**
> **and "Someone Comes to Town, Someone Leaves Town"**

"There's an old saying in the computer and videogame business – well, it can't be that old because the discipline is not all that old – and it goes something like this: Design is Life. What's particularly curious about this phrase is that even today almost no one who works at the craft of creating electronic games can agree on what it means to "design" a game. Is the designer a software engineer? An art director? A storyteller? An architect or a builder? A pitch person or a visionary? Can an individual indeed be in part all of these? And most importantly, who the %$!#&* cares?

It has been said that the "designed by" credit in interactive entertainment is akin to the "directed by" credit in filmmaking, which in fact allows it to share DNA with perhaps the single most controversial, overstated, and too often entirely lacking in humility credit grab ever propagated on commercial art. Good company, eh? Yet if Design is Life, then perhaps it is time we spent some quality cycles thinking about what it is.

Eric and Elisabeth Freeman have intrepidly volunteered to look behind the code curtain for us in "Head First Design Patterns." I'm not sure either of them cares all that much about the PlayStation or X-Box, nor should they. Yet they do address the notion of design at a significantly honest level such that anyone looking for ego reinforcement of his or her own brilliant auteurship is best advised not to go digging here where truth is stunningly revealed. Sophists and circus barkers need not apply. Next generation literati please come equipped with a pencil."

> — **Ken Goldstein, Executive Vice President & Managing Director,**
> **Disney Online**

"Just the right tone for the geeked-out, casual-cool guru coder in all of us. The right reference for practical development strategies—gets my brain going without having to slog through a bunch of tired, stale professor-speak."

> — **Travis Kalanick, Founder of Scour and Red Swoosh**
> **Member of the MIT TR100**

"This book combines good humors, great examples, and in-depth knowledge of Design Patterns in such a way that makes learning fun. Being in the entertainment technology industry, I am intrigued by the Hollywood Principle and the home theater Facade Pattern, to name a few. The understanding of Design Patterns not only helps us create reusable and maintainable quality software, but also helps sharpen our problem-solving skills across all problem domains. This book is a must read for all computer professionals and students."

> — **Newton Lee, Founder and Editor-in-Chief, Association for Computing**
> **Machinery's (ACM) Computers in Entertainment (acmcie.org)**

More Praise for *Head First Design Patterns*

"If there's one subject that needs to be taught better, needs to be more fun to learn, it's design patterns. Thank goodness for Head First Design Patterns.

From the awesome Head First Java folks, this book uses every conceivable trick to help you understand and remember. Not just loads of pictures: pictures of humans, which tend to interest other humans. Surprises everywhere. Stories, because humans love narrative. (Stories about things like pizza and chocolate. Need we say more?) Plus, it's darned funny.

It also covers an enormous swath of concepts and techniques, including nearly all the patterns you'll use most (observer, decorator, factory, singleton, command, adapter, façade, template method, iterator, composite, state, proxy). Read it, and those won't be 'just words': they'll be memories that tickle you, and tools you own."

> — **Bill Camarda, READ ONLY**

"After using Head First Java to teach our freshman how to start programming, I was eagerly waiting to see the next book in the series. Head First Design Patterns is that book and I am delighted. I am sure it will quickly become the standard first design patterns book to read, and is already the book I am recommending to students."

> — **Ben Bederson, Associate Professor of Computer Science & Director of the Human-Computer Interaction Lab, University of Maryland**

"Usually when reading through a book or article on design patterns I'd have to occasionally stick myself in the eye with something just to make sure I was paying attention. Not with this book. Odd as it may sound, this book makes learning about design patterns fun.

While other books on design patterns are saying, 'Buehler... Buehler... Buehler...' this book is on the float belting out 'Shake it up, baby!'"

> — **Eric Wuehler**

"I literally love this book. In fact, I kissed this book in front of my wife."

> — **Satish Kumar**

Praise for the *Head First* approach

"Java technology is everywhere—in mobile phones, cars, cameras, printers, games, PDAs, ATMs, smart cards, gas pumps, sports stadiums, medical devices, Web cams, servers, you name it. If you develop software and haven't learned Java, it's definitely time to dive in—Head First."

> — **Scott McNealy, Sun Microsystems Chairman, President and CEO**

"It's fast, irreverent, fun, and engaging. Be careful—you might actually learn something!"

> — **Ken Arnold, former Senior Engineer at Sun Microsystems Co-author (with James Gosling, creator of Java), "The Java Programming Language"**

Other related books from O'Reilly

Head First Java

Head First EJB

Head First Servlets & JSP

Learning Java

Java in a Nutshell

Java Enterprise in a Nutshell

Java Examples in a Nutshell

Java Cookbook

J2EE Design Patterns

Be watching for more books in the Head First series!

Head First Design Patterns

Wouldn't it be dreamy if there was a Design Patterns book that was more fun than going to the dentist, and more revealing than an IRS form? It's probably just a fantasy...

Eric Freeman
Elisabeth Freeman

with
Kathy Sierra
Bert Bates

O'REILLY®

Beijing · Cambridge · Köln · Paris · Sebastopol · Taipei · Tokyo

Head First Design Patterns

by Eric Freeman, Elisabeth Freeman, Kathy Sierra, and Bert Bates

Published by O'Reilly Media, Inc., 1005 Gravenstein Highway North, Sebastopol, CA 95472.

O'Reilly Media books may be purchased for educational, business, or sales promotional use. Online editions are also available for most titles (safari.oreilly.com). For more information, contact our corporate/institutional sales department: (800) 998-9938 or corporate@oreilly.com.

Editor:	Mike Loukides
Cover Designer:	Ellie Volckhausen
Pattern Wranglers:	Eric Freeman, Elisabeth Freeman
Facade Decoration:	Elisabeth Freeman
Strategy:	Kathy Sierra and Bert Bates
Observer:	Oliver 

Printing History:

October 2004: First Edition.

In other words, if you use anything in *Head First Design Patterns* to, say, run a nuclear power plant, you're on your own. We do, however, encourage you to use the DJ View app.

No ducks were harmed in the making of this book.

The original GoF agreed to have their photos in this book. Yes, they really *are* that good-looking.

ISBN: 0-596-00712-4

[M]   [3/06]

To the Gang of Four, whose insight and expertise in capturing and communicating Design Patterns has changed the face of software design forever, and bettered the lives of developers throughout the world.

But seriously, *when* are we going to see a second edition? After all, it's been only *ten years*!

Authors/Developers of Head First Design Patterns

Elisabeth Freeman

Eric Freeman

Elisabeth is an author, software developer and digital artist. She's been involved with the Internet since the early days, having co-founded The Ada Project (TAP), an award winning web site for women in computing now adopted by the ACM. More recently Elisabeth lead research and development efforts in digital media at the Walt Disney Company where she co-invented Motion, a content system that delivers terabytes of video every day to Disney, ESPN and Movies.com users.

Elisabeth is a computer scientist at heart and holds graduate degrees in Computer Science from Yale University and Indiana University. She's worked in a variety of areas including visual languages, RSS syndication and Internet systems. She's also been an active advocate for women in computing, developing programs that encourage woman to enter the field. These days you'll find her sipping some Java or Cocoa on her Mac, although she dreams of a day when the whole world is using Scheme.

Elisabeth has loved hiking and the outdoors since her days growing up in Scotland. When she's outdoors her camera is never far. She's also an avid cyclist, vegetarian and animal lover.

You can send her email at beth@wickedlysmart.com

Eric is a computer scientist with a passion for media and software architectures. He just wrapped up four years at a dream job – directing Internet broadband and wireless efforts at Disney – and is now back to writing, creating cool software and hacking Java and Macs.

Eric spent a lot of the '90s working on alternatives to the desktop metaphor with David Gelernter (and they're both *still* asking the question "why do I have to give a file a name?"). Based on this work, Eric landed a Ph.D. at Yale University in '97. He also co-founded Mirror Worlds Technologies (now acquired) to create a commercial version of his thesis work, Lifestreams.

In a previous life, Eric built software for networks and supercomputers. You might know him from such books as *JavaSpaces Principles Patterns and Practice*. Eric has fond memories of implementing tuple-space systems on Thinking Machine CM-5s and creating some of the first Internet information systems for NASA in the late 80s.

Eric is currently living in the high desert near Santa Fe. When he's not writing text or code you'll find him spending more time tweaking than watching his home theater and trying to restoring a circa 1980s Dragon's Lair video game. He also wouldn't mind moonlighting as an electronica DJ.

Write to him at eric@wickedlysmart.com or visit his blog at http://www.ericfreeman.com

Creators of the Head First series
(and co-conspirators on this book)

Kathy Sierra

Bert Bates

Kathy has been interested in learning theory since her days as a game designer (she wrote games for Virgin, MGM, and Amblin'). She developed much of the Head First format while teaching New Media Authoring for UCLA Extension's Entertainment Studies program. More recently, she's been a master trainer for Sun Microsystems, teaching Sun's Java instructors how to teach the latest Java technologies, and developing several of Sun's certification exams. Together with Bert Bates, she has been actively using the Head First concepts to teach throusands of developers. Kathy is the founder of javaranch.com, which won a 2003 and 2004 Software Development magazine Jolt Cola Productivity Award. You might catch her teaching Java on the Java Jam Geek Cruise (geekcruises.com).

She recently moved from California to Colorado, where she's had to learn new words like, "ice scraper" and "fleece", but the lightning there is fantastic.

Likes: runing, skiing, skateboarding, playing with her Icelandic horse, and weird science. Dislikes: entropy.

You can find her on javaranch, or occasionally blogging on java.net. Write to her at kathy@wickedlysmart.com.

Bert is a long-time software developer and architect, but a decade-long stint in artificial intelligence drove his interest in learning theory and technology-based training. He's been helping clients becoming better programmers ever since. Recently, he's been heading up the development team for several of Sun's Java Certification exams.

He spent the first decade of his software career travelling the world to help broadcast clients like Radio New Zealand, the Weather Channel, and the Arts & Entertainment Network (A & E). One of his all-time favorite projects was building a full rail system simulation for Union Pacific Railroad.

Bert is a long-time, hopelessly addicted *go* player, and has been working on a *go* program for way too long. He's a fair guitar player and is now trying his hand at banjo.

Look for him on javaranch, on the IGS go server, or you can write to him at terrapin@wickedlysmart.com.

Table of Contents (summary)

Table of Contents (the real thing)

Intro

Your brain on Design Patterns. Here *you* are trying to *learn* something, while here your *brain* is doing you a favor by making sure the learning doesn't *stick*. Your brain's thinking, "Better leave room for more important things, like which wild animals to avoid and whether naked snowboarding is a bad idea." So how *do* you trick your brain into thinking that your life depends on knowing Design Patterns?

1 Welcome to Design Patterns

Someone has already solved your problems. In this chapter, you'll learn why (and how) you can exploit the wisdom and lessons learned by other developers who've been down the same design problem road and survived the trip. Before we're done, we'll look at the use and benefits of design patterns, look at some key OO design principles, and walk through an example of how one pattern works. The best way to use patterns is to *load your brain* with them and then *recognize places* in your designs and existing applications where you can *apply them*. Instead of *code* reuse, with patterns you get *experience* reuse.

Remember, knowing concepts like abstraction, inheritance, and polymorphism do not make you a good object oriented designer. A design guru thinks about how to create flexible designs that are maintainable and that can cope with change.

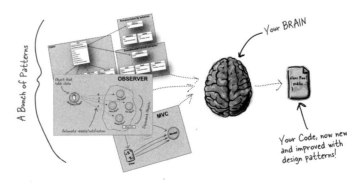

A Bunch of Patterns

OBSERVER

MVC

Your BRAIN

Your Code, now new and improved with design patterns!

the Observer Pattern

2 Keeping your Objects in the Know

Don't miss out when something interesting happens!

We've got a pattern that keeps your objects in the know when something they might care about happens. Objects can even decide at runtime whether they want to be kept informed. The Observer Pattern is one of the most heavily used patterns in the JDK, and it's incredibly useful. Before we're done, we'll also look at one to many relationships and loose coupling (yeah, that's right, we said coupling). With Observer, you'll be the life of the Patterns Party.

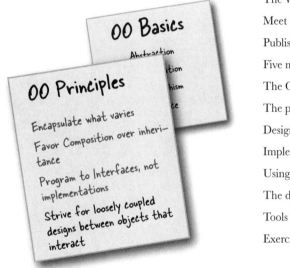

OO Basics

Abstraction
...tion
...hism
...e

OO Principles

Encapsulate what varies
Favor Composition over inheri-tance
Program to Interfaces, not implementations
Strive for loosely coupled designs between objects that interact

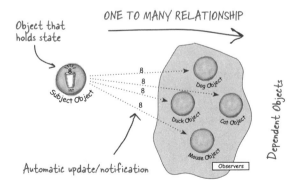

ONE TO MANY RELATIONSHIP

Object that holds state

Subject Object

Dog Object
Duck Object
Cat Object
Mouse Object

Observers

Dependent Objects

Automatic update/notification

3

Decorating Objects

Just call this chapter "Design Eye for the Inheritance Guy." We'll re-examine the typical overuse of inheritance and you'll learn how to decorate your classes at runtime using a form of object composition. Why? Once you know the techniques of decorating, you'll be able to give your (or someone else's) objects new responsibilities *without making any code changes to the underlying classes.*

I used to think real men subclassed everything. That was until I learned the power of extension at runtime, rather than at compile time. Now look at me!

the Factory Pattern

Baking with OO Goodness

Get ready to cook some loosely coupled OO designs.

There is more to making objects than just using the **new** operator. You'll learn that instantiation is an activity that shouldn't always be done in public and can often lead to *coupling problems*. And you don't want *that*, do you? Find out how Factory Patterns can help save you from embarrasing dependencies.

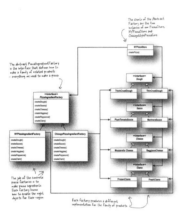

5 One of a Kind Objects

The Singleton Pattern: your ticket to creating one-of-a-kind objects, for which there is only one instance. You might be happy to know that of all patterns, the Singleton is the simplest in terms of its class diagram; in fact the diagram holds just a single class! But don't get too comfortable; despite its simplicity from a class design perspective, we'll encounter quite a few bumps and potholes in its implementation. So buckle up—this one's not as simple as it seems...

Hershey, PA

OO Patterns

Singleton - Ensure a class only has one instance and provide a global point of access to it.

the Command Pattern

6

Encapsulating Invocation

In this chapter we take encapsulation to a whole new level: we're going to encapsulate *method invocation*.

That's right, by encapsulating invocation we can crystallize pieces of computation so that the object invoking the computation doesn't need to worry about how to do things; it just uses our crystallized method to get it done. We can also do some wickedly smart things with these encapsulated method invocations, like save them away for logging or reuse them to implement undo in our code.

7 Being Adaptive

In this chapter we're going to attempt such impossible feats as putting a square peg in a round hole. Sound impossible? Not when we have Design Patterns. Remember the Decorator Pattern? We **wrapped objects** to give them new responsibilities. Now we're going to wrap some objects with a different purpose: to make their interfaces look like something they're not. Why would we do that? So we can adapt a design expecting one interface to a class that implements a different interface. That's not all, while we're at it we're going to look at another pattern that wraps objects to simplify their interface.

European Wall Outlet

AC Power Adapter

Standard AC Plug

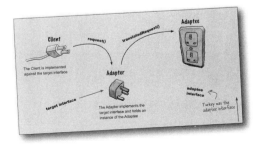

the Template Method Pattern

8

Encapsulating Algorithms

We've encapsulated object creation, method invocation, complex interfaces, ducks, pizzas... what could be next?

We're going to get down to encapsulating *pieces of algorithms* so that subclasses can hook themselves right into a computation anytime they want. We're even going to learn about a design principle inspired by Hollywood.

Tea
1. Boil some water
2. Steep the teabag in the water
3. Pour tea in a cup
4. Add lemon

Coffee
1. Boil some water
2. Brew the coffee grinds
3. Pour coffee in a cup
4. Add sugar and milk

We've recognized that the two recipes are essentially the same, although some of the steps require different implementations. So we've generalized the recipe and placed it in the base class.

generalize

Caffeine Beverage
1. Boil some water
2. Brew
3. Pour beverage in a cup
4. Add condiments

generalize

relies on subclass for some steps

relies on subclass for some steps

Tea subclass

Coffee subclass

2. Steep the teabag in the water
4. Add lemon

2. Brew the coffee grinds
4. Add sugar and milk

Caffeine Beverage knows, and controls the steps of the recipe, and performs steps 1 and 3 itself, but relies on Tea or Coffee to do steps 2 and 4.

9

Well-Managed Collections

There are lots of ways to stuff objects into a collection.

Put them in an Array, a Stack, a List, a Map, take your pick. Each has its own advantages and tradeoffs. But when your client wants to iterate over your objects, are you going to show him your implementation? We certainly hope not! That just *wouldn't* be professional. Don't worry—in this chapter you'll see how you can let your clients *iterate* through your objects without ever seeing how you *store* your objects. You're also going to learn how to create some *super collections* of objects that can leap over some impressive data structures in a single bound. You're also going to learn a thing or two about object responsibility.

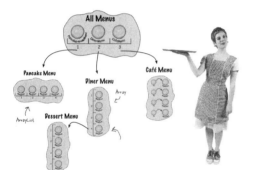

the State Pattern

10 The State of Things

A little known fact: the Strategy and State Patterns were twins separated at birth. As you know, the Strategy Pattern went on to create a wildly successful business around interchangeable algorithms. State, however, took the perhaps more noble path of helping objects learn to control their behavior by changing their internal state. He's often overheard telling his object clients, "just repeat after me, I'm good enough, I'm smart enough, and doggonit..."

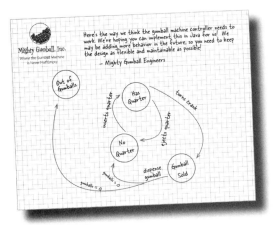

the Proxy Pattern

11 Controlling Object Access

Ever play good cop, bad cop? You're the good cop and you provide all your services in a nice and friendly manner, but you don't want *everyone* asking you for services, so you have the bad cop *control access* to you. That's what proxies do: control and manage access. As you're going to see there are *lots* of ways in which proxies stand in for the objects they proxy. Proxies have been known to haul entire method calls over the Internet for their proxied objects; they've also been known to patiently stand in the place for some pretty lazy objects.

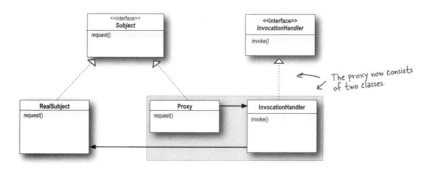

The proxy now consists of two classes.

Compound Patterns

12

Patterns of Patterns

Who would have ever guessed that Patterns could work together?
You've already witnessed the acrimonious Fireside Chats (and be thankful you didn't have to see the Pattern Death Match pages that the publisher forced us to remove from the book so we could avoid having to use a Parent's Advisory warning label), so who would have thought patterns can actually get along well together? Believe it or not, some of the most powerful OO designs use several patterns together. Get ready to take your pattern skills to the next level; it's time for Compound Patterns. Just be careful—your co-workers might kill you if you're struck with Pattern Fever.

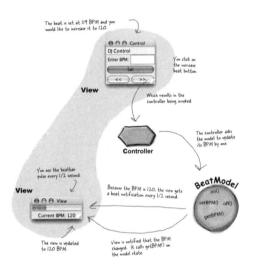

The beat is set at 119 BPM and you would like to increase it to 120

You click on the increase beat button.

View

Which results in the controller being invoked.

Controller

The controller asks the model to update its BPM by one.

You see the beatbar pulse every 1/2 second.

View

Because the BPM is 120, the view gets a beat notification every 1/2 second.

BeatModel
on()
setBPM() off()
getBPM()

View is notified that the BPM changed. It calls getBPM() on the model state.

The view is updated to 120 BPM.

Better Living with Patterns

13 Patterns in the Real World

Ahhhh, now you're ready for a bright new world filled with Design Patterns. But, before you go opening all those new doors of opportunity we need to cover a few details that you'll encounter out in the real world—things get a little more complex *out there* than they are here in Objectville. Come along, we've got a nice guide to help you through the transition...

Richard Helm

Ralph Johnson

Gang of Four

John Vlissides

Erich Gamma

14 Appendix: Leftover Patterns

Not everyone can be the most popular. A lot has changed in
the last 10 years. Since *Design Patterns: Elements of Reusable Object-Oriented
Software* first came out, developers have applied these patterns thousands of times.
The patterns we summarize in this appendix are full-fledged, card-carrying, official
GoF patterns, but aren't always used as often as the patterns we've explored so
far. But these patterns are awesome in their own right, and if your situation calls for
them, you should apply them with your head held high. Our goal in this appendix is
to give you a high level idea of what these patterns are all about.

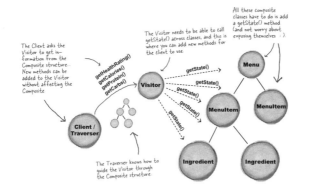

 **Index**

Intro

In this section, we answer the burning question: "So, why DID they put that in a design patterns book?"

Who is this book for?

If you can answer "yes" to all of these:

 Do you know Java? (You don't need to be a guru.)

You'll probably be okay if you know C# instead.

 Do you want to **learn, understand, remember, and apply** design patterns, including the OO design principles upon which design patterns are based?

 Do you prefer stimulating dinner party conversation to dry, dull, academic lectures?

this book is for you.

Who should probably back away from this book?

If you can answer "yes" to any one of these:

 Are you completely new to Java?

(You don't need to be advanced, and even if you *don't* know Java, but you know C#, you'll probably understand at least 80% of the code examples. You also *might* be okay with just a C++ background.)

 Are you a kick-butt OO designer/developer looking for **a *reference* book?**

 Are you an architect looking for ***enterprise*** design patterns?

 Are you **afraid to try something different**? Would you rather have a root canal than mix stripes with plaid? Do you believe that a technical book can't be serious if Java components are anthropomorphized?

this book is not for you.

[note from marketing: this book is for anyone with a credit card.]

We know what you're thinking.

"How can this be a serious programming book?"

"What's with all the graphics?"

"Can I actually learn it this way?"

your brain thinks THIS is important.

And we know what your *brain* is thinking.

Your brain craves novelty. It's always searching, scanning, *waiting* for something unusual. It was built that way, and it helps you stay alive.

Today, you're less likely to be a tiger snack. But your brain's still looking. You just never know.

So what does your brain do with all the routine, ordinary, normal things you encounter? Everything it *can* to stop them from interfering with the brain's *real* job—recording things that *matter*. It doesn't bother saving the boring things; they never make it past the "this is obviously not important" filter.

How does your brain *know* what's important? Suppose you're out for a day hike and a tiger jumps in front of you, what happens inside your head and body?

Neurons fire. Emotions crank up. *Chemicals surge.*

And that's how your brain knows...

This must be important! Don't forget it!

But imagine you're at home, or in a library. It's a safe, warm, tiger-free zone. You're studying. Getting ready for an exam. Or trying to learn some tough technical topic your boss thinks will take a week, ten days at the most.

Just one problem. Your brain's trying to do you a big favor. It's trying to make sure that this *obviously* non-important content doesn't clutter up scarce resources. Resources that are better spent storing the really *big* things. Like tigers. Like the danger of fire. Like how you should never again snowboard in shorts.

And there's no simple way to tell your brain, "Hey brain, thank you very much, but no matter how dull this book is, and how little I'm registering on the emotional Richter scale right now, I really *do* want you to keep this stuff around."

Great. Only 637 more dull, dry, boring pages.

your brain thinks THIS isn't worth saving.

We think of a "Head First" reader as a <u>learner</u>.

So what does it take to *learn* something? First, you have to *get* it, then make sure you don't *forget* it. It's not about pushing facts into your head. Based on the latest research in cognitive science, neurobiology, and educational psychology, *learning* takes a lot more than text on a page. We know what turns your brain on.

Some of the Head First learning principles:

Make it visual. Images are far more memorable than words alone, and make learning much more effective (up to 89% improvement in recall and transfer studies). It also makes things more understandable. **Put the words within or near the graphics** they relate to, rather than on the bottom or on another page, and learners will be up to *twice* as likely to solve problems related to the content.

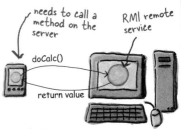

needs to call a method on the server

RMI remote service

doCalc()

return value

Use a conversational and personalized style. In recent studies, students performed up to 40% better on post-learning tests if the content spoke directly to the reader, using a first-person, conversational style rather than taking a formal tone. Tell stories instead of lecturing. Use casual language. Don't take yourself too seriously. Which would *you* pay more attention to: a stimulating dinner party companion, or a lecture?

It really sucks to be an abstract method. You don't have a body.

Get the learner to think more deeply. In other words, unless you actively flex your neurons, nothing much happens in your head. A reader has to be motivated, engaged, curious, and inspired to solve problems, draw conclusions, and generate new knowledge. And for that, you need challenges, exercises, and thought-provoking questions, and activities that involve both sides of the brain, and multiple senses.

Does it make sense to say Tub IS-A Bathroom? Bathroom IS-A Tub? Or is it a HAS-A relationship?

`abstract void roam();`

No method body! End it with a semicolon.

Get—and keep—the reader's attention. We've all had the "I really want to learn this but I can't stay awake past page one" experience. Your brain pays attention to things that are out of the ordinary, interesting, strange, eye-catching, unexpected. Learning a new, tough, technical topic doesn't have to be boring. Your brain will learn much more quickly if it's not.

Touch their emotions. We now know that your ability to remember something is largely dependent on its emotional content. You remember what you *care* about. You remember when you *feel* something. No, we're not talking heart-wrenching stories about a boy and his dog. We're talking emotions like surprise, curiosity, fun, "what the...?", and the feeling of "I Rule!" that comes when you solve a puzzle, learn something everybody else thinks is hard, or realize you know something that "I'm more technical than thou" Bob from engineering *doesn't*.

Metacognition: thinking about thinking

If you really want to learn, and you want to learn more quickly and more deeply, pay attention to how you pay attention. Think about how you think. Learn how you learn.

Most of us did not take courses on metacognition or learning theory when we were growing up. We were *expected* to learn, but rarely *taught* to learn.

But we assume that if you're holding this book, you really want to learn design patterns. And you probably don't want to spend a lot of time. And you want to *remember* what you read, and be able to apply it. And for that, you've got to *understand* it. To get the most from this book, or *any* book or learning experience, take responsibility for your brain. Your brain on *this* content.

The trick is to get your brain to see the new material you're learning as Really Important. Crucial to your well-being. As important as a tiger. Otherwise, you're in for a constant battle, with your brain doing its best to keep the new content from sticking.

> I wonder how I can trick my brain into remembering this stuff...

So how *DO* you get your brain to think Design Patterns are as important as a tiger?

There's the slow, tedious way, or the faster, more effective way. The slow way is about sheer repetition. You obviously know that you *are* able to learn and remember even the dullest of topics, if you keep pounding on the same thing. With enough repetition, your brain says, "This doesn't *feel* important to him, but he keeps looking at the same thing *over* and *over* and *over*, so I suppose it must be."

The faster way is to do ***anything that increases brain activity,*** especially different *types* of brain activity. The things on the previous page are a big part of the solution, and they're all things that have been proven to help your brain work in your favor. For example, studies show that putting words *within* the pictures they describe (as opposed to somewhere else in the page, like a caption or in the body text) causes your brain to try to makes sense of how the words and picture relate, and this causes more neurons to fire. More neurons firing = more chances for your brain to *get* that this is something worth paying attention to, and possibly recording.

A conversational style helps because people tend to pay more attention when they perceive that they're in a conversation, since they're expected to follow along and hold up their end. The amazing thing is, your brain doesn't necessarily *care* that the "conversation" is between you and a book! On the other hand, if the writing style is formal and dry, your brain perceives it the same way you experience being lectured to while sitting in a roomful of passive attendees. No need to stay awake.

But pictures and conversational style are just the beginning.

Here's what WE did:

We used **pictures**, because your brain is tuned for visuals, not text. As far as your brain's concerned, a picture really *is* worth 1024 words. And when text and pictures work together, we embedded the text *in* the pictures because your brain works more effectively when the text is *within* the thing the text refers to, as opposed to in a caption or buried in the text somewhere.

We used **redundancy**, saying the same thing in *different* ways and with different media types, and *multiple senses*, to increase the chance that the content gets coded into more than one area of your brain.

We used concepts and pictures in **unexpected** ways because your brain is tuned for novelty, and we used pictures and ideas with at least *some* **emotional** *content*, because your brain is tuned to pay attention to the biochemistry of emotions. That which causes you to *feel* something is more likely to be remembered, even if that feeling is nothing more than a little **humor**, **surprise**, or **interest.**

We used a personalized, **conversational style**, because your brain is tuned to pay more attention when it believes you're in a conversation than if it thinks you're passively listening to a presentation. Your brain does this even when you're *reading*.

The Patterns Guru

We included more than 40 **activities**, because your brain is tuned to learn and remember more when you **do** things than when you *read* about things. And we made the exercises challenging-yet-do-able, because that's what most *people* prefer.

We used **multiple learning styles**, because *you* might prefer step-by-step procedures, while someone else wants to understand the big picture first, while someone else just wants to see a code example. But regardless of your own learning preference, *everyone* benefits from seeing the same content represented in multiple ways.

BULLET POINTS

We include content for **both sides of your brain**, because the more of your brain you engage, the more likely you are to learn and remember, and the longer you can stay focused. Since working one side of the brain often means giving the other side a chance to rest, you can be more productive at learning for a longer period of time.

Puzzles

And we included **stories** and exercises that present **more than one point of view,** because your brain is tuned to learn more deeply when it's forced to make evaluations and judgements.

We included **challenges**, with exercises, and by asking **questions** that don't always have a straight answer, because your brain is tuned to learn and remember when it has to *work* at something. Think about it—you can't get your *body* in shape just by *watching* people at the gym. But we did our best to make sure that when you're working hard, it's on the *right* things. That **you're not spending one extra dendrite** processing a hard-to-understand example, or parsing difficult, jargon-laden, or overly terse text.

We used **people**. In stories, examples, pictures, etc., because, well, because *you're* a person. And your brain pays more attention to *people* than it does to *things*.

We used an **80/20** approach. We assume that if you're going for a PhD in software design, this won't be your only book. So we don't talk about *everything*. Just the stuff you'll actually *need*.

Here's what YOU can do to bend your brain into submission

So, we did our part. The rest is up to you. These tips are a starting point; listen to your brain and figure out what works for you and what doesn't.   Try new things.

cut this out and stick it on your refrigerator.

- -

(1) Slow down. The more you understand, the less you have to memorize.

Don't just *read*. Stop and think. When the book asks you a question, don't just skip to the answer. Imagine that someone really *is* asking the question. The more deeply you force your brain to think, the better chance you have of learning and remembering.

(2) Do the exercises. Write your own notes.

We put them in, but if we did them for you, that would be like having someone else do your workouts for you. And don't just *look* at the exercises. **Use a pencil.** There's plenty of evidence that physical activity *while* learning can increase the learning.

(3) Read the "There are No Dumb Questions"

That means all of them. They're not optional side-bars—*they're part of the core content!* Don't skip them.

(5) Make this the last thing you read before bed. Or at least the last *challenging* thing.

Part of the learning (especially the transfer to long-term memory) happens *after* you put the book down. Your brain needs time on its own, to do more processing. If you put in something new during that processing-time, some of what you just learned will be lost.

(6) Drink water. Lots of it.

Your brain works best in a nice bath of fluid. De-hydration (which can happen before you ever feel thirsty) decreases cognitive function.

(7) Talk about it. Out loud.

Speaking activates a different part of the brain. If you're trying to understand something, or increase your chance of remembering it later, say it out loud. Better still, try to explain it out loud to someone else. You'll learn more quickly, and you might uncover ideas you hadn't known were there when you were reading about it.

(8) Listen to your brain.

Pay attention to whether your brain is getting overloaded. If you find yourself starting to skim the surface or forget what you just read, it's time for a break. Once you go past a certain point, you won't learn faster by trying to shove more in, and you might even hurt the process.

(9) *Feel* something!

Your brain needs to know that this *matters*. Get involved with the stories. Make up your own captions for the photos. Groaning over a bad joke is *still* better than feeling nothing at all.

(10) *Design* something!

Apply this to something new you're designing, or refactor an older project. Just do *something* to get some experience beyond the exercises and activities in this book. All you need is a pencil and a problem to solve... a problem that might benefit from one or more design patterns.

Read Me

This is a learning experience, not a reference book. We deliberately stripped out everything that might get in the way of learning whatever it is we're working on at that point in the book. And the first time through, you need to begin at the beginning, because the book makes assumptions about what you've already seen and learned.

We use a simpler, modified faux-UML

Director
getMovies
getOscars()
getKevinBaconDegrees()

We use simple UML-like diagrams.

Although there's a good chance you've run across UML, it's not covered in the book, and it's not a prerequisite for the book. If you've never seen UML before, don't worry, we'll give you a few pointers along the way. So in other words, you won't have to worry about Design Patterns and UML at the same time. Our diagrams are "UML-*like*" -- while we try to be true to UML there are times we bend the rules a bit, usually for our own selfish artistic reasons.

We don't cover every single Design Pattern ever created.

There are a *lot* of Design Patterns: The original foundational patterns (known as the GoF patterns), Sun's J2EE patterns, JSP patterns, architectural patterns, game design patterns and a *lot* more. But our goal was to make sure the book weighed less than the person reading it, so we don't cover them all here. Our focus is on the core patterns that *matter* from the original GoF patterns, and making sure that you really, truly, deeply understand how and when to use them. You will find a brief look at some of the other patterns (the ones you're far less likely to use) in the appendix. In any case, once you're done with Head First Design Patterns, you'll be able to pick up any pattern catalog and get up to speed quickly.

The activities are NOT optional.

The exercises and activities are not add-ons; they're part of the core content of the book. Some of them are to help with memory, some for understanding, and some to help you apply what you've learned. ***Don't skip the exercises.*** The crossword puzzles are the only things you don't *have* to do, but they're good for giving your brain a chance to think about the words from a different context.

We use the word "composition" in the general OO sense, which is more flexible than the strict UML use of "composition".

When we say "one object is composed with another object" we mean that they are related by a HAS-A relationship. Our use reflects the traditional use of the term and is the one used in the GoF text (you'll learn what that is later). More recently, UML has refined this term into several types of composition. If you are an UML expert, you'll still be able to read the book and you should be able to easily map the use of composition to more refined terms as you read.

The redundancy is intentional and important.

One distinct difference in a Head First book is that we want you to *really* get it. And we want you to finish the book remembering what you've learned. Most reference books don't have retention and recall as a goal, but this book is about *learning*, so you'll see some of the same concepts come up more than once.

The code examples are as lean as possible.

Our readers tell us that it's frustrating to wade through 200 lines of code looking for the two lines they need to understand. Most examples in this book are shown within the smallest possible context, so that the part you're trying to learn is clear and simple. Don't expect all of the code to be robust, or even complete—the examples are written specifically for learning, and aren't always fully-functional.

In some cases, we haven't included all of the import statements needed, but we assume that if you're a Java programmer, you know that ArrayList is in java.util, for example. If the imports were not part of the normal core J2SE API, we mention it. We've also placed all the source code on the web so you can download it. You'll find it at
`http://www.headfirstlabs.com/books/hfdp/`

Also, for the sake of focusing on the learning side of the code, we did not put our classes into packages (in other words, they're all in the Java default package). We don't recommend this in the real world, and when you download the code examples from this book, you'll find that all classes *are* in packages.

The 'Brain Power' exercises don't have answers.

For some of them, there is no right answer, and for others, part of the learning experience of the Brain Power activities is for you to decide if and when your answers are right. In some of the Brain Power exercises you will find hints to point you in the right direction.

Tech Reviewers

Jef Cumps

Valentin Crettaz

Barney Marispini

Ike Van Atta ↘

Fearless leader of the HFDP Extreme Review Team.

Johannes deJong ↗

Jason Menard

Mark Spritzler →

Dirk Schreckmann

Philippe Maquet

In memory of Philippe Maquet

1960-2004

Your amazing technical expertise, relentless enthusiasm, and deep concern for the learner will inspire us always.

We will never forget you.

Acknowledgments

At O'Reilly:

Our biggest thanks to **Mike Loukides** at O'Reilly, for starting it all, and helping to shape the Head First concept into a series. And a big thanks to the driving force behind Head First, **Tim O'Reilly**. Thanks to the clever Head First "series mom" **Kyle Hart**, to rock and roll star **Ellie Volkhausen** for her inspired cover design and also to **Colleen Gorman** for her hardcore copyedit. Finally, thanks to **Mike Hendrickson** for championing this Design Patterns book, and building the team.

Our intrepid reviewers:

We are extremely grateful for our technical review director **Johannes deJong**. You are our hero, Johannes. And we deeply appreciate the contributions of the co-manager of the **Javaranch** review team, the late **Philippe Maquet**. You have single-handedly brightened the lives of thousands of developers, and the impact you've had on their (and our) lives is forever.
Jef Cumps is scarily good at finding problems in our draft chapters, and once again made a huge difference for the book. Thanks Jef! **Valentin Cretaz** (AOP guy), who has been with us from the very first Head First book, proved (as always) just how much we really need his technical expertise and insight. You rock Valentin (but lose the tie).

Two newcomers to the HF review team, Barney Marispini and Ike Van Atta did a kick butt job on the book—you guys gave us some *really* crucial feedback. Thanks for joining the team.

We also got some excellent technical help from Javaranch moderators/gurus **Mark Spritzler**, **Jason Menard**, **Dirk Schreckmann**, **Thomas Paul**, and **Margarita Isaeva**. And as always, thanks especially to the javaranch.com Trail Boss, **Paul Wheaton**.

Thanks to the finalists of the Javaranch "Pick the Head First Design Patterns Cover" contest. The winner, Si Brewster, submitted the winning essay that persuaded us to pick the woman you see on our cover. Other finalists include Andrew Esse, Gian Franco Casula, Helen Crosbie, Pho Tek, Helen Thomas, Sateesh Kommineni, and Jeff Fisher.

Even more people*

From Eric and Elisabeth

Writing a Head First book is a wild ride with two amazing tour guides: **Kathy Sierra** and **Bert Bates**. With Kathy and Bert you throw out all book writing convention and enter a world full of storytelling, learning theory, cognitive science, and pop culture, where the reader always rules. Thanks to both of you for letting us enter your amazing world; we hope we've done Head First justice. Seriously, this has been amazing. Thanks for all your careful guidance, for pushing us to go forward and most of all, for trusting us (with your baby). You're both certainly "wickedly smart" and you're also the hippest 29 year olds we know. So... what's next?

A big thank you to **Mike Loukides** and **Mike Hendrickson**. Mike L. was with us every step of the way. Mike, your insightful feedback helped shape the book and your encouragement kept us moving ahead. Mike H., thanks for your persistence over five years in trying to get us to write a patterns book; we finally did it and we're glad we waited for Head First.

A very special thanks to **Erich Gamma**, who went far beyond the call of duty in reviewing this book (he even took a draft with him on vacation). Erich, your interest in this book inspired us and your thorough technical review improved it immeasurably. Thanks as well to the entire **Gang of Four** for their support & interest, and for making a special appearance in Objectville. We are also indebted to **Ward Cunningham** and the patterns community who created the Portland Pattern Repository – an indespensible resource for us in writing this book.

It takes a village to write a technical book: **Bill Pugh** and **Ken Arnold** gave us expert advice on Singleton. **Joshua Marinacci** provided rockin' Swing tips and advice. **John Brewer's** "Why a Duck?" paper inspired SimUDuck (and we're glad he likes ducks too). **Dan Friedman** inspired the Little Singleton example. **Daniel Steinberg** acted as our "technical liason" and our emotional support network. And thanks to Apple's **James Dempsey** for allowing us to use his MVC song.

Last, a personal thank you to the **Javaranch review team** for their top-notch reviews and warm support. There's more of you in this book than you know.

From Kathy and Bert

We'd like to thank Mike Hendrickson for finding Eric and Elisabeth... but we can't. Because of these two, we discovered (to our horror) that we aren't the *only* ones who can do a Head First book. ;) However, if readers want to *believe* that it's really Kathy and Bert who did the cool things in the book, well, who are *we* to set them straight?

*The large number of acknowledgments is because we're testing the theory that everyone mentioned in a book acknowledgment will buy at least one copy, probably more, what with relatives and everything. If you'd like to be in the acknowledgment of our *next* book, and you have a large family, write to us.

1 Intro to Design Patterns

Welcome to
Design Patterns

> Now that we're living in Objectville, we've just got to get into Design Patterns... everyone is doing them. Soon we'll be the hit of Jim and Betty's Wednesday night patterns group!

Someone has already solved your problems. In this chapter, you'll learn why (and how) you can exploit the wisdom and lessons learned by other developers who've been down the same design problem road and survived the trip. Before we're done, we'll look at the use and benefits of design patterns, look at some key OO design principles, and walk through an example of how one pattern works. The best way to use patterns is to *load your brain* with them and then *recognize places* in your designs and existing applications where you can *apply them*. Instead of *code* reuse, with patterns you get *experience* reuse.

It started with a simple SimUDuck app

Joe works for a company that makes a highly successful duck pond simulation game, *SimUDuck*. The game can show a large variety of duck species swimming and making quacking sounds. The initial designers of the system used standard OO techniques and created one Duck superclass from which all other duck types inherit.

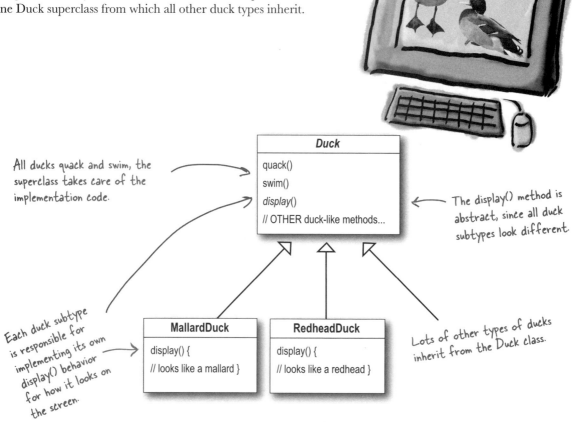

All ducks quack and swim, the superclass takes care of the implementation code.

Duck

quack()
swim()
display()
// OTHER duck-like methods...

The display() method is abstract, since all duck subtypes look different.

Each duck subtype is responsible for implementing its own display() behavior for how it looks on the screen.

MallardDuck

display() {
// looks like a mallard }

RedheadDuck

display() {
// looks like a redhead }

Lots of other types of ducks inherit from the Duck class.

In the last year, the company has been under increasing pressure from competitors. After a week long off-site brainstorming session over golf, the company executives think it's time for a big innovation. They need something *really* impressive to show at the upcoming shareholders meeting in Maui *next week*.

But now we need the ducks to FLY

The executives decided that flying ducks is just what the simulator needs to blow away the other duck sim competitors. And of course Joe's manager told them it'll be no problem for Joe to just whip something up in a week. "After all", said Joe's boss, "he's an OO programmer... *how hard can it be?*"

> I just need to add a fly() method in the Duck class and then all the ducks will inherit it. Now's my time to really show my true OO genius.

← Joe

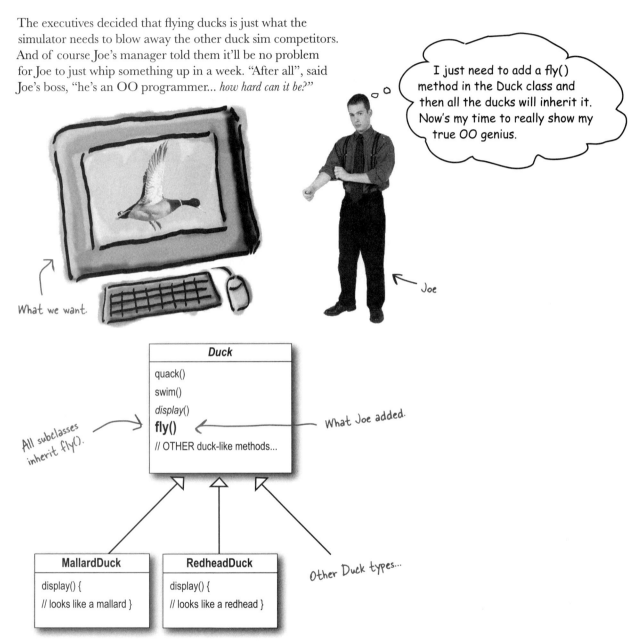

What we want.

Duck

quack()
swim()
display()
fly() ← What Joe added.
// OTHER duck-like methods...

All subclasses inherit fly().

MallardDuck

display() {
// looks like a mallard }

RedheadDuck

display() {
// looks like a redhead }

Other Duck types...

But something went horribly wrong...

*Joe, I'm at the shareholder's meeting. They just gave a demo and there were **rubber duckies** flying around the screen. Was this your idea of a joke? You might want to spend some time on Monster.com...*

What happened?

Joe failed to notice that not *all* subclasses of Duck should *fly*. When Joe added new behavior to the Duck superclass, he was also adding behavior that was *not* appropriate for some Duck subclasses. He now has flying inanimate objects in the SimUDuck program.

A localized update to the code caused a non-local side effect (flying rubber ducks)!

OK, so there's a slight flaw in my design. I don't see why they can't just call it a "feature". It's kind of cute...

What he thought was a great use of inheritance for the purpose of <u>reuse</u> hasn't turned out so well when it comes to <u>maintenance</u>.

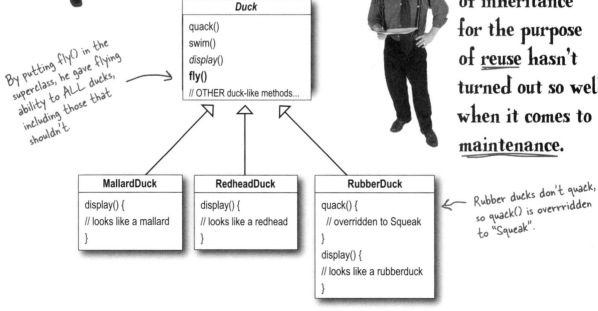

By putting fly() in the superclass, he gave flying ability to ALL ducks, including those that shouldn't.

```
            Duck
  quack()
  swim()
  display()
  fly()
  // OTHER duck-like methods...
```

```
   MallardDuck
 display() {
 // looks like a mallard
 }
```

```
   RedheadDuck
 display() {
 // looks like a redhead
 }
```

```
   RubberDuck
 quack() {
  // overridden to Squeak
 }
 display() {
 // looks like a rubberduck
 }
```

Rubber ducks don't quack, so quack() is overrridden to "Squeak".

Joe thinks about inheritance...

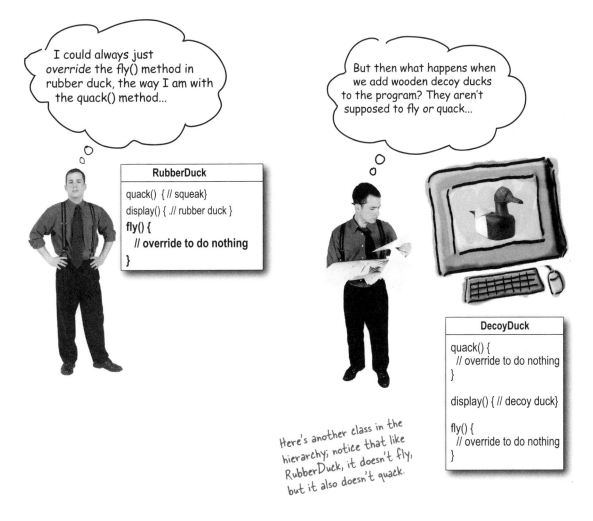

I could always just *override* the fly() method in rubber duck, the way I am with the quack() method...

RubberDuck

quack() { // squeak}

display() { .// rubber duck }

fly() {

// override to do nothing

}

But then what happens when we add wooden decoy ducks to the program? They aren't supposed to fly or quack...

DecoyDuck

quack() {
  // override to do nothing
}

display() { // decoy duck}

fly() {
  // override to do nothing
}

Here's another class in the hierarchy; notice that like RubberDuck, it doesn't fly, but it also doesn't quack.

Sharpen your pencil

Which of the following are disadvantages of using *inheritance* to provide Duck behavior? (Choose all that apply.)

❏ A. Code is duplicated across subclasses.

❏ B. Runtime behavior changes are difficult.

❏ C. We can't make ducks dance.

❏ D. Hard to gain knowledge of all duck behaviors.

❏ E. Ducks can't fly and quack at the same time.

❏ F. Changes can unintentionally affect other ducks.

How about an interface?

Joe realized that inheritance probably wasn't the answer, because he just got a memo that says that the executives now want to update the product every six months (in ways they haven't yet decided on). Joe knows the spec will keep changing and he'll be forced to look at and possibly override fly() and quack() for every new Duck subclass that's ever added to the program... *forever.*

So, he needs a cleaner way to have only *some* (but not *all*) of the duck types fly or quack.

I could take the fly() out of the Duck superclass, and make a **Flyable() interface** with a fly() method. That way, only the ducks that are *supposed* to fly will implement that interface and have a fly() method... and I might as well make a Quackable, too, since not all ducks can quack.

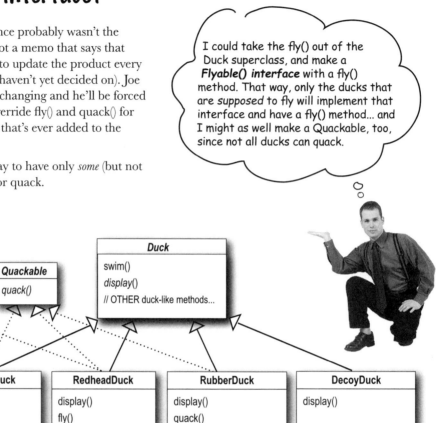

What do YOU think about this design?

That is, like, the dumbest idea you've come up with. **Can you say, "duplicate code"?** If you thought having to *override a few methods* was bad, how are you gonna feel when you need to make a little change to the flying behavior... *in all 48 of the flying Duck subclasses?!*

What would *you* do if you were Joe?

We know that not *all* of the subclasses should have flying or quacking behavior, so inheritance isn't the right answer. But while having the subclasses implement Flyable and/or Quackable solves *part* of the problem (no inappropriately flying rubber ducks), it completely destroys code reuse for those behaviors, so it just creates a *different* maintenance nightmare. And of course there might be more than one kind of flying behavior even among the ducks that *do* fly...

At this point you might be waiting for a Design Pattern to come riding in on a white horse and save the day. But what fun would that be? No, we're going to figure out a solution the old-fashioned way— *by applying good OO software design principles.*

Wouldn't it be dreamy if only there were a way to build software so that when we need to change it, we could do so with the least possible impact on the existing code? We could spend less time *reworking* code and more making the program do cooler things...

The one constant in software development

Okay, what's the one thing you can always count on in software development?

No matter where you work, what you're building, or what language you are programming in, what's the one true constant that will be with you always?

(use a mirror to see the answer)

No matter how well you design an application, over time an application must grow and change or it will *die*.

Lots of things can drive change. List some reasons you've had to change code in your applications (we put in a couple of our own to get you started).

My customers or users decide they want something else, or they want new functionality.

My company decided it is going with another database vendor and it is also purchasing its data from another supplier that uses a different data format. Argh!

Zeroing in on the problem...

So we know using inheritance hasn't worked out very well, since the duck behavior keeps changing across the subclasses, and it's not appropriate for *all* subclasses to have those behaviors. The Flyable and Quackable interface sounded promising at first—only ducks that really do fly will be Flyable, etc.—except Java interfaces have no implementation code, so no code reuse. And that means that whenever you need to modify a behavior, you're forced to track down and change it in all the different subclasses where that behavior is defined, probably introducing *new* bugs along the way!

Luckily, there's a design principle for just this situation.

> **Design Principle**
>
> *Identify the aspects of your application that vary and separate them from what stays the same.*

> Our first of many design principles. We'll spend more time on these thruoghout the book.

In other words, if you've got some aspect of your code that is changing, say with every new requirement, then you know you've got a behavior that needs to be pulled out and separated from all the stuff that doesn't change.

Here's another way to think about this principle: ***take the parts that vary and encapsulate them, so that later you can alter or extend the parts that vary without affecting those that don't.***

As simple as this concept is, it forms the basis for almost every design pattern. All patterns provide a way to let *some part of a system vary independently of all other parts*.

Okay, time to pull the duck behavior out of the Duck classes!

Take what varies and "encapsulate" it so it won't affect the rest of your code.

The result? Fewer unintended consequences from code changes and more flexibility in your systems!

Separating what changes from what stays the same

Where do we start? As far as we can tell, other than the problems with fly() and quack(), the Duck class is working well and there are no other parts of it that appear to vary or change frequently. So, other than a few slight changes, we're going to pretty much leave the Duck class alone.

Now, to separate the "parts that change from those that stay the same", we are going to create two *sets* of classes (totally apart from Duck), one for *fly* and one for *quack*. Each set of classes will hold all the implementations of their respective behavior. For instance, we might have *one* class that implements *quacking*, *another* that implements *squeaking*, and *another* that implements *silence*.

We know that fly() and quack() are the parts of the Duck class that vary across ducks.

To separate these behaviors from the Duck class, we'll pull both methods *out* of the Duck class and create a new set of classes to represent each behavior.

The Duck class is still the superclass of all ducks, but we are pulling out the fly and quack behaviors and putting them into another class structure.

Now flying and quacking each get their own set of classes.

Various behavior implementations are going to live here.

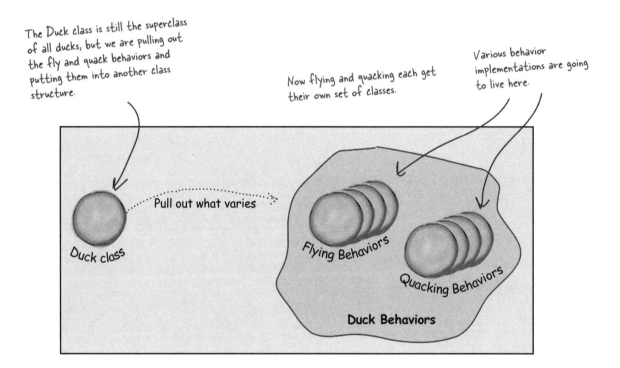

Pull out what varies

Duck class

Flying Behaviors

Quacking Behaviors

Duck Behaviors

Designing the Duck Behaviors

So how are we going to design the set of classes that implement the fly and quack behaviors?

We'd like to keep things flexible; after all, it was the inflexibility in the duck behaviors that got us into trouble in the first place. And we know that we want to *assign* behaviors to the instances of Duck. For example, we might want to instantiate a new MallardDuck instance and initialize it with a specific *type* of flying behavior. And while we're there, why not make sure that we can change the behavior of a duck dynamically? In other words, we should include behavior setter methods in the Duck classes so that we can, say, *change* the MallardDuck's flying behavior *at runtime*.

Given these goals, let's look at our second design principle:

> **Design Principle**
>
> *Program to an interface, not an implementation.*

We'll use an interface to represent each behavior – for instance, FlyBehavior and QuackBehavior – and each implementation of a *behavior* will implement one of those interfaces.

So this time it won't be the *Duck* classes that will implement the flying and quacking interfaces. Instead, we'll make a set of classes whose entire reason for living is to represent a behavior (for example, "squeaking"), and it's the *behavior* class, rather than the Duck class, that will implement the behavior interface.

This is in contrast to the way we were doing things before, where a behavior either came from a concrete implementation in the superclass Duck, or by providing a specialized implementation in the subclass itself. In both cases we were relying on an *implementation*. We were locked into using that specific implementation and there was no room for changing out the behavior (other than writing more code).

With our new design, the Duck subclasses will use a behavior represented by an *interface* (FlyBehavior and QuackBehavior), so that the actual *implementation* of the behavior (in other words, the specific concrete behavior coded in the class that implements the FlyBehavior or QuackBehavior) won't be locked into the Duck subclass.

From now on, the Duck behaviors will live in a separate class—a class that implements a particular behavior interface.

That way, the Duck classes won't need to know any of the implementation details for their own behaviors.

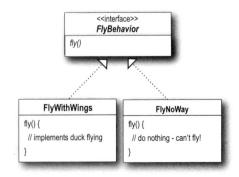

> I don't see why you have to use an *interface* for FlyBehavior. You can do the same thing with an abstract superclass. Isn't the whole point to use polymorphism?

"Program to an *interface*" really means "Program to a *supertype*."

The word *interface* is overloaded here. There's the *concept* of interface, but there's also the Java construct **interface**. You can *program to an interface*, without having to actually use a Java **interface**. The point is to exploit polymorphism by programming to a supertype so that the actual runtime object isn't locked into the code. And we could rephrase "program to a supertype" as "the declared type of the variables should be a supertype, usually an abstract class or interface, so that the objects assigned to those variables can be of any concrete implementation of the supertype, which means the class declaring them doesn't have to know about the actual object types!"

This is probably old news to you, but just to make sure we're all saying the same thing, here's a simple example of using a polymorphic type – imagine an abstract class Animal, with two concrete implementations, Dog and Cat.

Programming to an implementation would be:

```
Dog d = new Dog();
d.bark();
```
Declaring the variable "d" as type Dog (a concrete implementation of Animal) forces us to code to a concrete implementation.

But **programming to an interface/supertype** would be:

```
Animal animal = new Dog();
animal.makeSound();
```
We know it's a Dog, but we can now use the animal reference polymorphically.

Even better, rather than hard-coding the instantiation of the subtype (like new Dog()) into the code, **assign the concrete implementation object at runtime:**

```
a = getAnimal();
a.makeSound();
```
We don't know WHAT the actual animal subtype is... all we care about is that it knows how to respond to makeSound().

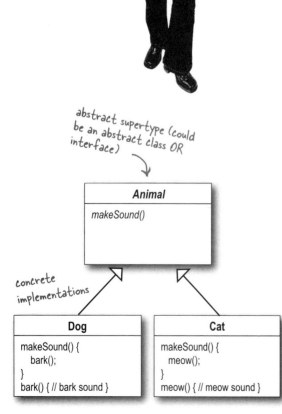

abstract supertype (could be an abstract class OR interface)

Animal

makeSound()

concrete implementations

Dog
makeSound() {
bark();
}
bark() { // bark sound }

Cat
makeSound() {
meow();
}
meow() { // meow sound }

Implementing the Duck Behaviors

Here we have the two interfaces, FlyBehavior and QuackBehavior along with the corresponding classes that implement each concrete behavior:

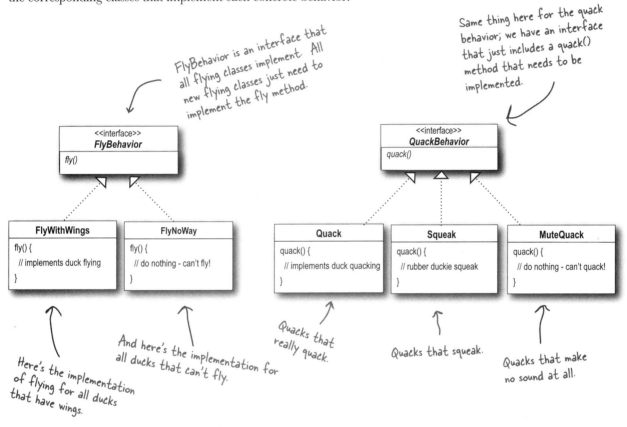

FlyBehavior is an interface that all flying classes implement. All new flying classes just need to implement the fly method.

Same thing here for the quack behavior; we have an interface that just includes a quack() method that needs to be implemented.

Here's the implementation of flying for all ducks that have wings.

And here's the implementation for all ducks that can't fly.

Quacks that really quack.

Quacks that squeak.

Quacks that make no sound at all.

> **With this design, other types of objects can reuse our fly and quack behaviors because these behaviors are no longer hidden away in our Duck classes!**
>
> **And we can add new behaviors without modifying any of our existing behavior classes or touching any of the Duck classes that *use* flying behaviors.**

So we get the benefit of REUSE without all the baggage that comes along with inheritance.

there are no
Dumb Questions

Q: Do I always have to implement my application first, see where things are changing, and then go back and separate & encapsulate those things?

A: Not always; often when you are designing an application, you anticipate those areas that are going to vary and then go ahead and build the flexibility to deal with it into your code. You'll find that the principles and patterns can be applied at any stage of the development lifecycle.

Q: Should we make Duck an interface too?

A: Not in this case. As you'll see once we've got everything hooked together, we do benefit by having Duck not be an interface and having specific ducks, like MallardDuck, inherit common properties and methods. Now that we've removed what varies from the Duck inheritance, we get the benefits of this structure without the problems.

Q: It feels a little weird to have a class that's just a behavior. Aren't classes supposed to represent *things? Aren't classes supposed to have both state AND behavior?*

A: In an OO system, yes, classes represent things that generally have both state (instance variables) and methods. And in this case, the *thing* happens to be a behavior. But even a behavior can still have state and methods; a flying behavior might have instance variables representing the attributes for the flying (wing beats per minute, max altitude and speed, etc.) behavior.

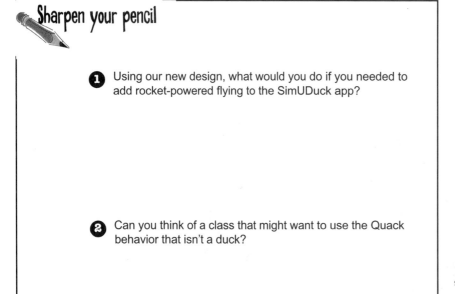

Sharpen your pencil

1 Using our new design, what would you do if you needed to add rocket-powered flying to the SimUDuck app?

2 Can you think of a class that might want to use the Quack behavior that isn't a duck?

Answers:
1) Create a FlyRocketPowered class that implements the FlyBehavior interface.
2) One example, a duck call (a device that makes duck sounds).

Integrating the Duck Behavior

The key is that a Duck will now *delegate* its flying and quacking behavior, instead of using quacking and flying methods defined in the Duck class (or subclass).

Here's how:

 First we'll add two instance variables to the Duck class called *flyBehavior* and *quackBehavior*, that are declared as the interface type (not a concrete class implementation type). Each duck object will set these variables polymorphically to reference the *specific* behavior type it would like at runtime (FlyWithWings, Squeak, etc.).

We'll also remove the fly() and quack() methods from the Duck class (and any subclasses) because we've moved this behavior out into the FlyBehavior and QuackBehavior classes.

We'll replace fly() and quack() in the Duck class with two similar methods, called performFly() and performQuack(); you'll see how they work next.

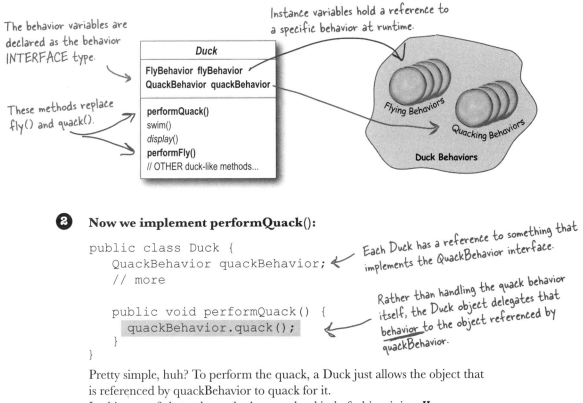

The behavior variables are declared as the behavior INTERFACE type.

These methods replace fly() and quack().

Instance variables hold a reference to a specific behavior at runtime.

Duck

FlyBehavior flyBehavior
QuackBehavior quackBehavior

performQuack()
swim()
display()
performFly()
// OTHER duck-like methods...

Flying Behaviors

Quacking Behaviors

Duck Behaviors

❷ **Now we implement performQuack():**

```
public class Duck {
   QuackBehavior quackBehavior;
   // more

   public void performQuack() {
      quackBehavior.quack();
   }
}
```

Each Duck has a reference to something that implements the QuackBehavior interface.

Rather than handling the quack behavior itself, the Duck object delegates that behavior to the object referenced by quackBehavior.

Pretty simple, huh? To perform the quack, a Duck just allows the object that is referenced by quackBehavior to quack for it.
In this part of the code we don't care what kind of object it is, **all we care about is that it knows how to quack()!**

More Integration...

3 Okay, time to worry about **how the flyBehavior and quackBehavior instance variables are set**. Let's take a look at the MallardDuck class:

```
public class MallardDuck extends Duck {

    public MallardDuck() {
        quackBehavior = new Quack();
        flyBehavior = new FlyWithWings();
    }

    public void display() {
        System.out.println("I'm a real Mallard duck");
    }
}
```

A MallardDuck uses the Quack class to handle its quack, so when performQuack is called, the responsibility for the quack is delegated to the Quack object and we get a real quack.

And it uses FlyWithWings as its FlyBehavior type.

Remember, MallardDuck inherits the quack-Behavior and flyBehavior instance variables from class Duck.

So MallardDuck's quack is a real live duck **quack**, not a **squeak** and not a **mute quack**. So what happens here? When a MallardDuck is instantiated, its constructor initializes the MallardDuck's inherited quackBehavior instance variable to a new instance of type Quack (a QuackBehavior concrete implementation class).

And the same is true for the duck's flying behavior—the MallardDuck's constructor initializes the flyBehavior instance variable with an instance of type FlyWithWings (a FlyBehavior concrete implementation class).

Wait a second, didn't you say we should NOT program to an implementation? But what are we doing in that constructor? We're making a new instance of a concrete Quack implementation class!

Good catch, that's exactly what we're doing... *for now.*

Later in the book we'll have more patterns in our toolbox that can help us fix it.

Still, notice that while we *are* setting the behaviors to concrete classes (by instantiating a behavior class like Quack or FlyWithWings and assigning it to our behavior reference variable), we could *easily* change that at runtime.

So, we still have a lot of flexibility here, but we're doing a poor job of initializing the instance variables in a flexible way. But think about it, since the quackBehavior instance variable is an interface type, we could (through the magic of polymorphism) dynamically assign a different QuackBehavior implementation class at runtime.

Take a moment and think about how you would implement a duck so that its behavior could change at runtime. (You'll see the code that does this a few pages from now.)

Testing the Duck code

❶ Type and compile the Duck class below (Duck.java), and the MallardDuck class from two pages back (MallardDuck.java).

```java
public abstract class Duck {

    FlyBehavior flyBehavior;
    QuackBehavior quackBehavior;
    public Duck() {
    }

    public abstract void display();

    public void performFly() {
        flyBehavior.fly();
    }

    public void performQuack() {
        quackBehavior.quack();
    }

    public void swim() {
        System.out.println("All ducks float, even decoys!");
    }
}
```

Declare two reference variables for the behavior interface types. All duck subclasses (in the same package) inherit these.

Delegate to the behavior class.

❷ Type and compile the FlyBehavior interface (FlyBehavior.java) and the two behavior implementation classes (FlyWithWings.java and FlyNoWay.java).

```java
public interface FlyBehavior {
    public void fly();
}
```

The interface that all flying behavior classes implement.

```java
public class FlyWithWings implements FlyBehavior {
    public void fly() {
        System.out.println("I'm flying!!");
    }
}
```

Flying behavior implementation for ducks that DO fly...

```java
public class FlyNoWay implements FlyBehavior {
    public void fly() {
        System.out.println("I can't fly");
    }
}
```

Flying behavior implementation for ducks that do NOT fly (like rubber ducks and decoy ducks).

Testing the Duck code continued...

3 **Type and compile the QuackBehavior interface (QuackBehavior.java) and the three behavior implementation classes (Quack.java, MuteQuack.java, and Sqeak.java).**

```java
public interface QuackBehavior {
    public void quack();
}
```

```java
public class Quack implements QuackBehavior {
    public void quack() {
        System.out.println("Quack");
    }
}
```

```java
public class MuteQuack implements QuackBehavior {
    public void quack() {
        System.out.println("<< Silence >>");
    }
}
```

```java
public class Squeak implements QuackBehavior {
    public void quack() {
        System.out.println("Squeak");
    }
}
```

4 **Type and compile the test class (MiniDuckSimulator.java).**

```java
public class MiniDuckSimulator {
    public static void main(String[] args) {
        Duck mallard = new MallardDuck();
        mallard.performQuack();
        mallard.performFly();
    }
}
```

This calls the MallardDuck's inherited performQuack() method, which then delegates to the object's QuackBehavior (i.e. calls quack() on the duck's inherited quackBehavior reference).

Then we do the same thing with MallardDuck's inherited performFly() method.

5 **Run the code!**

```
File Edit Window Help Yadayadayada
%java MiniDuckSimulator
Quack
I'm flying!!
```

Setting behavior dynamically

What a shame to have all this dynamic talent built into our ducks and not be using it! Imagine you want to set the duck's behavior type through a setter method on the duck subclass, rather than by instantiating it in the duck's constructor.

❶ Add two new methods to the Duck class:

```
public void setFlyBehavior(FlyBehavior fb) {
    flyBehavior = fb;
}

public void setQuackBehavior(QuackBehavior qb) {
    quackBehavior = qb;
}
```

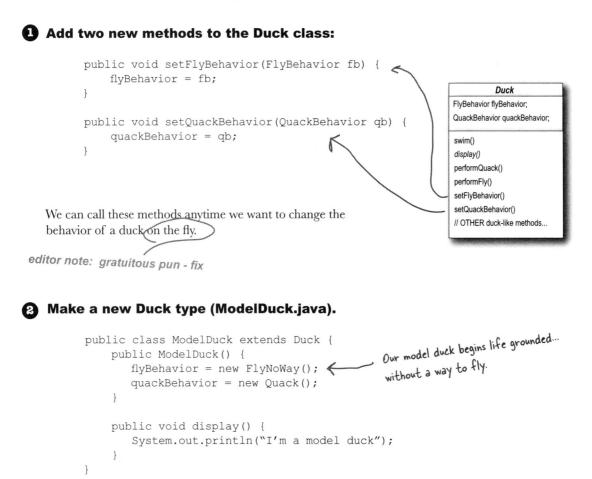

Duck
FlyBehavior flyBehavior;
QuackBehavior quackBehavior;
swim()
display()
performQuack()
performFly()
setFlyBehavior()
setQuackBehavior()
// OTHER duck-like methods...

We can call these methods anytime we want to change the behavior of a duck on the fly.

editor note: gratuitous pun - fix

❷ Make a new Duck type (ModelDuck.java).

```
public class ModelDuck extends Duck {
    public ModelDuck() {
        flyBehavior = new FlyNoWay();
        quackBehavior = new Quack();
    }

    public void display() {
        System.out.println("I'm a model duck");
    }
}
```

Our model duck begins life grounded... without a way to fly.

❸ Make a new FlyBehavior type (FlyRocketPowered.java).

That's okay, we're creating a rocket powered flying behavior.

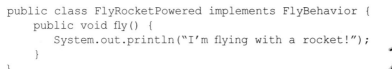

```
public class FlyRocketPowered implements FlyBehavior {
    public void fly() {
        System.out.println("I'm flying with a rocket!");
    }
}
```

❹ Change the test class (MiniDuckSimulator.java), add the ModelDuck, and make the ModelDuck rocket-enabled.

before

```java
public class MiniDuckSimulator {
    public static void main(String[] args) {
        Duck mallard = new MallardDuck();
        mallard.performQuack();
        mallard.performFly();

        Duck model = new ModelDuck();

        model.performFly();

        model.setFlyBehavior(new FlyRocketPowered());

        model.performFly();
    }
}
```

The first call to performFly() delegates to the flyBehavior object set in the ModelDuck's constructor, which is a FlyNoWay instance.

This invokes the model's inherited behavior setter method, and...voila! The model suddenly has rocket-powered flying capability!

If it worked, the model duck dynamically changed its flying behavior! You can't do THAT if the implementation lives inside the duck class.

after

❺ Run it!

```
File Edit Window Help Yabadabadoo
%java MiniDuckSimulator
Quack
I'm flying!!
I can't fly
I'm flying with a rocket
```

To change a duck's behavior at runtime, just call the duck's setter method for that behavior.

The Big Picture on encapsulated behaviors

Okay, now that we've done the deep dive on the duck simulator design, it's time to come back up for air and take a look at the big picture.

Below is the entire reworked class structure. We have everything you'd expect: ducks extending Duck, fly behaviors implementing FlyBehavior and quack behaviors implementing QuackBehavior.

Notice also that we've started to describe things a little differently. Instead of thinking of the duck behaviors as a *set of behaviors*, we'll start thinking of them as a *family of algorithms*. Think about it: in the SimUDuck design, the algorithms represent things a duck would do (different ways of quacking or flying), but we could just as easily use the same techniques for a set of classes that implement the ways to compute state sales tax by different states.

Pay careful attention to the *relationships* between the classes. In fact, grab your pen and write the appropriate relationship (IS-A, HAS-A and IMPLEMENTS) on each arrow in the class diagram.

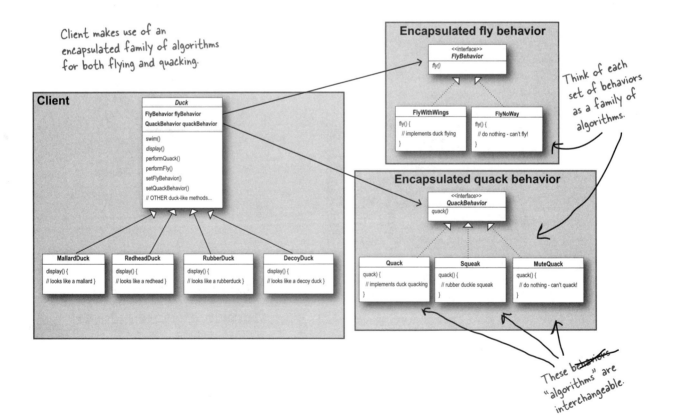

HAS-A can be better than IS-A

The HAS-A relationship is an interesting one: each duck has a FlyBehavior and a QuackBehavior to which it delegates flying and quacking.

When you put two classes together like this you're using **composition**. Instead of *inheriting* their behavior, the ducks get their behavior by being *composed* with the right behavior object.

This is an important technique; in fact, we've been using our third design principle:

Design Principle

Favor composition over inheritance.

As you've seen, creating systems using composition gives you a lot more flexibility. Not only does it let you encapsulate a family of algorithms into their own set of classes, but it also lets you ***change behavior at runtime*** as long as the object you're composing with implements the correct behavior interface.

Composition is used in <u>many</u> design patterns and you'll see a lot more about its advantages and disadvantages throughout the book.

A duck call is a device that hunters use to mimic the calls (quacks) of ducks. How would you implement your own duck call that does *not* inherit from the Duck class?

Master and Student...

Master: *Grasshopper, tell me what you have learned of the Object-Oriented ways.*

Student: *Master, I have learned that the promise of the object-oriented way is reuse.*

Master: *Grasshopper, continue...*

Student: *Master, through inheritance all good things may be reused and so we will come to drastically cut development time like we swiftly cut bamboo in the woods.*

Master: *Grasshopper, is more time spent on code **before** or **after** development is complete?*

Student: *The answer is **after**, Master. We always spend more time maintaining and changing software than initial development.*

Master: *So Grasshopper, should effort go into reuse **above** maintaintability and extensibility?*

Student: *Master, I believe that there is truth in this.*

Master: *I can see that you still have much to learn. I would like for you to go and meditate on inheritance further. As you've seen, inheritance has its problems, and there are other ways of achieving reuse.*

Speaking of Design Patterns...

Congratulations on your first pattern!

You just applied your first design pattern—the **STRATEGY** pattern. That's right, you used the Strategy Pattern to rework the SimUDuck app. Thanks to this pattern, the simulator is ready for any changes those execs might cook up on their next business trip to Vegas.

Now that we've made you take the long road to apply it, here's the formal definition of this pattern:

> **The Strategy Pattern** defines a family of algorithms, encapsulates each one, and makes them interchangeable. Strategy lets the algorithm vary independently from clients that use it.

Use THIS definition when you need to impress friends and influence key executives.

Design Puzzle

Below you'll find a mess of classes and interfaces for an action adventure game. You'll find classes for game characters along with classes for weapon behaviors the characters can use in the game. Each character can make use of one weapon at a time, but can change weapons at any time during the game. Your job is to sort it all out...

(Answers are at the end of the chapter.)

Your task:

1 Arrange the classes.

2 Identify one abstract class, one interface and eight classes.

3 Draw arrows between classes.

     a. Draw this kind of arrow for inheritance ("extends"). ⟶▷

     b. Draw this kind of arrow for interface ("implements"). ·········▷

     c. Draw this kind of arrow for "HAS-A". ⟶

4 Put the method setWeapon() into the right class.

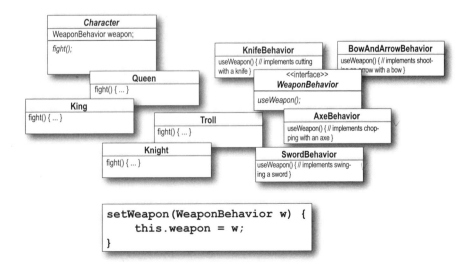

```
setWeapon(WeaponBehavior w) {
    this.weapon = w;
}
```

Overheard at the local diner...

What's the difference between these two orders? Not a thing! They're both the same order, except Alice is using twice the number of words and trying the patience of a grumpy short order cook.

What's Flo got that Alice doesn't? **A shared vocabulary** with the short order cook. Not only is it easier to communicate with the cook, but it gives the cook less to remember because he's got all the diner patterns in his head.

Design Patterns give you a shared vocabulary with other developers. Once you've got the vocabulary you can more easily communicate with other developers and inspire those who don't know patterns to start learning them. It also elevates your thinking about architectures by letting you **think at the *pattern* level**, not the nitty gritty *object* level.

Overheard in the next cubicle...

> So I created this broadcast class. It keeps track of all the objects listening to it and anytime a new piece of data comes along it sends a message to each listener. What's cool is that the listeners can join the broadcast at any time or they can even remove themselves. It is really dynamic and loosely-coupled!

Rick

BRAIN POWER

Can you think of other shared vocabularies that are used beyond OO design and diner talk? (Hint: how about auto mechanics, carpenters, gourmet chefs, air traffic control) What qualities are communicated along with the lingo?

Can you think of aspects of OO design that get communicated along with pattern names? What qualities get communicated along with the name "Strategy Pattern"?

> Rick, why didn't you just say you were using the **Observer** Pattern?

> Exactly. If you communicate in patterns, then other developers know immediately and *precisely* the design you're describing. Just don't get Pattern Fever... you'll know you have it when you start using patterns for Hello World...

The power of a shared pattern vocabulary

When you communicate using patterns you are doing <u>more</u> than just sharing LINGO.

Shared pattern vocabularies are POWERFUL.
When you communicate with another developer or your team using patterns, you are communicating not just a pattern name but a whole set of qualities, characteristics and constraints that the pattern represents.

"We're using the strategy pattern to implement the various behaviors of our ducks." This tells you the duck behavior has been encapsulated into its own set of classes that can be easily expanded and changed, even at runtime if needed.

Patterns allow you to say more with less. When you use a pattern in a description, other developers quickly know precisely the design you have in mind.

Talking at the pattern level allows you to stay "in the design" longer. Talking about software systems using patterns allows you to keep the discussion at the design level, without having to dive down to the nitty gritty details of implementing objects and classes.

How many design meetings have you been in that quickly degrade into implementation details?

Shared vocabularies can turbo charge your development team. A team well versed in design patterns can move more quickly with less room for misunderstanding.

As your team begins to share design ideas and experience in terms of patterns, you will build a community of patterns users.

Shared vocabularies encourage more junior developers to get up to speed. Junior developers look up to experienced developers. When senior developers make use of design patterns, junior developers also become motivated to learn them. Build a community of pattern users at your organization.

Think about starting a patterns study group at your organization, maybe you can even get paid while you're learning... ;)

How do I use Design Patterns?

We've all used off-the-shelf libraries and frameworks. We take them, write some code against their APIs, compile them into our programs, and benefit from a lot of code someone else has written. Think about the Java APIs and all the functionality they give you: network, GUI, IO, etc. Libraries and frameworks go a long way towards a development model where we can just pick and choose components and plug them right in. But... they don't help us structure our own applications in ways that are easier to understand, more maintainable and flexible. That's where Design Patterns come in.

Design patterns don't go directly into your code, they first go into your BRAIN. Once you've loaded your brain with a good working knowledge of patterns, you can then start to apply them to your new designs, and rework your old code when you find it's degrading into an inflexible mess of jungle spaghetti code.

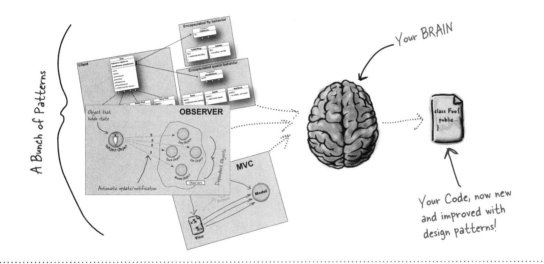

there are no Dumb Questions

Q: If design patterns are so great, why can't someone build a library of them so I don't have to?

A: Design patterns are higher level than libraries. Design patterns tell us how to structure classes and objects to solve certain problems and it is our job to adapt those designs to fit our particular application.

Q: Aren't libraries and frameworks also design patterns?

A: Frameworks and libraries are not design patterns; they provide specific implementations that we link into our code. Sometimes, however, libraries and frameworks make use of design patterns in their implementations. That's great, because once you understand design patterns, you'll more quickly understand APIs that are structured around design patterns.

Q: So, there are no libraries of design patterns?

A: No, but you will learn later about pattern catalogs with lists of patterns that you can apply to your applications.

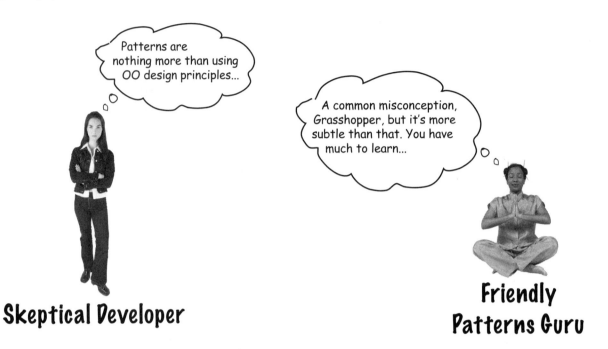

Skeptical Developer

Friendly Patterns Guru

Developer: Okay, hmm, but isn't this all just good object-oriented design; I mean as long as I follow encapsulation and I know about abstraction, inheritance, and polymorphism, do I really need to think about Design Patterns? Isn't it pretty straightforward? Isn't this why I took all those OO courses? I think Design Patterns are useful for people who don't know good OO design.

Guru: Ah, this is one of the true misunderstandings of object-oriented development: that by knowing the OO basics we are automatically going to be good at building flexible, reusable, and maintainable systems.

Developer: No?

Guru: No. As it turns out, constructing OO systems that have these properties is not always obvious and has been discovered only through hard work.

Developer: I think I'm starting to get it. These, sometimes non-obvious, ways of constructing object-oriented systems have been collected...

Guru: ...yes, into a set of patterns called Design Patterns.

Developer: So, by knowing patterns, I can skip the hard work and jump straight to designs that always work?

Guru: Yes, to an extent, but remember, design is an art. There will always be tradeoffs. But, if you follow well thought-out and time-tested design patterns, you'll be way ahead.

Developer: What do I do if I can't find a pattern?

Remember, knowing concepts like abstraction, inheritance, and polymorphism do not make you a good object oriented designer. A design guru thinks about how to create flexible designs that are maintainable and that can cope with change.

Guru: There are some object oriented-principles that underlie the patterns, and knowing these will help you to cope when you can't find a pattern that matches your problem.

Developer: Principles? You mean beyond abstraction, encapsulation, and...

Guru: Yes, one of the secrets to creating maintainable OO systems is thinking about how they might change in the future and these principles address those issues.

Tools for your Design Toolbox

You've nearly made it through the first chapter! You've already put a few tools in your OO toolbox; let's make a list of them before we move on to Chapter 2.

OO Basics

Abstraction

Encapsulation

Polymorphism

Inheritance

We assume you know the OO basics of using classes polymorphically, how inheritance is like design by contract, and how encapsulation works. If you are a little rusty on these, pull out your Head First Java and review, then skim this chapter again.

OO Principles

Encapsulate what varies.

Favor composition over inheritance.

Program to interfaces, not implementations.

We'll be taking a closer look at these down the road and also adding a few more to the list

OO Patterns

Strategy – defines a family of algorithms, encapsulates each one, and makes them interchangeable. Strategy lets the algorithm vary independently from clients that use it.

Throughout the book think about how patterns rely on OO basics and principles.

One down, many to go!

BULLET POINTS

- Knowing the OO basics does not make you a good OO designer.

- Good OO designs are reusable, extensible and maintainable.

- Patterns show you how to build systems with good OO design qualities.

- Patterns are proven object-oriented experience.

- Patterns don't give you code, they give you general solutions to design problems. You apply them to your specific application.

- Patterns aren't *invented*, they are *discovered*.

- Most patterns and principles address issues of *change* in software.

- Most patterns allow some part of a system to vary independently of all other parts.

- We often try to take what varies in a system and encapsulate it.

- Patterns provide a shared language that can maximize the value of your communication with other developers.

Let's give your right brain something to do.

It's your standard crossword; all of the solution words are from this chapter.

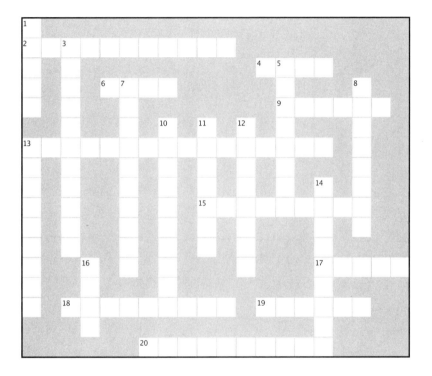

Across

2. _____ what varies
4. Design patterns _____
6. Java IO, Networking, Sound
9. Rubberducks make a
13. Bartender thought they were called
15. Program to this, not an implementation
17. Patterns go into your _____
18. Learn from the other guy's
19. Development constant
20. Patterns give us a shared _____

Down

1. Patterns _____ in many applications
3. Favor over inheritance
5. Dan was thrilled with this pattern
7. Most patterns follow from OO _____
8. Not your own
10. High level libraries
11. Joe's favorite drink
12. Pattern that fixed the simulator
13. Duck that can't quack
14. Grilled cheese with bacon
16. Duck demo was located where

Design Puzzle Solution

Character is the abstract class for all the other characters (King, Queen, Knight and Troll) while Weapon is an interface that all weapons implement. So all actual characters and weapons are concrete classes.

To switch weapons, each character calls the setWeapon() method, which is defined in the Character superclass. During a fight the useWeapon() method is called on the current weapon set for a given character to inflict great bodily damage on another character.

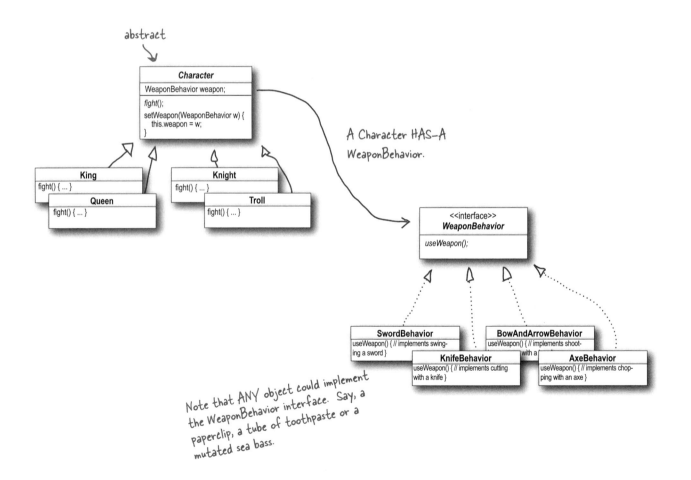

Solutions

Sharpen your pencil

Which of the following are disadvantages of using subclassing to provide specific Duck behavior? (Choose all that apply.)

- ☑ A. Code is duplicated across subclasses.
- ☑ B. Runtime behavior changes are difficult.
- ☐ C. We can't make duck's dance.
- ☑ C. Hard to gain knowledge of all duck behaviors.
- ☐ D. Ducks can't fly and quack at the same time.
- ☑ E. Changes can unintentionally affect other ducks.

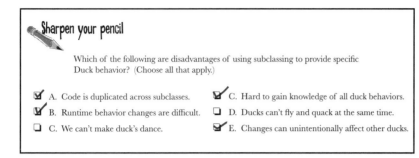

Crossword solution:

- 1 (down) R
- 2 (across) ENCAPSULATE
- 1 (down) RECURDUCK
- 3 (down) COMPOSITION
- 4 (across) ROCK
- 6 (across) APIS
- 5 (down) KBERWEIFIEL (KB...)
- 8 (down) FILURS
- 9 (across) SQUEAK
- 13 (across) DESIGNERPATTERNS
- 15 (across) INTERFACE
- 17 (across) BRAIN
- 18 (across) SUCCESSES
- 19 (across) CHANGE
- 20 (across) VOCABULARY

Sharpen your pencil

What are some factors that drive change in your applications? You might have a very different list, but here's a few of ours. Look familiar?

My customers or users decide they want something else, or they want new functionality.

My company decided it is going with another database vendor and it is also purchasing its data from another supplier that uses a different data format. Argh!

Well, technology changes and we've got to update our code to make use of protocols.

We've learned enough building our system that we'd like to go back and do things a little better.

2 the Observer Pattern

Keeping your Objects in the know

Hey Jerry, I'm notifying everyone that the Patterns Group meeting moved to Saturday night. We're going to be talking about the Observer Pattern. That pattern is the best! It's the BEST, Jerry!

Don't miss out when something interesting happens! We've got a pattern that keeps your objects in the know when something they might care about happens. Objects can even decide at runtime whether they want to be kept informed. The Observer Pattern is one of the most heavily used patterns in the JDK, and it's incredibly useful. Before we're done, we'll also look at one to many relationships and loose coupling (yeah, that's right, we said coupling). With Observer, you'll be the life of the Patterns Party.

Congratulations!

Your team has just won the contract to build Weather-O-Rama, Inc.'s next generation, Internet-based Weather Monitoring Station.

Weather-O-Rama, Inc.
100 Main Street
Tornado Alley, OK 45021

Statement of Work

Congratulations on being selected to build our next generation Internet-based Weather Monitoring Station!

The weather station will be based on our patent pending WeatherData object, which tracks current weather conditions (temperature, humidity, and barometric pressure). We'd like for you to create an application that initially provides three display elements: current conditions, weather statistics and a simple forecast, all updated in real time as the WeatherData object acquires the most recent measurements.

Further, this is an expandable weather station. Weather-O-Rama wants to release an API so that other developers can write their own weather displays and plug them right in. We'd like for you to supply that API!

Weather-O-Rama thinks we have a great business model: once the customers are hooked, we intend to charge them for each display they use. Now for the best part: we are going to pay you in stock options.

We look forward to seeing your design and alpha application.

Sincerely,

Johnny Hurricane

Johnny Hurricane, CEO
P.S. We are overnighting the WeatherData source files to you.

The Weather Monitoring application overview

The three players in the system are the weather station (the physical device that acquires the actual weather data), the WeatherData object (that tracks the data coming from the Weather Station and updates the displays), and the display that shows users the current weather conditions.

Current Conditions is one of three different displays. The user can also get weather stats and a forecast.

Humidity sensor device

Temperature sensor device

Pressure sensor device

Weather Station

pulls data

WeatherData object

displays

Current Conditions
Temp: 72°
Humidity: 60
Pressure: ↓

Display device

Weather-O-Rama provides

What we implement

The WeatherData object knows how to talk to the physical Weather Station, to get updated data. The WeatherData object then updates its displays for the three different display elements: Current Conditions (shows temperature, humidity, and pressure), Weather Statistics, and a simple forecast.

Our job, if we choose to accept it, is to create an app that uses the WeatherData object to update three displays for current conditions, weather stats, and a forecast.

Unpacking the WeatherData class

As promised, the next morning the WeatherData source files arrive. Peeking inside the code, things look pretty straightforward:

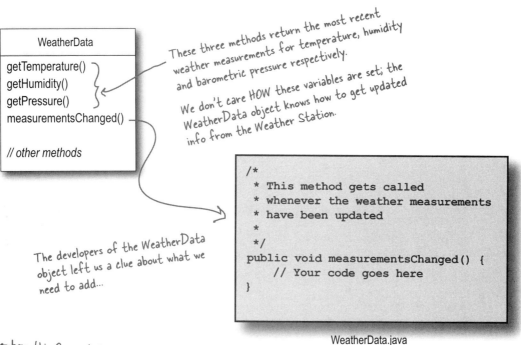

These three methods return the most recent weather measurements for temperature, humidity and barometric pressure respectively.

We don't care HOW these variables are set; the WeatherData object knows how to get updated info from the Weather Station.

```
WeatherData

getTemperature()
getHumidity()
getPressure()
measurementsChanged()

// other methods
```

The developers of the WeatherData object left us a clue about what we need to add...

```java
/*
 * This method gets called
 * whenever the weather measurements
 * have been updated
 *
 */
public void measurementsChanged() {
    // Your code goes here
}
```

WeatherData.java

Remember, this Current Conditions is just ONE of three different display screens.

↓

Current Conditions
Temp: 72°
Humidity: 60
Pressure: ↓

Display device

Our job is to implement measurementsChanged() so that it updates the three displays for current conditions, weather stats, and forecast.

What do we know so far?

The spec from Weather-O-Rama wasn't all that clear, but we have to figure out what we need to do. So, what do we know so far?

- ☼ The WeatherData class has getter methods for three measurement values: temperature, humidity and barometric pressure.

```
getTemperature()
getHumidity()
getPressure()
```

- ☼ The measurementsChanged() method is called any time new weather measurement data is available. (We don't know or care how this method is called; we just know that it *is*.)

```
measurementsChanged()
```

- ☼ We need to implement three display elements that use the weather data: a *current conditions* display, a *statistics display* and a *forecast* display. These displays must be updated each time WeatherData has new measurements.

Display Two

Display One

Display Three

- ☼ The system must be expandable—other developers can create new custom display elements and users can add or remove as many display elements as they want to the application. Currently, we know about only the initial *three* display types (current conditions, statistics and forecast).

Future displays

Taking a first, misguided SWAG at the Weather Station

Here's a first implementation possibility—we'll take the hint from the Weather-O-Rama developers and add our code to the measurementsChanged() method:

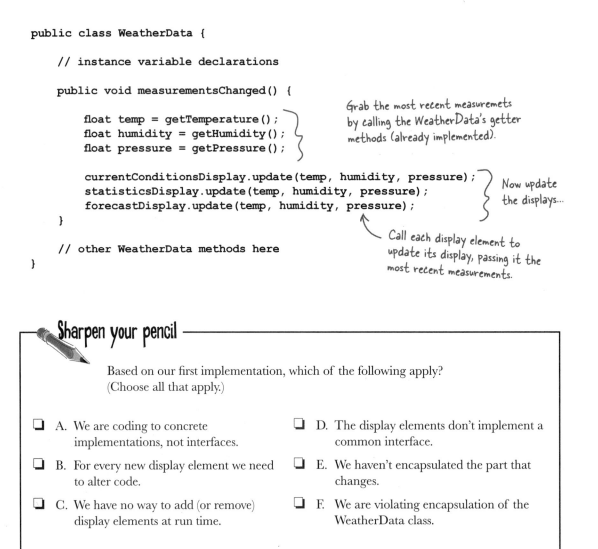

```
public class WeatherData {

    // instance variable declarations

    public void measurementsChanged() {

        float temp = getTemperature();
        float humidity = getHumidity();
        float pressure = getPressure();

        currentConditionsDisplay.update(temp, humidity, pressure);
        statisticsDisplay.update(temp, humidity, pressure);
        forecastDisplay.update(temp, humidity, pressure);
    }

    // other WeatherData methods here
}
```

Grab the most recent measuremets by calling the WeatherData's getter methods (already implemented).

Now update the displays...

Call each display element to update its display, passing it the most recent measurements.

Sharpen your pencil

Based on our first implementation, which of the following apply?
(Choose all that apply.)

❏ A. We are coding to concrete implementations, not interfaces.

❏ B. For every new display element we need to alter code.

❏ C. We have no way to add (or remove) display elements at run time.

❏ D. The display elements don't implement a common interface.

❏ E. We haven't encapsulated the part that changes.

❏ F. We are violating encapsulation of the WeatherData class.

Definition of SWAG: Scientific Wild A** Guess

What's wrong with our implementation?

Think back to all those Chapter 1 concepts and principles...

```
public void measurementsChanged() {

    float temp = getTemperature();
    float humidity = getHumidity();
    float pressure = getPressure();

    currentConditionsDisplay.update(temp, humidity, pressure);
    statisticsDisplay.update(temp, humidity, pressure);
    forecastDisplay.update(temp, humidity, pressure);
}
```

Area of change, we need to encapsulate this.

At least we seem to be using a common interface to talk to the display elements... they all have an update() method takes the temp, humidity, and pressure values.

By coding to concrete implementations we have no way to add or remove other display elements without making changes to the program.

Umm, I know I'm new here, but given that we are in the Observer Pattern chapter, maybe we should start using it?

We'll take a look at Observer, then come back and figure out how to apply it to the weather monitoring app.

Meet the Observer Pattern

You know how newspaper or magazine subscriptions work:

 1 A newspaper publisher goes into business and begins publishing newspapers.

 2 You subscribe to a particular publisher, and every time there's a new edition it gets delivered to you. As long as you remain a subscriber, you get new newspapers.

 3 You unsubscribe when you don't want papers anymore, and they stop being delivered.

 4 While the publisher remains in business, people, hotels, airlines and other businesses constantly subscribe and unsubscribe to the newspaper.

Miss what's going on in Objectville? No way, of course we subscribe!

Publishers + Subscribers = Observer Pattern

If you understand newspaper subscriptions, you pretty much understand the Observer Pattern, only we call the publisher the SUBJECT and the subscribers the OBSERVERS.

Let's take a closer look:

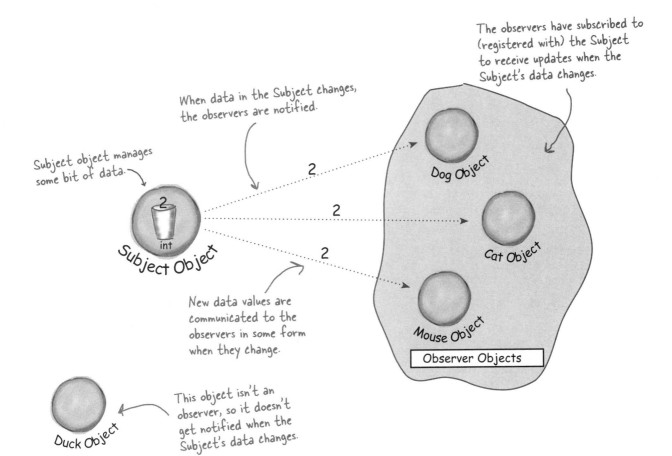

The observers have subscribed to (registered with) the Subject to receive updates when the Subject's data changes.

When data in the Subject changes, the observers are notified.

Subject object manages some bit of data.

New data values are communicated to the observers in some form when they change.

This object isn't an observer, so it doesn't get notified when the Subject's data changes.

A day in the life of the Observer Pattern

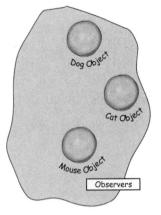

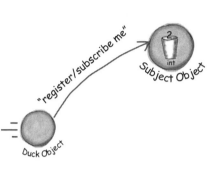

A Duck object comes along and tells the Subject that it wants to become an observer.

Duck really wants in on the action; those ints Subject is sending out whenever its state changes look pretty interesting...

The Duck object is now an official observer.

Duck is psyched... he's on the list and is waiting with great anticipation for the next notification so he can get an int.

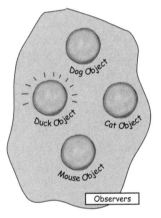

The Subject gets a new data value!

Now Duck and all the rest of the observers get a notification that the Subject has changed.

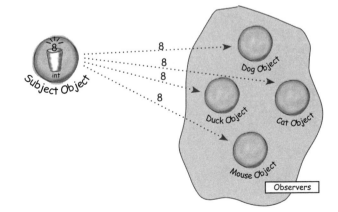

The Mouse object asks to be removed as an observer.

The Mouse object has been getting ints for ages and is tired of it, so it decides it's time to stop being an observer.

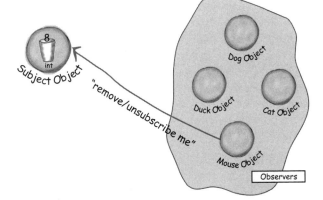

Mouse is outta here!

The Subject acknowledges the Mouse's request and removes it from the set of observers.

The Subject has another new int.

All the observers get another notification, except for the Mouse who is no longer included. Don't tell anyone, but the Mouse secretly misses those ints... maybe it'll ask to be an observer again some day.

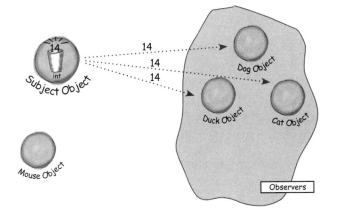

Five minute drama: a subject for observation

In today's skit, two post-bubble software developers encounter a real live head hunter...

5 Meanwhile for Ron and Jill life goes on; if a Java job comes along, they'll get notified, after all, they are observers.

Thanks, I'll send my resume right over.

This guy is a real jerk, who needs him. I'm looking for my own job.

Hey observers, there's a Java opening down at JavaBeans-R-Us, jump on it! Don't blow it!

Bwahaha, money in the bank, baby!

7

Observer

Observer

6

Subject

Jill lands her own job!

You can take me off your call list, I found my own job!

Arghhh!!! Mark my words Jill, you'll never work in this town again if I have anything to do with it. You're off my call list!!!

8

Observer

9

Subject

Two weeks later...

Jill's loving life, and no longer an observer. She's also enjoying the nice fat signing bonus that she got because the company didn't have to pay a headhunter.

But what has become of our dear Ron? We hear he's beating the headhunter at his own game. He's not only still an observer, he's got his own call list now, and he is notifying his own observers. Ron's a subject and an observer all in one.

The Observer Pattern defined

When you're trying to picture the Observer Pattern, a newspaper subscription service with its publisher and subscribers is a good way to visualize the pattern.

In the real world however, you'll typically see the Observer Pattern defined like this:

> **The Observer Pattern** defines a one-to-many dependency between objects so that when one object changes state, all of its dependents are notified and updated automatically.

Let's relate this definition to how we've been talking about the pattern:

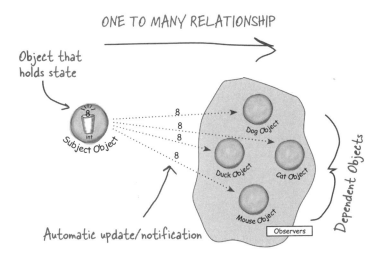

ONE TO MANY RELATIONSHIP

Object that holds state

Subject Object

Dog Object

Duck Object

Cat Object

Mouse Object

Observers

Dependent Objects

Automatic update/notification

The Observer Pattern defines a one-to-many relationship between a set of objects.

When the state of one object changes, all of its dependents are notified.

The subject and observers define the one-to-many relationship. The observers are dependent on the subject such that when the subject's state changes, the observers get notified. Depending on the style of notification, the observer may also be updated with new values.

As you'll discover, there are a few different ways to implement the Observer Pattern but most revolve around a class design that includes Subject and Observer interfaces.

Let's take a look...

The Observer Pattern defined: the class diagram

All potential observers need to implement the Observer interface. This interface just has one method, update(), that gets called when the Subject's state changes.

Here's the Subject interface. Objects use this interface to register as observers and also to remove themselves from being observers.

Each subject can have many observers.

<<interface>> **Subject**
registerObserver()
removeObserver()
notifyObservers()

observers →

<<interface>> **Observer**
update()

ConcreteSubject
registerObserver() {...}
removeObserver() {...}
notifyObservers() {...}
getState()
setState()

subject →

ConcreteObserver
update()
// other Observer specific
methods

A concrete subject always implements the Subject interface. In addition to the register and remove methods, the concrete subject implements a notifyObservers() method that is used to update all the current observers whenever state changes.

The concrete subject may also have methods for setting and getting its state (more about this later).

Concrete observers can be any class that implements the Observer interface. Each observer registers with a concrete subject to receive updates.

there are no Dumb Questions

Q: What does this have to do with one-to-many relationships?

A: With the Observer pattern, the Subject is the object that contains the state and controls it. So, there is ONE subject with state. The observers, on the other hand, use the state, even if they don't own it. There are many observers and they rely on the Subject to tell them when its state changes. So there is a relationship between the ONE Subject to the MANY Observers.

Q: How does dependence come into this?

A: Because the subject is the sole owner of that data, the observers are dependent on the subject to update them when the data changes. This leads to a cleaner OO design than allowing many objects to control the same data.

The power of Loose Coupling

When two objects are loosely coupled, they can interact, but have very little knowledge of each other.

The Observer Pattern provides an object design where subjects and observers are loosely coupled.

Why?

The only thing the subject knows about an observer is that it implements a certain interface (the Observer interface). It doesn't need to know the concrete class of the observer, what it does, or anything else about it.

We can add new observers at any time. Because the only thing the subject depends on is a list of objects that implement the Observer interface, we can add new observers whenever we want. In fact, we can replace any observer at runtime with another observer and the subject will keep purring along. Likewise, we can remove observers at any time.

We never need to modify the subject to add new types of observers. Let's say we have a new concrete class come along that needs to be an observer. We don't need to make any changes to the subject to accommodate the new class type, all we have to do is implement the Observer interface in the new class and register as an observer. The subject doesn't care; it will deliver notifications to any object that implements the Observer interface.

We can reuse subjects or observers independently of each other. If we have another use for a subject or an observer, we can easily reuse them because the two aren't tightly coupled.

Changes to either the subject or an observer will not affect the other. Because the two are loosely coupled, we are free to make changes to either, as long as the objects still meet their obligations to implement the subject or observer interfaces.

How many different kinds of change can you identify here?

> **Design Principle**
>
> *Strive for loosely coupled designs between objects that interact.*

Loosely coupled designs allow us to build flexible OO systems that can handle change because they minimize the interdependency between objects.

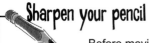

Sharpen your pencil

Before moving on, try sketching out the classes you'll need to implement the Weather Station, including the WeatherData class and its display elements. Make sure your diagram shows how all the pieces fit together and also how another developer might implement her own display element.

If you need a little help, read the next page; your teammates are already talking about how to design the Weather Station.

Cubicle conversation

Back to the Weather Station project, your teammates have already started thinking through the problem...

So, how are we going to build this thing?

Sue

Mary: Well, it helps to know we're using the Observer Pattern.

Sue: Right... but how do we apply it?

Mary: Hmm. Let's look at the definition again:

The Observer Pattern defines a one-to-many dependency between objects so that when one object changes state, all its dependents are notified and updated automatically.

Mary: That actually makes some sense when you think about it. Our WeatherData class is the "one" and our "many" is the various display elements that use the weather measurements.

Sue: That's right. The WeatherData class certainly has state... that's the temperature, humidity and barometric pressure, and those definitely change.

Mary: Yup, and when those measurements change, we have to notify all the display elements so they can do whatever it is they are going to do with the measurements.

Sue: Cool, I now think I see how the Observer Pattern can be applied to our Weather Station problem.

Mary: There are still a few things to consider that I'm not sure I understand yet.

Sue: Like what?

Mary: For one thing, how do we get the weather measurements to the display elements?

Sue: Well, looking back at the picture of the Observer Pattern, if we make the WeatherData object the subject, and the display elements the observers, then the displays will register themselves with the WeatherData object in order to get the information they want, right?

Mary: Yes... and once the Weather Station knows about a display element, then it can just call a method to tell it about the measurements.

Sue: We gotta remember that every display element can be different... so I think that's where having a common interface comes in. Even though every component has a different type, they should all implement the same interface so that the WeatherData object will know how to send them the measurements.

Mary: I see what you mean. So every display will have, say, an update() method that WeatherData will call.

Sue: And update() is defined in a common interface that all the elements implement...

Designing the Weather Station

How does this diagram compare with yours?

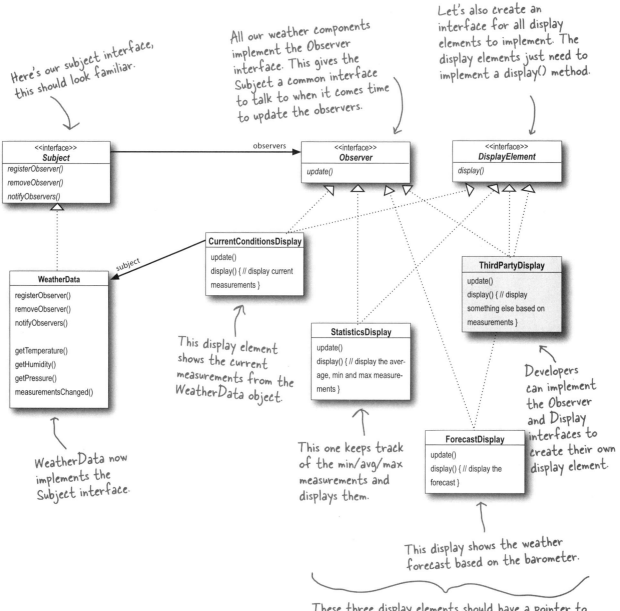

Here's our subject interface, this should look familiar.

All our weather components implement the Observer interface. This gives the Subject a common interface to talk to when it comes time to update the observers.

Let's also create an interface for all display elements to implement. The display elements just need to implement a display() method.

<<interface>>
Subject
registerObserver()
removeObserver()
notifyObservers()

observers

<<interface>>
Observer
update()

<<interface>>
DisplayElement
display()

subject

WeatherData
registerObserver()
removeObserver()
notifyObservers()

getTemperature()
getHumidity()
getPressure()
measurementsChanged()

CurrentConditionsDisplay
update()
display() { // display current measurements }

ThirdPartyDisplay
update()
display() { // display something else based on measurements }

StatisticsDisplay
update()
display() { // display the average, min and max measurements }

ForecastDisplay
update()
display() { // display the forecast }

This display element shows the current measurements from the WeatherData object.

WeatherData now implements the Subject interface.

This one keeps track of the min/avg/max measurements and displays them.

Developers can implement the Observer and Display interfaces to create their own display element.

This display shows the weather forecast based on the barometer.

These three display elements should have a pointer to WeatherData labeled "subject" too, but boy would this diagram start to look like spaghetti if they did.

Implementing the Weather Station

We're going to start our implementation using the class diagram and following Mary and Sue's lead (from a few pages back). You'll see later in this chapter that Java provides some built-in support for the Observer pattern, however, we're going to get our hands dirty and roll our own for now. While in some cases you can make use of Java's built-in support, in a lot of cases it's more flexible to build your own (and it's not all that hard). So, let's get started with the interfaces:

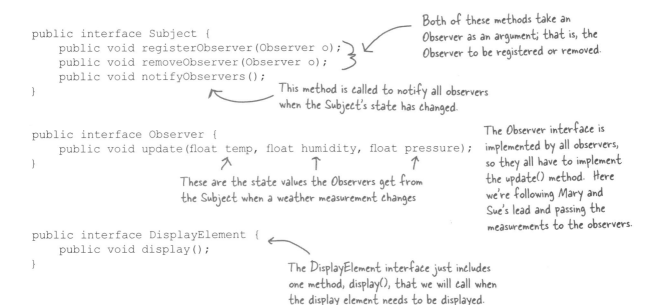

```java
public interface Subject {
    public void registerObserver(Observer o);
    public void removeObserver(Observer o);
    public void notifyObservers();
}
```

Both of these methods take an Observer as an argument; that is, the Observer to be registered or removed.

This method is called to notify all observers when the Subject's state has changed.

```java
public interface Observer {
    public void update(float temp, float humidity, float pressure);
}
```

These are the state values the Observers get from the Subject when a weather measurement changes

The Observer interface is implemented by all observers, so they all have to implement the update() method. Here we're following Mary and Sue's lead and passing the measurements to the observers.

```java
public interface DisplayElement {
    public void display();
}
```

The DisplayElement interface just includes one method, display(), that we will call when the display element needs to be displayed.

BRAIN POWER

Mary and Sue thought that passing the measurements directly to the observers was the most straightforward method of updating state. Do you think this is wise? Hint: is this an area of the application that might change in the future? If it did change, would the change be well encapsulated, or would it require changes in many parts of the code?

Can you think of other ways to approach the problem of passing the updated state to the observers?

Don't worry, we'll come back to this design decision after we finish the initial implementation.

Implementing the Subject interface in WeatherData

Remember our first attempt at implementing the WeatherData class at the beginning of the chapter? You might want to refresh your memory. Now it's time to go back and do things with the Observer Pattern in mind...

REMEMBER: we don't provide import and package statements in the code listings. Get the complete source code from the headfirstlabs web site. You'll find the URL on page xxxiii in the Intro.

```java
public class WeatherData implements Subject {
    private ArrayList observers;
    private float temperature;
    private float humidity;
    private float pressure;

    public WeatherData() {
        observers = new ArrayList();
    }

    public void registerObserver(Observer o) {
        observers.add(o);
    }

    public void removeObserver(Observer o) {
        int i = observers.indexOf(o);
        if (i >= 0) {
            observers.remove(i);
        }
    }

    public void notifyObservers() {
        for (int i = 0; i < observers.size(); i++) {
            Observer observer = (Observer)observers.get(i);
            observer.update(temperature, humidity, pressure);
        }
    }

    public void measurementsChanged() {
        notifyObservers();
    }

    public void setMeasurements(float temperature, float humidity, float pressure) {
        this.temperature = temperature;
        this.humidity = humidity;
        this.pressure = pressure;
        measurementsChanged();
    }

    // other WeatherData methods here
}
```

WeatherData now implements the Subject interface.

We've added an ArrayList to hold the Observers, and we create it in the constructor.

When an observer registers, we just add it to the end of the list.

Likewise, when an observer wants to un-register, we just take it off the list.

Here's the fun part; this is where we tell all the observers about the state. Because they are all Observers, we know they all implement update(), so we know how to notify them.

Here we implement the Subject Interface.

We notify the Observers when we get updated measurements from the Weather Station.

Okay, while we wanted to ship a nice little weather station with each book, the publisher wouldn't go for it. So, rather than reading actual weather data off a device, we're going to use this method to test our display elements. Or, for fun, you could write code to grab measurements off the web.

Now, let's build those display elements

Now that we've got our WeatherData class straightened out, it's time to build the Display Elements. Weather-O-Rama ordered three: the current conditions display, the statistics display and the forecast display. Let's take a look at the current conditions display; once you have a good feel for this display element, check out the statistics and forecast displays in the head first code directory. You'll see they are very similar.

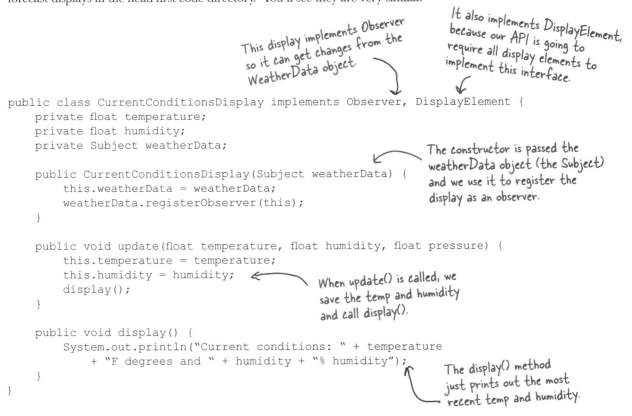

This display implements Observer so it can get changes from the WeatherData object.

It also implements DisplayElement, because our API is going to require all display elements to implement this interface.

```java
public class CurrentConditionsDisplay implements Observer, DisplayElement {
    private float temperature;
    private float humidity;
    private Subject weatherData;

    public CurrentConditionsDisplay(Subject weatherData) {
        this.weatherData = weatherData;
        weatherData.registerObserver(this);
    }

    public void update(float temperature, float humidity, float pressure) {
        this.temperature = temperature;
        this.humidity = humidity;
        display();
    }

    public void display() {
        System.out.println("Current conditions: " + temperature
            + "F degrees and " + humidity + "% humidity");
    }
}
```

The constructor is passed the weatherData object (the Subject) and we use it to register the display as an observer.

When update() is called, we save the temp and humidity and call display().

The display() method just prints out the most recent temp and humidity.

---

there are no
Dumb Questions

Q: **Is update() the best place to call display?**

A: In this simple example it made sense to call display() when the values changed. However, you are right, there are much better ways to design the way the data gets displayed. We are going to see this when we get to the model-view-controller pattern.

Q: **Why did you store a reference to the Subject? It doesn't look like you use it again after the constructor?**

A: True, but in the future we may want to un-register ourselves as an observer and it would be handy to already have a reference to the subject.

Power up the Weather Station

❶ First, let's create a test harness

The Weather Station is ready to go, all we need is some code to glue everything together. Here's our first attempt. We'll come back later in the book and make sure all the components are easily pluggable via a configuration file. For now here's how it all works:

```java
public class WeatherStation {
    public static void main(String[] args) {
        WeatherData weatherData = new WeatherData();

        CurrentConditionsDisplay currentDisplay =
            new CurrentConditionsDisplay(weatherData);
        StatisticsDisplay statisticsDisplay = new StatisticsDisplay(weatherData);
        ForecastDisplay forecastDisplay = new ForecastDisplay(weatherData);

        weatherData.setMeasurements(80, 65, 30.4f);
        weatherData.setMeasurements(82, 70, 29.2f);
        weatherData.setMeasurements(78, 90, 29.2f);
    }
}
```

First, create the WeatherData object.

If you don't want to download the code, you can comment out these two lines and run it.

Create the three displays and pass them the WeatherData object.

Simulate new weather measurements.

❷ Run the code and let the Observer Pattern do its magic

```
File  Edit  Window  Help  StormyWeather
%java WeatherStation
Current conditions: 80.0F degrees and 65.0% humidity
Avg/Max/Min temperature = 80.0/80.0/80.0
Forecast: Improving weather on the way!
Current conditions: 82.0F degrees and 70.0% humidity
Avg/Max/Min temperature = 81.0/82.0/80.0
Forecast: Watch out for cooler, rainy weather
Current conditions: 78.0F degrees and 90.0% humidity
Avg/Max/Min temperature = 80.0/82.0/78.0
Forecast: More of the same
%
```

Sharpen your pencil

Johnny Hurricane, Weather-O-Rama's CEO just called, they can't possibly ship without a Heat Index display element. Here are the details:

The heat index is an index that combines temperature and humidity to determine the apparent temperature (how hot it actually feels). To compute the heat index, you take the temperature, T, and the relative humidity, RH, and use this formula:

heatindex =

$$16.923 + 1.85212 * 10^{-1} * T + 5.37941 * RH - 1.00254 * 10^{-1} * T$$
$$* RH + 9.41695 * 10^{-3} * T^2 + 7.28898 * 10^{-3} * RH^2 + 3.45372 * 10^{-4}$$
$$* T^2 * RH - 8.14971 * 10^{-4} * T * RH^2 + 1.02102 * 10^{-5} * T^2 * RH^2 -$$
$$3.8646 * 10^{-5} * T^3 + 2.91583 * 10^{-5} * RH^3 + 1.42721 * 10^{-6} * T^3 * RH$$
$$+ 1.97483 * 10^{-7} * T * RH^3 - 2.18429 * 10^{-8} * T^3 * RH^2 + 8.43296 *$$
$$10^{-10} * T^2 * RH^3 - 4.81975 * 10^{-11} * T^3 * RH^3$$

So get typing!

Just kidding. Don't worry, you won't have to type that formula in; just create your own HeatIndexDisplay. java file and copy the formula from heatindex.txt into it.

↖ ——— You can get heatindex.txt from headfirstlabs.com

How does it work? You'd have to refer to *Head First Meteorology*, or try asking someone at the National Weather Service (or try a Google search).

When you finish, your output should look like this:

Here's what changed in this output.

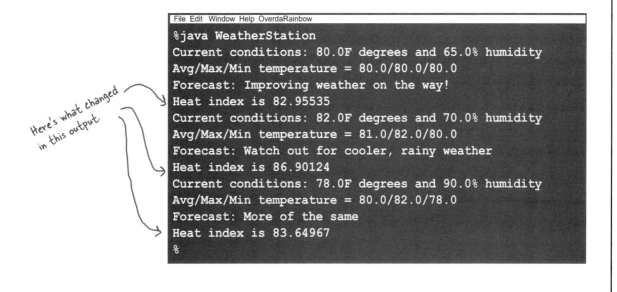

```
File Edit Window Help OverdaRainbow
%java WeatherStation
Current conditions: 80.0F degrees and 65.0% humidity
Avg/Max/Min temperature = 80.0/80.0/80.0
Forecast: Improving weather on the way!
Heat index is 82.95535
Current conditions: 82.0F degrees and 70.0% humidity
Avg/Max/Min temperature = 81.0/82.0/80.0
Forecast: Watch out for cooler, rainy weather
Heat index is 86.90124
Current conditions: 78.0F degrees and 90.0% humidity
Avg/Max/Min temperature = 80.0/82.0/78.0
Forecast: More of the same
Heat index is 83.64967
%
```

Fireside Chats

Tonight's talk: **A Subject and Observer spar over the right way to get state information to the Observer.**

Subject

I'm glad we're finally getting a chance to chat in person.

Well, I do my job, don't I? I always tell you what's going on... Just because I don't really know who you are doesn't mean I don't care. And besides, I do know the most important thing about you— you implement the Observer interface.

Oh yeah, like what?

Well *excuuuse* me. I have to send my state with my notifications so all you lazy Observers will know what happened!

Well... I guess that might work. I'd have to open myself up even more though to let all you Observers come in and get the state that you need. That might be kind of dangerous. I can't let you come in and just snoop around looking at everything I've got.

Observer

Really? I thought you didn't care much about us Observers.

Well yeah, but that's just a small part of who I am. Anyway, I know a lot more about you...

Well, you're always passing your state around to us Observers so we can see what's going on inside you. Which gets a little annoying at times...

Ok, wait just a minute here; first, we're not lazy, we just have other stuff to do in between your oh-so-important notifications, Mr. Subject, and second, why don't you let us come to you for the state we want rather than pushing it out to just everyone?

Subject

Yes, I could let you **pull** my state. But won't that be less convenient for you? If you have to come to me every time you want something, you might have to make multiple method calls to get all the state you want. That's why I like **push** better... then you have everything you need in one notification.

Well, I can see the advantages to doing it both ways. I have noticed that there is a built-in Java Observer Pattern that allows you to use either push or pull.

Great... maybe I'll get to see a good example of pull and change my mind.

Observer

Why don't you just write some public getter methods that will let us pull out the state we need?

Don't be so pushy! There's so many different kinds of us Observers, there's no way you can anticipate everything we need. Just let us come to you to get the state we need. That way, if some of us only need a little bit of state, we aren't forced to get it all. It also makes things easier to modify later. Say, for example, you expand yourself and add some more state, well if you use pull, you don't have to go around and change the update calls on every observer, you just need to change yourself to allow more getter methods to access our additional state.

Oh really? I think we're going to look at that next....

What, us agree on something? I guess there's always hope.

Using Java's built-in Observer Pattern

So far we've rolled our own code for the Observer Pattern, but Java has built-in support in several of its APIs. The most general is the Observer interface and the Observable class in the java.util package. These are quite similar to our Subject and Observer interface, but give you a lot of functionality out of the box. You can also implement either a push or pull style of update to your observers, as you will see.

To get a high level feel for java.util.Observer and java.util.Observable, check out this reworked OO design for the WeatherStation:

> With Java's built-in support, all you have to do is extend Observable and tell it when to notify the Observers. The API does the rest for you.

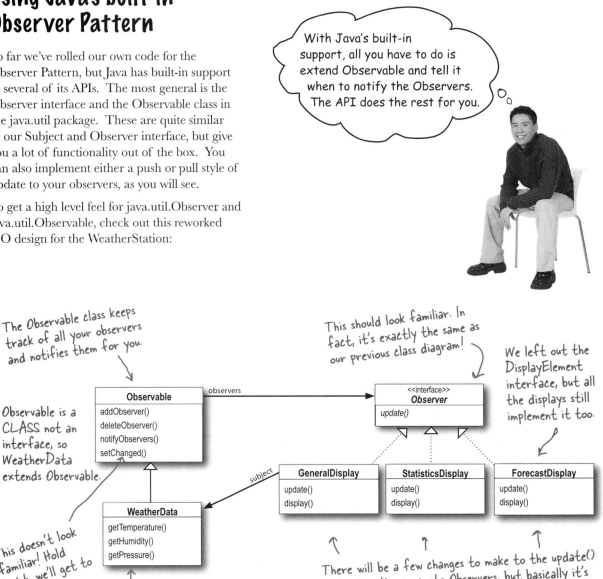

The Observable class keeps track of all your observers and notifies them for you.

Observable is a CLASS not an interface, so WeatherData extends Observable.

This should look familiar. In fact, it's exactly the same as our previous class diagram!

We left out the DisplayElement interface, but all the displays still implement it too.

This doesn't look familiar! Hold tight, we'll get to this in a sec...

Here's our Subject, which we can now also call the Observable. We don't need the register(), remove() and notifyObservers() methods anymore; we inherit that behavior from the superclass.

There will be a few changes to make to the update() method in the concrete Observers, but basically it's the same idea... we have a common Observer interface, with an update() method that's called by the Subject.

How Java's built-in Observer Pattern works

The built in Observer Pattern works a bit differently than the implementation that we used on the Weather Station. The most obvious difference is that WeatherData (our subject) now extends the Observable class and inherits the add, delete and notify Observer methods (among a few others). Here's how we use Java's version:

For an Object to become an observer...

As usual, implement the Observer interface (this time the java.util.Observer interface) and call addObserver() on any Observable object. Likewise, to remove yourself as an observer just call deleteObserver().

For the Observable to send notifications...

First of all you need to be Observable by extending the java.util.Observable superclass. From there it is a two step process:

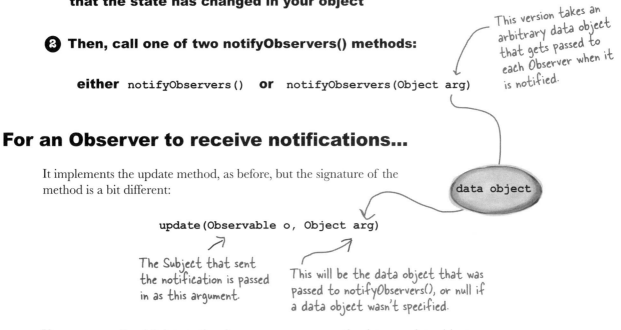

1 You first must call the setChanged() method to signify that the state has changed in your object

2 Then, call one of two notifyObservers() methods:

either notifyObservers() **or** notifyObservers(Object arg)

This version takes an arbitrary data object that gets passed to each Observer when it is notified.

For an Observer to receive notifications...

It implements the update method, as before, but the signature of the method is a bit different:

update(Observable o, Object arg)

data object

The Subject that sent the notification is passed in as this argument.

This will be the data object that was passed to notifyObservers(), or null if a data object wasn't specified.

If you want to "push" data to the observers you can pass the data as a data object to the notifyObserver(arg) method. If not, then the Observer has to "pull" the data it wants from the Observable object passed to it. How? Let's rework the Weather Station and you'll see.

Wait, before we get to that, why do we need this setChanged() method? We didn't need that before.

The setChanged() method is used to signify that the state has changed and that notifyObservers(), when it is called, should update its observers. If notifyObservers() is called without first calling setChanged(), the observers will NOT be notified. Let's take a look behind the scenes of Observable to see how this works:

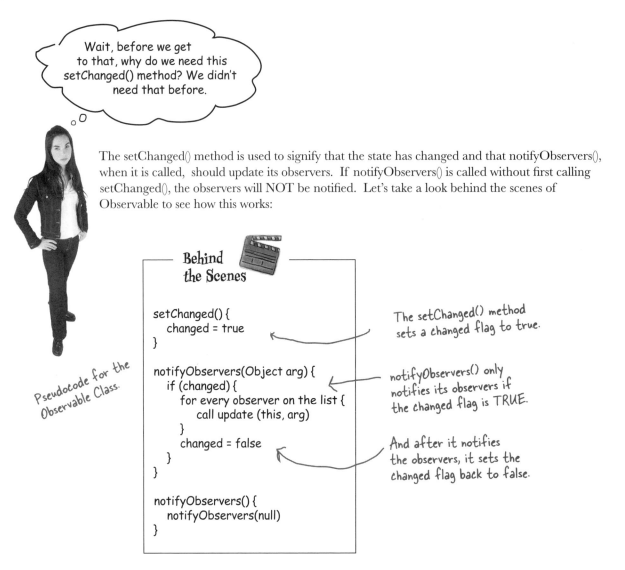

Behind the Scenes

```
setChanged() {
    changed = true
}

notifyObservers(Object arg) {
    if (changed) {
        for every observer on the list {
            call update (this, arg)
        }
        changed = false
    }
}

notifyObservers() {
    notifyObservers(null)
}
```

Pseudocode for the Observable Class.

The setChanged() method sets a changed flag to true.

notifyObservers() only notifies its observers if the changed flag is TRUE.

And after it notifies the observers, it sets the changed flag back to false.

Why is this necessary? The setChanged() method is meant to give you more flexibility in how you update observers by allowing you to optimize the notifications. For example, in our weather station, imagine if our measurements were so sensitive that the temperature readings were constantly fluctuating by a few tenths of a degree. That might cause the WeatherData object to send out notifications constantly. Instead, we might want to send out notifications only if the temperature changes more than half a degree and we could call setChanged() only after that happened.

You might not use this functionality very often, but it's there if you need it. In either case, you need to call setChanged() for notifications to work. If this functionality is something that is useful to you, you may also want to use the clearChanged() method, which sets the changed state back to false, and the hasChanged() method, which tells you the current state of the changed flag.

Reworking the Weather Station with the built-in support

First, let's rework WeatherData to use java.util.Observable

❶ Make sure we are importing the right Observer/Observable.

❷ We are now subclassing Observable.

❸ We don't need to keep track of our observers anymore, or manage their registration and removal, (the superclass will handle that) so we've removed the code for register, add and notify.

❹ Our constructor no longer needs to create a data structure to hold Observers.

✱ Notice we aren't sending a data object with the notifyObservers() call. That means we're using the PULL model.

❺ We now first call setChanged() to indicate the state has changed before calling notifyObservers().

❻ These methods aren't new, but because we are going to use "pull" we thought we'd remind you they are here. The Observers will use them to get at the WeatherData object's state.

```java
import java.util.Observable;
import java.util.Observer;

public class WeatherData extends Observable {
    private float temperature;
    private float humidity;
    private float pressure;

    public WeatherData() { }

    public void measurementsChanged() {
        setChanged();
        notifyObservers(); ✱
    }

    public void setMeasurements(float temperature, float humidity, float pressure) {
        this.temperature = temperature;
        this.humidity = humidity;
        this.pressure = pressure;
        measurementsChanged();
    }

    public float getTemperature() {
        return temperature;
    }

    public float getHumidity() {
        return humidity;
    }

    public float getPressure() {
        return pressure;
    }
}
```

Now, let's rework the CurrentConditionsDisplay

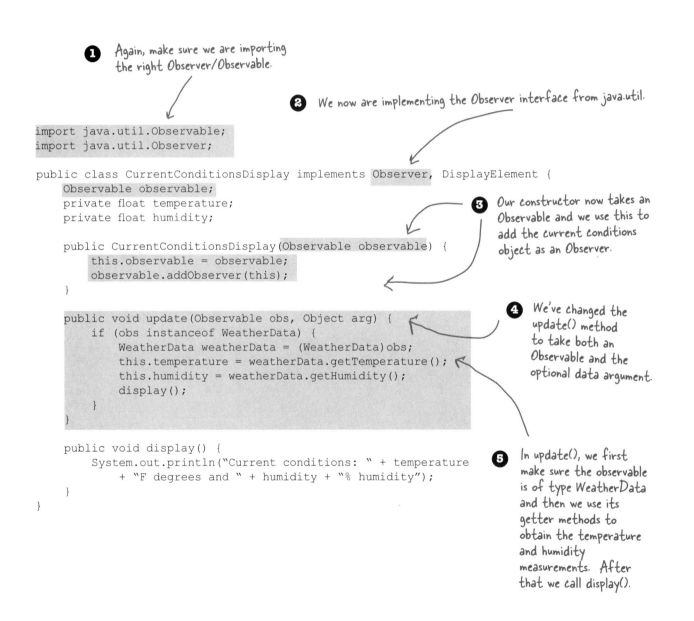

① Again, make sure we are importing the right Observer/Observable.

② We now are implementing the Observer interface from java.util.

```java
import java.util.Observable;
import java.util.Observer;

public class CurrentConditionsDisplay implements Observer, DisplayElement {
    Observable observable;
    private float temperature;
    private float humidity;

    public CurrentConditionsDisplay(Observable observable) {
        this.observable = observable;
        observable.addObserver(this);
    }

    public void update(Observable obs, Object arg) {
        if (obs instanceof WeatherData) {
            WeatherData weatherData = (WeatherData)obs;
            this.temperature = weatherData.getTemperature();
            this.humidity = weatherData.getHumidity();
            display();
        }
    }

    public void display() {
        System.out.println("Current conditions: " + temperature
            + "F degrees and " + humidity + "% humidity");
    }
}
```

③ Our constructor now takes an Observable and we use this to add the current conditions object as an Observer.

④ We've changed the update() method to take both an Observable and the optional data argument.

⑤ In update(), we first make sure the observable is of type WeatherData and then we use its getter methods to obtain the temperature and humidity measurements. After that we call display().

Code Magnets

Exercise

The ForecastDisplay class is all scrambled up on the fridge. Can you reconstruct the code snippets to make it work? Some of the curly braces fell on the floor and they were too small to pick up, so feel free to add as many of those as you need!

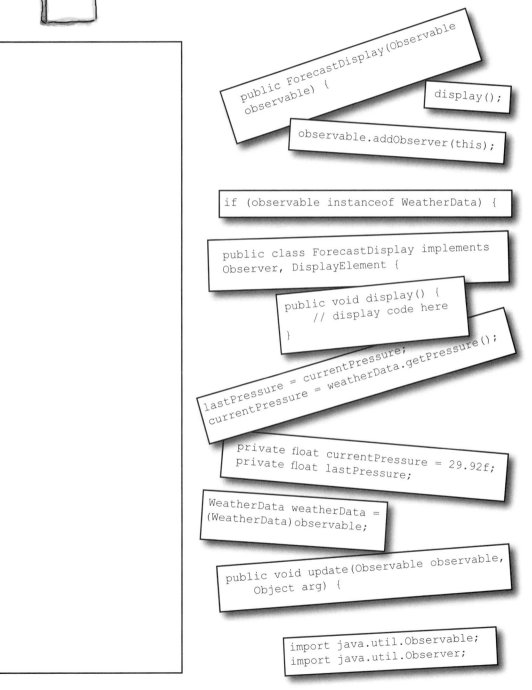

```
public ForecastDisplay(Observable
    observable) {
```

```
display();
```

```
observable.addObserver(this);
```

```
if (observable instanceof WeatherData) {
```

```
public class ForecastDisplay implements
Observer, DisplayElement {
```

```
public void display() {
    // display code here
}
```

```
lastPressure = currentPressure;
currentPressure = weatherData.getPressure();
```

```
private float currentPressure = 29.92f;
private float lastPressure;
```

```
WeatherData weatherData =
(WeatherData)observable;
```

```
public void update(Observable observable,
    Object arg) {
```

```
import java.util.Observable;
import java.util.Observer;
```

Running the new code

Just to be sure, let's run the new code...

```
File Edit  Window  Help  TryTihisAtHome
%java WeatherStation
Forecast: Improving weather on the way!
Avg/Max/Min temperature = 80.0/80.0/80.0
Current conditions: 80.0F degrees and 65.0% humidity
Forecast: Watch out for cooler, rainy weather
Avg/Max/Min temperature = 81.0/82.0/80.0
Current conditions: 82.0F degrees and 70.0% humidity
Forecast: More of the same
Avg/Max/Min temperature = 80.0/82.0/78.0
Current conditions: 78.0F degrees and 90.0% humidity
%
```

Hmm, do you notice anything different? Look again...

You'll see all the same calculations, but mysteriously, the order of the text output is different. Why might this happen? Think for a minute before reading on...

Never depend on order of evaluation of the Observer notifications

The java.util.Observable has implemented its notifyObservers() method such that the Observers are notified in a *different* order than our own implementation. Who's right? Neither; we just chose to implement things in different ways.

What would be incorrect, however, is if we wrote our code to *depend* on a specific notification order. Why? Because if you need to change Observable/Observer implementations, the order of notification could change and your application would produce incorrect results. Now that's definitely *not* what we'd consider loosely coupled.

> Doesn't java.util.Observable violate our OO design principle of programming to interfaces not implementations?

The dark side of java.util.Observable

Yes, good catch. As you've noticed, Observable is a *class*, not an *interface*, and worse, it doesn't even *implement* an interface. Unfortunately, the java.util.Observable implementation has a number of problems that limit its usefulness and reuse. That's not to say it doesn't provide some utility, but there are some large potholes to watch out for.

Observable is a class

You already know from our principles this is a bad idea, but what harm does it really cause?

First, because Observable is a *class*, you have to *subclass* it. That means you can't add on the Observable behavior to an existing class that already extends another superclass. This limits its reuse potential (and isn't that why we are using patterns in the first place?).

Second, because there isn't an Observable interface, you can't even create your own implementation that plays well with Java's built-in Observer API. Nor do you have the option of swapping out the java.util implementation for another (say, a new, multi-threaded implementation).

Observable protects crucial methods

If you look at the Observable API, the setChanged() method is protected. So what? Well, this means you can't call setChanged() unless you've subclassed Observable. This means you can't even create an instance of the Observable class and compose it with your own objects, you *have* to subclass. The design violates a second design principle here...*favor composition over inheritance.*

What to do?

Observable *may* serve your needs if you can extend java.util.Observable. On the other hand, you may need to roll your own implementation as we did at the beginning of the chapter. In either case, you know the Observer Pattern well and you're in a good position to work with any API that makes use of the pattern.

Other places you'll find the Observer Pattern in the JDK

The java.util implementation of Observer/Observable is not the only place you'll find the Observer Pattern in the JDK; both JavaBeans and Swing also provide their own implementations of the pattern. At this point you understand enough about observer to explore these APIs on your own; however, let's do a quick, simple Swing example just for the fun of it.

If you're curious about the Observer Pattern in JavaBeans check out the PropertyChangeListener interface.

A little background...

Let's take a look at a simple part of the Swing API, the JButton. If you look under the hood at JButton's superclass, AbstractButton, you'll see that it has a lot of add/remove listener methods. These methods allow you to add and remove observers, or as they are called in Swing, listeners, to listen for various types of events that occur on the Swing component. For instance, an ActionListener lets you "listen in" on any types of actions that might occur on a button, like a button press. You'll find various types of listeners all over the Swing API.

A little life-changing application

Okay, our application is pretty simple. You've got a button that says "Should I do it?" and when you click on that button the listeners (observers) get to answer the question in any way they want. We're implementing two such listeners, called the AngelListener and the DevilListener. Here's how the application behaves:

Here's our fancy interface.

Should I do it?

And here's the output when we click on the button.

File Edit Window Help HeMadeMeDolt

```
%java SwingObserverExample
Come on, do it!
Don't do it, you might regret it!
%
```

Devil answer →

Angel answer →

And the code...

This life-changing application requires very little code. All we need to do is
create a JButton object, add it to a JFrame and set up our listeners. We're going
to use inner classes for the listeners, which is a common technique in Swing
programming. If you aren't up on inner classes or Swing you might want to
review the "Getting GUI" chapter of Head First Java.

Simple Swing application that just creates a frame and throws a button in it.

```java
public class SwingObserverExample {
    JFrame frame;

    public static void main(String[] args) {
        SwingObserverExample example = new SwingObserverExample();
        example.go();
    }

    public void go() {
        frame = new JFrame();
        JButton button = new JButton("Should I do it?");
        button.addActionListener(new AngelListener());
        button.addActionListener(new DevilListener());
        frame.getContentPane().add(BorderLayout.CENTER, button);
        // Set frame properties here
    }

    class AngelListener implements ActionListener {
        public void actionPerformed(ActionEvent event) {
            System.out.println("Don't do it, you might regret it!");
        }
    }

    class DevilListener implements ActionListener {
        public void actionPerformed(ActionEvent event) {
            System.out.println("Come on, do it!");
        }
    }
}
```

Makes the devil and angel objects listeners (observers) of the button.

Here are the class definitions for the observers, defined as inner classes (but they don't have to be).

Rather than update(), the actionPerformed() method gets called when the state in the subject (in this case the button) changes.

Tools for your Design Toolbox

Welcome to the end of Chapter 2. You've added a few new things to your OO toolbox...

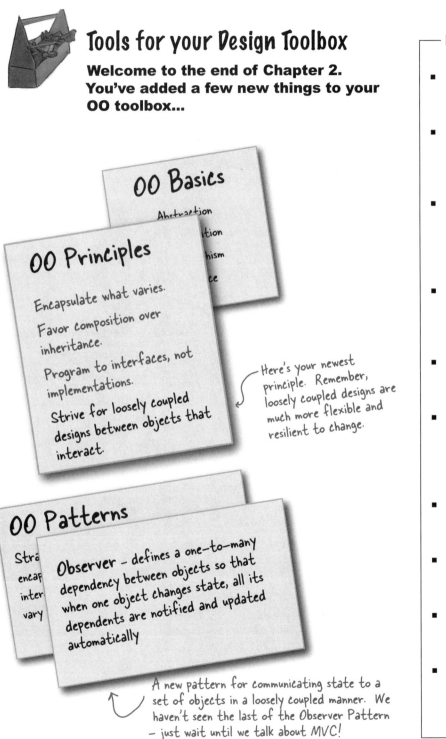

OO Basics

Abstraction
...tion
...hism
...ce

OO Principles

Encapsulate what varies.

Favor composition over inheritance.

Program to interfaces, not implementations.

Strive for loosely coupled designs between objects that interact.

> Here's your newest principle. Remember, loosely coupled designs are much more flexible and resilient to change.

OO Patterns

Stra...
encap...
inter...
vary...

Observer – defines a one–to–many dependency between objects so that when one object changes state, all its dependents are notified and updated automatically

> A new pattern for communicating state to a set of objects in a loosely coupled manner. We haven't seen the last of the Observer Pattern – just wait until we talk about MVC!

BULLET POINTS

- The Observer Pattern defines a one-to-many relationship between objects.

- Subjects, or as we also know them, Observables, update Observers using a common interface.

- Observers are loosely coupled in that the Observable knows nothing about them, other than that they implement the Observer Interface.

- You can push or pull data from the Observable when using the pattern (pull is considered more "correct").

- Don't depend on a specific order of notification for your Observers.

- Java has several implementations of the Observer Pattern, including the general purpose java.util.Observable.

- Watch out for issues with the java.util.Observable implementation.

- Don't be afraid to create your own Observable implementation if needed.

- Swing makes heavy use of the Observer Pattern, as do many GUI frameworks.

- You'll also find the pattern in many other places, including JavaBeans and RMI.

Exercise

Design Principle Challenge

For each design principle, describe how the Observer Pattern makes use of the principle.

_____

Design Principle

Identify the aspects of your application that vary and separate them from what stays the same.

_____
_____
_____
_____
_____
_____

Design Principle

Program to an interface, not an implementation.

_____
_____
_____
_____
_____
_____

This is a hard one, hint: think about how observers
and subjects work together.

_____

Design Principle

Favor composition over inheritance.

_____
_____
_____
_____

Time to give your right brain something to do again!

This time all of the solution words are from chapter 2.

Across

1. Observable is a _____ not an interface
3. Devil and Angel are _____ to the button
4. Implement this method to get notified
5. Jill got one of her own
6. CurrentConditionsDisplay implements this interface
8. How to get yourself off the Observer list
12. You forgot this if you're not getting notified when you think you should be
15. One Subject likes to talk to _____ observers
18. Don't count on this for notification
19. Temperature, humidity and _____
20. Observers are _____ on the Subject
21. Program to an _____ not an implementation
22. A Subject is similar to a _____

Down

2. Ron was both an Observer and a _____
3. You want to keep your coupling _____
7. He says you should go for it
9. _____ can manage your observers for you
10. Java framework with lots of Observers
11. Weather-O-Rama's CEO named after this kind of storm
13. Observers like to be _____ when something new happens
14. The WeatherData class _____ the Subject interface
16. He didn't want any more ints, so he removed himself
17. CEO almost forgot the _____ index display
19. Subject initially wanted to ____ all the data to Observer

Exercise solutions

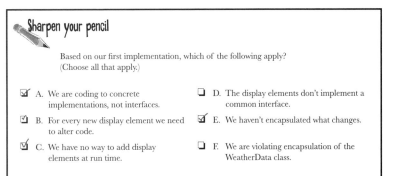

✏️ **Sharpen your pencil**

Based on our first implementation, which of the following apply?
(Choose all that apply.)

☑ A. We are coding to concrete implementations, not interfaces.

☐ D. The display elements don't implement a common interface.

☑ B. For every new display element we need to alter code.

☑ E. We haven't encapsulated what changes.

☑ C. We have no way to add display elements at run time.

☐ F. We are violating encapsulation of the WeatherData class.

Design Principle Challenge

Design Principle

Identify the aspects of your application that vary and separate them from what stays the same.

The thing that varies in the Observer Pattern is the state of the Subject and the number and types of Observers. With this pattern, you can vary the objects that are dependent on the state of the Subject, without having to change that Subject. That's called planning ahead!

Design Principle

Program to an interface, not an implementation.

Both the Subject and Observer use interfaces. The Subject keeps track of objects implementing the Observer interface, while the observers register with, and get notified by, the Subject interface. As we've seen, this keeps things nice and loosely coupled.

Design Principle

Favor composition over inheritance.

The Observer Pattern uses composition to compose any number of Observers with their Subjects. These relationships aren't set up by some kind of inheritance hierarchy. No, they are set up at runtime by composition!

Exercise solutions

Code Magnets

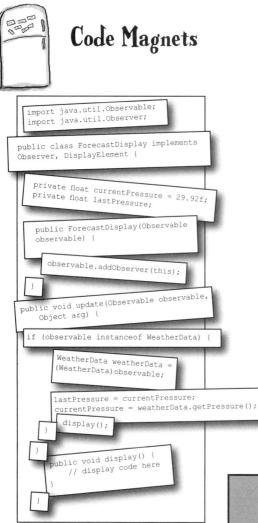

```java
import java.util.Observable;
import java.util.Observer;

public class ForecastDisplay implements
Observer, DisplayElement {

    private float currentPressure = 29.92f;
    Private float lastPressure;

    public ForecastDisplay(Observable
    observable) {
        observable.addObserver(this);
    }

    public void update(Observable observable,
        Object arg) {
        if (observable instanceof WeatherData) {
            WeatherData weatherData =
            (WeatherData)observable;
            lastPressure = currentPressure;
            currentPressure = weatherData.getPressure();
            display();
        }
    }

    public void display() {
        // display code here
    }
}
```

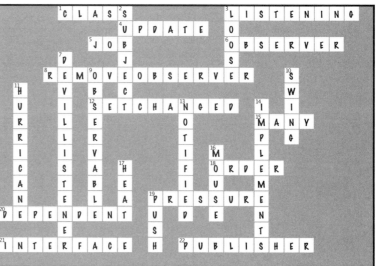

3 the Decorator Pattern

Decorating Objects

I used to think real men subclassed everything. That was until I learned the power of extension at runtime, rather than at compile time. Now look at me!

Just call this chapter "Design Eye for the Inheritance Guy."

We'll re-examine the typical overuse of inheritance and you'll learn how to decorate your classes at runtime using a form of object composition. Why? Once you know the techniques of decorating, you'll be able to give your (or someone else's) objects new responsibilities *without making any code changes to the underlying classes.*

Welcome to Starbuzz Coffee

Starbuzz Coffee has made a name for itself as the fastest growing coffee shop around. If you've seen one on your local corner, look across the street; you'll see another one.

Because they've grown so quickly, they're scrambling to update their ordering systems to match their beverage offerings.

When they first went into business they designed their classes like this...

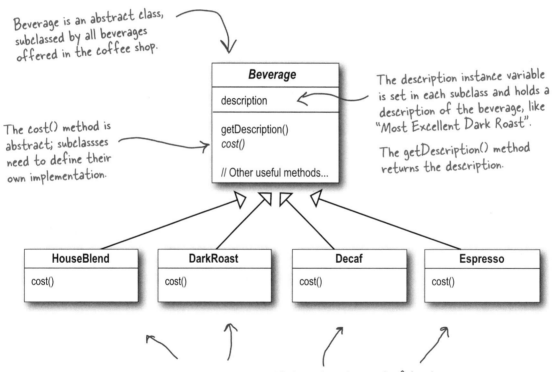

Beverage is an abstract class, subclassed by all beverages offered in the coffee shop.

The cost() method is abstract; subclasses need to define their own implementation.

Beverage

description

getDescription()
cost()

// Other useful methods...

The description instance variable is set in each subclass and holds a description of the beverage, like "Most Excellent Dark Roast".

The getDescription() method returns the description.

HouseBlend	DarkRoast	Decaf	Espresso
cost()	cost()	cost()	cost()

Each subclass implements cost() to return the cost of the beverage.

In addition to your coffee, you can also ask for several condiments like steamed milk, soy, and mocha (otherwise known as chocolate), and have it all topped off with whipped milk. Starbuzz charges a bit for each of these, so they really need to get them built into their order system.

Here's their first attempt...

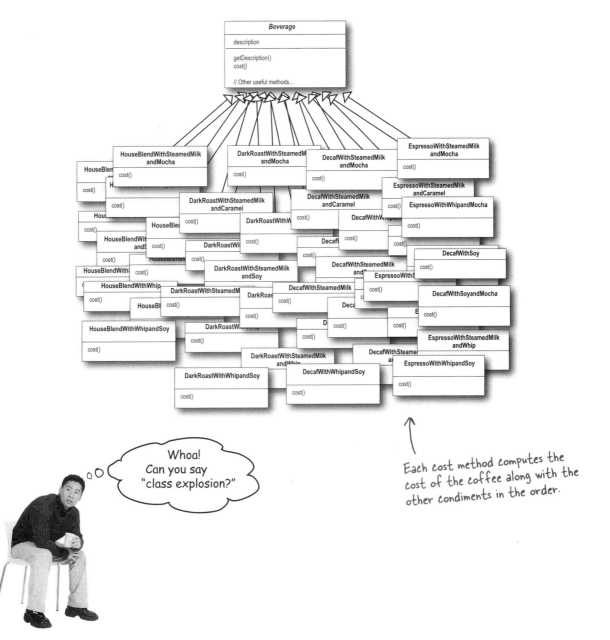

Each cost method computes the cost of the coffee along with the other condiments in the order.

Whoa! Can you say "class explosion?"

⚛ BRAIN POWER

It's pretty obvious that Starbuzz has created a maintenance nightmare for themselves. What happens when the price of milk goes up? What do they do when they add a new caramel topping?

Thinking beyond the maintenance problem, which of the design principles that we've covered so far are they violating?

Hint: they're violating two of them in a big way!

This is stupid; why do we need all these classes? Can't we just use instance variables and inheritance in the superclass to keep track of the condiments?

Well, let's give it a try. Let's start with the Beverage base class and add instance variables to represent whether or not each beverage has milk, soy, mocha and whip...

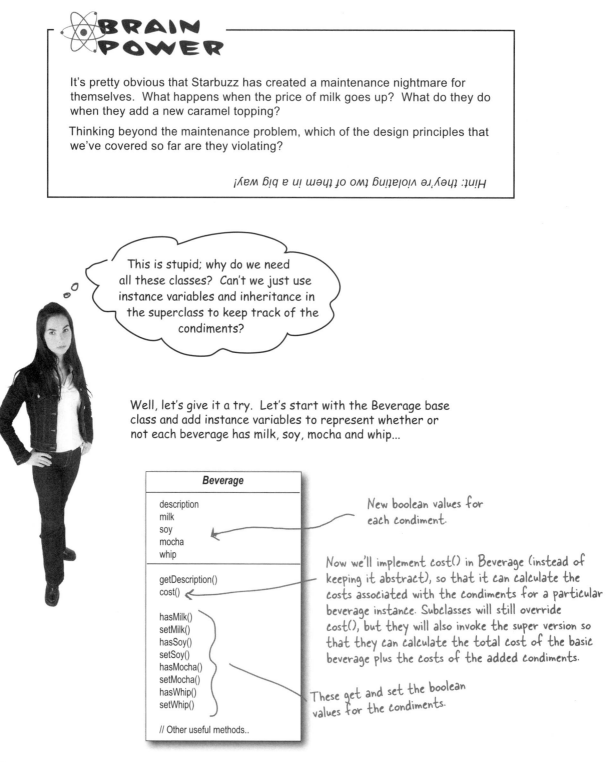

Beverage
description milk soy mocha whip
getDescription() cost()
hasMilk() setMilk() hasSoy() setSoy() hasMocha() setMocha() hasWhip() setWhip() // Other useful methods..

New boolean values for each condiment.

Now we'll implement cost() in Beverage (instead of keeping it abstract), so that it can calculate the costs associated with the condiments for a particular beverage instance. Subclasses will still override cost(), but they will also invoke the super version so that they can calculate the total cost of the basic beverage plus the costs of the added condiments.

These get and set the boolean values for the condiments.

Now let's add in the subclasses, one for each beverage on the menu:

The superclass cost() will calculate the costs for all of the condiments, while the overridden cost() in the subclasses will extend that functionality to include costs for that specific beverage type.

Each cost() method needs to compute the cost of the beverage and then add in the condiments by calling the superclass implementation of cost().

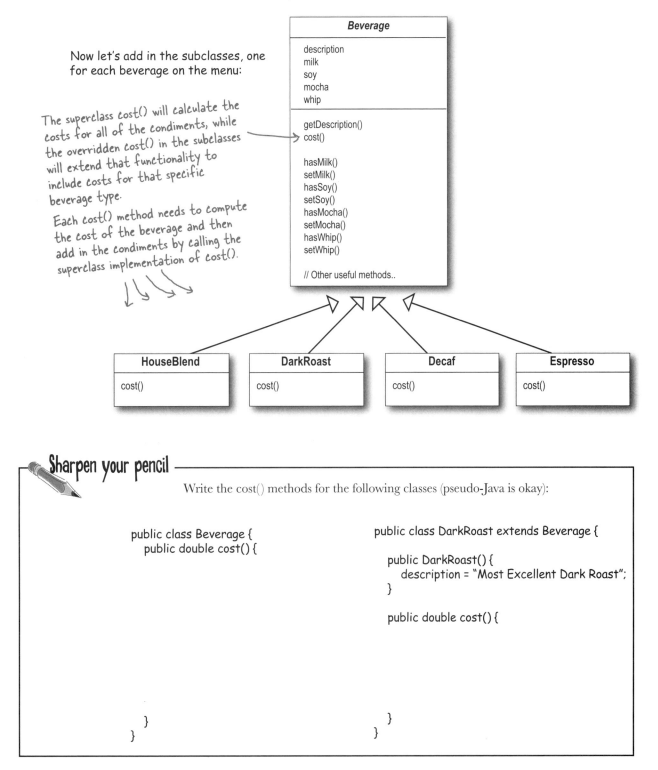

Beverage

description
milk
soy
mocha
whip

getDescription()
cost()

hasMilk()
setMilk()
hasSoy()
setSoy()
hasMocha()
setMocha()
hasWhip()
setWhip()

// Other useful methods..

HouseBlend	**DarkRoast**	**Decaf**	**Espresso**
cost()	cost()	cost()	cost()

Sharpen your pencil

Write the cost() methods for the following classes (pseudo-Java is okay):

```
public class Beverage {
    public double cost() {




        }
    }
```

```
public class DarkRoast extends Beverage {

    public DarkRoast() {
        description = "Most Excellent Dark Roast";
    }

    public double cost() {




        }
    }
```

See, five classes total. This is definitely the way to go.

I'm not so sure; I can see some potential problems with this approach by thinking about how the design might need to change in the future.

Sharpen your pencil

What requirements or other factors might change that will impact this design?

Price changes for condiments will force us to alter existing code.

New condiments will force us to add new methods and alter the cost method in the superclass.

We may have new beverages. For some of these beverages (iced tea?), the condiments may not be appropriate, yet the Tea subclass will still inherit methods like hasWhip().

What if a customer wants a double mocha?

As we saw in Chapter 1, this is a very bad idea!

Your turn:

_____

_____

Master and Student...

Master: *Grasshopper, it has been some time since our last meeting. Have you been deep in meditation on inheritance?*

Student: *Yes, Master. While inheritance is powerful, I have learned that it doesn't always lead to the most flexible or maintainable designs.*

Master: *Ah yes, you have made some progress. So, tell me my student, how then will you achieve reuse if not through inheritance?*

Student: *Master, I have learned there are ways of "inheriting" behavior at runtime through composition and delegation.*

Master: *Please, go on...*

Student: *When I inherit behavior by subclassing, that behavior is set statically at compile time. In addition, all subclasses must inherit the same behavior. If however, I can extend an object's behavior through composition, then I can do this dynamically at runtime.*

Master: *Very good, Grasshopper, you are beginning to see the power of composition.*

Student: *Yes, it is possible for me to add multiple new responsibilities to objects through this technique, including responsibilities that were not even thought of by the designer of the superclass. And, I don't have to touch their code!*

Master: *What have you learned about the effect of composition on maintaining your code?*

Student: *Well, that is what I was getting at. By dynamically composing objects, I can add new functionality by writing new code rather than altering existing code. Because I'm not changing existing code, the chances of introducing bugs or causing unintended side effects in pre-existing code are much reduced.*

Master: *Very good. Enough for today, Grasshopper. I would like for you to go and meditate further on this topic... Remember, code should be closed (to change) like the lotus flower in the evening, yet open (to extension) like the lotus flower in the morning.*

The Open-Closed Principle

Grasshopper is on to one of the most important design principles:

Design Principle

Classes should be open
for extension, but closed for
modification.

Come on in; we're
open. Feel free to extend
our classes with any new behavior you
like. If your needs or requirements change (and we
know they will), just go ahead and make your own
extensions.

Sorry, we're *closed*.
That's right, we spent
a lot of time getting this code correct and
bug free, so we can't let you alter the existing code.
It must remain closed to modification. If you don't
like it, you can speak to the manager.

**Our goal is to allow classes to be easily extended to
incorporate new behavior without modifying existing code.
What do we get if we accomplish this? Designs that are
resilient to change and flexible enough to take on new
functionality to meet changing requirements.**

there are no
Dumb Questions

Q: Open for extension and closed for modification? That sounds very contradictory. How can a design be both?

A: That's a very good question. It certainly sounds contradictory at first. After all, the less modifiable something is, the harder it is to extend, right?

As it turns out, though, there are some clever OO techniques for allowing systems to be extended, even if we can't change the underlying code. Think about the Observer Pattern (in Chapter 2)... by adding new Observers, we can extend the Subject at any time, without adding code to the Subject. You'll see quite a few more ways of extending behavior with other OO design techniques.

Q: Okay, I understand Observable, but how do I generally design something to be extensible, yet closed for modification?

A: Many of the patterns give us time tested designs that protect your code from being modified by supplying a means of extension. In this chapter you'll see a good example of using the Decorator pattern to follow the Open-Closed principle.

Q: How can I make every part of my design follow the Open-Closed Principle?

A: Usually, you can't. Making OO design flexible and open to extension without the modification of existing code takes time and effort. In general, we don't have the luxury of tying down every part of our designs (and it would probably be wasteful). Following the Open-Closed Principle usually introduces new levels of abstraction, which adds complexity to our code. You want to concentrate on those areas that are most likely to change in your designs and apply the principles there.

Q: How do I know which areas of change are more important?

A: That is partly a matter of experience in designing OO systems and also a matter of knowing the domain you are working in. Looking at other examples will help you learn to identify areas of change in your own designs.

While it may seem like a contradiction, there are techniques for allowing code to be extended without direct modification.

Be careful when choosing the areas of code that need to be extended; applying the Open-Closed Principle EVERYWHERE is wasteful, unnecessary, and can lead to complex, hard to understand code.

Meet the Decorator Pattern

Okay, enough of the "Object Oriented Design Club." We have real problems here! Remember us? Starbuzz Coffee? Do you think you could use some of those design principles to actually help us?

Okay, we've seen that representing our beverage plus condiment pricing scheme with inheritance has not worked out very well – we get class explosions, rigid designs, or we add functionality to the base class that isn't appropriate for some of the subclasses.

So, here's what we'll do instead: we'll start with a beverage and "decorate" it with the condiments at runtime. For example, if the customer wants a Dark Roast with Mocha and Whip, then we'll:

① Take a DarkRoast object

② Decorate it with a Mocha object

③ Decorate it with a Whip object

④ Call the cost() method and rely on delegation to add on the condiment costs

Okay, but how do you "decorate" an object, and how does delegation come into this? A hint: think of decorator objects as "wrappers." Let's see how this works...

Constructing a drink order with Decorators

① **We start with our DarkRoast object.**

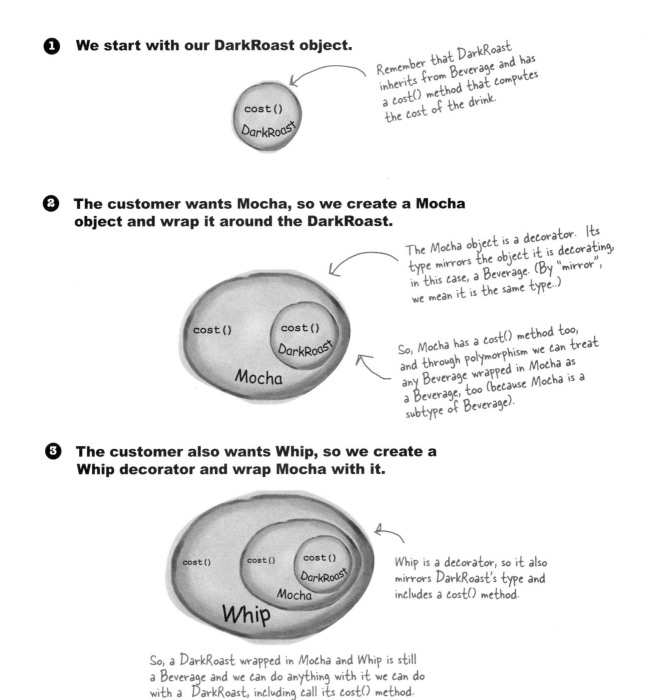

Remember that DarkRoast inherits from Beverage and has a cost() method that computes the cost of the drink.

② **The customer wants Mocha, so we create a Mocha object and wrap it around the DarkRoast.**

The Mocha object is a decorator. Its type mirrors the object it is decorating, in this case, a Beverage. (By "mirror", we mean it is the same type..)

So, Mocha has a cost() method too, and through polymorphism we can treat any Beverage wrapped in Mocha as a Beverage, too (because Mocha is a subtype of Beverage).

③ **The customer also wants Whip, so we create a Whip decorator and wrap Mocha with it.**

Whip is a decorator, so it also mirrors DarkRoast's type and includes a cost() method.

So, a DarkRoast wrapped in Mocha and Whip is still a Beverage and we can do anything with it we can do with a DarkRoast, including call its cost() method.

④ **Now it's time to compute the cost for the customer. We do this by calling cost() on the outermost decorator, Whip, and Whip is going to delegate computing the cost to the objects it decorates. Once it gets a cost, it will add on the cost of the Whip.**

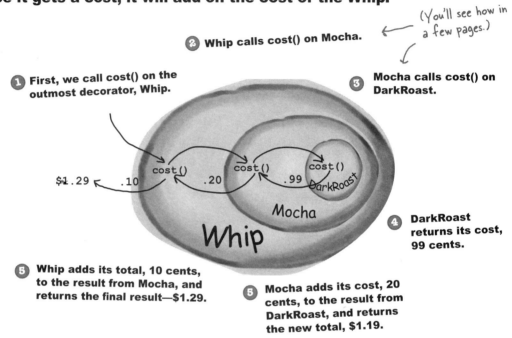

② Whip calls cost() on Mocha.

(You'll see how in a few pages.)

① First, we call cost() on the outmost decorator, Whip.

③ Mocha calls cost() on DarkRoast.

$1.29 ← .10 cost() .20 cost() .99 cost() DarkRoast

Mocha

Whip

④ DarkRoast returns its cost, 99 cents.

⑤ Whip adds its total, 10 cents, to the result from Mocha, and returns the final result—$1.29.

⑤ Mocha adds its cost, 20 cents, to the result from DarkRoast, and returns the new total, $1.19.

Okay, here's what we know so far...

- Decorators have the same supertype as the objects they decorate.

- You can use one or more decorators to wrap an object.

- Given that the decorator has the same supertype as the object it decorates, we can pass around a decorated object in place of the original (wrapped) object.

- The decorator adds its own behavior either before and/or after delegating to the object it decorates to do the rest of the job.   *Key Point!*

- Objects can be decorated at any time, so we can decorate objects dynamically at runtime with as many decorators as we like.

Now let's see how this all really works by looking at the Decorator Pattern definition and writing some code.

The Decorator Pattern defined

Let's first take a look at the Decorator Pattern description:

> **The Decorator Pattern** attaches additional responsibilities to an object dynamically. Decorators provide a flexible alternative to subclassing for extending functionality.

While that describes the *role* of the Decorator Pattern, it doesn't give us a lot of insight into how we'd *apply* the pattern to our own implementation. Let's take a look at the class diagram, which is a little more revealing (on the next page we'll look at the same structure applied to the beverage problem).

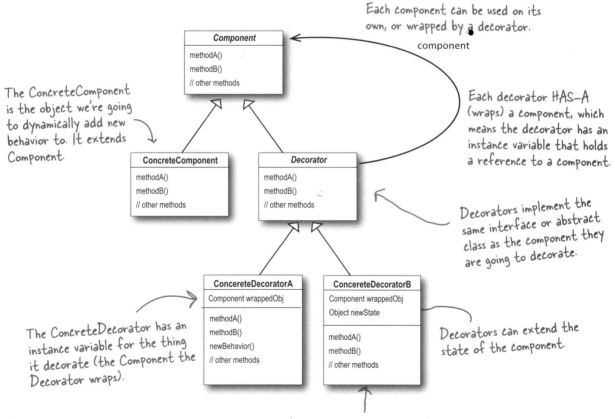

Each component can be used on its own, or wrapped by a decorator.

The ConcreteComponent is the object we're going to dynamically add new behavior to. It extends Component.

Each decorator HAS-A (wraps) a component, which means the decorator has an instance variable that holds a reference to a component.

Decorators implement the same interface or abstract class as the component they are going to decorate.

The ConcreteDecorator has an instance variable for the thing it decorate (the Component the Decorator wraps).

Decorators can extend the state of the component.

Decorators can add new methods; however, new behavior is typically added by doing computation before or after an existing method in the component.

Decorating our Beverages

Okay, let's work our Starbuzz beverages into this framework...

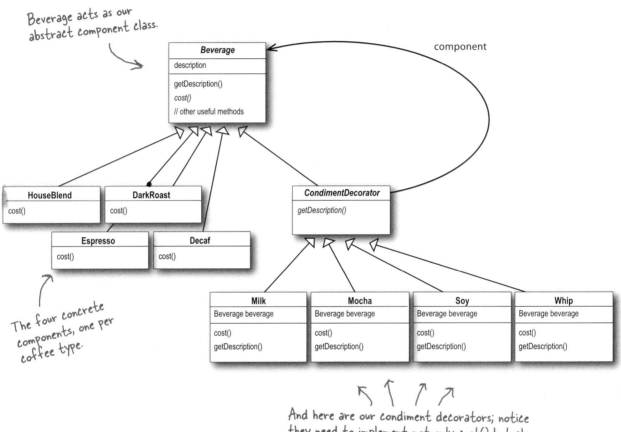

Beverage acts as our abstract component class.

component

The four concrete components, one per coffee type.

And here are our condiment decorators; notice they need to implement not only cost() but also getDescription(). We'll see why in a moment...

BRAIN POWER

Before going further, think about how you'd implement the cost() method of the coffees and the condiments. Also think about how you'd implement the getDescription() method of the condiments.

Cubicle Conversation

Some confusion over Inheritance versus Composition

> Okay, I'm a little confused...I thought we weren't going to use inheritance in this pattern, but rather we were going to rely on composition instead.

Mary

Sue: What do you mean?

Mary: Look at the class diagram. The CondimentDecorator is extending the Beverage class. That's inheritance, right?

Sue: True. I think the point is that it's vital that the decorators have the same type as the objects they are going to decorate. So here we're using inheritance to achieve the *type matching*, but we aren't using inheritance to get *behavior*.

Mary: Okay, I can see how decorators need the same "interface" as the components they wrap because they need to stand in place of the component. But where does the behavior come in?

Sue: When we compose a decorator with a component, we are adding new behavior. We are acquiring new behavior not by inheriting it from a superclass, but by composing objects together.

Mary: Okay, so we're subclassing the abstract class Beverage in order to have the correct type, not to inherit its behavior. The behavior comes in through the composition of decorators with the base components as well as other decorators.

Sue: That's right.

Mary: Ooooh, I see. And because we are using object composition, we get a whole lot more flexibility about how to mix and match condiments and beverages. Very smooth.

Sue: Yes, if we rely on inheritance, then our behavior can only be determined statically at compile time. In other words, we get only whatever behavior the superclass gives us or that we override. With composition, we can mix and match decorators any way we like... *at runtime*.

Mary: And as I understand it, we can implement new decorators at any time to add new behavior. If we relied on inheritance, we'd have to go in and change existing code any time we wanted new behavior.

Sue: Exactly.

Mary: I just have one more question. If all we need to inherit is the type of the component, how come we didn't use an interface instead of an abstract class for the Beverage class?

Sue: Well, remember, when we got this code, Starbuzz already *had* an abstract Beverage class. Traditionally the Decorator Pattern does specify an abstract component, but in Java, obviously, we could use an interface. But we always try to avoid altering existing code, so don't "fix" it if the abstract class will work just fine.

New barista training

Make a picture for what happens when the order is for a "double mocha soy latte with whip" beverage. Use the menu to get the correct prices, and draw your picture using the same format we used earlier (from a few pages back):

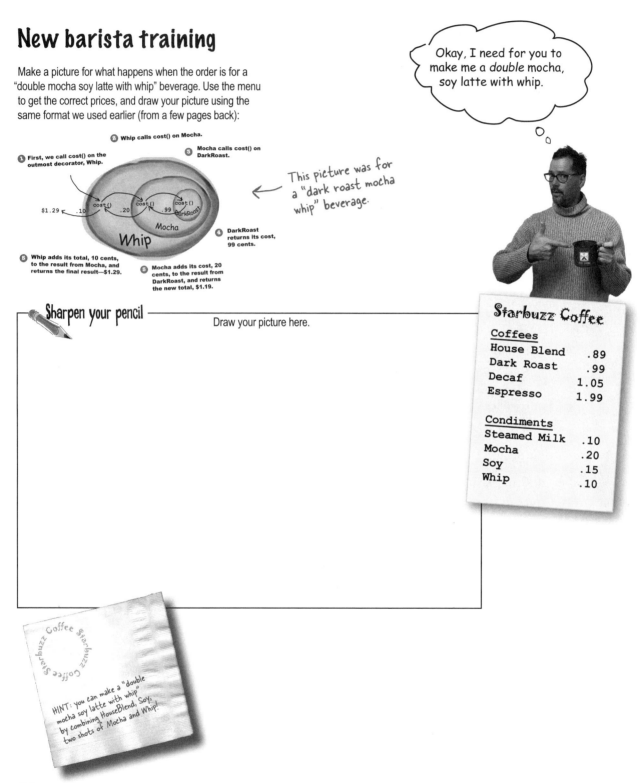

Okay, I need for you to make me a *double* mocha, soy latte with whip.

② Whip calls cost() on Mocha.

③ Mocha calls cost() on DarkRoast.

① First, we call cost() on the outmost decorator, Whip.

This picture was for a "dark roast mocha whip" beverage.

$1.29 ← .10 .20 .99 cost() DarkRoast

Mocha

Whip

④ DarkRoast returns its cost, 99 cents.

⑥ Whip adds its total, 10 cents, to the result from Mocha, and returns the final result—$1.29.

⑤ Mocha adds its cost, 20 cents, to the result from DarkRoast, and returns the new total, $1.19.

Sharpen your pencil

Draw your picture here.

Starbuzz Coffee

Coffees

House Blend	.89
Dark Roast	.99
Decaf	1.05
Espresso	1.99

Condiments

Condiment	Price
Steamed Milk	.10
Mocha	.20
Soy	.15
Whip	.10

HINT: You can make a "double mocha soy latte with whip" by combining HouseBlend, Soy, two shots of Mocha and Whip!

Writing the Starbuzz code

It's time to whip this design into some real code.

Let's start with the Beverage class, which doesn't need to change from Starbuzz's original design. Let's take a look:

```java
public abstract class Beverage {
    String description = "Unknown Beverage";

    public String getDescription() {
        return description;
    }

    public abstract double cost();
}
```

Beverage is an abstract class with the two methods getDescription() and cost().

getDescription is already implemented for us, but we need to implement cost() in the subclasses.

Beverage is simple enough. Let's implement the abstract class for the Condiments (Decorator) as well:

First, we need to be interchangeable with a Beverage, so we extend the Beverage class.

```java
public abstract class CondimentDecorator extends Beverage {
    public abstract String getDescription();
}
```

We're also going to require that the condiment decorators all reimplement the getDescription() method. Again, we'll see why in a sec...

Coding beverages

Now that we've got our base classes out of the way, let's implement some beverages. We'll start with Espresso. Remember, we need to set a description for the specific beverage and also implement the cost() method.

First we extend the Beverage class, since this is a beverage.

```
public class Espresso extends Beverage {

    public Espresso() {
        description = "Espresso";
    }

    public double cost() {
        return 1.99;
    }
}
```

To take care of the description, we set this in the constructor for the class. Remember the description instance variable is inherited from Beverage.

Finally, we need to compute the cost of an Espresso. We don't need to worry about adding in condiments in this class, we just need to return the price of an Espresso: $1.99.

```
public class HouseBlend extends Beverage {
    public HouseBlend() {
        description = "House Blend Coffee";
    }

    public double cost() {
        return .89;
    }
}
```

Okay, here's another Beverage. All we do is set the appropriate description, "House Blend Coffee," and then return the correct cost: 89¢.

You can create the other two Beverage classses (DarkRoast and Decaf) in exactly the same way.

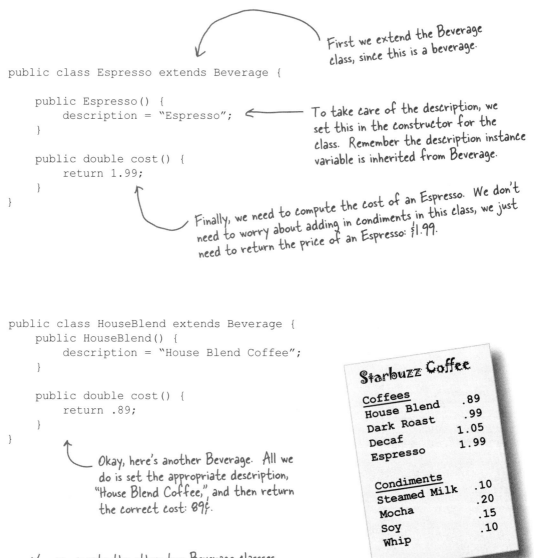

Starbuzz Coffee

Coffees	
House Blend	.89
Dark Roast	.99
Decaf	1.05
Espresso	1.99

Condiments	
Steamed Milk	.10
Mocha	.20
Soy	.15
Whip	.10

Coding condiments

If you look back at the Decorator Pattern class diagram, you'll see we've now written our abstract component (Beverage), we have our concrete components (HouseBlend), and we have our abstract decorator (CondimentDecorator). Now it's time to implement the concrete decorators. Here's Mocha:

Mocha is a decorator, so we extend CondimentDecorator.

Remember, CondimentDecorator extends Beverage.

We're going to instantiate Mocha with a reference to a Beverage using:

(1) An instance variable to hold the beverage we are wrapping.

(2) A way to set this instance variable to the object we are wrapping. Here, we're going to to pass the beverage we're wrapping to the decorator's constructor.

```java
public class Mocha extends CondimentDecorator {
    Beverage beverage;

    public Mocha(Beverage beverage) {
        this.beverage = beverage;
    }

    public String getDescription() {
        return beverage.getDescription() + ", Mocha";
    }

    public double cost() {
        return .20 + beverage.cost();
    }
}
```

Now we need to compute the cost of our beverage with Mocha. First, we delegate the call to the object we're decorating, so that it can compute the cost; then, we add the cost of Mocha to the result.

We want our description to not only include the beverage – say "Dark Roast" – but also to include each item decorating the beverage, for instance, "Dark Roast, Mocha". So we first delegate to the object we are decorating to get its description, then append ", Mocha" to that description.

On the next page we'll actually instantiate the beverage and wrap it with all its condiments (decorators), but first...

 **Sharpen your pencil**

Write and compile the code for the other Soy and Whip condiments. You'll need them to finish and test the application.

Serving some coffees

Congratulations. It's time to sit back, order a few coffees and marvel at the flexible design you created with the Decorator Pattern.

Here's some test code* to make orders:

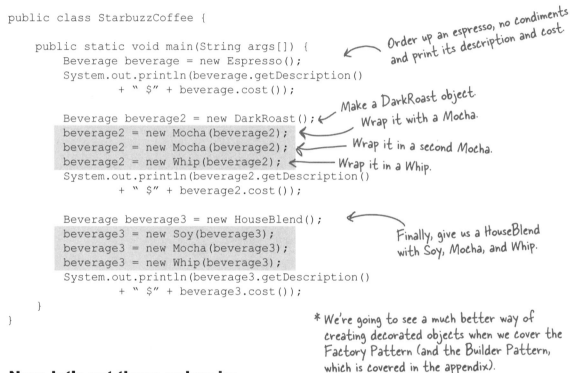

```java
public class StarbuzzCoffee {

    public static void main(String args[]) {
        Beverage beverage = new Espresso();
        System.out.println(beverage.getDescription()
                + " $" + beverage.cost());

        Beverage beverage2 = new DarkRoast();
        beverage2 = new Mocha(beverage2);
        beverage2 = new Mocha(beverage2);
        beverage2 = new Whip(beverage2);
        System.out.println(beverage2.getDescription()
                + " $" + beverage2.cost());

        Beverage beverage3 = new HouseBlend();
        beverage3 = new Soy(beverage3);
        beverage3 = new Mocha(beverage3);
        beverage3 = new Whip(beverage3);
        System.out.println(beverage3.getDescription()
                + " $" + beverage3.cost());
    }
}
```

Order up an espresso, no condiments and print its description and cost.

Make a DarkRoast object. Wrap it with a Mocha.

Wrap it in a second Mocha.

Wrap it in a Whip.

Finally, give us a HouseBlend with Soy, Mocha, and Whip.

* We're going to see a much better way of creating decorated objects when we cover the Factory Pattern (and the Builder Pattern, which is covered in the appendix).

Now, let's get those orders in:

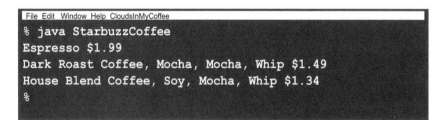

```
File Edit Window Help CloudsInMyCoffee
% java StarbuzzCoffee
Espresso $1.99
Dark Roast Coffee, Mocha, Mocha, Whip $1.49
House Blend Coffee, Soy, Mocha, Whip $1.34
%
```

there are no Dumb Questions

Q: I'm a little worried about code that might test for a specfic concrete component – say, HouseBlend – and do something, like issue a discount. Once I've wrapped the HouseBlend with decorators, this isn't going to work anymore.

A: That is exactly right. If you have code that relies on the concrete component's type, decorators will break that code. As long as you only write code against the abstract component type, the use of decorators will remain transparent to your code. However, once you start writing code against concrete components, you'll want to rethink your application design and your use of decorators.

Q: Wouldn't it be easy for some client of a beverage to end up with a decorator that isn't the outermost decorator? Like if I had a DarkRoast with Mocha, Soy, and Whip, it would be easy to write code that somehow ended up with a reference to Soy instead of Whip, which means it would not include Whip in the order.

A: You could certainly argue that you have to manage more objects with the Decorator Pattern and so there is an increased chance that coding errors will introduce the kinds of problems you suggest. However, decorators are typically created by using other patterns like Factory and Builder. Once we've covered these patterns, you'll see that the creation of the concrete component with its decorator is "well encapsulated" and doesn't lead to these kinds of problems.

Q: Can decorators know about the other decorations in the chain? Say, I wanted my getDecription() method to print "Whip, Double Mocha" instead of "Mocha, Whip, Mocha"? That would require that my outermost decorator know all the decorators it is wrapping.

A: Decorators are meant to add behavior to the object they wrap. When you need to peek at multiple layers into the decorator chain, you are starting to push the decorator beyond its true intent. Nevertheless, such things are possible. Imagine a CondimentPrettyPrint decorator that parses the final decription and can print "Mocha, Whip, Mocha" as "Whip, Double Mocha." Note that getDecription() could return an ArrayList of descriptions to make this easier.

Sharpen your pencil

Our friends at Starbuzz have introduced sizes to their menu. You can now order a coffee in tall, grande, and venti sizes (translation: small, medium, and large). Starbuzz saw this as an intrinsic part of the coffee class, so they've added two methods to the Beverage class: setSize() and getSize(). They'd also like for the condiments to be charged according to size, so for instance, Soy costs 10¢, 15¢ and 20¢ respectively for tall, grande, and venti coffees.

How would you alter the decorator classes to handle this change in requirements?

Real World Decorators: Java I/O

The large number of classes in the java.io package is... *overwhelming*. Don't feel alone if you said "whoa" the first (and second and third) time you looked at this API. But now that you know the Decorator Pattern, the I/O classes should make more sense since the java.io package is largely based on Decorator. Here's a typical set of objects that use decorators to add functionality to reading data from a file:

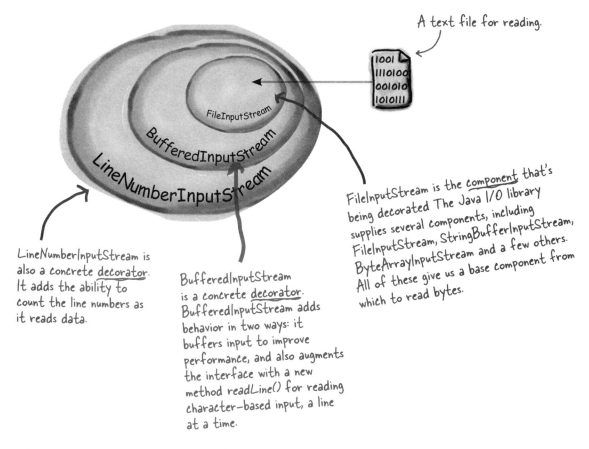

A text file for reading.

FilelnputStream is the **component** that's being decorated The Java I/O library supplies several components, including FilelnputStream, StringBufferInputStream, ByteArrayInputStream and a few others. All of these give us a base component from which to read bytes.

LineNumberInputStream is also a concrete decorator. It adds the ability to count the line numbers as it reads data.

BufferedInputStream is a concrete decorator. BufferedInputStream adds behavior in two ways: it buffers input to improve performance, and also augments the interface with a new method readLine() for reading character-based input, a line at a time.

BufferedInputStream and **LineNumber**InputStream both extend **Filter**InputStream, which acts as the abstract decorator class.

Decorating the java.io classes

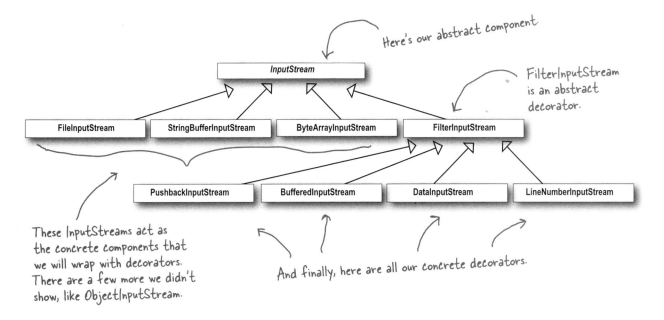

Here's our abstract component.

FilterInputStream is an abstract decorator.

These InputStreams act as the concrete components that we will wrap with decorators. There are a few more we didn't show, like ObjectInputStream.

And finally, here are all our concrete decorators.

You can see that this isn't so different from the Starbuzz design. You should now be in a good position to look over the java.io API docs and compose decorators on the various *input* streams.

And you'll see that the *output* streams have the same design. And you've probably already found that the Reader/Writer streams (for character-based data) closely mirror the design of the streams classes (with a few differences and inconsistencies, but close enough to figure out what's going on).

But Java I/O also points out one of the *downsides* of the Decorator Pattern: designs using this pattern often result in a large number of small classes that can be overwhelming to a developer trying to use the Decorator-based API. But now that you know how Decorator works, you can keep things in perspective and when you're using someone else's Decorator-heavy API, you can work through how their classes are organized so that you can easily use wrapping to get the behavior you're after.

Writing your own Java I/O Decorator

Okay, you know the Decorator Pattern, you've seen the I/O class diagram. You should be ready to write your own input decorator.

How about this: write a decorator that converts all uppercase characters to lowercase in the input stream. In other words, if we read in "I know the Decorator Pattern therefore I RULE!" then your decorator converts this to "i know the decorator pattern therefore i rule!"

> No problem. I just have to extend the FilterInputStream class and override the read() methods.

Don't forget to import java.io... (not shown)

First, extend the FilterInputStream, the abstract decorator for all InputStreams.

```java
public class LowerCaseInputStream extends FilterInputStream {
    public LowerCaseInputStream(InputStream in) {
        super(in);
    }

    public int read() throws IOException {
        int c = super.read();
        return (c == -1 ? c : Character.toLowerCase((char)c));
    }

    public int read(byte[] b, int offset, int len) throws IOException {
        int result = super.read(b, offset, len);
        for (int i = offset; i < offset+result; i++) {
            b[i] = (byte)Character.toLowerCase((char)b[i]);
        }
        return result;
    }
}
```

Now we need to implement two read methods. They take a byte (or an array of bytes) and convert each byte (that represents a character) to lowercase if it's an uppercase character.

REMEMBER: we don't provide import and package statements in the code listings. Get the complete source code from the headfirstlabs web site. You'll find the URL on page xxxiii in the Intro.

Test out your new Java I/O Decorator

Write some quick code to test the I/O decorator:

```java
public class InputTest {
    public static void main(String[] args) throws IOException {
        int c;
        try {
            InputStream in =
                new LowerCaseInputStream(
                    new BufferedInputStream(
                        new FileInputStream("test.txt")));

            while((c = in.read()) >= 0) {
                System.out.print((char)c);
            }

            in.close();
        } catch (IOException e) {
            e.printStackTrace();
        }
    }
}
```

Set up the FileInputStream and decorate it, first with a BufferedInputStream and then our brand new LowerCaseInputStream filter.

Just use the stream to read characters until the end of file and print as we go.

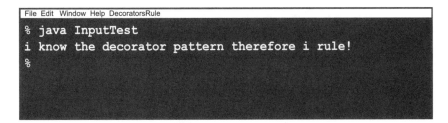

I know the Decorator Pattern therefore I RULE!

test.txt file

You need to make this file.

Give it a spin:

```
File Edit Window Help DecoratorsRule
% java InputTest
i know the decorator pattern therefore i rule!
%
```

Patterns Exposed

This week's interview:
Confessions of a Decorator

HeadFirst: Welcome Decorator Pattern. We've heard that you've been a bit down on yourself lately?

Decorator: Yes, I know the world sees me as the glamorous design pattern, but you know, I've got my share of problems just like everyone.

HeadFirst: Can you perhaps share some of your troubles with us?

Decorator: Sure. Well, you know I've got the power to add flexibility to designs, that much is for sure, but I also have a *dark side*. You see, I can sometimes add a lot of small classes to a design and this occasionally results in a design that's less than straightforward for others to understand.

HeadFirst: Can you give us an example?

Decorator: Take the Java I/O libraries. These are notoriously difficult for people to understand at first. But if they just saw the classes as a set of wrappers around an InputStream, life would be much easier.

HeadFirst: That doesn't sound so bad. You're still a great pattern, and improving this is just a matter of public education, right?

Decorator: There's more, I'm afraid. I've got typing problems: you see, people sometimes take a piece of client code that relies on specific types and introduce decorators without thinking through everything. Now, one great thing about me is that ***you can usually insert decorators transparently and the client never has to know it's dealing with a decorator.*** But like I said, some code is dependent on specific types and when you start introducing decorators, boom! Bad things happen.

HeadFirst: Well, I think everyone understands that you have to be careful when inserting decorators, I don't think this is a reason to be too down on yourself.

Decorator: I know, I try not to be. I also have the problem that introducing decorators can increase the complexity of the code needed to instantiate the component. Once you've got decorators, you've got to not only instantiate the component, but also wrap it with who knows how many decorators.

HeadFirst: I'll be interviewing the Factory and Builder patterns next week – I hear they can be very helpful with this?

Decorator: That's true; I should talk to those guys more often.

HeadFirst: Well, we all think you're a great pattern for creating flexible designs and staying true to the Open-Closed Principle, so keep your chin up and think positively!

Decorator: I'll do my best, thank you.

Tools for your Design Toolbox

You've got another chapter under your belt and a new principle and pattern in the toolbox.

OO Basics

...ction
...ulation
...rphism
...ance

OO Principles

Encapsulate what varies.

Favor composition over inheritance.

Program to interfaces, not implementations.

Strive for loosely coupled designs between objects that interact.

Classes should be open for extension but closed for modification.

↙ We now have the Open–Closed Principle to guide us. We're going to strive to design our system so that the closed parts are isolated from our new extensions.

OO Patterns

Stra...
encap...
inter...
vary...

Decorator – Attach additional responsibilities to an object dynamically. Decorators provide a flexible alternative to subclassing for extending functionality.

↙ And here's our first pattern for creating designs that satisfy the Open–Closed Principle. Or was it really the first? Is there another pattern we've used that follows this principle as well?

BULLET POINTS

- Inheritance is one form of extension, but not necessarily the best way to achieve flexibility in our designs.

- In our designs we should allow behavior to be extended without the need to modify existing code.

- Composition and delegation can often be used to add new behaviors at runtime.

- The Decorator Pattern provides an alternative to subclassing for extending behavior.

- The Decorator Pattern involves a set of decorator classes that are used to wrap concrete components.

- Decorator classes mirror the type of the components they decorate. (In fact, they are the same type as the components they decorate, either through inheritance or interface implementation.)

- Decorators change the behavior of their components by adding new functionality before and/or after (or even in place of) method calls to the component.

- You can wrap a component with any number of decorators.

- Decorators are typically transparent to the client of the component; that is, unless the client is relying on the component's concrete type.

- Decorators can result in many small objects in our design, and overuse can be complex.

Exercise solutions

```
public class Beverage {

    // declare instance variables for milkCost,
    // soyCost, mochaCost, and whipCost, and
    // getters and setters for milk, soy, mocha
    // and whip.

    public double cost() {

        double condimentCost = 0.0;
        if (hasMilk()) {
            condimentCost += milkCost;
        }
        if (hasSoy()) {
            condimentCost += soyCost;
        }
        if (hasMocha()) {
            condimentCost += mochaCost;
        }
        if (hasWhip()) {
            condimentCost += whipCost;
        }
        return condimentCost;
    }
}
```

```
public class DarkRoast extends Beverage {

    public DarkRoast() {
        description = "Most Excellent Dark Roast";
    }

    public double cost() {

        return 1.99 + super.cost();

    }
}
```

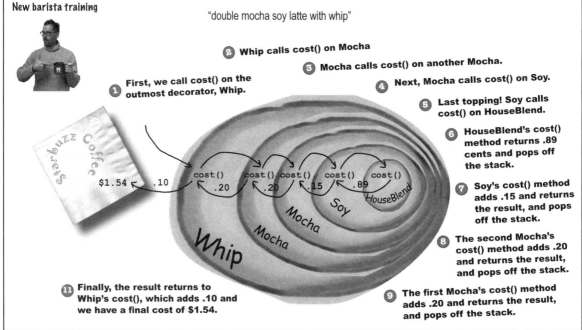

New barista training

"double mocha soy latte with whip"

2 Whip calls cost() on Mocha

3 Mocha calls cost() on another Mocha.

1 First, we call cost() on the outmost decorator, Whip.

4 Next, Mocha calls cost() on Soy.

5 Last topping! Soy calls cost() on HouseBlend.

6 HouseBlend's cost() method returns .89 cents and pops off the stack.

7 Soy's cost() method adds .15 and returns the result, and pops off the stack.

8 The second Mocha's cost() method adds .20 and returns the result, and pops off the stack.

9 The first Mocha's cost() method adds .20 and returns the result, and pops off the stack.

11 Finally, the result returns to Whip's cost(), which adds .10 and we have a final cost of $1.54.

$1.54   .10   cost()   .20   cost()   cost()   .20   .15   cost()   .89   cost()

Whip   Mocha   Mocha   Soy   HouseBlend

Exercise solutions

Our friends at Starbuzz have introduced sizes to their menu. You can now order a coffee in tall, grande, and venti sizes (for us normal folk: small, medium, and large). Starbuzz saw this as an intrinsic part of the coffee class, so they've added two methods to the Beverage class: setSize() and getSize(). They'd also like for the condiments to be charged according to size, so for instance, Soy costs 10¢, 15¢, and 20¢ respectively for tall, grande, and venti coffees.

How would you alter the decorator classes to handle this change in requirements?

```java
public class Soy extends CondimentDecorator {
    Beverage beverage;

    public Soy(Beverage beverage) {
        this.beverage = beverage;
    }

    public int getSize() {
        return beverage.getSize();
    }

    public String getDescription() {
        return beverage.getDescription() + ", Soy";
    }

    public double cost() {
        double cost = beverage.cost();
        if (getSize() == Beverage.TALL) {
            cost += .10;
        } else if (getSize() == Beverage.GRANDE) {
            cost += .15;
        } else if (getSize() == Beverage.VENTI) {
            cost += .20;
        }
        return cost;
    }
}
```

Now we need to propagate the getSize() method to the wrapped beverage. We should also move this method to the abstract class since it's used in all condiment decorators.

Here we get the size (which propagates all the way to the concrete beverage) and then add the appropriate cost.

4 the Factory Pattern

Baking with OO Goodness

Get ready to bake some loosely coupled OO designs. There is more to making objects than just using the **new** operator. You'll learn that instantiation is an activity that shouldn't always be done in public and can often lead to *coupling problems*. And you don't want *that*, do you? Find out how Factory Patterns can help save you from embarrasing dependencies.

Okay, it's been three chapters and you still haven't answered my question about **new**. We aren't supposed to program to an implementation but every time I use **new**, that's exactly what I'm doing, right?

When you see "new", think "concrete".

Yes, when you use **new** you are certainly instantiating a concrete class, so that's definitely an implementation, not an interface. And it's a good question; you've learned that tying your code to a concrete class can make it more fragile and less flexible.

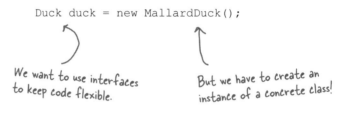

```
Duck duck = new MallardDuck();
```

We want to use interfaces to keep code flexible.

But we have to create an instance of a concrete class!

When you have a whole set of related concrete classes, often you're forced to write code like this:

```
Duck duck;

if (picnic) {
    duck = new MallardDuck();
} else if (hunting) {
    duck = new DecoyDuck();
} else if (inBathTub) {
    duck = new RubberDuck();
}
```

We have a bunch of different duck classes, and we don't know until runtime which one we need to instantiate.

Here we've got several concrete classes being instantiated, and the decision of which to instantiate is made at runtime depending on some set of conditions.

When you see code like this, you know that when it comes time for changes or extensions, you'll have to reopen this code and examine what needs to be added (or deleted). Often this kind of code ends up in several parts of the application making maintenance and updates more difficult and error-prone.

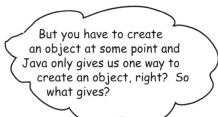

> But you have to create an object at some point and Java only gives us one way to create an object, right? So what gives?

What's wrong with "new"?

Technically there's nothing wrong with **new**, after all, it's a fundamental part of Java. The real culprit is our old friend CHANGE and how change impacts our use of **new**.

By coding to an interface, you know you can insulate yourself from a lot of changes that might happen to a system down the road. Why? If your code is written to an interface, then it will work with any new classes implementing that interface through polymorphism. However, when you have code that makes use of lots of concrete classes, you're looking for trouble because that code may have to be changed as new concrete classes are added. So, in other words, your code will not be "closed for modification." To extend it with new concrete types, you'll have to reopen it.

Remember that designs should be "open for extension but closed for modification" – see Chapter 3 for a review.

So what can you do? It's times like these that you can fall back on OO Design Principles to look for clues. Remember, our first principle deals with change and guides us to *identify the aspects that vary and separate them from what stays the same.*

☀ BRAIN POWER

How might you take all the parts of your application that instantiate concrete classes and separate or encapsulate them from the rest of your application?

Identifying the aspects that vary

Let's say you have a pizza shop, and as a cutting-edge pizza store owner in Objectville you might end up writing some code like this:

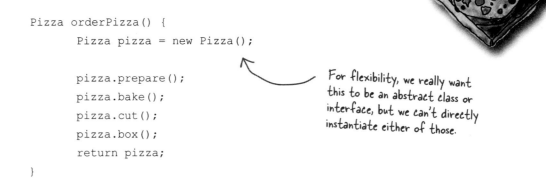

```
Pizza orderPizza() {
    Pizza pizza = new Pizza();

    pizza.prepare();
    pizza.bake();
    pizza.cut();
    pizza.box();
    return pizza;
}
```

For flexibility, we really want this to be an abstract class or interface, but we can't directly instantiate either of those.

But you need more than one type of pizza...

So then you'd add some code that *determines* the appropriate type of pizza and then goes about *making* the pizza:

```
Pizza orderPizza(String type) {
    Pizza pizza;

    if (type.equals("cheese")) {
        pizza = new CheesePizza();
    } else if (type.equals("greek") {
        pizza = new GreekPizza();
    } else if (type.equals("pepperoni") {
        pizza = new PepperoniPizza();
    }

    pizza.prepare();
    pizza.bake();
    pizza.cut();
    pizza.box();
    return pizza;
}
```

We're now passing in the type of pizza to orderPizza.

Based on the type of pizza, we instantiate the correct concrete class and assign it to the pizza instance variable. Note that each pizza here has to implement the Pizza interface.

Once we have a Pizza, we prepare it (you know, roll the dough, put on the sauce and add the toppings & cheese), then we bake it, cut it and box it!

Each Pizza subtype (CheesePizza, VeggiePizza, etc.) knows how to prepare itself.

But the pressure is on to add more pizza types

You realize that all of your competitors have added a couple of trendy pizzas to their menus: the Clam Pizza and the Veggie Pizza. Obviously you need to keep up with the competition, so you'll add these items to your menu. And you haven't been selling many Greek Pizzas lately, so you decide to take that off the menu:

```java
Pizza orderPizza(String type) {
    Pizza pizza;

    if (type.equals("cheese")) {
        pizza = new CheesePizza();
    } else if (type.equals("greek") {
        pizza = new GreekPizza();
    } else if (type.equals("pepperoni") {
        pizza = new PepperoniPizza();
    } else if (type.equals("clam") {
        pizza = new ClamPizza();
    } else if (type.equals("veggie") {
        pizza = new VeggiePizza();
    }

    pizza.prepare();
    pizza.bake();
    pizza.cut();
    pizza.box();
    return pizza;
}
```

This code is NOT closed for modification. If the Pizza Shop changes its pizza offerings, we have to get into this code and modify it.

This is what varies. As the pizza selection changes over time, you'll have to modify this code over and over.

This is what we expect to stay the same. For the most part, preparing, cooking, and packaging a pizza has remained the same for years and years. So, we don't expect this code to change, just the pizzas it operates on.

Clearly, dealing with *which* concrete class is instantiated is really messing up our orderPizza() method and preventing it from being closed for modification. But now that we know what is varying and what isn't, it's probably time to encapsulate it.

Encapsulating object creation

So now we know we'd be better off moving the object creation out of the orderPizza() method. But how? Well, what we're going to do is take the creation code and move it out into another object that is only going to be concerned with creating pizzas.

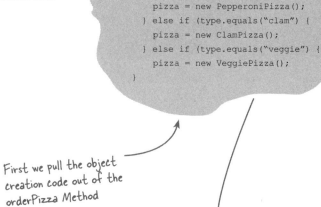

```
if (type.equals("cheese")) {
    pizza = new CheesePizza();
} else if (type.equals("pepperoni") {
    pizza = new PepperoniPizza();
} else if (type.equals("clam") {
    pizza = new ClamPizza();
} else if (type.equals("veggie")) {
    pizza = new VeggiePizza();
}
```

```
Pizza orderPizza(String type) {
    Pizza pizza;



    pizza.prepare();
    pizza.bake();
    pizza.cut();
    pizza.box();
    return pizza;
}
```

First we pull the object creation code out of the orderPizza Method

What's going to go here?

Then we place that code in an object that is only going to worry about how to create pizzas. If any other object needs a pizza created, this is the object to come to.

SimplePizzaFactory

We've got a name for this new object: we call it a Factory.

Factories handle the details of object creation. Once we have a SimplePizzaFactory, our orderPizza() method just becomes a client of that object. Any time it needs a pizza it asks the pizza factory to make one. Gone are the days when the orderPizza() method needs to know about Greek versus Clam pizzas. Now the orderPizza() method just cares that it gets a pizza, which implements the Pizza interface so that it can call prepare(), bake(), cut(), and box().

We've still got a few details to fill in here; for instance, what does the orderPizza() method replace its creation code with? Let's implement a simple factory for the pizza store and find out...

Building a simple pizza factory

We'll start with the factory itself. What we're going to do is define a class that encapsulates the object creation for all pizzas. Here it is...

Here's our new class, the SimplePizzaFactory. It has one job in life: creating pizzas for its clients.

First we define a createPizza() method in the factory. This is the method all clients will use to instantiate new objects.

```java
public class SimplePizzaFactory {
    public Pizza createPizza(String type) {
        Pizza pizza = null;

        if (type.equals("cheese")) {
            pizza = new CheesePizza();
        } else if (type.equals("pepperoni")) {
            pizza = new PepperoniPizza();
        } else if (type.equals("clam")) {
            pizza = new ClamPizza();
        } else if (type.equals("veggie")) {
            pizza = new VeggiePizza();
        }
        return pizza;
    }
}
```

Here's the code we plucked out of the orderPizza() method.

This code is still parameterized by the type of the pizza, just like our original orderPizza() method was.

Dumb Questions
there are no

Q: **What's the advantage of this? It looks like we are just pushing the problem off to another object.**

A: One thing to remember is that the SimplePizzaFactory may have many clients. We've only seen the orderPizza() method; however, there may be a PizzaShopMenu class that uses the factory to get pizzas for their current description and price. We might also have a HomeDelivery class that handles pizzas in a different way than our

PizzaShop class but is also a client of the factory.

So, by encapsulating the pizza creating in one class, we now have only one place to make modifications when the implementation changes.

Don't forget, we are also just about to remove the concrete instantiations from our client code!

Q: **I've seen a similar design where a factory like this is defined as a static method. What is the difference?**

A: Defining a simple factory as a static method is a common technique and is often called a static factory. Why use a static method? Because you don't need to instantiate an object to make use of the create method. But remember it also has the disadvanage that you can't subclass and change the behavior of the create method.

Reworking the PizzaStore class

Now it's time to fix up our client code. What we want to do is rely on the factory to create the pizzas for us. Here are the changes:

Now we give PizzaStore a reference to a SimplePizzaFactory.

```
public class PizzaStore {
    SimplePizzaFactory factory;

    public PizzaStore(SimplePizzaFactory factory) {
        this.factory = factory;
    }

    public Pizza orderPizza(String type) {
        Pizza pizza;

        pizza = factory.createPizza(type);

        pizza.prepare();
        pizza.bake();
        pizza.cut();
        pizza.box();
        return pizza;
    }

    // other methods here
}
```

PizzaStore gets the factory passed to it in the constructor.

And the orderPizza() method uses the factory to create its pizzas by simply passing on the type of the order.

Notice that we've replaced the new operator with a create method on the factory object. No more concrete instantiations here!

BRAIN POWER

We know that object composition allows us to change behavior dynamically at runtime (among other things) because we can swap in and out implementations. How might we be able to use that in the PizzaStore? What factory implementations might we be able to swap in and out?

We don't know about you, but we're thinking New York, Chicago, and California style pizza factories (let's not forget New Haven, too)

The Simple Factory defined

Pattern
Honorable
Mention

The Simple Factory isn't actually a Design Pattern; it's more of a programming idiom. But it is commonly used, so we'll give it a Head First Pattern Honorable Mention. Some developers do mistake this idiom for the "Factory Pattern," so the next time there is an awkward silence between you and another developer, you've got a nice topic to break the ice.

Just because Simple Factory isn't a REAL pattern doesn't mean we shouldn't check out how it's put together. Let's take a look at the class diagram of our new Pizza Store:

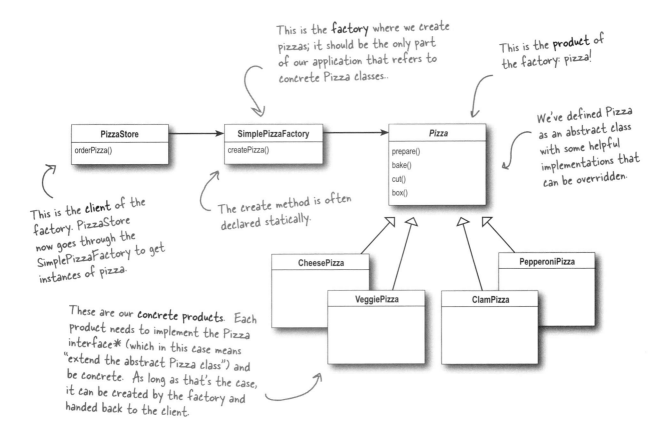

This is the **factory** where we create pizzas; it should be the only part of our application that refers to concrete Pizza classes..

This is the **product** of the factory: pizza!

We've defined Pizza as an abstract class with some helpful implementations that can be overridden.

This is the **client** of the factory. PizzaStore now goes through the SimplePizzaFactory to get instances of pizza.

The create method is often declared statically.

These are our **concrete products**. Each product needs to implement the Pizza interface* (which in this case means "extend the abstract Pizza class") and be concrete. As long as that's the case, it can be created by the factory and handed back to the client.

Think of Simple Factory as a warm up. Next, we'll explore two heavy duty patterns that are both factories. But don't worry, there's more pizza to come!

*Just another reminder: in design patterns, the phrase "implement an interface" does NOT always mean "write a class the implements a Java interface, by using the "implements" keyword in the class declaration." In the general use of the phrase, a concrete class implementing a method from a supertype (which could be a class OR interface) is still considered to be "implementing the interface" of that supertype.

Franchising the pizza store

Your Objectville PizzaStore has done so well that you've trounced the competition and now everyone wants a PizzaStore in their own neighborhood.   As the franchiser, you want to ensure the quality of the franchise operations and so you want them to use your time-tested code.

But what about regional differences? Each franchise might want to offer different styles of pizzas (New York, Chicago, and California, to name a few), depending on where the franchise store is located and the tastes of the local pizza connoisseurs.

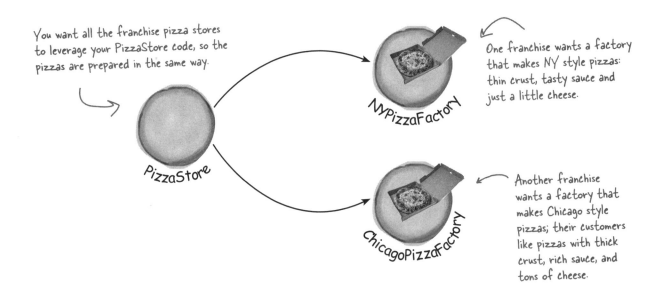

You want all the franchise pizza stores to leverage your PizzaStore code, so the pizzas are prepared in the same way.

PizzaStore

NYPizzaFactory

One franchise wants a factory that makes NY style pizzas: thin crust, tasty sauce and just a little cheese.

ChicagoPizzaFactory

Another franchise wants a factory that makes Chicago style pizzas; their customers like pizzas with thick crust, rich sauce, and tons of cheese.

We've seen one approach...

If we take out SimplePizzaFactory and create three different factories, NYPizzaFactory, ChicagoPizzaFactory and CaliforniaPizzaFactory, then we can just compose the PizzaStore with the appropriate factory and a franchise is good to go. That's one approach.

Let's see what that would look like...

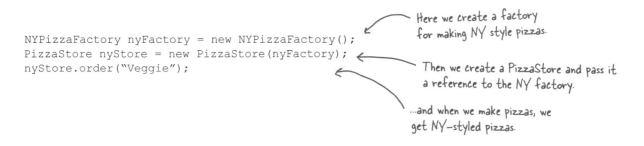

```
NYPizzaFactory nyFactory = new NYPizzaFactory();
PizzaStore nyStore = new PizzaStore(nyFactory);
nyStore.order("Veggie");
```

Here we create a factory for making NY style pizzas.

Then we create a PizzaStore and pass it a reference to the NY factory.

...and when we make pizzas, we get NY-styled pizzas.

```
ChicagoPizzaFactory chicagoFactory = new ChicagoPizzaFactory();
PizzaStore chicagoStore = new PizzaStore(chicagoFactory);
chicagoStore.order("Veggie");
```

Likewise for the Chicago pizza stores: we create a factory for Chicago pizzas and create a store that is composed with a Chicago factory. When we make pizzas, we get the Chicago flavored ones

But you'd like a little more quality control...

So you test marketed the SimpleFactory idea, and what you found was that the franchises were using your factory to create pizzas, but starting to employ their own home grown procedures for the rest of the process: they'd bake things a little differently, they'd forget to cut the pizza and they'd use third-party boxes.

Rethinking the problem a bit, you see that what you'd really like to do is create a framework that ties the store and the pizza creation together, yet still allows things to remain flexible.

In our early code, before the SimplePizzaFactory, we had the pizza-making code tied to the PizzaStore, but it wasn't flexible. So, how can we have our pizza and eat it too?

I've been making pizza for years so I thought I'd add my own "improvements" to the PizzaStore procedures...

Not what you want in a good franchise. You do NOT want to know what he puts on his pizzas.

A framework for the pizza store

There *is* a way to localize all the pizza making activities to the PizzaStore class, and yet give the franchises freedom to have their own regional style.

What we're going to do is put the createPizza() method back into PizzaStore, but this time as an **abstract method**, and then create a PizzaStore subclass for each regional style.

First, let's look at the changes to the PizzaStore:

PizzaStore is now abstract (see why below).

```
public abstract class PizzaStore {

    public Pizza orderPizza(String type) {
        Pizza pizza;

        pizza = createPizza(type);

        pizza.prepare();
        pizza.bake();
        pizza.cut();
        pizza.box();

        return pizza;
    }

    abstract Pizza createPizza(String type);
}
```

Now createPizza is back to being a call to a method in the PizzaStore rather than on a factory object.

All this looks just the same...

Now we've moved our factory object to this method.

Our "factory method" is now abstract in PizzaStore.

Now we've got a store waiting for subclasses; we're going to have a subclass for each regional type (NYPizzaStore, ChicagoPizzaStore, CaliforniaPizzaStore) and each subclass is going to make the decision about what makes up a pizza. Let's take a look at how this is going to work.

Allowing the subclasses to decide

Remember, the PizzaStore already has a well-honed order system in the orderPizza() method and you want to ensure that it's consistent across all franchises.

What varies among the regional PizzaStores is the style of pizzas they make – New York Pizza has thin crust, Chicago Pizza has thick, and so on – and we are going to push all these variations into the createPizza() method and make it responsible for creating the right kind of pizza. The way we do this is by letting each subclass of PizzaStore define what the createPizza() method looks like. So, we will have a number of concrete subclasses of PizzaStore, each with its own pizza variations, all fitting within the PizzaStore framework and still making use of the well-tuned orderPizza() method.

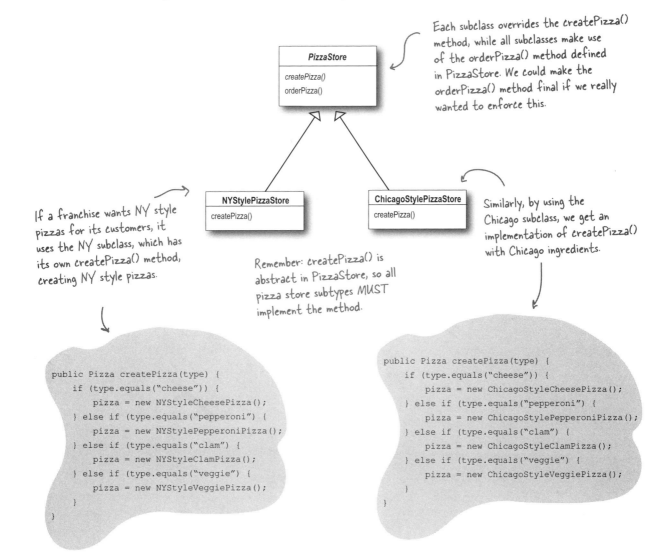

Each subclass overrides the createPizza() method, while all subclasses make use of the orderPizza() method defined in PizzaStore. We could make the orderPizza() method final if we really wanted to enforce this.

If a franchise wants NY style pizzas for its customers, it uses the NY subclass, which has its own createPizza() method, creating NY style pizzas.

Remember: createPizza() is abstract in PizzaStore, so all pizza store subtypes MUST implement the method.

Similarly, by using the Chicago subclass, we get an implementation of createPizza() with Chicago ingredients.

```
public Pizza createPizza(type) {
    if (type.equals("cheese")) {
        pizza = new NYStyleCheesePizza();
    } else if (type.equals("pepperoni") {
        pizza = new NYStylePepperoniPizza();
    } else if (type.equals("clam") {
        pizza = new NYStyleClamPizza();
    } else if (type.equals("veggie") {
        pizza = new NYStyleVeggiePizza();
    }
}
```

```
public Pizza createPizza(type) {
    if (type.equals("cheese")) {
        pizza = new ChicagoStyleCheesePizza();
    } else if (type.equals("pepperoni") {
        pizza = new ChicagoStylePepperoniPizza();
    } else if (type.equals("clam") {
        pizza = new ChicagoStyleClamPizza();
    } else if (type.equals("veggie") {
        pizza = new ChicagoStyleVeggiePizza();
    }
}
```

I don't get it. The PizzaStore subclasses are just subclasses. How are they *deciding* anything? I don't see any logical decision-making code in NYStylePizzaStore....

Well, think about it from the point of view of the PizzaStore's orderPizza() method: it is defined in the abstract PizzaStore, but concrete types are only created in the subclasses.

PizzaStore
createPizza()
orderPizza()

orderPizza() is defined in the abstract PizzaStore, not the subclasses. So, the method has no idea which subclass is actually running the code and making the pizzas.

Now, to take this a little further, the orderPizza() method does a lot of things with a Pizza object (like prepare, bake, cut, box), but because Pizza is abstract, orderPizza() has no idea what real concrete classes are involved. In other words, it's decoupled!

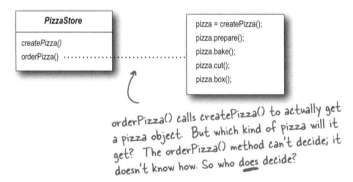

orderPizza() calls createPizza() to actually get a pizza object. But which kind of pizza will it get? The orderPizza() method can't decide; it doesn't know how. So who <u>does</u> decide?

When orderPizza() calls createPizza(), one of your subclasses will be called into action to create a pizza. Which kind of pizza will be made? Well, that's decided by the choice of pizza store you order from, NYStylePizzaStore or ChicagoStylePizzaStore.

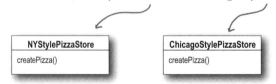

So, is there a real-time decision that subclasses make? No, but from the perspective of orderPizza(), if you chose a NYStylePizzaStore, that subclass gets to determine which pizza is made. So the subclasses aren't really "deciding" – it was *you* who decided by choosing which store you wanted – but they do determine which kind of pizza gets made.

Let's make a PizzaStore

Being a franchise has its benefits. You get all the PizzaStore functionality for free. All the regional stores need to do is subclass PizzaStore and supply a createPizza() method that implements their style of Pizza. We'll take care of the big three pizza styles for the franchisees.

Here's the New York regional style:

createPizza() returns a Pizza, and the subclass is fully responsible for which concrete Pizza it instantiates

The NYPizzaStore extends PizzaStore, so it inherits the orderPizza() method (among others).

```java
public class NYPizzaStore extends PizzaStore {
    Pizza createPizza(String item) {
        if (item.equals("cheese")) {
            return new NYStyleCheesePizza();
        } else if (item.equals("veggie")) {
            return new NYStyleVeggiePizza();
        } else if (item.equals("clam")) {
            return new NYStyleClamPizza();
        } else if (item.equals("pepperoni")) {
            return new NYStylePepperoniPizza();
        } else return null;
    }
}
```

We've got to implement createPizza(), since it is abstract in PizzaStore.

Here's where we create our concrete classes. For each type of Pizza we create the NY style.

✳ Note that the orderPizza() method in the superclass has no clue which Pizza we are creating; it just knows it can prepare, bake, cut, and box it!

Once we've got our PizzaStore subclasses built, it will be time to see about ordering up a pizza or two. But before we do that, why don't you take a crack at building the Chicago Style and California Style pizza stores on the next page.

Sharpen your pencil

We've knocked out the NYPizzaStore, just two more to go and we'll be ready to franchise!
Write the Chicago and California PizzaStore implementations here:

Declaring a factory method

With just a couple of transformations to the PizzaStore we've gone from
having an object handle the instantiation of our concrete classes to a set of
subclasses that are now taking on that responsibility. Let's take a closer look:

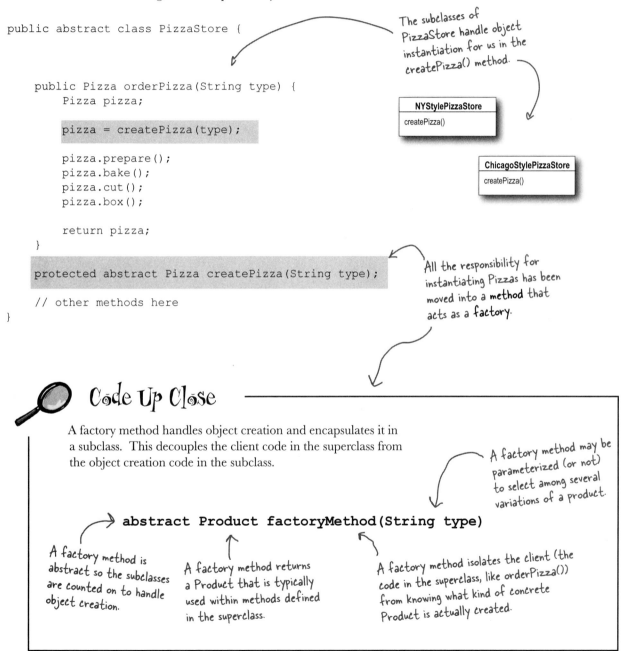

```
public abstract class PizzaStore {

    public Pizza orderPizza(String type) {
        Pizza pizza;

        pizza = createPizza(type);

        pizza.prepare();
        pizza.bake();
        pizza.cut();
        pizza.box();

        return pizza;
    }

    protected abstract Pizza createPizza(String type);

    // other methods here
}
```

The subclasses of
PizzaStore handle object
instantiation for us in the
createPizza() method.

NYStylePizzaStore

createPizza()

ChicagoStylePizzaStore

createPizza()

All the responsibility for
instantiating Pizzas has been
moved into a **method** that
acts as a **factory**.

Code Up Close

A factory method handles object creation and encapsulates it in
a subclass. This decouples the client code in the superclass from
the object creation code in the subclass.

A factory method may be
parameterized (or not)
to select among several
variations of a product.

abstract Product factoryMethod(String type)

A factory method is
abstract so the subclasses
are counted on to handle
object creation.

A factory method returns
a Product that is typically
used within methods defined
in the superclass.

A factory method isolates the client (the
code in the superclass, like orderPizza())
from knowing what kind of concrete
Product is actually created.

Let's see how it works: ordering pizzas with the pizza factory method

I like NY Style pizza... you know, thin, crispy crust with a little cheese and really good sauce.

I like Chicago style deep dish pizza with thick crust and tons of cheese.

Ethan

Joel

Ethan needs to order his pizza from a NY pizza store.

Joel needs to order his pizza from a Chicago pizza store. Same pizza ordering method, but different kind of pizza!

So how do they order?

1 First, Joel and Ethan need an instance of a PizzaStore. Joel needs to instantiate a ChicagoPizzaStore and Ethan needs a NYPizzaStore.

2 With a PizzaStore in hand, both Ethan and Joel call the orderPizza() method and pass in the type of pizza they want (cheese, veggie, and so on).

3 To create the pizzas, the createPizza() method is called, which is defined in the two subclasses NYPizzaStore and ChicagoPizzaStore. As we defined them, the NYPizzaStore instantiates a NY style pizza, and the ChicagoPizzaStore instantiates Chicago style pizza. In either case, the Pizza is returned to the orderPizza() method.

4 The orderPizza() method has no idea what kind of pizza was created, but it knows it is a pizza and it prepares, bakes, cuts, and boxes it for Ethan and Joel.

Let's check out how these pizzas are really made to order...

Behind the Scenes

1 **Let's follow Ethan's order: first we need a NY PizzaStore:**

```
PizzaStore nyPizzaStore = new NYPizzaStore();
```

Creates a instance of NYPizzaStore.

nyPizzaStore

2 **Now that we have a store, we can take an order:**

```
nyPizzaStore.orderPizza("cheese");
```

The orderPizza() method is called on the nyPizzaStore instance (the method defined inside PizzaStore runs).

createPizza("cheese")

3 **The orderPizza() method then calls the createPizza() method:**

```
Pizza pizza  = createPizza("cheese");
```

Remember, createPizza(), the factory method, is implemented in the subclass. In this case it returns a NY Cheese Pizza.

Pizza

4 **Finally we have the unprepared pizza in hand and the orderPizza() method finishes preparing it:**

```
pizza.prepare();
pizza.bake();
pizza.cut();
pizza.box();
```

All of these methods are defined in the specific pizza returned from the factory method createPizza(), defined in the NYPizzaStore.

The orderPizza() method gets back a Pizza, without knowing exactly what concrete class it is.

We're just missing one thing: PIZZA!

Our PizzaStore isn't going to be very popular without some pizzas, so let's implement them:

We'll start with an abstract Pizza class and all the concrete pizzas will derive from this.

Each Pizza has a name, a type of dough, a type of sauce, and a set of toppings.

```java
public abstract class Pizza {
    String name;
    String dough;
    String sauce;
    ArrayList toppings = new ArrayList();

    void prepare() {
        System.out.println("Preparing " + name);
        System.out.println("Tossing dough...");
        System.out.println("Adding sauce...");
        System.out.println("Adding toppings: ");
        for (int i = 0; i < toppings.size(); i++) {
            System.out.println("   " + toppings.get(i));
        }
    }

    void bake() {
        System.out.println("Bake for 25 minutes at 350");
    }

    void cut() {
        System.out.println("Cutting the pizza into diagonal slices");
    }

    void box() {
        System.out.println("Place pizza in official PizzaStore box");
    }

    public String getName() {
        return name;
    }
}
```

The abstract class provides some basic defaults for baking, cutting and boxing.

Preparation follows a number of steps in a particular sequence.

REMEMBER: we don't provide import and package statements in the code listings. Get the complete source code from the headfirstlabs web site. You'll find the URL on page xxxiii in the Intro.

Now we just need some concrete subclasses... how about defining New York and Chicago style cheese pizzas?

```
public class NYStyleCheesePizza extends Pizza {
    public NYStyleCheesePizza() {
        name = "NY Style Sauce and Cheese Pizza";
        dough = "Thin Crust Dough";
        sauce = "Marinara Sauce";

        toppings.add("Grated Reggiano Cheese");
    }
}
```

The NY Pizza has its own marinara style sauce and thin crust.

And one topping, reggiano cheese!

```
public class ChicagoStyleCheesePizza extends Pizza {
    public ChicagoStyleCheesePizza() {
        name = "Chicago Style Deep Dish Cheese Pizza";
        dough = "Extra Thick Crust Dough";
        sauce = "Plum Tomato Sauce";

        toppings.add("Shredded Mozzarella Cheese");
    }

    void cut() {
        System.out.println("Cutting the pizza into square slices");
    }
}
```

The Chicago Pizza uses plum tomatoes as a sauce along with extra thick crust.

The Chicago style deep dish pizza has lots of mozzarella cheese!

The Chicago style pizza also overrides the cut() method so that the pieces are cut into squares.

You've waited long enough, time for some pizzas!

```java
public class PizzaTestDrive {

    public static void main(String[] args) {
        PizzaStore nyStore = new NYPizzaStore();
        PizzaStore chicagoStore = new ChicagoPizzaStore();

        Pizza pizza = nyStore.orderPizza("cheese");
        System.out.println("Ethan ordered a " + pizza.getName() + "\n");

        pizza = chicagoStore.orderPizza("cheese");
        System.out.println("Joel ordered a " + pizza.getName() + "\n");
    }
}
```

First we create two different stores.

Then use one one store to make Ethan's order.

And the other for Joel's.

```
File Edit Window Help YouWantMootzOnThatPizza?
%java PizzaTestDrive

Preparing NY Style Sauce and Cheese Pizza
Tossing dough...
Adding sauce...
Adding toppings:
    Grated Regiano cheese
Bake for 25 minutes at 350
Cutting the pizza into diagonal slices
Place pizza in official PizzaStore box
Ethan ordered a NY Style Sauce and Cheese Pizza

Preparing Chicago Style Deep Dish Cheese Pizza
Tossing dough...
Adding sauce...
Adding toppings:
    Shredded Mozzarella Cheese
Bake for 25 minutes at 350
Cutting the pizza into square slices
Place pizza in official PizzaStore box
Joel ordered a Chicago Style Deep Dish Cheese Pizza
```

Both pizzas get prepared, the toppings added, and the pizzas baked, cut and boxed. Our superclass never had to know the details, the subclass handled all that just by instantiating the right pizza.

It's finally time to meet the Factory Method Pattern

All factory patterns encapsulate object creation. The Factory Method Pattern encapsulates object creation by letting subclasses decide what objects to create. Let's check out these class diagrams to see who the players are in this pattern:

The Creator classes

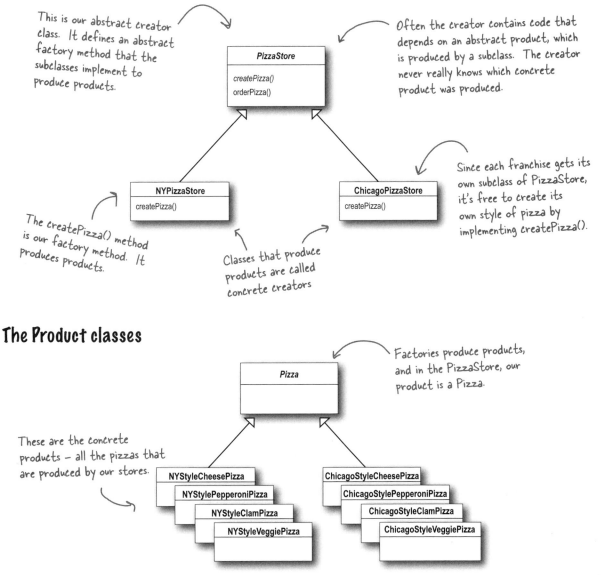

This is our abstract creator class. It defines an abstract factory method that the subclasses implement to produce products.

Often the creator contains code that depends on an abstract product, which is produced by a subclass. The creator never really knows which concrete product was produced.

Since each franchise gets its own subclass of PizzaStore, it's free to create its own style of pizza by implementing createPizza().

The createPizza() method is our factory method. It produces products.

Classes that produce products are called concrete creators

The Product classes

Factories produce products, and in the PizzaStore, our product is a Pizza.

These are the concrete products – all the pizzas that are produced by our stores.

Another perspective: parallel class hierarchies

We've seen that the factory method provides a framework by supplying an orderPizza() method that is combined with a factory method. Another way to look at this pattern as a framework is in the way it encapsulates product knowledge into each creator.

Let's look at the two parallel class hierarchies and see how they relate:

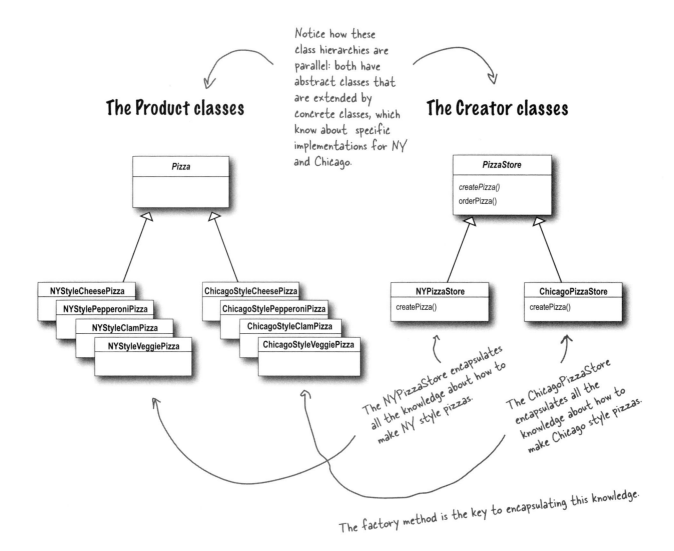

The Product classes

Notice how these class hierarchies are parallel: both have abstract classes that are extended by concrete classes, which know about specific implementations for NY and Chicago.

The Creator classes

The NYPizzaStore encapsulates all the knowledge about how to make NY style pizzas.

The ChicagoPizzaStore encapsulates all the knowledge about how to make Chicago style pizzas.

The factory method is the key to encapsulating this knowledge.

 Design Puzzle

We need another kind of pizza for those crazy Californians (crazy in a *good* way of course). Draw another parallel set of classes that you'd need to add a new California region to our PizzaStore.

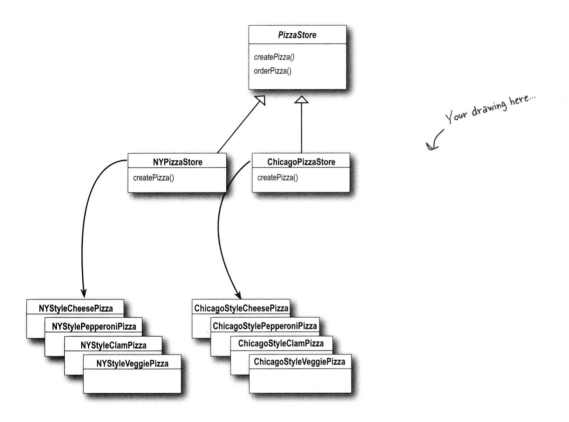

Your drawing here...

Okay, now write the five *most bizarre* things you can think of to put on a pizza. Then, you'll be ready to go into business making pizza in California!

_____

_____

_____

_____

_____

Factory Method Pattern defined

It's time to roll out the official definition of the Factory Method Pattern:

> **The Factory Method Pattern** defines an interface
> for creating an object, but lets subclasses decide which
> class to instantiate. Factory Method lets a class defer
> instantiation to subclasses.

As with every factory, the Factory Method Pattern gives us a way to encapsulate the instantiations of concrete types. Looking at the class diagram below, you can see that the abstract Creator gives you an interface with a method for creating objects, also known as the "factory method." Any other methods implemented in the abstract Creator are written to operate on products produced by the factory method. Only subclasses actually implement the factory method and create products.

As in the official definition, you'll often hear developers say that the Factory Method lets subclasses decide which class to instantiate. They say "decides" not because the pattern allows subclasses themselves to decide at runtime, but because the creator class is written without knowledge of the actual products that will be created, which is decided purely by the choice of the subclass that is used.

You could ask them what "decides" means, but we bet you now understand this better than they do!

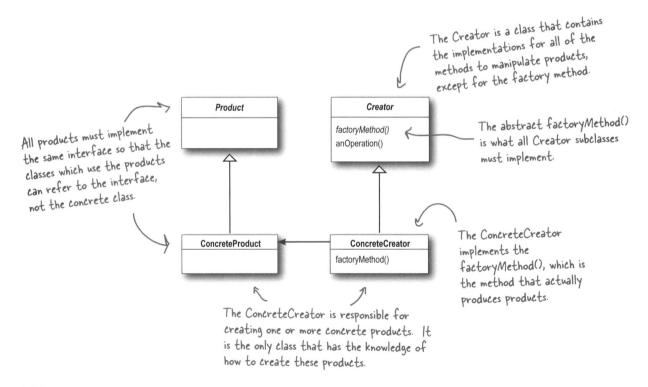

The Creator is a class that contains the implementations for all of the methods to manipulate products, except for the factory method.

The abstract factoryMethod() is what all Creator subclasses must implement.

All products must implement the same interface so that the classes which use the products can refer to the interface, not the concrete class.

The ConcreteCreator implements the factoryMethod(), which is the method that actually produces products.

The ConcreteCreator is responsible for creating one or more concrete products. It is the only class that has the knowledge of how to create these products.

there are no
Dumb Questions

Q: What's the advantage of the Factory Method Pattern when you only have one ConcreteCreator?

A: The Factory Method Pattern is useful if you've only got one concrete creator because you are decoupling the implementation of the product from its use. If you add additional products or change a product's implementation, it will not affect your Creator (because the Creator is not tightly coupled to any ConcreteProduct).

Q: Would it be correct to say that our NY and Chicago stores are implemented using Simple Factory? They look just like it.

A: They're similar, but used in different ways. Even though the implementation of each concrete store looks a lot like the SimplePizzaFactory, remember that the concrete stores are extending a class which has defined createPizza() as an abstract method. It is up to each store to define the behavior of the createPizza() method. In Simple Factory, the factory is another object that is composed with the PizzaStore.

Q: Are the factory method and the Creator always abstract?

A: No, you can define a default factory method to produce some concrete product. Then you always have a means of creating products even if there are no subclasses of the Creator.

Q: Each store can make four different kinds of pizzas based on the type passed in. Do all concrete creators make multiple products, or do they sometimes just make one?

A: We implemented what is known as the parameterized factory method. It can make more than one object based on a parameter passed in, as you noticed. Often, however, a factory just produces one object and is not parameterized. Both are valid forms of the pattern.

Q: Your parameterized types don't seem "type-safe." I'm just passing in a String! What if I asked for a "CalmPizza"?

A: You are certainly correct and that would cause, what we call in the business, a "runtime error." There are several other more sophisticated techniques that can be used to make parameters more "type safe", or, in other words, to ensure errors in parameters can be caught at compile time. For instance, you can create objects that represent the parameter types, use static constants, or, in Java 5, you can use *enums*.

Q: I'm still a bit confused about the difference between Simple Factory and Factory Method. They look very similar, except that in Factory Method, the class that returns the pizza is a subclass. Can you explain?

A: You're right that the subclasses do look a lot like Simple Factory, however think of Simple Factory as a one shot deal, while with Factory Method you are creating a framework that let's the subclasses decide which implementation will be used. For example, the orderPizza() method in the Factory Method provides a general framework for creating pizzas that relies on a factory method to actually create the concrete classes that go into making a pizza. By subclassing the PizzaStore class, you decide what concrete products go into making the pizza that orderPizza() returns. Compare that with SimpleFactory, which gives you a way to encapsulate object creation, but doesn't give you the flexibility of the Factory Method because there is no way to vary the products you're creating.

Master and Student...

Master: *Grasshopper, tell me how your training is going?*

Student: *Master, I have taken my study of "encapsulate what varies" further.*

Master: *Go on...*

Student: *I have learned that one can encapsulate the code that creates objects. When you have code that instantiates concrete classes, this is an area of frequent change. I've learned a technique called "factories" that allows you to encapsulate this behavior of instantiation.*

Master: *And these "factories," of what benefit are they?*

Student: *There are many. By placing all my creation code in one object or method, I avoid duplication in my code and provide one place to perform maintenance. That also means clients depend only upon interfaces rather than the concrete classes required to instantiate objects. As I have learned in my studies, this allows me to program to an interface, not an implementation, and that makes my code more flexible and extensible in the future.*

Master: *Yes Grasshopper, your OO instincts are growing. Do you have any questions for your master today?*

Student: *Master, I know that by encapsulating object creation I am coding to abstractions and decoupling my client code from actual implementations. But my factory code must still use concrete classes to instantiate real objects. Am I not pulling the wool over my own eyes?*

Master: *Grasshopper, object creation is a reality of life; we must create objects or we will never create a single Java program. But, with knowledge of this reality, we can design our code so that we have corralled this creation code like the sheep whose wool you would pull over your eyes. Once corralled, we can protect and care for the creation code. If we let our creation code run wild, then we will never collect its "wool."*

Student: *Master, I see the truth in this.*

Master: *As I knew you would. Now, please go and meditate on object dependencies.*

A very dependent PizzaStore

Sharpen your pencil

Let's pretend you've never heard of an OO factory. Here's a version of the PizzaStore that doesn't use a factory; make a count of the number of concrete pizza objects this class is dependent on. If you added California style pizzas to this PizzaStore, how many objects would it be dependent on then?

```java
public class DependentPizzaStore {

    public Pizza createPizza(String style, String type) {
        Pizza pizza = null;
        if (style.equals("NY")) {
            if (type.equals("cheese")) {
                pizza = new NYStyleCheesePizza();
            } else if (type.equals("veggie")) {
                pizza = new NYStyleVeggiePizza();
            } else if (type.equals("clam")) {
                pizza = new NYStyleClamPizza();
            } else if (type.equals("pepperoni")) {
                pizza = new NYStylePepperoniPizza();
            }
        } else if (style.equals("Chicago")) {
            if (type.equals("cheese")) {
                pizza = new ChicagoStyleCheesePizza();
            } else if (type.equals("veggie")) {
                pizza = new ChicagoStyleVeggiePizza();
            } else if (type.equals("clam")) {
                pizza = new ChicagoStyleClamPizza();
            } else if (type.equals("pepperoni")) {
                pizza = new ChicagoStylePepperoniPizza();
            }
        } else {
            System.out.println("Error: invalid type of pizza");
            return null;
        }
        pizza.prepare();
        pizza.bake();
        pizza.cut();
        pizza.box();
        return pizza;
    }
}
```

Handles all the NY style pizzas

Handles all the Chicago style pizzas

You can write your answers here: _____ number   _____ number with California too

Looking at object dependencies

When you directly instantiate an object, you are depending on its concrete class. Take a look at our very dependent PizzaStore one page back. It creates all the pizza objects right in the PizzaStore class instead of delegating to a factory.

If we draw a diagram representing that version of the PizzaStore and all the objects it depends on, here's what it looks like:

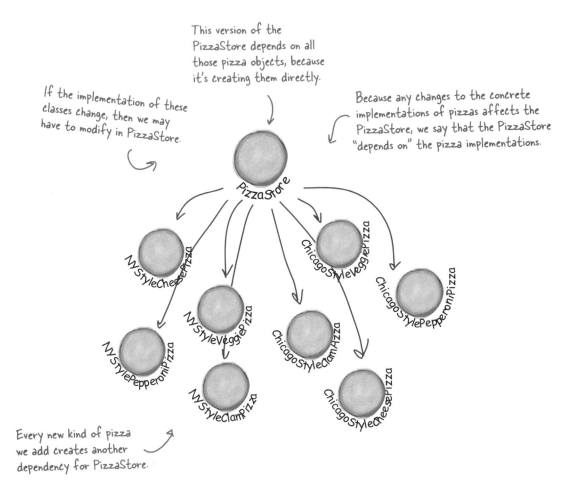

This version of the PizzaStore depends on all those pizza objects, because it's creating them directly.

If the implementation of these classes change, then we may have to modify in PizzaStore.

Because any changes to the concrete implementations of pizzas affects the PizzaStore, we say that the PizzaStore "depends on" the pizza implementations.

Every new kind of pizza we add creates another dependency for PizzaStore.

The Dependency Inversion Principle

It should be pretty clear that reducing dependencies to concrete classes in our code is a "good thing." In fact, we've got an OO design principle that formalizes this notion; it even has a big, formal name: *Dependency Inversion Principle*.

Here's the general principle:

Yet another phrase you can use to impress the execs in the room! Your raise will more than offset the cost of this book, and you'll gain the admiration of your fellow developers.

Design Principle

Depend upon abstractions. Do not depend upon concrete classes.

At first, this principle sounds a lot like "Program to an interface, not an implementation," right? It is similar; however, the Dependency Inversion Principle makes an even stronger statement about abstraction. It suggests that our high-level components should not depend on our low-level components; rather, they should *both* depend on abstractions.

A "high-level" component is a class with behavior defined in terms of other, "low level" components.

For example, PizzaStore is a high-level component because its behavior is defined in terms of pizzas — it creates all the different pizza objects, prepares, bakes, cuts, and boxes them, while the pizzas it uses are low-level components.

But what the heck does that mean?

Well, let's start by looking again at the pizza store diagram on the previous page. PizzaStore is our "high-level component" and the pizza implementations are our "low-level components," and clearly the PizzaStore is dependent on the concrete pizza classes.

Now, this principle tells us we should instead write our code so that we are depending on abstractions, not concrete classes. That goes for both our high level modules and our low-level modules.

But how do we do this? Let's think about how we'd apply this principle to our Very Dependent PizzaStore implementation...

Applying the Principle

Now, the main problem with the Very Dependent PizzaStore is that it depends on every type of pizza because it actually instantiates concrete types in its orderPizza() method.

While we've created an abstraction, Pizza, we're nevertheless creating concrete Pizzas in this code, so we don't get a lot of leverage out of this abstraction.

How can we get those instantiations out of the orderPizza() method? Well, as we know, the Factory Method allows us to do just that.

So, after we've applied the Factory Method, our diagram looks like this:

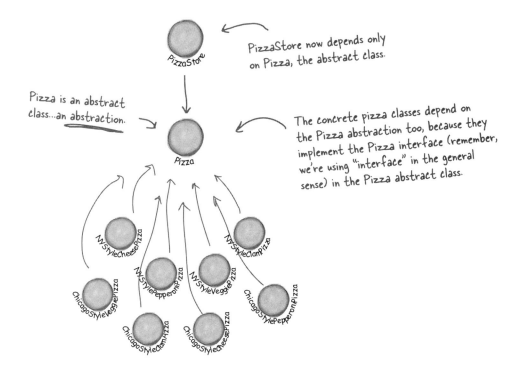

PizzaStore now depends only on Pizza, the abstract class.

Pizza is an abstract class...an abstraction.

The concrete pizza classes depend on the Pizza abstraction too, because they implement the Pizza interface (remember, we're using "interface" in the general sense) in the Pizza abstract class.

After applying the Factory Method, you'll notice that our high-level component, the PizzaStore, and our low-level components, the pizzas, both depend on Pizza, the abstraction. Factory Method is not the only technique for adhering to the Dependency Inversion Principle, but it is one of the more powerful ones.

Okay, I get the dependency part, but why is it called dependency **inversion**?

Where's the "inversion" in Dependency Inversion Principle?

The "inversion" in the name Dependency Inversion Principle is there because it inverts the way you typically might think about your OO design. Look at the diagram on the previous page, notice that the low-level components now depend on a higher level abstraction. Likewise, the high-level component is also tied to the same abstraction. So, the top-to-bottom dependency chart we drew a couple of pages back has inverted itself, with both high-level and low-level modules now depending on the abstraction.

Let's also walk through the thinking behind the typical design process and see how introducing the principle can invert the way we think about the design...

Inverting your thinking...

Okay, so you need to implement a PizzaStore. What's the first thought that pops into your head?

> Hmmm, Pizza Stores prepare, bake and box pizzas. So, my store needs to be able to make a bunch of different pizzas: CheesePizza, VeggiePizza, ClamPizza, and so on...

Right, you start at top and follow things down to the concrete classes. But, as you've seen, you don't want your store to know about the concrete pizza types, because then it'll be dependent on all those concrete classes!

Now, let's "invert" your thinking... instead of starting at the top, start at the Pizzas and think about what you can abstract.

> Well, a CheesePizza and a VeggiePizza and a ClamPizza are all just Pizzas, so they should share a Pizza interface.

Right! You are thinking about the abstraction *Pizza*. So now, go back and think about the design of the Pizza Store again.

> Since I now have a Pizza abstraction, I can design my Pizza Store and not worry about the concrete pizza classes.

Close. But to do that you'll have to rely on a factory to get those concrete classes out of your Pizza Store. Once you've done that, your different concrete pizza types depend only on an abstraction and so does your store. We've taken a design where the store depended on concrete classes and inverted those dependencies (along with your thinking).

A few guidelines to help you follow the Principle...

The following guidelines can help you avoid OO designs that violate the Dependency Inversion Principle:

- No variable should hold a reference to a concrete class.

  > If you use **new**, you'll be holding a reference to a concrete class. Use a factory to get around that!

- No class should derive from a concrete class.

  > If you derive from a concrete class, you're depending on a concrete class. Derive from an abstraction, like an interface or an abstract class.

- No method should override an implemented method of any of its base classes.

  > If you override an implemented method, then your base class wasn't really an abstraction to start with. Those methods implemented in the base class are meant to be shared by all your subclasses.

> But wait, aren't these guidelines impossible to follow? If I follow these, I'll never be able to write a single program!

You're exactly right! Like many of our principles, this is a guideline you should strive for, rather than a rule you should follow all the time. Clearly, every single Java program ever written violates these guidelines!

But, if you internalize these guidelines and have them in the back of your mind when you design, you'll know when you are violating the principle and you'll have a good reason for doing so. For instance, if you have a class that isn't likely to change, and you know it, then it's not the end of the world if you instantiate a concrete class in your code. Think about it; we instantiate String objects all the time without thinking twice. Does that violate the principle? Yes. Is that okay? Yes. Why? Because String is very unlikely to change.

If, on the other hand, a class you write is likely to change, you have some good techniques like Factory Method to encapsulate that change.

Meanwhile, back at the PizzaStore...

The design for the PizzaStore is really shaping up: it's got a flexible framework and it does a good job of adhering to design principles.

Now, the key to Objectville Pizza's success has always been fresh, quality ingredients, and what you've discovered is that with the new framework your franchises have been following your *procedures*, but a few franchises have been substituting inferior ingredients in their pies to lower costs and increase their margins. You know you've got to do something, because in the long term this is going to hurt the Objectville brand!

Dough

Pepperoni

Veggies

Cheese

Sauce

Ensuring consistency in your ingredients

So how are you going to ensure each franchise is using quality ingredients? You're going to build a factory that produces them and ships them to your franchises!

Now there is only one problem with this plan: the franchises are located in different regions and what is red sauce in New York is not red sauce in Chicago. So, you have one set of ingredients that need to be shipped to New York and a *different* set that needs to shipped to Chicago. Let's take a closer look:

Chicago PizzaMenu

Cheese Pizza
    Plum Tomato Sauce, Mozzarella, Parmesan, Oregano

Veggie Pizza
    Plum Tomato Sauce, Mozzarella, Parmesan, Eggplant, Spinach, Black Olives

Clam Pizza
    Plum Tomato Sauce, Mozzarella, Parmesan, Clams

Pepperoni Pizza
    Plum Tomato Sauce, Mozzarella, Parmesan, Eggplant, Spinach, Black Olives, Pepperoni

We've got the same product families (dough, sauce, cheese, veggies, meats) but different implementations based on region.

New York PizzaMenu

Cheese Pizza
    Marinara Sauce, Reggiano, Garlic

Veggie Pizza
    Marinara Sauce, Reggiano, Mushrooms, Onions, Red Peppers

Clam Pizza
    Marinara Sauce, Reggiano, Fresh Clams

Pepperoni Pizza
    Marinara Sauce, Reggiano, Mushrooms, Onions, Red Peppers, Pepperoni

Families of ingredients...

New York uses one set of
ingredients and Chicago another.
Given the popularity of Objectville
Pizza it won't be long before you
also need to ship another set of
regional ingredients to California,
and what's next? Seattle?

For this to work, you are going to
have to figure out how to handle
families of ingredients.

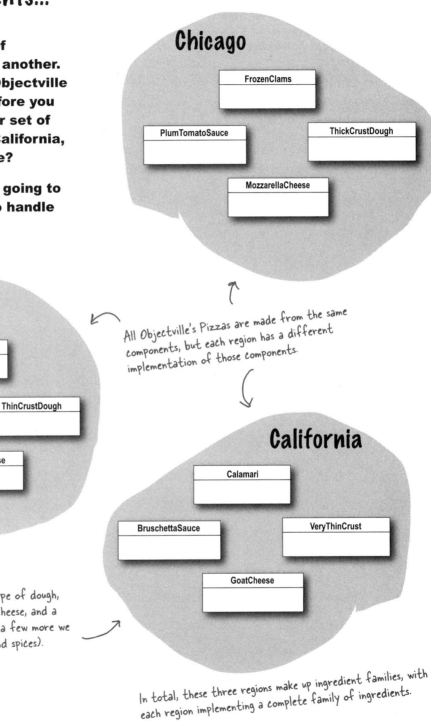

Chicago

FrozenClams

PlumTomatoSauce

ThickCrustDough

MozzarellaCheese

New York

FreshClams

MarinaraSauce

ThinCrustDough

ReggianoCheese

California

Calamari

BruschettaSauce

VeryThinCrust

GoatCheese

All Objectville's Pizzas are made from the same
components, but each region has a different
implementation of those components.

Each family consists of a type of dough,
a type of sauce, a type of cheese, and a
seafood topping (along with a few more we
haven't shown, like veggies and spices).

In total, these three regions make up ingredient families, with
each region implementing a complete family of ingredients.

Building the ingredient factories

Now we're going to build a factory to create our ingredients; the factory will be responsible for creating each ingredient in the ingredient family. In other words, the factory will need to create dough, sauce, cheese, and so on... You'll see how we are going to handle the regional differences shortly.

Let's start by defining an interface for the factory that is going to create all our ingredients:

```
public interface PizzaIngredientFactory {

    public Dough createDough();
    public Sauce createSauce();
    public Cheese createCheese();
    public Veggies[] createVeggies();
    public Pepperoni createPepperoni();
    public Clams createClam();

}
```

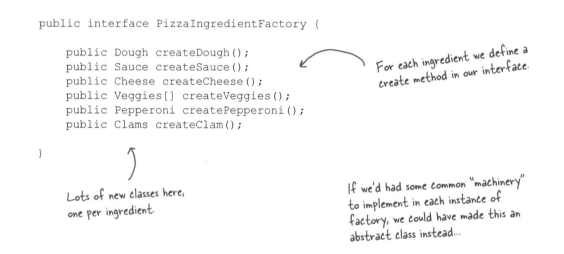

For each ingredient we define a create method in our interface.

Lots of new classes here, one per ingredient.

If we'd had some common "machinery" to implement in each instance of factory, we could have made this an abstract class instead...

Here's what we're going to do:

 Build a factory for each region. To do this, you'll create a subclass of PizzaIngredientFactory that implements each create method

 Implement a set of ingredient classes to be used with the factory, like ReggianoCheese, RedPeppers, and ThickCrustDough. These classes can be shared among regions where appropriate.

③ Then we still need to hook all this up by working our new ingredient factories into our old PizzaStore code.

Building the New York ingredient factory

Okay, here's the implementation for the New York ingredient factory. This factory specializes in Marinara sauce, Reggiano Cheese, Fresh Clams...

The NY ingredient factory implements the interface for all ingredient factories

```
public class NYPizzaIngredientFactory implements PizzaIngredientFactory {

    public Dough createDough() {
        return new ThinCrustDough();
    }

    public Sauce createSauce() {
        return new MarinaraSauce();
    }

    public Cheese createCheese() {
        return new ReggianoCheese();
    }

    public Veggies[] createVeggies() {
        Veggies veggies[] = { new Garlic(), new Onion(), new Mushroom(), new RedPepper() };
        return veggies;
    }

    public Pepperoni createPepperoni() {
        return new SlicedPepperoni();
    }
    public Clams createClam() {
        return new FreshClams();
    }
}
```

For each ingredient in the ingredient family, we create the New York version.

For veggies, we return an array of Veggies. Here we've hardcoded the veggies. We could make this more sophisticated, but that doesn't really add anything to learning the factory pattern, so we'll keep it simple.

New York is on the coast; it gets fresh clams. Chicago has to settle for frozen.

The best sliced pepperoni. This is shared between New York and Chicago. Make sure you use it on the next page when you get to implement the Chicago factory yourself

Sharpen your pencil

Write the ChicagoPizzaIngredientFactory. You can reference the classes below in your implementation:

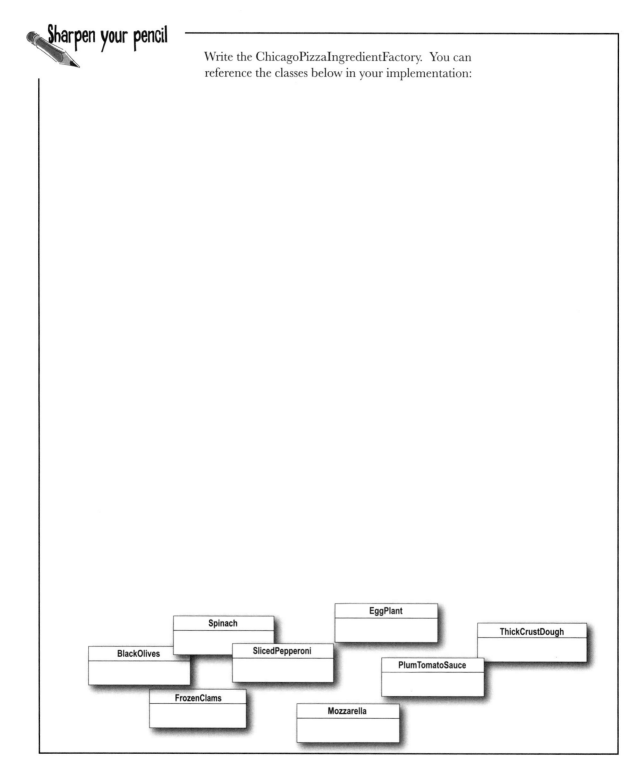

EggPlant

Spinach

ThickCrustDough

BlackOlives

SlicedPepperoni

PlumTomatoSauce

FrozenClams

Mozzarella

Reworking the pizzas...

We've got our factories all fired up and ready to produce quality ingredients; now we just need to rework our Pizzas so they only use factory-produced ingredients. We'll start with our abstract Pizza class:

```java
public abstract class Pizza {
    String name;
    Dough dough;
    Sauce sauce;
    Veggies veggies[];
    Cheese cheese;
    Pepperoni pepperoni;
    Clams clam;

    abstract void prepare();

    void bake() {
        System.out.println("Bake for 25 minutes at 350");
    }

    void cut() {
        System.out.println("Cutting the pizza into diagonal slices");
    }

    void box() {
        System.out.println("Place pizza in official PizzaStore box");
    }

    void setName(String name) {
        this.name = name;
    }

    String getName() {
        return name;
    }

    public String toString() {
        // code to print pizza here
    }
}
```

Each pizza holds a set of ingredients that are used in its preparation.

We've now made the prepare method abstract. This is where we are going to collect the ingredients needed for the pizza, which of course will come from the ingredient factory.

Our other methods remain the same, with the exception of the prepare method.

Reworking the pizzas, continued...

Now that you've got an abstract Pizza to work from, it's time to create the New York and Chicago style Pizzas – only this time around they will get their ingredients straight from the factory. The franchisees' days of skimping on ingredients are over!

When we wrote the Factory Method code, we had a NYCheesePizza and a ChicagoCheesePizza class. If you look at the two classes, the only thing that differs is the use of regional ingredients. The pizzas are made just the same (dough + sauce + cheese). The same goes for the other pizzas: Veggie, Clam, and so on. They all follow the same preparation steps; they just have different ingredients.

So, what you'll see is that we really don't need two classes for each pizza; the ingredient factory is going to handle the regional differences for us. Here's the Cheese Pizza:

```java
public class CheesePizza extends Pizza {
    PizzaIngredientFactory ingredientFactory;

    public CheesePizza(PizzaIngredientFactory ingredientFactory) {
        this.ingredientFactory = ingredientFactory;
    }

    void prepare() {
        System.out.println("Preparing " + name);
        dough = ingredientFactory.createDough();
        sauce = ingredientFactory.createSauce();
        cheese = ingredientFactory.createCheese();
    }
}
```

To make a pizza now, we need a factory to provide the ingredients. So each Pizza class gets a factory passed into its constructor, and it's stored in an instance variable.

← Here's where the magic happens!

The prepare() method steps through creating a cheese pizza, and each time it needs an ingredient, it asks the factory to produce it.

Code Up Close

The Pizza code uses the factory it has been composed with to produce the ingredients used in the pizza. The ingredients produced depend on which factory we're using. The Pizza class doesn't care; it knows how to make pizzas. Now, it's decoupled from the differences in regional ingredients and can be easily reused when there are factories for the Rockies, the Pacific Northwest, and beyond.

```
sauce = ingredientFactory.createSauce();
```

We're setting the Pizza instance variable to refer to the specific sauce used in this pizza.

This is our ingredient factory. The Pizza doesn't care which factory is used, as long as it is an ingredient factory.

The createSauce() method returns the sauce that is used in its region. If this is a NY ingredient factory, then we get marinara sauce.

Let's check out the ClamPizza as well:

```java
public class ClamPizza extends Pizza {
    PizzaIngredientFactory ingredientFactory;

    public ClamPizza(PizzaIngredientFactory ingredientFactory) {
        this.ingredientFactory = ingredientFactory;
    }

    void prepare() {
        System.out.println("Preparing " + name);
        dough = ingredientFactory.createDough();
        sauce = ingredientFactory.createSauce();
        cheese = ingredientFactory.createCheese();
        clam = ingredientFactory.createClam();
    }
}
```

ClamPizza also stashes an ingredient factory.

To make a clam pizza, the prepare method collects the right ingredients from its local factory.

If it's a New York factory, the clams will be fresh; if it's Chicago, they'll be frozen.

Revisiting our pizza stores

We're almost there; we just need to make a quick trip to our franchise stores to make sure they are using the correct Pizzas. We also need to give them a reference to their local ingredient factories:

```java
public class NYPizzaStore extends PizzaStore {

    protected Pizza createPizza(String item) {
        Pizza pizza = null;
        PizzaIngredientFactory ingredientFactory =
            new NYPizzaIngredientFactory();

        if (item.equals("cheese")) {

            pizza = new CheesePizza(ingredientFactory);
            pizza.setName("New York Style Cheese Pizza");

        } else if (item.equals("veggie")) {

            pizza = new VeggiePizza(ingredientFactory);
            pizza.setName("New York Style Veggie Pizza");

        } else if (item.equals("clam")) {

            pizza = new ClamPizza(ingredientFactory);
            pizza.setName("New York Style Clam Pizza");

        } else if (item.equals("pepperoni")) {
            pizza = new PepperoniPizza(ingredientFactory);
            pizza.setName("New York Style Pepperoni Pizza");

        }
        return pizza;
    }
}
```

The NY Store is composed with a NY pizza ingredient factory. This will be used to produce the ingredients for all NY style pizzas.

We now pass each pizza the factory that should be used to produce its ingredients.

Look back one page and make sure you understand how the pizza and the factory work together!

For each type of Pizza, we instantiate a new Pizza and give it the factory it needs to get its ingredients.

Compare this version of the createPizza() method to the one in the Factory Method implementation earlier in the chapter.

What have we done?

That was quite a series of code changes; what exactly did we do?

We provided a means of creating a family of ingredients for pizzas by introducing a new type of factory called an Abstract Factory.

An Abstract Factory gives us an interface for creating a family of products. By writing code that uses this interface, we decouple our code from the actual factory that creates the products. That allows us to implement a variety of factories that produce products meant for different contexts – such as different regions, different operating systems, or different look and feels.

Because our code is decoupled from the actual products, we can substitute different factories to get different behaviors (like getting marinara instead of plum tomatoes).

An Abstract Factory provides an interface for a family of products. What's a family? In our case it's all the things we need to make a pizza: dough, sauce, cheese, meats and veggies.

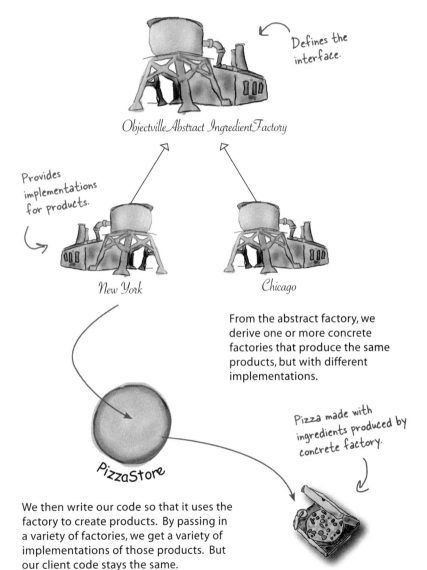

Defines the interface.

Objectville Abstract IngredientFactory

Provides implementations for products.

New York   *Chicago*

From the abstract factory, we derive one or more concrete factories that produce the same products, but with different implementations.

Pizza made with ingredients produced by concrete factory.

PizzaStore

We then write our code so that it uses the factory to create products. By passing in a variety of factories, we get a variety of implementations of those products. But our client code stays the same.

More pizza for Ethan and Joel...

Ethan and Joel can't get enough Objectville Pizza! What they don't know is that now their orders are making use of the new ingredient factories. So now when they order...

Behind the Scenes

> I'm still lovin' NY Style.

> I'm stickin' with Chicago.

The first part of the order process hasn't changed at all. Let's follow Ethan's order again:

1 **First we need a NY PizzaStore:**

```
PizzaStore nyPizzaStore = new NYPizzaStore();
```

Creates an instance of NYPizzaStore.

nyPizzaStore

2 **Now that we have a store, we can take an order:**

```
nyPizzaStore.orderPizza("cheese");
```

the orderPizza() method is called on the nyPizzaStore instance.

```
createPizza("cheese")
```

3 **The orderPizza() method first calls the createPizza() method:**

```
Pizza pizza  = createPizza("cheese");
```

From here things change, because we are using an ingredient factory

Behind the Scenes

4 **When the createPizza() method is called, that's when our ingredient factory gets involved:**

The ingredient factory is chosen and instantiated in the PizzaStore and then passed into the constructor of each pizza.

```
Pizza pizza = new CheesePizza(nyIngredientFactory);
```

holds

Creates a instance of Pizza that is composed with the New York ingredient factory.

myIngredientFactory

Pizza

5 **Next we need to prepare the pizza. Once the prepare() method is called, the factory is asked to prepare ingredients:**

prepare()

```
void prepare() {
    dough = factory.createDough();
    sauce = factory.createSauce();
    cheese = factory.createCheese();
}
```

→ Thin crust

→ Marinara

↘ Reggiano

For Ethan's pizza the New York ingredient factory is used, and so we get the NY ingredients.

6 **Finally we have the prepared pizza in hand and the orderPizza() method bakes, cuts, and boxes the pizza.**

Abstract Factory Pattern defined

We're adding yet another factory pattern to our pattern family, one that lets us create families of products. Let's check out the official definition for this pattern:

> **The Abstract Factory Pattern** provides an interface for creating families of related or dependent objects without specifying their concrete classes.

We've certainly seen that Abstract Factory allows a client to use an abstract interface to create a set of related products without knowing (or caring) about the concrete products that are actually produced. In this way, the client is decoupled from any of the specifics of the concrete products. Let's look at the class diagram to see how this all holds together:

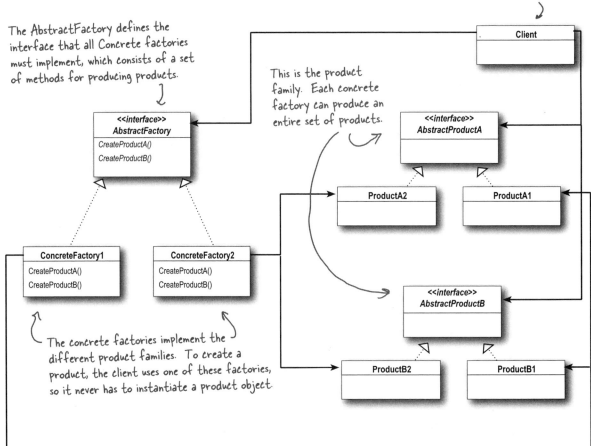

The Client is written against the abstract factory and then composed at runtime with an actual factory.

The AbstractFactory defines the interface that all Concrete factories must implement, which consists of a set of methods for producing products.

This is the product family. Each concrete factory can produce an entire set of products.

The concrete factories implement the different product families. To create a product, the client uses one of these factories, so it never has to instantiate a product object.

That's a fairly complicated class diagram; let's look at it all in terms of our PizzaStore:

The clients of the Abstract Factory are the concrete instances of the Pizza abstract class.

The abstract PizzaIngredientFactory is the interface that defines how to make a family of related products — everything we need to make a pizza.

The job of the concrete pizza factories is to make pizza ingredients. Each factory knows how to create the right objects for their region.

Each factory produces a different implementation for the family of products.

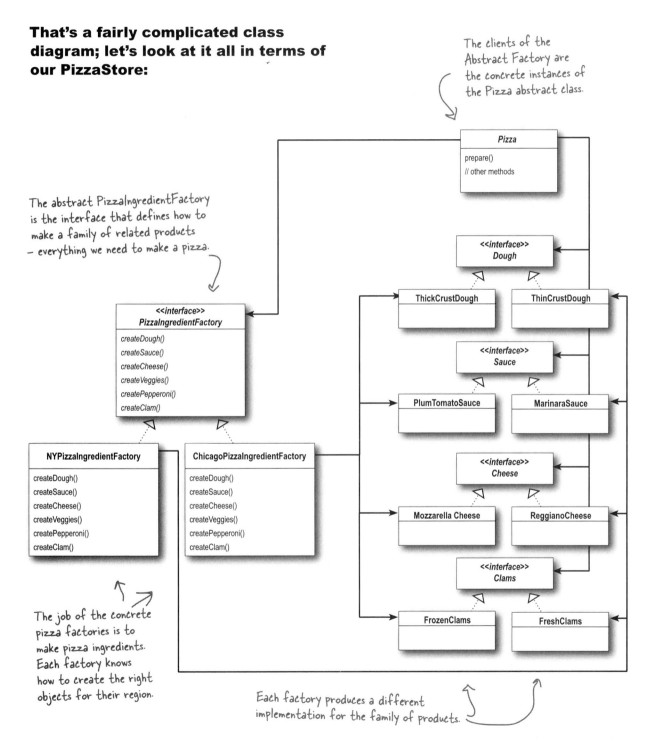

> I noticed that each method in the Abstract Factory actually looks like a Factory Method (createDough(), createSauce(), etc.). Each method is declared abstract and the subclasses override it to create some object. Isn't that Factory Method?

Is that a Factory Method lurking inside the Abstract Factory?

Good catch! Yes, often the methods of an Abstract Factory are implemented as factory methods. It makes sense, right? The job of an Abstract Factory is to define an interface for creating a set of products. Each method in that interface is responsible for creating a concrete product, and we implement a subclass of the Abstract Factory to supply those implementations. So, factory methods are a natural way to implement your product methods in your abstract factories.

Patterns Exposed

This week's interview:
Factory Method and Abstract Factory, on each other

HeadFirst: Wow, an interview with two patterns at once! This is a first for us.

Factory Method: Yeah, I'm not so sure I like being lumped in with Abstract Factory, you know. Just because we're both factory patterns doesn't mean we shouldn't get our own interviews.

HeadFirst: Don't be miffed, we wanted to interview you together so we could help clear up any confusion about who's who for the readers. You do have similarities, and I've heard that people sometimes get you confused.

Abstract Factory: It is true, there have been times I've been mistaken for Factory Method, and I know you've had similar issues, Factory Method. We're both really good at decoupling applications from specific implementations; we just do it in different ways. So I can see why people might sometimes get us confused.

Factory Method: Well, it still ticks me off. After all, I use classes to create and you use objects; that's totally different!

HeadFirst: Can you explain more about that, Factory Method?

Factory Method: Sure. Both Abstract Factory and I create objects – that's our jobs. But I do it through inheritance...

Abstract Factory: ...and I do it through object composition.

Factory Method: Right. So that means, to create objects using Factory Method, you need to extend a class and override a factory method.

HeadFirst: And that factory method does what?

Factory Method: It creates objects, of course! I mean, the whole point of the Factory Method Pattern is that you're using a subclass to do your creation for you. In that way, clients only need to know the abstract type they are using, the subclass worries about the concrete type. So, in other words, I keep clients decoupled from the concrete types.

Abstract Factory: And I do too, only I do it in a different way.

HeadFirst: Go on, Abstract Factory... you said something about object composition?

Abstract Factory: I provide an abstract type for creating a family of products. Subclasses of this type define how those products are produced. To use the factory, you instantiate one and pass it into some code that is written against the abstract type. So, like Factory Method, my clients are decoupled from the actual concrete products they use.

HeadFirst: Oh, I see, so another advantage is that you group together a set of related products.

Abstract Factory: That's right.

HeadFirst: What happens if you need to extend that set of related products, to say add another one? Doesn't that require changing your interface?

Abstract Factory: That's true; my interface has to change if new products are added, which I know people don't like to do....

Factory Method: <snicker>

Abstract Factory: What are you snickering at, Factory Method?

Factory Method: Oh, come on, that's a big deal! Changing your interface means you have to go in and change the interface of every subclass! That sounds like a lot of work.

Abstract Factory: Yeah, but I need a big interface because I am used to create entire families of products. You're only creating one product, so you don't really need a big interface, you just need one method.

HeadFirst: Abstract Factory, I heard that you often use factory methods to implement your concrete factories?

Abstract Factory: Yes, I'll admit it, my concrete factories often implement a factory method to create their products. In my case, they are used purely to create products...

Factory Method: ...while in my case I usually implement code in the abstract creator that makes use of the concrete types the subclasses create.

HeadFirst: It sounds like you both are good at what you do. I'm sure people like having a choice; after all, factories are so useful, they'll want to use them in all kinds of different situations. You both encapsulate object creation to keep applications loosely coupled and less dependent on implementations, which is really great, whether you're using Factory Method or Abstract Factory. May I allow you each a parting word?

Abstract Factory: Thanks. Remember me, Abstract Factory, and use me whenever you have families of products you need to create and you want to make sure your clients create products that belong together.

Factory Method: And I'm Factory Method; use me to decouple your client code from the concrete classes you need to instantiate, or if you don't know ahead of time all the concrete classes you are going to need. To use me, just subclass me and implement my factory method!

Factory Method and Abstract Factory compared

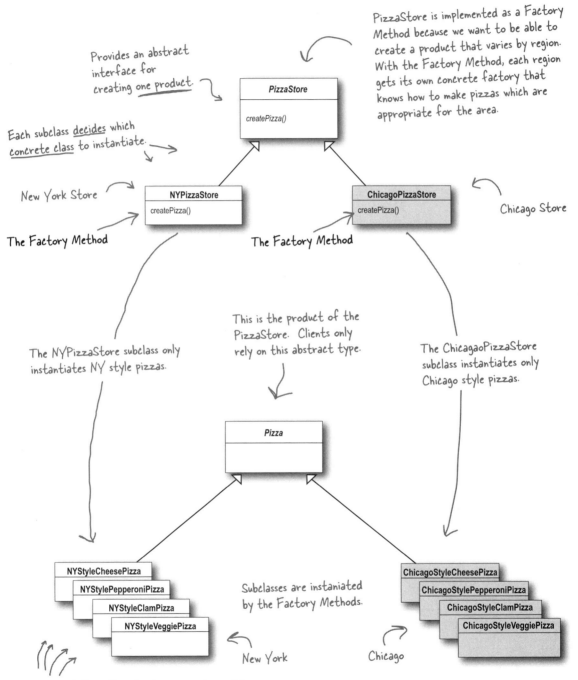

Provides an abstract interface for creating one <u>product</u>.

PizzaStore is implemented as a Factory Method because we want to be able to create a product that varies by region. With the Factory Method, each region gets its own concrete factory that knows how to make pizzas which are appropriate for the area.

PizzaStore

createPizza()

Each subclass <u>decides</u> which <u>concrete class</u> to instantiate.

New York Store

NYPizzaStore

createPizza()

The Factory Method

ChicagoPizzaStore

createPizza()

Chicago Store

The Factory Method

The NYPizzaStore subclass only instantiates NY style pizzas.

This is the product of the PizzaStore. Clients only rely on this abstract type.

The ChicagaoPizzaStore subclass instantiates only Chicago style pizzas.

Pizza

NYStyleCheesePizza
NYStylePepperoniPizza
NYStyleClamPizza
NYStyleVeggiePizza

Subclasses are instaniated by the Factory Methods.

ChicagoStyleCheesePizza
ChicagoStylePepperoniPizza
ChicagoStyleClamPizza
ChicagoStyleVeggiePizza

New York

Chicago

The createPizza() method is parameterized by pizza type, so we can return many types of pizza products.

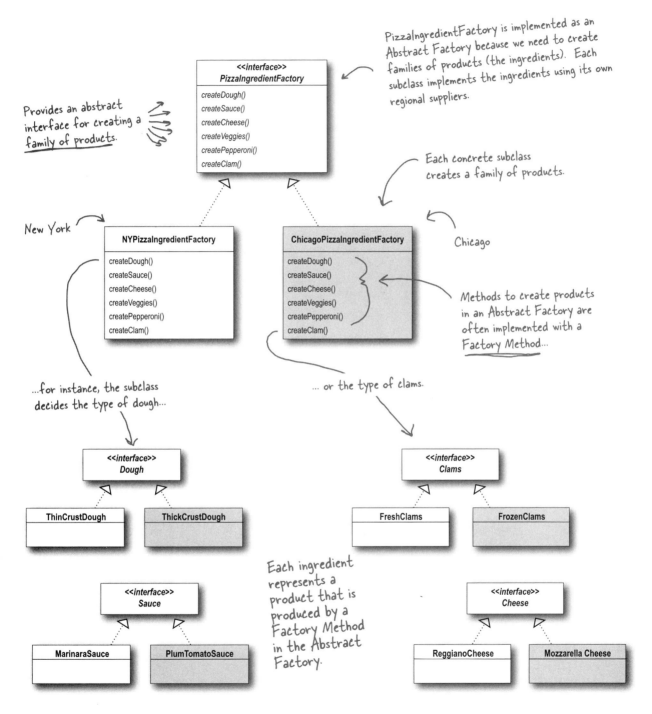

PizzaIngredientFactory is implemented as an Abstract Factory because we need to create families of products (the ingredients). Each subclass implements the ingredients using its own regional suppliers.

Provides an abstract interface for creating a family of products.

Each concrete subclass creates a family of products.

New York

Chicago

Methods to create products in an Abstract Factory are often implemented with a Factory Method...

...for instance, the subclass decides the type of dough...

... or the type of clams.

Each ingredient represents a product that is produced by a Factory Method in the Abstract Factory.

The product subclasses create parallel sets of product families. Here we have a New York ingredient family and a Chicago family.

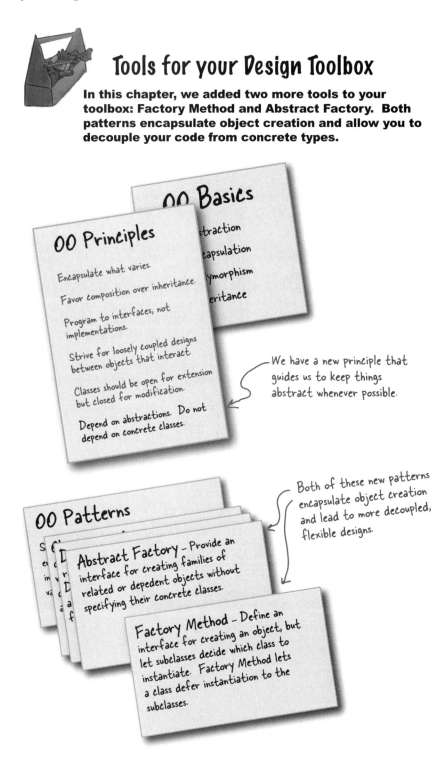

Tools for your Design Toolbox

In this chapter, we added two more tools to your toolbox: Factory Method and Abstract Factory. Both patterns encapsulate object creation and allow you to decouple your code from concrete types.

OO Basics

straction

capsulation

ymorphism

eritance

OO Principles

Encapsulate what varies.

Favor composition over inheritance.

Program to interfaces, not implementations.

Strive for loosely coupled designs between objects that interact.

Classes should be open for extension but closed for modification.

Depend on abstractions. Do not depend on concrete classes.

— We have a new principle that guides us to keep things abstract whenever possible.

Both of these new patterns encapsulate object creation and lead to more decoupled, flexible designs.

OO Patterns

S
e
in
va
D
a
f

Abstract Factory – Provide an interface for creating families of related or depedent objects without specifying their concrete classes.

Factory Method – Define an interface for creating an object, but let subclasses decide which class to instantiate. Factory Method lets a class defer instantiation to the subclasses.

It's been a long chapter. Grab a slice of Pizza and relax while doing this crossword; all of the solution words are from this chapter.

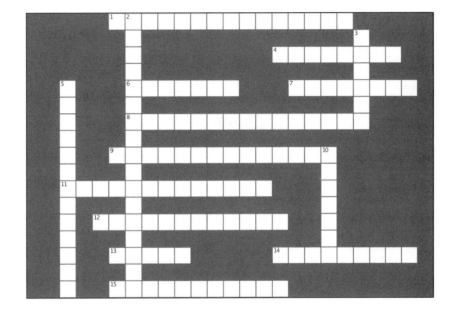

Across

1. In Factory Method, each franchise is a _____

4. In Factory Method, who decides which class to instantiate?

6. Role of PizzaStore in Factory Method Pattern

7. All New York Style Pizzas use this kind of cheese

8. In Abstract Factory, each ingredient factory is a _____

9. When you use new, you are programming to an _____

11. createPizza() is a _____ (two words)

12. Joel likes this kind of pizza

13. In Factory Method, the PizzaStore and the concrete Pizzas all depend on this abstraction

14. When a class instantiates an object from a concrete class, it's _____ on that object

15. All factory patterns allow us to _____ object creation

Down

2. We used _____ in Simple Factory and Abstract Factory and inheritance in Factory Method

3. Abstract Factory creates a _____ of products

5. Not a REAL factory pattern, but handy nonetheless

10. Ethan likes this kind of pizza

Exercise solutions

We've knocked out the NYPizzaStore; just two more to go and we'll be ready to franchise! Write the Chicago and California PizzaStore implementations here:

> Both of these stores are almost exactly like the New York store... they just create different kinds of pizzas

```
public class ChicagoPizzaStore extends PizzaStore {
    protected Pizza createPizza(String item) {
        if (item.equals("cheese")) {
            return new ChicagoStyleCheesePizza();
        } else if (item.equals("veggie")) {
            return new ChicagoStyleVeggiePizza();
        } else if (item.equals("clam")) {
            return new ChicagoStyleClamPizza();
        } else if (item.equals("pepperoni")) {
            return new ChicagoStylePepperoniPizza();
        } else return null;
    }
}
```

For the Chicago pizza store, we just have to make sure we create Chicago style pizzas...

```
public class CaliforniaPizzaStore extends PizzaStore {
    protected Pizza createPizza(String item) {
        if (item.equals("cheese")) {
            return new CaliforniaStyleCheesePizza();
        } else if (item.equals("veggie")) {
            return new CaliforniaStyleVeggiePizza();
        } else if (item.equals("clam")) {
            return new CaliforniaStyleClamPizza();
        } else if (item.equals("pepperoni")) {
            return new CaliforniaStylePepperoniPizza();
        } else return null;
    }
}
```

and for the California pizza store, we create California style pizzas.

Design Puzzle Solution

We need another kind of pizza for those crazy Californians (crazy in a GOOD way of course). Draw another parallel set of classes that you'd need to add a new California region to our PizzaStore.

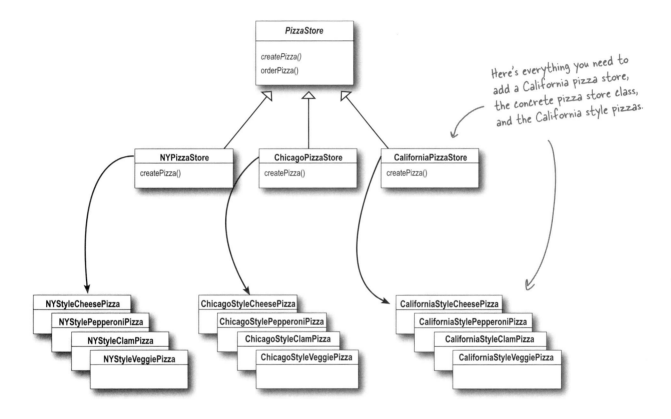

Here's everything you need to add a California pizza store, the concrete pizza store class, and the California style pizzas.

Okay, now write the five silliest things you can think of to put on a pizza. Then, you'll be ready to go into business making pizza in California!

Here are our suggestions...

Mashed Potatoes with Roasted Garlic

BBQ Sauce

Artichoke Hearts

M&M's

Peanuts

A very dependent PizzaStore

Sharpen your pencil

Let's pretend you've never heard of an OO factory. Here's a version of the PizzaStore that doesn't use a factory; make a count of the number of concrete pizza objects this class is dependent on. If you added California style pizzas to this PizzaStore, how many objects would it be dependent on then?

```java
public class DependentPizzaStore {

    public Pizza createPizza(String style, String type) {
        Pizza pizza = null;
        if (style.equals("NY")) {
            if (type.equals("cheese")) {
                pizza = new NYStyleCheesePizza();
            } else if (type.equals("veggie")) {
                pizza = new NYStyleVeggiePizza();
            } else if (type.equals("clam")) {
                pizza = new NYStyleClamPizza();
            } else if (type.equals("pepperoni")) {
                pizza = new NYStylePepperoniPizza();
            }
        } else if (style.equals("Chicago")) {
            if (type.equals("cheese")) {
                pizza = new ChicagoStyleCheesePizza();
            } else if (type.equals("veggie")) {
                pizza = new ChicagoStyleVeggiePizza();
            } else if (type.equals("clam")) {
                pizza = new ChicagoStyleClamPizza();
            } else if (type.equals("pepperoni")) {
                pizza = new ChicagoStylePepperoniPizza();
            }
        } else {
            System.out.println("Error: invalid type of pizza");
            return null;
        }
        pizza.prepare();
        pizza.bake();
        pizza.cut();
        pizza.box();
        return pizza;
    }
}
```

Handles all the NY style pizzas

Handles all the Chicago style pizzas

You can write your answers here:

_____8_____ number

_____12_____ number with California too

Sharpen your pencil

Go ahead and write the ChicagoPizzaIngredientFactory; you can reference the classes below in your implementation:

```java
public class ChicagoPizzaIngredientFactory
    implements PizzaIngredientFactory
{
    public Dough createDough() {
        return new ThickCrustDough();
    }

    public Sauce createSauce() {
        return new PlumTomatoSauce();
    }

    public Cheese createCheese() {
        return new MozzarellaCheese();
    }

    public Veggies[] createVeggies() {
        Veggies veggies[] = { new BlackOlives(),
                              new Spinach(),
                              new Eggplant() };
        return veggies;
    }

    public Pepperoni createPepperoni() {
        return new SlicedPepperoni();
    }

    public Clams createClam() {
        return new FrozenClams();
    }
}
```

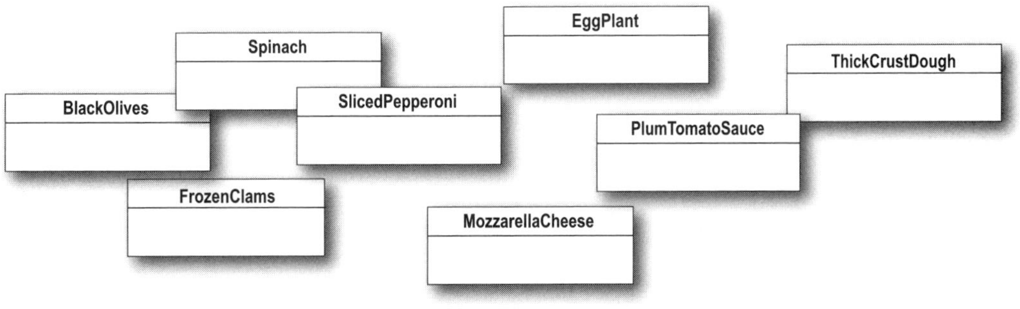

EggPlant	

Spinach	

ThickCrustDough	

BlackOlives	

SlicedPepperoni	

PlumTomatoSauce	

FrozenClams	

MozzarellaCheese	

Puzzle Solution

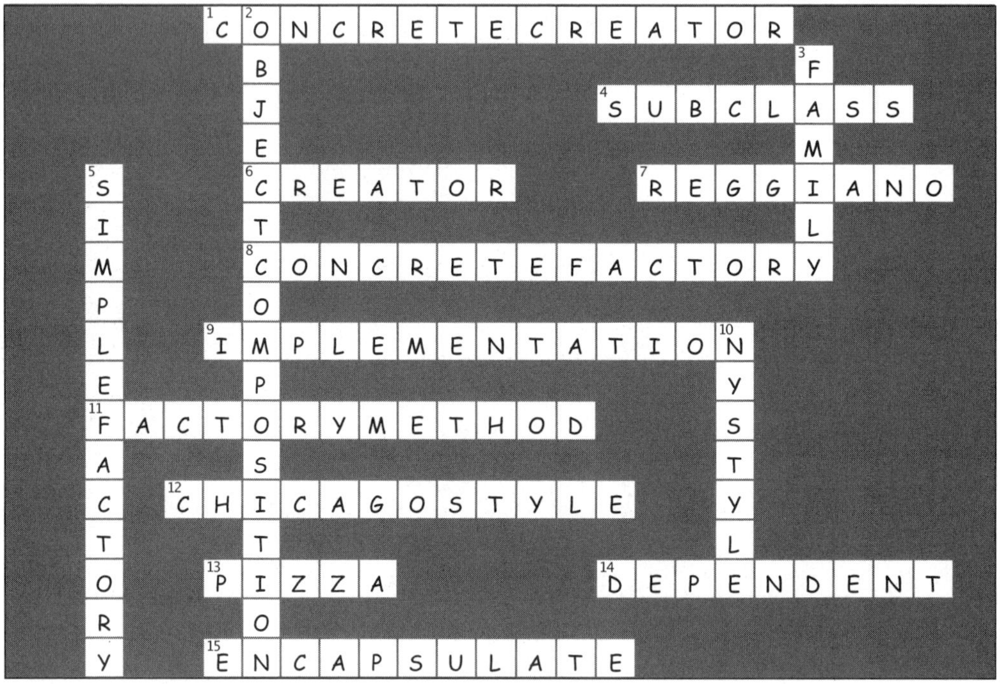
1 CONCRETECREATOR
2 OBJECTCOMPOSITION
3 FAMILY
4 SUBCLASS
5 SIMPLEFACTORY
6 CREATOR
7 REGGIANO
8 CONCRETEFACTORY
9 IMPLEMENTATION
10 NYSTYLE
11 FACTORYMETHOD
12 CHICAGOSTYLE
13 PIZZA
14 DEPENDENT
15 ENCAPSULATE

5 the Singleton Pattern

✳ *One of a Kind Objects* ✳

I tell ya she's ONE OF A KIND. Look at the lines, the curves, the body, the headlights!

You talkin' to me or the car? Oh, and when can I get my oven mitt back?

Our next stop is the Singleton Pattern, our ticket to creating one-of-a-kind objects for which there is only one instance. You might be happy to know that of all patterns, the Singleton is the simplest in terms of its class diagram; in fact, the diagram holds just a single class! But don't get too comfortable; despite its simplicity from a class design perspective, we are going to encounter quite a few bumps and potholes in its implementation. So buckle up.

Developer: What use is that?

Guru: There are many objects we only need one of: thread pools, caches, dialog boxes, objects that handle preferences and registry settings, objects used for logging, and objects that act as device drivers to devices like printers and graphics cards. In fact, for many of these types of objects, if we were to instantiate more than one we'd run into all sorts of problems like incorrect program behavior, overuse of resources, or inconsistent results.

Developer: Okay, so maybe there are classes that should only be instantiated once, but do I need a whole chapter for this? Can't I just do this by convention or by global variables? You know, like in Java, I could do it with a static variable.

Guru: In many ways, the Singleton Pattern **is a convention** for ensuring one and only one object is instantiated for a given class. If you've got a better one, the world would like to hear about it; but remember, like all patterns, the Singleton Pattern is a time-tested method for ensuring only one object gets created. The Singleton Pattern also gives us a global point of access, just like a global variable, but without the downsides.

Developer: What downsides?

Guru: Well, here's one example: if you assign an object to a global variable, then that object might be created when your application begins. Right? What if this object is resource intensive and your application never ends up using it? As you will see, with the Singleton Pattern, we can create our objects only when they are needed.

Developer: This still doesn't seem like it should be so difficult.

Guru: If you've got a good handle on static class variables and methods as well as access modifiers, it's not. But, in either case, it is interesting to see how a Singleton works, and, as simple as it sounds, Singleton code is hard to get right. Just ask yourself: how do I prevent more than one object from being instantiated? It's not so obvious, is it?

The Little Singleton

A small Socratic exercise in the style of The Little Lisper

How would you create a single object?	`new MyObject();`

And, what if another object wanted to create a MyObject? Could it call new on MyObject again?	Yes, of course.

So as long as we have a class, can we always instantiate it one or more times?	Yes. Well, only if it's a public class.

And if not?	Well, if it's not a public class, only classes in the same package can instantiate it. But they can still instantiate it more than once.

Hmm, interesting. Did you know you could do this?	No, I'd never thought of it, but I guess it makes sense because it is a legal definition.

```
public MyClass {

    private MyClass() {}

}
```

What does it mean?	I suppose it is a class that can't be instantiated because it has a private constructor.

Well, is there ANY object that could use the private constructor?	Hmm, I think the code in MyClass is the only code that could call it. But that doesn't make much sense.

Why not ?	Because I'd have to have an instance of the class to call it, but I can't have an instance because no other class can instantiate it. It's a chicken and egg problem: I can use the constructor from an object of type MyClass, but I can never instantiate that object because no other object can use "new MyClass()".

Okay. It was just a thought. What does this mean?	MyClass is a class with a static method. We can call the static method like this: `MyClass.getInstance();`

```
public MyClass {

    public static MyClass getInstance() {
    }
}
```

Why did you use MyClass, instead of some object name?	Well, getInstance() is a static method; in other words, it is a CLASS method. You need to use the class name to reference a static method.

Very interesting. What if we put things together. *Now* can I instantiate a MyClass?	Wow, you sure can.

```
public MyClass {

    private MyClass() {}

    public static MyClass getInstance() {
        return new MyClass();
    }
}
```

So, now can you think of a second way to instantiate an object?	`MyClass.getInstance();`

Can you finish the code so that only ONE instance of MyClass is ever created?	Yes, I think so...
	(You'll find the code on the next page.)

Dissecting the classic Singleton Pattern implementation

Let's rename MyClass to Singleton.

We have a static variable to hold our one instance of the class Singleton.

```
public class Singleton {
    private static Singleton uniqueInstance;

    // other useful instance variables here

    private Singleton() {}

    public static Singleton getInstance() {
        if (uniqueInstance == null) {
            uniqueInstance = new Singleton();
        }
        return uniqueInstance;
    }

    // other useful methods here
}
```

Our constructor is declared private; only Singleton can instantiate this class!

The getInstance() method gives us a way to instantiate the class and also to return an instance of it.

Of course, Singleton is a normal class; it has other useful instance variables and methods.

Watch it!

If you're just flipping through the book, don't blindly type in this code, you'll see a it has a few issues later in the chapter.

Code Up Close

uniqueInstance holds our ONE instance; remember, it is a static variable.

If uniqueInstance is null, then we haven't created the instance yet...

...and, if it doesn't exist, we instantiate Singleton through its private constructor and assign it to uniqueInstance. Note that if we never need the instance, it never gets created; this is lazy instantiation.

```
if (uniqueInstance == null) {
    uniqueInstance = new MyClass();
}
return uniqueInstance;
```

By the time we hit this code, we have an instance and we return it.

If uniqueInstance wasn't null, then it was previously created. We just fall through to the return statement.

Patterns Exposed

This week's interview:
Confessions of a Singleton

HeadFirst: Today we are pleased to bring you an interview with a Singleton object. Why don't you begin by telling us a bit about yourself.

Singleton: Well, I'm totally unique; there is just one of me!

HeadFirst: One?

Singleton: Yes, one. I'm based on the Singleton Pattern, which assures that at any one time there is only one instance of me.

HeadFirst: Isn't that sort of a waste? Someone took the time to develop a full-blown class and now all we can get is one object out of it?

Singleton: Not at all! There is power in ONE. Let's say you have an object that contains registry settings. You don't want multiple copies of that object and its values running around – that would lead to chaos. By using an object like me you can assure that every object in your application is making use of the same global resource.

HeadFirst: Tell us more…

Singleton: Oh, I'm good for all kinds of things. Being single sometimes has its advantages you know. I'm often used to manage pools of resources, like connection or thread pools.

HeadFirst: Still, only one of your kind? That sounds lonely.

Singleton: Because there's only one of me, I do keep busy, but it would be nice if more developers knew me – many developers run into bugs because they have multiple copies of objects floating around they're not even aware of.

HeadFirst: So, if we may ask, how do you know there is only one of you? Can't anyone with a new operator create a "new you"?

Singleton: Nope! I'm truly unique.

HeadFirst: Well, do developers swear an oath not to instantiate you more than once?

Singleton: Of course not. The truth be told… well, this is getting kind of personal but… I have no public constructor.

HeadFirst: NO PUBLIC CONSTRUCTOR! Oh, sorry, no public constructor?

Singleton: That's right. My constructor is declared private.

HeadFirst: How does that work? How do you EVER get instantiated?

Singleton: You see, to get a hold of a Singleton object, you don't instantiate one, you just ask for an instance. So my class has a static method called getInstance(). Call that, and I'll show up at once, ready to work. In fact, I may already be helping other objects when you request me.

HeadFirst: Well, Mr. Singleton, there seems to be a lot under your covers to make all this work. Thanks for revealing yourself and we hope to speak with you again soon!

The Chocolate Factory

Everyone knows that all modern chocolate factories have computer controlled chocolate boilers. The job of the boiler is to take in chocolate and milk, bring them to a boil, and then pass them on to the next phase of making chocolate bars.

Here's the controller class for Choc-O-Holic, Inc.'s industrial strength Chocolate Boiler. Check out the code; you'll notice they've tried to be very careful to ensure that bad things don't happen, like draining 500 gallons of unboiled mixture, or filling the boiler when it's already full, or boiling an empty boiler!

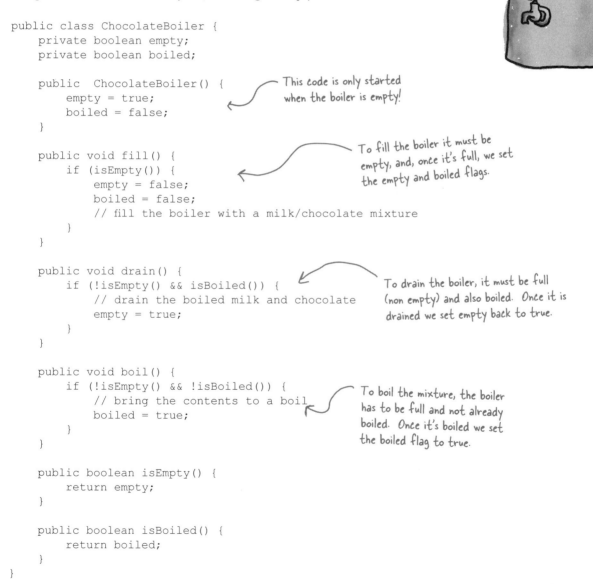

```java
public class ChocolateBoiler {
    private boolean empty;
    private boolean boiled;

    public ChocolateBoiler() {
        empty = true;
        boiled = false;
    }

    public void fill() {
        if (isEmpty()) {
            empty = false;
            boiled = false;
            // fill the boiler with a milk/chocolate mixture
        }
    }

    public void drain() {
        if (!isEmpty() && isBoiled()) {
            // drain the boiled milk and chocolate
            empty = true;
        }
    }

    public void boil() {
        if (!isEmpty() && !isBoiled()) {
            // bring the contents to a boil
            boiled = true;
        }
    }

    public boolean isEmpty() {
        return empty;
    }

    public boolean isBoiled() {
        return boiled;
    }
}
```

This code is only started when the boiler is empty!

To fill the boiler it must be empty, and, once it's full, we set the empty and boiled flags.

To drain the boiler, it must be full (non empty) and also boiled. Once it is drained we set empty back to true.

To boil the mixture, the boiler has to be full and not already boiled. Once it's boiled we set the boiled flag to true.

BRAIN POWER

Choc-O-Holic has done a decent job of ensuring bad things don't happen, don't ya think? Then again, you probably suspect that if two ChocolateBoiler instances get loose, some very bad things can happen.

How might things go wrong if more than one instance of ChocolateBoiler is created in an application?

Sharpen your pencil Can you help Choc-O-Holic improve their ChocolateBoiler class by turning it into a singleton?

```java
public class ChocolateBoiler {
    private boolean empty;
    private boolean boiled;

    ┌─────────────────────────────────────────────────┐
    │                                                 │
    └─────────────────────────────────────────────────┘

    [        ] ChocolateBoiler() {
        empty = true;
        boiled = false;
    }

    ┌─────────────────────────────────────────────────┐
    │                                                 │
    │                                                 │
    │                                                 │
    │                                                 │
    └─────────────────────────────────────────────────┘

    public void fill() {
        if (isEmpty()) {
            empty = false;
            boiled = false;
            // fill the boiler with a milk/chocolate mixture
        }
    }
    // rest of ChocolateBoiler code...
}
```

Singleton Pattern defined

Now that you've got the classic implementation of Singleton in your head, it's time to sit back, enjoy a bar of chocolate, and check out the finer points of the Singleton Pattern.

Let's start with the concise definition of the pattern:

> **The Singleton Pattern** ensures a class has only one instance, and provides a global point of access to it.

No big surprises there. But, let's break it down a bit more:

- What's really going on here? We're taking a class and letting it manage a single instance of itself. We're also preventing any other class from creating a new instance on its own. To get an instance, you've got to go through the class itself.

- We're also providing a global access point to the instance: whenever you need an instance, just query the class and it will hand you back the single instance. As you've seen, we can implement this so that the Singleton is created in a lazy manner, which is especially important for resource intensive objects.

Okay, let's check out the class diagram:

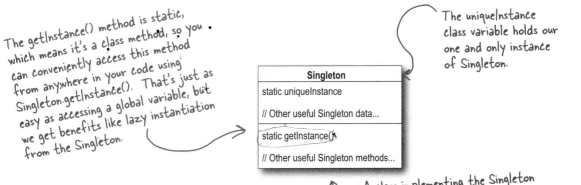

The getInstance() method is static, which means it's a class method, so you can conveniently access this method from anywhere in your code using Singleton.getInstance(). That's just as easy as accessing a global variable, but we get benefits like lazy instantiation from the Singleton.

The uniqueInstance class variable holds our one and only instance of Singleton.

```
              Singleton
static uniqueInstance

// Other useful Singleton data...

static getInstance()

// Other useful Singleton methods...
```

A class implementing the Singleton Pattern is more than a Singleton; it is a general purpose class with its own set of data and methods.

Hershey, PA
~~Houston,~~ we have a problem...

It looks like the Chocolate Boiler has let us down; despite the fact we improved the code using Classic Singleton, somehow the ChocolateBoiler's fill() method was able to start filling the boiler even though a batch of milk and chocolate was already boiling! That's 500 gallons of spilled milk (and chocolate)! What happened!?

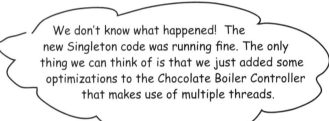

We don't know what happened! The new Singleton code was running fine. The only thing we can think of is that we just added some optimizations to the Chocolate Boiler Controller that makes use of multiple threads.

CAUTION
WATCH OUT FOR
HOT CHOCOLATE

Could the addition of threads have caused this? Isn't it the case that once we've set the uniqueInstance variable to the sole instance of ChocolateBoiler, all calls to getInstance() should return the same instance? Right?

BE the JVM

We have two threads, each executing this code. Your job is to play the JVM and determine whether there is a case in which two threads might get ahold of different boiler objects. Hint: you really just need to look at the sequence of operations in the getInstance() method and the value of uniqueInstance to see how they might overlap. Use the code Magnets to help you study how the code might interleave to create two boiler objects.

```
ChocolateBoiler boiler =
        ChocolateBoiler.getInstance();
fill();
boil();
drain();
```

```
public static ChocolateBoiler
        getInstance() {
```

```
if (uniqueInstance == null) {
```

```
uniqueInstance =
        new ChocolateBoiler();
```

```
}
```

```
return uniqueInstance;
```

```
}
```

Make sure you check your answer on page 188 before turning the page!

	Thread One		Thread Two	Value of uniqueInstance

Dealing with multithreading

Our multithreading woes are almost trivially fixed by making getInstance() a synchronized method:

```
public class Singleton {
    private static Singleton uniqueInstance;

    // other useful instance variables here

    private Singleton() {}

    public static synchronized Singleton getInstance() {
        if (uniqueInstance == null) {
            uniqueInstance = new Singleton();
        }
        return uniqueInstance;
    }

    // other useful methods here
}
```

By adding the synchronized keyword to getInstance(), we force every thread to wait its turn before it can enter the method. That is, no two threads may enter the method at the same time.

> I agree this fixes the problem. But synchronization is expensive; is this an issue?

Good point, and it's actually a little worse than you make out: the only time synchronization is relevant is the first time through this method. In other words, once we've set the uniqueInstance variable to an instance of Singleton, we have no further need to synchronize this method. After the first time through, synchronization is totally unneeded overhead!

Can we improve multithreading?

For most Java applications, we obviously need to ensure that the Singleton works in the presence of multiple threads. But, it looks fairly expensive to synchronize the getInstance() method, so what do we do?

Well, we have a few options...

1. Do nothing if the performance of getInstance() isn't critical to your application

That's right; if calling the getInstance() method isn't causing substantial overhead for your application, forget about it. Synchronizing getInstance() is straightforward and effective. Just keep in mind that synchronizing a method can decrease performance by a factor of 100, so if a high traffic part of your code begins using getInstance(), you may have to reconsider.

2. Move to an eagerly created instance rather than a lazily created one

If your application always creates and uses an instance of the Singleton or the overhead of creation and runtime aspects of the Singleton are not onerous, you may want to create your Singleton eagerly, like this:

```
public class Singleton {
    private static Singleton uniqueInstance = new Singleton();

    private Singleton() {}

    public static Singleton getInstance() {
        return uniqueInstance;
    }
}
```

Go ahead and create an instance of Singleton in a static initializer. This code is guaranteed to be thread safe!

We've already got an instance, so just return it.

Using this approach, we rely on the JVM to create the unique instance of the Singleton when the class is loaded. The JVM guarantees that the instance will be created before any thread accesses the static uniqueInstance variable.

3. Use "double-checked locking" to reduce the use of synchronization in getInstance()

With double-checked locking, we first check to see if an instance is created, and if not, THEN we synchronize. This way, we only synchronize the first time through, just what we want.

Let's check out the code:

```java
public class Singleton {
    private volatile static Singleton uniqueInstance;

    private Singleton() {}

    public static Singleton getInstance() {
        if (uniqueInstance == null) {
            synchronized (Singleton.class) {
                if (uniqueInstance == null) {
                    uniqueInstance = new Singleton();
                }
            }
        }
        return uniqueInstance;
    }
}
```

Check for an instance and if there isn't one, enter a synchronized block.

Note we only synchronize the first time through!

Once in the block, check again and if still null, create an instance.

* The volatile keyword ensures that multiple threads handle the uniqueInstance variable correctly when it is being initialized to the Singleton instance.

If performance is an issue in your use of the getInstance() method then this method of implementing the Singleton can drastically reduce the overhead.

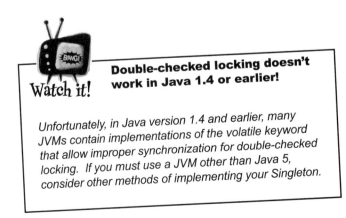

Double-checked locking doesn't work in Java 1.4 or earlier!

Unfortunately, in Java version 1.4 and earlier, many JVMs contain implementations of the volatile keyword that allow improper synchronization for double-checked locking. If you must use a JVM other than Java 5, consider other methods of implementing your Singleton.

Meanwhile, back at the Chocolate Factory...

While we've been off diagnosing the multithreading problems, the chocolate boiler has been cleaned up and is ready to go. But first, we have to fix the multithreading problems. We have a few solutions at hand, each with different tradeoffs, so which solution are we going to employ?

Sharpen your pencil

For each solution, describe its applicability to the problem of fixing the Chocolate Boiler code:

Synchronize the getInstance() method:

_____

_____

Use eager instantiation:

_____

_____

Double-checked locking:

_____

_____

Congratulations!

At this point, the Chocolate Factory is a happy customer and Choc-O-Holic was glad to have some expertise applied to their boiler code. No matter which multithreading solution you applied, the boiler should be in good shape with no more mishaps. Congratulations. You've not only managed to escape 500lbs of hot chocolate in this chapter, but you've been through all the potential problems of the Singleton.

there are no
Dumb Questions

Q: **For such a simple pattern consisting of only one class, Singletons sure seem to have some problems.**

A: Well, we warned you up front! But don't let the problems discourage you; while implementing Singletons *correctly* can be tricky, after reading this chapter you are now well informed on the techniques for creating Singletons and should use them wherever you need to control the number of instances you are creating.

Q: **Can't I just create a class in which all methods and variables are defined as static? Wouldn't that be the same as a Singleton?**

A: Yes, if your class is self-contained and doesn't depend on complex initialization. However, because of the way static initializations are handled in Java, this can get very messy, especially if multiple classes are involved. Often this scenario can result in subtle, hard to find bugs involving order of initialization. Unless there is a compelling need to implement your "singleton" this way, it is far better to stay in the object world.

Q: **What about class loaders? I heard there is a chance that two class loaders could each end up with their own instance of Singleton.**

A: Yes, that is true as each class loader defines a namespace. If you have two or more classloaders, you can load the same class multiple times (once in each classloader). Now, if that class happens to be a Singleton, then since we have more than one version of the class, we also have more than one instance of the Singleton. So, if you are using multiple classloaders and Singletons, be careful. One way around this problem is to specify the classloader yourself.

Relax *Rumors of Singletons being eaten by the garbage collectors are greatly exaggerated*

Prior to Java 1.2, a bug in the garbage collector allowed Singletons to be prematurely collected if there was no global reference to them. In other words, you could create a Singleton and if the only reference to the Singleton was in the Singleton itself, it would be collected and destroyed by the garbage collector. This leads to confusing bugs because after the Singleton is "collected," the next call to getInstance() produced a shiny new Singleton. In many applications, this can cause confusing behavior as state is mysteriously reset to initial values or things like network connections are reset.

Since Java 1.2 this bug has been fixed and a global reference is no longer required. If you are, for some reason, still using a pre-Java 1.2 JVM, then be aware of this issue, otherwise, you can sleep well knowing your Singletons won't be prematurely collected.

Q: **I've always been taught that a class should do one thing and one thing only. For a class to do two things is considered bad OO design. Isn't a Singleton violating this?**

A: You would be referring to the "One Class, One Responsibility" principle, and yes, you are correct, the Singleton is not only responsible for managing its one instance (and providing global access), it is also responsible for whatever its main role is in your application. So, certainly it can be argued it is taking on two responsibilities. Nevertheless, it isn't hard to see that there is utility in a class managing its own instance; it certainly makes the overall design simpler. In addition, many developers are familiar with the Singleton pattern as it is in wide use. That said, some developers do feel the need to abstract out the Singleton functionality.

Q: **I wanted to subclass my Singleton code, but I ran into problems. Is it okay to subclass a Singleton?**

A: One problem with subclassing Singleton is that the constructor is private. You can't extend a class with a private constructor. So, the first thing you'll have to do is change your constructor so that it's public or protected. But then, it's not *really* a Singleton anymore, because other classes can instantiate it.

If you do change your constructor, there's another issue. The implementation of Singleton is based on a static variable, so if you do a straightforward subclass, all of your derived classes will share the same instance variable. This is probably not what you had in mind. So, for subclassing to work, implementing registry of sorts is required in the base class.

Before implementing such a scheme, you should ask yourself what you are really gaining from subclassing a Singleton. Like most patterns, the Singleton is not necessarily meant to be a solution that can fit into a library. In addition, the Singleton code is trivial to add to any existing class. Last, if you are using a large number of Singletons in your application, you should take a hard look at your design. Singletons are meant to be used sparingly.

Q: **I still don't totally understand why global variables are worse than a Singleton.**

A: In Java, global variables are basically static references to objects. There are a couple of disadvantages to using global variables in this manner. We've already mentioned one: the issue of lazy versus eager instantiation. But we need to keep in mind the intent of the pattern: to ensure only one instance of a class exists and to provide global access. A global variable can provide the latter, but not the former. Global variables also tend to encourage developers to pollute the namespace with lots of global references to small objects. Singletons don't encourage this in the same way, but can be abused nonetheless.

Tools for your Design Toolbox

You've now added another pattern to your toolbox. Singleton gives you another method of creating objects – in this case, unique objects.

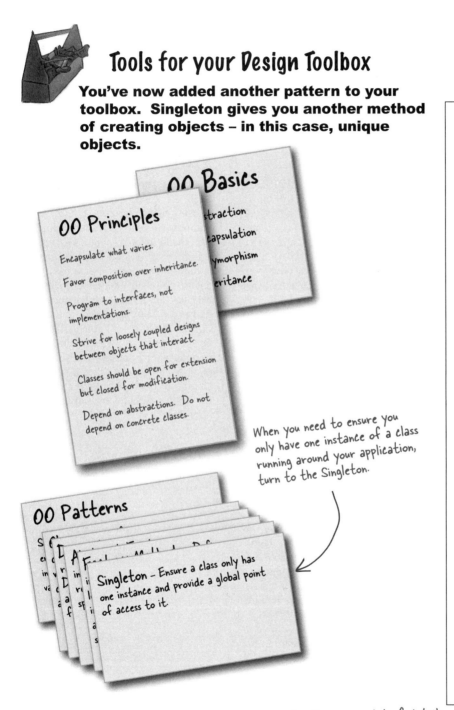

OO Basics

straction

apsulation

ymorphism

eritance

OO Principles

Encapsulate what varies.

Favor composition over inheritance.

Program to interfaces, not implementations.

Strive for loosely coupled designs between objects that interact.

Classes should be open for extension but closed for modification.

Depend on abstractions. Do not depend on concrete classes.

When you need to ensure you only have one instance of a class running around your application, turn to the Singleton.

OO Patterns

Singleton – Ensure a class only has one instance and provide a global point of access to it.

BULLET POINTS

- The Singleton Pattern ensures you have at most one instance of a class in your application.

- The Singleton Pattern also provides a global access point to that instance.

- Java's implementation of the Singleton Pattern makes use of a private constructor, a static method combined with a static variable.

- Examine your performance and resource constraints and carefully choose an appropriate Singleton implementation for multithreaded applications (and we should consider all applications multithreaded!).

- Beware of the double-checked locking implementation; it is not thread-safe in versions before Java 2, version 5.

- Be careful if you are using multiple class loaders; this could defeat the Singleton implementation and result in multiple instances.

- If you are using a JVM earlier than 1.2, you'll need to create a registry of Singletons to defeat the garbage collector.

As you've seen, despite its apparent simplicity, there are a lot of details involved in the Singleton's implementation. After reading this chapter, though, you are ready to go out and use Singleton in the wild.

Sit back, open that case of chocolate that you were sent for solving the multithreading problem, and have some downtime working on this little crossword puzzle; all of the solution words are from this chapter.

Across

1. It was "one of a kind"
2. Added to chocolate in the boiler
8. An incorrect implementation caused this to overflow
10. Singleton provides a single instance and _____ (three words)
12. Flawed multithreading approach if not using Java 1.5
13. Chocolate capital of the US
14. One advantage over global variables: _____ creation
15. Company that produces boilers
16. To totally defeat the new constructor, we have to declare the constructor _____

Down

1. Multiple _____ can cause problems
3. A Singleton is a class that manages an instance of _____
4. If you don't need to worry about lazy instantiation, you can create your instance _____
5. Prior to 1.2, this can eat your Singletons (two words)
6. The Singleton was embarassed it had no public _____
7. The classic implementation doesn't handle this
9. Singleton ensures only one of these exist
11. The Singleton Pattern has one

Exercise solutions

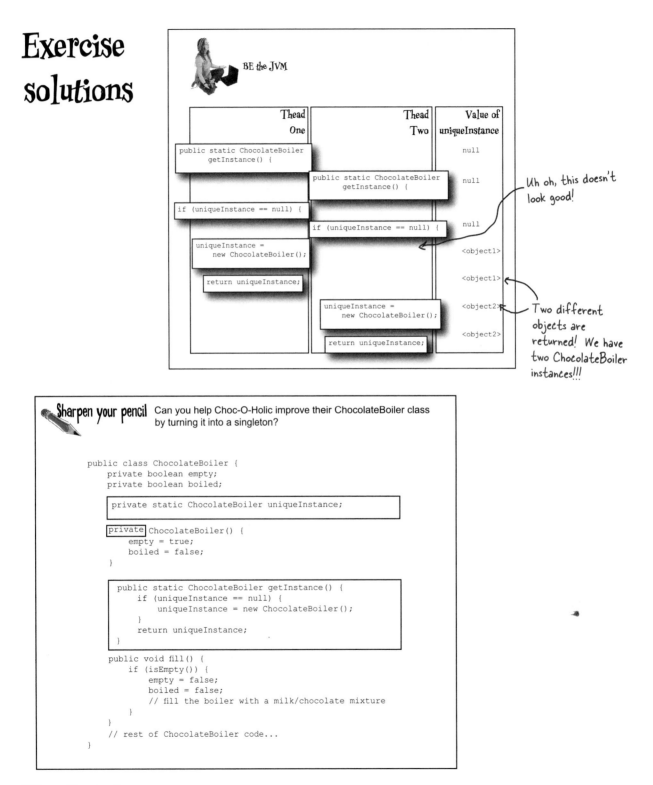

BE the JVM

	Thead One	Thead Two	Value of uniqueInstance
	`public static ChocolateBoiler getInstance() {`		null
		`public static ChocolateBoiler getInstance() {`	null
	`if (uniqueInstance == null) {`		null
		`if (uniqueInstance == null) {`	null
	`uniqueInstance = new ChocolateBoiler();`		<object1>
	`return uniqueInstance;`		<object1>
		`uniqueInstance = new ChocolateBoiler();`	<object2>
		`return uniqueInstance;`	<object2>

Uh oh, this doesn't look good!

Two different objects are returned! We have two ChocolateBoiler instances!!!

Sharpen your pencil Can you help Choc-O-Holic improve their ChocolateBoiler class by turning it into a singleton?

```java
public class ChocolateBoiler {
    private boolean empty;
    private boolean boiled;

    private static ChocolateBoiler uniqueInstance;

    private ChocolateBoiler() {
        empty = true;
        boiled = false;
    }

    public static ChocolateBoiler getInstance() {
        if (uniqueInstance == null) {
            uniqueInstance = new ChocolateBoiler();
        }
        return uniqueInstance;
    }

    public void fill() {
        if (isEmpty()) {
            empty = false;
            boiled = false;
            // fill the boiler with a milk/chocolate mixture
        }
    }
    // rest of ChocolateBoiler code...
}
```

Exercise solutions

Sharpen your pencil

For each solution, describe its applicability to the problem of fixing the Chocolate Boiler code:

Synchronize the getInstance() method:

A straightforward technique that is guaranteed to work. We don't seem to have any

performance concerns with the chocolate boiler, so this would be a good choice.

Use eager instantiation:

We are always going to instantiate the chocolate boiler in our code, so statically inializing the

instance would cause no concerns. This solution would work as well as the synchronized method,

although perhaps be less obvious to a developer familar with the standard pattern.

Double checked locking:

Given we have no performance concerns, double-checked locking seems like overkill. In addition, we'd

have to ensure that we are running at least Java 5.

 Exercise solutions

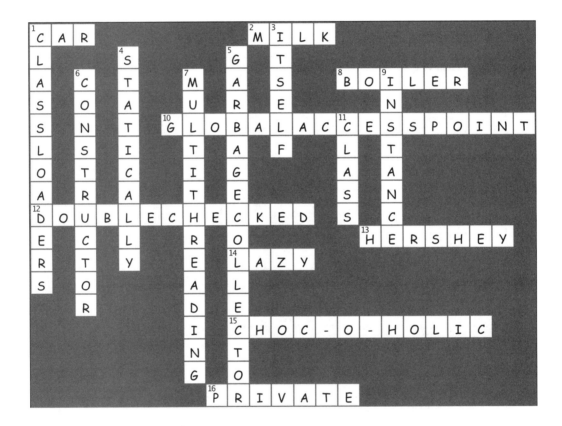

6 the Command Pattern

✳ Encapsulating Invocation ✳

These top secret drop boxes have revolutionized the spy industry. I just drop in my request and people disappear, governments change overnight and my dry cleaning gets done. I don't have to worry about when, where, or how; it just happens!

DROP ALL TOP SECRET INSTRUCTIONS HERE

In this chapter, we take encapsulation to a whole new level: we're going to encapsulate method invocation. That's right, by encapsulating method invocation, we can crystallize pieces of computation so that the object invoking the computation doesn't need to worry about how to do things, it just uses our crystallized method to get it done. We can also do some wickedly smart things with these encapsulated method invocations, like save them away for logging or reuse them to implement undo in our code.

Home Automation or Bust, Inc.
1221 Industrial Avenue, Suite 2000
Future City, IL 62914

Greetings!

I recently received a demo and briefing from Johnny Hurricane, CEO of Weather-O-Rama, on their new expandable weather station. I have to say, I was so impressed with the software architecture that I'd like to ask you to design the API for our new Home Automation Remote Control. In return for your services we'd be happy to handsomely reward you with stock options in Home Automation or Bust, Inc.

I'm enclosing a prototype of our ground-breaking remote control for your perusal. The remote control features seven programmable slots (each can be assigned to a different household device) along with corresponding on/off buttons for each. The remote also has a global undo button.

I'm also enclosing a set of Java classes on CD-R that were created by various vendors to control home automation devices such as lights, fans, hot tubs, audio equipment, and other similar controllable appliances.

We'd like you to create an API for programming the remote so that each slot can be assigned to control a device or set of devices. Note that it is important that we be able to control the current devices on the disc, and also any future devices that the vendors may supply.

Given the work you did on the Weather-O-Rama weather station, we know you'll do a great job on our remote control!

We look forward to seeing your design.

Sincerely,

Bill "X-10" Thompson, CEO

HOME AUTOMATION
VENDOR CLASSES

Free hardware! Let's check out the Remote Control...

There are "on" and "off" buttons for each of the seven slots.

We've got seven slots to program. We can put a different device in each slot and control it via the buttons.

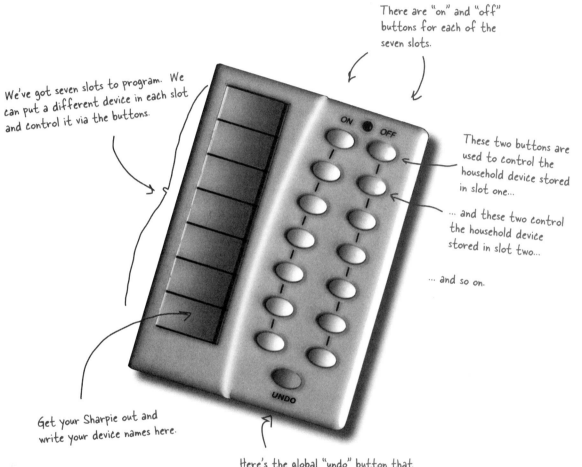

These two buttons are used to control the household device stored in slot one...

... and these two control the household device stored in slot two...

... and so on.

Get your Sharpie out and write your device names here.

Here's the global "undo" button that undoes the last button pressed.

Taking a look at the vendor classes

Check out the vendor classes on the CD-R. These should give you some idea of the interfaces of the objects we need to control from the remote.

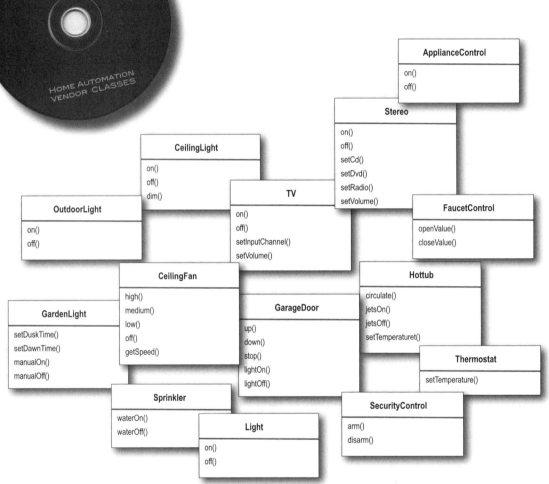

It looks like we have quite a set of classes here, and not a lot of industry effort to come up with a set of common interfaces. Not only that, it sounds like we can expect more of these classes in the future. Designing a remote control API is going to be interesting. Let's get on to the design.

Cubicle Conversation

Your teammates are already discussing how to design the remote control API...

> Well, we've got another design to do. My first observation is that we've got a simple remote with on and off buttons but a set of vendor classes that are quite diverse.

Sue

Mary: Yes, I thought we'd see a bunch of classes with on() and off() methods, but here we've got methods like dim(), setTemperature(), setVolume(), setDirection().

Sue: Not only that, it sounds like we can expect more vendor classes in the future with just as diverse methods.

Mary: I think it's important we view this as a separation of concerns: the remote should know how to interpret button presses and make requests, but it shouldn't know a lot about home automation or how to turn on a hot tub.

Sue: Sounds like good design. But if the remote is dumb and just knows how to make generic requests, how do we design the remote so that it can invoke an action that, say, turns on a light or opens a garage door?

Mary: I'm not sure, but we don't want the remote to have to know the specifics of the vendor classes.

Sue: What do you mean?

Mary: We don't want the remote to consist of a set of if statements, like "if slot1 == Light, then light.on(), else if slot1 = Hottub then hottub.jetsOn()". We know that is a bad design.

Sue: I agree. Whenever a new vendor class comes out, we'd have to go in and modify the code, potentially creating bugs and more work for ourselves!

Hey, I couldn't help overhearing. Since Chapter 1 I've been boning up on Design Patterns. There's a pattern called "Command Pattern" I think might help.

Mary: Yeah? Tell us more.

Joe: The Command Pattern allows you to decouple the requester of an action from the object that actually performs the action. So, here the requester would be the remote control and the object that performs the action would be an instance of one of your vendor classes.

Sue: How is that possible? How can we decouple them? After all, when I press a button, the remote has to turn on a light.

Joe: You can do that by introducing "command objects" into your design. A command object encapsulates a request to do something (like turn on a light) on a specific object (say, the living room light object). So, if we store a command object for each button, when the button is pressed we ask the command object to do some work. The remote doesn't have any idea what the work is, it just has a command object that knows how to talk to the right object to get the work done. So, you see, the remote is decoupled from the light object!

Sue: This certainly sounds like it's going in the right direction.

Mary: Still, I'm having a hard time wrapping my head around the pattern.

Joe: Given that the objects are so decoupled, it's a little difficult to picture how the pattern actually works.

Mary: Let me see if I at least have the right idea: using this pattern we, could create an API in which these command objects can be loaded into button slots, allowing the remote code to stay very simple. And, the command objects encapsulate how to do a home automation task along with the object that needs to do it.

Joe: Yes, I think so. I also think this pattern can help you with that Undo button, but I haven't studied that part yet.

Mary: This sounds really encouraging, but I think I have a bit of work to do to really "get" the pattern.

Sue: Me too.

Meanwhile, back at the Diner...,
or, A brief introduction to the Command Pattern

As Joe said, it is a little hard to understand the Command Pattern by just hearing its description. But don't fear, we have some friends ready to help: remember our friendly diner from Chapter 1? It's been a while since we visited Alice, Flo, and the short-order cook, but we've got good reason for returning (well, beyond the food and great conversation): the diner is going to help us understand the Command Pattern.

So, let's take a short detour back to the diner and study the interactions between the customers, the waitress, the orders and the short-order cook. Through these interactions, you're going to understand the objects involved in the Command Pattern and also get a feel for how the decoupling works. After that, we're going to knock out that remote control API.

Checking in at the Objectville Diner...

Okay, we all know how the Diner operates:

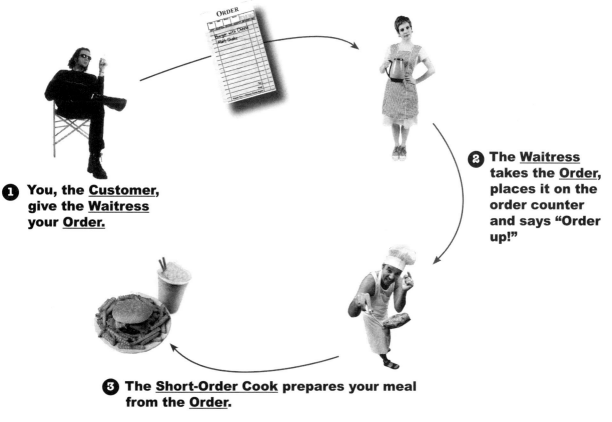

① You, the **Customer**, give the **Waitress** your **Order.**

② The **Waitress** takes the **Order**, places it on the order counter and says "Order up!"

③ The **Short-Order Cook** prepares your meal from the **Order.**

Let's study the interaction in a little more detail...

...and given this Diner is in Objectville, let's think about the object and method calls involved, too!

The Order consists of an order slip and the customer's menu items that are written on it.

createOrder()

I'll have a Burger with Cheese and a Malt Shake.

Start Here

The customer knows what he wants and creates an order.

takeOrder()

The Waitress takes the Order, and when she gets around to it, she calls its orderUp() method to begin the Order's preparation.

orderUp()

The Order has all the instructions needed to prepare the meal. The Order directs the Short Order Cook with methods like makeBurger().

The Short Order Cook follows the instructions of the Order and produces the meal.

makeBurger(), makeShake()

output

The Objectville Diner roles and responsibilities

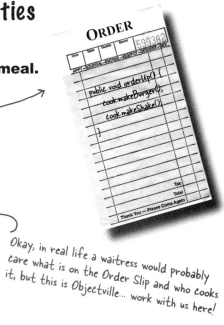

An Order Slip encapsulates a request to prepare a meal.

Think of the Order Slip as an object, an object that acts as a request to prepare a meal. Like any object, it can be passed around – from the Waitress to the order counter, or to the next Waitress taking over her shift. It has an interface that consists of only one method, orderUp(), that encapsulates the actions needed to prepare the meal. It also has a reference to the object that needs to prepare it (in our case, the Cook). It's encapsulated in that the Waitress doesn't have to know what's in the order or even who prepares the meal; she only needs to pass the slip through the order window and call "Order up!"

Okay, in real life a waitress would probably care what is on the Order Slip and who cooks it, but this is Objectville... work with us here!

The Waitress's job is to take Order Slips and invoke the orderUp() method on them.

The Waitress has it easy: take an order from the customer, continue helping customers until she makes it back to the order counter, then invoke the orderUp() method to have the meal prepared. As we've already discussed, in Objectville, the Waitress really isn't worried about what's on the order or who is going to prepare it; she just knows order slips have an orderUp() method she can call to get the job done.

Now, throughout the day, the Waitress's takeOrder() method gets parameterized with different order slips from different customers, but that doesn't phase her; she knows all Order slips support the orderUp() method and she can call orderUp() any time she needs a meal prepared.

The Short Order Cook has the knowledge required to prepare the meal.

The Short Order Cook is the object that really knows how to prepare meals. Once the Waitress has invoked the orderUp() method; the Short Order Cook takes over and implements all the methods that are needed to create meals. Notice the Waitress and the Cook are totally decoupled: the Waitress has Order Slips that encapsulate the details of the meal; she just calls a method on each order to get it prepared. Likewise, the Cook gets his instructions from the Order Slip; he never needs to directly communicate with the Waitress.

Don't ask me to cook, I just take orders and yell "Order up!"

You can definitely say the waitress and I are decoupled. She's not even my type!

Okay, we have a Diner with a Waitress who is decoupled from the Cook by an Order Slip, so what? Get to the point!

Patience, we're getting there...

Think of the Diner as a model for an OO design pattern that allows us to separate an object making a request from the objects that receive and execute those requests. For instance, in our remote control API, we need to separate the code that gets invoked when we press a button from the objects of the vendor-specific classes that carry out those requests. What if each slot of the remote held an object like the Diner's order slip object? Then, when a button is pressed, we could just call the equivalent of the "orderUp()" method on this object and have the lights turn on without the remote knowing the details of how to make those things happen or what objects are making them happen.

Now, let's switch gears a bit and map all this Diner talk to the Command Pattern...

BRAIN POWER

Before we move on, spend some time studying the diagram two pages back along with Diner roles and responsibilities until you think you've got a handle on the Objectville Diner objects and relationships. Once you've done that, get ready to nail the Command Pattern!

From the Diner to the Command Pattern

Okay, we've spent enough time in the Objectville Diner that we know all the personalities and their responsibilities quite well. Now we're going to rework the Diner diagram to reflect the Command Pattern. You'll see that all the players are the same; only the names have changed.

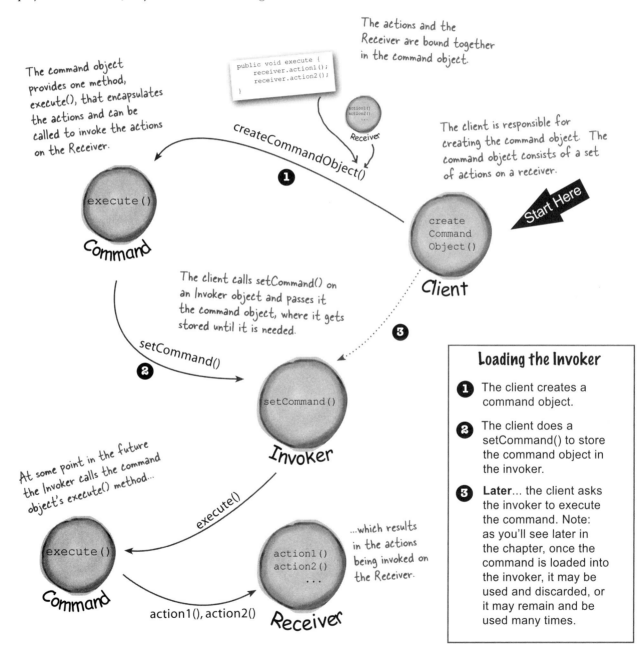

The actions and the Receiver are bound together in the command object.

```
public void execute {
    receiver.action1();
    receiver.action2();
}
```

The command object provides one method, execute(), that encapsulates the actions and can be called to invoke the actions on the Receiver.

The client is responsible for creating the command object. The command object consists of a set of actions on a receiver.

The client calls setCommand() on an Invoker object and passes it the command object, where it gets stored until it is needed.

At some point in the future the Invoker calls the command object's execute() method...

...which results in the actions being invoked on the Receiver.

Loading the Invoker

1 The client creates a command object.

2 The client does a setCommand() to store the command object in the invoker.

3 **Later**... the client asks the invoker to execute the command. Note: as you'll see later in the chapter, once the command is loaded into the invoker, it may be used and discarded, or it may remain and be used many times.

WHO DOES WHAT?

Match the diner objects and methods with the corresponding names from the Command Pattern.

Diner	Command Pattern
Waitress	Command
Short Order Cook	execute()
orderUp()	Client
Order	Invoker
Customer	Receiver
takeOrder()	setCommand()

Our first command object

Isn't it about time we build our first command object? Let's go ahead and write some code for the remote control. While we haven't figured out how to design the remote control API yet, building a few things from the bottom up may help us...

Implementing the Command interface

First things first: all command objects implement the same interface, which consists of one method. In the Diner we called this method orderUp(); however, we typically just use the name execute().

Here's the Command interface:

```
public interface Command {
    public void execute();
}
```

Simple. All we need is one method called execute().

Implementing a Command to turn a light on

Now, let's say you want to implement a command for turning a light on. Referring to our set of vendor classes, the Light class has two methods: on() and off(). Here's how you can implement this as a command:

Light
on()
off()

This is a command, so we need to implement the Command interface.

```
public class LightOnCommand implements Command {
    Light light;

    public LightOnCommand(Light light) {
        this.light = light;
    }

    public void execute() {
        light.on();
    }
}
```

The constructor is passed the specific light that this command is going to control – say the living room light – and stashes it in the light instance variable. When execute gets called, this is the light object that is going to be the Receiver of the request.

The execute method calls the on() method on the receiving object, which is the light we are controlling.

Now that you've got a LightOnCommand class, let's see if we can put it to use...

Using the command object

Okay, let's make things simple: say we've got a remote control with only one button and corresponding slot to hold a device to control:

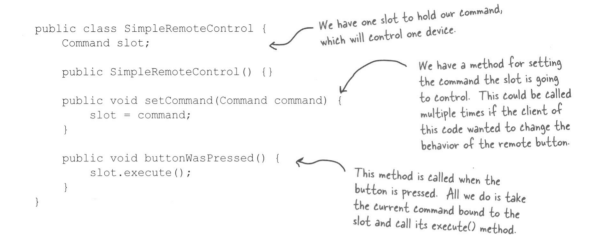

```java
public class SimpleRemoteControl {
    Command slot;

    public SimpleRemoteControl() {}

    public void setCommand(Command command) {
        slot = command;
    }

    public void buttonWasPressed() {
        slot.execute();
    }
}
```

We have one slot to hold our command, which will control one device.

We have a method for setting the command the slot is going to control. This could be called multiple times if the client of this code wanted to change the behavior of the remote button.

This method is called when the button is pressed. All we do is take the current command bound to the slot and call its execute() method.

Creating a simple test to use the Remote Control

Here's just a bit of code to test out the simple remote control. Let's take a look and we'll point out how the pieces match the Command Pattern diagram:

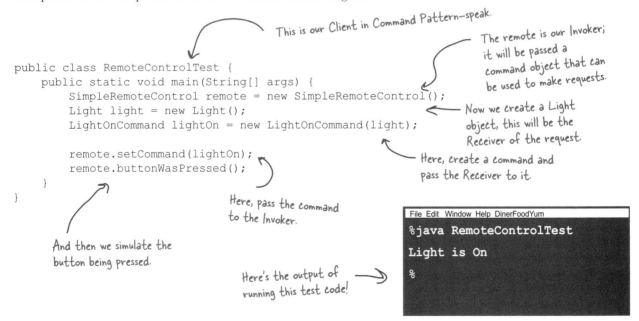

```java
public class RemoteControlTest {
    public static void main(String[] args) {
        SimpleRemoteControl remote = new SimpleRemoteControl();
        Light light = new Light();
        LightOnCommand lightOn = new LightOnCommand(light);

        remote.setCommand(lightOn);
        remote.buttonWasPressed();
    }
}
```

This is our Client in Command Pattern-speak.

The remote is our Invoker; it will be passed a command object that can be used to make requests.

Now we create a Light object, this will be the Receiver of the request.

Here, create a command and pass the Receiver to it.

Here, pass the command to the Invoker.

And then we simulate the button being pressed.

Here's the output of running this test code!

```
File  Edit  Window  Help  DinerFoodYum
%java RemoteControlTest
Light is On
%
```

Sharpen your pencil

Okay, it's time for you to implement the
**GarageDoorOpenCommand class. First, supply the code for
the class below. You'll need the GarageDoor class diagram.**

```
public class GarageDoorOpenCommand
        implements Command {




}
```

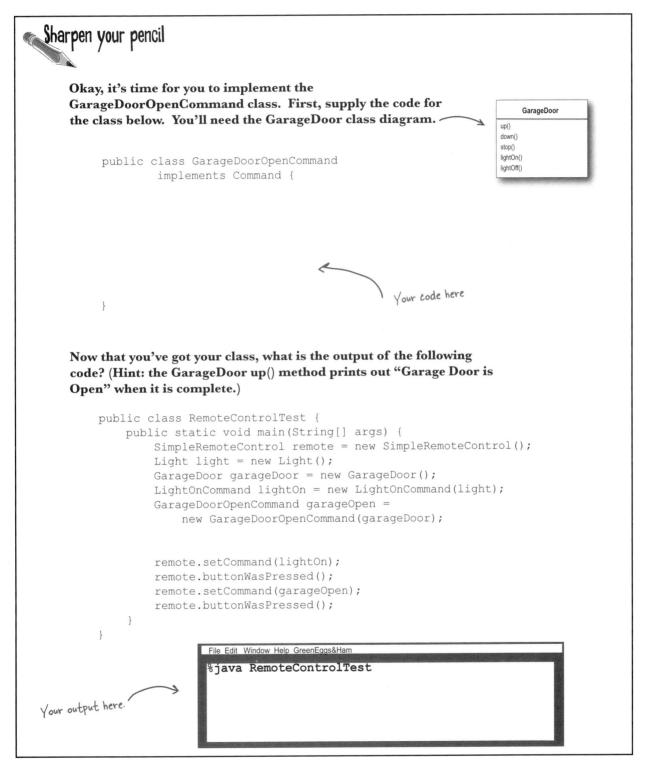

GarageDoor
up()
down()
stop()
lightOn()
lightOff()

Your code here

**Now that you've got your class, what is the output of the following
code? (Hint: the GarageDoor up() method prints out "Garage Door is
Open" when it is complete.)**

```
public class RemoteControlTest {
    public static void main(String[] args) {
        SimpleRemoteControl remote = new SimpleRemoteControl();
        Light light = new Light();
        GarageDoor garageDoor = new GarageDoor();
        LightOnCommand lightOn = new LightOnCommand(light);
        GarageDoorOpenCommand garageOpen =
            new GarageDoorOpenCommand(garageDoor);


        remote.setCommand(lightOn);
        remote.buttonWasPressed();
        remote.setCommand(garageOpen);
        remote.buttonWasPressed();
    }
}
```

File Edit Window Help GreenEggs&Ham

%**java RemoteControlTest**

Your output here.

The Command Pattern defined

You've done your time in the Objectville Diner, you've partly implemented the remote control API, and in the process you've got a fairly good picture of how the classes and objects interact in the Command Pattern. Now we're going to define the Command Pattern and nail down all the details.

Let's start with its official definition:

> **The Command Pattern** encapsulates a request as an object, thereby letting you parameterize other objects with different requests, queue or log requests, and support undoable operations.

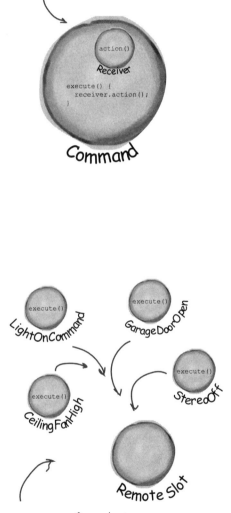

An encapsulated request.

```
action()
```
Receiver
```
execute() {
    receiver.action();
}
```
Command

An invoker — for instance one slot of the remote — can be parameterized with different requests.

Let's step through this. We know that a command object *encapsulates a request* by binding together a set of actions on a specific receiver. To achieve this, it packages the actions and the receiver up into an object that exposes just one method, execute(). When called, execute() causes the actions to be invoked on the receiver. From the outside, no other objects really know what actions get performed on what receiver; they just know that if they call the execute() method, their request will be serviced.

We've also seen a couple examples of *parameterizing an object* with a command. Back at the diner, the Waitress was parameterized with multiple orders throughout the day. In the simple remote control, we first loaded the button slot with a "light on" command and then later replaced it with a "garage door open" command. Like the Waitress, your remote slot didn't care what command object it had, as long as it implemented the Command interface.

What we haven't encountered yet is using commands to implement *queues and logs and support undo operations*. Don't worry, those are pretty straightforward extensions of the basic Command Pattern and we will get to them soon. We can also easily support what's known as the Meta Command Pattern once we have the basics in place. The Meta Command Pattern allows you to create macros of commands so that you can execute multiple commands at once.

The Command Pattern defined:
the class diagram

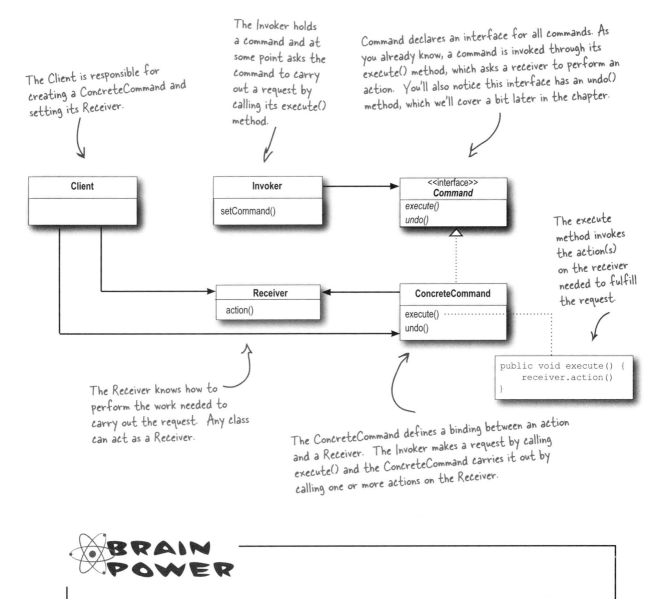

The Invoker holds a command and at some point asks the command to carry out a request by calling its execute() method.

Command declares an interface for all commands. As you already know, a command is invoked through its execute() method, which asks a receiver to perform an action. You'll also notice this interface has an undo() method, which we'll cover a bit later in the chapter.

The Client is responsible for creating a ConcreteCommand and setting its Receiver.

The execute method invokes the action(s) on the receiver needed to fulfill the request.

The Receiver knows how to perform the work needed to carry out the request. Any class can act as a Receiver.

The ConcreteCommand defines a binding between an action and a Receiver. The Invoker makes a request by calling execute() and the ConcreteCommand carries it out by calling one or more actions on the Receiver.

```
public void execute() {
    receiver.action()
}
```

Client

Invoker
setCommand()

<<interface>>
Command
execute()
undo()

Receiver
action()

ConcreteCommand
execute()
undo()

BRAIN POWER

How does the design of the Command Pattern support the decoupling of the invoker of a request and the receiver of the request?

Okay, I think I've got a good feel for the Command Pattern now. Great tip Joe, I think we are going to look like superstars after finishing off the Remote Control API.

Mary: Me too. So where do we begin?

Sue: Like we did in the SimpleRemote, we need to provide a way to assign commands to slots. In our case we have seven slots, each with an "on" and "off" button. So we might assign commands to the remote something like this:

```
onCommands[0] = onCommand;
offCommands[0] = offCommand;
```

Mary: That makes sense, except for the Light objects. How does the remote know the living room from the kitchen light?

Sue: Ah, that's just it, it doesn't! The remote doesn't know anything but how to call execute() on the corresponding command object when a button is pressed.

Mary: Yeah, I sorta got that, but in the implementation, how do we make sure the right objects are turning on and off the right devices?

Sue: When we create the commands to be loaded into the remote, we create one LightCommand that is bound to the living room light object and another that is bound to the kitchen light object. Remember, the receiver of the request gets bound to the command it's encapsulated in. So, by the time the button is pressed, no one cares which light is which, the right thing just happens when the execute() method is called.

Mary: I think I've got it. Let's implement the remote and I think this will get clearer!

Sue: Sounds good. Let's give it a shot...

Assigning Commands to slots

So we have a plan: We're going to assign each slot to a command in the remote control. This makes the remote control our *invoker*. When a button is pressed the execute() method is going to be called on the corresponding command, which results in actions being invoked on the receiver (like lights, ceiling fans, stereos).

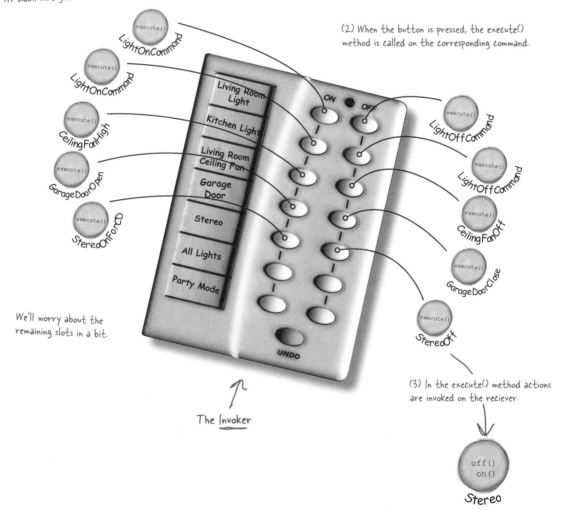

(1) Each slot gets a command.

(2) When the button is pressed, the execute() method is called on the corresponding command.

We'll worry about the remaining slots in a bit.

The Invoker

(3) In the execute() method actions are invoked on the receiver.

Implementing the Remote Control

```
public class RemoteControl {
    Command[] onCommands;
    Command[] offCommands;

    public RemoteControl() {
        onCommands = new Command[7];
        offCommands = new Command[7];

        Command noCommand = new NoCommand();
        for (int i = 0; i < 7; i++) {
            onCommands[i] = noCommand;
            offCommands[i] = noCommand;
        }
    }

    public void setCommand(int slot, Command onCommand, Command offCommand) {
        onCommands[slot] = onCommand;
        offCommands[slot] = offCommand;
    }

    public void onButtonWasPushed(int slot) {
        onCommands[slot].execute();
    }

    public void offButtonWasPushed(int slot) {
        offCommands[slot].execute();
    }


    public String toString() {
        StringBuffer stringBuff = new StringBuffer();
        stringBuff.append("\n------ Remote Control -------\n");
        for (int i = 0; i < onCommands.length; i++) {
            stringBuff.append("[slot " + i + "] " + onCommands[i].getClass().getName()
                + "    " + offCommands[i].getClass().getName() + "\n");
        }
        return stringBuff.toString();
    }
}
```

This time around the remote is going to handle seven On and Off commands, which we'll hold in corresponding arrays.

In the constructor all we need to do is instantiate and initialize the on and off arrays.

The setCommand() method takes a slot position and an On and Off command to be stored in that slot. It puts these commands in the on and off arrays for later use.

When an On or Off button is pressed, the hardware takes care of calling the corresponding methods onButtonWasPushed() or offButtonWasPushed().

We've overwritten toString() to print out each slot and its corresponding command. You'll see us use this when we test the remote control.

Implementing the Commands

Well, we've already gotten our feet wet implementing the LightOnCommand for the SimpleRemoteControl. We can plug that same code in here and everything works beautifully. Off commands are no different; in fact the LightOffCommand looks like this:

```java
public class LightOffCommand implements Command {
    Light light;

    public LightOffCommand(Light light) {
        this.light = light;
    }

    public void execute() {
        light.off();
    }
}
```

The LightOffCommand works exactly the same way as the LightOnCommand, except that we are binding the receiver to a different action: the off() method.

Let's try something a little more challenging; how about writing on and off commands for the Stereo? Okay, off is easy, we just bind the Stereo to the off() method in the StereoOffCommand. On is a little more complicated; let's say we want to write a StereoOnWithCDCommand...

Stereo
on()
off()
setCd()
setDvd()
setRadio()
setVolume()

```java
public class StereoOnWithCDCommand implements Command {
    Stereo stereo;

    public StereoOnWithCDCommand(Stereo stereo) {
        this.stereo = stereo;
    }

    public void execute() {
        stereo.on();
        stereo.setCD();
        stereo.setVolume(11);
    }
}
```

Just like the LightOnCommand, we get passed the instance of the stereo we are going to be controlling and we store it in a local instance variable.

To carry out this request, we need to call three methods on the stereo: first, turn it on, then set it to play the CD, and finally set the volume to 11. Why 11? Well, it's better than 10, right?

Not too bad. Take a look at the rest of the vendor classes; by now, you can definitely knock out the rest of the Command classes we need for those.

Putting the Remote Control through its paces

Our job with the remote is pretty much done; all we need to do is run some tests and get some documentation together to describe the API. Home Automation or Bust, Inc. sure is going to be impressed, don't you think? We've managed to come up with a design that is going to allow them to produce a remote that is easy to maintain and they're going to have no trouble convincing the vendors to write some simple command classes in the future since they are so easy to write.

Let's get to testing this code!

```java
public class RemoteLoader {

    public static void main(String[] args) {
        RemoteControl remoteControl = new RemoteControl();

        Light livingRoomLight = new Light("Living Room");
        Light kitchenLight = new Light("Kitchen");
        CeilingFan ceilingFan= new CeilingFan("Living Room");
        GarageDoor garageDoor = new GarageDoor("");
        Stereo stereo = new Stereo("Living Room");

        LightOnCommand livingRoomLightOn =
                new LightOnCommand(livingRoomLight);
        LightOffCommand livingRoomLightOff =
                new LightOffCommand(livingRoomLight);
        LightOnCommand kitchenLightOn =
                new LightOnCommand(kitchenLight);
        LightOffCommand kitchenLightOff =
                new LightOffCommand(kitchenLight);

        CeilingFanOnCommand ceilingFanOn =
                new CeilingFanOnCommand(ceilingFan);
        CeilingFanOffCommand ceilingFanOff =
                new CeilingFanOffCommand(ceilingFan);

        GarageDoorUpCommand garageDoorUp =
                new GarageDoorUpCommand(garageDoor);
        GarageDoorDownCommand garageDoorDown =
                new GarageDoorDownCommand(garageDoor);

        StereoOnWithCDCommand stereoOnWithCD =
                new StereoOnWithCDCommand(stereo);
        StereoOffCommand  stereoOff =
                new StereoOffCommand(stereo);
```

Create all the devices in their proper locations.

Create all the Light Command objects.

Create the On and Off for the ceiling fan.

Create the Up and Down commands for the Garage.

Create the stereo On and Off commands.

```
remoteControl.setCommand(0, livingRoomLightOn, livingRoomLightOff);
remoteControl.setCommand(1, kitchenLightOn, kitchenLightOff);
remoteControl.setCommand(2, ceilingFanOn, ceilingFanOff);
remoteControl.setCommand(3, stereoOnWithCD, stereoOff);

System.out.println(remoteControl);

remoteControl.onButtonWasPushed(0);
remoteControl.offButtonWasPushed(0);
remoteControl.onButtonWasPushed(1);
remoteControl.offButtonWasPushed(1);
remoteControl.onButtonWasPushed(2);
remoteControl.offButtonWasPushed(2);
remoteControl.onButtonWasPushed(3);
remoteControl.offButtonWasPushed(3);
    }
}
```

Now that we've got all our commands, we can load them into the remote slots.

Here's where we use our toString() method to print each remote slot and the command that it is assigned to.

All right, we are ready to roll! Now, we step through each slot and push its On and Off button.

Now, let's check out the execution of our remote control test...

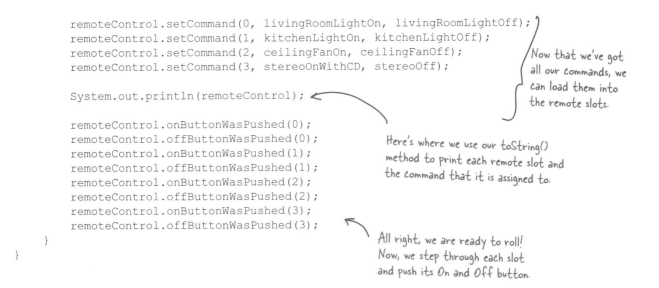

```
File Edit Window Help CommandsGetThingsDone

% java RemoteLoader
------ Remote Control -------
[slot 0] headfirst.command.remote.LightOnCommand          headfirst.command.remote.LightOffCommand
[slot 1] headfirst.command.remote.LightOnCommand          headfirst.command.remote.LightOffCommand
[slot 2] headfirst.command.remote.CeilingFanOnCommand     headfirst.command.remote.CeilingFanOffCommand
[slot 3] headfirst.command.remote.StereoOnWithCDCommand   headfirst.command.remote.StereoOffCommand
[slot 4] headfirst.command.remote.NoCommand               headfirst.command.remote.NoCommand
[slot 5] headfirst.command.remote.NoCommand               headfirst.command.remote.NoCommand
[slot 6] headfirst.command.remote.NoCommand               headfirst.command.remote.NoCommand

Living Room light is on
Living Room light is off
Kitchen light is on
Kitchen light is off
Living Room ceiling fan is on high
Living Room ceiling fan is off
Living Room stereo is on
Living Room stereo is set for CD input
Living Room Stereo volume set to 11
Living Room stereo is off

%
```

On slots

Off Slots

Our commands in action! Remember, the output from each device comes from the vendor classes. For instance, when a light object is turned on it prints "Living Room light is on."

> Wait a second, what is with that NoCommand that is loaded in slots four through six? Trying to pull a fast one?

Good catch. We did sneak a little something in there. In the remote control, we didn't want to check to see if a command was loaded every time we referenced a slot. For instance, in the onButtonWasPushed() method, we would need code like this:

```
public void onButtonWasPushed(int slot) {
    if (onCommands[slot] != null) {
        onCommands[slot].execute();
    }
}
```

So, how do we get around that? Implement a command that does nothing!

```
public class NoCommand implements Command {
    public void execute() { }
}
```

Then, in our RemoteControl constructor, we assign every slot a NoCommand object by default and we know we'll always have some command to call in each slot.

```
Command noCommand = new NoCommand();
for (int i = 0; i < 7; i++) {
    onCommands[i] = noCommand;
    offCommands[i] = noCommand;
}
```

So in the output of our test run, you are seeing slots that haven't been assigned to a command, other than the default NoCommand object which we assigned when we created the RemoteControl.

Pattern Honorable Mention

The NoCommand object is an example of a *null object*. A null object is useful when you don't have a meaningful object to return, and yet you want to remove the responsibility for handling **null** from the client. For instance, in our remote control we didn't have a meaningful object to assign to each slot out of the box, so we provided a NoCommand object that acts as a surrogate and does nothing when its execute method is called.

You'll find uses for Null Objects in conjunction with many Design Patterns and sometimes you'll even see Null Object listed as a Design Pattern.

Time to write that documentation...

Remote Control API Design for Home Automation or Bust, Inc.,

We are pleased to present you with the following design and application programming interface for your Home Automation Remote Control. Our primary design goal was to keep the remote control code as simple as possible so that it doesn't require changes as new vendor classes are produced. To this end we have employed the Command Pattern to logically decouple the RemoteControl class from the Vendor Classes. We believe this will reduce the cost of producing the remote as well as drastically reduce your ongoing maintenance costs.

The following class diagram provides an overview of our design:

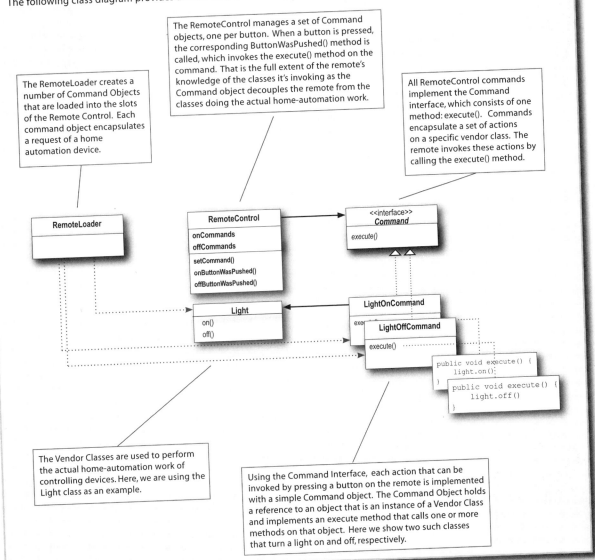

The RemoteLoader creates a number of Command Objects that are loaded into the slots of the Remote Control. Each command object encapsulates a request of a home automation device.

The RemoteControl manages a set of Command objects, one per button. When a button is pressed, the corresponding ButtonWasPushed() method is called, which invokes the execute() method on the command. That is the full extent of the remote's knowledge of the classes it's invoking as the Command object decouples the remote from the classes doing the actual home-automation work.

All RemoteControl commands implement the Command interface, which consists of one method: execute(). Commands encapsulate a set of actions on a specific vendor class. The remote invokes these actions by calling the execute() method.

The Vendor Classes are used to perform the actual home-automation work of controlling devices. Here, we are using the Light class as an example.

Using the Command Interface, each action that can be invoked by pressing a button on the remote is implemented with a simple Command object. The Command Object holds a reference to an object that is an instance of a Vendor Class and implements an execute method that calls one or more methods on that object. Here we show two such classes that turn a light on and off, respectively.

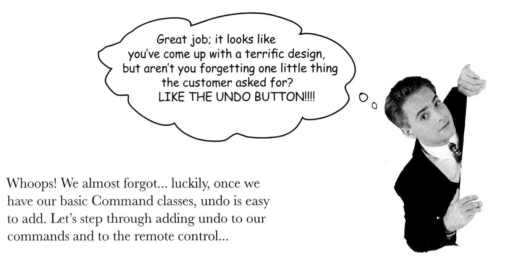

Whoops! We almost forgot... luckily, once we have our basic Command classes, undo is easy to add. Let's step through adding undo to our commands and to the remote control...

What are we doing?

Okay, we need to add functionality to support the undo button on the remote. It works like this: say the Living Room Light is off and you press the on button on the remote. Obviously the light turns on. Now if you press the undo button then the last action will be reversed – in this case the light will turn off. Before we get into more complex examples, let's get the light working with the undo button:

 When commands support undo, they have an undo() method that mirrors the execute() method. Whatever execute() last did, undo() reverses. So, before we can add undo to our commands, we need to add an undo() method to the Command interface:

```
public interface Command {
    public void execute();
    public void undo();
}
```
Here's the new undo() method.

That was simple enough.

Now, let's dive into the Light command and implement the undo() method.

❷ Let's start with the LightOnCommand: if the LightOnCommand's execute() method was called, then the on() method was last called. We know that undo() needs to do the opposite of this by calling the off() method.

```java
public class LightOnCommand implements Command {
    Light light;

    public LightOnCommand(Light light) {
        this.light = light;
    }

    public void execute() {
        light.on();
    }

    public void undo() {
        light.off();
    }
}
```

execute() turns the light on, so undo() simply turns the light back off.

Piece of cake! Now for the LightOffCommand. Here the undo() method just needs to call the Light's on() method.

```java
public class LightOffCommand implements Command {
    Light light;

    public LightOffCommand(Light light) {
        this.light = light;
    }

    public void execute() {
        light.off();
    }

    public void undo() {
        light.on();
    }
}
```

And here, undo() turns the light back on!

Could this be any easier? Okay, we aren't done yet; we need to work a little support into the Remote Control to handle tracking the last button pressed and the undo button press.

③ To add support for the undo button we only have to make a few small changes to the Remote Control class. Here's how we're going to do it: we'll add a new instance variable to track the last command invoked; then, whenever the undo button is pressed, we retrieve that command and invoke its undo() method.

```java
public class RemoteControlWithUndo {
    Command[] onCommands;
    Command[] offCommands;
    Command undoCommand;

    public RemoteControlWithUndo() {
        onCommands = new Command[7];
        offCommands = new Command[7];

        Command noCommand = new NoCommand();
        for(int i=0;i<7;i++) {
            onCommands[i] = noCommand;
            offCommands[i] = noCommand;
        }
        undoCommand = noCommand;
    }

    public void setCommand(int slot, Command onCommand, Command offCommand) {
        onCommands[slot] = onCommand;
        offCommands[slot] = offCommand;
    }

    public void onButtonWasPushed(int slot) {
        onCommands[slot].execute();
        undoCommand = onCommands[slot];
    }

    public void offButtonWasPushed(int slot) {
        offCommands[slot].execute();
        undoCommand = offCommands[slot];
    }

    public void undoButtonWasPushed() {
        undoCommand.undo();
    }

    public String toString() {
        // toString code here...
    }
}
```

This is where we'll stash the last command executed for the undo button.

Just like the other slots, undo starts off with a NoCommand, so pressing undo before any other button won't do anything at all.

When a button is pressed, we take the command and first execute it; then we save a reference to it in the undoCommand instance variable. We do this for both "on" commands and "off" commands.

When the undo button is pressed, we invoke the undo() method of the command stored in undoCommand. This reverses the operation of the last command executed.

Time to QA that Undo button!

Okay, let's rework the test harness a bit to test the undo button:

```java
public class RemoteLoader {

    public static void main(String[] args) {
        RemoteControlWithUndo remoteControl = new RemoteControlWithUndo();

        Light livingRoomLight = new Light("Living Room");

        LightOnCommand livingRoomLightOn =
                new LightOnCommand(livingRoomLight);
        LightOffCommand livingRoomLightOff =
                new LightOffCommand(livingRoomLight);

        remoteControl.setCommand(0, livingRoomLightOn, livingRoomLightOff);

        remoteControl.onButtonWasPushed(0);
        remoteControl.offButtonWasPushed(0);
        System.out.println(remoteControl);
        remoteControl.undoButtonWasPushed();
        remoteControl.offButtonWasPushed(0);
        remoteControl.onButtonWasPushed(0);
        System.out.println(remoteControl);
        remoteControl.undoButtonWasPushed();
    }
}
```

← Create a Light, and our new undo() enabled Light On and Off Commands.

⤺ Add the light Commands to the remote in slot 0.

← Turn the light on, then off and then undo.

← Then, turn the light off, back on and undo.

And here's the test results...

```
File Edit Window Help UndoCommandsDefyEntropy
% java RemoteLoader
Light is on          Turn the light on, then off.
Light is off

------ Remote Control ------                                        Here's the Light commands.
[slot 0] headfirst.command.undo.LightOnCommand    headfirst.command.undo.LightOffCommand
[slot 1] headfirst.command.undo.NoCommand         headfirst.command.undo.NoCommand
[slot 2] headfirst.command.undo.NoCommand         headfirst.command.undo.NoCommand
[slot 3] headfirst.command.undo.NoCommand         headfirst.command.undo.NoCommand
[slot 4] headfirst.command.undo.NoCommand         headfirst.command.undo.NoCommand
[slot 5] headfirst.command.undo.NoCommand         headfirst.command.undo.NoCommand
[slot 6] headfirst.command.undo.NoCommand         headfirst.command.undo.NoCommand
[undo] headfirst.command.undo.LightOffCommand
                                                        Now undo holds the
Light is on          Undo was pressed... the LightOffCommand      LightOffCommand, the last
                     undo() turns the light back on.             command invoked.
Light is off
Light is on          Then we turn the light off then back on.

------ Remote Control ------
[slot 0] headfirst.command.undo.LightOnCommand    headfirst.command.undo.LightOffCommand
[slot 1] headfirst.command.undo.NoCommand         headfirst.command.undo.NoCommand
[slot 2] headfirst.command.undo.NoCommand         headfirst.command.undo.NoCommand
[slot 3] headfirst.command.undo.NoCommand         headfirst.command.undo.NoCommand
[slot 4] headfirst.command.undo.NoCommand         headfirst.command.undo.NoCommand
[slot 5] headfirst.command.undo.NoCommand         headfirst.command.undo.NoCommand
[slot 6] headfirst.command.undo.NoCommand         headfirst.command.undo.NoCommand
[undo] headfirst.command.undo.LightOnCommand
                                                        Now undo holds the LightOnCommand, the last
Light is off    Undo was pressed, the light is back off.           command invoked.
```

Using state to implement Undo

Okay, implementing undo on the Light was instructive but a little too easy. Typically, we need to manage a bit of state to implement undo. Let's try something a little more interesting, like the CeilingFan from the vendor classes. The ceiling fan allows a number of speeds to be set along with an off method.

Here's the source code for the CeilingFan:

CeilingFan
high()
medium()
low()
off()
getSpeed()

```java
public class CeilingFan {
    public static final int HIGH = 3;
    public static final int MEDIUM = 2;
    public static final int LOW = 1;
    public static final int OFF = 0;
    String location;
    int speed;

    public CeilingFan(String location) {
        this.location = location;
        speed = OFF;
    }

    public void high() {
        speed = HIGH;
        // code to set fan to high
    }

    public void medium() {
        speed = MEDIUM;
        // code to set fan to medium
    }

    public void low() {
        speed = LOW;
        // code to set fan to low
    }

    public void off() {
        speed = OFF;
        // code to turn fan off
    }

    public int getSpeed() {
        return speed;
    }
}
```

Notice that the CeilingFan class holds local state representing the speed of the ceiling fan.

These methods set the speed of the ceiling fan.

We can get the current speed of the ceiling fan using getSpeed().

Hmm, so to properly implement undo, I'd have to take the previous speed of the ceiling fan into account...

Adding Undo to the ceiling fan commands

Now let's tackle adding undo to the various CeilingFan commands. To do so, we need to track the last speed setting of the fan and, if the undo() method is called, restore the fan to its previous setting. Here's the code for the CeilingFanHighCommand:

```java
public class CeilingFanHighCommand implements Command {
    CeilingFan ceilingFan;
    int prevSpeed;

    public CeilingFanHighCommand(CeilingFan ceilingFan) {
        this.ceilingFan = ceilingFan;
    }

    public void execute() {
        prevSpeed = ceilingFan.getSpeed();
        ceilingFan.high();
    }

    public void undo() {
        if (prevSpeed == CeilingFan.HIGH) {
            ceilingFan.high();
        } else if (prevSpeed == CeilingFan.MEDIUM) {
            ceilingFan.medium();
        } else if (prevSpeed == CeilingFan.LOW) {
            ceilingFan.low();
        } else if (prevSpeed == CeilingFan.OFF) {
            ceilingFan.off();
        }
    }
}
```

We've added local state to keep track of the previous speed of the fan.

In execute, before we change the speed of the fan, we need to first record its previous state, just in case we need to undo our actions.

To undo, we set the speed of the fan back to its previous speed.

We've got three more ceiling fan commands to write: low, medium, and off. Can you see how these are implemented?

Get ready to test the ceiling fan

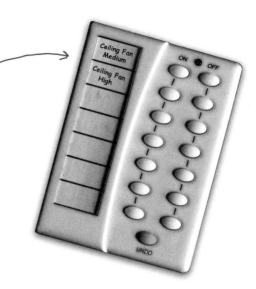

Time to load up our remote control with the ceiling fan
commands. We're going to load slot zero's on button with
the medium setting for the fan and slot one with the high
setting. Both corresponding off buttons will hold the ceiling
fan off command.

Here's our test script:

```
public class RemoteLoader {

    public static void main(String[] args) {
        RemoteControlWithUndo remoteControl = new RemoteControlWithUndo();

        CeilingFan ceilingFan = new CeilingFan("Living Room");

        CeilingFanMediumCommand ceilingFanMedium =
                new CeilingFanMediumCommand(ceilingFan);
        CeilingFanHighCommand ceilingFanHigh =
                new CeilingFanHighCommand(ceilingFan);
        CeilingFanOffCommand ceilingFanOff =
                new CeilingFanOffCommand(ceilingFan);

        remoteControl.setCommand(0, ceilingFanMedium, ceilingFanOff);
        remoteControl.setCommand(1, ceilingFanHigh, ceilingFanOff);

        remoteControl.onButtonWasPushed(0);
        remoteControl.offButtonWasPushed(0);
        System.out.println(remoteControl);
        remoteControl.undoButtonWasPushed();

        remoteControl.onButtonWasPushed(1);
        System.out.println(remoteControl);
        remoteControl.undoButtonWasPushed();
    }
}
```

Here we instantiate three commands: high, medium, and off.

Here we put medium in slot zero, and high in slot one. We also load up the off commands.

First, turn the fan on medium.

Then turn it off.

Undo! It should go back to medium...

Turn it on to high this time.

And, one more undo; it should go back to medium.

Testing the ceiling fan...

Okay, let's fire up the remote, load it with commands, and push some buttons!

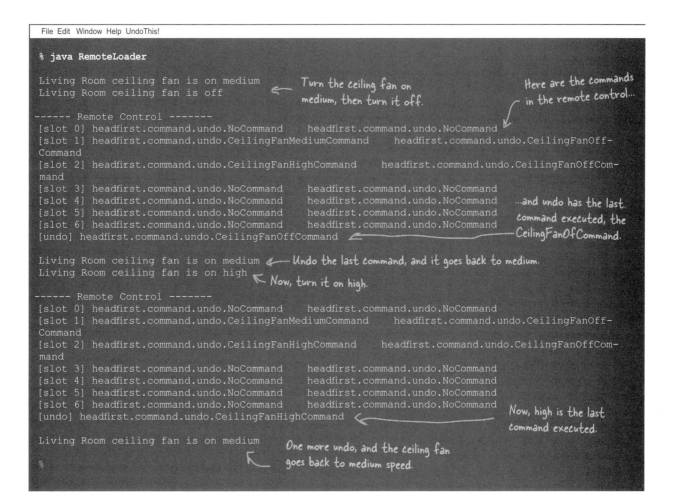

```
File  Edit  Window  Help  UndoThis!

% java RemoteLoader

Living Room ceiling fan is on medium
Living Room ceiling fan is off

------ Remote Control -------
[slot 0] headfirst.command.undo.NoCommand         headfirst.command.undo.NoCommand
[slot 1] headfirst.command.undo.CeilingFanMediumCommand    headfirst.command.undo.CeilingFanOff-
Command
[slot 2] headfirst.command.undo.CeilingFanHighCommand    headfirst.command.undo.CeilingFanOffCom-
mand
[slot 3] headfirst.command.undo.NoCommand         headfirst.command.undo.NoCommand
[slot 4] headfirst.command.undo.NoCommand         headfirst.command.undo.NoCommand
[slot 5] headfirst.command.undo.NoCommand         headfirst.command.undo.NoCommand
[slot 6] headfirst.command.undo.NoCommand         headfirst.command.undo.NoCommand
[undo] headfirst.command.undo.CeilingFanOffCommand

Living Room ceiling fan is on medium
Living Room ceiling fan is on high

------ Remote Control -------
[slot 0] headfirst.command.undo.NoCommand         headfirst.command.undo.NoCommand
[slot 1] headfirst.command.undo.CeilingFanMediumCommand    headfirst.command.undo.CeilingFanOff-
Command
[slot 2] headfirst.command.undo.CeilingFanHighCommand    headfirst.command.undo.CeilingFanOffCom-
mand
[slot 3] headfirst.command.undo.NoCommand         headfirst.command.undo.NoCommand
[slot 4] headfirst.command.undo.NoCommand         headfirst.command.undo.NoCommand
[slot 5] headfirst.command.undo.NoCommand         headfirst.command.undo.NoCommand
[slot 6] headfirst.command.undo.NoCommand         headfirst.command.undo.NoCommand
[undo] headfirst.command.undo.CeilingFanHighCommand

Living Room ceiling fan is on medium
%
```

Turn the ceiling fan on medium, then turn it off.

Here are the commands in the remote control...

...and undo has the last command executed, the CeilingFanOfCommand.

Undo the last command, and it goes back to medium.

Now, turn it on high.

Now, high is the last command executed.

One more undo, and the ceiling fan goes back to medium speed.

Every remote needs a Party Mode!

What's the point of having a remote if you can't push one button and have the lights dimmed, the stereo and TV turned on and set to a DVD and the hot tub fired up?

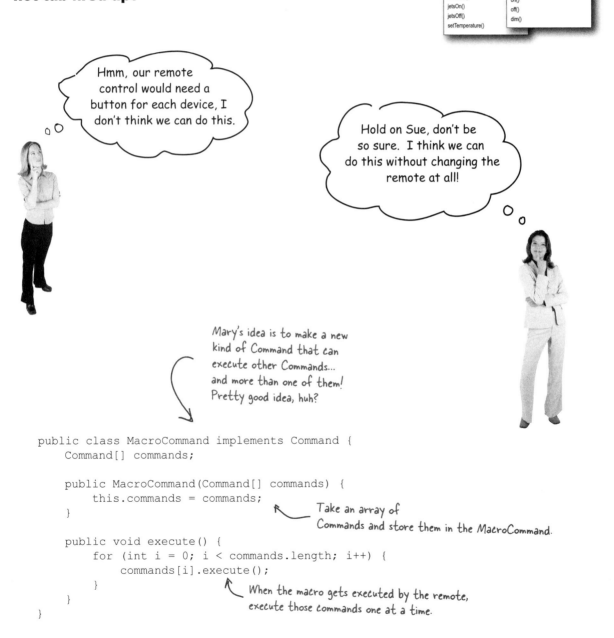

> Hmm, our remote control would need a button for each device, I don't think we can do this.

> Hold on Sue, don't be so sure. I think we can do this without changing the remote at all!

Mary's idea is to make a new kind of Command that can execute other Commands... and more than one of them! Pretty good idea, huh?

```java
public class MacroCommand implements Command {
    Command[] commands;

    public MacroCommand(Command[] commands) {
        this.commands = commands;
    }

    public void execute() {
        for (int i = 0; i < commands.length; i++) {
            commands[i].execute();
        }
    }
}
```

Take an array of Commands and store them in the MacroCommand.

When the macro gets executed by the remote, execute those commands one at a time.

The devices shown:

Stereo
on()
off()
setCd()
setDvd()
setRadio()
setVolume()

TV
on()
off()
setInputChannel()
setVolume()

Hottub
on()
off()
circulate()
jetsOn()
jetsOff()
setTemperature()

Light
on()
off()
dim()

Using a macro command

Let's step through how we use a macro command:

1 First we create the set of commands we want to go into the macro:

```
Light light = new Light("Living Room");
TV tv = new TV("Living Room");
Stereo stereo = new Stereo("Living Room");
Hottub hottub = new Hottub();

LightOnCommand lightOn = new LightOnCommand(light);
StereoOnCommand stereoOn = new StereoOnCommand(stereo);
TVOnCommand tvOn = new TVOnCommand(tv);
HottubOnCommand hottubOn = new HottubOnCommand(hottub);
```

Create all the devices, a light, tv, stereo, and hot tub.

Now create all the On commands to control them.

> **Sharpen your pencil**
>
> **We will also need commands for the off buttons, write the code to create those here:**

2 Next we create two arrays, one for the On commands and one for the Off commands, and load them with the corresponding commands:

Create an array for On and an array for Off commands...

```
Command[] partyOn = { lightOn, stereoOn, tvOn, hottubOn};
Command[] partyOff = { lightOff, stereoOff, tvOff, hottubOff};

MacroCommand partyOnMacro = new MacroCommand(partyOn);
MacroCommand partyOffMacro = new MacroCommand(partyOff);
```

...and create two corresponding macros to hold them.

3 Then we assign MacroCommand to a button like we always do:

```
remoteControl.setCommand(0, partyOnMacro, partyOffMacro);
```

Assign the macro command to a button as we would any command.

4 Finally, we just need to push some buttons and see if this works.

```
System.out.println(remoteControl);
System.out.println("--- Pushing Macro On---");
remoteControl.onButtonWasPushed(0);
System.out.println("--- Pushing Macro Off---");
remoteControl.offButtonWasPushed(0);
```

Here's the output.

File Edit Window Help You Can'tBeatABabka

```
% java RemoteLoader
------ Remote Control -------
[slot 0] headfirst.command.party.MacroCommand    headfirst.command.party.MacroCommand
[slot 1] headfirst.command.party.NoCommand       headfirst.command.party.NoCommand
[slot 2] headfirst.command.party.NoCommand       headfirst.command.party.NoCommand
[slot 3] headfirst.command.party.NoCommand       headfirst.command.party.NoCommand
[slot 4] headfirst.command.party.NoCommand       headfirst.command.party.NoCommand
[slot 5] headfirst.command.party.NoCommand       headfirst.command.party.NoCommand
[slot 6] headfirst.command.party.NoCommand       headfirst.command.party.NoCommand
[undo] headfirst.command.party.NoCommand

--- Pushing Macro On---
Light is on
Living Room stereo is on
Living Room TV is on
Living Room TV channel is set for DVD
Hottub is heating to a steaming 104 degrees
Hottub is bubbling!

--- Pushing Macro Off---
Light is off
Living Room stereo is off
Living Room TV is off
Hottub is cooling to 98 degrees

%
```

Here are the two macro commands.

All the Commands in the macro are executed when we invoke the on macro...

...and when we invoke the off macro. Looks like it works.

Exercise

The only thing our MacroCommand is missing its undo functionality. When the undo button is pressed after a macro command, all the commands that were invoked in the macro must undo their previous actions. Here's the code for MacroCommand; go ahead and implement the undo() method:

```java
public class MacroCommand implements Command {
    Command[] commands;

    public MacroCommand(Command[] commands) {
        this.commands = commands;
    }

    public void execute() {
        for (int i = 0; i < commands.length; i++) {
            commands[i].execute();
        }
    }

    public void undo() {



    }
}
```

Q: Do I always need a receiver? Why can't the command object implement the details of the execute() method?

A: In general, we strive for "dumb" command objects that just invoke an action on a receiver; however, there are many examples of "smart" command objects that implement most, if not all, of the logic needed to carry out a request. Certainly you can do this; just keep in mind you'll no longer have the same level of decoupling between the invoker and receiver, nor will you be able to parameterize your commands with receivers.

Q: How can I implement a history of undo operations? In other words, I want to be able to press the undo button multiple times.

A: Great question! It's pretty easy actually; instead of keeping just a reference to the last Command executed, you keep a stack of previous commands. Then, whenever undo is pressed, your invoker pops the first item off the stack and calls its undo() method.

Q: Could I have just implemented Party Mode as a Command by creating a PartyCommand and putting the calls to execute the other Commands in the PartyCommand's execute() method?

A: You could; however, you'd essentially be "hardcoding" the party mode into the PartyCommand. Why go to the trouble? With the MacroCommand, you can decide dynamically which Commands you want to go into the PartyCommand, so you have more flexibility using MacroCommands. In general, the MacroCommand is a more elegant solution and requires less new code.

More uses of the Command Pattern: queuing requests

Commands give us a way to package a piece of computation (a receiver and a set of actions) and pass it around as a first-class object. Now, the computation itself may be invoked long after some client application creates the command object. In fact, it may even be invoked by a different thread. We can take this scenario and apply it to many useful applications such as schedulers, thread pools and job queues, to name a few.

Imagine a job queue: you add commands to the queue on one end, and on the other end sit a group of threads. Threads run the following script: they remove a command from the queue, call its execute() method, wait for the call to finish, then discard the command object and retrieve a new one.

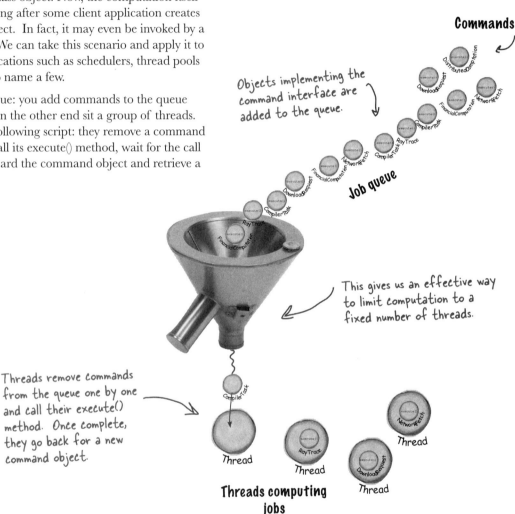

Commands

Objects implementing the command interface are added to the queue.

Job queue

This gives us an effective way to limit computation to a fixed number of threads.

Threads remove commands from the queue one by one and call their execute() method. Once complete, they go back for a new command object.

Threads computing jobs

Note that the job queue classes are totally decoupled from the objects that are doing the computation. One minute a thread may be computing a financial computation, and the next it may be retrieving something from the network. The job queue objects don't care; they just retrieve commands and call execute(). Likewise, as long as you put objects into the queue that implement the Command Pattern, your execute() method will be invoked when a thread is available.

How might a web server make use of such a queue? What other applications can you think of?

More uses of the Command Pattern: logging requests

The semantics of some applications require that we log all actions and be able to recover after a crash by reinvoking those actions. The Command Pattern can support these semantics with the addition of two methods: store() and load(). In Java we could use object serialization to implement these methods, but the normal caveats for using serialization for persistence apply.

How does this work? As we execute commands, we store a history of them on disk. When a crash occurs, we reload the command objects and invoke their execute() methods in batch and in order.

Now, this kind of logging wouldn't make sense for a remote control; however, there are many applications that invoke actions on large data structures that can't be quickly saved each time a change is made. By using logging, we can save all the operations since the last check point, and if there is a system failure, apply those operations to our checkpoint. Take, for example, a spreadsheet application: we might want to implement our failure recovery by logging the actions on the spreadsheet rather than writing a copy of the spreadsheet to disk every time a change occurs. In more advanced applications, these techniques can be extended to apply to sets of operations in a transactional manner so that all of the operations complete, or none of them do.

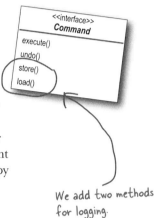

We add two methods for logging.

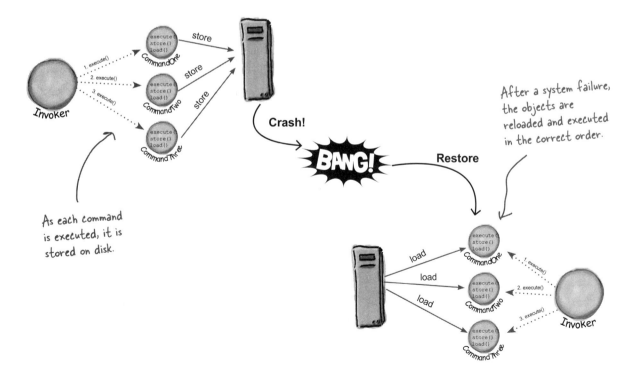

As each command is executed, it is stored on disk.

After a system failure, the objects are reloaded and executed in the correct order.

Tools for your Design Toolbox

Your toolbox is starting to get heavy! In this chapter we've added a pattern that allows us to encapsulate methods into Command objects: store them, pass them around, and invoke them when you need them.

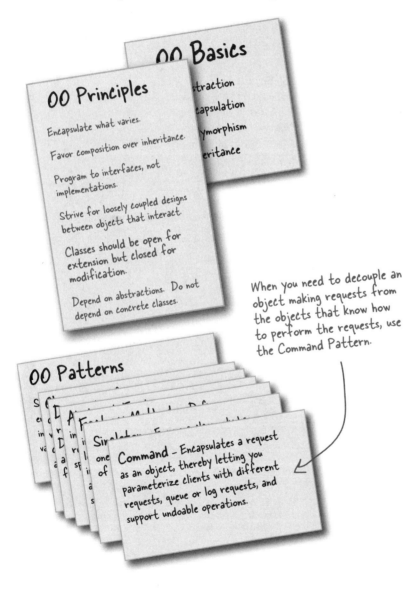

OO Basics

st: ...traction

...capsulation

...lymorphism

...eritance

OO Principles

Encapsulate what varies.

Favor composition over inheritance.

Program to interfaces, not implementations.

Strive for loosely coupled designs between objects that interact.

Classes should be open for extension but closed for modification.

Depend on abstractions. Do not depend on concrete classes.

When you need to decouple an object making requests from the objects that know how to perform the requests, use the Command Pattern.

OO Patterns

Command – Encapsulates a request as an object, thereby letting you parameterize clients with different requests, queue or log requests, and support undoable operations.

BULLET POINTS

- The Command Pattern decouples an object, making a request from the one that knows how to perform it.

- A Command object is at the center of this decoupling and encapsulates a receiver with an action (or set of actions) .

- An invoker makes a request of a Command object by calling its execute() method, which invokes those actions on the receiver.

- Invokers can be parameterized with Commands, even dynamically at runtime.

- Commands may support undo by implementing an undo method that restores the object to its previous state before the execute() method was last called.

- Macro Commands are a simple extension of Command that allow multiple commands to be invoked. Likewise, Macro Commands can easily support undo().

- In practice, it is not uncommon for "smart" Command objects to implement the request themselves rather than delegating to a receiver.

- Commands may also be used to implement logging and transactional systems.

Time to take a breather and let it all sink in.

It's another crossword; all of the solution words are from this chapter.

Across

3. The Waitress was one
4. A command _____ a set of actions and a receiver
7. Dr. Seuss diner food
8. Our favorite city
9. Act as the receivers in the remote control
13. Object that knows the actions and the receiver
14. Another thing Command can do
15. Object that knows how to get things done
17. A command encapsulates this

Down

1. Role of customer in the command pattern
2. Our first command object controlled this
5. Invoker and receiver are _____
6. Company that got us word of mouth business
10. All commands provide this
11. The cook and this person were definitely decoupled
12. Carries out a request
16. Waitress didn't do this

Exercise
solutions

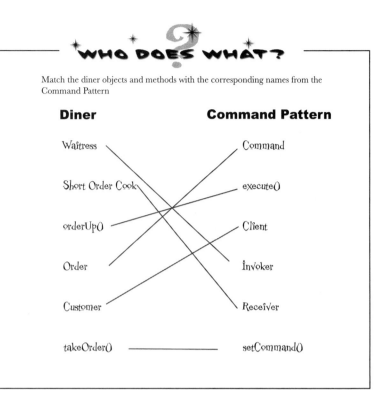

WHO DOES WHAT?

Match the diner objects and methods with the corresponding names from the Command Pattern

Diner	Command Pattern
Waitress	Command
Short Order Cook	execute()
orderUp()	Client
Order	Invoker
Customer	Receiver
takeOrder()	setCommand()

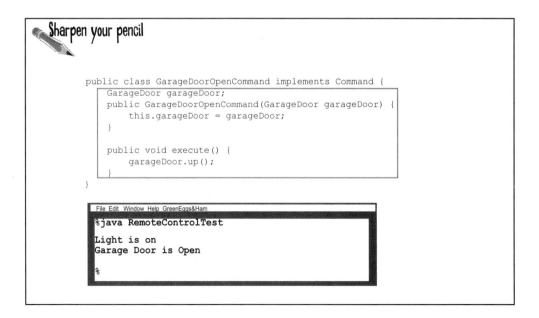

Sharpen your pencil

```java
public class GarageDoorOpenCommand implements Command {
    GarageDoor garageDoor;
    public GarageDoorOpenCommand(GarageDoor garageDoor) {
        this.garageDoor = garageDoor;
    }

    public void execute() {
        garageDoor.up();
    }
}
```

```
File Edit Window Help GreenEggs&Ham
%java RemoteControlTest

Light is on
Garage Door is Open

%
```

Exercise
solutions

Write the undo() method for MacroCommand

```java
public class MacroCommand implements Command {
    Command[] commands;
    public MacroCommand(Command[] commands) {
        this.commands = commands;
    }

    public void execute() {
        for (int i = 0; i < commands.length; i++) {
            commands[i].execute();
        }
    }

    public void undo() {
        for (int i = 0; i < commands.length; i++) {
            commands[i].undo();
        }
    }
}
```

Sharpen your pencil   **We will also need commands for the off button. Write the code to create those here:**

```java
LightOffCommand lightOff = new LightOffCommand(light);
StereoOffCommand stereoOff = new StereoOffCommand(stereo);
TVOffCommand tvOff = new TVOffCommand(tv);
HottubOffCommand hottubOff = new HottubOffCommand(hottub);
```

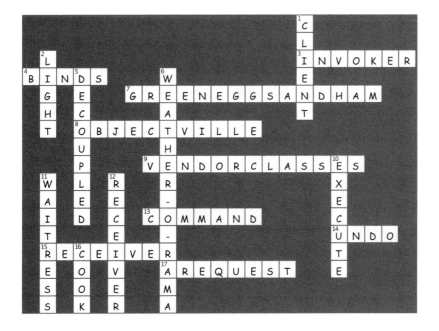

7 the Adapter and Facade Patterns

Being Adaptive

In this chapter we're going to attempt such impossible feats as putting a square peg in a round hole. Sound impossible? Not when we have Design Patterns. Remember the Decorator Pattern? We **wrapped objects** to give them new responsibilities. Now we're going to wrap some objects with a different purpose: to make their interfaces look like something they're not. Why would we do that? So we can adapt a design expecting one interface to a class that implements a different interface. That's not all; while we're at it, we're going to look at another pattern that wraps objects to simplify their interface.

Adapters all around us

You'll have no trouble understanding what an OO adapter is because the real world is full of them. How's this for an example: Have you ever needed to use a US-made laptop in a European country? Then you've probably needed an AC power adapter...

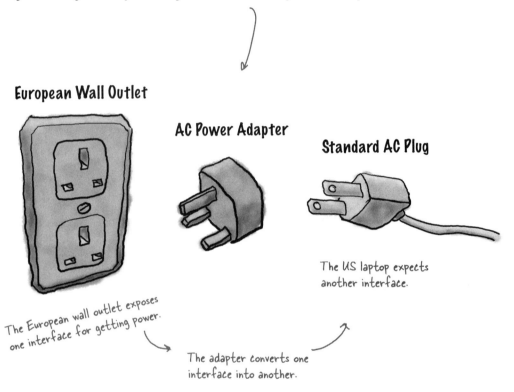

European Wall Outlet

AC Power Adapter

Standard AC Plug

The US laptop expects another interface.

The European wall outlet exposes one interface for getting power.

The adapter converts one interface into another.

You know what the adapter does: it sits in between the plug of your laptop and the European AC outlet; its job is to adapt the European outlet so that you can plug your laptop into it and receive power. Or look at it this way: the adapter changes the interface of the outlet into one that your laptop expects.

How many other real world adapters can you think of?

Some AC adapters are simple – they only change the shape of the outlet so that it matches your plug, and they pass the AC current straight through – but other adapters are more complex internally and may need to step the power up or down to match your devices' needs.

Okay, that's the real world, what about object oriented adapters? Well, our OO adapters play the same role as their real world counterparts: they take an interface and adapt it to one that a client is expecting.

Object oriented adapters

Say you've got an existing software system that you need to work a new vendor class library into, but the new vendor designed their interfaces differently than the last vendor:

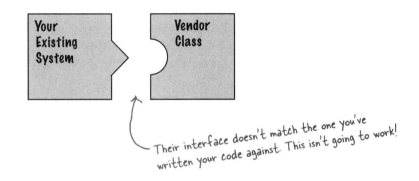

Their interface doesn't match the one you've written your code against. This isn't going to work!

Okay, you don't want to solve the problem by changing your existing code (and you can't change the vendor's code). So what do you do? Well, you can write a class that adapts the new vendor interface into the one you're expecting.

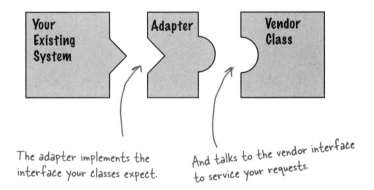

The adapter implements the interface your classes expect.

And talks to the vendor interface to service your requests.

The adapter acts as the middleman by receiving requests from the client and converting them into requests that make sense on the vendor classes.

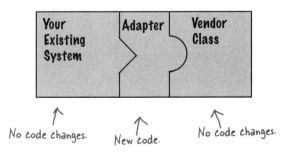

No code changes.   New code.   No code changes.

Can you think of a solution that doesn't require YOU to write ANY additional code to integrate the new vendor classes? How about making the vendor supply the adapter class.

If it walks like a duck and quacks like a duck, then it ~~must~~ might be a ~~duck~~ turkey wrapped with a duck adapter...

It's time to see an adapter in action. Remember our ducks from Chapter 1? Let's review a slightly simplified version of the Duck interfaces and classes:

```java
public interface Duck {
    public void quack();
    public void fly();
}
```

This time around, our ducks implement a Duck interface that allows Ducks to quack and fly.

Here's a subclass of Duck, the MallardDuck.

```java
public class MallardDuck implements Duck {
    public void quack() {
        System.out.println("Quack");
    }

    public void fly() {
        System.out.println("I'm flying");
    }
}
```

Simple implementations: the duck just prints out what it is doing.

Now it's time to meet the newest fowl on the block:

Turkeys don't quack, they gobble.

```java
public interface Turkey {
    public void gobble();
    public void fly();
}
```

Turkeys can fly, although they can only fly short distances.

```
public class WildTurkey implements Turkey {
    public void gobble() {
        System.out.println("Gobble gobble");
    }

    public void fly() {
        System.out.println("I'm flying a short distance");
    }
}
```

Here's a concrete implementation of Turkey; like Duck, it just prints out its actions.

Now, let's say you're short on Duck objects and you'd like to use some Turkey objects in their place. Obviously we can't use the turkeys outright because they have a different interface.

So, let's write an Adapter:

Code Up Close

First, you need to implement the interface of the type you're adapting to. This is the interface your client expects to see.

```
public class TurkeyAdapter implements Duck {
    Turkey turkey;

    public TurkeyAdapter(Turkey turkey) {
        this.turkey = turkey;
    }

    public void quack() {
        turkey.gobble();
    }

    public void fly() {
        for(int i=0; i < 5; i++) {
            turkey.fly();
        }
    }
}
```

Next, we need to get a reference to the object that we are adapting; here we do that through the constructor.

Now we need to implement all the methods in the interface; the quack() translation between classes is easy: just call the gobble() method.

Even though both interfaces have a fly() method, Turkeys fly in short spurts — they can't do long-distance flying like ducks. To map between a Duck's fly() method and a Turkey's, we need to call the Turkey's fly() method five times to make up for it.

Test drive the adapter

Now we just need some code to test drive our adapter:

```java
public class DuckTestDrive {
    public static void main(String[] args) {
        MallardDuck duck = new MallardDuck();

        WildTurkey turkey = new WildTurkey();
        Duck turkeyAdapter = new TurkeyAdapter(turkey);

        System.out.println("The Turkey says...");
        turkey.gobble();
        turkey.fly();

        System.out.println("\nThe Duck says...");
        testDuck(duck);

        System.out.println("\nThe TurkeyAdapter says...");
        testDuck(turkeyAdapter);
    }

    static void testDuck(Duck duck) {
        duck.quack();
        duck.fly();
    }
}
```

Let's create a Duck... and a Turkey.

And then wrap the turkey in a TurkeyAdapter, which makes it look like a Duck.

Then, let's test the Turkey: make it gobble, make it fly.

Now let's test the duck by calling the testDuck() method, which expects a Duck object.

Now the big test: we try to pass off the turkey as a duck...

Here's our testDuck() method; it gets a duck and calls its quack() and fly() methods.

Test run

```
File Edit Window Help Don'tForgetToDuck
%java RemoteControlTest
The Turkey says...

Gobble gobble

I'm flying a short distance

The Duck says...
Quack
I'm flying

The TurkeyAdapter says...
Gobble gobble
I'm flying a short distance
I'm flying a short distance
I'm flying a short distance
I'm flying a short distance
I'm flying a short distance
```

The Turkey gobbles and flies a short distance.

The Duck quacks and flies just like you'd expect.

And the adapter gobbles when quack() is called and flies a few times when fly() is called. The testDuck() method never knows it has a turkey disguised as a duck!

The Adapter Pattern explained

Now that we have an idea of what an Adapter is, let's step back and look at all the pieces again.

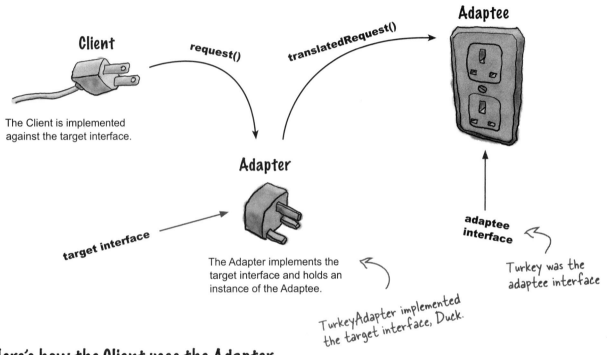

Client

The Client is implemented against the target interface.

request()

translatedRequest()

Adaptee

Adapter

target interface

The Adapter implements the target interface and holds an instance of the Adaptee.

TurkeyAdapter implemented the target interface, Duck.

adaptee interface

Turkey was the adaptee interface

Here's how the Client uses the Adapter

❶ **The client makes a request to the adapter by calling a method on it using the target interface.**

❷ **The adapter translates the request into one or more calls on the adaptee using the adaptee interface.**

❸ **The client receives the results of the call and never knows there is an adapter doing the translation.**

Note that the Client and Adaptee are decoupled — neither knows about the other.

 **Sharpen your pencil**

Let's say we also need an Adapter that converts a Duck to a Turkey. Let's call it DuckAdapter. Write that class:

How did you handle the fly method (after all we know ducks fly longer than turkeys)? Check the answers at the end of the chapter for our solution. Did you think of a better way?

there are no Dumb Questions

Q: How much "adapting" does an adapter need to do? It seems like if I need to implement a large target interface, I could have a LOT of work on my hands.

A: You certainly could. The job of implementing an adapter really is proportional to the size of the interface you need to support as your target interface. Think about your options, however. You could rework all your client-side calls to the interface, which would result in a lot of investigative work and code changes. Or, you can cleanly provide one class that encapsulates all the changes in one class.

Q: Does an adapter always wrap one and only one class?

A: The Adapter Pattern's role is to convert one interface into another. While most examples of the adapter pattern show an adapter wrapping one adaptee, we both know the world is often a bit more messy. So, you may well have situations where an adapter holds two or more adaptees that are needed to implement the target interface.

This relates to another pattern called the Facade Pattern; people often confuse the two. Remind us to revisit this point when we talk about facades later in this chapter.

Q: What if I have old and new parts of my system, the old parts expect the old vendor interface, but we've already written the new parts to use the new vendor interface? It is going to get confusing using an adapter here and the unwrapped interface there. Wouldn't I be better off just writing my older code and forgetting the adapter?

A: Not necessarily. One thing you can do is create a Two Way Adapter that supports both interfaces. To create a Two Way Adapter, just implement both interfaces involved, so the adapter can act as an old interface or a new interface.

Adapter Pattern defined

Enough ducks, turkeys and AC power adapters; let's get real and look at the official definition of the Adapter Pattern:

> **The Adapter Pattern** converts the interface of a class into another interface the clients expect. Adapter lets classes work together that couldn't otherwise because of incompatible interfaces.

Now, we know this pattern allows us to use a client with an incompatible interface by creating an Adapter that does the conversion. This acts to decouple the client from the implemented interface, and if we expect the interface to change over time, the adapter encapsulates that change so that the client doesn't have to be modified each time it needs to operate against a different interface.

We've taken a look at the runtime behavior of the pattern; let's take a look at its class diagram as well:

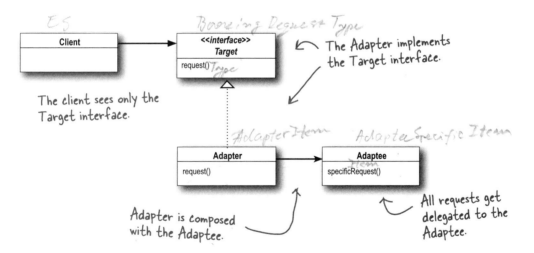

The Adapter Pattern is full of good OO design principles: check out the use of object composition to wrap the adaptee with an altered interface. This approach has the added advantage that we can use an adapter with any subclass of the adaptee.

Also check out how the pattern binds the client to an interface, not an implementation; we could use several adapters, each converting a different backend set of classes. Or, we could add new implementations after the fact, as long as they adhere to the Target interface.

Object and class adapters

Now despite having defined the pattern, we haven't told you the whole story yet. There are actually *two* kinds of adapters: *object* adapters and *class* adapters. This chapter has covered object adapters and the class diagram on the previous page is a diagram of an object adapter.

So what's a *class* adapter and why haven't we told you about it? Because you need multiple inheritance to implement it, which isn't possible in Java. But, that doesn't mean you might not encounter a need for class adapters down the road when using your favorite multiple inheritance language! Let's look at the class diagram for multiple inheritance.

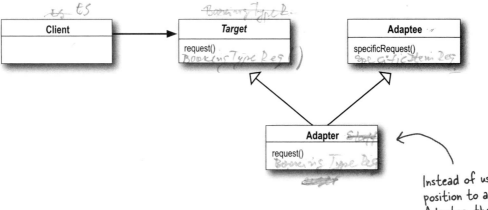

Instead of using composition to adapt the Adaptee, the Adapter now subclasses the Adaptee and the Target classes.

Look familiar? That's right – the only difference is that with class adapter we subclass the Target and the Adaptee, while with object adapter we use composition to pass requests to an Adaptee.

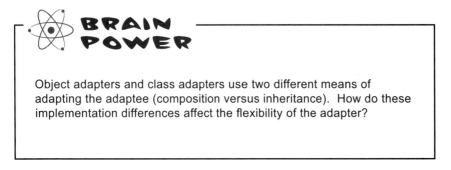

Object adapters and class adapters use two different means of adapting the adaptee (composition versus inheritance). How do these implementation differences affect the flexibility of the adapter?

Duck Magnets

Your job is to take the duck and turkey magnets and drag them over the part of the diagram that describes the role played by that bird, in our earlier example. (Try not to flip back through the pages.) Then add your own annotations to describe how it works.

Class Adapter

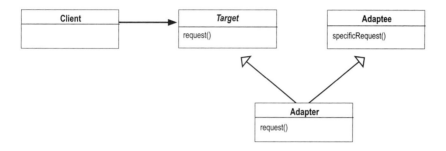

Object Adapter

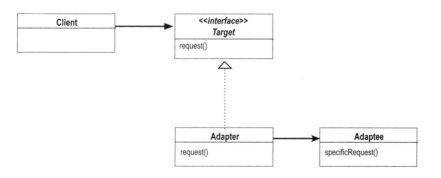

Drag these onto the class diagram, to show which part of the diagram represents the Duck and which represents the Turkey.

Duck Magnets Answer

Note: the class adapter uses multiple inheritance, so you can't do it in Java...

Class Adapter

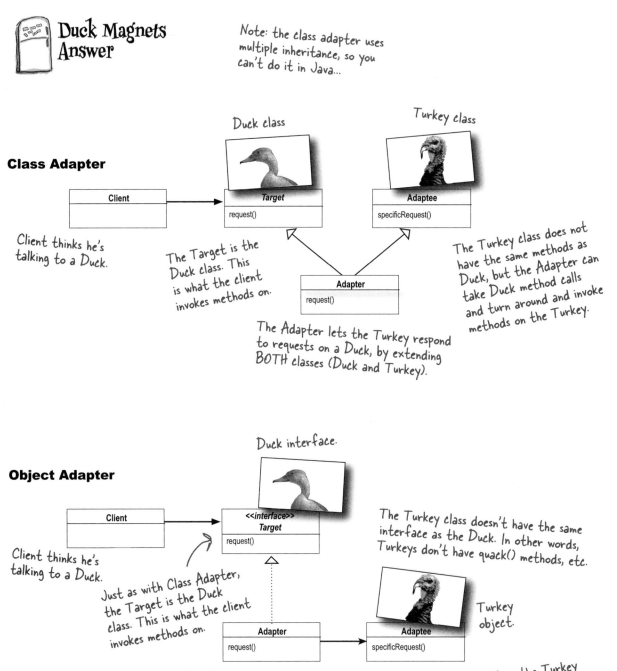

Duck class

Turkey class

Client thinks he's talking to a Duck.

Client ──→ Target
request()

Adaptee
specificRequest()

The Target is the Duck class. This is what the client invokes methods on.

The Turkey class does not have the same methods as Duck, but the Adapter can take Duck method calls and turn around and invoke methods on the Turkey.

Adapter
request()

The Adapter lets the Turkey respond to requests on a Duck, by extending BOTH classes (Duck and Turkey).

Object Adapter

Duck interface.

Client thinks he's talking to a Duck.

Client ──→ <<interface>>
Target
request()

Just as with Class Adapter, the Target is the Duck class. This is what the client invokes methods on.

The Turkey class doesn't have the same interface as the Duck. In other words, Turkeys don't have quack() methods, etc.

Turkey object.

Adapter
request()
──→ Adaptee
specificRequest()

The Adapter implements the Duck interface, but when it gets a method call it turns around and delegates the calls to a Turkey.

Thanks to the Adapter, the Turkey (Adaptee) will get calls that the client makes on the Duck interface.

Fireside Chats

Tonight's talk: **The Object Adapter and Class Adapter meet face to face.**

Object Adapter	**Class Adapter**
Because I use composition I've got a leg up. I can not only adapt an adaptee class, but any of its subclasses.	
	That's true, I do have trouble with that because I am committed to one specific adaptee class, but I have a huge advantage because I don't have to reimplement my entire adaptee. I can also override the behavior of my adaptee if I need to because I'm just subclassing.
In my part of the world, we like to use composition over inheritance; you may be saving a few lines of code, but all I'm doing is writing a little code to delegate to the adaptee. We like to keep things flexible.	
	Flexible maybe, efficient? No. Using a class adapter there is just one of me, not an adapter and an adaptee.
You're worried about one little object? You might be able to quickly override a method, but any behavior I add to my adapter code works with my adaptee class *and* all its subclasses.	
	Yeah, but what if a subclass of adaptee adds some new behavior. Then what?
Hey, come on, cut me a break, I just need to compose with the subclass to make that work.	
	Sounds messy...
You wanna see messy? Look in the mirror!	

Real world adapters

Let's take a look at the use of a simple Adapter in the real world (something more serious than Ducks at least)...

Old world Enumerators

If you've been around Java for a while you probably remember that the early collections types (Vector, Stack, Hashtable, and a few others) implement a method elements(), which returns an Enumeration. The Enumeration interface allows you to step through the elements of a collection without knowing the specifics of how they are managed in the collection.

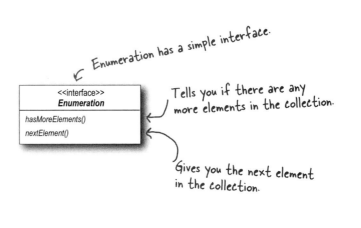

← Enumeration has a simple interface.

Tells you if there are any more elements in the collection.

Gives you the next element in the collection.

New world Iterators

When Sun released their more recent Collections classes they began using an Iterator interface that, like Enumeration, allows you to iterate through a set of items in a collection, but also adds the ability to remove items.

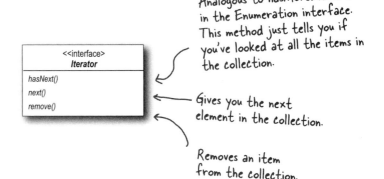

Analogous to hasMoreElements() in the Enumeration interface. This method just tells you if you've looked at all the items in the collection.

Gives you the next element in the collection.

Removes an item from the collection.

And today...

We are often faced with legacy code that exposes the Enumerator interface, yet we'd like for our new code to use only Iterators. It looks like we need to build an adapter.

Adapting an Enumeration to an Iterator

First we'll look at the two interfaces to figure out how the methods map from one to the other. In other words, we'll figure out what to call on the adaptee when the client invokes a method on the target.

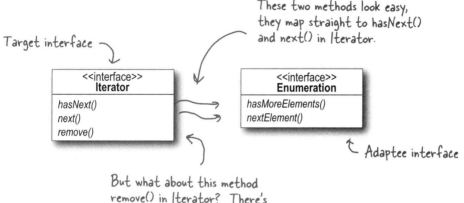

These two methods look easy, they map straight to hasNext() and next() in Iterator.

Target interface

<<interface>>
Iterator
hasNext()
next()
remove()

<<interface>>
Enumeration
hasMoreElements()
nextElement()

Adaptee interface

But what about this method remove() in Iterator? There's nothing like that in Enumeration.

Designing the Adapter

Here's what the classes should look like: we need an adapter that implements the Target interface and that is composed with an adaptee. The hasNext() and next() methods are going to be straightforward to map from target to adaptee: we just pass them right through. But what do you do about remove()? Think about it for a moment (and we'll deal with it on the next page). For now, here's the class diagram:

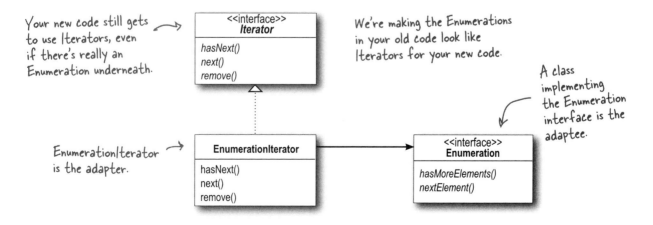

Your new code still gets to use Iterators, even if there's really an Enumeration underneath.

We're making the Enumerations in your old code look like Iterators for your new code.

A class implementing the Enumeration interface is the adaptee.

EnumerationIterator is the adapter.

<<interface>>
Iterator
hasNext()
next()
remove()

EnumerationIterator
hasNext()
next()
remove()

<<interface>>
Enumeration
hasMoreElements()
nextElement()

Dealing with the remove() method

Well, we know Enumeration just doesn't support remove. It's a "read only" interface. There's no way to implement a fully functioning remove() method on the adapter. The best we can do is throw a runtime exception. Luckily, the designers of the Iterator interface foresaw this need and defined the remove() method so that it supports an UnsupportedOperationException.

This is a case where the adapter isn't perfect; clients will have to watch out for potential exceptions, but as long as the client is careful and the adapter is well documented this is a perfectly reasonable solution.

Writing the EnumerationIterator adapter

Here's simple but effective code for all those legacy classes still producing Enumerations:

```java
public class EnumerationIterator implements Iterator
{
    Enumeration enum;

    public EnumerationIterator(Enumeration enum) {
        this.enum = enum;
    }

    public boolean hasNext() {
        return enum.hasMoreElements();
    }

    public Object next() {
        return enum.nextElement();
    }

    public void remove() {
        throw new UnsupportedOperationException();
    }
}
```

Since we're adapting Enumeration to Iterator, our Adapter implements the Iterator interface... it has to look like an Iterator.

The Enumeration we're adapting. We're using composition so we stash it in an instance variable.

The Iterator's hasNext() method is delegated to the Enumeration's hasMoreElements() method...

... and the Iterator's next() method is delegated to the Enumerations's nextElement() method.

Unfortunately, we can't support Iterator's remove() method, so we have to punt (in other words, we give up!). Here we just throw an exception.

Exercise

While Java has gone in the direction of the Iterator, there is nevertheless a lot of legacy **client code** that depends on the Enumeration interface, so an Adapter that converts an Iterator to an Enumeration is also quite useful.

Write an Adapter that adapts an Iterator to an Enumeration. You can test your code by adapting an ArrayList. The ArrayList class supports the Iterator interface but doesn't support Enumerations (well, not yet anyway).

BRAIN POWER

Some AC adapters do more than just change the interface – they add other features like surge protection, indicator lights and other bells and whistles.

If you were going to implement these kinds of features, what pattern would you use?

Fireside Chats

Tonight's talk: **The Decorator Pattern and the Adapter Pattern discuss their differences.**

Decorator	**Adapter**
I'm important. My job is all about *responsibility* – you know that when a Decorator is involved there's going to be some new responsibilities or behaviors added to your design.	
	You guys want all the glory while us adapters are down in the trenches doing the dirty work: converting interfaces. Our jobs may not be glamorous, but our clients sure do appreciate us making their lives simpler.
That may be true, but don't think we don't work hard. When we have to decorate a big interface, whoa, that can take a lot of code.	
	Try being an adapter when you've got to bring several classes together to provide the interface your client is expecting. Now that's tough. But we have a saying: "an uncoupled client is a happy client."
Cute. Don't think we get all the glory; sometimes I'm just one decorator that is being wrapped by who knows how many other decorators. When a method call gets delegated to you, you have no idea how many other decorators have already dealt with it and you don't know that you'll ever get noticed for your efforts servicing the request.	
	Hey, if adapters are doing their job, our clients never even know we're there. It can be a thankless job.

Decorator

Adapter

But, the great thing about us adapters is that we allow clients to make use of new libraries and subsets without changing *any* code, they just rely on us to do the conversion for them. Hey, it's a niche, but we're good at it.

Well us decorators do that as well, only we allow *new behavior* to be added to classes without altering existing code. I still say that adapters are just fancy decorators – I mean, just like us, you wrap an object.

No, no, no, not at all. We *always* convert the interface of what we wrap, you *never* do. I'd say a decorator is like an adapter; it is just that you don't change the interface!

Uh, no. Our job in life is to extend the behaviors or responsibilities of the objects we wrap, we aren't a *simple pass through*.

Hey, who are you calling a simple pass through? Come on down and we'll see how long *you* last converting a few interfaces!

Maybe we should agree to disagree. We seem to look somewhat similar on paper, but clearly we are *miles* apart in our *intent*.

Oh yeah, I'm with you there.

And now for something different...

There's another pattern in this chapter.

You've seen how the Adapter Pattern converts the interface of a class into one that a client is expecting. You also know we achieve this in Java by wrapping the object that has an incompatible interface with an object that implements the correct one.

We're going to look at a pattern now that alters an interface, but for a different reason: to simplify the interface. It's aptly named the Facade Pattern because this pattern hides all the complexity of one or more classes behind a clean, well-lit facade.

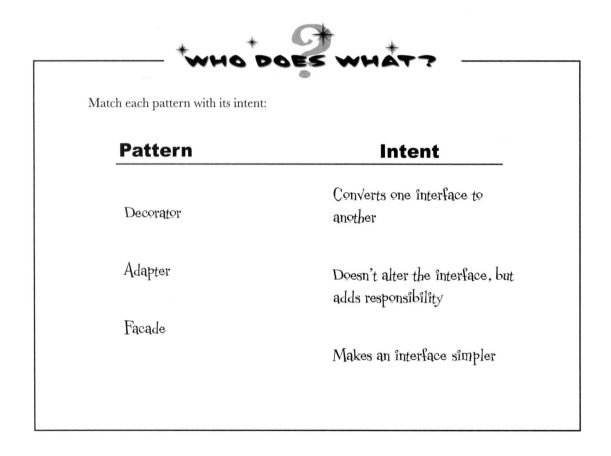

WHO DOES WHAT?

Match each pattern with its intent:

Pattern	Intent
Decorator	Converts one interface to another
Adapter	Doesn't alter the interface, but adds responsibility
Facade	Makes an interface simpler

Home Sweet Home Theater

Before we dive into the details of the Facade Pattern, let's take a look at a growing national obsession: building your own home theater.

You've done your research and you've assembled a killer system complete with a DVD player, a projection video system, an automated screen, surround sound and even a popcorn popper.

Check out all the components you've put together:

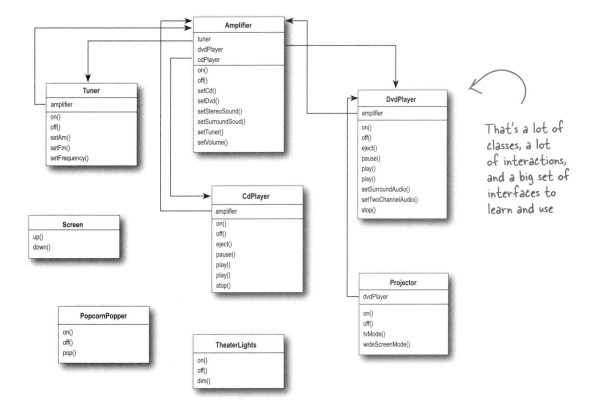

That's a lot of classes, a lot of interactions, and a big set of interfaces to learn and use

You've spent weeks running wire, mounting the projector, making all the connections and fine tuning. Now it's time to put it all in motion and enjoy a movie...

Watching a movie (the hard way)

Pick out a DVD, relax, and get ready for movie magic. Oh, there's just one thing – to watch the movie, you need to perform a few tasks:

❶ Turn on the popcorn popper

❷ Start the popper popping

❸ Dim the lights

❹ Put the screen down

❺ Turn the projector on

❻ Set the projector input to DVD

❼ Put the projector on wide-screen mode

❽ Turn the sound amplifier on

❾ Set the amplifier to DVD input

❿ Set the amplifier to surround sound

⓫ Set the amplifier volume to medium (5)

⓬ Turn the DVD Player on

⓭ Start the DVD Player playing

I'm already exhausted and all I've done is turn everything on!

Let's check out those same tasks in terms of the classes and the method calls needed to perform them:

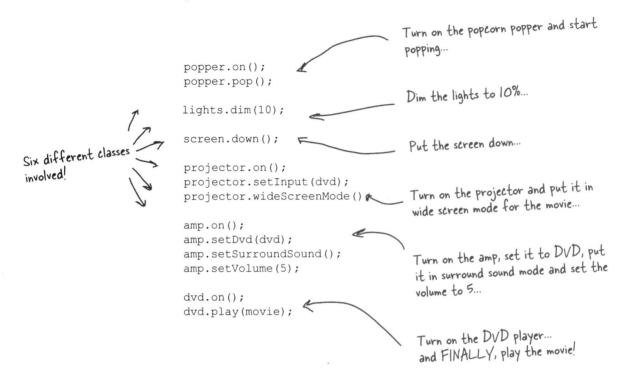

```
popper.on();
popper.pop();

lights.dim(10);

screen.down();

projector.on();
projector.setInput(dvd);
projector.wideScreenMode();

amp.on();
amp.setDvd(dvd);
amp.setSurroundSound();
amp.setVolume(5);

dvd.on();
dvd.play(movie);
```

Turn on the popcorn popper and start popping...

Dim the lights to 10%...

Put the screen down...

Turn on the projector and put it in wide screen mode for the movie...

Six different classes involved!

Turn on the amp, set it to DVD, put it in surround sound mode and set the volume to 5...

Turn on the DVD player... and FINALLY, play the movie!

But there's more...

- When the movie is over, how do you turn everything off? Wouldn't you have to do all of this over again, in reverse?

- Wouldn't it be as complex to listen to a CD or the radio?

- If you decide to upgrade your system, you're probably going to have to learn a slightly different procedure.

So what to do? The complexity of using your home theater is becoming apparent!

Let's see how the Facade Pattern can get us out of this mess so we can enjoy the movie...

Lights, Camera, Facade!

A Facade is just what you need: with the Facade Pattern you can take a complex subsystem and make it easier to use by implementing a Facade class that provides one, more reasonable interface. Don't worry; if you need the power of the complex subsystem, it's still there for you to use, but if all you need is a straightforward interface, the Facade is there for you.

Let's take a look at how the Facade operates:

1 Okay, time to create a Facade for the home theater system. To do this we create a new class HomeTheaterFacade, which exposes a few simple methods such as watchMovie().

2 The Facade class treats the home theater components as a subsystem, and calls on the subsystem to implement its watchMovie() method.

The Facade

The subsystem the Facade is simplifying.

play()

on()

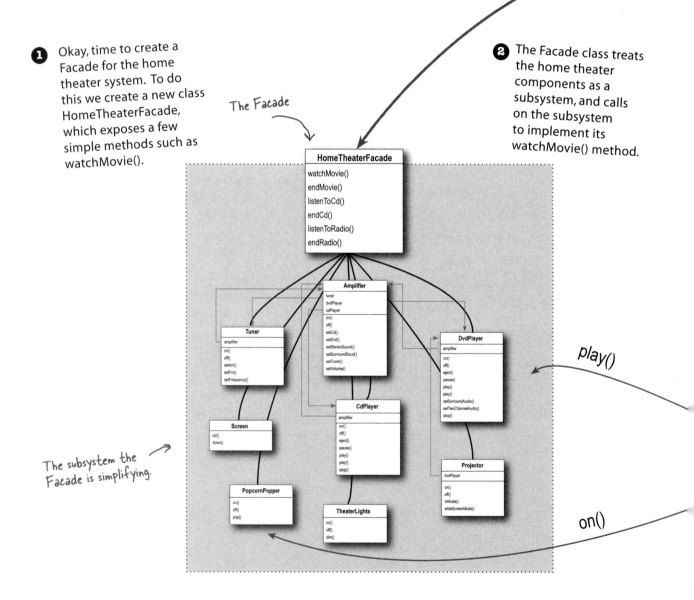

watchMovie()

A client of the ~~subsystem~~ facade

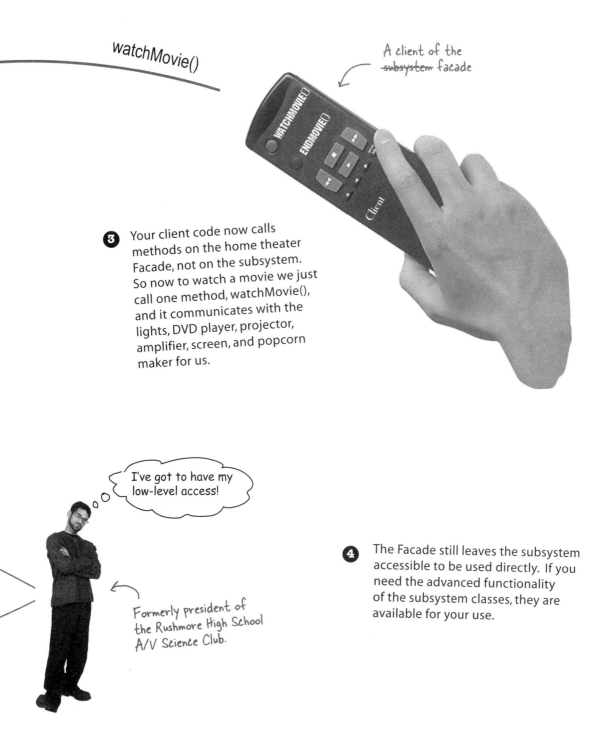

3 Your client code now calls methods on the home theater Facade, not on the subsystem. So now to watch a movie we just call one method, watchMovie(), and it communicates with the lights, DVD player, projector, amplifier, screen, and popcorn maker for us.

I've got to have my low-level access!

Formerly president of the Rushmore High School A/V Science Club.

4 The Facade still leaves the subsystem accessible to be used directly. If you need the advanced functionality of the subsystem classes, they are available for your use.

there are no
Dumb Questions

Q: If the Facade encapsulates the subsystem classes, how does a client that needs lower-level functionality gain access to them?

A: Facades don't "encapsulate" the subsystem classes; they merely provide a simplified interface to their functionality. The subsystem classes still remain available for direct use by clients that need to use more specific interfaces. This is a nice property of the Facade Pattern: it provides a simplified interface while still exposing the full functionality of the system to those who may need it.

Q: Does the facade add any functionality or does it just pass through each request to the subsystem?

A: A facade is free to add its own "smarts" in addition to making use of the subsystem. For instance, while our home theater facade doesn't implement any new behavior, it is smart enough to know that the popcorn popper has to be turned on before it can pop (as well as the details of how to turn on and stage a movie showing).

Q: Does each subsystem have only one facade?

A: Not necessarily. The pattern certainly allows for any number of facades to be created for a given subsystem.

Q: What is the benefit of the facade other than the fact that I now have a simpler interface?

A: The Facade Pattern also allows you to decouple your client implementation from any one subsystem. Let's say for instance that you get a big raise and decide to upgrade your home theater to all new components that have different interfaces. Well, if you coded your client to the facade rather than the subsystem, your client code doesn't need to change, just the facade (and hopefully the manufacturer is supplying that!).

Q: So the way to tell the difference between the Adapter Pattern and the Facade Pattern is that the adapter wraps one class and the facade may represent many classes?

A: No! Remember, the Adapter Pattern changes the interface of one or more classes into one interface that a client is expecting. While most textbook examples show the adapter adapting one class, you may need to adapt many classes to provide the interface a client is coded to. Likewise, a Facade may provide a simplified interface to a single class with a very complex interface.

The difference between the two is not in terms of how many classes they "wrap," it is in their **intent**. The intent of the Adapter Pattern is to **alter** an interface so that it matches one a client is expecting. The intent of the Facade Pattern is to provide a **simplified** interface to a subsystem.

A facade not only simplifies an interface, it decouples a client from a subsystem of components.

Facades and adapters may wrap multiple classes, but a facade's intent is to simplify, while an adapter's is to convert the interface to something different.

Constructing your home theater facade

Let's step through the construction of the HomeTheaterFacade: The
first step is to use composition so that the facade has access to all the
components of the subsystem:

```java
public class HomeTheaterFacade {
    Amplifier amp;
    Tuner tuner;
    DvdPlayer dvd;
    CdPlayer cd;
    Projector projector;
    TheaterLights lights;
    Screen screen;
    PopcornPopper popper;

    public HomeTheaterFacade(Amplifier amp,
                Tuner tuner,
                DvdPlayer dvd,
                CdPlayer cd,
                Projector projector,
                Screen screen,
                TheaterLights lights,
                PopcornPopper popper) {

        this.amp = amp;
        this.tuner = tuner;
        this.dvd = dvd;
        this.cd = cd;
        this.projector = projector;
        this.screen = screen;
        this.lights = lights;
        this.popper = popper;
    }

    // other methods here
}
```

Here's the composition; these
are all the components of the
subsystem we are going to use.

The facade is passed a
reference to each component
of the subsystem in its
constructor. The facade
then assigns each to the
corresponding instance variable.

We're just about to fill these in...

Implementing the simplified interface

Now it's time to bring the components of the subsystem together into a unified interface.
Let's implement the watchMovie() and endMovie() methods:

```java
public void watchMovie(String movie) {
    System.out.println("Get ready to watch a movie...");
    popper.on();
    popper.pop();
    lights.dim(10);
    screen.down();
    projector.on();
    projector.wideScreenMode();
    amp.on();
    amp.setDvd(dvd);
    amp.setSurroundSound();
    amp.setVolume(5);
    dvd.on();
    dvd.play(movie);
}

public void endMovie() {
    System.out.println("Shutting movie theater down...");
    popper.off();
    lights.on();
    screen.up();
    projector.off();
    amp.off();
    dvd.stop();
    dvd.eject();
    dvd.off();
}
```

watchMovie() follows the same sequence we had to do by hand before, but wraps it up in a handy method that does all the work. Notice that for each task we are delegating the responsibility to the corresponding component in the subsystem.

And endMovie() takes care of shutting everything down for us. Again, each task is delegated to the appropriate component in the subsystem.

BRAIN POWER

Think about the facades you've encountered in the Java API.
Where would you like to have a few new ones?

Time to watch a movie (the easy way)

It's SHOWTIME!

```
public class HomeTheaterTestDrive {
    public static void main(String[] args) {
        // instantiate components here

        HomeTheaterFacade homeTheater =
                new HomeTheaterFacade(amp, tuner, dvd, cd,
                        projector, screen, lights, popper);

        homeTheater.watchMovie("Raiders of the Lost Ark");
        homeTheater.endMovie();
    }
}
```

Here we're creating the components right in the test drive. Normally the client is given a facade, it doesn't have to construct one itself.

First you instantiate the Facade with all the components in the subsystem.

Use the simplified interface to first start the movie up, and then shut it down.

Here's the output.

Calling the Facade's watchMovie() does all this work for us...

...and here, we're done watching the movie, so calling endMovie() turns everything off.

```
File Edit Window Help SnakesWhy'dItHaveToBeSnakes?
%java HomeTheaterTestDrive

Get ready to watch a movie...
Popcorn Popper on
Popcorn Popper popping popcorn!
Theater Ceiling Lights dimming to 10%
Theater Screen going down
Top-O-Line Projector on
Top-O-Line Projector in widescreen mode (16x9 aspect ratio)
Top-O-Line Amplifier on
Top-O-Line Amplifier setting DVD player to Top-O-Line DVD Player
Top-O-Line Amplifier surround sound on (5 speakers, 1 subwoofer)
Top-O-Line Amplifier setting volume to 5
Top-O-Line DVD Player on
Top-O-Line DVD Player playing "Raiders of the Lost Ark"
Shutting movie theater down...
Popcorn Popper off
Theater Ceiling Lights on
Theater Screen going up
Top-O-Line Projector off
Top-O-Line Amplifier off
Top-O-Line DVD Player stopped "Raiders of the Lost Ark"
Top-O-Line DVD Player eject
Top-O-Line DVD Player off
%
```

Facade Pattern defined

To use the Facade Pattern, we create a class that simplifies and unifies a set of more complex classes that belong to some subsystem. Unlike a lot of patterns, Facade is fairly straightforward; there are no mind bending abstractions to get your head around. But that doesn't make it any less powerful: the Facade Pattern allows us to avoid tight coupling between clients and subsystems, and, as you will see shortly, also helps us adhere to a new object oriented principle.

Before we introduce that new principle, let's take a look at the official definition of the pattern:

> **The Facade Pattern** provides a unified interface to a set of interfaces in a subsytem. Facade defines a higher-level interface that makes the subsystem easier to use.

There isn't a lot here that you don't already know, but one of the most important things to remember about a pattern is its intent. This definition tells us loud and clear that the purpose of the facade it to make a subsystem easier to use through a simplified interface. You can see this in the pattern's class diagram:

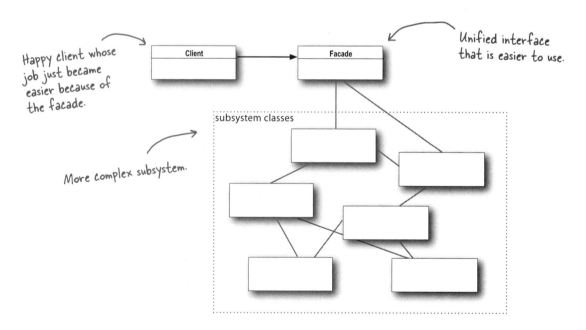

Happy client whose job just became easier because of the facade.

Unified interface that is easier to use.

More complex subsystem.

That's it; you've got another pattern under your belt! Now, it's time for that new OO principle. Watch out, this one can challenge some assumptions!

The Principle of Least Knowledge

The Principle of Least Knowledge guides us to reduce the interactions between objects to just a few close "friends." The principle is usually stated as:

Design Principle

Principle of Least Knowledge - talk only to your immediate friends.

But what does this mean in real terms? It means when you are designing a system, for any object, be careful of the number of classes it interacts with and also how it comes to interact with those classes.

This principle prevents us from creating designs that have a large number of classes coupled together so that changes in one part of the system cascade to other parts. When you build a lot of dependencies between many classes, you are building a fragile system that will be costly to maintain and complex for others to understand.

BRAIN POWER

How many classes is this code coupled to?

```
public float getTemp() {
    return station.getThermometer().getTemperature();
}
```

How NOT to Win Friends and Influence Objects

Okay, but how do you keep from doing this? The principle provides some guidelines: take any object; now from any method in that object, the principle tells us that we should only invoke methods that belong to:

- The object itself

- Objects passed in as a parameter to the method

- Any object the method creates or instantiates

- Any components of the object

Notice that these guidelines tell us not to call methods on objects that were returned from calling other methods!!

Think of a "component" as any object that is referenced by an instance variable. In other words think of this as a HAS–A relationship.

This sounds kind of stringent doesn't it? What's the harm in calling the method of an object we get back from another call? Well, if we were to do that, then we'd be making a request of another object's subpart (and increasing the number of objects we directly know). In such cases, the principle forces us to ask the object to make the request for us; that way we don't have to know about its component objects (and we keep our circle of friends small). For example:

Without the Principle

```java
public float getTemp() {
    Thermometer thermometer = station.getThermometer();
    return thermometer.getTemperature();
}
```

Here we get the thermometer object from the station and then call the getTemperature() method ourselves.

With the Principle

```java
public float getTemp() {
    return station.getTemperature();
}
```

When we apply the principle, we add a method to the Station class that makes the request to the thermometer for us. This reduces the number of classes we're dependent on.

Keeping your method calls in bounds...

Here's a Car class that demonstrates all the ways you can call methods and still adhere to the Principle of Least Knowledge:

```java
public class Car {
    Engine engine;
    // other instance variables

    public Car() {
        // initialize engine, etc.
    }

    public void start(Key key) {
        Doors doors = new Doors();

        boolean authorized = key.turns();

        if (authorized) {
            engine.start();
            updateDashboardDisplay();
            doors.lock();
        }
    }

    public void updateDashboardDisplay() {
        // update display
    }
}
```

Here's a component of this class. We can call its methods.

Here we're creating a new object, its methods are legal.

You can call a method on an object passed as a parameter.

You can call a method on a component of the object.

You can call a local method within the object.

You can call a method on an object you create or instantiate.

there are no Dumb Questions

Q: There is another principle called the Law of Demeter; how are they related?

A: The two are one and the same and you'll encounter these terms being intermixed. We prefer to use the Principle of Least Knowledge for a couple of reasons: (1) the name is more intuitive and (2) the use of the word "Law" implies we always have to apply this principle. In fact, no principle is a law, all principles should be used when and where they are helpful. All design involves tradeoffs (abstractions versus speed, space versus time, and so on) and while principles provide guidance, all factors should be taken into account before applying them.

Q: Are there any disadvantages to applying the Principle of Least Knowledge?

A: Yes; while the principle reduces the dependencies between objects and studies have shown this reduces software maintenance, it is also the case that applying this principle results in more "wrapper" classes being written to handle method calls to other components. This can result in increased complexity and development time as well as decreased runtime performance.

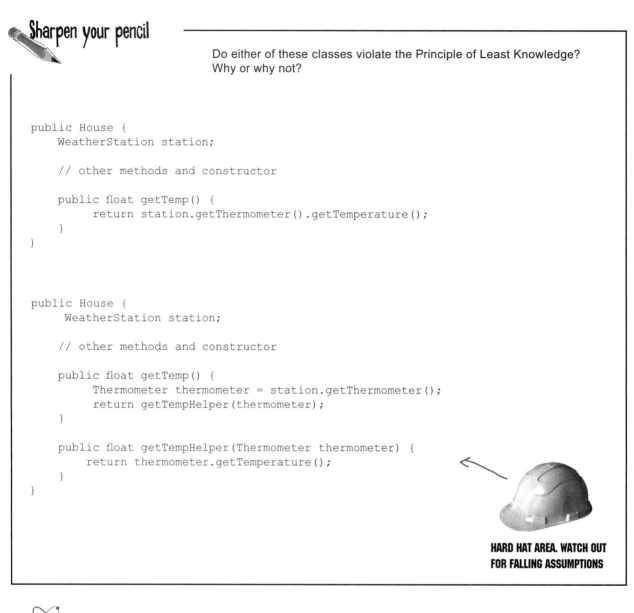

Sharpen your pencil

Do either of these classes violate the Principle of Least Knowledge? Why or why not?

```java
public House {
    WeatherStation station;

    // other methods and constructor

    public float getTemp() {
        return station.getThermometer().getTemperature();
    }
}
```

```java
public House {
    WeatherStation station;

    // other methods and constructor

    public float getTemp() {
        Thermometer thermometer = station.getThermometer();
        return getTempHelper(thermometer);
    }

    public float getTempHelper(Thermometer thermometer) {
        return thermometer.getTemperature();
    }
}
```

HARD HAT AREA. WATCH OUT
FOR FALLING ASSUMPTIONS

BRAIN POWER

Can you think of a common use of Java that violates the Principle of Least Knowledge?

Should you care?

Answer: How about System.out.println()?

The Facade and the Principle of Least Knowledge

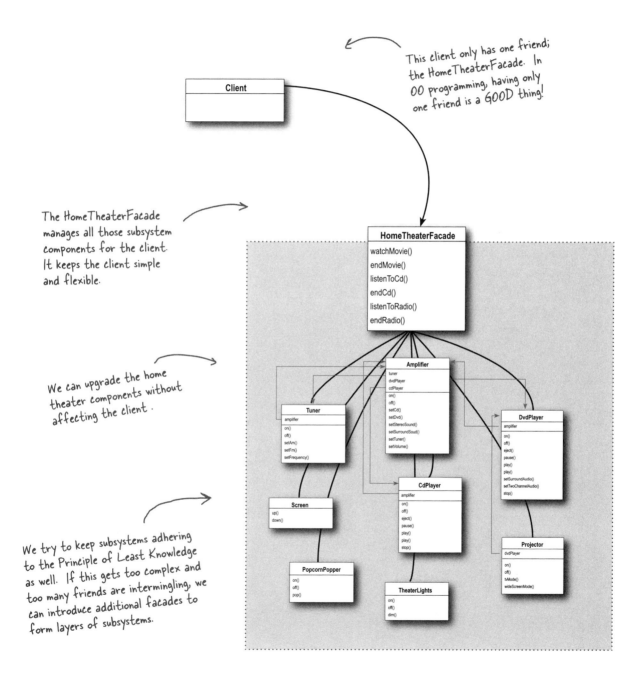

This client only has one friend; the HomeTheaterFacade. In OO programming, having only one friend is a GOOD thing!

The HomeTheaterFacade manages all those subsystem components for the client. It keeps the client simple and flexible.

We can upgrade the home theater components without affecting the client.

We try to keep subsystems adhering to the Principle of Least Knowledge as well. If this gets too complex and too many friends are intermingling, we can introduce additional facades to form layers of subsystems.

Tools for your Design Toolbox

Your toolbox is starting to get heavy! In this chapter we've added a couple of patterns that allow us to alter interfaces and reduce coupling between clients and the systems they use.

OO Basics

straction
apsulation
ymorphism
eritance

OO Principles

Encapsulate what varies

Favor composition over inheritance

Program to interfaces, not implementations

Strive for loosely coupled designs between objects that interact

Classes should be open for extension but closed for modification

Depend on abstractions. Do not depend on concretions

Only talk to your friends

We have a new technique for maintaining a low level of coupling in our designs. (remember, talk only to your friends)...

...and TWO new patterns. Each changes an interface, the adapter to convert and the facade to unify and simplify

OO Patterns

Adapter – Converts the interface of a class into another interface clients expect. Lets classes work together that couldn't otherwise because of incompatible interfaces.

Facade – Provides a unified interface to a set of interfaces in a subsystem. Facade defines a higher-level interface that makes the subsystem easier to use.

BULLET POINTS

- When you need to use an existing class and its interface is not the one you need, use an adapter.

- When you need to simplify and unify a large interface or complex set of interfaces, use a facade.

- An adapter changes an interface into one a client expects.

- A facade decouples a client from a complex subsystem.

- Implementing an adapter may require little work or a great deal of work depending on the size and complexity of the target interface.

- Implementing a facade requires that we compose the facade with its subsystem and use delegation to perform the work of the facade.

- There are two forms of the Adapter Pattern: object and class adapters. Class adapters require multiple inheritance.

- You can implement more than one facade for a subsystem.

- An adapter wraps an object to change its interface, a decorator wraps an object to add new behaviors and responsibilities, and a facade "wraps" a set of objects to simplify.

Yes, it's another crossword. All of the solution words are from this chapter.

Across

1. True or false, Adapters can only wrap one object
5. An Adapter _____ an interface
6. Movie we watched (5 words)
10. If in Europe you might need one of these (two words)
11. Adapter with two roles (two words)
14. Facade still _____ low level access
15. Ducks do it better than Turkeys
16. Disadvantage of the Principle of Least Knowledge: too many _____
17. A _____ simplifies an interface
19. New American dream (two words)

Down

2. Decorator called Adapter this (3 words)
3. One advantage of Facade
4. Principle that wasn't as easy as it sounded (two words)
7. A _____ adds new behavior
8. Masquerading as a Duck
9. Example that violates the Principle of Least Knowledge: System.out._____
12. No movie is complete without this
13. Adapter client uses the _____ interface
18. An Adapter and a Decorator can be said to _____ an object

Exercise solutions

Let's say we also need an adapter that converts a Duck to a Turkey.
Let's call it DuckAdapter. Write that class:

Now we are adapting Turkeys
to Ducks, so we implement the
Turkey interface.

```java
public class DuckAdapter implements Turkey {
    Duck duck;
    Random rand;

    public DuckAdapter(Duck duck) {
        this.duck = duck;
        rand = new Random();
    }

    public void gobble() {
        duck.quack();
    }

    public void fly() {
        if (rand.nextInt(5)  == 0) {
            duck.fly();
        }
    }
}
```

We stash a reference to the Duck we are adapting.

We also recreate a random object;
take a look at the fly() method
to see how it is used.

A gobble just becomes a quack.

Since ducks fly a lot longer than
turkeys, we decided to only fly the
duck on average one of five times.

Do either of these classes violate the Principle of Least Knowledge?
For each, why or why not?

```java
public House {
    WeatherStation station;

    // other methods and constructor

    public float getTemp() {
        return station.getThermometer().getTemperature();
    }
}
```

Violates the Principle of Least Knowledge!
You are calling the method of an object
returned from another call.

```java
public House {
    WeatherStation station;

    // other methods and constructor

    public float getTemp() {
        Thermometer thermometer = station.getThermometer();
        return getTempHelper(thermometer);
    }

    public float getTempHelper(Thermometer thermometer) {
        return thermometer.getTemperature();
    }
}
```

Doesn't violate Principle of Least Knowledge!
This seems like hacking our way around the
principle. Has anything really changed since we
just moved out the call to another method?

Exercise solutions

You've seen how to implement an adapter that adapts an Enumeration to an Iterator; now write an adapter that adapts an Iterator to an Enumaration.

```java
public class IteratorEnumeration implements Enumeration {
    Iterator iterator;

    public IteratorEnumeration(Iterator iterator) {
        this.iterator = iterator;
    }

    public boolean hasMoreElements() {
        return iterator.hasNext();
    }

    public Object nextElement() {
        return iterator.next();
    }
}
```

WHO DOES WHAT?

Match each pattern with its intent:

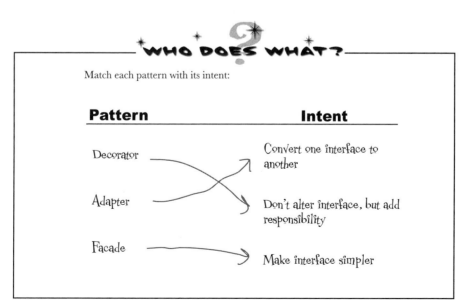

Pattern	Intent
Decorator	Convert one interface to another
Adapter	Don't alter interface, but add responsibility
Facade	Make interface simpler

Exercise solutions

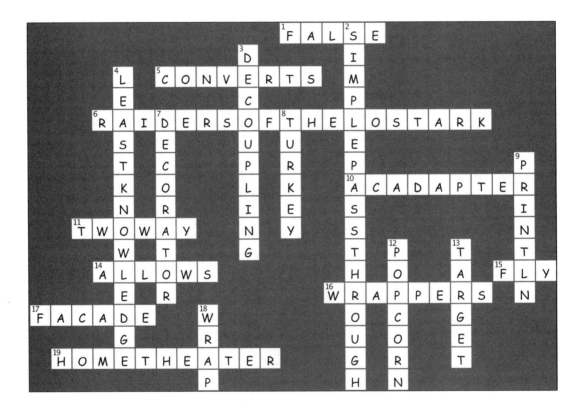

8 the Template Method Pattern

Encapsulating Algorithms

We're on an encapsulation roll; we've encapsulated object creation, method invocation, complex interfaces, ducks, pizzas... what could be next? We're going to get down to encapsulating pieces of algorithms so that subclasses can hook themselves right into a computation anytime they want. We're even going to learn about a design principle inspired by Hollywood.

It's time for some more caffeine

Some people can't live without their coffee; some people can't live without their tea. The common ingredient? Caffeine of course!

But there's more; tea and coffee are made in very similar ways. Let's check it out:

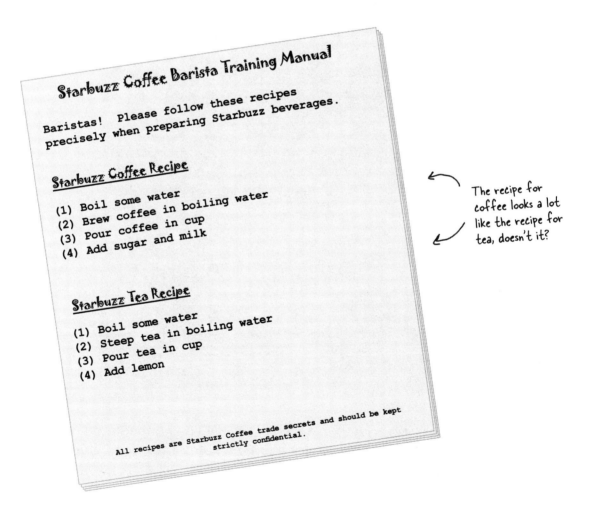

Starbuzz Coffee Barista Training Manual

Baristas! Please follow these recipes precisely when preparing Starbuzz beverages.

Starbuzz Coffee Recipe

(1) Boil some water
(2) Brew coffee in boiling water
(3) Pour coffee in cup
(4) Add sugar and milk

Starbuzz Tea Recipe

(1) Boil some water
(2) Steep tea in boiling water
(3) Pour tea in cup
(4) Add lemon

All recipes are Starbuzz Coffee trade secrets and should be kept strictly confidential.

The recipe for coffee looks a lot like the recipe for tea, doesn't it?

Whipping up some coffee and tea classes (in Java)

Let's play "coding barista" and write some code for creating coffee and tea.

Here's the coffee:

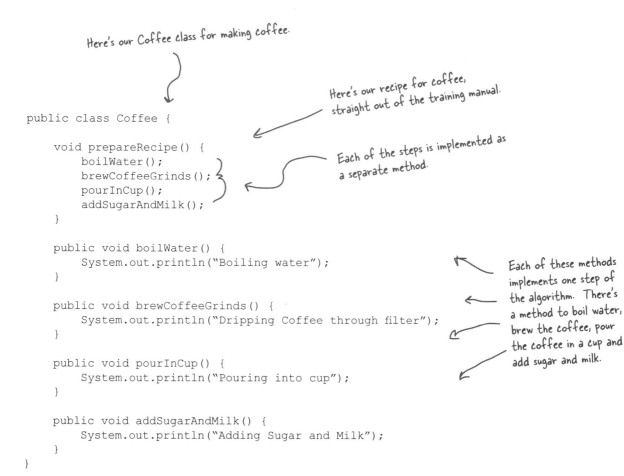

Here's our Coffee class for making coffee.

Here's our recipe for coffee, straight out of the training manual.

Each of the steps is implemented as a separate method.

```java
public class Coffee {

    void prepareRecipe() {
        boilWater();
        brewCoffeeGrinds();
        pourInCup();
        addSugarAndMilk();
    }

    public void boilWater() {
        System.out.println("Boiling water");
    }

    public void brewCoffeeGrinds() {
        System.out.println("Dripping Coffee through filter");
    }

    public void pourInCup() {
        System.out.println("Pouring into cup");
    }

    public void addSugarAndMilk() {
        System.out.println("Adding Sugar and Milk");
    }
}
```

Each of these methods implements one step of the algorithm. There's a method to boil water, brew the coffee, pour the coffee in a cup and add sugar and milk.

and now the Tea...

```java
public class Tea {

    void prepareRecipe() {
        boilWater();
        steepTeaBag();
        pourInCup();
        addLemon();
    }

    public void boilWater() {
        System.out.println("Boiling water");
    }

    public void steepTeaBag() {
        System.out.println("Steeping the tea");
    }

    public void addLemon() {
        System.out.println("Adding Lemon");
    }

    public void pourInCup() {
        System.out.println("Pouring into cup");
    }
}
```

This looks very similar to the one we just implemented in Coffee; the second and forth steps are different, but it's basically the same recipe.

These two methods are specialized to Tea.

Notice that these two methods are exactly the same as they are in Coffee! So we definitely have some code duplication going on here.

When we've got code duplication, that's a good sign we need to clean up the design. It seems like here we should abstract the commonality into a base class since coffee and tea are so similar?

Design Puzzle

You've seen that the Coffee and Tea classes have a fair bit of code duplication. Take another look at the Coffee and Tea classes and draw a class diagram showing how you'd redesign the classes to remove redundancy:

Sir, may I abstract your Coffee, Tea?

It looks like we've got a pretty straightforward design exercise on our hands with the Coffee and Tea classes. Your first cut might have looked something like this:

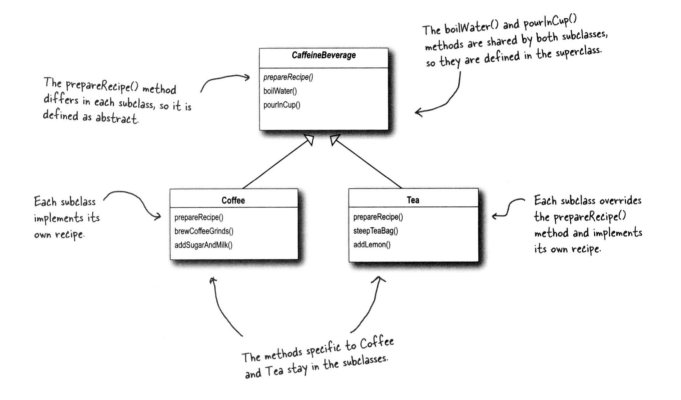

The prepareRecipe() method differs in each subclass, so it is defined as abstract.

The boilWater() and pourInCup() methods are shared by both subclasses, so they are defined in the superclass.

Each subclass implements its own recipe.

Each subclass overrides the prepareRecipe() method and implements its own recipe.

The methods specific to Coffee and Tea stay in the subclasses.

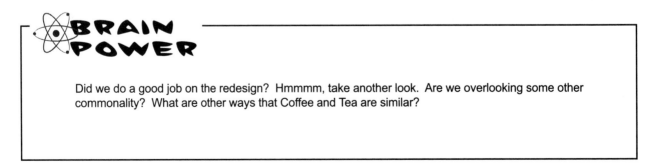

BRAIN POWER

Did we do a good job on the redesign? Hmmmm, take another look. Are we overlooking some other commonality? What are other ways that Coffee and Tea are similar?

Taking the design further...

So what else do Coffee and Tea have in common? Let's start with the recipes.

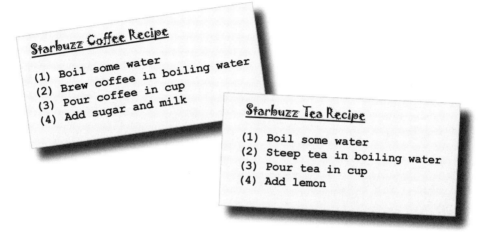

Notice that both recipes follow the same algorithm:

1 Boil some water.

2 Use the hot water to extract the coffee or tea.

3 Pour the resulting beverage into a cup.

4 Add the appropriate condiments to the beverage.

These aren't abstracted, but are the same, they just apply to different beverages.

These two are already abstracted into the base class.

So, can we find a way to abstract prepareRecipe() too? Yes, let's find out...

Abstracting prepareRecipe()

Let's step through abstracting prepareRecipe() from each subclass (that is, the Coffee and Tea classes)...

 The first problem we have is that Coffee uses brewCoffeeGrinds() and addSugarAndMilk() methods while Tea uses steepTeaBag() and addLemon() methods.

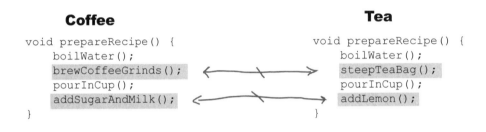

Let's think through this: steeping and brewing aren't so different; they're pretty analogous. So let's make a new method name, say, brew(), and we'll use the same name whether we're brewing coffee or steeping tea.

Likewise, adding sugar and milk is pretty much the same as adding a lemon: both are adding condiments to the beverage. Let's also make up a new method name, addCondiments(), to handle this. So, our new prepareRecipe() method will look like this:

```
void prepareRecipe() {
    boilWater();
    brew();
    pourInCup();
    addCondiments();
}
```

 Now we have a new prepareRecipe() method, but we need to fit it into the code. To do this we are going to start with the CaffeineBeverage superclass:

CaffeineBeverage is abstract, just like in the class design.

Now, the same prepareRecipe() method will be used to make both Tea and Coffee. prepareRecipe() is declared final because we don't want our subclasses to be able to override this method and change the recipe! We've generalized steps 2 and 4 to brew() the beverage and addCondiments().

```java
public abstract class CaffeineBeverage {

    final void prepareRecipe() {
        boilWater();
        brew();
        pourInCup();
        addCondiments();
    }

    abstract void brew();

    abstract void addCondiments();

    void boilWater() {
        System.out.println("Boiling water");
    }

    void pourInCup() {
        System.out.println("Pouring into cup");
    }
}
```

Because Coffee and Tea handle these methods in different ways, they're going to have to be declared as abstract. Let the subclasses worry about that stuff!

Remember, we moved these into the CaffeineBeverage class (back in our class diagram).

3 Finally we need to deal with the Coffee and Tea classes. They now rely on CaffeineBeverage to handle the recipe, so they just need to handle brewing and condiments:

As in our design, Tea and Coffee now extend CaffeineBeverage.

```java
public class Tea extends CaffeineBeverage {
    public void brew() {
        System.out.println("Steeping the tea");
    }
    public void addCondiments() {
        System.out.println("Adding Lemon");
    }
}
```

Tea needs to define brew() and addCondiments() — the two abstract methods from Beverage.

Same for Coffee, except Coffee deals with coffee, and sugar and milk instead of tea bags and lemon.

```java
public class Coffee extends CaffeineBeverage {
    public void brew() {
        System.out.println("Dripping Coffee through filter");
    }
    public void addCondiments() {
        System.out.println("Adding Sugar and Milk");
    }
}
```

Sharpen your pencil

Draw the new class diagram now that we've moved the implementation of prepareRecipe() into the CaffeineBeverage class:

What have we done?

We've recognized that the two recipes are essentially the same, although some of the steps require different implementations. So we've generalized the recipe and placed it in the base class.

Tea

1. Boil some water
2. Steep the teabag in the water
3. Pour tea in a cup
4. Add lemon

Coffee

1. Boil some water
2. Brew the coffee grinds
3. Pour coffee in a cup
4. Add sugar and milk

generalize

Caffeine Beverage

1. Boil some water
2. Brew
3. Pour beverage in a cup
4. Add condiments

generalize

relies on subclass for some steps

relies on subclass for some steps

Tea subclass

Coffee subclass

2. Steep the teabag in the water
4. Add lemon

2. Brew the coffee grinds
4. Add sugar and milk

Caffeine Beverage knows and controls the steps of the recipe, and performs steps 1 and 3 itself, but relies on Tea or Coffee to do steps 2 and 4.

Meet the Template Method

We've basically just implemented the Template Method Pattern. What's that? Let's look at the structure of the CaffeineBeverage class; it contains the actual "template method:"

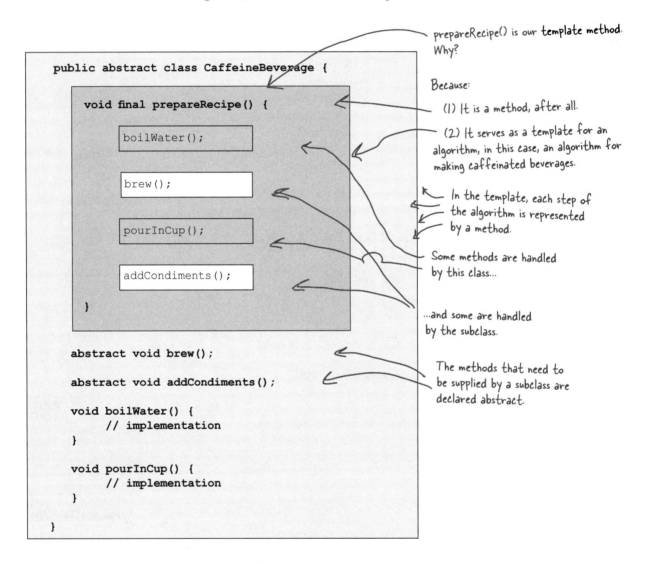

prepareRecipe() is our **template method**. Why?

Because:

(1) It is a method, after all.

(2) It serves as a template for an algorithm, in this case, an algorithm for making caffeinated beverages.

In the template, each step of the algorithm is represented by a method.

Some methods are handled by this class...

...and some are handled by the subclass.

The methods that need to be supplied by a subclass are declared abstract.

```
public abstract class CaffeineBeverage {

    void final prepareRecipe() {

        boilWater();

        brew();

        pourInCup();

        addCondiments();

    }

    abstract void brew();

    abstract void addCondiments();

    void boilWater() {
        // implementation
    }

    void pourInCup() {
        // implementation
    }

}
```

The Template Method defines the steps of an algorithm and allows subclasses to provide the implementation for one or more steps.

Let's make some tea...

**Let's step through making a tea and trace through
how the template method works. You'll see that
the template method controls the algorithm; at
certain points in the algorithm, it lets the subclass
supply the implementation of the steps...**

**Behind
the Scenes**

```
boilWater();
brew();
pourInCup();
addCondiments();
```

1 Okay, first we need a Tea object...

```
Tea myTea = new Tea();
```

2 Then we call the template method:

```
myTea.prepareRecipe();
```

which follows the algorithm for making caffeine
beverages...

The prepareRecipe()
method controls the
algorithm, no one can
change this, and it
counts on subclasses to
provide some or all of
the implementation.

3 First we boil water:

```
boilWater();
```

which happens in CaffeineBeverage.

4 Next we need to brew the tea, which only the subclass knows
how to do:

```
brew();
```

5 Now we pour the tea in the cup; this is the same for all beverages so it
happens in CaffeineBeverage:

```
pourInCup();
```

6 Finally, we add the condiments, which are specific to each beverage, so
the subclass implements this:

```
addCondiments();
```

CaffeineBeverage

prepareRecipe()
boilWater()
pourInCup()

Tea

brew()
addCondiments();

What did the Template Method get us?

Underpowered Tea & Coffee implementation	New, hip CaffeineBeverage powered by Template Method
Coffee and Tea are running the show; they control the algorithm.	The CaffeineBeverage class runs the show; it has the algorithm, and protects it.
Code is duplicated across Coffee and Tea.	The CaffeineBeverage class maximizes reuse among the subclasses.
Code changes to the algorithm require opening the subclasses and making multiple changes.	The algorithm lives in one place and code changes only need to be made there.
Classes are organized in a structure that requires a lot of work to add a new caffeine beverage.	The Template Method version provides a framework that other caffeine beverages can be plugged into. New caffeine beverages only need to implement a couple of methods.
Knowledge of the algorithm and how to implement it is distributed over many classes.	The CaffeineBeverage class concentrates knowledge about the algorithm and relies on subclasses to provide complete implementations.

Template Method Pattern defined

You've seen how the Template Method Pattern works in our Tea and Coffee example; now, check out the official definition and nail down all the details:

> **The Template Method Pattern** defines the skeleton of an algorithm in a method, deferring some steps to subclasses. Template Method lets subclasses redefine certain steps of an algorithm without changing the algorithm's structure.

This pattern is all about creating a template for an algorithm. What's a template? As you've seen it's just a method; more specifically, it's a method that defines an algorithm as a set of steps. One or more of these steps is defined to be abstract and implemented by a subclass. This ensures the algorithm's structure stays unchanged, while subclasses provide some part of the implementation.

Let's check out the class diagram:

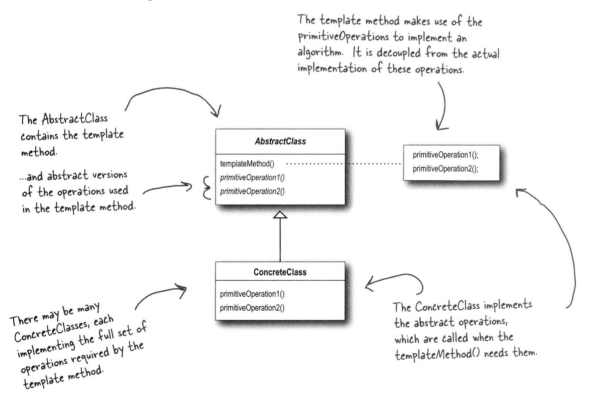

The template method makes use of the primitiveOperations to implement an algorithm. It is decoupled from the actual implementation of these operations.

The AbstractClass contains the template method.

...and abstract versions of the operations used in the template method.

There may be many ConcreteClasses, each implementing the full set of operations required by the template method.

The ConcreteClass implements the abstract operations, which are called when the templateMethod() needs them.

AbstractClass

templateMethod() ....
primitiveOperation1()
primitiveOperation2()

primitiveOperation1();
primitiveOperation2();

ConcreteClass

primitiveOperation1()
primitiveOperation2()

Code Up Close

Let's take a closer look at how the AbstractClass is defined, including the template method and primitive operations.

Here we have our abstract class; it is declared abstract and meant to be subclassed by classes that provide implementations of the operations.

Here's the template method. It's declared final to prevent subclasses from reworking the sequence of steps in the algorithm.

```java
abstract class AbstractClass {

    final void templateMethod() {
        primitiveOperation1();
        primitiveOperation2();
        concreteOperation();
    }

    abstract void primitiveOperation1();

    abstract void primitiveOperation2();

    void concreteOperation() {
        // implementation here
    }
}
```

The template method defines the sequence of steps, each represented by a method.

In this example, two of the primitive operations must be implemented by concrete subclasses.

We also have a concrete operation defined in the abstract class. More about these kinds of methods in a bit...

Code Way Up Close

Now we're going to look even closer at the types of method that can go in the abstract class:

We've changed the templateMethod() to include a new method call.

```
abstract class AbstractClass {

    final void templateMethod() {
        primitiveOperation1();
        primitiveOperation2();
        concreteOperation();
        hook();
    }

    abstract void primitiveOperation1();

    abstract void primitiveOperation2();

    final void concreteOperation() {
        // implementation here
    }

    void hook() {}

}
```

We still have our primitive methods; these are abstract and implemented by concrete subclasses.

A concrete operation is defined in the abstract class. This one is declared final so that subclasses can't override it. It may be used in the template method directly, or used by subclasses.

A concrete method, but it does nothing!

We can also have concrete methods that do nothing by default; we call these "hooks." Subclasses are free to override these but don't have to. We're going to see how these are useful on the next page.

Hooked on Template Method...

A hook is a method that is declared in the abstract class, but only given an empty or default implementation. This gives subclasses the ability to "hook into" the algorithm at various points, if they wish; a subclass is also free to ignore the hook.

There are several uses of hooks; let's take a look at one now. We'll talk about a few other uses later:

> With a hook, I can override the method, or not. It's my choice. If I don't, the abstract class provides a default implementation.

```java
public abstract class CaffeineBeverageWithHook {

    final void prepareRecipe() {
        boilWater();
        brew();
        pourInCup();
        if (customerWantsCondiments()) {
            addCondiments();
        }
    }

    abstract void brew();

    abstract void addCondiments();

    void boilWater() {
        System.out.println("Boiling water");
    }

    void pourInCup() {
        System.out.println("Pouring into cup");
    }

    boolean customerWantsCondiments() {
        return true;
    }
}
```

We've added a little conditional statement that bases its success on a concrete method, customerWantsCondiments(). If the customer WANTS condiments, only then do we call addCondiments().

Here we've defined a method with a (mostly) empty default implementation. This method just returns true and does nothing else.

This is a **hook** because the subclass can override this method, but doesn't have to.

Using the hook

To use the hook, we override it in our subclass. Here, the hook controls whether the CaffeineBeverage evaluates a certain part of the algorithm; that is, whether it adds a condiment to the beverage.

How do we know whether the customer wants the condiment? Just ask !

```java
public class CoffeeWithHook extends CaffeineBeverageWithHook {

    public void brew() {
        System.out.println("Dripping Coffee through filter");
    }

    public void addCondiments() {
        System.out.println("Adding Sugar and Milk");
    }

    public boolean customerWantsCondiments() {
        String answer = getUserInput();

        if (answer.toLowerCase().startsWith("y")) {
            return true;
        } else {
            return false;
        }
    }

    private String getUserInput() {
        String answer = null;

        System.out.print("Would you like milk and sugar with your coffee (y/n)? ");

        BufferedReader in = new BufferedReader(new InputStreamReader(System.in));
        try {
            answer = in.readLine();
        } catch (IOException ioe) {
            System.err.println("IO error trying to read your answer");
        }
        if (answer == null) {
            return "no";
        }
        return answer;
    }
}
```

Here's where you override the hook and provide your own functionality.

Get the user's input on the condiment decision and return true or false, depending on the input.

This code asks the user if he'd like milk and sugar and gets his input from the command line.

Let's run the TestDrive

Okay, the water's boiling... Here's the test code where we create a hot tea and a hot coffee

```java
public class BeverageTestDrive {
    public static void main(String[] args) {

        TeaWithHook teaHook = new TeaWithHook();
        CoffeeWithHook coffeeHook = new CoffeeWithHook();

        System.out.println("\nMaking tea...");
        teaHook.prepareRecipe();

        System.out.println("\nMaking coffee...");
        coffeeHook.prepareRecipe();
    }
}
```

← Create a tea.

← A coffee.

And call prepareRecipe() on both!

And let's give it a run...

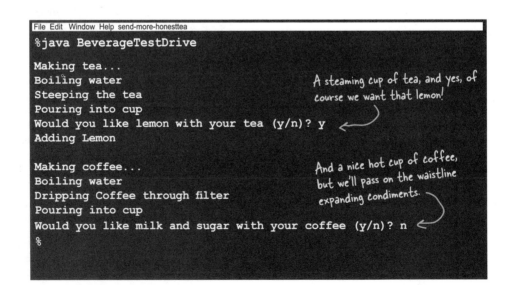

```
File Edit Window Help send-more-honesttea
%java BeverageTestDrive

Making tea...
Boiling water
Steeping the tea
Pouring into cup
Would you like lemon with your tea (y/n)? y
Adding Lemon

Making coffee...
Boiling water
Dripping Coffee through filter
Pouring into cup
Would you like milk and sugar with your coffee (y/n)? n
%
```

A steaming cup of tea, and yes, of course we want that lemon!

And a nice hot cup of coffee, but we'll pass on the waistline expanding condiments.

Now, I would have thought that functionality like asking the customer could have been used by all subclasses?

You know what? We agree with you. But you have to admit before you thought of that it was a pretty cool example of how a hook can be used to conditionally control the flow of the algorithm in the abstract class. Right?

We're sure you can think of many other more realistic scenarios where you could use the template method and hooks in your own code.

---

there are no
Dumb Questions

Q: When I'm creating a template method, how do I know when to use abstract methods and when to use hooks?

A: Use abstract methods when your subclass MUST provide an implementation of the method or step in the algorithm. Use hooks when that part of the algorithm is optional. With hooks, a subclass may choose to implement that hook, but it doesn't have to.

Q: What are hooks really supposed to be used for?

A: There are a few uses of hooks. As we just said, a hook may provide a way for a subclass to implement an optional part

of an algorithm, or if it isn't important to the subclass' implementation, it can skip it. Another use is to give the subclass a chance to react to some step in the template method that is about to happen, or just happened. For instance, a hook method like justReOrderedList() allows the subclass to perform some activity (such as redisplaying an onscreen representation) after an internal list is reordered. As you've seen a hook can also provide a subclass with the ability to make a decision for the abstract class.

Q: Does a subclass have to implement all the abstract methods in the AbstractClass?

A: Yes, each concrete subclass defines the entire set of abstract methods and

provides a complete implementation of the undefined steps of the template method's algorithm.

Q: It seems like I should keep my abstract methods small in number, otherwise it will be a big job to implement them in the subclass.

A: That's a good thing to keep in mind when you write template methods. Sometimes this can be done by not making the steps of your algorithm too granular. But it's obviously a trade off: the less granularity, the less flexibility.

Remember, too, that some steps will be optional; so you can implement these as hooks rather than abstract methods, easing the burden on the subclasses of your abstract class.

The Hollywood Principle

We've got another design principle for you; it's called the Hollywood Principle:

The Hollywood Principle

Don't call us, we'll call you.

Easy to remember, right? But what has it got to do with OO design?

The Hollywood principle gives us a way to prevent "dependency rot." Dependency rot happens when you have high-level components depending on low-level components depending on high-level components depending on sideways components depending on low-level components, and so on. When rot sets in, no one can easily understand the way a system is designed.

With the Hollywood Principle, we allow low-level components to hook themselves into a system, but the high-level components determine when they are needed, and how. In other words, the high-level components give the low-level components a "don't call us, we'll call you" treatment.

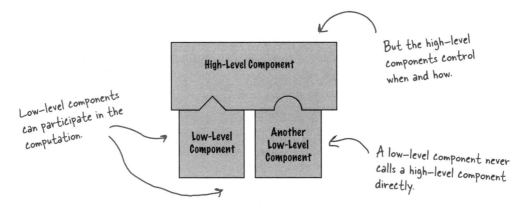

The Hollywood Principle and Template Method

The connection between the Hollywood Principle and the Template Method Pattern is probably somewhat apparent: when we design with the Template Method Pattern, we're telling subclasses, "don't call us, we'll call you." How? Let's take another look at our CaffeineBeverage design:

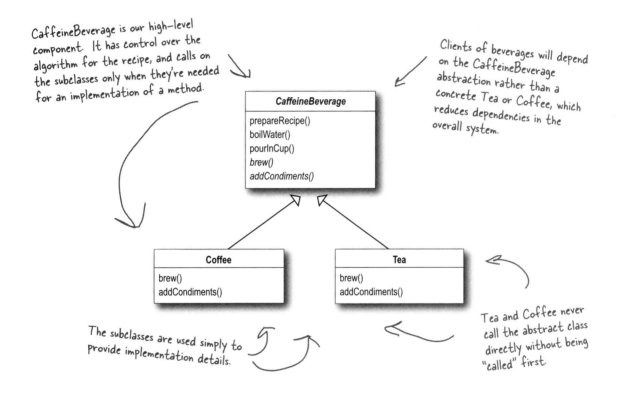

CaffeineBeverage is our high-level component. It has control over the algorithm for the recipe, and calls on the subclasses only when they're needed for an implementation of a method.

Clients of beverages will depend on the CaffeineBeverage abstraction rather than a concrete Tea or Coffee, which reduces dependencies in the overall system.

CaffeineBeverage
prepareRecipe()
boilWater()
pourInCup()
brew()
addConditments()

Coffee
brew()
addConditments()

Tea
brew()
addConditments()

The subclasses are used simply to provide implementation details.

Tea and Coffee never call the abstract class directly without being "called" first.

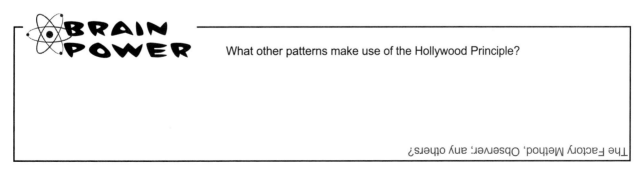

BRAIN POWER

What other patterns make use of the Hollywood Principle?

The Factory Method, Observer; any others?

there are no Dumb Questions

Q: How does the Hollywood Principle relate to the Dependency Inversion Principle that we learned a few chapters back?

A: The Dependency Inversion Principle teaches us to avoid the use of concrete classes and instead work as much as possible with abstractions. The Hollywood Principle is a technique for building frameworks or components so that lower-level components can be hooked into the computation, but without creating dependencies between the lower-level components and the higher-level layers. So, they both have the goal of decoupling, but the Dependency Inversion Principle makes a much stronger and general statement about how to avoid dependencies in design.

The Hollywood Principle gives us a technique for creating designs that allow low-level structures to interoperate while preventing other classes from becoming too dependent on them.

Q: Is a low-level component disallowed from calling a method in a higher-level component?

A: Not really. In fact, a low level component will often end up calling a method defined above it in the inheritance hierarchy purely through inheritance. But we want to avoid creating explicit circular dependencies between the low-level component and the high-level ones.

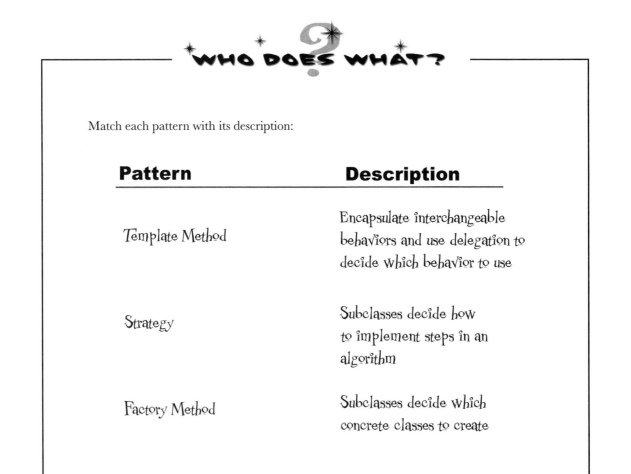

WHO DOES WHAT?

Match each pattern with its description:

Pattern	Description
Template Method	Encapsulate interchangeable behaviors and use delegation to decide which behavior to use
Strategy	Subclasses decide how to implement steps in an algorithm
Factory Method	Subclasses decide which concrete classes to create

Template Methods in the Wild

The Template Method Pattern is a very common pattern and you're going to find lots of it in the wild. You've got to have a keen eye, though, because there are many implementations of the template methods that don't quite look like the textbook design of the pattern.

This pattern shows up so often because it's a great design tool for creating frameworks, where the framework controls how something gets done, but leaves you (the person using the framework) to specify your own details about what is actually happening at each step of the framework's algorithm.

Let's take a little safari through a few uses in the wild (well, okay, in the Java API)...

In training, we study the classic patterns. However, when we are out in the real world, we must learn to recognize the patterns out of context. We must also learn to recognize variations of patterns, because in the real world a square hole is not always truly square.

Sorting with Template Method

What's something we often need to do with arrays?
Sort them!

Recognizing that, the designers of the Java Arrays class
have provided us with a handy template method for
sorting. Let's take a look at how this method operates:

We've pared down this
code a little to make it
easier to explain. If you'd
like to see it all, grab
the source from Sun and
check it out...

We actually have two methods here and they act together to
provide the sort functionality.

The first method, sort(), is just a helper method
that creates a copy of the array and passes it along
as the destination array to the mergeSort() method.
It also passes along the length of the array and tells
the sort to start at the first element.

```java
public static void sort(Object[] a) {
    Object aux[] = (Object[])a.clone();
    mergeSort(aux, a, 0, a.length, 0);
}
```

The mergeSort() method contains the sort algorithm, and relies
on an implementation of the compareTo() method to complete the
algorithm. If you're interested in the nitty gritty of how the
sorting happens, you'll want to check out the Sun source code.

Think of this as the
template method.

```java
private static void mergeSort(Object src[], Object dest[],
            int low, int high, int off)
{

    for (int i=low; i<high; i++){
        for (int j=i; j>low &&
            ((Comparable)dest[j-1]).compareTo((Comparable)dest[j])>0; j--)
        {
            swap(dest, j, j-1);
        }
    }
    return;
}
```

This is a concrete method, already
defined in the Arrays class.

compareTo() is the method we
need to implement to "fill out"
the template method.

We've got some ducks to sort...

Let's say you have an array of ducks that you'd like to sort. How do you do it? Well, the sort template method in Arrays gives us the algorithm, but you need to tell it how to compare ducks, which you do by implementing the compareTo() method... Make sense?

We've got an array of Ducks we need to sort.

> No, it doesn't. Aren't we supposed to be subclassing something? I thought that was the point of Template Method. An array doesn't subclass anything, so I don't get how we'd use sort().

Good point. Here's the deal: the designers of sort() wanted it to be useful across all arrays, so they had to make sort() a static method that could be used from anywhere. But that's okay, it works almost the same as if it were in a superclass. Now, here is one more detail: because sort() really isn't defined in our superclass, the sort() method needs to know that you've implemented the compareTo() method, or else you don't have the piece needed to complete the sort algorithm.

To handle this, the designers made use of the Comparable interface. All you have to do is implement this interface, which has one method (surprise): compareTo().

What is compareTo()?

The compareTo() method compares two objects and returns whether one is less than, greater than, or equal to the other. sort() uses this as the basis of its comparison of objects in the array.

> Am I greater than you?

> I don't know, that's what compareTo() tells us.

Comparing Ducks and Ducks

Okay, so you know that if you want to sort Ducks, you're going to have to implement this compareTo() method; by doing that you'll give the Arrays class what it needs to complete the algorithm and sort your ducks.

Here's the duck implementation:

Remember, we need to implement the Comparable interface since we aren't really subclassing.

```java
public class Duck implements Comparable {
    String name;
    int weight;

    public Duck(String name, int weight) {
        this.name = name;
        this.weight = weight;
    }

    public String toString() {
        return name + " weighs " + weight;
    }

    public int compareTo(Object object) {

        Duck otherDuck = (Duck)object;

        if (this.weight < otherDuck.weight) {
            return -1;
        } else if (this.weight == otherDuck.weight) {
            return 0;
        } else { // this.weight > otherDuck.weight
            return 1;
        }
    }
}
```

Our Ducks have a name and a weight

We're keepin' it simple; all Ducks do is print their name and weight!

Okay, here's what sort needs...

compareTo() takes another Duck to compare THIS Duck to.

Here's where we specify how Ducks compare. If THIS Duck weighs less than otherDuck then we return –1; if they are equal, we return 0; and if THIS Duck weighs more, we return 1.

Let's sort some Ducks

Here's the test drive for sorting Ducks...

```java
public class DuckSortTestDrive {
    public static void main(String[] args) {
        Duck[] ducks = {
                          new Duck("Daffy", 8),
                          new Duck("Dewey", 2),
                          new Duck("Howard", 7),
                          new Duck("Louie", 2),
                          new Duck("Donald", 10),
                          new Duck("Huey", 2)
        };

        System.out.println("Before sorting:");
        display(ducks);

        Arrays.sort(ducks);

        System.out.println("\nAfter sorting:");
        display(ducks);
    }

    public static void display(Duck[] ducks) {
        for (int i = 0; i < ducks.length; i++) {
            System.out.println(ducks[i]);
        }
    }
}
```

We need an array of Ducks; these look good.

Notice that we call Arrays' static method sort, and pass it our Ducks.

Let's print them to see their names and weights.

It's sort time!

Let's print them (again) to see their names and weights.

Let the sorting commence!

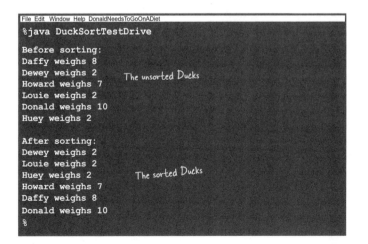

```
File Edit Window Help DonaldNeedsToGoOnADiet
%java DuckSortTestDrive

Before sorting:
Daffy weighs 8
Dewey weighs 2          The unsorted Ducks
Howard weighs 7
Louie weighs 2
Donald weighs 10
Huey weighs 2

After sorting:
Dewey weighs 2
Louie weighs 2
Huey weighs 2           The sorted Ducks
Howard weighs 7
Daffy weighs 8
Donald weighs 10
%
```

The making of the sorting duck machine

Let's trace through how the Arrays sort() template method works. We'll check out how the template method controls the algorithm, and at certain points in the algorithm, how it asks our Ducks to supply the implementation of a step...

Behind
the Scenes

```
for (int i=low; i<high; i++){
    ... compareTo() ...
    ... swap() ...
}
```

❶ First, we need an array of Ducks:

```
Duck[] ducks = {new Duck("Daffy", 8), ... };
```

The sort() method controls the algorithm, no class can change this. sort() counts on a Comparable class to provide the implementation of compareTo()

❷ Then we call the sort() template method in the Array class and pass it our ducks:

```
Arrays.sort(ducks);
```

The sort() method (and its helper mergeSort()) control the sort procedure.

❸ To sort an array, you need to compare two items one by one until the entire list is in sorted order.

When it comes to comparing two ducks, the sort method relies on the Duck's compareTo() method to know how to do this. The compareTo() method is called on the first duck and passed the duck to be compared to:

```
ducks[0].compareTo(ducks[1]);
```

First Duck

Duck to compare it to

Duck
compareTo()
toString()

No inheritance, unlike a typical template method.

❹ If the Ducks are not in sorted order, they're swapped with the concrete swap() method in Arrays:

```
swap()
```

Arrays
sort()
swap()

❺ The sort method continues comparing and swapping Ducks until the array is in the correct order!

there are no
Dumb Questions

Q: **Is this really the Template Method Pattern, or are you trying too hard?**

A: The pattern calls for implementing an algorithm and letting subclasses supply the implementation of the steps – and the Arrays sort is clearly not doing that! But, as we know, patterns in the wild aren't always just like the textbook patterns. They have to be modified to fit the context and implementation constraints.

The designers of the Arrays sort() method had a few constraints. In general, you can't subclass a Java array and they wanted the sort to be used on all arrays (and each array is a different class). So they defined a static method and deferred the comparison part of the algorithm to the items being sorted.

So, while it's not a textbook template method, this implementation is still in the spirit of the Template Method Pattern. Also, by eliminating the requirement that you have to subclass Arrays to use this algorithm, they've made sorting in some ways more flexible and useful.

Q: **This implementation of sorting actually seems more like the Strategy Pattern than the Template Method Pattern. Why do we consider it Template Method?**

A: You're probably thinking that because the Strategy Pattern uses object composition. You're right in a way – we're *using* the Arrays object to sort our array, so that's similar to Strategy. But remember, in Strategy, the class that you compose with implements the *entire* algorithm. The algorithm that Arrays implements for sort is incomplete; it needs a class to fill in the missing compareTo() method. So, in that way, it's more like Template Method.

Q: **Are there other examples of template methods in the Java API?**

A: Yes, you'll find them in a few places. For example, java.io has a read() method in InputStream that subclasses must implement and is used by the tempate method read(byte b[], int off, int len).

We know that we should favor composition over inheritance, right? Well, the implementers of the sort() template method decided not to use inheritance and instead to implement sort() as a static method that is composed with a Comparable at runtime. How is this better? How is it worse? How would you approach this problem? Do Java arrays make this particularly tricky?

Think of another pattern that is a specialization of the template method. In this specialization, primitive operations are used to create and return objects. What pattern is this?

Swingin' with Frames

Up next on our Template Method safari... keep your eye out for swinging JFrames!

If you haven't encountered JFrame, it's the most basic Swing container and inherits a paint() method. By default, paint() does nothing because it's a *hook*! By overriding paint(), you can insert yourself into JFrame's algorithm for displaying its area of the screen and have your own graphic output incorporated into the JFrame. Here's an embarrassingly simple example of using a JFrame to override the paint() hook method:

> We're extending JFrame, which contains a method update() that controls the algorithm for updating the screen. We can hook into that algorithm by overriding the paint() hook method.

```java
public class MyFrame extends JFrame {

    public MyFrame(String title) {
        super(title);
        this.setDefaultCloseOperation(JFrame.EXIT_ON_CLOSE);

        this.setSize(300,300);
        this.setVisible(true);
    }

    public void paint(Graphics graphics) {
        super.paint(graphics);
        String msg = "I rule!!";
        graphics.drawString(msg, 100, 100);
    }

    public static void main(String[] args) {
        MyFrame myFrame = new MyFrame("Head First Design Patterns");
    }
}
```

> Don't look behind the curtain! Just some initialization here...

> JFrame's update algorithm calls paint(). By default, paint() does nothing... it's a hook. We're overriding paint(), and telling the JFrame to draw a message in the window.

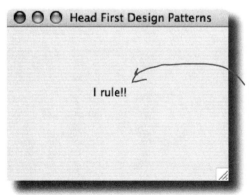

⬤ ⬤ ⬤ **Head First Design Patterns**

I rule!!

> Here's the message that gets painted in the frame because we've hooked into the paint() method.

Applets

Our final stop on the safari: the applet.

You probably know an applet is a small program that runs in a web page. Any applet must subclass Applet, and this class provides several hooks. Let's take a look at a few of them:

```java
public class MyApplet extends Applet {
    String message;

    public void init() {
        message = "Hello World, I'm alive!";
        repaint();
    }

    public void start() {
        message = "Now I'm starting up...";
        repaint();
    }

    public void stop() {
        message = "Oh, now I'm being stopped...";
        repaint();
    }

    public void destroy() {
        // applet is going away...
    }

    public void paint(Graphics g) {
        g.drawString(message, 5, 15);
    }
}
```

The init hook allows the applet to do whatever it wants to initialize the applet the first time.

repaint() is a concrete method in the Applet class that lets upper-level components know the applet needs to be redrawn.

The start hook allows the applet to do something when the applet is just about to be displayed on the web page.

If the user goes to another page, the stop hook is used, and the applet can do whatever it needs to do to stop its actions.

And the destroy hook is used when the applet is going to be destroyed, say, when the browser pane is closed. We could try to display something here, but what would be the point?

Well looky here! Our old friend the paint() method! Applet also makes use of this method as a hook.

Concrete applets make extensive use of hooks to supply their own behaviors. Because these methods are implemented as hooks, the applet isn't required to implement them.

Fireside Chats

Tonight's talk: **Template Method and Strategy compare methods.**

Template Method

Hey Strategy, what are you doing in my chapter? I figured I'd get stuck with someone boring like Factory Method.

I was just kidding! But seriously, what are you doing here? We haven't heard from you in eight chapters!

You might want to remind the reader what you're all about, since it's been so long.

Hey, that does sound a lot like what I do. But my intent's a little different from yours; my job is to define the outline of an algorithm, but let my subclasses do some of the work. That way, I can have different implementations of an algorithm's individual steps, but keep control over the algorithm's structure. Seems like you have to give up control of your algorithms.

Strategy

Nope, it's me, although be careful – you and Factory Method are related, aren't you?

I'd heard you were on the final draft of your chapter and I thought I'd swing by to see how it was going. We have a lot in common, so I thought I might be able to help...

I don't know, since Chapter 1, people have been stopping me in the street saying, "Aren't you that pattern..." So I think they know who I am. But for your sake: I define a family of algorithms and make them interchangeable. Since each algorithm is encapsulated, the client can use different algorithms easily.

I'm not sure I'd put it quite like *that*... and anyway, I'm not stuck using inheritance for algorithm implementations. I offer clients a choice of algorithm implementation through object composition.

Template Method

I remember that. But I have more control over my algorithm and I don't duplicate code. In fact, if every part of my algorithm is the same except for, say, one line, then my classes are much more efficient than yours. All my duplicated code gets put into the superclass, so all the subclasses can share it.

Strategy

You *might* be a little more efficient (just a little) and require fewer objects. *And* you might also be a little less complicated in comparison to my delegation model, but I'm more flexible because I use object composition. With me, clients can change their algorithms at runtime simply by using a different strategy object. Come on, they didn't choose *me* for Chapter 1 for nothing!

Yeah, well, I'm *real* happy for ya, but don't forget I'm the most used pattern around. Why? Because I provide a fundamental method for code reuse that allows subclasses to specify behavior. I'm sure you can see that this is perfect for creating frameworks.

Yeah, I guess... but, what about dependency? You're way more dependent than me.

How's that? My superclass is abstract.

But you have to depend on methods implemented in your superclass, which are part of your algorithm. I don't depend on anyone; I can do the entire algorithm myself!

Like I said Strategy, I'm *real* happy for you. Thanks for stopping by, but I've got to get the rest of this chapter done.

Okay, okay, don't get touchy. I'll let you work, but let me know if you need my special techniques anyway, I'm always glad to help.

Got it. Don't call us, we'll call you...

It's that time again....

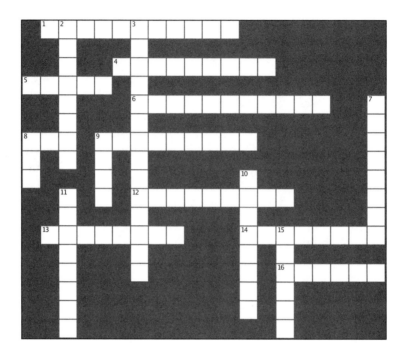

Across

1. Strategy uses _____ rather than inheritance
4. Type of sort used in Arrays
5. The JFrame hook method that we overrode to print "I Rule"
6. The Template Method Pattern uses _____ to defer implementation to other classes
8. Coffee and _____
9. Don't call us, we'll call you is known as the _____ Principle
12. A template method defines the steps of an _____
13. In this chapter we gave you more _____
14. The template method is usually defined in an _____ class
16. Class that likes web pages

Down

2. _____ algorithm steps are implemented by hook methods
3. Factory Method is a _____ of Template Method
7. The steps in the algorithm that must be supplied by the subclasses are usually declared _____
8. Huey, Louie and Dewey all weigh _____ pounds
9. A method in the abstract superclass that does nothing or provides default behavior is called a _____ method
10. Big headed pattern
11. Our favorite coffee shop in Objectville
15. The Arrays class implements its template method as a _____ method

Tools for your Design Toolbox

We've added Template Method to your toolbox. With Template Method you can reuse code like a pro while keeping control of your algorithms.

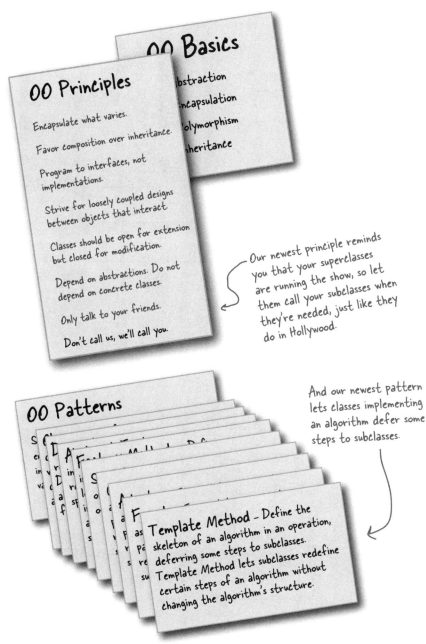

OO Basics

- Abstraction
- Encapsulation
- Polymorphism
- Inheritance

OO Principles

Encapsulate what varies.

Favor composition over inheritance.

Program to interfaces, not implementations.

Strive for loosely coupled designs between objects that interact.

Classes should be open for extension but closed for modification.

Depend on abstractions. Do not depend on concrete classes.

Only talk to your friends.

Don't call us, we'll call you.

> Our newest principle reminds you that your superclasses are running the show, so let them call your subclasses when they're needed, just like they do in Hollywood.

OO Patterns

> And our newest pattern lets classes implementing an algorithm defer some steps to subclasses.

Template Method – Define the skeleton of an algorithm in an operation, deferring some steps to subclasses. Template Method lets subclasses redefine certain steps of an algorithm without changing the algorithm's structure.

Exercise
solutions

Sharpen your pencil

Draw the new class diagram now that we've moved prepareRecipe() into the CaffeineBeverage class:

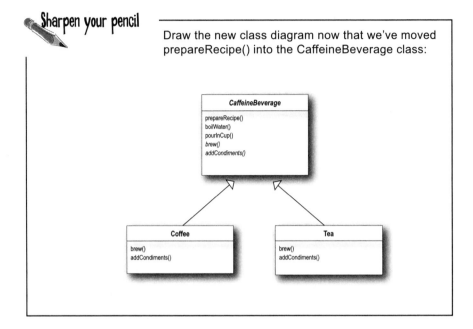

WHO DOES WHAT?

Match each pattern with its description:

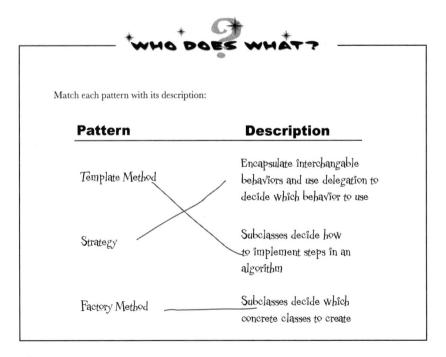

Pattern	Description
Template Method	Encapsulate interchangable behaviors and use delegation to decide which behavior to use
Strategy	Subclasses decide how to implement steps in an algorithm
Factory Method	Subclasses decide which concrete classes to create

Exercise solutions

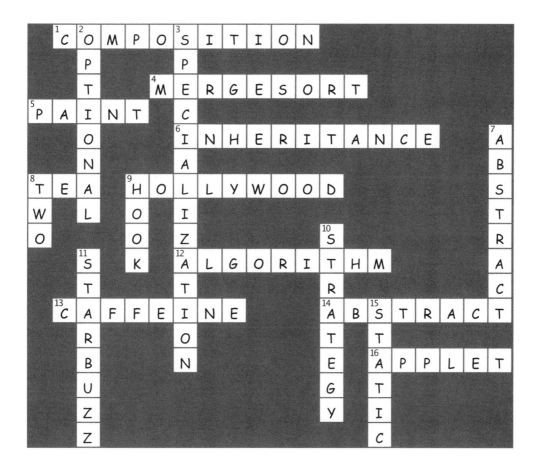

9 the Iterator and Composite Patterns

Well-Managed ✳ ✳ *Collections* ✳

You bet I keep my collections well encapsulated!

There are lots of ways to stuff objects into a collection. Put them in an Array, a Stack, a List, a Hashtable, take your pick. Each has its own advantages and tradeoffs. But at some point your client is going to want to iterate over those objects, and when he does, are you going to show him your implementation? We certainly hope not! That just wouldn't be professional. Well, you don't have to risk your career; you're going to see how you can allow your clients to iterate through your objects without ever getting a peek at how you store your objects. You're also going to learn how to create some *super collections* of objects that can leap over some impressive data structures in a single bound. And if that's not enough, you're also going to learn a thing or two about object responsibility.

Breaking News: Objectville Diner and Objectville Pancake House Merge

That's great news! Now we can get those delicious pancake breakfasts at the Pancake House and those yummy lunches at the Diner all in one place. But, there seems to be a slight problem...

They want to use my Pancake House menu as the breakfast menu and the Diner's menu as the lunch menu. We've agreed on an implementation for the menu items...

Lou

... but we can't agree on how to implement our menus. That joker over there used an ArrayList to hold his menu items, and I used an Array. Neither one of us is willing to change our implementations... we just have too much code written that depends on them.

Mel

Check out the Menu Items

At least Lou and Mel agree on the
implementation of the MenuItems.
Let's check out the items on each
menu, and also take a look at the
implementation.

> The Diner menu has lots of lunch items, while the Pancake House consists of breakfast items. Every menu item has a name, a description, and a price

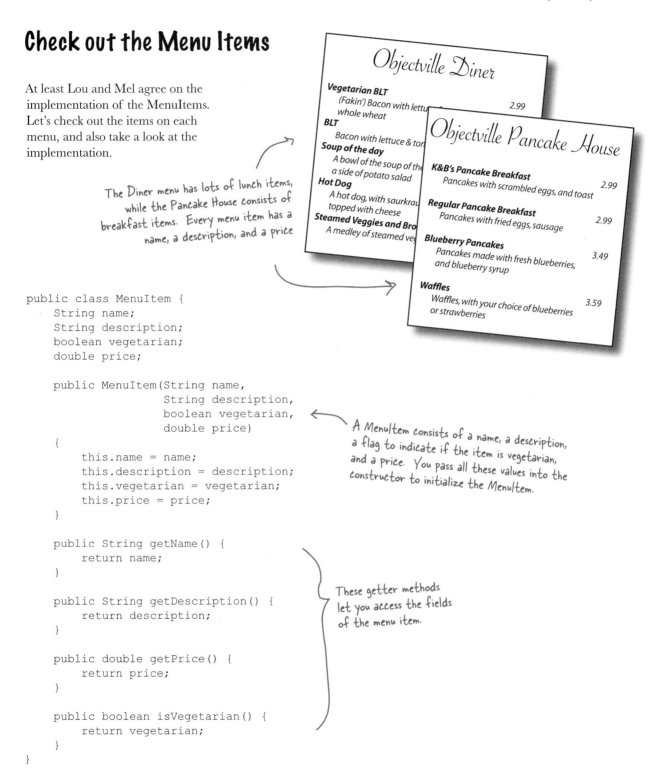

Objectville Diner

Vegetarian BLT
(Fakin') Bacon with lettu[ce]   2.99
whole wheat
BLT
Bacon with lettuce & to[mato]
Soup of the day
A bowl of the soup of the [day,]
a side of potato salad
Hot Dog
A hot dog, with saurkrau[t,]
topped with cheese
Steamed Veggies and Bro[...]
A medley of steamed ve[...]

Objectville Pancake House

K&B's Pancake Breakfast
Pancakes with scrambled eggs, and toast   2.99

Regular Pancake Breakfast
Pancakes with fried eggs, sausage   2.99

Blueberry Pancakes
Pancakes made with fresh blueberries,
and blueberry syrup   3.49

Waffles
Waffles, with your choice of blueberries
or strawberries   3.59

```java
public class MenuItem {
    String name;
    String description;
    boolean vegetarian;
    double price;

    public MenuItem(String name,
                    String description,
                    boolean vegetarian,
                    double price)
    {
        this.name = name;
        this.description = description;
        this.vegetarian = vegetarian;
        this.price = price;
    }

    public String getName() {
        return name;
    }

    public String getDescription() {
        return description;
    }

    public double getPrice() {
        return price;
    }

    public boolean isVegetarian() {
        return vegetarian;
    }
}
```

> A MenuItem consists of a name, a description, a flag to indicate if the item is vegetarian, and a price. You pass all these values into the constructor to initialize the MenuItem.

> These getter methods let you access the fields of the menu item.

Lou and Mel's Menu implementations

Now let's take a look at what Lou and Mel are arguing about. They both have lots of time and code invested in the way they store their menu items in a menu, and lots of other code that depends on it.

> I used an ArrayList so I can easily expand my menu.

Here's Lou's implementation of the Pancake House menu.

```java
public class PancakeHouseMenu {
    ArrayList menuItems;

    public PancakeHouseMenu() {
        menuItems = new ArrayList();

        addItem("K&B's Pancake Breakfast",
            "Pancakes with scrambled eggs, and toast",
            true,
            2.99);

        addItem("Regular Pancake Breakfast",
            "Pancakes with fried eggs, sausage",
            false,
            2.99);

        addItem("Blueberry Pancakes",
            "Pancakes made with fresh blueberries",
            true,
            3.49);

        addItem("Waffles",
            "Waffles, with your choice of blueberries or strawberries",
            true,
            3.59);
    }
    public void addItem(String name, String description,
                        boolean vegetarian, double price)
    {
        MenuItem menuItem = new MenuItem(name, description, vegetarian, price);
        menuItems.add(menuItem);
    }

    public ArrayList getMenuItems() {
        return menuItems;
    }

    // other menu methods here
}
```

Lou's using an ArrayList to store his menu items

Each menu item is added to the ArrayList here, in the constructor

Each MenuItem has a name, a description, whether or not it's a vegetarian item, and the price

To add a menu item, Lou creates a new MenuItem object, passing in each argument, and then adds it to the ArrayList

The getMenuItems() method returns the list of menu items

Lou has a bunch of other menu code that depends on the ArrayList implementation. He doesn't want to have to rewrite all that code!

Haah! An Arraylist... I used a REAL Array so I can control the maximum size of my menu and get my MenuItems without having to use a cast.

And here's Mel's implementation of the Diner menu.

```java
public class DinerMenu {
    static final int MAX_ITEMS = 6;
    int numberOfItems = 0;
    MenuItem[] menuItems;

    public DinerMenu() {
        menuItems = new MenuItem[MAX_ITEMS];

        addItem("Vegetarian BLT",
            "(Fakin') Bacon with lettuce & tomato on whole wheat", true, 2.99);
        addItem("BLT",
            "Bacon with lettuce & tomato on whole wheat", false, 2.99);
        addItem("Soup of the day",
            "Soup of the day, with a side of potato salad", false, 3.29);
        addItem("Hotdog",
            "A hot dog, with saurkraut, relish, onions, topped with cheese",
            false, 3.05);
        // a couple of other Diner Menu items added here
    }

    public void addItem(String name, String description,
                        boolean vegetarian, double price)
    {
        MenuItem menuItem = new MenuItem(name, description, vegetarian, price);
        if (numberOfItems >= MAX_ITEMS) {
            System.err.println("Sorry, menu is full!  Can't add item to menu");
        } else {
            menuItems[numberOfItems] = menuItem;
            numberOfItems = numberOfItems + 1;
        }
    }

    public MenuItem[] getMenuItems() {
        return menuItems;
    }

    // other menu methods here

}
```

Mel takes a different approach; he's using an Array so he can control the max size of the menu and retrieve menu items out without having to cast his objects.

Like Lou, Mel creates his menu items in the constructor, using the addItem() helper method.

addItem() takes all the parameters necessary to create a MenuItem and instantiates one. It also checks to make sure we haven't hit the menu size limit.

Mel specifically wants to keep his menu under a certain size (presumably so he doesn't have to remember too many recipes).

getMenuItems() returns the array of menu items.

Like Lou, Mel has a bunch of code that depends on the implementation of his menu being an Array. He's too busy cooking to rewrite all of this.

What's the problem with having two different menu representations?

To see why having two different menu representations complicates things, let's try implementing a client that uses the two menus. Imagine you have been hired by the new company formed by the merger of the Diner and the Pancake House to create a Java-enabled waitress (this *is* Objectville, after all). The spec for the Java-enabled waitress specifies that she can print a custom menu for customers on demand, and even tell you if a menu item is vegetarian without having to ask the cook – now that's an innovation!

Let's check out the spec, and then step through what it might take to implement her...

The Waitress is getting Java-enabled.

The Java-Enabled Waitress Specification

Java-Enabled Waitress: code-name "Alice"

```
printMenu()
    - prints every item on the menu

printBreakfastMenu()
    - prints just breakfast items

printLunchMenu()
    - prints just lunch items

printVegetarianMenu()
    - prints all vegetarian menu items

isItemVegetarian(name)
    - given the name of an item, returns true
      if the items is vegetarian, otherwise,
      returns false
```

The spec for the Waitress

Let's start by stepping through how we'd implement the printMenu() method:

1 To print all the items on each menu, you'll need to call the getMenuItem() method on the PancakeHouseMenu and the DinerMenu to retrieve their respective menu items. Note that each returns a different type:

The method looks the same, but the calls are returning different types.

```
PancakeHouseMenu pancakeHouseMenu = new PancakeHouseMenu();
ArrayList breakfastItems = pancakeHouseMenu.getMenuItems();

DinerMenu dinerMenu = new DinerMenu();
MenuItem[] lunchItems = dinerMenu.getMenuItems();
```

The implementation is showing through, breakfast items are in an ArrayList, lunch items are in an Array.

2 Now, to print out the items from the PancakeHouseMenu, we'll loop through the items on the breakfastItems ArrayList. And to print out the Diner items we'll loop through the Array.

```
for (int i = 0; i < breakfastItems.size(); i++) {
    MenuItem menuItem = (MenuItem)breakfastItems.get(i);
    System.out.print(menuItem.getName() + " ");
    System.out.println(menuItem.getPrice() + " ");
    System.out.println(menuItem.getDescription());
}
for (int i = 0; i < lunchItems.length; i++) {
    MenuItem menuItem = lunchItems[i];
    System.out.print(menuItem.getName() + " ");
    System.out.println(menuItem.getPrice() + " ");
    System.out.println(menuItem.getDescription());
}
```

Now, we have to implement two different loops to step through the two implementations of the menu items...

...one loop for the ArrayList...

and another for the Array.

3 Implementing every other method in the Waitress is going to be a variation of this theme. We're always going to need to get both menus and use two loops to iterate through their items. If another restaurant with a different implementation is acquired then we'll have *three* loops.

Sharpen your pencil

Based on our implementation of printMenu(), which of the following apply?

❑ A. We are coding to the PancakeHouseMenu and DinerMenu concrete implementations, not to an interface.

❑ B. The Waitress doesn't implement the Java Waitress API and so she isn't adhering to a standard.

❑ C. If we decided to switch from using DinerMenu to another type of menu that implemented its list of menu items with a Hashtable, we'd have to modify a lot of code in the Waitress.

❑ D. The Waitress needs to know how each menu represents its internal collection of menu items; this violates encapsulation.

❑ E. We have duplicate code: the printMenu() method needs two separate loops to iterate over the two different kinds of menus. And if we added a third menu, we'd have yet another loop.

❑ F. The implementation isn't based on MXML (Menu XML) and so isn't as interoperable as it should be.

What now?

Mel and Lou are putting us in a difficult position. They don't want to change their implementations because it would mean rewriting a lot of code that is in each respective menu class. But if one of them doesn't give in, then we're going to have the job of implementing a Waitress that is going to be hard to maintain and extend.

It would really be nice if we could find a way to allow them to implement the same interface for their menus (they're already close, except for the return type of the getMenuItems() method). That way we can minimize the concrete references in the Waitress code and also hopefully get rid of the multiple loops required to iterate over both menus.

Sound good? Well, how are we going to do that?

Can we encapsulate the iteration?

If we've learned one thing in this book, it's encapsulate what varies. It's obvious what is changing here: the iteration caused by different collections of objects being returned from the menus. But can we encapsulate this? Let's work through the idea...

1 To iterate through the breakfast items we use the size() and get() methods on the ArrayList:

```
for (int i = 0; i < breakfastItems.size(); i++) {
    MenuItem menuItem = (MenuItem)breakfastItems.get(i);
}
```

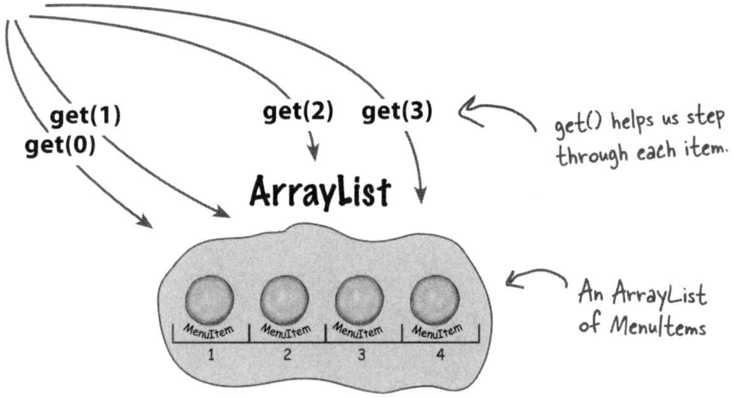

get(1)
get(0)

get(2)   get(3)   ← get() helps us step through each item.

ArrayList

← An ArrayList of MenuItems

MenuItem MenuItem MenuItem MenuItem
1   2   3   4

2 And to iterate through the lunch items we use the Array length field and the array subscript notation on the MenuItem Array.

Array

lunchItems[0]

```
for (int i = 0; i < lunchItems.length; i++) {
    MenuItem menuItem = lunchItems[i];
}
```

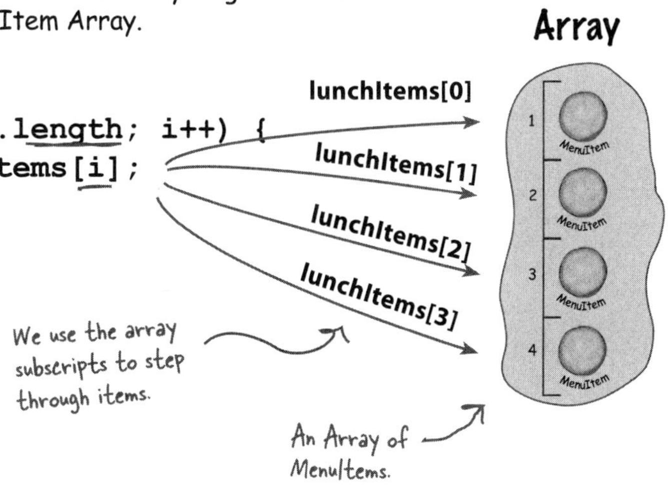

lunchItems[1]

lunchItems[2]

lunchItems[3]

We use the array subscripts to step through items.

An Array of MenuItems.

1 MenuItem
2 MenuItem
3 MenuItem
4 MenuItem

3 Now what if we create an object, let's call it an Iterator, that encapsulates the way we iterate through a collection of objects? Let's try this on the ArrayList

We ask the breakfastMenu for an iterator of its MenuItems.

```
Iterator iterator = breakfastMenu.createIterator();
```

```
while (iterator.hasNext()) {
    MenuItem menuItem = (MenuItem)iterator.next();
}
```

And while there are more items left...

next()

We get the next item.

The client just calls hasNext() and next(); behind the scenes the iterator calls get() on the ArrayList.

get(2)   **get(3)**

get(1)

get(0)

Iterator

ArrayList

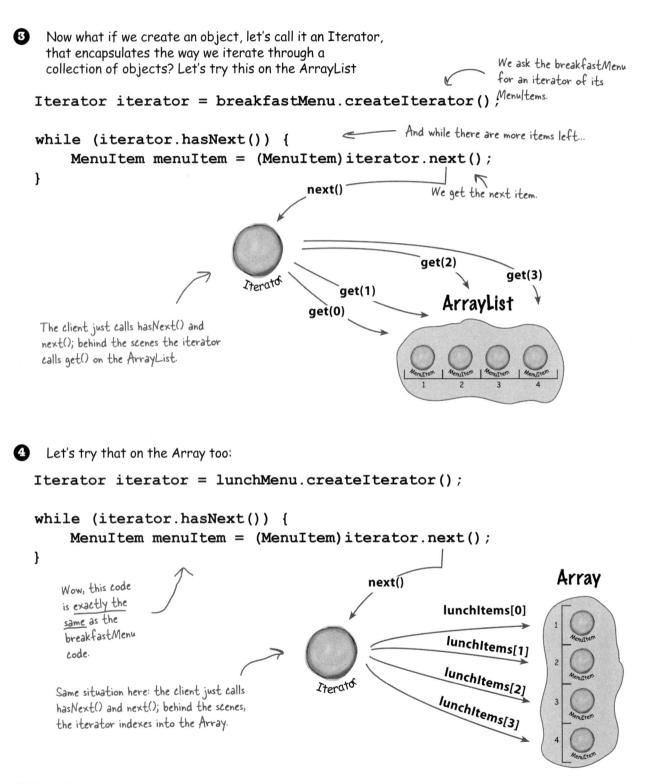

4 Let's try that on the Array too:

```
Iterator iterator = lunchMenu.createIterator();
```

```
while (iterator.hasNext()) {
    MenuItem menuItem = (MenuItem)iterator.next();
}
```

Wow, this code is exactly the same as the breakfastMenu code.

Same situation here: the client just calls hasNext() and next(); behind the scenes, the iterator indexes into the Array.

next()

Iterator

Array

lunchItems[0]

lunchItems[1]

lunchItems[2]

lunchItems[3]

Meet the Iterator Pattern

Well, it looks like our plan of encapsulating iteration just might actually work; and as you've probably already guessed, it is a Design Pattern called the Iterator Pattern.

The first thing you need to know about the Iterator Pattern is that it relies on an interface called Iterator. Here's one possible Iterator interface:

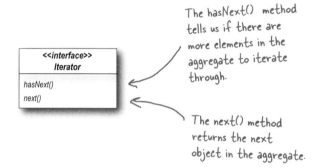

The hasNext() method tells us if there are more elements in the aggregate to iterate through.

The next() method returns the next object in the aggregate.

Now, once we have this interface, we can implement Iterators for any kind of collection of objects: arrays, lists, hashtables, ...pick your favorite collection of objects. Let's say we wanted to implement the Iterator for the Array used in the DinerMenu. It would look like this:

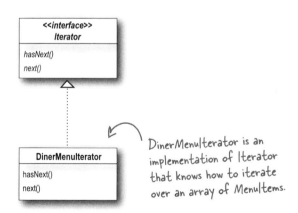

DinerMenuIterator is an implementation of Iterator that knows how to iterate over an array of MenuItems.

When we say COLLECTION we just mean a group of objects. They might be stored in very different data structures like lists, arrays, hashtables, but they're still collections. We also sometimes call these AGGREGATES.

Let's go ahead and implement this Iterator and hook it into the DinerMenu to see how this works...

Adding an Iterator to DinerMenu

To add an Iterator to the DinerMenu we first need to define the Iterator Interface:

Here's our two methods:

The hasNext() method returns a boolean indicating whether or not there are more elements to iterate over...

```java
public interface Iterator {
    boolean hasNext();
    Object next();
}
```

...and the next() method returns the next element.

And now we need to implement a concrete Iterator that works for the Diner menu:

We implement the Iterator interface.

position maintains the current position of the iteration over the array.

The constructor takes the array of menu items we are going to iterate over.

The next() method returns the next item in the array and increments the position.

```java
public class DinerMenuIterator implements Iterator {
    MenuItem[] items;
    int position = 0;

    public DinerMenuIterator(MenuItem[] items) {
        this.items = items;
    }

    public Object next() {
        MenuItem menuItem = items[position];
        position = position + 1;
        return menuItem;
    }

    public boolean hasNext() {
        if (position >= items.length || items[position] == null) {
            return false;
        } else {
            return true;
        }
    }
}
```

The hasNext() method checks to see if we've seen all the elements of the array and returns true if there are more to iterate through.

Because the diner chef went ahead and allocated a max sized array, we need to check not only if we are at the end of the array, but also if the next item is null, which indicates there are no more items.

Reworking the Diner Menu with Iterator

Okay, we've got the iterator. Time to work it into the DinerMenu; all we need to do is add one method to create a DinerMenuIterator and return it to the client:

```
public class DinerMenu {
    static final int MAX_ITEMS = 6;
    int numberOfItems = 0;
    MenuItem[] menuItems;

    // constructor here

    // addItem here

    public MenuItem[] getMenuItems() {
        return menuItems;
    }

    public Iterator createIterator() {
        return new DinerMenuIterator(menuItems);
    }

    // other menu methods here
}
```

We're not going to need the getMenuItems() method anymore and in fact, we don't want it because it exposes our internal implementation!

Here's the createIterator() method. It creates a DinerMenuIterator from the menuItems array and returns it to the client.

We're returning the Iterator interface. The client doesn't need to know how the menuItems are maintained in the DinerMenu, nor does it need to know how the DinerMenuIterator is implemented. It just needs to use the iterators to step through the items in the menu.

Exercise

Go ahead and implement the PancakeHouseIterator yourself and make the changes needed to incorporate it into the PancakeHouseMenu.

Fixing up the Waitress code

Now we need to integrate the iterator code into the Waitress. We should be able to get rid of some of the redundancy in the process. Integration is pretty straightforward: first we create a printMenu() method that takes an Iterator, then we use the createIterator() method on each menu to retrieve the Iterator and pass it to the new method.

New and improved with Iterator.

```java
public class Waitress {
    PancakeHouseMenu pancakeHouseMenu;
    DinerMenu dinerMenu;

    public Waitress(PancakeHouseMenu pancakeHouseMenu, DinerMenu dinerMenu) {
        this.pancakeHouseMenu = pancakeHouseMenu;
        this.dinerMenu = dinerMenu;
    }

    public void printMenu() {
        Iterator pancakeIterator = pancakeHouseMenu.createIterator();
        Iterator dinerIterator = dinerMenu.createIterator();
        System.out.println("MENU\n----\nBREAKFAST");
        printMenu(pancakeIterator);
        System.out.println("\nLUNCH");
        printMenu(dinerIterator);
    }

    private void printMenu(Iterator iterator) {
        while (iterator.hasNext()) {
            MenuItem menuItem = (MenuItem)iterator.next();
            System.out.print(menuItem.getName() + ", ");
            System.out.print(menuItem.getPrice() + " -- ");
            System.out.println(menuItem.getDescription());
        }
    }

    // other methods here
}
```

In the constructor the Waitress takes the two menus.

The printMenu() method now creates two iterators, one for each menu.

And then calls the overloaded printMenu() with each iterator.

Test if there are any more items.

Get the next item.

The overloaded printMenu() method uses the Iterator to step through the menu items and print them.

Use the item to get name, price and description and print them.

Note that we're down to one loop.

Testing our code

It's time to put everything to a test.   Let's write some
test drive code and see how the Waitress works...

First we create the new menus.

```java
public class MenuTestDrive {
    public static void main(String args[]) {
        PancakeHouseMenu pancakeHouseMenu = new PancakeHouseMenu();
        DinerMenu dinerMenu = new DinerMenu();

        Waitress waitress = new Waitress(pancakeHouseMenu, dinerMenu);

        waitress.printMenu();
    }
}
```

*Then we create a
Waitress and pass
her the menus.*

Then we print them.

Here's the test run...

```
File  Edit  Window  Help  GreenEggs&Ham
% java DinerMenuTestDrive
MENU
----
BREAKFAST
K&B's Pancake Breakfast, 2.99 -- Pancakes with scrambled eggs, and toast
Regular Pancake Breakfast, 2.99 -- Pancakes with fried eggs, sausage
Blueberry Pancakes, 3.49 -- Pancakes made with fresh blueberries
Waffles, 3.59 -- Waffles, with your choice of blueberries or strawberries

LUNCH
Vegetarian BLT, 2.99 -- (Fakin') Bacon with lettuce & tomato on whole wheat
BLT, 2.99 -- Bacon with lettuce & tomato on whole wheat
Soup of the day, 3.29 -- Soup of the day, with a side of potato salad
Hotdog, 3.05 -- A hot dog, with saurkraut, relish, onions, topped with cheese
Steamed Veggies and Brown Rice, 3.99 -- Steamed vegetables over brown rice
Pasta, 3.89 -- Spaghetti with Marinara Sauce, and a slice of sourdough bread

%
```

*First we iterate
through the pancake
menu.*

*And then
the lunch
menu, all
with the
same
iteration
code.*

What have we done so far?

For starters, we've made our Objectville cooks very happy. They settled their differences and kept their own implementations. Once we gave them a PancakeHouseMenuIterator and a DinerMenuIterator, all they had to do was add a createIterator() method and they were finished.

We've also helped ourselves in the process. The Waitress will be much easier to maintain and extend down the road. Let's go through exactly what we did and think about the consequences:

Woohoo! No code changes other than adding the createIterator() method.

Veggie burger

Hard to Maintain Waitress Implementation

The Menus are not well encapsulated; we can see the Diner is using an Array and the Pancake House an ArrayList.

We need two loops to iterate through the MenuItems.

The Waitress is bound to concrete classes (MenuItem[] and ArrayList).

The Waitress is bound to two different concrete Menu classes, despite their interfaces being almost identical.

New, Hip Waitress Powered by Iterator

The Menu implementations are now encapsulated. The Waitress has no idea how the Menus hold their collection of menu items.

All we need is a loop that polymorphically handles any collection of items as long as it implements Iterator.

The Waitress now uses an interface (Iterator).

The Menu interfaces are now exactly the same and, uh oh, we still don't have a common interface, which means the Waitress is still bound to two concrete Menu classes. We'd better fix that.

What we have so far...

Before we clean things up, let's get a bird's eye view of our current design.

These two menus implement the same exact set of methods, but they aren't implementing the same Interface. We're going to fix this and free the Waitress from any dependencies on concrete Menus.

The Iterator allows the Waitress to be decoupled from the actual implementation of the concrete classes. She doesn't need to know if a Menu is implemented with an Array, an ArrayList, or with PostIt™ notes. All she cares is that she can get an Iterator to do her iterating.

We're now using a common Iterator interface and we've implemented two concrete classes.

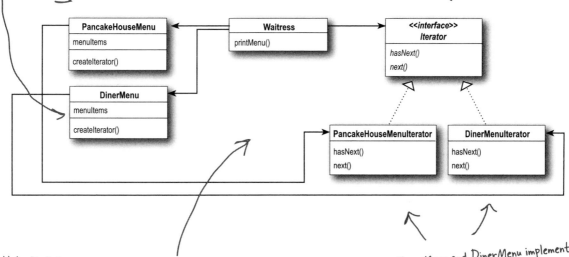

Note that the iterator give us a way to step through the elements of an aggregate without forcing the aggregate to clutter its own interface with a bunch of methods to support traversal of its elements. It also allows the implementation of the iterator to live outside of the aggregate; in other words, we've encapsulated the interation.

PancakeHouseMenu and DinerMenu implement the new createIterator() method; they are responsible for creating the iterator for their respective menu items implementations.

Making some improvements...

Okay, we know the interfaces of PancakeHouseMenu and DinerMenu are exactly the same and yet we haven't defined a common interface for them. So, we're going to do that and clean up the Waitress a little more.

You may be wondering why we're not using the Java Iterator interface – we did that so you could see how to build an iterator from scratch. Now that we've done that, we're going to switch to using the Java Iterator interface, because we'll get a lot of leverage by implementing that instead of our home grown Iterator interface. What kind of leverage? You'll soon see.

First, let's check out the java.util.Iterator interface:

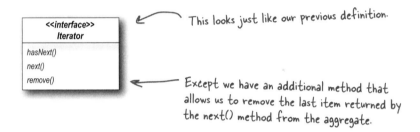

This is going to be a piece of cake: We just need to change the interface that both PancakeHouseMenuIterator and DinerMenuIterator extend, right? Almost... actually, it's even easier than that. Not only does java.util have its own Iterator interface, but ArrayList has an iterator() method that returns an iterator. In other words, we never needed to implement our own iterator for ArrayList. However, we'll still need our implementation for the DinerMenu because it relies on an Array, which doesn't support the iterator() method (or any other way to create an array iterator).

---

there are no
Dumb Questions

Q: What if I don't want to provide the ability to remove something from the underlying collection of objects?

A: The remove() method is considered optional. You don't have to provide remove functionality. But, obviously you do need to provide the method because it's part of the Iterator interface. If you're not going to allow remove() in your iterator you'llwant to throw the runtime exception java.lang.UnsupportedOperationException. The Iterator API documentation specifies that this exception may be thrown from remove() and any client that is a good citizen will check for this exception when calling the remove() method.

Q: How does remove() behave under multiple threads that may be using different iterators over the same collection of objects?

A: The behavior of the remove() is unspecified if the collection changes while you are iterating over it. So you should be careful in designing your own multithreaded code when accessing a collection concurrently.

Cleaning things up with java.util.Iterator

Let's start with the PancakeHouseMenu, changing it over to java.util.Iterator is going to be easy. We just delete the PancakeHouseMenuIterator class, add an import java.util.Iterator to the top of PancakeHouseMenu and change one line of the PancakeHouseMenu:

```java
public Iterator createIterator() {
    return menuItems.iterator();
}
```

Instead of creating our own iterator now, we just call the iterator() method on the menuItems ArrayList.

And that's it, PancakeHouseMenu is done.

Now we need to make the changes to allow the DinerMenu to work with java.util.Iterator.

```java
import java.util.Iterator;

public class DinerMenuIterator implements Iterator {
    MenuItem[] list;
    int position = 0;

    public DinerMenuIterator(MenuItem[] list) {
        this.list = list;
    }

    public Object next() {
        //implementation here
    }

    public boolean hasNext() {
        //implementation here
    }

    public void remove() {
        if (position <= 0) {
            throw new IllegalStateException
                ("You can't remove an item until you've done at least one next()");
        }
        if (list[position-1] != null) {
            for (int i = position-1; i < (list.length-1); i++) {
                list[i] = list[i+1];
            }
            list[list.length-1] = null;
        }
    }
}
```

First we import java.util.Iterator, the interface we're going to implement.

None of our current implementation changes...

...but we do need to implement remove(). Here, because the chef is using a fixed sized Array, we just shift all the elements up one when remove() is called.

We are almost there...

We just need to give the Menus a common interface and rework the Waitress a little. The Menu interface is quite simple: we might want to add a few more methods to it eventually, like addItem(), but for now we will let the chefs control their menus by keeping that method out of the public interface:

```java
public interface Menu {
    public Iterator createIterator();
}
```

This is a simple interface that just lets clients get an iterator for the items in the menu.

Now we need to add an `implements` `Menu` to both the PancakeHouseMenu and the DinerMenu class definitions and update the Waitress:

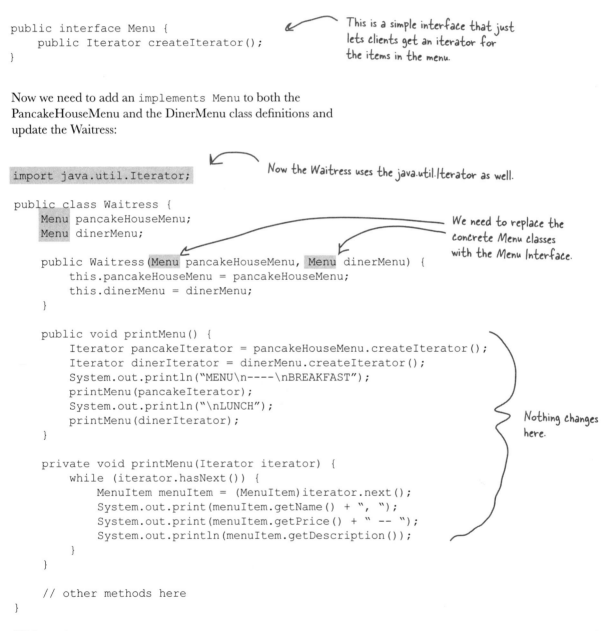

```java
import java.util.Iterator;
```

Now the Waitress uses the java.util.Iterator as well.

```java
public class Waitress {
    Menu pancakeHouseMenu;
    Menu dinerMenu;

    public Waitress(Menu pancakeHouseMenu, Menu dinerMenu) {
        this.pancakeHouseMenu = pancakeHouseMenu;
        this.dinerMenu = dinerMenu;
    }

    public void printMenu() {
        Iterator pancakeIterator = pancakeHouseMenu.createIterator();
        Iterator dinerIterator = dinerMenu.createIterator();
        System.out.println("MENU\n----\nBREAKFAST");
        printMenu(pancakeIterator);
        System.out.println("\nLUNCH");
        printMenu(dinerIterator);
    }

    private void printMenu(Iterator iterator) {
        while (iterator.hasNext()) {
            MenuItem menuItem = (MenuItem)iterator.next();
            System.out.print(menuItem.getName() + ", ");
            System.out.print(menuItem.getPrice() + " -- ");
            System.out.println(menuItem.getDescription());
        }
    }

    // other methods here
}
```

We need to replace the concrete Menu classes with the Menu Interface.

Nothing changes here.

What does this get us?

The PancakeHouseMenu and DinerMenu classes implement an interface, Menu. Waitress can refer to each menu object using the interface rather than the concrete class. So, we're reducing the dependency between the Waitress and the concrete classes by "programming to an interface, not an implementation."

This solves the problem of the Waitress depending on the concrete Menus.

The new Menu interface has one method, createIterator(), that is implemented by PancakeHouseMenu and DinerMenu. Each menu class assumes the responsibility of creating a concrete Iterator that is appropriate for its internal implementation of the menu items.

This solves the problem of the Waitress depending on the implementation of the MenuItems.

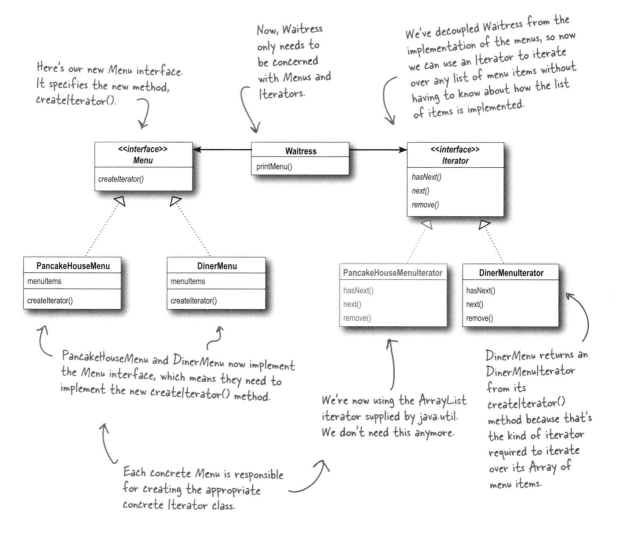

Now, Waitress only needs to be concerned with Menus and Iterators.

We've decoupled Waitress from the implementation of the menus, so now we can use an Iterator to iterate over any list of menu items without having to know about how the list of items is implemented.

Here's our new Menu interface. It specifies the new method, createIterator().

PancakeHouseMenu and DinerMenu now implement the Menu interface, which means they need to implement the new createIterator() method.

Each concrete Menu is responsible for creating the appropriate concrete Iterator class.

We're now using the ArrayList iterator supplied by java.util. We don't need this anymore.

DinerMenu returns an DinerMenuIterator from its createIterator() method because that's the kind of iterator required to iterate over its Array of menu items.

Iterator Pattern defined

You've already seen how to implement the Iterator Pattern with your very own iterator. You've also seen how Java supports iterators in some of its collection oriented classes (the ArrayList). Now it's time to check out the official definition of the pattern:

> **The Iterator Pattern** provides a way to access the elements of an aggregate object sequentially without exposing its underlying representation.

This makes a lot of sense: the pattern gives you a way to step through the elements of an aggregate without having to know how things are represented under the covers. You've seen that with the two implementations of Menus. But the effect of using iterators in your design is just as important: once you have a uniform way of accessing the elements of all your aggregate objects, you can write polymorphic code that works with *any* of these aggregates – just like the printMenu() method, which doesn't care if the menu items are held in an Array or ArrayList (or anything else that can create an Iterator), as long as it can get hold of an Iterator.

The other important impact on your design is that the Iterator Pattern takes the responsibility of traversing elements and gives that responsibility to the iterator object, not the aggregate object. This not only keeps the aggregate interface and implementation simpler, it removes the responsibility for iteration from the aggregate and keeps the aggregate focused on the things it should be focused on (managing a collection of objects), not on iteration.

Let's check out the class diagram to put all the pieces in context...

The Iterator Pattern allows traversal of the elements of an aggregate without exposing the underlying implementation.

It also places the task of traversal on the iterator object, not on the aggregate, which simplifies the aggregate interface and implementation, and places the responsibility where it should be.

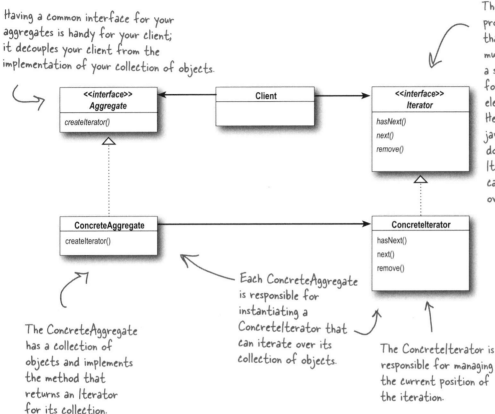

Having a common interface for your aggregates is handy for your client; it decouples your client from the implementation of your collection of objects.

The Iterator interface provides the interface that all iterators must implement, and a set of methods for traversing over elements of a collection. Here we're using the java.util.Iterator. If you don't want to use Java's Iterator interface, you can always create your own.

The ConcreteAggregate has a collection of objects and implements the method that returns an Iterator for its collection.

Each ConcreteAggregate is responsible for instantiating a ConcreteIterator that can iterate over its collection of objects.

The ConcreteIterator is responsible for managing the current position of the iteration.

BRAIN POWER

The class diagram for the Iterator Pattern looks very similar to another Pattern you've studied; can you think of what it is? Hint: A subclass decides which object to create.

Dumb Questions
there are no

Q: **I've seen other books show the Iterator class diagram with the methods first(), next(), isDone() and currentItem(). Why are these methods different?**

A: Those are the "classic" method names that have been used. These names have changed over time and we now have next(), hasNext() and even remove() in java.util.Iterator.

Let's look at the classic methods. The next() and currentItem() have been merged into one method in java.util. The isDone() method has obviously become hasNext(); but we have no method corresponding to first(). That's because in Java we tend to just get a new iterator whenever we need to start the traversal over. Nevertheless, you can see there is very little difference in these interfaces. In fact, there is a whole range of behaviors you can give your iterators. The remove() method is an example of an extension in java.util.Iterator.

Q: **I've heard about "internal" iterators and "external" iterators. What are they? Which kind did we implement in the example?**

A: We implemented an external iterator, which means that the client controls the iteration by calling next() to get the next element. An internal iterator is controlled by the iterator itself. In that case, because it's the iterator that's stepping through the elements, you have to tell the iterator what to do with those elements as it goes through them. That means you need a way to pass an operation to an iterator. Internal iterators are less flexible that external iterators because the client doesn't have control of the iteration. However, some might argue

that they are easier to use because you just hand them an operation and tell them to iterate, and they do all the work for you.

Q: **Could I implement an Iterator that can go backwards as well as forwards?**

A: Definitely. In that case, you'd probably want to add two methods, one to get to the previous element, and one to tell you when you're at the beginning of the collection of elements. Java's Collection Framework provides another type of iterator interface called ListIterator. This iterator adds previous() and a few other methods to the standard Iterator interface. It is supported by any Collection that implements the List interface.

Q: **Who defines the ordering of the iteration in a collection like Hashtable, which are inherently unordered?**

A: Iterators imply no ordering. The underlying collections may be unordered as in a hashtable or in a bag; they may even contain duplicates. So ordering is related to both the properties of the underlying collection and to the implementation. In general, you should make no assumptions about ordering unless the Collection documentation indicates otherwise.

Q: **You said we can write "polymorphic code" using an iterator; can you explain that more?**

A: When we write methods that take Iterators as parameters, we are using polymorphic iteration. That means we are creating code that can iterate over any

collection as long as it supports Iterator. We don't care about how the collection is implemented, we can still write code to iterate over it.

Q: **If I'm using Java, won't I always want to use the java.util.Iterator interface so I can use my own iterator implementations with classes that are already using the Java iterators?**

A: Probably. If you have a common Iterator interface, it will certainly make it easier for you to mix and match your own aggregates with Java aggregates like ArrayList and Vector. But remember, if you need to add functionality to your Iterator interface for your aggregates, you can always extend the Iterator interface.

Q: **I've seen an Enumeration interface in Java; does that implement the Iterator Pattern?**

A: We talked about this in the Adapter Chapter. Remember? The java.util.Enumeration is an older implementation of Iterator that has since been replaced by java.util.Iterator. Enumeration has two methods, hasMoreElements(), corresponding to hasNext(), and nextElement(), corresponding to next(). However, you'll probably want to use Iterator over Enumeration as more Java classes support it. If you need to convert from one to another, review the Adapter Chapter again where you implemented the adapter for Enumeration and Iterator.

Single Responsibility

What if we allowed our aggregates to implement their internal collections and related operations AND the iteration methods? Well, we already know that would expand the number of methods in the aggregate, but so what? Why is that so bad?

Well, to see why, you first need to recognize that when we allow a class to not only take care of its own business (managing some kind of aggregate) but also take on more responsibilities (like iteration) then we've given the class two reasons to change. Two? Yup, two: it can change if the collection changes in some way, and it can change if the way we iterate changes. So once again our friend CHANGE is at the center of another design principle:

Design Principle

A class should have only one reason to change.

We know we want to avoid change in a class like the plague – modifying code provides all sorts of opportunities for problems to creep in. Having two ways to change increases the probability the class will change in the future, and when it does, it's going to affect two aspects of your design.

The solution? The principle guides us to assign each responsibility to one class, and only one class.

That's right, it's as easy as that, and then again it's not: separating responsibility in design is one of the most difficult things to do. Our brains are just too good at seeing a set of behaviors and grouping them together even when there are actually two or more responsibilities. The only way to succeed is to be diligent in examining your designs and to watch out for signals that a class is changing in more than one way as your system grows.

Every responsibility of a class is an area of potential change. More than one responsibility means more than one area of change.

This principle guides us to keep each class to a single responsibility.

Cohesion is a term you'll hear used as a measure of how closely a class or a module supports a single purpose or responsibility.

We say that a module or class has *high cohesion* when it is designed around a set of related functions, and we say it has *low cohesion* when it is designed around a set of unrelated functions.

Cohesion is a more general concept than the Single Responsibility Principle, but the two are closely related. Classes that adhere to the principle tend to have high cohesion and are more maintainable than classes that take on multiple responsibilities and have low cohesion.

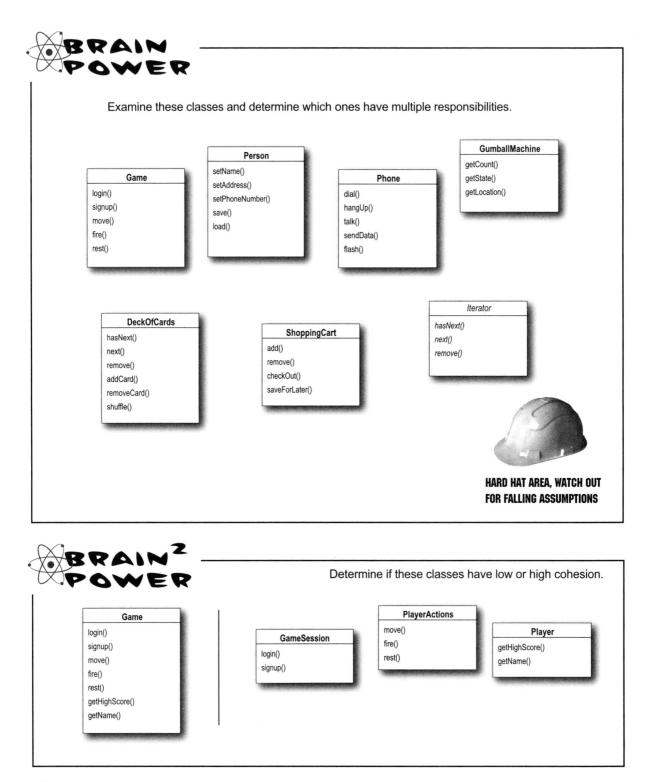

BRAIN POWER

Examine these classes and determine which ones have multiple responsibilities.

Person
setName()
setAddress()
setPhoneNumber()
save()
load()

GumballMachine
getCount()
getState()
getLocation()

Game
login()
signup()
move()
fire()
rest()

Phone
dial()
hangUp()
talk()
sendData()
flash()

DeckOfCards
hasNext()
next()
remove()
addCard()
removeCard()
shuffle()

ShoppingCart
add()
remove()
checkOut()
saveForLater()

Iterator
hasNext()
next()
remove()

HARD HAT AREA, WATCH OUT FOR FALLING ASSUMPTIONS

BRAIN² POWER

Determine if these classes have low or high cohesion.

Game
login()
signup()
move()
fire()
rest()
getHighScore()
getName()

GameSession
login()
signup()

PlayerActions
move()
fire()
rest()

Player
getHighScore()
getName()

Taking a look at the Café Menu

Here's the Café Menu. It doesn't look like too much trouble to integrate the Cafe Menu into our framework... let's check it out.

CafeMenu doesn't implement our new Menu interface, but this is easily fixed.

The Café is storing their menu items in a Hashtable. Does that support Iterator? We'll see shortly...

Like the other Menus, the menu items are initialized in the constructor.

```java
public class CafeMenu {
    Hashtable menuItems = new Hashtable();

    public CafeMenu() {
        addItem("Veggie Burger and Air Fries",
            "Veggie burger on a whole wheat bun, lettuce, tomato, and fries",
            true, 3.99);
        addItem("Soup of the day",
            "A cup of the soup of the day, with a side salad",
            false, 3.69);
        addItem("Burrito",
            "A large burrito, with whole pinto beans, salsa, guacamole",
            true, 4.29);
    }

    public void addItem(String name, String description,
                        boolean vegetarian, double price)
    {
        MenuItem menuItem = new MenuItem(name, description, vegetarian, price);
        menuItems.put(menuItem.getName(), menuItem);
    }

    public Hashtable getItems() {
        return menuItems;
    }
}
```

Here's where we create a new MenuItem and add it to the menuItems hashtable.

the key is the item name.

the value is the menuItem object.

We're not going to need this anymore.

✏️ Sharpen your pencil

Before looking at the next page, quickly jot down the three things we have to do to this code to fit it into our framework:

1. _____

2. _____

3. _____

Reworking the Café Menu code

Integrating the Cafe Menu into our framework is easy. Why? Because Hashtable is one of those Java collections that supports Iterator. But it's not quite the same as ArrayList...

```
public class CafeMenu implements Menu {
    Hashtable menuItems = new Hashtable();

    public CafeMenu() {
        // constructor code here
    }

    public void addItem(String name, String description,
                        boolean vegetarian, double price)
    {
        MenuItem menuItem = new MenuItem(name, description, vegetarian, price);
        menuItems.put(menuItem.getName(), menuItem);
    }

    public Hashtable getItems() {
        return menuItems;
    }

    public Iterator createIterator() {
        return menuItems.values().iterator();
    }
}
```

CafeMenu implements the Menu interface, so the Waitress can use it just like the other two Menus.

We're using Hashtable because it's a common data structure for storing values; you could also use the newer HashMap.

Just like before, we can get rid of getItems() so we don't expose the implementation of menuItems to the Waitress.

And here's where we implement the createIterator() method. Notice that we're not getting an Iterator for the whole Hashtable, just for the values.

Code Up Close

Hashtable is a little more complex than the ArrayList because it supports both keys and values, but we can still get an Iterator for the values (which are the MenuItems).

```
public Iterator createIterator() {
    return menuItems.values().iterator();
}
```

First we get the values of the Hashtable, which is just a collection of all the objects in the hashtable.

Luckily that collection supports the iterator() method, which returns a object of type java.util.Iterator.

Adding the Café Menu to the Waitress

That was easy; how about modifying the Waitress to support our new Menu? Now that the Waitress expects Iterators, that should be easy too.

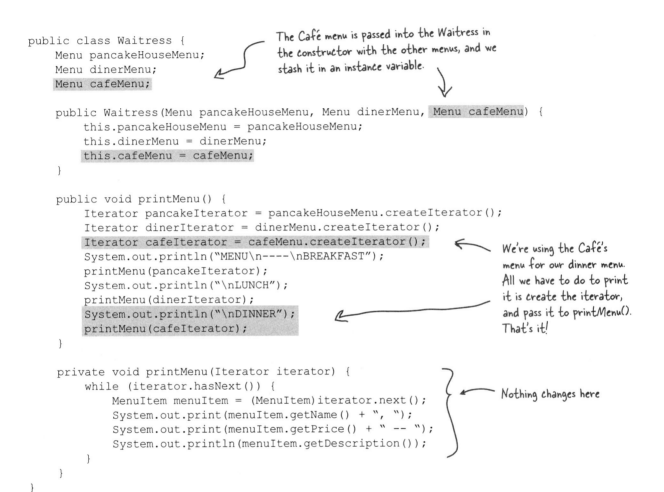

```java
public class Waitress {
    Menu pancakeHouseMenu;
    Menu dinerMenu;
    Menu cafeMenu;

    public Waitress(Menu pancakeHouseMenu, Menu dinerMenu, Menu cafeMenu) {
        this.pancakeHouseMenu = pancakeHouseMenu;
        this.dinerMenu = dinerMenu;
        this.cafeMenu = cafeMenu;
    }

    public void printMenu() {
        Iterator pancakeIterator = pancakeHouseMenu.createIterator();
        Iterator dinerIterator = dinerMenu.createIterator();
        Iterator cafeIterator = cafeMenu.createIterator();
        System.out.println("MENU\n----\nBREAKFAST");
        printMenu(pancakeIterator);
        System.out.println("\nLUNCH");
        printMenu(dinerIterator);
        System.out.println("\nDINNER");
        printMenu(cafeIterator);
    }

    private void printMenu(Iterator iterator) {
        while (iterator.hasNext()) {
            MenuItem menuItem = (MenuItem)iterator.next();
            System.out.print(menuItem.getName() + ", ");
            System.out.print(menuItem.getPrice() + " -- ");
            System.out.println(menuItem.getDescription());
        }
    }
}
```

The Café menu is passed into the Waitress in the constructor with the other menus, and we stash it in an instance variable.

We're using the Café's menu for our dinner menu. All we have to do to print it is create the iterator, and pass it to printMenu(). That's it!

Nothing changes here

Breakfast, lunch AND dinner

Let's update our test drive to make sure this all works.

```
public class MenuTestDrive {
    public static void main(String args[]) {
        PancakeHouseMenu pancakeHouseMenu = new PancakeHouseMenu();
        DinerMenu dinerMenu = new DinerMenu();
        CafeMenu cafeMenu = new CafeMenu();

        Waitress waitress = new Waitress(pancakeHouseMenu, dinerMenu, cafeMenu);

        waitress.printMenu();
    }
}
```

Create a CafeMenu...

... and pass it to the waitress.

Now, when we print we should see all three menus.

Here's the test run; check out the new dinner menu from the Café!

```
File Edit Window Help Kathy&BertLikePancakes
% java DinerMenuTestDrive
MENU
----
BREAKFAST
K&B's Pancake Breakfast, 2.99 -- Pancakes with scrambled eggs, and toast
Regular Pancake Breakfast, 2.99 -- Pancakes with fried eggs, sausage
Blueberry Pancakes, 3.49 -- Pancakes made with fresh blueberries
Waffles, 3.59 -- Waffles, with your choice of blueberries or strawberries

LUNCH
Vegetarian BLT, 2.99 -- (Fakin') Bacon with lettuce & tomato on whole wheat
BLT, 2.99 -- Bacon with lettuce & tomato on whole wheat
Soup of the day, 3.29 -- Soup of the day, with a side of potato salad
Hotdog, 3.05 -- A hot dog, with saurkraut, relish, onions, topped with cheese
Steamed Veggies and Brown Rice, 3.99 -- Steamed vegetables over brown rice
Pasta, 3.89 -- Spaghetti with Marinara Sauce, and a slice of sourdough bread

DINNER
Soup of the day, 3.69 -- A cup of the soup of the day, with a side salad
Burrito, 4.29 -- A large burrito, with whole pinto beans, salsa, guacamole
Veggie Burger and Air Fries, 3.99 -- Veggie burger on a whole wheat bun,
  lettuce, tomato, and fries
%
```

First we iterate through the pancake menu.

And then the diner menu.

And finally the new café menu, all with the same iteration code.

What did we do?

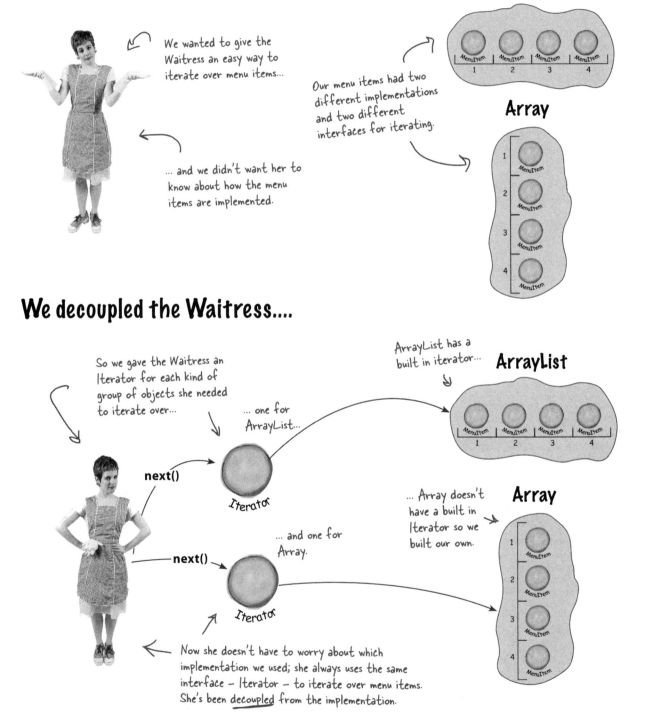

We wanted to give the Waitress an easy way to iterate over menu items...

... and we didn't want her to know about how the menu items are implemented.

Our menu items had two different implementations and two different interfaces for iterating.

ArrayList

MenuItem 1   MenuItem 2   MenuItem 3   MenuItem 4

Array

1 MenuItem
2 MenuItem
3 MenuItem
4 MenuItem

We decoupled the Waitress....

So we gave the Waitress an Iterator for each kind of group of objects she needed to iterate over...

... one for ArrayList...

next()

Iterator

ArrayList has a built in iterator...

ArrayList

MenuItem 1   MenuItem 2   MenuItem 3   MenuItem 4

... and one for Array.

next()

Iterator

... Array doesn't have a built in Iterator so we built our own.

Array

1 MenuItem
2 MenuItem
3 MenuItem
4 MenuItem

Now she doesn't have to worry about which implementation we used; she always uses the same interface - Iterator - to iterate over menu items. She's been <u>decoupled</u> from the implementation.

... and we made the Waitress more extensible

By giving her an Iterator we have decoupled her from the implementation of the menu items, so we can easily add new Menus if we want.

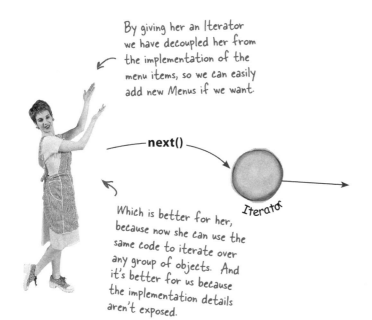

next()

Iterator

Which is better for her, because now she can use the same code to iterate over any group of objects. And it's better for us because the implementation details aren't exposed.

We easily added another implementation of menu items, and since we provided an Iterator, the Waitress knew what to do.

Hashtable

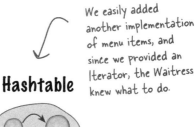

key MenuItem

key MenuItem

key MenuItem

key MenuItem

Making an Iterator for the Hashtable values was easy; when you call values.iterator() you get an Iterator.

But there's more!

Java gives you a lot of "collection" classes that allow you to store and retrieve groups of objects. For example, Vector and LinkedList.

Most have different interfaces.

But almost all of them support a way to obtain an Iterator.

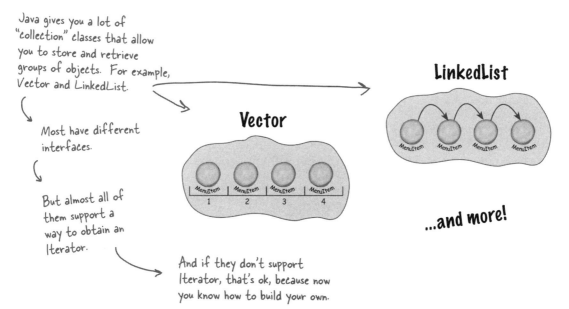

Vector

MenuItem 1 MenuItem 2 MenuItem 3 MenuItem 4

LinkedList

MenuItem MenuItem MenuItem MenuItem

...and more!

And if they don't support Iterator, that's ok, because now you know how to build your own.

Iterators and Collections

We've been using a couple of classes that are part of the Java Collections Framework. This "framework" is just a set of classes and interfaces, including ArrayList, which we've been using, and many others like Vector, LinkedList, Stack, and PriorityQueue. Each of these classes implements the java.util.Collection interface, which contains a bunch of useful methods for manipulating groups of objects.

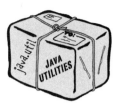

Let's take a quick look at the interface:

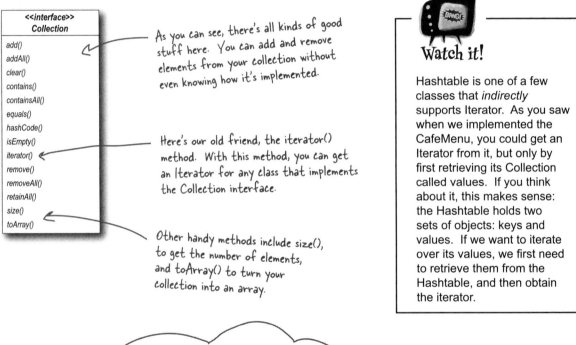

<<interface>> Collection
add()
addAll()
clear()
contains()
containsAll()
equals()
hashCode()
isEmpty()
iterator()
remove()
removeAll()
retainAll()
size()
toArray()

As you can see, there's all kinds of good stuff here. You can add and remove elements from your collection without even knowing how it's implemented.

Here's our old friend, the iterator() method. With this method, you can get an Iterator for any class that implements the Collection interface.

Other handy methods include size(), to get the number of elements, and toArray() to turn your collection into an array.

Watch it!

Hashtable is one of a few classes that *indirectly* supports Iterator. As you saw when we implemented the CafeMenu, you could get an Iterator from it, but only by first retrieving its Collection called values. If you think about it, this makes sense: the Hashtable holds two sets of objects: keys and values. If we want to iterate over its values, we first need to retrieve them from the Hashtable, and then obtain the iterator.

> The nice thing about Collections and Iterator is that each Collection object knows how to create its own Iterator. Calling iterator() on an ArrayList returns a concrete Iterator made for ArrayLists, but you never need to see or worry about the concrete class it uses; you just use the Iterator interface.

Iterators and Collections in Java 5

Check this out, in Java 5 they've added support for iterating over Collections so that you don't even have to ask for an iterator.

Java 5 includes a new form of the **for** statement, called **for/in**, that lets you iterate over a collection or an array without creating an iterator explicitly.

To use **for/in**, you use a **for** statement that looks like:

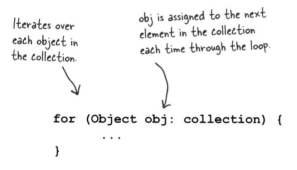

Iterates over each object in the collection.

obj is assigned to the next element in the collection each time through the loop.

```
for (Object obj: collection) {
    . . .
}
```

Here's how you iterate over an ArrayList using **for/in**:

Load up an ArrayList of MenuItems.

```
ArrayList items = new ArrayList();
items.add(new MenuItem("Pancakes", "delicious pancakes", true, 1.59);
items.add(new MenuItem("Waffles", "yummy waffles", true, 1.99);
items.add(new MenuItem("Toast", "perfect toast", true, 0.59);

for (MenuItem item: items) {
    System.out.println("Breakfast item: " + item);
}
```

Iterate over the list and print each item.

Watch it!

You need to use Java 5's new generics feature to ensure for/in type safety. Make sure you read up on the details before using generics and for/in.

Code Magnets

The Chefs have decided that they want to be able to alternate their lunch menu items; in other words, they will offer some items on Monday, Wednesday, Friday and Sunday, and other items on Tuesday, Thursday, and Saturday. Someone already wrote the code for a new "Alternating" DinerMenu Iterator so that it alternates the menu items, but they scrambled it up and put it on the fridge in the Diner as a joke. Can you put it back together? Some of the curly braces fell on the floor and they were too small to pick up, so feel free to add as many of those as you need.

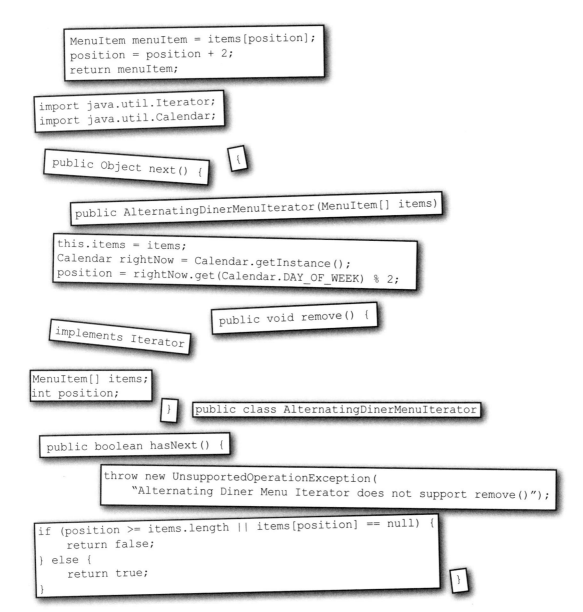

```java
MenuItem menuItem = items[position];
position = position + 2;
return menuItem;
```

```java
import java.util.Iterator;
import java.util.Calendar;
```

```java
public Object next() {
```

```
{
```

```java
public AlternatingDinerMenuIterator(MenuItem[] items)
```

```java
this.items = items;
Calendar rightNow = Calendar.getInstance();
position = rightNow.get(Calendar.DAY_OF_WEEK) % 2;
```

```java
public void remove() {
```

```java
implements Iterator
```

```java
MenuItem[] items;
int position;
```

```
}
```

```java
public class AlternatingDinerMenuIterator
```

```java
public boolean hasNext() {
```

```java
throw new UnsupportedOperationException(
    "Alternating Diner Menu Iterator does not support remove()");
```

```java
if (position >= items.length || items[position] == null) {
    return false;
} else {
    return true;
}
```

```
}
```

Is the Waitress ready for prime time?

The Waitress has come a long way, but you've gotta admit those three calls to printMenu() are looking kind of ugly.

Let's be real, every time we add a new menu we are going to have to open up the Waitress implementation and add more code. Can you say "violating the Open Closed Principle?"

Three createIterator() calls.

```java
public void printMenu() {
    Iterator pancakeIterator = pancakeHouseMenu.createIterator();
    Iterator dinerIterator = dinerMenu.createIterator();
    Iterator cafeIterator = cafeMenu.createIterator();

    System.out.println("MENU\n----\nBREAKFAST");
    printMenu(pancakeIterator);

    System.out.println("\nLUNCH");
    printMenu(dinerIterator);

    System.out.println("\nDINNER");
    printMenu(cafeIterator);
}
```

Three calls to printMenu.

Everytime we add or remove a menu we're going to have to open this code up for changes.

It's not the Waitress' fault. We have done a great job of decoupling the menu implementation and extracting the iteration into an iterator. But we still are handling the menus with separate, independent objects – we need a way to manage them together.

BRAIN POWER

The Waitress still needs to make three calls to printMenu(), one for each menu. Can you think of a way to combine the menus so that only one call needs to be made? Or perhaps so that one Iterator is passed to the Waitress to iterate over all the menus?

Sounds like the chef is on to something. Let's give it a try:

```
public class Waitress {
    ArrayList menus;

    public Waitress(ArrayList menus) {
        this.menus = menus;
    }

    public void printMenu() {
        Iterator menuIterator = menus.iterator();
        while(menuIterator.hasNext()) {
            Menu menu = (Menu)menuIterator.next();
            printMenu(menu.createIterator());
        }
    }

    void printMenu(Iterator iterator) {
        while (iterator.hasNext()) {
            MenuItem menuItem = (MenuItem)iterator.next();
            System.out.print(menuItem.getName() + ", ");
            System.out.print(menuItem.getPrice() + " -- ");
            System.out.println(menuItem.getDescription());
        }
    }
}
```

> Now we just take an ArrayList of menus.

> And we iterate through the menus, passing each menu's iterator to the overloaded printMenu() method.

> No code changes here.

This looks pretty good, although we've lost the names of the menus, but we could add the names to each menu.

Just when we thought it was safe...

Now they want to add a dessert submenu.

Okay, now what? Now we have to support not only multiple menus, but menus within menus.

It would be nice if we could just make the dessert menu an element of the DinerMenu collection, but that won't work as it is now implemented.

What we want (something like this):

> I just heard the Diner is going to be creating a dessert menu that is going to be an insert into their regular menu.

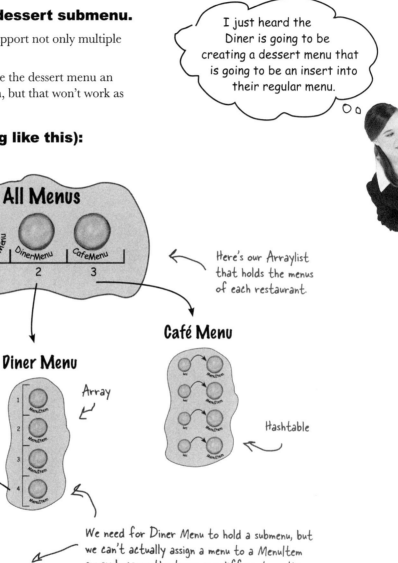

Here's our Arraylist that holds the menus of each restaurant.

All Menus

Pancake Menu — ArrayList

Diner Menu — Array

Café Menu — Hashtable

Dessert Menu

We need for Diner Menu to hold a submenu, but we can't actually assign a menu to a MenuItem array because the types are different, so this isn't going to work.

But this won't work!

We can't assign a dessert menu to a MenuItem array.

Time for a change!

What do we need?

The time has come to make an executive decision to rework the chef's implementation into something that is general enough to work over all the menus (and now sub menus). That's right, we're going to tell the chefs that the time as come for us to reimplement their menus.

The reality is that we've reached a level of complexity such that if we don't rework the design now, we're never going to have a design that can accommodate further acquisitions or submenus.

So, what is it we really need out of our new design?

- We need some kind of a tree shaped structure that will accommodate menus, submenus and menu items.

- We need to make sure we maintain a way to traverse the items in each menu that is at least as convenient as what we are doing now with iterators.

- We may need to be able to traverse the items in a more flexible manner. For instance, we might need to iterate over only the Diner's dessert menu, or we might need to iterate over the Diner's entire menu, including the dessert submenu.

There comes a time when we must refactor our code in order for it to grow. To not do so would leave us with rigid, inflexible code that has no hope of ever sprouting new life.

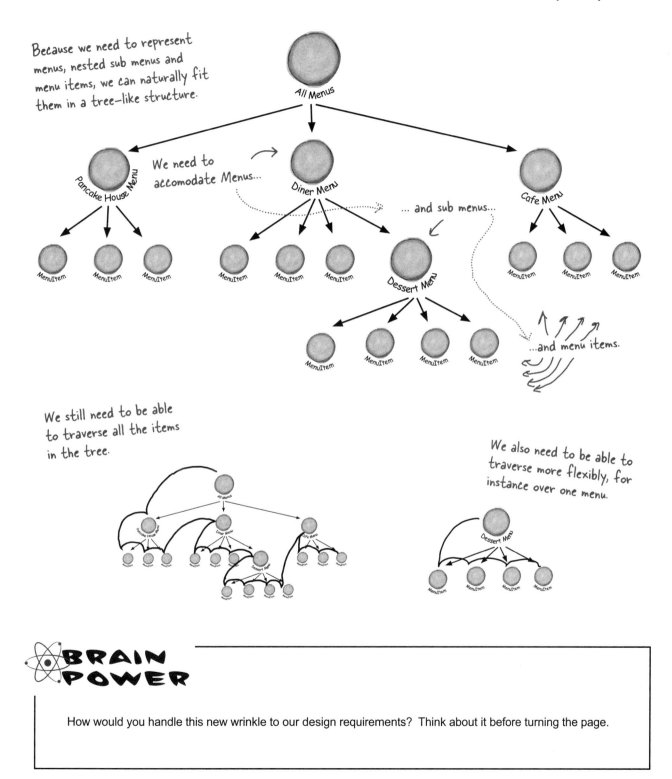

Because we need to represent menus, nested sub menus and menu items, we can naturally fit them in a tree-like structure.

We need to accomodate Menus...

... and sub menus...

...and menu items.

We still need to be able to traverse all the items in the tree.

We also need to be able to traverse more flexibly, for instance over one menu.

⚛️ **BRAIN POWER**

How would you handle this new wrinkle to our design requirements? Think about it before turning the page.

The Composite Pattern defined

That's right, we're going to introduce another pattern to solve this problem. We didn't give up on Iterator – it will still be part of our solution – however, the problem of managing menus has taken on a new dimension that Iterator doesn't solve. So, we're going to step back and solve it with the Composite Pattern.

We're not going to beat around the bush on this pattern, we're going to go ahead and roll out the official definition now:

> **The Composite Pattern** allows you to compose objects into tree structures to represent part-whole hierarchies. Composite lets clients treat individual objects and compositions of objects uniformly.

Let's think about this in terms of our menus: this pattern gives us a way to create a tree structure that can handle a nested group of menus *and* menu items in the same structure. By putting menus and items in the same structure we create a part-whole hierarchy; that is, a tree of objects that is made of parts (menus and menu items) but that can be treated as a whole, like one big über menu.

Once we have our über menu, we can use this pattern to treat "individual objects and compositions uniformly." What does that mean? It means if we have a tree structure of menus, submenus, and perhaps subsubmenus along with menu items, then any menu is a "composition" because it can contain both other menus and menu items. The individual objects are just the menu items – they don't hold other objects. As you'll see, using a design that follows the Composite Pattern is going to allow us to write some simple code that can apply the same operation (like printing!) over the entire menu structure.

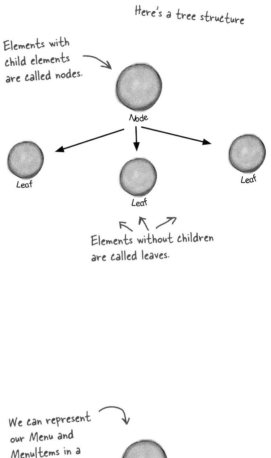

Here's a tree structure

Elements with child elements are called nodes.

Elements without children are called leaves.

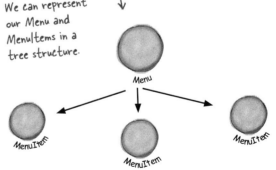

We can represent our Menu and MenuItems in a tree structure.

Menus are nodes and MenuItems are leaves.

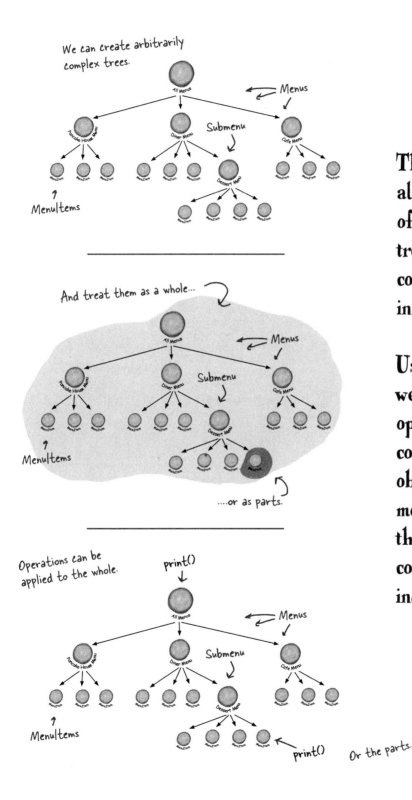

We can create arbitrarily complex trees.

Menus

Submenu

MenuItems

And treat them as a whole...

Menus

Submenu

MenuItems

....or as parts.

Operations can be applied to the whole.

print()

Menus

Submenu

MenuItems

print()

Or the parts.

The Composite Pattern allows us to build structures of objects in the form of trees that contain both compositions of objects and individual objects as nodes.

Using a composite structure, we can apply the same operations over both composites and individual objects. In other words, in most cases we can ignore the differences between compositions of objects and individual objects.

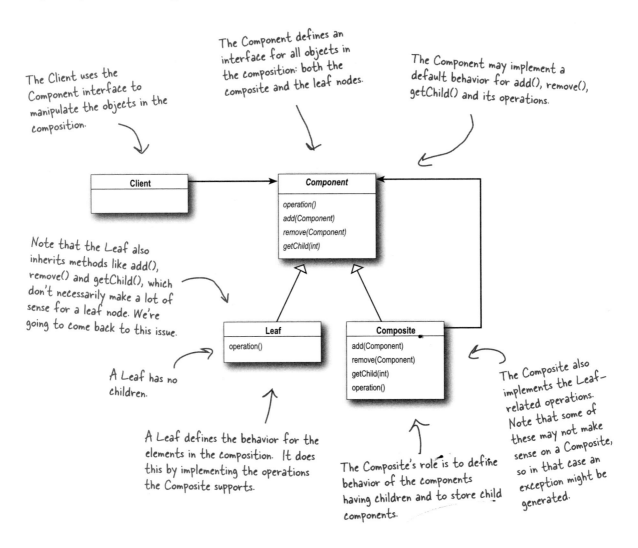

The Client uses the Component interface to manipulate the objects in the composition.

The Component defines an interface for all objects in the composition: both the composite and the leaf nodes.

The Component may implement a default behavior for add(), remove(), getChild() and its operations.

Note that the Leaf also inherits methods like add(), remove() and getChild(), which don't necessarily make a lot of sense for a leaf node. We're going to come back to this issue.

A Leaf has no children.

A Leaf defines the behavior for the elements in the composition. It does this by implementing the operations the Composite supports.

The Composite's role is to define behavior of the components having children and to store child components.

The Composite also implements the Leaf-related operations. Note that some of these may not make sense on a Composite, so in that case an exception might be generated.

Client

Component
operation()
add(Component)
remove(Component)
getChild(int)

Leaf
operation()

Composite
add(Component)
remove(Component)
getChild(int)
operation()

there are no Dumb Questions

Q: Component, Composite, Trees? I'm confused.

A: A composite contains components. Components come in two flavors: composites and leaf elements. Sound recursive? It is. A composite holds a set of children, those children may be other composites or leaf elements.

When you organize data in this way you end up with a tree structure (actually an upside down tree structure) with a composite at the root and branches of composites growing up to leaf nodes.

Q: How does this relate to iterators?

A: Remember, we're taking a new approach. We're going to re-implement the menus with a new solution: the Composite Pattern. So don't look for some magical transformation from an iterator to a composite. That said, the two work very nicely together. You'll soon see that we can use iterators in a couple of ways in the composite implementation.

Designing Menus with Composite

So, how do we apply the Composite Pattern to our menus? To start with, we need to create a component interface; this acts as the common interface for both menus and menu items and allows us to treat them uniformly. In other words we can call the *same* method on menus or menu items.

Now, it may not make *sense* to call some of the methods on a menu item or a menu, but we can deal with that, and we will in just a moment. But for now, let's take a look at a sketch of how the menus are going to fit into a Composite Pattern structure:

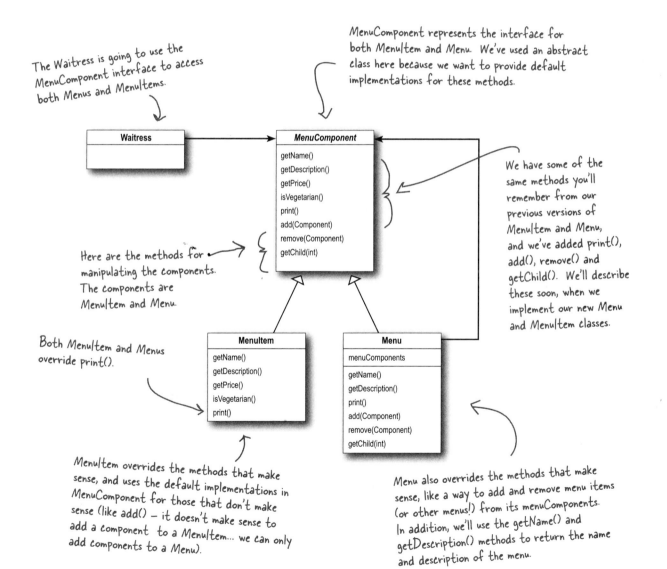

The Waitress is going to use the MenuComponent interface to access both Menus and MenuItems.

MenuComponent represents the interface for both MenuItem and Menu. We've used an abstract class here because we want to provide default implementations for these methods.

Waitress

MenuComponent

getName()
getDescription()
getPrice()
isVegetarian()
print()
add(Component)
remove(Component)
getChild(int)

Here are the methods for manipulating the components. The components are MenuItem and Menu.

We have some of the same methods you'll remember from our previous versions of MenuItem and Menu, and we've added print(), add(), remove() and getChild(). We'll describe these soon, when we implement our new Menu and MenuItem classes.

Both MenuItem and Menus override print().

MenuItem

getName()
getDescription()
getPrice()
isVegetarian()
print()

Menu

menuComponents

getName()
getDescription()
print()
add(Component)
remove(Component)
getChild(int)

MenuItem overrides the methods that make sense, and uses the default implementations in MenuComponent for those that don't make sense (like add() – it doesn't make sense to add a component to a MenuItem... we can only add components to a Menu).

Menu also overrides the methods that make sense, like a way to add and remove menu items (or other menus!) from its menuComponents. In addition, we'll use the getName() and getDescription() methods to return the name and description of the menu.

Implementing the Menu Component

Okay, we're going to start with the MenuComponent abstract class; remember, the role of the menu component is to provide an interface for the leaf nodes and the composite nodes. Now you might be asking, "Isn't the MenuComponent playing two roles?" It might well be and we'll come back to that point. However, for now we're going to provide a default implementation of the methods so that if the MenuItem (the leaf) or the Menu (the composite) doesn't want to implement some of the methods (like getChild() for a leaf node) they can fall back on some basic behavior:

All components must implement the MenuComponent interface; however, because leaves and nodes have different roles we can't always define a default implementation for each method that makes sense. Sometimes the best you can do is throw a runtime exception.

MenuComponent provides default implementations for every method.

↓

```java
public abstract class MenuComponent {

    public void add(MenuComponent menuComponent) {
        throw new UnsupportedOperationException();
    }
    public void remove(MenuComponent menuComponent) {
        throw new UnsupportedOperationException();
    }
    public MenuComponent getChild(int i) {
        throw new UnsupportedOperationException();
    }

    public String getName() {
        throw new UnsupportedOperationException();
    }
    public String getDescription() {
        throw new UnsupportedOperationException();
    }
    public double getPrice() {
        throw new UnsupportedOperationException();
    }
    public boolean isVegetarian() {
        throw new UnsupportedOperationException();
    }

    public void print() {
        throw new UnsupportedOperationException();
    }
}
```

Because some of these methods only make sense for MenuItems, and some only make sense for Menus, the <u>default implementation</u> is UnsupportedOperationException. That way, if MenuItem or Menu doesn't support an operation, they don't have to do anything, they can just <u>inherit</u> the <u>default implementation</u>.

We've grouped together the "composite" methods — that is, methods to add, remove and get MenuComponents.

Here are the "operation" methods; these are used by the MenuItems. It turns out we can also use a couple of them in Menu too, as you'll see in a couple of pages when we show the Menu code.

print() is an "operation" method that both our Menus and MenuItems will implement, but we provide a default operation here.

Implementing the Menu Item

Okay, let's give the MenuItem class a shot. Remember, this is the leaf class in the Composite diagram and it implements the behavior of the elements of the composite.

> I'm glad we're going in this direction, I'm thinking this is going to give me the flexibility I need to implement that crêpe menu I've always wanted.

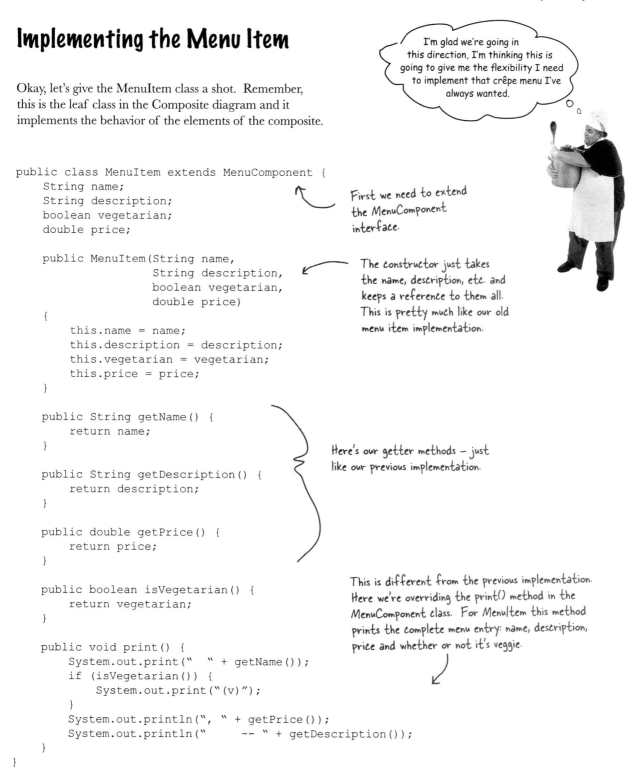

```java
public class MenuItem extends MenuComponent {
    String name;
    String description;
    boolean vegetarian;
    double price;

    public MenuItem(String name,
                    String description,
                    boolean vegetarian,
                    double price)
    {
        this.name = name;
        this.description = description;
        this.vegetarian = vegetarian;
        this.price = price;
    }

    public String getName() {
        return name;
    }

    public String getDescription() {
        return description;
    }

    public double getPrice() {
        return price;
    }

    public boolean isVegetarian() {
        return vegetarian;
    }

    public void print() {
        System.out.print("  " + getName());
        if (isVegetarian()) {
            System.out.print("(v)");
        }
        System.out.println(", " + getPrice());
        System.out.println("     -- " + getDescription());
    }
}
```

First we need to extend the MenuComponent interface.

The constructor just takes the name, description, etc. and keeps a reference to them all. This is pretty much like our old menu item implementation.

Here's our getter methods – just like our previous implementation.

This is different from the previous implementation. Here we're overriding the print() method in the MenuComponent class. For MenuItem this method prints the complete menu entry: name, description, price and whether or not it's veggie.

Implementing the Composite Menu

Now that we have the MenuItem, we just need the composite class, which we're calling Menu. Remember, the composite class can hold MenuItems *or* other Menus. There's a couple of methods from MenuComponent this class doesn't implement: getPrice() and isVegetarian(), because those don't make a lot of sense for a Menu.

Menu is also a MenuComponent, just like MenuItem.

Menu can have any number of children of type MenuComponent, we'll use an internal ArrayList to hold these.

```java
public class Menu extends MenuComponent {
    ArrayList menuComponents = new ArrayList();
    String name;
    String description;

    public Menu(String name, String description) {
        this.name = name;
        this.description = description;
    }

    public void add(MenuComponent menuComponent) {
        menuComponents.add(menuComponent);
    }

    public void remove(MenuComponent menuComponent) {
        menuComponents.remove(menuComponent);
    }

    public MenuComponent getChild(int i) {
        return (MenuComponent)menuComponents.get(i);
    }

    public String getName() {
        return name;
    }

    public String getDescription() {
        return description;
    }

    public void print() {
        System.out.print("\n" + getName());
        System.out.println(", " + getDescription());
        System.out.println("--------------------");
    }
}
```

This is different than our old implementation: we're going to give each Menu a name and a description. Before, we just relied on having different classes for each menu.

Here's how you add MenuItems or other Menus to a Menu. Because both MenuItems and Menus are MenuComponents, we just need one method to do both.

You can also remove a MenuComponent or get a MenuComponent.

Here are the getter methods for getting the name and description.

Notice, we aren't overriding getPrice() or isVegetarian() because those methods don't make sense for a Menu (although you could argue that isVegetarian() might make sense). If someone tries to call those methods on a Menu, they'll get an UnsupportedOperationException.

To print the Menu, we print the Menu's name and description.

Wait a sec, I don't understand the implementation of print(). I thought I was supposed to be able to apply the same operations to a composite that I could to a leaf. If I apply print() to a composite with this implementation, all I get is a simple menu name and description. I don't get a printout of the COMPOSITE.

Excellent catch. Because menu is a composite and contains both Menu Items and other Menus, its print() method should print everything it contains. If it didn't we'd have to iterate through the entire composite and print each item ourselves. That kind of defeats the purpose of having a composite structure.

As you're going to see, implementing print() correctly is easy because we can rely on each component to be able to print itself. It's all wonderfully recursive and groovy. Check it out:

Fixing the print() method

```
public class Menu extends MenuComponent {
    ArrayList menuComponents = new ArrayList();
    String name;
    String description;

    // constructor code here

    // other methods here

    public void print() {
        System.out.print("\n" + getName());
        System.out.println(", " + getDescription());
        System.out.println("--------------------");

        Iterator iterator = menuComponents.iterator();
        while (iterator.hasNext()) {
            MenuComponent menuComponent =
                (MenuComponent)iterator.next();
            menuComponent.print();
        }
    }
}
```

All we need to do is change the print() method to make it print not only the information about this Menu, but all of this Menu's components: other Menus and MenuItems.

Look! We get to use an Iterator. We use it to iterate through all the Menu's components... those could be other Menus, or they could be MenuItems. Since both Menus and MenuItems implement print(), we just call print() and the rest is up to them.

NOTE: If, during this iteration, we encounter another Menu object, its print() method will start another iteration, and so on.

Getting ready for a test drive...

It's about time we took this code for a test drive, but we need to update the Waitress code before we do – after all she's the main client of this code:

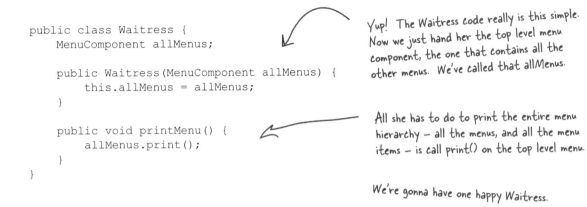

```
public class Waitress {
    MenuComponent allMenus;

    public Waitress(MenuComponent allMenus) {
        this.allMenus = allMenus;
    }

    public void printMenu() {
        allMenus.print();
    }
}
```

Yup! The Waitress code really is this simple. Now we just hand her the top level menu component, the one that contains all the other menus. We've called that allMenus.

All she has to do to print the entire menu hierarchy – all the menus, and all the menu items – is call print() on the top level menu.

We're gonna have one happy Waitress.

Okay, one last thing before we write our test drive. Let's get an idea of what the menu composite is going to look like at runtime:

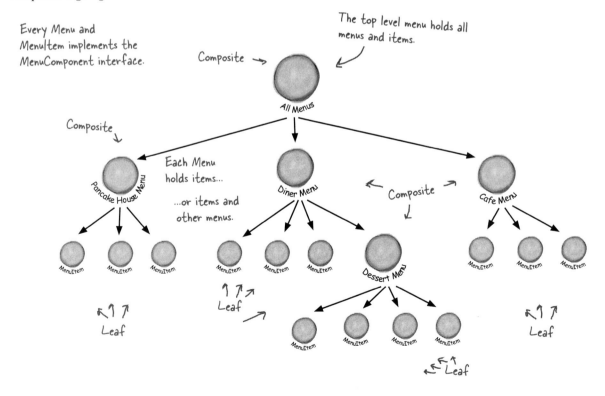

Every Menu and MenuItem implements the MenuComponent interface.

The top level menu holds all menus and items.

Composite →

All Menus

Composite ↓

Pancake House Menu

Each Menu holds items...

...or items and other menus.

Diner Menu

← Composite →

Cafe Menu

MenuItem MenuItem MenuItem

↑ ↑ ↗
Leaf

MenuItem MenuItem MenuItem

↖ ↑ ↗
Leaf

Dessert Menu

MenuItem MenuItem MenuItem MenuItem

MenuItem MenuItem MenuItem MenuItem

↖ ↑
Leaf

↖ ↑ ↗
Leaf

Now for the test drive...

Okay, now we just need a test drive. Unlike our previous version, we're going to handle all the menu creation in the test drive. We could ask each chef to give us his new menu, but let's get it all tested first. Here's the code:

```java
public class MenuTestDrive {
    public static void main(String args[]) {
        MenuComponent pancakeHouseMenu =
            new Menu("PANCAKE HOUSE MENU", "Breakfast");
        MenuComponent dinerMenu =
            new Menu("DINER MENU", "Lunch");
        MenuComponent cafeMenu =
            new Menu("CAFE MENU", "Dinner");
        MenuComponent dessertMenu =
            new Menu("DESSERT MENU", "Dessert of course!");

        MenuComponent allMenus = new Menu("ALL MENUS", "All menus combined");

        allMenus.add(pancakeHouseMenu);
        allMenus.add(dinerMenu);
        allMenus.add(cafeMenu);

        // add menu items here

        dinerMenu.add(new MenuItem(
            "Pasta",
            "Spaghetti with Marinara Sauce, and a slice of sourdough bread",
            true,
            3.89));

        dinerMenu.add(dessertMenu);

        dessertMenu.add(new MenuItem(
            "Apple Pie",
            "Apple pie with a flakey crust, topped with vanilla icecream",
            true,
            1.59));

        // add more menu items here

        Waitress waitress = new Waitress(allMenus);

        waitress.printMenu();
    }
}
```

Let's first create all the menu objects.

We also need two top level menu now that we'll name allMenus.

We're using the Composite add() method to add each menu to the top level menu, allMenus.

Now we need to add all the menu items, here's one example, for the rest, look at the complete source code.

And we're also adding a menu to a menu. All dinerMenu cares about is that everything it holds, whether it's a menu item or a menu, is a MenuComponent.

Add some apple pie to the dessert menu...

Once we've constructed our entire menu hierarchy, we hand the whole thing to the Waitress, and as you've seen, it's easy as apple pie for her to print it out.

Getting ready for a test drive...

NOTE: this output is based on the complete source.

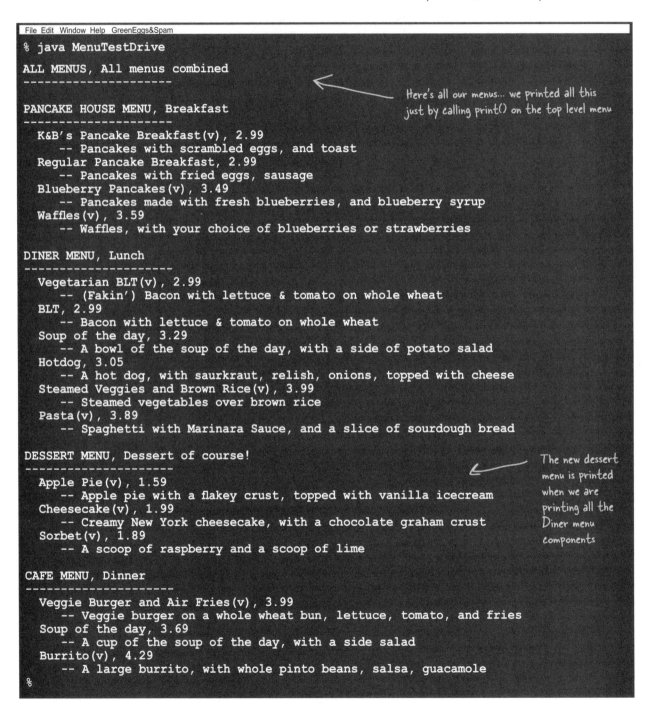

```
File Edit Window Help GreenEggs&Spam
% java MenuTestDrive
ALL MENUS, All menus combined
--------------------

PANCAKE HOUSE MENU, Breakfast
--------------------
   K&B's Pancake Breakfast(v), 2.99
      -- Pancakes with scrambled eggs, and toast
   Regular Pancake Breakfast, 2.99
      -- Pancakes with fried eggs, sausage
   Blueberry Pancakes(v), 3.49
      -- Pancakes made with fresh blueberries, and blueberry syrup
   Waffles(v), 3.59
      -- Waffles, with your choice of blueberries or strawberries

DINER MENU, Lunch
--------------------
   Vegetarian BLT(v), 2.99
      -- (Fakin') Bacon with lettuce & tomato on whole wheat
   BLT, 2.99
      -- Bacon with lettuce & tomato on whole wheat
   Soup of the day, 3.29
      -- A bowl of the soup of the day, with a side of potato salad
   Hotdog, 3.05
      -- A hot dog, with saurkraut, relish, onions, topped with cheese
   Steamed Veggies and Brown Rice(v), 3.99
      -- Steamed vegetables over brown rice
   Pasta(v), 3.89
      -- Spaghetti with Marinara Sauce, and a slice of sourdough bread

DESSERT MENU, Dessert of course!
--------------------
   Apple Pie(v), 1.59
      -- Apple pie with a flakey crust, topped with vanilla icecream
   Cheesecake(v), 1.99
      -- Creamy New York cheesecake, with a chocolate graham crust
   Sorbet(v), 1.89
      -- A scoop of raspberry and a scoop of lime

CAFE MENU, Dinner
--------------------
   Veggie Burger and Air Fries(v), 3.99
      -- Veggie burger on a whole wheat bun, lettuce, tomato, and fries
   Soup of the day, 3.69
      -- A cup of the soup of the day, with a side salad
   Burrito(v), 4.29
      -- A large burrito, with whole pinto beans, salsa, guacamole
%
```

Here's all our menus... we printed all this just by calling print() on the top level menu

The new dessert menu is printed when we are printing all the Diner menu components

What's the story? First you tell us One Class, One Responsibility, and now you are giving us a pattern with two responsibilities in one class. The Composite Pattern manages a hierarchy AND it performs operations related to Menus.

There is some truth to that observation. We could say that the Composite Pattern takes the Single Responsibility design principle and trades it for *transparency*. What's transparency? Well, by allowing the Component interface to contain the child management operations *and* the leaf operations, a client can treat both composites and leaf nodes uniformly; so whether an element is a composite or leaf node becomes transparent to the client.

Now given we have both types of operations in the Component class, we lose a bit of *safety* because a client might try to do something inappropriate or meaningless on an element (like try to add a menu to a menu item). This is a design decision; we could take the design in the other direction and separate out the responsibilities into interfaces. This would make our design safe, in the sense that any inappropriate calls on elements would be caught at compile time or runtime, but we'd lose transparency and our code would have to use conditionals and the `instanceof` operator.

So, to return to your question, this is a classic case of tradeoff. We are guided by design principles, but we always need to observe the effect they have on our designs. Sometimes we purposely do things in a way that seems to violate the principle. In some cases, however, this is a matter of perspective; for instance, it might seem incorrect to have child management operations in the leaf nodes (like add(), remove() and getChild()), but then again you can always shift your perspective and see a leaf as a node with zero children.

Flashback to Iterator

We promised you a few pages back that we'd show you how to use Iterator with a Composite. You know that we are already using Iterator in our internal implementation of the print() method, but we can also allow the Waitress to iterate over an entire composite if she needs to, for instance, if she wants to go through the entire menu and pull out vegetarian items.

To implement a Composite iterator, let's add a createIterator() method in every component. We'll start with the abstract MenuComponent class:

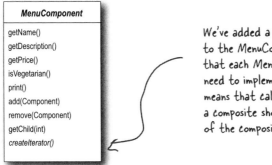

MenuComponent
getName()
getDescription()
getPrice()
isVegetarian()
print()
add(Component)
remove(Component)
getChild(int)
createIterator()

We've added a createIterator() method to the MenuComponent. This means that each Menu and MenuItem will need to implement this method. It also means that calling createIterator() on a composite should apply to all children of the composite.

Now we need to implement this method in the Menu and MenuItem classes:

Here we're using a new iterator called CompositeIterator. It knows how to iterate over any composite.

```
public class Menu extends MenuComponent {
    Iterator iterator = null;                    ←———  We only need one
    // other code here doesn't change               iterator per Menu.

    public Iterator createIterator() {
        if (iterator == null) {
            iterator = new CompositeIterator(menuComponents.iterator());
        }
        return iterator;
    }
}
```

We pass it the current composite's iterator.

```
public class MenuItem extends MenuComponent {

    // other code here doesn't change

    public Iterator createIterator() {
        return new NullIterator();
    }

}
```

Now for the MenuItem...

Whoa! What's this NullIterator? You'll see in two pages.

The Composite Iterator

The CompositeIterator is a SERIOUS iterator. It's got the job of iterating over the MenuItems in the component, and of making sure all the child Menus (and child child Menus, and so on) are included.

Here's the code. Watch out, this isn't a lot of code, but it can be a little mind bending. Just repeat to yourself as you go through it "recursion is my friend, recursion is my friend."

WATCH OUT: RECURSION ZONE AHEAD

```java
import java.util.*;
```
Like all iterators, we're implementing the java.util.Iterator interface.

```java
public class CompositeIterator implements Iterator {
    Stack stack = new Stack();

    public CompositeIterator(Iterator iterator) {
        stack.push(iterator);
    }
```
The iterator of the top level composite we're going to iterate over is passed in. We throw that in a stack data structure.

```java
    public Object next() {
        if (hasNext()) {
            Iterator iterator = (Iterator) stack.peek();
            MenuComponent component = (MenuComponent) iterator.next();
            if (component instanceof Menu) {
                stack.push(component.createIterator());
            }
            return component;
        } else {
            return null;
        }
    }
```
Okay, when the client wants to get the next element we first make sure there is one by calling hasNext()...

If there is a next element, we get the current iterator off the stack and get its next element.

If that element is a menu, we have another composite that needs to be included in the iteration, so we throw it on the stack. In either case, we return the component.

```java
    public boolean hasNext() {
        if (stack.empty()) {
            return false;
        } else {
            Iterator iterator = (Iterator) stack.peek();
            if (!iterator.hasNext()) {
                stack.pop();
                return hasNext();
            } else {
                return true;
            }
        }
    }
```
To see if there is a next element, we check to see if the stack is empty; if so, there isn't.

Otherwise, we get the iterator off the top of the stack and see if it has a next element. If it doesn't we pop it off the stack and call hasNext() recursively.

Otherwise there is a next element and we return true.

```java
    public void remove() {
        throw new UnsupportedOperationException();
    }
}
```
We're not supporting remove, just traversal.

That is serious code... I'm trying to understand why iterating over a composite like this is more difficult than the iteration code we wrote for print() in the MenuComponent class?

When we wrote the print() method in the MenuComponent class we used an iterator to step through each item in the component and if that item was a Menu (rather than a MenuItem), then we recursively called the print() method to handle it. In other words, the MenuComponent handled the iteration itself, *internally*.

With this code we are implementing an *external* iterator so there is a lot more to keep track of. For starters, an external iterator must maintain its position in the iteration so that an outside client can drive the iteration by calling hasNext() and next(). But in this case, our code also needs to maintain that position over a composite, recursive structure. That's why we use stacks to maintain our position as we move up and down the composite hierarchy.

Draw a diagram of the Menus and MenuItems. Then pretend you are the CompositeIterator, and your job is to handle calls to hasNext() and next(). Trace the way the CompositeIterator traverses the structure as this code is executed:

```
public void testCompositeIterator(MenuComponent component) {
        CompositeIterator iterator = new CompositeIterator(component.iterator);

        while(iterator.hasNext()) {
                MenuComponent component = iterator.next();
        }
}
```

The Null Iterator

Okay, now what is this Null Iterator all about? Think about it this way: a MenuItem has nothing to iterate over, right? So how do we handle the implementation of its createIterator() method? Well, we have two choices:

NOTE: Another example of the Null Object "Design Pattern."

Choice one:
Return null

We could return null from createIterator(), but then we'd need conditional code in the client to see if null was returned or not.

Choice two:
Return an iterator that always returns false when hasNext() is called

This seems like a better plan. We can still return an iterator, but the client doesn't have to worry about whether or not null is ever returned. In effect, we're creating an iterator that is a "no op".

The second choice certainly seems better. Let's call it NullIterator and implement it.

This is the laziest Iterator you've ever seen, at every step of the way it punts.

```java
import java.util.Iterator;

public class NullIterator implements Iterator {

    public Object next() {
        return null;
    }

    public boolean hasNext() {
        return false;
    }

    public void remove() {
        throw new UnsupportedOperationException();
    }
}
```

← When next() is called, we return null.

← Most importantly when hasNext() is called we always return false.

← And the NullIterator wouldn't think of supporting remove.

Give me the vegetarian menu

Now we've got a way to iterate over every item of the Menu. Let's take that and give our Waitress a method that can tell us exactly which items are vegetarian.

```java
public class Waitress {
    MenuComponent allMenus;

    public Waitress(MenuComponent allMenus) {
        this.allMenus = allMenus;
    }

    public void printMenu() {
        allMenus.print();
    }

    public void printVegetarianMenu() {
        Iterator iterator = allMenus.createIterator();
        System.out.println("\nVEGETARIAN MENU\n----");
        while (iterator.hasNext()) {
            MenuComponent menuComponent =
                    (MenuComponent)iterator.next();
            try {
                if (menuComponent.isVegetarian()) {
                    menuComponent.print();
                }
            } catch (UnsupportedOperationException e) {}
        }
    }
}
```

The printVegetarianMenu() method takes the allMenu's composite and gets its iterator. That will be our CompositeIterator.

Iterate through every element of the composite.

Call each element's isVegetarian() method and if true, we call its print() method.

print() is only called on MenuItems, never composites. Can you see why?

We implemented isVegetarian() on the Menus to always throw an exception. If that happens we catch the exception, but continue with our iteration.

The magic of Iterator & Composite together...

Whooo! It's been quite a development effort to get our code to this point. Now we've got a general menu structure that should last the growing Diner empire for some time. Now it's time to sit back and order up some veggie food:

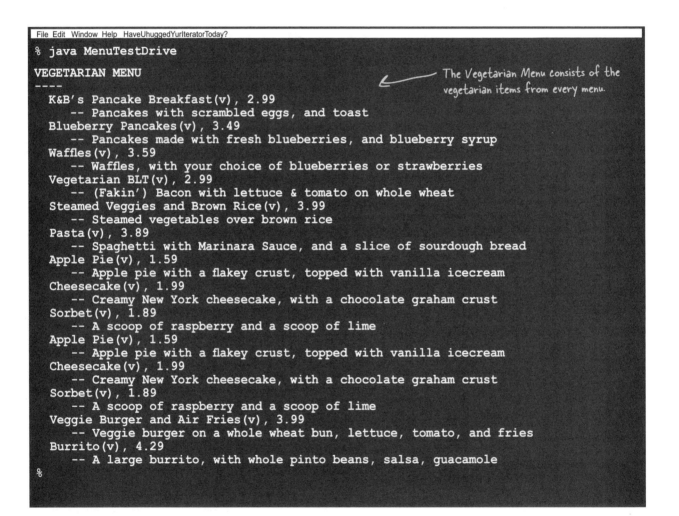

```
File  Edit  Window  Help  HaveUhuggedYurIteratorToday?
% java MenuTestDrive
VEGETARIAN MENU
----
  K&B's Pancake Breakfast(v), 2.99
     -- Pancakes with scrambled eggs, and toast
  Blueberry Pancakes(v), 3.49
     -- Pancakes made with fresh blueberries, and blueberry syrup
  Waffles(v), 3.59
     -- Waffles, with your choice of blueberries or strawberries
  Vegetarian BLT(v), 2.99
     -- (Fakin') Bacon with lettuce & tomato on whole wheat
  Steamed Veggies and Brown Rice(v), 3.99
     -- Steamed vegetables over brown rice
  Pasta(v), 3.89
     -- Spaghetti with Marinara Sauce, and a slice of sourdough bread
  Apple Pie(v), 1.59
     -- Apple pie with a flakey crust, topped with vanilla icecream
  Cheesecake(v), 1.99
     -- Creamy New York cheesecake, with a chocolate graham crust
  Sorbet(v), 1.89
     -- A scoop of raspberry and a scoop of lime
  Apple Pie(v), 1.59
     -- Apple pie with a flakey crust, topped with vanilla icecream
  Cheesecake(v), 1.99
     -- Creamy New York cheesecake, with a chocolate graham crust
  Sorbet(v), 1.89
     -- A scoop of raspberry and a scoop of lime
  Veggie Burger and Air Fries(v), 3.99
     -- Veggie burger on a whole wheat bun, lettuce, tomato, and fries
  Burrito(v), 4.29
     -- A large burrito, with whole pinto beans, salsa, guacamole
%
```

The Vegetarian Menu consists of the vegetarian items from every menu.

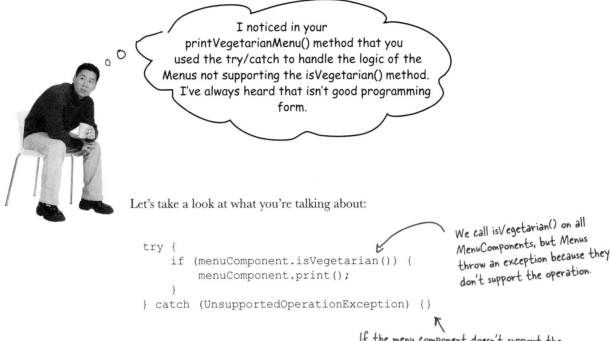

I noticed in your printVegetarianMenu() method that you used the try/catch to handle the logic of the Menus not supporting the isVegetarian() method. I've always heard that isn't good programming form.

Let's take a look at what you're talking about:

```
try {
    if (menuComponent.isVegetarian()) {
        menuComponent.print();
    }
} catch (UnsupportedOperationException) {}
```

We call isVegetarian() on all MenuComponents, but Menus throw an exception because they don't support the operation.

If the menu component doesn't support the operation, we just throw away the exception and ignore it.

In general we agree; try/catch is meant for error handling, not program logic. What are our other options? We could have checked the runtime type of the menu component with instanceof to make sure it's a MenuItem before making the call to isVegetarian(). But in the process we'd lose *transparency* because we wouldn't be treating Menus and MenuItems uniformly.

We could also change isVegetarian() in the Menus so that it returns false. This provides a simple solution and we keep our transparency.

In our solution we are going for clarity: we really want to communicate that this is an unsupported operation on the Menu (which is different than saying isVegetarian() is false). It also allows for someone to come along and actually implement a reasonable isVegetarian() method for Menu and have it work with the existing code.

That's our story and we're stickin' to it.

Patterns Exposed

This week's interview:
The Composite Pattern, on Implementation issues

HeadFirst: We're here tonight speaking with the Composite Pattern. Why don't you tell us a little about yourself, Composite?

Composite: Sure... I'm the pattern to use when you have collections of objects with whole-part relationships and you want to be able to treat those objects uniformly.

HeadFirst: Okay, let's dive right in here... what do you mean by whole-part relationships?

Composite: Imagine a graphical user interface; there you'll often find a top level component like a Frame or a Panel, containing other components, like menus, text panes, scrollbars and buttons. So your GUI consists of several parts, but when you display it, you generally think of it as a whole. You tell the top level component to display, and count on that component to display all its parts. We call the components that contain other components, composite objects, and components that don't contain other components, leaf objects.

HeadFirst: Is that what you mean by treating the objects uniformly? Having common methods you can call on composites and leaves?

Composite: Right. I can tell a composite object to display or a leaf object to display and they will do the right thing. The composite object will display by telling all its components to display.

HeadFirst: That implies that every object has the same interface. What if you have objects in your composite that do different things?

Composite: Well, in order for the composite to work transparently to the client, you must implement the same interface for all objects in the composite, otherwise, the client has to worry about which interface each object is implementing, which kind of defeats the purpose. Obviously that means that at times you'll have objects for which some of the method calls don't make sense.

HeadFirst: So how do you handle that?

Composite: Well there's a couple of ways to handle it; sometimes you can just do nothing, or return null or false – whatever makes sense in your application. Other times you'll want to be more proactive and throw an exception. Of course, then the client has to be willing to do a little work and make sure that the method call didn't do something unexpected.

HeadFirst: But if the client doesn't know which kind of object they're dealing with, how would they ever know which calls to make without checking the type?

Composite: If you're a little creative you can structure your methods so that the default implementations do something that does make sense. For instance, if the client is calling getChild(), on the composite this makes sense. And it makes sense on a leaf too, if you think of the leaf as an object with no children.

HeadFirst: Ah... smart. But, I've heard some clients are so worried about this issue, that they require separate interfaces for different objects so they aren't allowed to make nonsensical method calls. Is that still the Composite Pattern?

Composite: Yes. It's a much safer version of the Composite Pattern, but it requires the client to check the type of every object before making a call so the object can be cast correctly.

HeadFirst: Tell us a little more about how these composite and leaf objects are structured.

Composite: Usually it's a tree structure, some kind of hierarchy. The root is the top level composite, and all its children are either composites or leaf nodes.

HeadFirst: Do children ever point back up to their parents?

Composite: Yes, a component can have a pointer to a parent to make traversal of the structure easier. And, if you have a reference to a child, and you need to delete it, you'll need to get the parent to remove the child. Having the parent reference makes that easier too.

HeadFirst: There's really quite a lot to consider in your implementation. Are there other issues we should think about when implementing the Composite Pattern?

Composite: Actually there are... one is the ordering of children. What if you have a composite that needs to keep its children in a particular order? Then you'll need a more sophisticated management scheme for adding and removing children, and you'll have to be careful about how you traverse the hierarchy.

HeadFirst: A good point I hadn't thought of.

Composite: And did you think about caching?

HeadFirst: Caching?

Composite: Yeah, caching. Sometimes, if the composite structure is complex or expensive to traverse, it's helpful to implement caching of the composite nodes. For instance, if you are constantly traversing a composite and all its children to compute some result, you could implement a cache that stores the result temporarily to save traversals.

HeadFirst: Well, there's a lot more to the Composite Patterns than I ever would have guessed. Before we wrap this up, one more question: What do you consider your greatest strength?

Composite: I think I'd definitely have to say simplifying life for my clients. My clients don't have to worry about whether they're dealing with a composite object or a leaf object, so they don't have to write if statements everywhere to make sure they're calling the right methods on the right objects. Often, they can make one method call and execute an operation over an entire structure.

HeadFirst: That does sound like an important benefit. There's no doubt you're a useful pattern to have around for collecting and managing objects. And, with that, we're out of time... Thanks so much for joining us and come back soon for another Patterns Exposed.

It's that time again....

Across

1. User interface packages often use this pattern for their components.
3. Collection and Iterator are in this package
5. We encapsulated this.
6. A separate object that can traverse a collection.
10. Merged with the Diner.
12. Has no children.
13. Name of principle that states only one responsibility per class.
14. Third company acquired.
15. A class should have only one reason to do this.
16. This class indirectly supports Iterator.
17. This menu caused us to change our entire implementation.

Down

1. A composite holds this.
2. We java-enabled her.
4. We deleted PancakeHouseMenuIterator because this class already provides an iterator.
5. The Iterator Pattern decouples the client from the aggregates _____.
7. CompositeIterator used a lot of this.
8. Iterators are usually created using this pattern.
9. A component can be a composite or this.
11. Hashtable and ArrayList both implement this interface.

Match each pattern with its description:

Pattern	Description
Strategy	Clients treat collections of objects and individual objects uniformly
Adapter	Provides a way to traverse a collection of objects without exposing the collection's implementation
Iterator	Simplifies the interface of a group of classes
Facade	Changes the interface of one or more classes
Composite	Allows a group of objects to be notified when some state changes
Observer	Encapsulates interchangeable behaviors and uses delegation to decide which one to uses

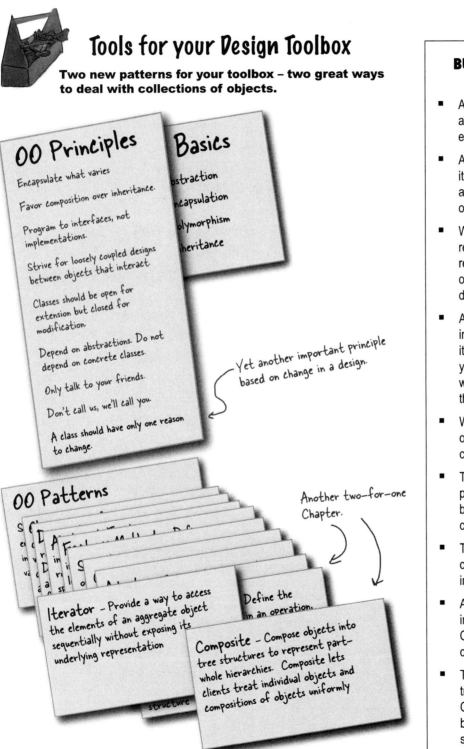

Tools for your Design Toolbox

Two new patterns for your toolbox – two great ways to deal with collections of objects.

OO Principles

Encapsulate what varies

Favor composition over inheritance.

Program to interfaces, not implementations.

Strive for loosely coupled designs between objects that interact.

Classes should be open for extension but closed for modification.

Depend on abstractions. Do not depend on concrete classes.

Only talk to your friends.

Don't call us, we'll call you.

A class should have only one reason to change.

Basics

bstraction

ncapsulation

olymorphism

nheritance

Yet another important principle based on change in a design.

OO Patterns

S C
e D A F M D
in v r in i S
va a r l
a sh o
r p

Iterator – Provide a way to access the elements of an aggregate object sequentially without exposing its underlying representation

Define the
in an operation.

Composite – Compose objects into tree structures to represent part-whole hierarchies. Composite lets clients treat individual objects and compositions of objects uniformly

structure

Another two-for-one Chapter.

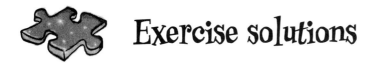

Exercise solutions

Sharpen your pencil

Based on our implementation of printMenu(), which of the following apply?

☑ A. We are coding to the PancakeHouseMenu and DinerMenu concrete implementations, not to an interface.

☐ B. The Waitress doesn't implement the Java Waitress API and so isn't adhering to a standard.

☑ C. If we decided to switch from using DinerMenu to another type of menu that implemented its list of menu items with a Hashtable, we'd have to modify a lot of code in the Waitress.

☑ D. The Waitress needs to know how each menu represents its internal collection of menu items is implemented, this violates encapsulation.

☑ E. We have duplicate code: the printMenu() method needs two separate loop implementations to iterate over the two different kinds of menus. And if we added a third menu, we might have to add yet another loop.

☐ F. The implementation isn't based on MXML (Menu XML) and so isn't as interoperable as it should be.

Sharpen your pencil

Before turning the page, quickly jot down the three things we have to do to this code to fit it into our framework:

1.   implement the Menu interface

2.   get rid of getItems()

3.   add createIterator() and return an Iterator that can step through the Hashtable values

Code Magnets Solution

The unscrambled "Alternating" DinerMenu Iterator

```java
import java.util.Iterator;
import java.util.Calendar;

public class AlternatingDinerMenuIterator    implements Iterator    {

    MenuItem[] items;
    int position;

    public AlternatingDinerMenuIterator(MenuItem[] items)    {

        this.items = items;
        Calendar rightNow = Calendar.getInstance();
        position = rightNow.get(Calendar.DAY_OF_WEEK) % 2;

    }

    public boolean hasNext() {

        if (position >= items.length || items[position] == null) {
            return false;
        } else {
            return true;
        }

    }

    public Object next() {

        MenuItem menuItem = items[position];
        position = position + 2;
        return menuItem;

    }

    public void remove() {

        throw new UnsupportedOperationException(
            "Alternating Diner Menu Iterator does not support remove()");

    }
}
```

Notice that this Iterator implementation does not support remove()

WHO DOES WHAT?

Match each pattern with its description:

Pattern

Description

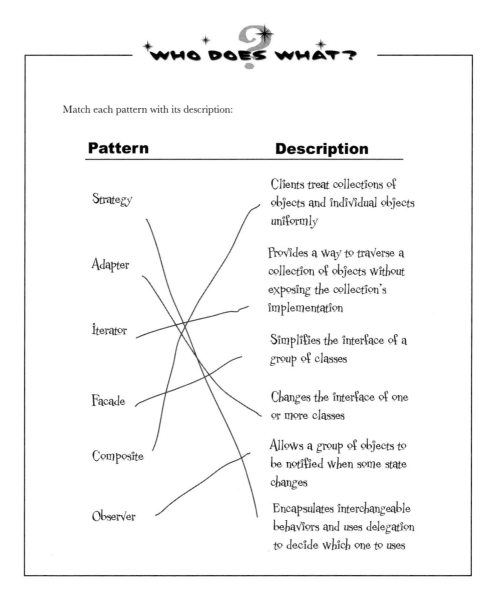

Strategy

Adapter

Iterator

Facade

Composite

Observer

Clients treat collections of objects and individual objects uniformly

Provides a way to traverse a collection of objects without exposing the collection's implementation

Simplifies the interface of a group of classes

Changes the interface of one or more classes

Allows a group of objects to be notified when some state changes

Encapsulates interchangeable behaviors and uses delegation to decide which one to uses

Exercise solutions

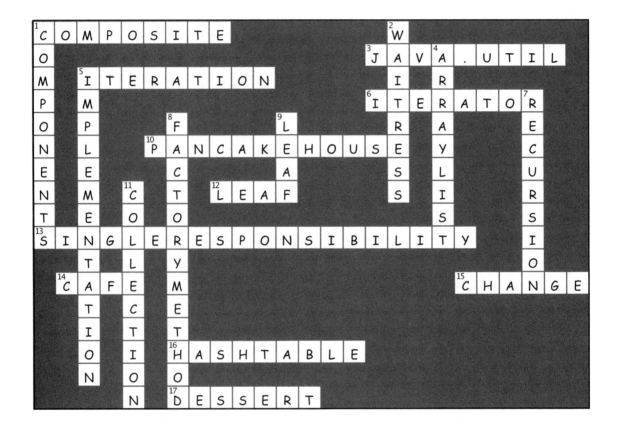

The State of Things

I thought things in Objectville were going to be so easy, but now every time I turn around there's another change request coming in. I'm to the breaking point! Oh, maybe I should have been going to Betty's Wednesday night patterns group all along. I'm in such a state!

A little known fact: the Strategy and State Patterns were twins separated at birth. As you know, the Strategy Pattern went on to create a wildly successful business around interchangeable algorithms. State, however, took the perhaps more noble path of helping objects to control their behavior by changing their internal state. He's often overheard telling his object clients, "Just repeat after me: I'm good enough, I'm smart enough, and doggonit..."

Ja~~wa~~ Breakers

Java toasters are so '90s. Today people are building Java into *real* devices, like gumball machines. That's right, gumball machines have gone high tech; the major manufacturers have found that by putting CPUs into their machines, they can increase sales, monitor inventory over the network and measure customer satisfaction more accurately.

At least that's their story — we think they just got bored with the circa 1800's technology and needed to find a way to make their jobs more exciting.

But these manufacturers are gumball machine experts, not software developers, and they've asked for your help:

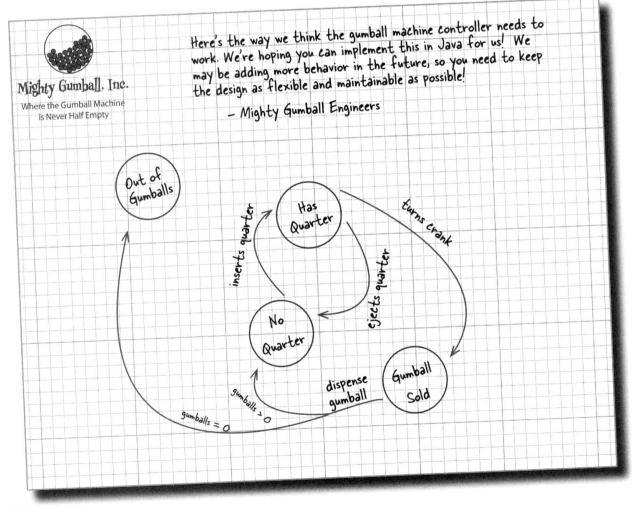

Mighty Gumball, Inc.
Where the Gumball Machine is Never Half Empty

Here's the way we think the gumball machine controller needs to work. We're hoping you can implement this in Java for us! We may be adding more behavior in the future, so you need to keep the design as flexible and maintainable as possible!

— Mighty Gumball Engineers

Cubicle Conversation

Let's take a look at this diagram and see what the Mighty Gumball guys want...

Joe   Anne   Frank

Anne: This diagram looks like a state diagram.

Joe: Right, each of those circles is a state...

Anne: ... and each of the arrows is a state transition.

Frank: Slow down, you two, it's been too long since I studied state diagrams. Can you remind me what they're all about?

Anne: Sure, Frank. Look at the circles; those are states. "No Quarter" is probably the starting state for the gumball machine because it's just sitting there waiting for you to put your quarter in. All states are just different configurations of the machine that behave in a certain way and need some action to take them to another state.

Joe: Right. See, to go to another state, you need to do something like put a quarter in the machine. See the arrow from "No Quarter" to "Has Quarter?"

Frank: Yes...

Joe: That just means that if the gumball machine is in the "No Quarter" state and you put a quarter in, it will change to the "Has Quarter" state. That's the state transition.

Frank: Oh, I see! And if I'm in the "Has Quarter" state, I can turn the crank and change to the "Gumball Sold" state, or eject the quarter and change back to the "No Quarter" state.

Anne: You got it!

Frank: This doesn't look too bad then. We've obviously got four states, and I think we also have four actions: "inserts quarter," "ejects quarter," "turns crank" and "dispense." But... when we dispense, we test for zero or more gumballs in the "Gumball Sold" state, and then either go to the "Out of Gumballs" state or the "No Quarter" state. So we actually have five transitions from one state to another.

Anne: That test for zero or more gumballs also implies we've got to keep track of the number of gumballs too. Any time the machine gives you a gumball, it might be the last one, and if it is, we need to transition to the "Out of Gumballs" state.

Joe: Also, don't forget that you could do nonsensical things, like try to eject the quarter when the gumball machine is in the "No Quarter" state, or insert two quarters.

Frank: Oh, I didn't think of that; we'll have to take care of those too.

Joe: For every possible action we'll just have to check to see which state we're in and act appropriately. We can do this! Let's start mapping the state diagram to code...

State machines 101

How are we going to get from that state diagram to actual code? Here's a quick introduction to implementing state machines:

1 First, gather up your states:

Here are the states — four in total.

2 Next, create an instance variable to hold the current state, and define values for each of the states:

Let's just call "Out of Gumballs" "Sold Out" for short.

```
final static int SOLD_OUT = 0;
final static int NO_QUARTER = 1;
final static int HAS_QUARTER = 2;
final static int SOLD = 3;

int state = SOLD_OUT;
```

Here's each state represented as a unique integer...

...and here's an instance variable that holds the current state. We'll go ahead and set it to "Sold Out" since the machine will be unfilled when it's first taken out of its box and turned on.

3 Now we gather up all the actions that can happen in the system:

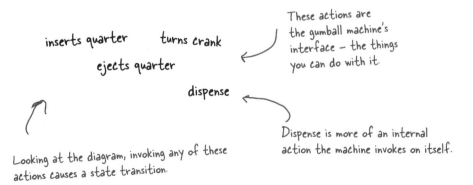

inserts quarter   turns crank

ejects quarter

dispense

These actions are the gumball machine's interface — the things you can do with it.

Dispense is more of an internal action the machine invokes on itself.

Looking at the diagram, invoking any of these actions causes a state transition.

4 Now we create a class that acts as the state machine. For each action, we create a method that uses conditional statements to determine what behavior is appropriate in each state. For instance, for the insert quarter action, we might write a method like this:

```
public void insertQuarter() {

    if (state == HAS_QUARTER) {

        System.out.println("You can't insert another quarter");

    } else if (state == SOLD_OUT) {

        System.out.println("You can't insert a quarter, the machine is sold out");

    } else if (state == SOLD) {

        System.out.println("Please wait, we're already giving you a gumball");

    } else if (state == NO_QUARTER) {

        state = HAS_QUARTER;
        System.out.println("You inserted a quarter");

    }
}
```

Each possible state is checked with a conditional statement...

...and exhibits the appropriate behavior for each possible state...

...but can also transition to other states, just as depicted in the diagram.

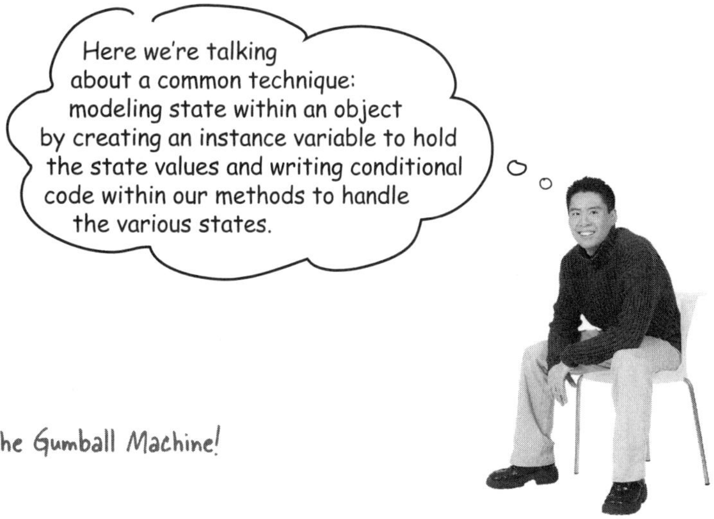

> Here we're talking about a common technique: modeling state within an object by creating an instance variable to hold the state values and writing conditional code within our methods to handle the various states.

With that quick review, let's go implement the Gumball Machine!

Writing the code

It's time to implement the Gumball Machine. We know we're going to have an instance variable that holds the current state. From there, we just need to handle all the actions, behaviors and state transitions that can happen. For actions, we need to implement inserting a quarter, removing a quarter, turning the crank and dispensing a gumball; we also have the empty gumball condition to implement as well.

Here are the four states; they match the states in Mighty Gumball's state diagram.

Here's the instance variable that is going to keep track of the current state we're in. We start in the SOLD_OUT state.

We have a second instance variable that keeps track of the number of gumballs in the machine.

The constructor takes an initial inventory of gumballs. If the inventory isn't zero, the machine enters state NO_QUARTER, meaning it is waiting for someone to insert a quarter, otherwise it stays in the SOLD_OUT state.

```java
public class GumballMachine {

    final static int SOLD_OUT = 0;
    final static int NO_QUARTER = 1;
    final static int HAS_QUARTER = 2;
    final static int SOLD = 3;

    int state = SOLD_OUT;
    int count = 0;

    public GumballMachine(int count) {
        this.count = count;
        if (count > 0) {
            state = NO_QUARTER;
        }
    }
```

Now we start implementing the actions as methods....

When a quarter is inserted, if....

a quarter is already inserted we tell the customer;

otherwise we accept the quarter and transition to the HAS_QUARTER state.

```java
    public void insertQuarter() {
        if (state == HAS_QUARTER) {
            System.out.println("You can't insert another quarter");
        } else if (state == NO_QUARTER) {
            state = HAS_QUARTER;
            System.out.println("You inserted a quarter");
        } else if (state == SOLD_OUT) {
            System.out.println("You can't insert a quarter, the machine is sold out");
        } else if (state == SOLD) {
            System.out.println("Please wait, we're already giving you a gumball");
        }
    }
}
```

If the customer just bought a gumball he needs to wait until the transaction is complete before inserting another quarter.

and if the machine is sold out, we reject the quarter.

```java
public void ejectQuarter() {
    if (state == HAS_QUARTER) {
        System.out.println("Quarter returned");
        state = NO_QUARTER;
    } else if (state == NO_QUARTER) {
        System.out.println("You haven't inserted a quarter");
    } else if (state == SOLD) {
        System.out.println("Sorry, you already turned the crank");
    } else if (state == SOLD_OUT) {
        System.out.println("You can't eject, you haven't inserted a quarter yet");
    }
}
```

Now, if the customer tries to remove the quarter...

If there is a quarter, we return it and go back to the NO_QUARTER state.

Otherwise, if there isn't one we can't give it back.

If the customer just turned the crank, we can't give a refund; he already has the gumball!

You can't eject if the machine is sold out, it doesn't accept quarters!

The customer tries to turn the crank...

```java
public void turnCrank() {
    if (state == SOLD) {
        System.out.println("Turning twice doesn't get you another gumball!");
    } else if (state == NO_QUARTER) {
        System.out.println("You turned but there's no quarter");
    } else if (state == SOLD_OUT) {
        System.out.println("You turned, but there are no gumballs");
    } else if (state == HAS_QUARTER) {
        System.out.println("You turned...");
        state = SOLD;
        dispense();
    }
}
```

Someone's trying to cheat the machine.

We need a quarter first.

We can't deliver gumballs; there are none.

Success! They get a gumball. Change the state to SOLD and call the machine's dispense() method.

Called to dispense a gumball.

```java
public void dispense() {
    if (state == SOLD) {
        System.out.println("A gumball comes rolling out the slot");
        count = count - 1;
        if (count == 0) {
            System.out.println("Oops, out of gumballs!");
            state = SOLD_OUT;
        } else {
            state = NO_QUARTER;
        }
    } else if (state == NO_QUARTER) {
        System.out.println("You need to pay first");
    } else if (state == SOLD_OUT) {
        System.out.println("No gumball dispensed");
    } else if (state == HAS_QUARTER) {
        System.out.println("No gumball dispensed");
    }
}

// other methods here like toString() and refill()
}
```

We're in the SOLD state; give 'em a gumball!

Here's where we handle the "out of gumballs" condition: If this was the last one, we set the machine's state to SOLD_OUT; otherwise, we're back to not having a quarter.

None of these should ever happen, but if they do, we give 'em an error, not a gumball.

In-house testing

That feels like a nice solid design using a well-thought out methodology doesn't it? Let's do a little in-house testing before we hand it off to Mighty Gumball to be loaded into their actual gumball machines. Here's our test harness:

```
public class GumballMachineTestDrive {
    public static void main(String[] args) {
        GumballMachine gumballMachine = new GumballMachine(5);

        System.out.println(gumballMachine);

        gumballMachine.insertQuarter();
        gumballMachine.turnCrank();

        System.out.println(gumballMachine);

        gumballMachine.insertQuarter();
        gumballMachine.ejectQuarter();
        gumballMachine.turnCrank();

        System.out.println(gumballMachine);

        gumballMachine.insertQuarter();
        gumballMachine.turnCrank();
        gumballMachine.insertQuarter();
        gumballMachine.turnCrank();
        gumballMachine.ejectQuarter();

        System.out.println(gumballMachine);

        gumballMachine.insertQuarter();
        gumballMachine.insertQuarter();
        gumballMachine.turnCrank();
        gumballMachine.insertQuarter();
        gumballMachine.turnCrank();
        gumballMachine.insertQuarter();
        gumballMachine.turnCrank();

        System.out.println(gumballMachine);
    }
}
```

Load it up with five gumballs total.

Print out the state of the machine.

Throw a quarter in...
Turn the crank; we should get our gumball.

Print out the state of the machine, again.

Throw a quarter in...
Ask for it back.
Turn the crank; we shouldn't get our gumball.

Print out the state of the machine, again.

Throw a quarter in...
Turn the crank; we should get our gumball
Throw a quarter in...
Turn the crank; we should get our gumball
Ask for a quarter back we didn't put in.

Print out the state of the machine, again.

Throw TWO quarters in...
Turn the crank; we should get our gumball.

Now for the stress testing... ☺

Print that machine state one more time.

```
File Edit  Window  Help  mightygumball.com
%java GumballMachineTestDrive

Mighty Gumball, Inc.
Java-enabled Standing Gumball Model #2004
Inventory: 5 gumballs
Machine is waiting for quarter

You inserted a quarter
You turned...
A gumball comes rolling out the slot

Mighty Gumball, Inc.
Java-enabled Standing Gumball Model #2004
Inventory: 4 gumballs
Machine is waiting for quarter

You inserted a quarter
Quarter returned
You turned but there's no quarter

Mighty Gumball, Inc.
Java-enabled Standing Gumball Model #2004
Inventory: 4 gumballs
Machine is waiting for quarter

You inserted a quarter
You turned...
A gumball comes rolling out the slot
You inserted a quarter
You turned...
A gumball comes rolling out the slot
You haven't inserted a quarter

Mighty Gumball, Inc.
Java-enabled Standing Gumball Model #2004
Inventory: 2 gumballs
Machine is waiting for quarter

You inserted a quarter
You can't insert another quarter
You turned...
A gumball comes rolling out the slot
You inserted a quarter
You turned...
A gumball comes rolling out the slot
Oops, out of gumballs!
You can't insert a quarter, the machine is sold out
You turned, but there are no gumballs

Mighty Gumball, Inc.
Java-enabled Standing Gumball Model #2004
Inventory: 0 gumballs
Machine is sold out
```

You knew it was coming... a change request!

Mighty Gumball, Inc. has loaded your code into their new-est machine and their quality assurance experts are putting it through its paces. So far, everything's looking great from their perspective.

In fact, things have gone so smoothly they'd like to take things to the next level...

We think that by turning "gumball buying" into a game we can significantly increase our sales. We're going to put one of these stickers on every machine. We're so glad we've got Java in the machines because this is going to be easy, right?

Be a Winner! One in Ten get a FREE GUMBALL

CEO, Mighty Gumball, Inc.

JawBreaker or Gumdrop?

10% of the time, when the crank is turned, the customer gets two gumballs instead of one.

Gumballs

Design Puzzle

Draw a state diagram for a Gumball Machine that handles the 1 in 10 contest. In this contest, 10% of the time the Sold state leads to two balls being released, not one. Check your answer with ours (at the end of the chapter) to make sure we agree before you go further...

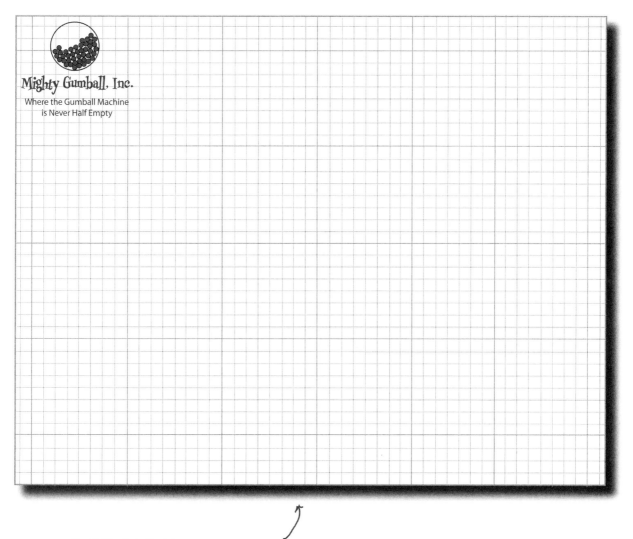

Use Mighty Gumball's stationary to draw your state diagram.

The messy STATE of things...

Just because you've written your gumball machine using a well-thought out methodology doesn't mean it's going to be easy to extend. In fact, when you go back and look at your code and think about what you'll have to do to modify it, well...

```
final static int SOLD_OUT = 0;
final static int NO_QUARTER = 1;
final static int HAS_QUARTER = 2;
final static int SOLD = 3;


public void insertQuarter() {
    // insert quarter code here
}

public void ejectQuarter() {
    // eject quarter code here
}

public void turnCrank() {
    // turn crank code here
}

public void dispense() {
    // dispense code here
}
```

First, you'd have to add a new WINNER state here. That isn't too bad...

... but then, you'd have to add a new conditional in every single method to handle the WINNER state; that's a lot of code to modify.

turnCrank() will get especially messy, because you'd have to add code to check to see whether you've got a WINNER and then switch to either the WINNER state or the SOLD state.

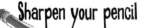 **Sharpen your pencil**

Which of the following describe the state of our implementation?
(Choose all that apply.)

❏ A. This code certainly isn't adhering to the Open Closed Principle.

❏ B. This code would make a FORTRAN programmer proud.

❏ C. This design isn't even very object oriented.

❏ C. State transitions aren't explicit; they are buried in the middle of a bunch of conditional statements.

❏ D. We haven't encapsulated anything that varies here.

❏ E. Further additions are likely to cause bugs in working code.

Okay, this isn't good. I think our first version was great, but it isn't going to hold up over time as Mighty Gumball keeps asking for new behavior. The rate of bugs is just going to make us look bad, not to mention that CEO will drive us crazy.

Joe: You're right about that! We need to refactor this code so that it's easy to maintain and modify.

Anne: We really should try to localize the behavior for each state so that if we make changes to one state, we don't run the risk of messing up the other code.

Joe: Right; in other words, follow that ol' "encapsulate what varies" principle.

Anne: Exactly.

Joe: If we put each state's behavior in its own class, then every state just implements its own actions.

Anne: Right. And maybe the Gumball Machine can just delegate to the state object that represents the current state.

Joe: Ah, you're good: favor composition... more principles at work.

Anne: Cute. Well, I'm not 100% sure how this is going to work, but I think we're on to something.

Joe: I wonder if this will this make it easier to add new states?

Anne: I think so... We'll still have to change code, but the changes will be much more limited in scope because adding a new state will mean we just have to add a new class and maybe change a few transitions here and there.

Joe: I like the sound of that. Let's start hashing out this new design!

The new design

It looks like we've got a new plan: instead of maintaining our existing code, we're going to rework it to encapsulate state objects in their own classes and then delegate to the current state when an action occurs.

We're following our design principles here, so we should end up with a design that is easier to maintain down the road. Here's how we're going to do it:

1 **First, we're going to define a State interface that contains a method for every action in the Gumball Machine.**

2 **Then we're going to implement a State class for every state of the machine. These classes will be responsible for the behavior of the machine when it is in the corresponding state.**

3 **Finally, we're going to get rid of all of our conditional code and instead delegate to the state class to do the work for us.**

Not only are we following design principles, as you'll see, we're actually implementing the State Pattern. But we'll get to all the official State Pattern stuff after we rework our code...

> Now we're going put all the behavior of a state into one class. That way, we're localizing the behavior and making things a lot easier to change and understand.

Defining the State interfaces and classes

First let's create an interface for State, which all our states implement:

Here's the interface for all states. The methods map directly to actions that could happen to the Gumball Machine (these are the same methods as in the previous code).

Then take each state in our design and encapsulate it in a class that implements the State interface.

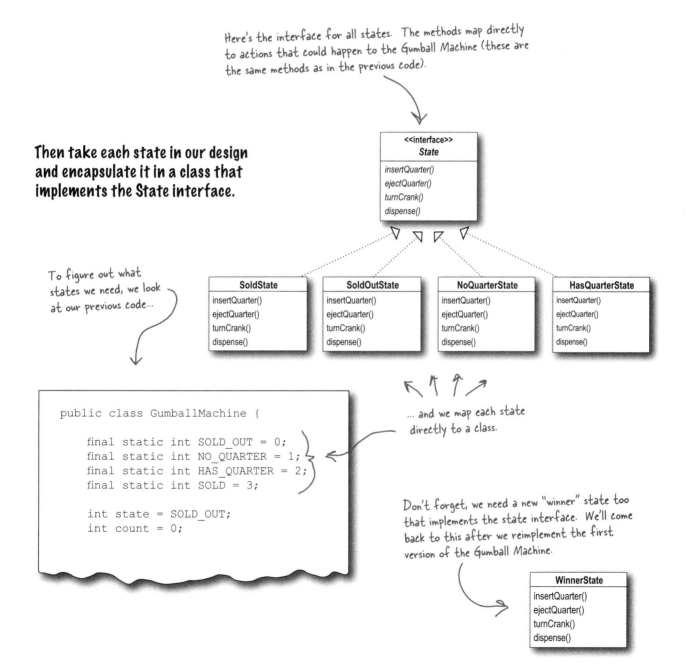

```
<<interface>>
State

insertQuarter()
ejectQuarter()
turnCrank()
dispense()
```

To figure out what states we need, we look at our previous code...

SoldState
insertQuarter()
ejectQuarter()
turnCrank()
dispense()

SoldOutState
insertQuarter()
ejectQuarter()
turnCrank()
dispense()

NoQuarterState
insertQuarter()
ejectQuarter()
turnCrank()
dispense()

HasQuarterState
insertQuarter()
ejectQuarter()
turnCrank()
dispense()

... and we map each state directly to a class.

```
public class GumballMachine {

    final static int SOLD_OUT = 0;
    final static int NO_QUARTER = 1;
    final static int HAS_QUARTER = 2;
    final static int SOLD = 3;

    int state = SOLD_OUT;
    int count = 0;
```

Don't forget, we need a new "winner" state too that implements the state interface. We'll come back to this after we reimplement the first version of the Gumball Machine.

WinnerState
insertQuarter()
ejectQuarter()
turnCrank()
dispense()

Sharpen your pencil

To implement our states, we first need to specify the behavior of the classes when each action is called. Annotate the diagram below with the behavior of each action in each class; we've already filled in a few for you.

Go to HasQuarterState

Tell the customer, "You haven't inserted a quarter."

NoQuarterState
insertQuarter()
ejectQuarter()
turnCrank()
dispense()

HasQuarterState
insertQuarter()
ejectQuarter()
turnCrank()
dispense()

Go to SoldState

Tell the customer, "Please wait, we're already giving you a gumball."

SoldState
insertQuarter()
ejectQuarter()
turnCrank()
dispense()

Dispense one gumball. Check number of gumballs; if > 0, go to NoQuarterState, otherwise, go to SoldOutState

SoldOutState
insertQuarter()
ejectQuarter()
turnCrank()
dispense()

Tell the customer, "There are no gumballs."

WinnerState
insertQuarter()
ejectQuarter()
turnCrank()
dispense()

Go ahead and fill this out even though we're implementing it later.

Implementing our State classes

Time to implement a state: we know what behaviors we want; we just need to get it down in code. We're going to closely follow the state machine code we wrote, but this time everything is broken out into different classes.

Let's start with the NoQuarterState:

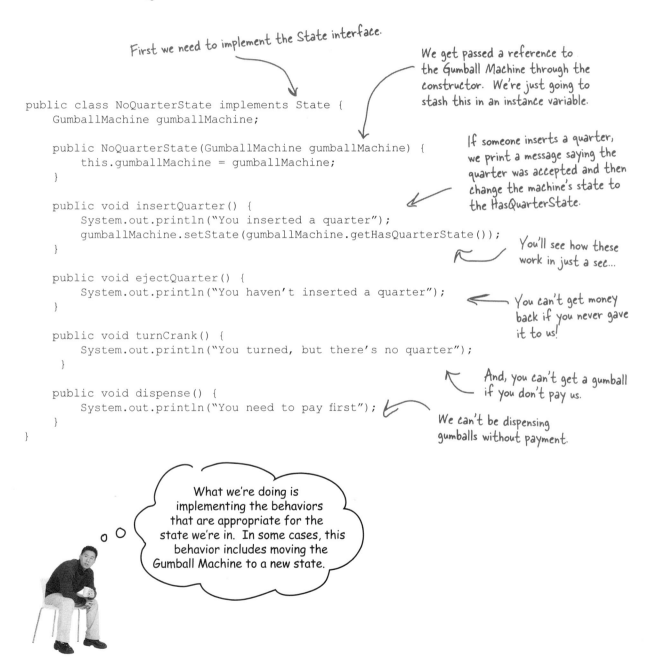

First we need to implement the State interface.

We get passed a reference to the Gumball Machine through the constructor. We're just going to stash this in an instance variable.

```java
public class NoQuarterState implements State {
    GumballMachine gumballMachine;

    public NoQuarterState(GumballMachine gumballMachine) {
        this.gumballMachine = gumballMachine;
    }

    public void insertQuarter() {
        System.out.println("You inserted a quarter");
        gumballMachine.setState(gumballMachine.getHasQuarterState());
    }

    public void ejectQuarter() {
        System.out.println("You haven't inserted a quarter");
    }

    public void turnCrank() {
        System.out.println("You turned, but there's no quarter");
    }

    public void dispense() {
        System.out.println("You need to pay first");
    }
}
```

If someone inserts a quarter, we print a message saying the quarter was accepted and then change the machine's state to the HasQuarterState.

You'll see how these work in just a sec...

You can't get money back if you never gave it to us!

And, you can't get a gumball if you don't pay us.

We can't be dispensing gumballs without payment.

What we're doing is implementing the behaviors that are appropriate for the state we're in. In some cases, this behavior includes moving the Gumball Machine to a new state.

Reworking the Gumball Machine

Before we finish the State classes, we're going to rework the Gumball Machine – that way you can see how it all fits together. We'll start with the state-related instance variables and switch the code from using integers to using state objects:

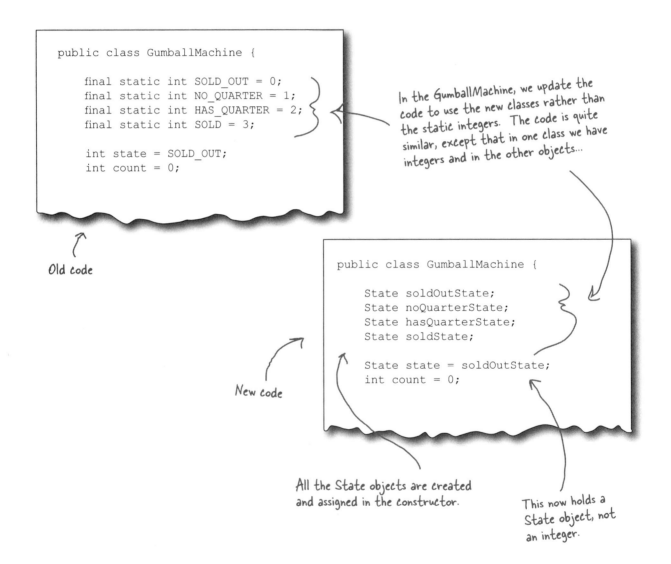

```java
public class GumballMachine {

    final static int SOLD_OUT = 0;
    final static int NO_QUARTER = 1;
    final static int HAS_QUARTER = 2;
    final static int SOLD = 3;

    int state = SOLD_OUT;
    int count = 0;
```

In the GumballMachine, we update the code to use the new classes rather than the static integers. The code is quite similar, except that in one class we have integers and in the other objects...

Old code

```java
public class GumballMachine {

    State soldOutState;
    State noQuarterState;
    State hasQuarterState;
    State soldState;

    State state = soldOutState;
    int count = 0;
```

New code

All the State objects are created and assigned in the constructor.

This now holds a State object, not an integer.

Now, let's look at the complete GumballMachine class...

```java
public class GumballMachine {

    State soldOutState;
    State noQuarterState;
    State hasQuarterState;
    State soldState;

    State state = soldOutState;
    int count = 0;

    public GumballMachine(int numberGumballs) {
        soldOutState = new SoldOutState(this);
        noQuarterState = new NoQuarterState(this);
        hasQuarterState = new HasQuarterState(this);
        soldState = new SoldState(this);
        this.count = numberGumballs;
        if (numberGumballs > 0) {
            state = noQuarterState;
        }
    }

    public void insertQuarter() {
        state.insertQuarter();
    }

    public void ejectQuarter() {
        state.ejectQuarter();
    }

    public void turnCrank() {
        state.turnCrank();
        state.dispense();
    }

    void setState(State state) {
        this.state = state;
    }

    void releaseBall() {
        System.out.println("A gumball comes rolling out the slot...");
        if (count != 0) {
            count = count - 1;
        }
    }

    // More methods here including getters for each State...
}
```

Here are all the States again...

...and the State instance variable.

The count instance variable holds the count of gumballs — initially the machine is empty.

Our constructor takes the initial number of gumballs and stores it in an instance variable.

It also creates the State instances, one of each.

If there are more than 0 gumballs we set the state to the NoQuarterState.

Now for the actions. These are VERY EASY to implement now. We just delegate to the current state.

Note that we don't need an action method for dispense() in GumballMachine because it's just an internal action; a user can't ask the machine to dispense directly. But we do call dispense() on the State object from the turnCrank() method.

This method allows other objects (like our State objects) to transition the machine to a different state.

The machine supports a releaseBall() helper method that releases the ball and decrements the count instance variable.

This includes methods like getNoQuarterState() for getting each state object, and getCount() for getting the gumball count.

Implementing more states

Now that you're starting to get a feel for how the Gumball Machine and the states
fit together, let's implement the HasQuarterState and the SoldState classes...

```java
public class HasQuarterState implements State {
    GumballMachine gumballMachine;

    public HasQuarterState(GumballMachine gumballMachine) {
        this.gumballMachine = gumballMachine;
    }

    public void insertQuarter() {
        System.out.println("You can't insert another quarter");
    }

    public void ejectQuarter() {
        System.out.println("Quarter returned");
        gumballMachine.setState(gumballMachine.getNoQuarterState());
    }

    public void turnCrank() {
        System.out.println("You turned...");
        gumballMachine.setState(gumballMachine.getSoldState());
    }
    public void dispense() {
        System.out.println("No gumball dispensed");
    }
}
```

When the state is instantiated
we pass it a reference to the
GumballMachine. This is used
to transition the machine to a
different state.

An inappropriate
action for this
state.

Return the customer's
quarter and
transition back to the
NoQuarterState.

When the crank is
turned we transition
the machine to the
SoldState state by
calling its setState()
method and passing it
the SoldState object.
The SoldState object
is retrieved by the
getSoldState()
getter method
(there is one of these
getter methods for
each state).

Another
inappropriate
action for this
state.

Now, let's check out the SoldState class...

Here are all the inappropriate actions for this state

```java
public class SoldState implements State {
    //constructor and instance variables here

    public void insertQuarter() {
        System.out.println("Please wait, we're already giving you a gumball");
    }

    public void ejectQuarter() {
        System.out.println("Sorry, you already turned the crank");
    }

    public void turnCrank() {
        System.out.println("Turning twice doesn't get you another gumball!");
    }

    public void dispense() {
        gumballMachine.releaseBall();
        if (gumballMachine.getCount() > 0) {
            gumballMachine.setState(gumballMachine.getNoQuarterState());
        } else {
            System.out.println("Oops, out of gumballs!");
            gumballMachine.setState(gumballMachine.getSoldOutState());
        }
    }
}
```

And here's where the real work begins...

We're in the SoldState, which means the customer paid. So, we first need to ask the machine to release a gumball.

Then we ask the machine what the gumball count is, and either transition to the NoQuarterState or the SoldOutState.

BRAIN POWER

Look back at the GumballMachine implementation. If the crank is turned and not successful (say the customer didn't insert a quarter first), we call dispense anyway, even though it's unnecessary. How might you fix this?

Sharpen your pencil

We have one remaining class we haven't implemented: SoldOutState. Why don't you implement it? To do this, carefully think through how the Gumball Machine should behave in each situation. Check your answer before moving on...

```java
public class SoldOutState implements [          ] {
    GumballMachine gumballMachine;

    public SoldOutState(GumballMachine gumballMachine) {


    }

    public void insertQuarter() {


    }

    public void ejectQuarter() {


    }

    public void turnCrank() {



    }

    public void dispense() {



    }
}
```

Let's take a look at what we've done so far...

For starters, you now have a Gumball Machine implementation that is *structurally* quite different from your first version, and yet *functionally it is exactly the same*. By structurally changing the implemention you've:

- Localized the behavior of each state into its own class.

- Removed all the troublesome **if** statements that would have been difficult to maintain.

- Closed each state for modification, and yet left the Gumball Machine open to extension by adding new state classes (and we'll do this in a second).

- Created a code base and class structure that maps much more closely to the Mighty Gumball diagram and is easier to read and understand.

Now let's look a little more at the functional aspect of what we did:

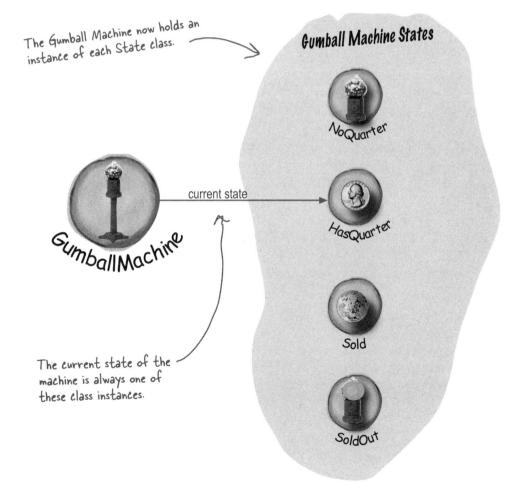

The Gumball Machine now holds an instance of each State class.

Gumball Machine States

NoQuarter

current state

HasQuarter

GumballMachine

The current state of the machine is always one of these class instances.

Sold

SoldOut

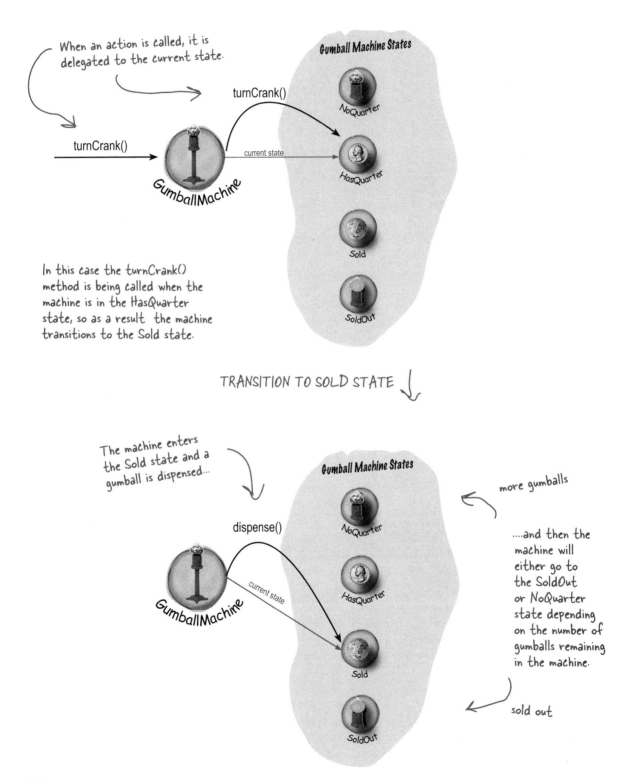

When an action is called, it is delegated to the current state.

turnCrank()

turnCrank()

GumballMachine

current state

Gumball Machine States

NoQuarter

HasQuarter

Sold

SoldOut

In this case the turnCrank() method is being called when the machine is in the HasQuarter state, so as a result the machine transitions to the Sold state.

TRANSITION TO SOLD STATE

The machine enters the Sold state and a gumball is dispensed...

dispense()

GumballMachine

current state

Gumball Machine States

NoQuarter

HasQuarter

Sold

SoldOut

more gumballs

....and then the machine will either go to the SoldOut or NoQuarter state depending on the number of gumballs remaining in the machine.

sold out

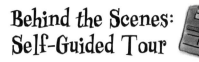

Sharpen your pencil

Behind the Scenes: Self-Guided Tour

Trace the steps of the Gumball Machine starting with the NoQuarter state. Also annotate the diagram with actions and output of the machine. For this exercise you can assume there are plenty of gumballs in the machine.

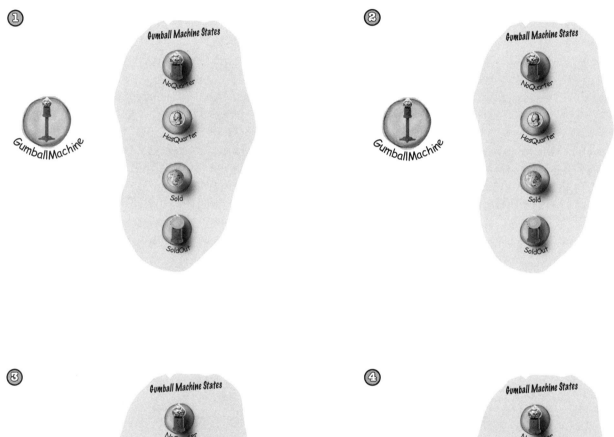

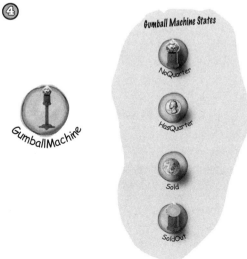

The State Pattern defined

Yes, it's true, we just implemented the State Pattern! So now, let's take a look at what it's all about:

> **The State Pattern** allows an object to alter its behavior when its internal state changes. The object will appear to change its class.

The first part of this description makes a lot of sense, right? Because the pattern encapsulates state into separate classes and delegates to the object representing the current state, we know that behavior changes along with the internal state. The Gumball Machine provides a good example: when the gumball machine is in the NoQuarterState and you insert a quarter, you get different behavior (the machine accepts the quarter) than if you insert a quarter when it's in the HasQuarterState (the machine rejects the quarter).

What about the second part of the definition? What does it mean for an object to "appear to change its class?" Think about it from the perspective of a client: if an object you're using can completely change its behavior, then it appears to you that the object is actually instantiated from another class. In reality, however, you know that we are using composition to give the appearance of a class change by simply referencing different state objects.

Okay, now it's time to check out the State Pattern class diagram:

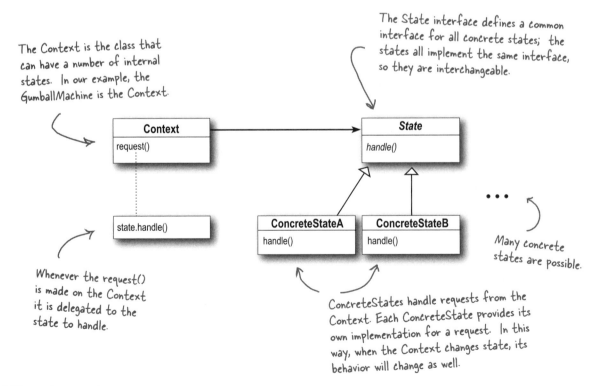

The Context is the class that can have a number of internal states. In our example, the GumballMachine is the Context.

The State interface defines a common interface for all concrete states; the states all implement the same interface, so they are interchangeable.

Context
request()

State
handle()

state.handle()

Whenever the request() is made on the Context it is delegated to the state to handle.

ConcreteStateA
handle()

ConcreteStateB
handle()

Many concrete states are possible.

ConcreteStates handle requests from the Context. Each ConcreteState provides its own implementation for a request. In this way, when the Context changes state, its behavior will change as well.

Wait a sec, from what I remember of the Strategy Pattern, this class diagram is EXACTLY the same.

You've got a good eye! Yes, the class diagrams are essentially the same, but the two patterns differ in their *intent*.

With the State Pattern, we have a set of behaviors encapsulated in state objects; at any time the context is delegating to one of those states. Over time, the current state changes across the set of state objects to reflect the internal state of the context, so the context's behavior changes over time as well. The client usually knows very little, if anything, about the state objects.

With Strategy, the client usually specifies the strategy object that the context is composed with. Now, while the pattern provides the flexibility to change the strategy object at runtime, often there is a strategy object that is most appropriate for a context object. For instance, in Chapter 1, some of our ducks were configured to fly with typical flying behavior (like mallard ducks), while others were configured with a fly behavior that kept them grounded (like rubber ducks and decoy ducks).

In general, think of the Strategy Pattern as a flexible alternative to subclassing; if you use inheritance to define the behavior of a class, then you're stuck with that behavior even if you need to change it. With Strategy you can change the behavior by composing with a different object.

Think of the State Pattern as an alternative to putting lots of conditionals in your context; by encapsulating the behaviors within state objects, you can simply change the state object in context to change its behavior.

there are no
Dumb Questions

Q: In the GumballMachine, the states decide what the next state should be. Do the ConcreteStates always decide what state to go to next?

A: No, not always. The alternative is to let the Context decide on the flow of state transitions.

As a general guideline, when the state transitions are fixed they are appropriate for putting in the Context; however, when the transitions are more dynamic, they are typically placed in the state classes themselves (for instance, in the GumballMachine the choice of the transition to NoQuarter or SoldOut depended on the runtime count of gumballs).

The disadvantage of having state transitions in the state classes is that we create dependencies between the state classes. In our implementation of the GumballMachine we tried to minimize this by using getter methods on the Context, rather than hardcoding explicit concrete state classes.

Notice that by making this decision, you are making a decision as to which classes are closed for modification – the Context or the state classes – as the system evolves.

Q: Do clients ever interact directly with the states?

A: No. The states are used by the Context to represent its internal state and behavior, so all requests to the states come from the Context. Clients don't directly change the state of the Context. It is the Context's job to oversee its state, and you don't usually want a client changing the state of a Context without that Context's knowledge.

Q: If I have lots of instances of the Context in my application, is it possible to share the state objects across them?

A: Yes, absolutely, and in fact this is a very common scenario. The only requirement is that your state objects do not keep their own internal state; otherwise, you'd need a unique instance per context.

To share your states, you'll typically assign each state to a static instance variable. If your state needs to make use of methods or instance variables in your Context, you'll also have to give it a reference to the Context in each handler() method.

Q: It seems like using the State Pattern always increases the number of classes in our designs. Look how many more classes our GumballMachine had than the original design!

A: You're right, by encapsulating state behavior into separate state classes, you'll always end up with more classes in your design. That's often the price you pay for flexibility. Unless your code is some "one off" implementation you're going to throw away (yeah, right), consider building it with the additional classes and you'll probably thank yourself down the road. Note that often what is important is the number of classes that you expose to your clients, and there are ways to hide these extra classes from your clients (say, by declaring them package visible).

Also, consider the alternative: if you have an application that has a lot of state and you decide not to use separate objects, you'll instead end up with very large, monolithic conditional statements. This makes your code hard to maintain and understand. By using objects, you make states explicit and reduce the effort needed to understand and maintain your code.

Q: The State Pattern class diagram shows that State is an abstract class. But didn't you use an interface in the implementation of the gumball machine's state?

A: Yes. Given we had no common functionality to put into an abstract class, we went with an interface. In your own implementation, you might want to consider an abstract class. Doing so has the benefit of allowing you to add methods to the abstract class later, without breaking the concrete state implementations.

We still need to finish the Gumball 1 in 10 game

Remember, we're not done yet. We've got a game to implement; but now that we've got the State Pattern implemented, it should be a breeze. First, we need to add a state to the GumballMachine class:

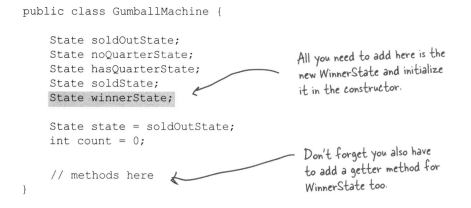

```
public class GumballMachine {

    State soldOutState;
    State noQuarterState;
    State hasQuarterState;
    State soldState;
    State winnerState;

    State state = soldOutState;
    int count = 0;

    // methods here
}
```

All you need to add here is the new WinnerState and initialize it in the constructor.

Don't forget you also have to add a getter method for WinnerState too.

Now let's implement the WinnerState class itself, it's remarkably similar to the SoldState class:

```
public class WinnerState implements State {

    // instance variables and constructor

    // insertQuarter error message

    // ejectQuarter error message

    // turnCrank error message

    public void dispense() {
        System.out.println("YOU'RE A WINNER! You get two gumballs for your quarter");
        gumballMachine.releaseBall();
        if (gumballMachine.getCount() == 0) {
            gumballMachine.setState(gumballMachine.getSoldOutState());
        } else {
            gumballMachine.releaseBall();
            if (gumballMachine.getCount() > 0) {
                gumballMachine.setState(gumballMachine.getNoQuarterState());
            } else {
                System.out.println("Oops, out of gumballs!");
                gumballMachine.setState(gumballMachine.getSoldOutState());
            }
        }
    }
}
```

Just like SoldState.

Here we release two gumballs and then either go to the NoQuarterState or the SoldOutState.

As long as we have a second gumball we release it.

Finishing the game

We've just got one more change to make: we need to implement the random
chance game and add a transition to the WinnerState. We're going to add both to
the HasQuarterState since that is where the customer turns the crank:

```java
public class HasQuarterState implements State {
    Random randomWinner = new Random(System.currentTimeMillis());
    GumballMachine gumballMachine;

    public HasQuarterState(GumballMachine gumballMachine) {
        this.gumballMachine = gumballMachine;
    }

    public void insertQuarter() {
        System.out.println("You can't insert another quarter");
    }

    public void ejectQuarter() {
        System.out.println("Quarter returned");
        gumballMachine.setState(gumballMachine.getNoQuarterState());
    }

    public void turnCrank() {
        System.out.println("You turned...");
        int winner = randomWinner.nextInt(10);
        if ((winner == 0) && (gumballMachine.getCount() > 1)) {
            gumballMachine.setState(gumballMachine.getWinnerState());
        } else {
            gumballMachine.setState(gumballMachine.getSoldState());
        }
    }
    public void dispense() {
        System.out.println("No gumball dispensed");
    }
}
```

First we add a random number generator to generate the 10% chance of winning...

...then we determine if this customer won.

If they won, and there's enough gumballs left for them to get two, we go to the WinnerState; otherwise, we go to the SoldState (just like we always did).

Wow, that was pretty simple to implement! We just added a new state to the GumballMachine
and then implemented it. All we had to do from there was to implement our chance game and
transition to the correct state. It looks like our new code strategy is paying off...

Demo for the CEO of Mighty Gumball, Inc.

The CEO of Mighty Gumball has dropped by for a demo of your new gumball game code. Let's hope those states are all in order! We'll keep the demo short and sweet (the short attention span of CEOs is well documented), but hopefully long enough so that we'll win at least once.

This code really hasn't changed at all; we just shortened it a bit.

Once, again, start with a gumball machine with 5 gumballs.

```java
public class GumballMachineTestDrive {
    public static void main(String[] args) {
        GumballMachine gumballMachine = new GumballMachine(5);

        System.out.println(gumballMachine);

        gumballMachine.insertQuarter();
        gumballMachine.turnCrank();

        System.out.println(gumballMachine);

        gumballMachine.insertQuarter();
        gumballMachine.turnCrank();
        gumballMachine.insertQuarter();
        gumballMachine.turnCrank();

        System.out.println(gumballMachine);
    }
}
```

We want to get a winning state, so we just keep pumping in those quarters and turning the crank. We print out the state of the gumball machine every so often...

The whole engineering team is waiting outside the conference room to see if the new State Pattern-based design is going to work!!

Yes! That rocks!

```
File Edit Window Help Whenisagumballajawbreaker?
%java GumballMachineTestDrive
Mighty Gumball, Inc.
Java-enabled Standing Gumball Model #2004
Inventory: 5 gumballs
Machine is waiting for quarter

You inserted a quarter
You turned...
YOU'RE A WINNER! You get two gumballs for your quarter
A gumball comes rolling out the slot...
A gumball comes rolling out the slot...

Mighty Gumball, Inc.
Java-enabled Standing Gumball Model #2004
Inventory: 3 gumballs
Machine is waiting for quarter

You inserted a quarter
You turned...
A gumball comes rolling out the slot...
You inserted a quarter
You turned...
YOU'RE A WINNER! You get two gumballs for your quarter
A gumball comes rolling out the slot...
A gumball comes rolling out the slot...
Oops, out of gumballs!

Mighty Gumball, Inc.
Java-enabled Standing Gumball Model #2004
Inventory: 0 gumballs
Machine is sold out
%
```

Gee, did we get lucky or what? In our demo to the CEO, we won not once, but twice!

there are no
Dumb Questions

Q: Why do we need the WinnerState? Couldn't we just have the SoldState dispense two gumballs?

A: That's a great question. SoldState and WinnerState are almost identical, except that WinnerState dispenses two gumballs instead of one. You certainly could put the code to dispense two gumballs into the SoldState. The downside is, of course, that now you've got TWO states represented in one State class: the state in which you're a winner, and the state in which you're not. So you are sacrificing clarity in your State class to reduce code duplication. Another thing to consider is the principle you learned in the previous chapter: One class, One responsibility. By putting the WinnerState responsibility into the SoldState, you've just given the SoldState TWO responsibilities. What happens when the promotion ends? Or the stakes of the contest change? So, it's a tradeoff and comes down to a design decision.

> Bravo! Great job, gang. Our sales are already going through the roof with the new game. You know, we also make soda machines, and I was thinking we could put one of those slot machine arms on the side and make that a game too. We've got four year olds gambling with the gumball machines; why stop there?

Sanity check...

Yes, the CEO of Mighty Gumball probably needs a sanity check, but that's not what we're talking about here. Let's think through some aspects of the GumballMachine that we might want to shore up before we ship the gold version:

- We've got a lot of duplicate code in the Sold and Winning states and we might want to clean those up. How would we do it? We could make State into an abstract class and build in some default behavior for the methods; after all, error messages like, "You already inserted a quarter," aren't going to be seen by the customer. So all "error response" behavior could be generic and inherited from the abstract State class.

    Dammit Jim, I'm a gumball machine, not a computer!

- The dispense() method always gets called, even if the crank is turned when there is no quarter. While the machine operates correctly and doesn't dispense unless it's in the right state, we could easily fix this by having turnCrank() return a boolean, or by introducing exceptions. Which do you think is a better solution?

- All of the intelligence for the state transitions is in the State classes. What problems might this cause? Would we want to move that logic into the Gumball Machine? What would be the advantages and disadvantages of that?

- Will you be instantiating a lot of GumballMachine objects? If so, you may want to move the state instances into static instance variables and share them. What changes would this require to the GumballMachine and the States?

Fireside Chats

Tonight: **A Strategy and State Pattern Reunion.**

Strategy

Hey bro. Did you hear I was in Chapter 1?

I was just over giving the Template Method guys a hand – they needed me to help them finish off their chapter. So, anyway, what is my noble brother up to?

I don't know, you always sound like you've just copied what I do and you're using different words to describe it. Think about it: I allow objects to incorporate different behaviors or algorithms through composition and delegation. You're just copying me.

Oh yeah? How so? I don't get it.

Yeah, that was some *fine* work... and I'm sure you can see how that's more powerful than inheriting your behavior, right?

Sorry, you're going to have to explain that.

State

Yeah, word is definitely getting around.

Same as always – helping classes to exhibit different behaviors in different states.

I admit that what we do is definitely related, but my intent is totally different than yours. And, the way I teach my clients to use composition and delegation is totally different.

Well if you spent a little more time thinking about something other than *yourself*, you might. Anyway, think about how you work: you have a class you're instantiating and you usually give it a strategy object that implements some behavior. Like, in Chapter 1 you were handing out quack behaviors, right? Real ducks got a real quack, rubber ducks got a quack that squeaked.

Yes, of course. Now, think about how I work; it's totally different.

Strategy

Hey, come on, I can change behavior at runtime too; that's what composition is all about!

Well, I admit, I don't encourage my objects to have a well-defined set of transitions between states. In fact, I typically like to control what strategy my objects are using.

Yeah, yeah, keep living your pipe dreams brother. You act like you're a big pattern like me, but check it out: I'm in Chapter 1; they stuck you way out in Chapter 10. I mean, how many people are actually going to read this far?

That's my brother, always the dreamer.

State

Okay, when my Context objects get created, I may tell them the state to start in, but then they change their own state over time.

Sure you can, but the way I work is built around discrete states; my Context objects change state over time according to some well defined state transitions. In other words, changing behavior is built in to my scheme – it's how I work!

Look, we've already said we're alike in structure, but what we do is quite different in intent. Face it, the world has uses for both of us.

Are you kidding? This is a Head First book and Head First readers rock. Of course they're going to get to Chapter 10!

We almost forgot!

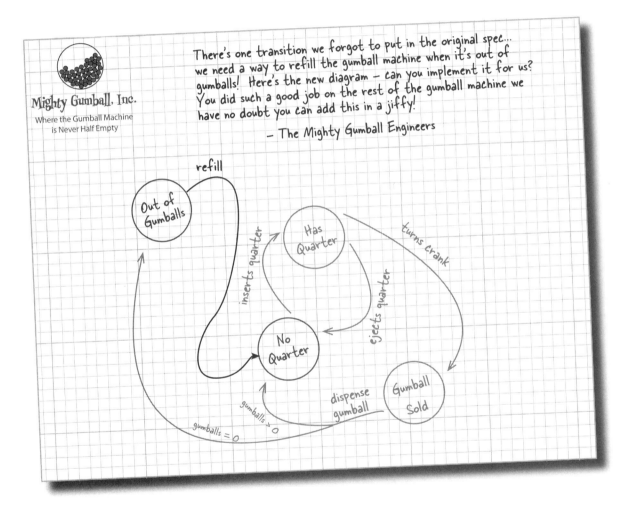

There's one transition we forgot to put in the original spec...
we need a way to refill the gumball machine when it's out of
gumballs! Here's the new diagram — can you implement it for us?
You did such a good job on the rest of the gumball machine we
have no doubt you can add this in a jiffy!

— The Mighty Gumball Engineers

Sharpen your pencil

We need you to write the refill() method for the Gumball machine. It has one argument – the number of gumballs you're adding to the machine – and should update the gumball machine count and reset the machine's state.

> You've done some amazing work! I've got some more ideas that are going to change the gumball industry and I need you to implement them. Shhhhh! I'll let you in on these ideas in the next chapter.

WHO DOES WHAT?

Match each pattern with its description:

Pattern	Description
State	Encapsulate interchangeable behaviors and use delegation to decide which behavior to use
Strategy	Subclasses decide how to implement steps in an algorithm
Template Method	Encapsulate state-based behavior and delegate behavior to the current state

Tools for your Design Toolbox

It's the end of another chapter; you've got enough patterns here to breeze through any job interview!

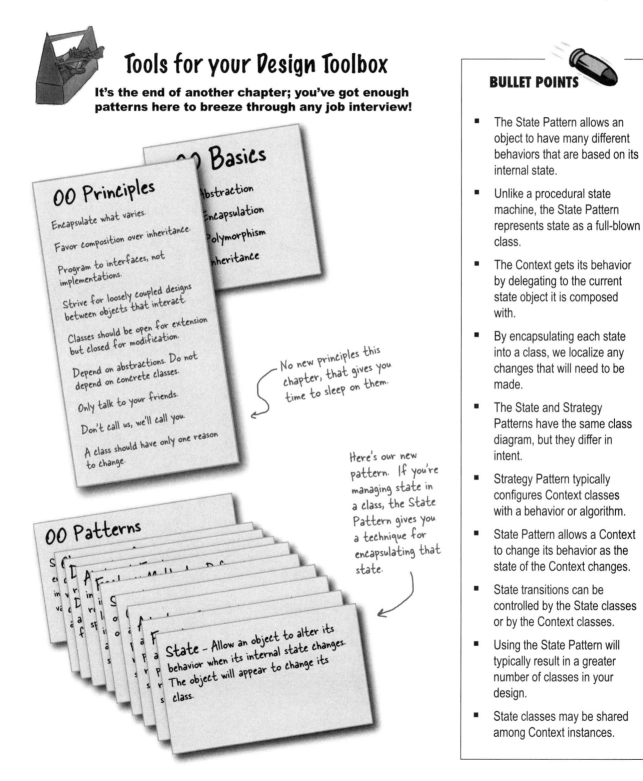

OO Basics

Abstraction

Encapsulation

Polymorphism

Inheritance

OO Principles

Encapsulate what varies.

Favor composition over inheritance.

Program to interfaces, not implementations.

Strive for loosely coupled designs between objects that interact.

Classes should be open for extension but closed for modification.

Depend on abstractions. Do not depend on concrete classes.

Only talk to your friends.

Don't call us, we'll call you.

A class should have only one reason to change.

No new principles this chapter, that gives you time to sleep on them.

Here's our new pattern. If you're managing state in a class, the State Pattern gives you a technique for encapsulating that state.

OO Patterns

State – Allow an object to alter its behavior when its internal state changes. The object will appear to change its class.

Exercise solutions

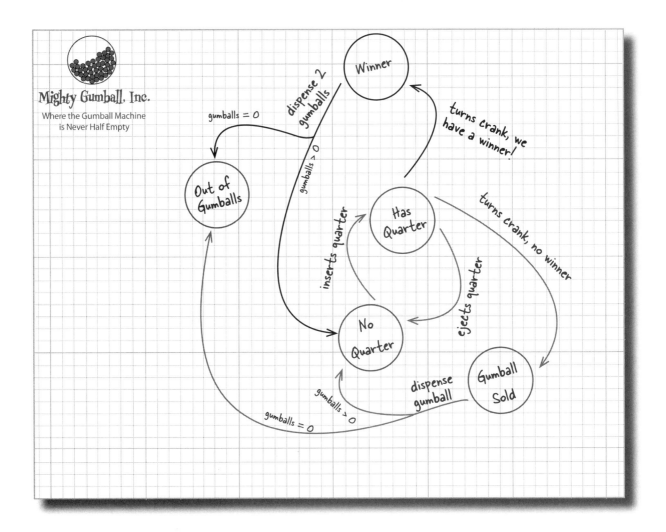

Exercise solutions

Sharpen your pencil

Based on our first implementation, which of the following apply?
(Choose all that apply.)

☑ A. This code certainly isn't adhering to the
Open Closed Principle!

☑ B. This code would make a FORTRAN
programmer proud.

☑ C. This design isn't even very object
oriented.

☑ C. State transitions aren't explicit; they
are buried in the middle of a bunch of
conditional code.

☑ D. We haven't encapsulated anything that
varies here.

☑ E. Further additions are likely to cause bugs
in working code.

Sharpen your pencil

We have one remaining class we haven't implemented: SoldOutState.
Why don't you implement it? To do this, carefully think through how
the Gumball Machine should behave in each situation. Check your
answer before moving on...

In the Sold Out state, we really can't do anything until someone refills the Gumball Machine.

```java
public class SoldOutState implements State {
    GumballMachine gumballMachine;

    public SoldOutState(GumballMachine gumballMachine) {
        this.gumballMachine = gumballMachine;
    }

    public void insertQuarter() {
        System.out.println("You can't insert a quarter, the machine is sold out");
    }

    public void ejectQuarter() {
        System.out.println("You can't eject, you haven't inserted a quarter yet");
    }

    public void turnCrank() {
        System.out.println("You turned, but there are no gumballs");
    }

    public void dispense() {
        System.out.println("No gumball dispensed");
    }

}
```

Sharpen your pencil

To implement the states, we first need to define what the behavior will be when the corresponding action is called. Annotate the diagram below with the behavior of each action in each class; we've already filled in a few for you.

Go to HasQuarterState

Tell the customer "you haven't inserted a quarter"

Tell the customer "you turned, but there's no quarter"

Tell the customer "you need to pay first"

NoQuarterState

insertQuarter()
ejectQuarter()
turnCrank()
dispense()

Tell the customer "you can't insert another quarter"

Give back quarter, go to No Quarter state

Go to SoldState

Tell the customer, "no gumball dispensed"

HasQuarterState

insertQuarter()
ejectQuarter()
turnCrank()
dispense()

Tell the customer "please wait, we're already giving you a gumball"

Tell the customer "sorry, you already turned the crank"

Tell the customer "turning twice doesn't get you another gumball"

Dispense one gumball. Check number of gumballs; if > 0, go to NoQuarter state, otherwise, go to Sold Out state

SoldState

insertQuarter()
ejectQuarter()
turnCrank()
dispense()

Tell the customer "the machine is sold out"

Tell the customer "you haven't inserted a quarter yet"

Tell the customer "There are no gumballs"

Tell the customer "no gumball dispensed"

SoldOutState

insertQuarter()
ejectQuarter()
turnCrank()
dispense()

Tell the customer "please wait, we're already giving you a gumball"

Tell the customer "sorry, you already turned the crank"

Tell the customer "turning twice doesn't get you another gumball"

Dispense two gumballs. Check number of gumballs; if > 0, go to NoQuarter state, otherwise, go to SoldOutState

WinnerState

insertQuarter()
ejectQuarter()
turnCrank()
dispense()

Behind the Scenes: Self-Guided Tour Solution

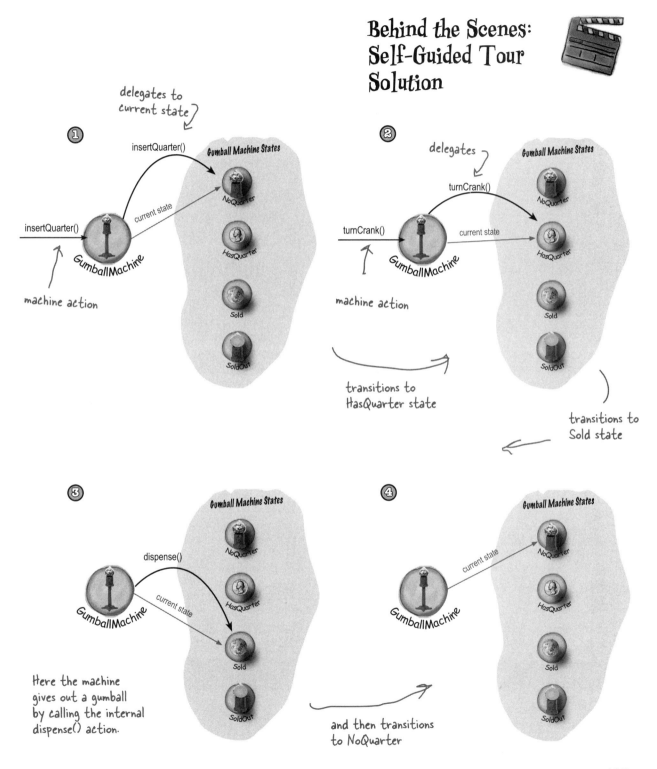

① insertQuarter()

delegates to current state

Gumball Machine States

insertQuarter()

current state

GumballMachine

machine action

NoQuarter

HasQuarter

Sold

SoldOut

② delegates

turnCrank()

Gumball Machine States

turnCrank()

current state

GumballMachine

machine action

NoQuarter

HasQuarter

Sold

SoldOut

transitions to HasQuarter state

transitions to Sold state

③ dispense()

Gumball Machine States

current state

GumballMachine

Here the machine gives out a gumball by calling the internal dispense() action.

NoQuarter

HasQuarter

Sold

SoldOut

④ current state

GumballMachine

Gumball Machine States

NoQuarter

HasQuarter

Sold

SoldOut

and then transitions to NoQuarter

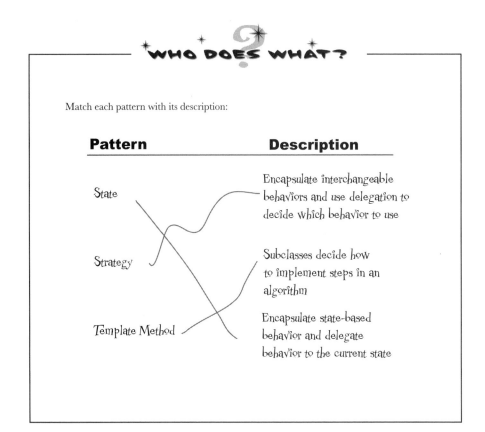

WHO DOES WHAT?

Match each pattern with its description:

Pattern	Description
State	Encapsulate interchangeable behaviors and use delegation to decide which behavior to use
Strategy	Subclasses decide how to implement steps in an algorithm
Template Method	Encapsulate state-based behavior and delegate behavior to the current state

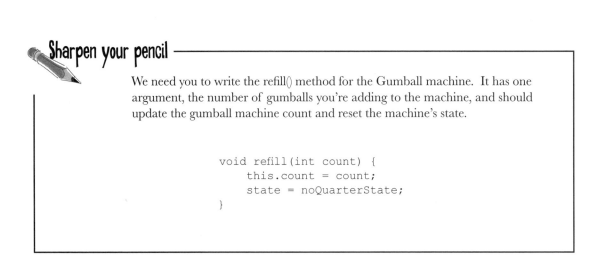

Sharpen your pencil

We need you to write the refill() method for the Gumball machine. It has one argument, the number of gumballs you're adding to the machine, and should update the gumball machine count and reset the machine's state.

```
void refill(int count) {
    this.count = count;
    state = noQuarterState;
}
```

11 the Proxy Pattern

Controlling Object Access

With you as my Proxy, I'll be able to triple the amount of lunch money I can extract from friends!

Ever play good cop, bad cop? You're the good cop and you provide all your services in a nice and friendly manner, but you don't want *everyone* asking you for services, so you have the bad cop *control access* to you. That's what proxies do: control and manage access. As you're going to see, there are *lots* of ways in which proxies stand in for the objects they proxy. Proxies have been known to haul entire method calls over the Internet for their proxied objects; they've also been known to patiently stand in the place for some pretty lazy objects.

Hey team, I'd
really like to get
some better monitoring for
my gumball machines. Can you
find a way to get me a report of
inventory and machine state?

Remember the CEO of
Mighty Gumball, Inc.?

Sounds easy enough. If you remember, we've already
got methods in the gumball machine code for getting the
count of gumballs (getCount()), and getting the current
state of the machine (getState()).

All we need to do is create a report that can be printed out
and sent back to the CEO. Hmmm, we should probably
add a location field to each gumball machine as well; that
way the CEO can keep the machines straight.

Let's just jump in and code this. We'll impress the CEO
with a very fast turnaround.

Coding the Monitor

Let's start by adding support to the GumballMachine class so that it can handle locations:

```java
public class GumballMachine {
    // other instance variables
    String location;

    public GumballMachine(String location, int count) {
        // other constructor code here
        this.location = location;
    }

    public String getLocation() {
        return location;
    }

    // other methods here
}
```

A location is just a String.

The location is passed into the constructor and stored in the instance variable.

Let's also add a getter method to grab the location when we need it.

Now let's create another class, GumballMonitor, that retrieves the machine's location, inventory of gumballs and the current machine state and prints them in a nice little report:

```java
public class GumballMonitor {
    GumballMachine machine;

    public GumballMonitor(GumballMachine machine) {
        this.machine = machine;
    }

    public void report() {
        System.out.println("Gumball Machine: " + machine.getLocation());
        System.out.println("Current inventory: " + machine.getCount() + " gumballs");
        System.out.println("Current state: " + machine.getState());
    }
}
```

The monitor takes the machine in its constructor and assigns it to the machine instance variable.

Our report method just prints a report with location, inventory and the machine's state.

Testing the Monitor

We implemented that in no time. The CEO is going to be thrilled and amazed by our development skills.

Now we just need to instantiate a GumballMonitor and give it a machine to monitor:

```java
public class GumballMachineTestDrive {
    public static void main(String[] args) {
        int count = 0;

        if (args.length < 2) {
            System.out.println("GumballMachine <name> <inventory>");
            System.exit(1);
        }

        count = Integer.parseInt(args[1]);
        GumballMachine gumballMachine = new GumballMachine(args[0], count);

        GumballMonitor monitor = new GumballMonitor(gumballMachine);


        // rest of test code here

        monitor.report();
    }
}
```

Pass in a location and initial # of gumballs on the command line.

Don't forget to give the constructor a location and count...

...and instantiate a monitor and pass it a machine to provide a report on.

When we need a report on the machine, we call the report() method.

```
File  Edit  Window  Help  FlyingFish
%java GumballMachineTestDrive Seattle 112

Gumball Machine: Seattle
Current Inventory: 112 gumballs
Current State: waiting for quarter
```

And here's the output!

> The monitor output looks great, but I guess I wasn't clear. I need to monitor gumball machines REMOTELY! In fact, we already have the networks in place for monitoring. Come on guys, you're supposed to be the Internet generation!

Joe: A remote what?

Frank: *Remote proxy*. Think about it: we've already got the monitor code written, right? We give the GumballMonitor a reference to a machine and it gives us a report. The problem is that monitor runs in the same JVM as the gumball machine and the CEO wants to sit at his desk and *remotely* monitor the machines! So what if we left our GumballMonitor class as is, but handed it a proxy to a *remote* object?

Joe: I'm not sure I get it.

Jim: Me neither.

Frank: Let's start at the beginning... a proxy is a stand in for a *real* object. In this case, the proxy acts just like it is a Gumball Machine object, but behind the scenes it is communicating over the network to talk to the real, remote GumballMachine.

Jim: So you're saying we keep our code as it is, and we give the monitor a reference to a proxy version of the GumballMachine...

Joe: And this proxy pretends it's the real object, but it's really just communicating over the net to the real object.

Frank: Yeah, that's pretty much the story.

Joe: It sounds like something that is easier said than done.

Frank: Perhaps, but I don't think it'll be that bad. We have to make sure that the gumball machine can act as a service and accept requests over the network; we also need to give our monitor a way to get a reference to a proxy object, but we've got some great tools already built into Java to help us. Let's talk a little more about remote proxies first...

The role of the 'remote proxy'

A remote proxy acts as a *local representative to a remote object*. What's a "remote object?" It's an object that lives in the heap of a different Java Virtual Machine (or more generally, a remote object that is running in a different address space). What's a "local representative?" It's an object that you can call local methods on and have them forwarded on to the remote object.

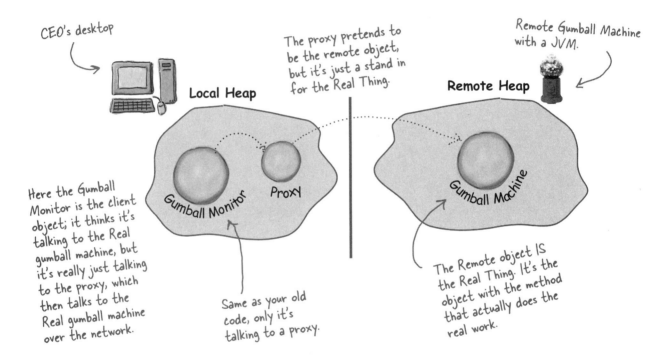

CEO's desktop

The proxy pretends to be the remote object, but it's just a stand in for the Real Thing.

Remote Gumball Machine with a JVM.

Local Heap

Remote Heap

Gumball Monitor

Proxy

Gumball Machine

Here the Gumball Monitor is the client object; it thinks it's talking to the Real gumball machine, but it's really just talking to the proxy, which then talks to the Real gumball machine over the network.

Same as your old code, only it's talking to a proxy.

The Remote object IS the Real Thing. It's the object with the method that actually does the real work.

Your client object acts like it's making remote method calls. But what it's really doing is calling methods on a heap-local 'proxy' object that handles all the low-level details of network communication.

This is a pretty slick idea. We're going to write some code that takes a method invocation, somehow transfers it over the network and invokes the same method on a remote object. Then I presume when the call is complete, the result gets sent back over the network to our client. But it seems to me this code is going to be very tricky to write.

Hold on now, we aren't going to write that code ourselves, it's pretty much built into Java's remote invocation functionality. All we have to do is retrofit our code so that it takes advantage of RMI.

BRAIN POWER

Before going further, think about how you'd design a system to enable remote method invocation. How would you make it easy on the developer so that she has to write as little code as possible? How would you make the remote invocation look seamless?

BRAIN² POWER

Should making remote calls be totally transparent? Is that a good idea? What might be a problem with that approach?

Adding a remote proxy to the Gumball Machine monitoring code

On paper this looks good, but how do we create a proxy that knows how to invoke a method on an object that lives in another JVM?

Hmmm. Well, you can't get a reference to something on another heap, right? In other words, you can't say:

```
Duck d = <object in another heap>
```

Whatever the variable **d** is referencing must be in the same heap space as the code running the statement. So how do we approach this? Well, that's where Java's Remote Method Invocation comes in... RMI gives us a way to find objects in a remote JVM and allows us to invoke their methods.

You may have encountered RMI in Head First Java; if not, we're going to take a slight detour and come up to speed on RMI before adding the proxy support to the Gumball Machine code.

So, here's what we're going to do:

❶ **First, we're going to take the RMI Detour and check RMI out. Even if you are familiar with RMI, you might want to follow along and check out the scenery.**

An RMI Detour

If you're new to RMI, take the detour that runs over the next few pages; otherwise, you might want to just quickly thumb through the detour as a review.

❷ **Then we're going to take our GumballMachine and make it a remote service that provides a set of methods calls that can be invoked remotely.**

❸ **Then, we going to create a proxy that can talk to a remote GumballMachine, again using RMI, and put the monitoring system back together so that the CEO can monitor any number of remote machines.**

Remote methods 101

Let's say we want to design a system that allows us to call a local object that forwards each request to a remote object. How would we design it? We'd need a couple of helper objects that actually do the communicating for us. The helpers make it possible for the client to act as though it's calling a method on a local object (which in fact, it is). The client calls a method on the client helper, as if the client helper were the actual service. The client helper then takes care of forwarding that request for us.

In other words, the client object thinks it's calling a method on the remote service, because the client helper is pretending to be the service object. Pretending to be the thing with the method the client wants to call.

But the client helper isn't really the remote service. Although the client helper acts like it (because it has the same method that the service is advertising), the client helper doesn't have any of the actual method logic the client is expecting. Instead, the client helper contacts the server, transfers information about the method call (e.g., name of the method, arguments, etc.), and waits for a return from the server.

On the server side, the service helper receives the request from the client helper (through a Socket connection), unpacks the information about the call, and then invokes the real method on the real service object. So, to the service object, the call is local. It's coming from the service helper, not a remote client.

The service helper gets the return value from the service, packs it up, and ships it back (over a Socket's output stream) to the client helper. The client helper unpacks the information and returns the value to the client object.

This should look familiar...

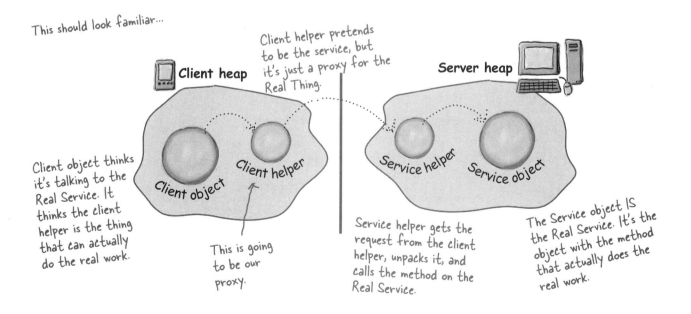

How the method call happens

① Client object calls doBigThing() on the client helper object.

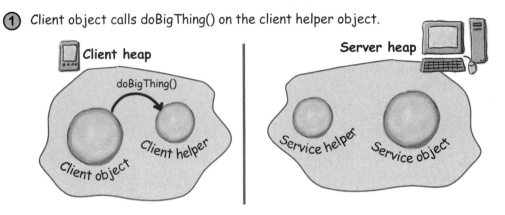

② Client helper packages up information about the call (arguments, method name, etc.) and ships it over the network to the service helper.

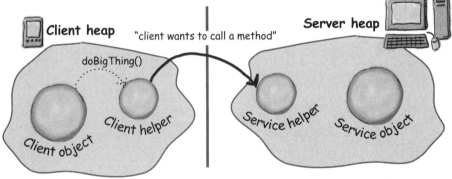

③ Service helper unpacks the information from the client helper, finds out which method to call (and on which object) and invokes the <u>real</u> method on the <u>real</u> service object.

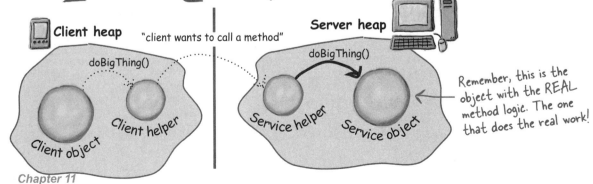

Remember, this is the object with the REAL method logic. The one that does the real work!

An RMI Detour

④ The method is invoked on the service object, which returns some result to the service helper.

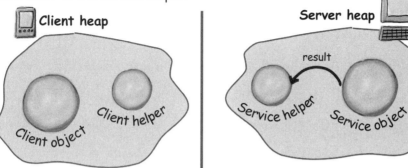

⑤ Service helper packages up information returned from the call and ships it back over the network to the client helper.

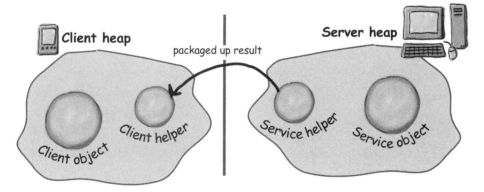

⑥ Client helper unpackages the returned values and returns them to the client object. To the client object, this was all transparent.

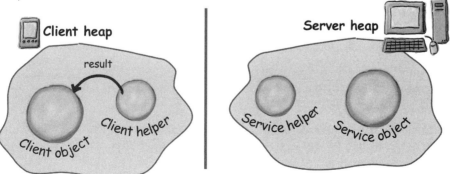

Java RMI, the Big Picture

Okay, you've got the gist of how remote methods work; now you just need to understand how to use RMI to enable remote method invocation.

What RMI does for you is build the client and service helper objects, right down to creating a client helper object with the same methods as the remote service. The nice thing about RMI is that you don't have to write any of the networking or I/O code yourself. With your client, you call remote methods (i.e., the ones the Real Service has) just like normal method calls on objects running in the client's own local JVM.

RMI also provides all the runtime infrastructure to make it all work, including a lookup service that the client can use to find and access the remote objects.

There is one difference between RMI calls and local (normal) method calls. Remember that even though to the client it looks like the method call is local, the client helper sends the method call across the network. So there is networking and I/O. And what do we know about networking and I/O methods?

They're risky! They can fail! And so, they throw exceptions all over the place. As a result, the client does have to acknowledge the risk. We'll see how in a few pages.

RMI Nomenclature: in RMI, the client helper is a 'stub' and the service helper is a 'skeleton'.

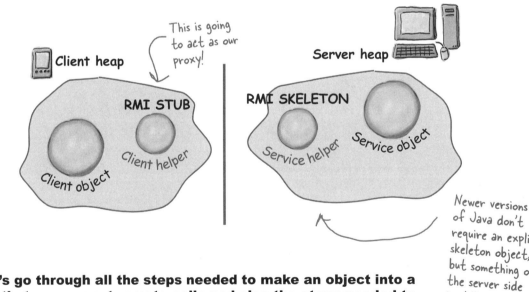

This is going to act as our proxy!

Client heap

RMI STUB

Client helper

Client object

Server heap

RMI SKELETON

Service helper

Service object

Newer versions of Java don't require an explicit skeleton object, but something on the server side is still handling skeleton behavior.

Now let's go through all the steps needed to make an object into a service that can accept remote calls and also the steps needed to allow a client to make remote calls.

You might want to make sure your seat belt is fastened; there are a lot of steps and a few bumps and curves – but nothing to be too worried about.

Making the Remote service

This is an **overview** of the five steps for making the remote service. In other words, the steps needed to take an ordinary object and supercharge it so it can be called by a remote client. We'll be doing this later to our GumballMachine. For now, let's get the steps down and then we'll explain each one in detail.

Step one:

Make a **Remote Interface**

The remote interface defines the methods that a client can call remotely. It's what the client will use as the class type for your service. Both the Stub and actual service will implement this!

MyService.java

← This interface defines the remote methods that you want clients to call.

Step two:

Make a **Remote Implementation**

This is the class that does the Real Work. It has the real implementation of the remote methods defined in the remote interface. It's the object that the client wants to call methods on (e.g., our GumballMachine!).

MyServiceImpl.java

← The Real Service; the class with the methods that do the real work. It implements the remote interface.

Step three:

Generate the **stubs** and **skeletons** using rmic

These are the client and server 'helpers'. You don't have to create these classes or ever look at the source code that generates them. It's all handled automatically when you run the rmic tool that ships with your Java development kit.

Running rmic against the actual service implementation class...

...spits out two new classes for the helper objects.

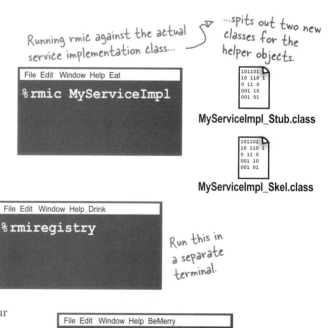

```
File  Edit  Window  Help  Eat
%rmic MyServiceImpl
```

MyServiceImpl_Stub.class

MyServiceImpl_Skel.class

Step four:

Start the **RMI registry** (rmiregistry)

The *rmiregistry* is like the white pages of a phone book. It's where the client goes to get the proxy (the client stub/helper object).

```
File  Edit  Window  Help  Drink
%rmiregistry
```

Run this in a separate terminal.

Step five:

Start the **remote service**

You have to get the service object up and running. Your service implementation class instantiates an instance of the service and registers it with the RMI registry. Registering it makes the service available for clients.

```
File  Edit  Window  Help  BeMerry
%java MyServiceImpl
```

Step one: make a Remote interface

① Extend java.rmi.Remote

Remote is a 'marker' interface, which means it has no methods. It has special meaning for RMI, though, so you must follow this rule. Notice that we say 'extends' here. One interface is allowed to *extend* another interface.

```
public interface MyRemote extends Remote {
```

This tells us that the interface is going to be used to support remote calls.

② Declare that all methods throw a RemoteException

The remote interface is the one the client uses as the type for the service. In other words, the client invokes methods on something that implements the remote interface. That something is the stub, of course, and since the stub is doing networking and I/O, all kinds of Bad Things can happen. The client has to acknowledge the risks by handling or declaring the remote exceptions. If the methods in an interface declare exceptions, any code calling methods on a reference of that type (the interface type) must handle or declare the exceptions.

```
import java.rmi.*;          ← Remote interface is in java.rmi

public interface MyRemote extends Remote {
    public String sayHello() throws RemoteException;
}
```

Every remote method call is considered 'risky'. Declaring RemoteException on every method forces the client to pay attention and acknowledge that things might not work.

③ Be sure arguments and return values are primitives or Serializable

Arguments and return values of a remote method must be either primitive or Serializable. Think about it. Any argument to a remote method has to be packaged up and shipped across the network, and that's done through Serialization. Same thing with return values. If you use primitives, Strings, and the majority of types in the API (including arrays and collections), you'll be fine. If you are passing around your own types, just be sure that you make your classes implement Serializable.

Check out Head First Java if you need to refresh your memory on Serializable.

```
public String sayHello() throws RemoteException;
```

This return value is gonna be shipped over the wire from the server back to the client, so it must be Serializable. That's how args and return values get packaged up and sent.

Step two: make a Remote implementation

An RMI Detour

(1) Implement the Remote interface

Your service has to implement the remote interface—the one with the methods your client is going to call.

```java
public class MyRemoteImpl extends UnicastRemoteObject implements MyRemote {
    public String sayHello() {
        return "Server says, 'Hey'";
    }
    // more code in class
}
```

The compiler will make sure that you've implemented all the methods from the interface you implement. In this case, there's only one.

(2) Extend UnicastRemoteObject

In order to work as a remote service object, your object needs some functionality related to 'being remote'. The simplest way is to extend UnicastRemoteObject (from the java.rmi.server package) and let that class (your superclass) do the work for you.

```java
public class MyRemoteImpl extends UnicastRemoteObject implements MyRemote {
```

(3) Write a no-arg constructor that declares a RemoteException

Your new superclass, UnicastRemoteObject, has one little problem—its constructor throws a RemoteException. The only way to deal with this is to declare a constructor for your remote implementation, just so that you have a place to declare the RemoteException. Remember, when a class is instantiated, its superclass constructor is always called. If your superclass constructor throws an exception, you have no choice but to declare that your constructor also throws an exception.

```java
public MyRemoteImpl() throws RemoteException { }
```

You don't have to put anything in the constructor. You just need a way to declare that your superclass constructor throws an exception.

(4) Register the service with the RMI registry

Now that you've got a remote service, you have to make it available to remote clients. You do this by instantiating it and putting it into the RMI registry (which must be running or this line of code fails). When you register the implementation object, the RMI system actually puts the *stub* in the registry, since that's what the client really needs. Register your service using the static rebind() method of the java.rmi.Naming class.

```java
try {
    MyRemote service = new MyRemoteImpl();
    Naming.rebind("RemoteHello", service);
} catch(Exception ex) {...}
```

Give your service a name (that clients can use to look it up in the registry) and register it with the RMI registry. When you bind the service object, RMI swaps the service for the stub and puts the stub in the registry.

Step three: generate stubs and skeletons

(1) Run rmic on the remote implementation class (not the remote interface)

The rmic tool, which comes with the Java software development kit, takes a service implementation and creates two new classes, the stub and the skeleton. It uses a naming convention that is the name of your remote implementation, with either _Stub or _Skel added to the end. There are other options with rmic, including not generating skeletons, seeing what the source code for these classes looked like, and even using IIOP as the protocol. The way we're doing it here is the way you'll usually do it. The classes will land in the current directory (i.e. whatever you did a cd to). Remember, rmic must be able to see your implementation class, so you'll probably run rmic from the directory where your remote implementation is located. (We're deliberately not using packages here, to make it simpler. In the Real World, you'll need to account for package directory structures and fully-qualified names).

Notice that you don't say ".class" on the end. Just the class name.

RMIC generates two new classes for the helper objects.

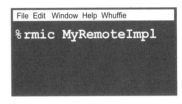

MyRemoteImpl_Stub.class

MyRemoteImpl_Skel.class

Step four: run rmiregistry

(1) Bring up a terminal and start the rmiregistry.

Be sure you start it from a directory that has access to your classes. The simplest way is to start it from your 'classes' directory.

File Edit Window Help Huh?
```
%rmiregistry
```

Step five: start the service

(1) Bring up another terminal and start your service

This might be from a main() method in your remote implementation class, or from a separate launcher class. In this simple example, we put the starter code in the implementation class, in a main method that instantiates the object and registers it with RMI registry.

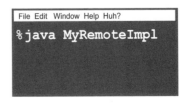

An RMI Detour

Complete code for the server side

The Remote interface:

```java
import java.rmi.*;

public interface MyRemote extends Remote {

    public String sayHello() throws RemoteException;
}
```

RemoteException and Remote interface are in java.rmi package.

Your interface MUST extend java.rmi.Remote

All of your remote methods must declare a RemoteException.

The Remote service (the implementation):

```java
import java.rmi.*;
import java.rmi.server.*;

public class MyRemoteImpl extends UnicastRemoteObject implements MyRemote {

    public String sayHello() {
        return "Server says, 'Hey'";
    }

    public MyRemoteImpl() throws RemoteException { }

    public static void main (String[] args) {

        try {
            MyRemote service = new MyRemoteImpl();
            Naming.rebind("RemoteHello", service);
        } catch(Exception ex) {
            ex.printStackTrace();
        }
    }
}
```

UnicastRemoteObject is in the java.rmi.server package.

Extending UnicastRemoteObject is the easiest way to make a remote object.

You MUST implement your remote interface!!

You have to implement all the interface methods, of course. But notice that you do NOT have to declare the RemoteException.

Your superclass constructor (for UnicastRemoteObject) declares an exception, so YOU must write a constructor, because it means that your constructor is calling risky code (its super constructor).

Make the remote object, then 'bind' it to the rmiregistery using the static Naming.rebind(). The name you register it under is the name clients will use to look it up in the RMI registry.

How does the client get the stub object?

The client has to get the stub object (our proxy), since that's the thing the client will call methods on. And that's where the RMI registry comes in. The client does a 'lookup', like going to the white pages of a phone book, and essentially says, "Here's a name, and I'd like the stub that goes with that name."

Let's take a look at the code we need to lookup and retrieve a stub object.

Here's how it works.

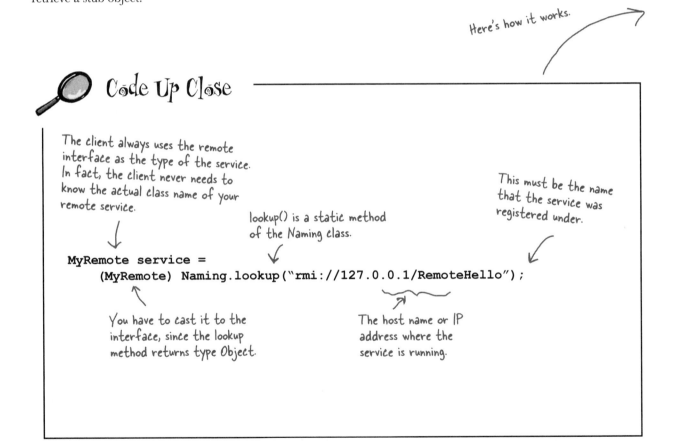

Code Up Close

The client always uses the remote interface as the type of the service. In fact, the client never needs to know the actual class name of your remote service.

lookup() is a static method of the Naming class.

This must be the name that the service was registered under.

```
MyRemote service =
    (MyRemote) Naming.lookup("rmi://127.0.0.1/RemoteHello");
```

You have to cast it to the interface, since the lookup method returns type Object.

The host name or IP address where the service is running.

An RMI Detour

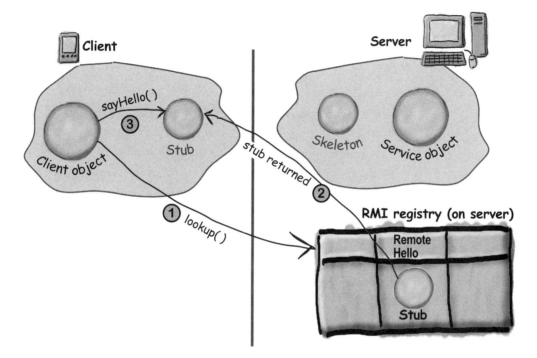

How it works...

① **Client does a lookup on the RMI registry**

```
Naming.lookup("rmi://127.0.0.1/RemoteHello");
```

② **RMI registry returns the stub object**
(as the return value of the lookup method) and RMI deserializes the stub
automatically. You MUST have the stub class (that rmic generated for you)
on the client or the stub won't be deserialized.

③ **Client invokes a method on the stub, as if the
stub IS the real service**

Complete client code

```
import java.rmi.*;

public class MyRemoteClient {
    public static void main (String[] args) {
        new MyRemoteClient().go();
    }

    public void go() {

        try {
            MyRemote service = (MyRemote) Naming.lookup("rmi://127.0.0.1/RemoteHello");

            String s = service.sayHello();

            System.out.println(s);
        } catch(Exception ex) {
            ex.printStackTrace();
        }
    }
}
```

The Naming class (for doing the rmiregistry lookup) is in the java.rmi package.

It comes out of the registry as type Object, so don't forget the cast.

You need the IP address or hostname.

and the name used to bind/rebind the service.

It looks just like a regular old method call! (Except it must acknowledge the RemoteException.)

Geek Bits

How does the client get the stub class?

Now we get to the interesting question. Somehow, some way, the client must have the stub class (that you generated earlier using rmic) at the time the client does the lookup, or else the stub won't be deserialized on the client and the whole thing blows up. The client also needs classes for any serialized objects returned by method calls to the remote object. In a simple system, you can simply hand-deliver the these classes to the client.

There's a much cooler way, although it's beyond the scope of this book. But just in case you're interested, the cooler way is called "dynamic class downloading". With dynamic class downloading, Serialized objects (like the stub) are "stamped" with a URL that tells the RMI system on the client where to find the class file for that object. Then, in the process of deserializing an object, if RMI can't find the class locally, it uses that URL to do an HTTP Get to retrieve the class file. So you'd need a simple web server to serve up class files, and you'd also need to change some security parameters on the client. There are a few other tricky issues with dynamic class downloading, but that's the overview.

For the stub object specifically, there's *another* way the client can get the class. This is only available in Java 5, though. We'll briefly talk about this near the end of the chapter.

An RMI Detour

Watch it!

The top three things programmers do wrong with RMI are:

1) Forget to start rmiregistry before starting remote service (when the service is registered using Naming.rebind(), the rmiregistry must be running!)

2) Forget to make arguments and return types serializable (you won't know until runtime; this is not something the compiler will detect.)

3) Forget to give the stub class to the client.

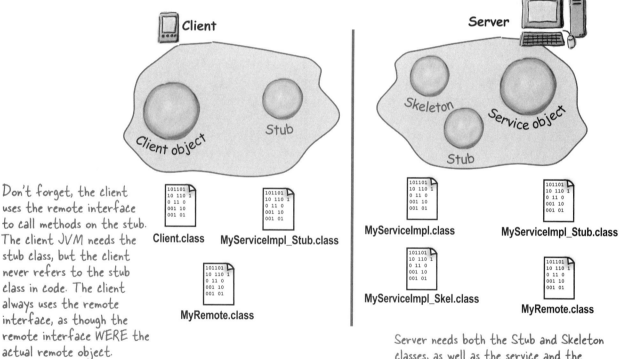

Don't forget, the client uses the remote interface to call methods on the stub. The client JVM needs the stub class, but the client never refers to the stub class in code. The client always uses the remote interface, as though the remote interface WERE the actual remote object.

Server needs both the Stub and Skeleton classes, as well as the service and the remote interface. It needs the stub class because remember, the stub is substituted for the real service when the real service is bound to the RMI registry.

Back to our GumballMachine remote proxy

Okay, now that you have the RMI basics down, you've got the tools you need to implement the gumball machine remote proxy. Let's take a look at how the GumballMachine fits into this framework:

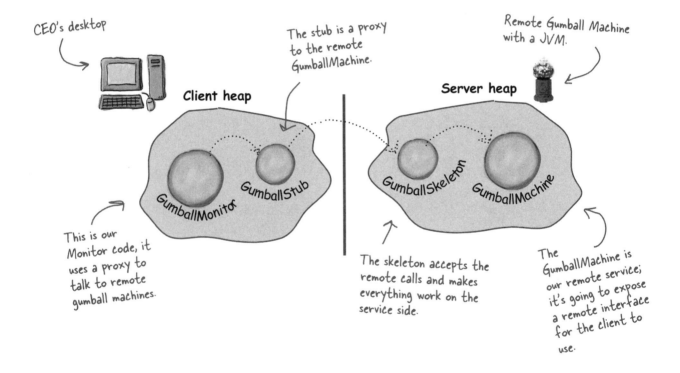

CEO's desktop

The stub is a proxy to the remote GumballMachine.

Remote Gumball Machine with a JVM.

Client heap

Server heap

GumballMonitor

GumballStub

GumballSkeleton

GumballMachine

This is our Monitor code, it uses a proxy to talk to remote gumball machines.

The skeleton accepts the remote calls and makes everything work on the service side.

The GumballMachine is our remote service; it's going to expose a remote interface for the client to use.

Getting the GumballMachine ready to be a remote service

The first step in converting our code to use the remote proxy is to enable the GumballMachine to service remote requests from clients. In other words, we're going to make it into a service. To do that, we need to:

1) Create a remote interface for the GumballMachine. This will provide a set of methods that can be called remotely.

2) Make sure all the return types in the interface are serializable.

3) Implement the interface in a concrete class.

We'll start with the remote interface:

Don't forget to import java.rmi.*

This is the remote interface.

```java
import java.rmi.*;

public interface GumballMachineRemote extends Remote {
    public int getCount() throws RemoteException;
    public String getLocation() throws RemoteException;
    public State getState() throws RemoteException;
}
```

All return types need to be primitive or Serializable...

Here are the methods were going to support. Each one throws RemoteException.

We have one return type that isn't Serializable: the State class. Let's fix it up...

```java
import java.io.*;

public interface State extends Serializable {
    public void insertQuarter();
    public void ejectQuarter();
    public void turnCrank();
    public void dispense();
}
```

Serializable is in the java.io package.

Then we just extend the Serializable interface (which has no methods in it). And now State in all the subclasses can be transferred over the network.

Actually, we're not done with Serializable yet; we have one problem with State. As you may remember, each State object maintains a reference to a gumball machine so that it can call the gumball machine's methods and change its state. We don't want the entire gumball machine serialized and transferred with the State object. There is an easy way to fix this:

```
public class NoQuarterState implements State {
    transient GumballMachine gumballMachine;

    // all other methods here
}
```

In each implementation of State, we add the transient keyword to the GumballMachine instance variable. This tells the JVM not to serialize this field. Note that this can be slightly dangerous if you try to access this field once its been serialized and transferred.

We've already implemented our GumballMachine, but we need to make sure it can act as a service and handle requests coming from over the network. To do that, we have to make sure the GumballMachine is doing everything it needs to implement the GumballMachineRemote interface.

As you've already seen in the RMI detour, this is quite simple, all we need to do is add a couple of things...

First, we need to import the rmi packages.

GumballMachine is going to subclass the UnicastRemoteObject; this gives it the ability to act as a remote service.

GumballMachine also needs to implement the remote interface...

```
import java.rmi.*;
import java.rmi.server.*;

public class GumballMachine
        extends UnicastRemoteObject implements GumballMachineRemote
{
    // instance variables here

    public GumballMachine(String location, int numberGumballs) throws RemoteException {
        // code here
    }

    public int getCount() {
        return count;
    }

    public State getState() {
        return state;
    }

    public String getLocation() {
        return location;
    }

    // other methods here
}
```

...and the constructor needs to throw a remote exception, because the superclass does.

That's it! Nothing changes here at all!

Registering with the RMI registry...

That completes the gumball machine service. Now we just need to fire it up so it can receive requests. First, we need to make sure we register it with the RMI registry so that clients can locate it.

We're going to add a little code to the test drive that will take care of this for us:

```
public class GumballMachineTestDrive {

    public static void main(String[] args) {
        GumballMachineRemote gumballMachine = null;
        int count;
        if (args.length < 2) {
            System.out.println("GumballMachine <name> <inventory>");
            System.exit(1);
        }

        try {
            count = Integer.parseInt(args[1]);

            gumballMachine =
                new GumballMachine(args[0], count);
            Naming.rebind("//" + args[0] + "/gumballmachine", gumballMachine);
        } catch (Exception e) {
            e.printStackTrace();
        }
    }
}
```

First we need to add a try/catch block around the gumball instantiation because our constructor can now throw exceptions.

We also add the call to Naming.rebind, which publishes the GumballMachine stub under the name gumballmachine.

Let's go ahead and get this running...

Run this first.

This gets the RMI registry service up and running.

We're using the "official" Mighty Gumball machines, you should substitute your own machine name here.

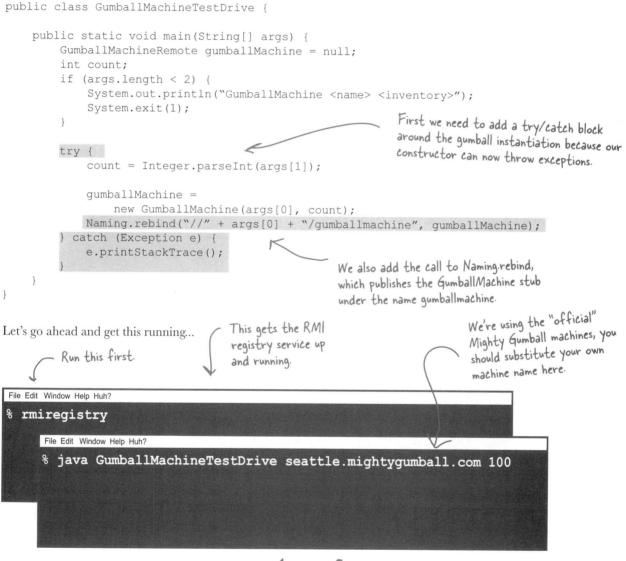

```
File Edit  Window Help Huh?
% rmiregistry
```

```
File Edit  Window Help Huh?
% java GumballMachineTestDrive seattle.mightygumball.com 100
```

Run this second.

This gets the GumballMachine up and running and registers it with the RMI registry.

Now for the GumballMonitor client...

Remember the GumballMonitor? We wanted to reuse it without
having to rewrite it to work over a network. Well, we're pretty much
going to do that, but we do need to make a few changes.

*We need to import the RMI package because we are
using the RemoteException class below...*

```java
import java.rmi.*;

public class GumballMonitor {
    GumballMachineRemote machine;

    public GumballMonitor(GumballMachineRemote machine) {
        this.machine = machine;
    }

    public void report() {
        try {
            System.out.println("Gumball Machine: " + machine.getLocation());
            System.out.println("Current inventory: " + machine.getCount() + " gumballs");
            System.out.println("Current state: " + machine.getState());
        } catch (RemoteException e) {
            e.printStackTrace();
        }
    }
}
```

*Now we're going to rely on the remote
interface rather than the concrete
GumballMachine class.*

*We also need to catch any remote exceptions
that might happen as we try to invoke methods
that are ultimately happening over the network.*

Frank was right; this
is working out quite
nicely!

Writing the Monitor test drive

Now we've got all the pieces we need. We just need to write some code so the CEO can monitor a bunch of gumball machines:

Here's the monitor test drive. The CEO is going to run this!

```java
import java.rmi.*;

public class GumballMonitorTestDrive {

    public static void main(String[] args) {
        String[] location = {"rmi://santafe.mightygumball.com/gumballmachine",
                             "rmi://boulder.mightygumball.com/gumballmachine",
                             "rmi://seattle.mightygumball.com/gumballmachine"};

        GumballMonitor[] monitor = new GumballMonitor[location.length];

        for (int i=0;i < location.length; i++) {
            try {
                GumballMachineRemote machine =
                        (GumballMachineRemote) Naming.lookup(location[i]);
                monitor[i] = new GumballMonitor(machine);
                System.out.println(monitor[i]);
            } catch (Exception e) {
                e.printStackTrace();
            }
        }

        for(int i=0; i < monitor.length; i++) {
            monitor[i].report();
        }
    }
}
```

Here's all the locations were going to monitor.

We create an array of locations, one for each machine.

We also create an array of monitors.

Now we need to get a proxy to each remote machine.

Then we iterate through each machine and print out its report.

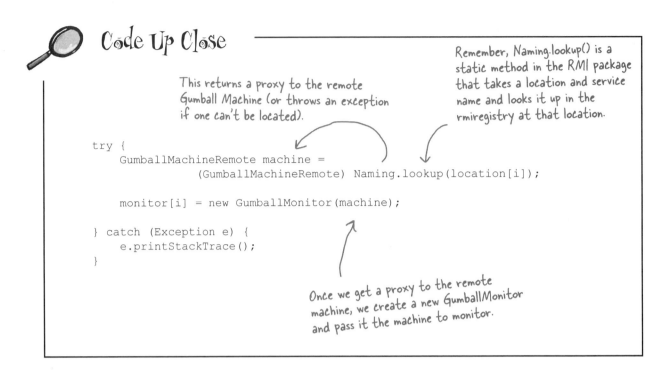

Code Up Close

This returns a proxy to the remote Gumball Machine (or throws an exception if one can't be located).

Remember, Naming.lookup() is a static method in the RMI package that takes a location and service name and looks it up in the rmiregistry at that location.

```
try {
    GumballMachineRemote machine =
            (GumballMachineRemote) Naming.lookup(location[i]);

    monitor[i] = new GumballMonitor(machine);

} catch (Exception e) {
    e.printStackTrace();
}
```

Once we get a proxy to the remote machine, we create a new GumballMonitor and pass it the machine to monitor.

Another demo for the CEO of Mighty Gumball...

Okay, it's time to put all this work together and give another demo. First let's make sure a few gumball machines are running the new code:

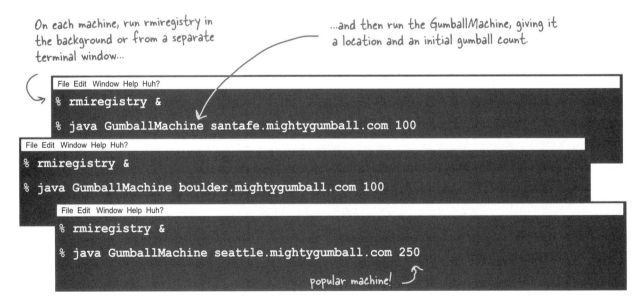

On each machine, run rmiregistry in the background or from a separate terminal window...

...and then run the GumballMachine, giving it a location and an initial gumball count.

```
File Edit Window Help Huh?
% rmiregistry &
% java GumballMachine santafe.mightygumball.com 100
```

```
File Edit Window Help Huh?
% rmiregistry &
% java GumballMachine boulder.mightygumball.com 100
```

```
File Edit Window Help Huh?
% rmiregistry &
% java GumballMachine seattle.mightygumball.com 250
```

popular machine!

And now let's put the monitor in the hands of the CEO.
Hopefully this time he'll love it:

```
File Edit  Window Help  GumballsAndBeyond
% java GumballMonitor
Gumball Machine: santafe.mightygumball.com
Current inventory: 99 gumballs
Current state: waiting for quarter


Gumball Machine: boulder.mightygumball.com
Current inventory: 44 gumballs
Current state: waiting for turn of crank


Gumball Machine: seattle.mightygumball.com
Current inventory: 187 gumballs
Current state: waiting for quarter
%
```

The monitor iterates over each remote machine and calls its getLocation(), getCount() and getState() methods.

This is amazing; it's going to revolutionize my business and blow away the competition!

By invoking methods on the proxy, a remote call is made across the wire and a String, an integer and a State object are returned. Because we are using a proxy, the GumballMonitor doesn't know, or care, that calls are remote (other than having to worry about remote exceptions).

❶ The CEO runs the monitor, which first grabs the proxies to the remote gumball machines and then calls getState() on each one (along with getCount() and getLocation()).

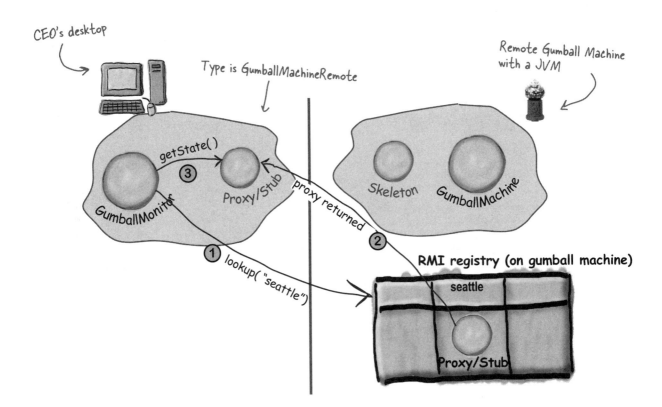

2 getState() is called on the proxy, which forwards the call to the remote service. The skeleton receives the request and then forwards it to the gumball machine.

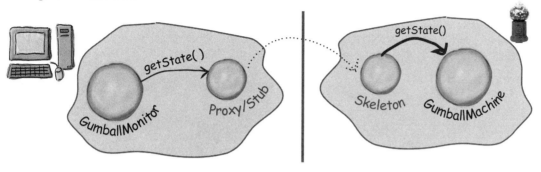

3 GumballMachine returns the state to the skeleton, which serializes it and transfers it back over the wire to the proxy. The proxy deserializes it and returns it as an object to the monitor.

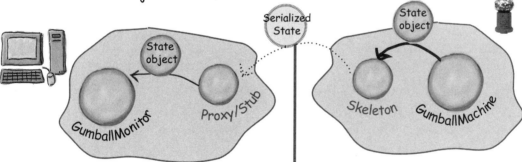

The monitor hasn't changed at all, except it knows it may encounter remote exceptions. It also uses the GumballMachineRemote interface rather than a concrete implementation.

Likewise, the GumballMachine implements another interface and may throw a remote exception in its constructor, but other than that, the code hasn't changed.

We also have a small bit of code to register and locate stubs using the RMI registry. But no matter what, if we were writing something to work over the Internet, we'd need some kind of locator service.

The Proxy Pattern defined

We've already put a lot of pages behind us in this chapter; as you can see, explaining the Remote Proxy is quite involved. Despite that, you'll see that the definition and class diagram for the Proxy Pattern is actually fairly straightforward. Note that Remote Proxy is one implementation of the general Proxy Pattern; there are actually quite a few variations of the pattern, and we'll talk about them later. For now, let's get the details of the general pattern down.

Here's the Proxy Pattern definition:

> **The Proxy Pattern** provides a surrogate or placeholder for another object to control access to it.

Well, we've seen how the Proxy Pattern provides a surrogate or placeholder for another object. We've also described the proxy as a "representative" for another object.

But what about a proxy controlling access? That sounds a little strange. No worries. In the case of the gumball machine, just think of the proxy controlling access to the remote object. The proxy needed to control access because our client, the monitor, didn't know how to talk to a remote object. So in some sense the remote proxy controlled access so that it could handle the network details for us. As we just discussed, there are many variations of the Proxy Pattern, and the variations typically revolve around the way the proxy "controls access." We're going to talk more about this later, but for now here are a few ways proxies control access:

- As we know, a remote proxy controls access to a remote object.

- A virtual proxy controls access to a resource that is expensive to create.

- A protection proxy controls access to a resource based on access rights.

Now that you've got the gist of the general pattern, check out the class diagram...

Use the Proxy Pattern to create a representative object that controls access to another object, which may be remote, expensive to create or in need of securing.

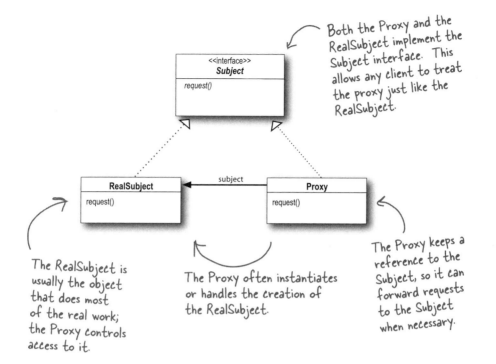

Both the Proxy and the RealSubject implement the Subject interface. This allows any client to treat the proxy just like the RealSubject.

The RealSubject is usually the object that does most of the real work; the Proxy controls access to it.

The Proxy often instantiates or handles the creation of the RealSubject.

The Proxy keeps a reference to the Subject, so it can forward requests to the Subject when necessary.

Let's step through the diagram...

First we have a Subject, which provides an interface for the RealSubject and the Proxy. By implementing the same interface, the Proxy can be substituted for the RealSubject anywhere it occurs.

The RealSubject is the object that does the real work. It's the object that the Proxy represents and controls access to.

The Proxy holds a reference to the RealSubject. In some cases, the Proxy may be responsible for creating and destroying the RealSubject. Clients interact with the RealSubject through the Proxy. Because the Proxy and RealSubject implement the same interface (Subject), the Proxy can be substituted anywhere the subject can be used. The Proxy also controls access to the RealSubject; this control may be needed if the Subject is running on a remote machine, if the Subject is expensive to create in some way or if access to the subject needs to be protected in some way.

Now that you understand the general pattern, let's look at some other ways of using proxy beyond the Remote Proxy...

Get ready for Virtual Proxy

Okay, so far you've seen the definition of the Proxy Pattern and you've taken a look at one specific example: the *Remote Proxy*. Now we're going to take a look at a different type of proxy, the *Virtual Proxy*. As you'll discover, the Proxy Pattern can manifest itself in many forms, yet all the forms follow roughly the general proxy design. Why so many forms? Because the proxy pattern can be applied to a lot of different use cases. Let's check out the Virtual Proxy and compare it to Remote Proxy:

Remote Proxy

With Remote Proxy, the proxy acts as a local representative for an object that lives in a different JVM. A method call on the proxy results in the call being transferred over the wire, invoked remotely, and the result being returned back to the proxy and then to the Client.

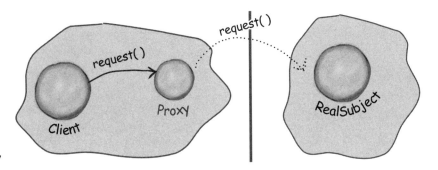

We know this diagram pretty well by now...

Virtual Proxy

Virtual Proxy acts as a representative for an object that may be expensive to create. The Virtual Proxy often defers the creation of the object until it is needed; the Virtual Proxy also acts as a surrogate for the object before and while it is being created. After that, the proxy delegates requests directly to the RealSubject.

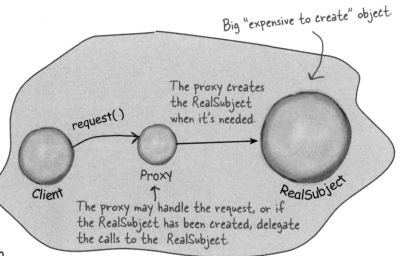

Big "expensive to create" object.

The proxy creates the RealSubject when it's needed.

The proxy may handle the request, or if the RealSubject has been created, delegate the calls to the RealSubject.

Displaying CD covers

Let's say you want to write an application that displays your favorite compact disc covers. You might create a menu of the CD titles and then retrieve the images from an online service like Amazon.com. If you're using Swing, you might create an Icon and ask it to load the image from the network. The only problem is, depending on the network load and the bandwidth of your connection, retrieving a CD cover might take a little time, so your application should display something while you are waiting for the image to load. We also don't want to hang up the entire application while it's waiting on the image. Once the image is loaded, the message should go away and you should see the image.

An easy way to achieve this is through a virtual proxy. The virtual proxy can stand in place of the icon, manage the background loading, and before the image is fully retrieved from the network, display "Loading CD cover, please wait...". Once the image is loaded, the proxy delegates the display to the Icon.

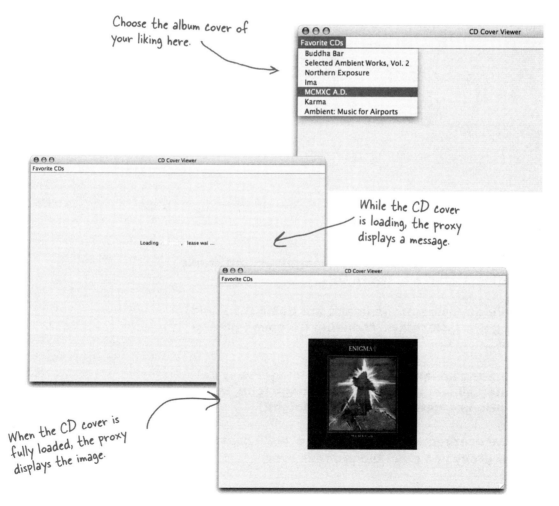

Choose the album cover of your liking here.

While the CD cover is loading, the proxy displays a message.

When the CD cover is fully loaded, the proxy displays the image.

Designing the CD cover Virtual Proxy

Before writing the code for the CD Cover Viewer, let's look at the class diagram.
You'll see this looks just like our Remote Proxy class diagram, but here the proxy is
used to hide an object that is expensive to create (because we need to retrieve the data
for the Icon over the network) as opposed to an object that actually lives somewhere
else on the network.

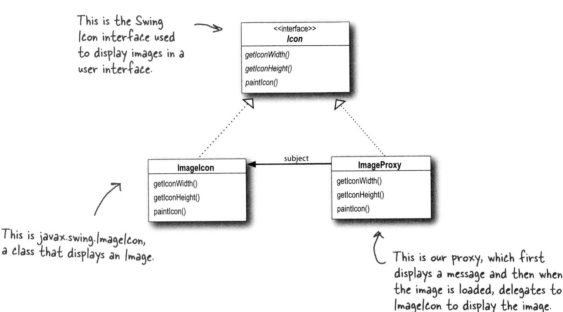

This is the Swing Icon interface used to display images in a user interface.

This is javax.swing.ImageIcon, a class that displays an Image.

This is our proxy, which first displays a message and then when the image is loaded, delegates to ImageIcon to display the image.

How ImageProxy is going to work:

❶ **ImageProxy first creates an ImageIcon and starts loading it from a network URL.**

❷ **While the bytes of the image are being retrieved, ImageProxy displays "Loading CD cover, please wait...".**

❸ **When the image is fully loaded, ImageProxy delegates all method calls to the image icon, including paintIcon(), getWidth() and getHeight().**

❹ **If the user requests a new image, we'll create a new proxy and start the process over.**

Writing the Image Proxy

The ImageProxy implements the Icon interface.

<<interface>>
Icon
getIconWidth()
getIconHeight()
paintIcon()

```
class ImageProxy implements Icon {
    ImageIcon imageIcon;
    URL imageURL;
    Thread retrievalThread;
    boolean retrieving = false;

    public ImageProxy(URL url) { imageURL = url; }

    public int getIconWidth() {
        if (imageIcon != null) {
            return imageIcon.getIconWidth();
        } else {
            return 800;
        }
    }

    public int getIconHeight() {
        if (imageIcon != null) {
            return imageIcon.getIconHeight();
        } else {
            return 600;
        }
    }

    public void paintIcon(final Component c, Graphics  g, int x,  int y) {
        if (imageIcon != null) {
            imageIcon.paintIcon(c, g, x, y);
        } else {
            g.drawString("Loading CD cover, please wait...", x+300, y+190);
            if (!retrieving) {
                retrieving = true;
                retrievalThread = new Thread(new Runnable() {
                    public void run() {
                        try {
                            imageIcon = new ImageIcon(imageURL, "CD Cover");
                            c.repaint();
                        } catch (Exception e) {
                            e.printStackTrace();
                        }
                    }
                });
                retrievalThread.start();
            }
        }
    }
}
```

The imageIcon is the REAL icon that we eventually want to display when it's loaded.

We pass the URL of the image into the constructor. This is the image we need to display once it's loaded!

We return a default width and height until the imageIcon is loaded; then we turn it over to the imageIcon.

Here's where things get interesting. This code paints the icon on the screen (by delegating to the imageIcon). However, if we don't have a fully created ImageIcon, then we create one. Let's look at this closer on the next page...

Code Up Close

⌐ This method is called when it's time to paint the icon on the screen.

```
public void paintIcon(final Component c, Graphics  g, int x,  int y) {
    if (imageIcon != null) {

        imageIcon.paintIcon(c, g, x, y);

    } else {

        g.drawString("Loading CD cover, please wait...", x+300, y+190);
        if (!retrieving) {

            retrieving = true;
            retrievalThread = new Thread(new Runnable() {
                public void run() {
                    try {
                        imageIcon = new ImageIcon(imageURL, "CD Cover");
                        c.repaint();
                    } catch (Exception e) {
                        e.printStackTrace();
                    }
                }
            });

            retrievalThread.start();
        }
    }
}
```

← If we've got an icon already, we go ahead and tell it to paint itself.

↖ Otherwise we display the "loading" message.

Here's where we load the REAL icon image. Note that the image loading with IconImage is synchronous: the ImageIcon constructor doesn't return until the image is loaded. That doesn't give us much of a chance to do screen updates and have our message displayed, so we're going to do this asynchronously. See the "Code Way Up Close" on the next page for more...

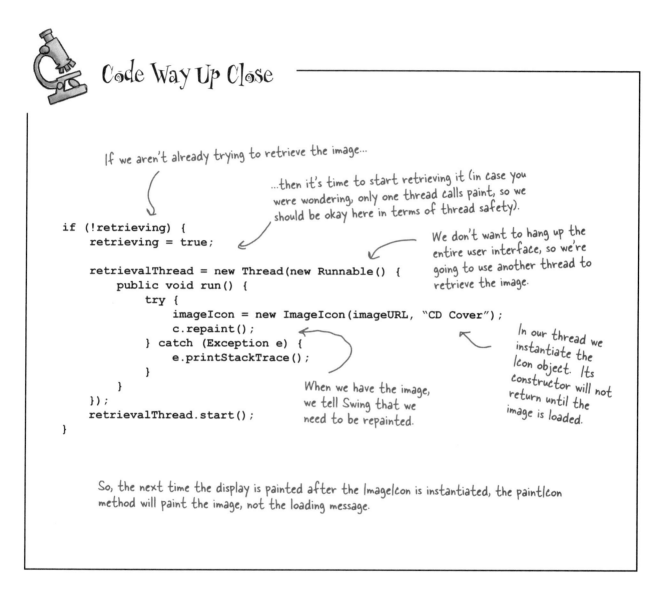

Code Way Up Close

If we aren't already trying to retrieve the image…

…then it's time to start retrieving it (in case you were wondering, only one thread calls paint, so we should be okay here in terms of thread safety).

```
if (!retrieving) {
    retrieving = true;

    retrievalThread = new Thread(new Runnable() {
        public void run() {
            try {
                imageIcon = new ImageIcon(imageURL, "CD Cover");
                c.repaint();
            } catch (Exception e) {
                e.printStackTrace();
            }
        }
    });
    retrievalThread.start();
}
```

We don't want to hang up the entire user interface, so we're going to use another thread to retrieve the image.

In our thread we instantiate the icon object. Its constructor will not return until the image is loaded.

When we have the image, we tell Swing that we need to be repainted.

So, the next time the display is painted after the ImageIcon is instantiated, the paintIcon method will paint the image, not the loading message.

Design Puzzle

The ImageProxy class appears to have two states that are controlled by conditional statements. Can you think of another pattern that might clean up this code? How would you redesign ImageProxy?

```java
class ImageProxy implements Icon {
    // instance variables & constructor here

    public int getIconWidth() {
        if (imageIcon != null) {
            return imageIcon.getIconWidth();
        } else {
            return 800;
        }
    }

    public int getIconHeight() {
        if (imageIcon != null) {
            return imageIcon.getIconHeight();
        } else {
            return 600;
        }
    }

    public void paintIcon(final Component c, Graphics  g, int x,  int y) {
        if (imageIcon != null) {
            imageIcon.paintIcon(c, g, x, y);
        } else {
            g.drawString("Loading CD cover, please wait...", x+300, y+190);
            // more code here
        }
    }
}
```

Two states

Two states

Two states

Testing the CD Cover Viewer

Ready-bake Code

Okay, it's time to test out this fancy new virtual proxy. Behind the scenes we've been baking up a new ImageProxyTestDrive that sets up the window, creates a frame, installs the menus and creates our proxy. We don't go through all that code in gory detail here, but you can always grab the source code and have a look, or check it out at the end of the chapter where we list all the source code for the Virtual Proxy.

Here's a partial view of the test drive code:

```java
public class ImageProxyTestDrive {
    ImageComponent imageComponent;
    public static void main (String[] args) throws Exception {
        ImageProxyTestDrive testDrive = new ImageProxyTestDrive();
    }

    public ImageProxyTestDrive() throws Exception{

        // set up frame and menus

        Icon icon = new ImageProxy(initialURL);
        imageComponent = new ImageComponent(icon);
        frame.getContentPane().add(imageComponent);
    }
}
```

Here we create an image proxy and set it to an initial URL. Whenever you choose a selection from the CD menu, you'll get a new image proxy.

Next we wrap our proxy in a component so it can be added to the frame. The component will take care of the proxy's width, height and similar details.

Finally we add the proxy to the frame so it can be displayed.

Now let's run the test drive:

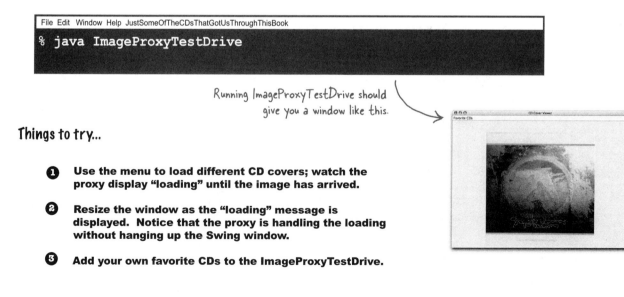

File Edit Window Help JustSomeOfTheCDsThatGotUsThroughThisBook

```
% java ImageProxyTestDrive
```

Running ImageProxyTestDrive should give you a window like this.

Things to try...

1 **Use the menu to load different CD covers; watch the proxy display "loading" until the image has arrived.**

2 **Resize the window as the "loading" message is displayed. Notice that the proxy is handling the loading without hanging up the Swing window.**

3 **Add your own favorite CDs to the ImageProxyTestDrive.**

What did we do?

Behind the Scenes

1 We created an ImageProxy for the display. The paintIcon() method is called and ImageProxy fires off a thread to retrieve the image and create the ImageIcon.

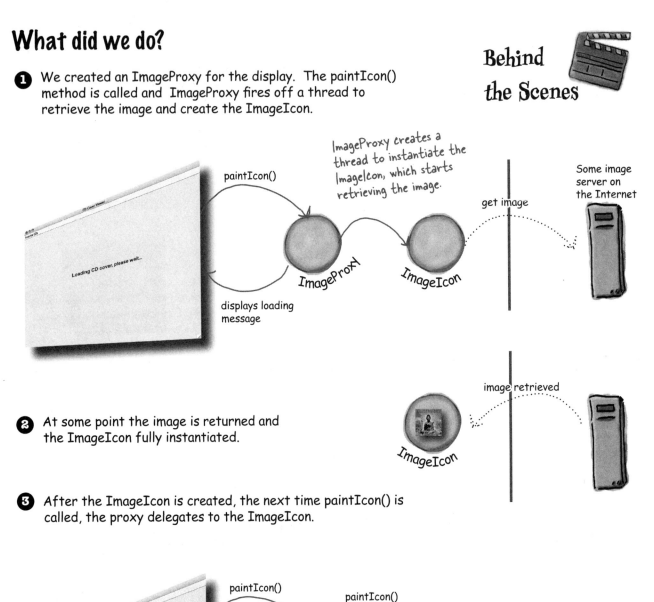

ImageProxy creates a thread to instantiate the ImageIcon, which starts retrieving the image.

paintIcon()

get image

Some image server on the Internet

Loading CD cover, please wait...

displays loading message

ImageProxy

ImageIcon

image retrieved

2 At some point the image is returned and the ImageIcon fully instantiated.

ImageIcon

3 After the ImageIcon is created, the next time paintIcon() is called, the proxy delegates to the ImageIcon.

paintIcon()

paintIcon()

ImageProxy

ImageIcon

displays the real image

there are no
Dumb Questions

Q: **The Remote Proxy and Virtual Proxy seem so different to me; are they really ONE pattern?**

A: You'll find a lot of variants of the Proxy Pattern in the real world; what they all have in common is that they intercept a method invocation that the client is making on the subject. This level of indirection allows us to do many things, including dispatching requests to a remote subject, providing a representative for an expensive object as it is created, or, as you'll see, providing some level of protection that can determine which clients should be calling which methods. That's just the beginning; the general Proxy Pattern can be applied in many different ways, and we'll cover some of the other ways at the end of the chapter.

Q: **ImageProxy seems just like a Decorator to me. I mean, we are basically wrapping one object with another and then delegating the calls to the ImageIcon. What am I missing?**

A: Sometimes Proxy and Decorator look very similar, but their purposes are different: a decorator adds behavior to a class, while a proxy controls access to it. You might say, "Isn't the loading message adding behavior?" In some

ways it is; however, more importantly, the ImageProxy is controlling access to an ImageIcon. How does it control access? Well, think about it this way: the proxy is decoupling the client from the ImageIcon. If they were coupled the client would have to wait until each image is retrieved before it could paint it entire interface. The proxy controls access to the ImageIcon so that before it is fully created, the proxy provides another on screen representation. Once the ImageIcon is created the proxy allows access.

Q: **How do I make clients use the Proxy rather than the Real Subject?**

A: Good question. One common technique is to provide a factory that instantiates and returns the subject. Because this happens in a factory method we can then wrap the subject with a proxy before returning it. The client never knows or cares that it's using a proxy instead of the real thing.

Q: **I noticed in the ImageProxy example, you always create a new ImageIcon to get the image, even if the image has already been retrieved. Could you implement something similar to the ImageProxy that caches past retrievals?**

A: You are talking about a specialized form of a Virtual Proxy called a Caching Proxy. A caching proxy maintains a cache of previous created objects and when a request is made it returns cached object, if possible.

We're going to look this and at several other variants of the Proxy Pattern at the end of the chapter.

Q: **I see how Decorator and Proxy relate, but what about Adapter? An adapter seems very similar as well.**

A: Both Proxy and Adapter sit in front of other objects and forward requests to them. Remember that Adapter changes the interface of the objects it adapts, while the Proxy implements the same interface.

There is one additional similarity that relates to the Protection Proxy. A Protection Proxy may allow or disallow a client access to particular methods in an object based on the role of the client. In this way a Protection Proxy may only provide a partial interface to a client, which is quite similar to some Adapters. We are going to take a look at Protection Proxy in a few pages.

Fireside Chats

Tonight's talk: **Proxy and Decorator get intentional.**

Proxy

Hello, Decorator. I presume you're here because people sometimes get us confused?

Me copying *your* ideas? Please. I control access to objects. You just decorate them. My job is so much more important than yours it's just not even funny.

Fine, so maybe you're not entirely frivolous... but I still don't get why you think I'm copying all your ideas. I'm all about representing my subjects, not decorating them.

I don't think you get it, Decorator. I stand in for my Subjects; I don't just add behavior. Clients use me as a surrogate of a Real Subject, because I can protect them from unwanted access, or keep their GUIs from hanging up while they're waiting for big objects to load, or hide the fact that their Subjects are running on remote machines. I'd say that's a very different intent from yours!

Decorator

Well, I think the reason people get us confused is that you go around pretending to be an entirely different pattern, when in fact, you're just a Decorator in disguise. I really don't think you should be copying all my ideas.

"Just" decorate? You think decorating is some frivolous unimportant pattern? Let me tell you buddy, I add *behavior*. That's the most important thing about objects - what they *do*!

You can call it "representation" but if it looks like a duck and walks like a duck... I mean, just look at your Virtual Proxy; it's just another way of adding behavior to do something while some big expensive object is loading, and your Remote Proxy is a way of talking to remote objects so your clients don't have to bother with that themselves. It's all about behavior, just like I said.

Call it what you want. I implement the same interface as the objects I wrap; so do you.

Proxy

Okay, let's review that statement. You wrap an object. While sometimes we informally say a proxy wraps its Subject, that's not really an accurate term.

Think about a remote proxy... what object am I wrapping? The object I'm representing and controlling access to lives on another machine! Let's see you do that.

Sure, okay, take a virtual proxy... think about the CD viewer example. When the client first uses me as a proxy the subject doesn't even exist! So what am I wrapping there?

I never knew decorators were so dumb! Of course I sometimes create objects, how do you think a virtual proxy gets its subject! Okay, you just pointed out a big difference between us: we both know decorators only add window dressing; they never get to instantiate anything.

Hey, after this conversation I'm convinced you're just a dumb proxy!

Very seldom will you ever see a proxy get into wrapping a subject multiple times; in fact, if you're wrapping something 10 times, you better go back reexamine your design.

Decorator

Oh yeah? Why not?

Okay, but we all know remote proxies are kinda weird. Got a second example? I doubt it.

Uh huh, and the next thing you'll be saying is that you actually get to create objects.

Oh yeah? Instantiate this!

Dumb proxy? I'd like to see you recursively wrap an object with 10 decorators and keep your head straight at the same time.

Just like a proxy, acting all real when in fact you just stand in for the objects doing the real work. You know, I actually feel sorry for you.

Using the Java API's Proxy to create a protection proxy

Java's got its own proxy support right in the java.lang.reflect package. With this package, Java lets you create a proxy class *on the fly* that implements one or more interfaces and forwards method invocations to a class that you specify. Because the actual proxy class is created at runtime, we refer to this Java technology as a *dynamic proxy*.

We're going to use Java's dynamic proxy to create our next proxy implementation (a protection proxy), but before we do that, let's quickly look at a class diagram that shows how dynamic proxies are put together. Like most things in the real world, it differs slightly from the classic definition of the pattern:

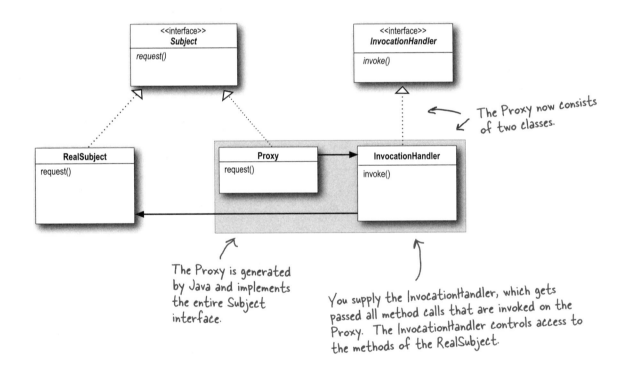

The Proxy now consists of two classes.

The Proxy is generated by Java and implements the entire Subject interface.

You supply the InvocationHandler, which gets passed all method calls that are invoked on the Proxy. The InvocationHandler controls access to the methods of the RealSubject.

Because Java creates the Proxy class *for you*, you need a way to tell the Proxy class what to do. You can't put that code into the Proxy class like we did before, because you're not implementing one directly. So, if you can't put this code in the Proxy class, where do you put it? In an InvocationHandler. The job of the InvocationHandler is to respond to any method calls on the proxy. Think of the InvocationHandler as the object the Proxy asks to do all the real work after it's received the method calls.

Okay, let's step through how to use the dynamic proxy...

Matchmaking in Objectville

Every town needs a matchmaking service, right? You've risen to the task and implemented a dating service for Objectville. You've also tried to be innovative by including a "Hot or Not" feature in the service where participants can rate each other – you figure this keeps your customers engaged and looking through possible matches; it also makes things a lot more fun.

Your service revolves around a Person bean that allows you to set and get information about a person:

This is the interface; we'll get to the implementation in just a sec...

Here we can get information about the person's name, gender, interests and HotOrNot rating (1–10).

```java
public interface PersonBean {

    String getName();
    String getGender();
    String getInterests();
    int getHotOrNotRating();

    void setName(String name);
    void setGender(String gender);
    void setInterests(String interests);
    void setHotOrNotRating(int rating);

}
```

We can also set the same information through the respective method calls.

setHotOrNotRating() takes an integer and adds it to the running average for this person.

Now let's check out the implementation...

The PersonBean implementation

The PersonBeanImpl implements the PersonBean interface
↙

```java
public class PersonBeanImpl implements PersonBean {
    String name;
    String gender;
    String interests;          ←———  The instance variables.
    int rating;
    int ratingCount = 0;

    public String getName() {
        return name;
    }

    public String getGender() {
        return gender;
    }

    public String getInterests() {
        return interests;
    }

    public int getHotOrNotRating() {
        if (ratingCount == 0) return 0;
        return (rating/ratingCount);
    }


    public void setName(String name) {
        this.name = name;
    }

    public void setGender(String gender) {
        this.gender = gender;
    }

    public void setInterests(String interests) {
        this.interests = interests;
    }

    public void setHotOrNotRating(int rating) {
        this.rating += rating;
        ratingCount++;
    }
}
```

All the getter methods; they each return the appropriate instance variable…

…except for getHotOrNotRating(), which computes the average of the ratings by dividing the ratings by the ratingCount.

And here's all the setter methods, which set the corresponding instance variable.

Finally, the setHotOrNotRating() method increments the total ratingCount and adds the rating to the running total.

I wasn't very successful finding dates. Then I noticed someone had changed my interests. I also noticed that a lot of people are bumping up their HotOrNot scores by giving themselves high ratings. You shouldn't be able to change someone else's interests or give yourself a rating!

Elroy

While we suspect other factors may be keeping Elroy from getting dates, he is right: you shouldn't be able to vote for yourself or to change another customer's data. The way our PersonBean is defined, any client can call any of the methods.

This is a perfect example of where we might be able to use a Protection Proxy. What's a Protection Proxy? It's a proxy that controls access to an object based on access rights. For instance, if we had an employee object, a protection proxy might allow the employee to call certain methods on the object, a manager to call additional methods (like setSalary()), and a human resources employee to call any method on the object.

In our dating service we want to make sure that a customer can set his own information while preventing others from altering it. We also want to allow just the opposite with the HotOrNot ratings: we want the other customers to be able to set the rating, but not that particular customer. We also have a number of getter methods in the PersonBean, and because none of these return private information, any customer should be able to call them.

Five minute drama: protecting subjects

The Internet bubble seems a distant memory; those were the days when all you needed to do to find a better, higher-paying job was to walk across the street. Even agents for software developers were in vogue...

I'd like to make an offer, can we get her on the phone?

She's tied up ... uh ... in a meeting right now, what did you have in mind?

Like a protection proxy, the agent protects access to his subject, only letting certain calls through...

Joe DotCom

Agent

We think we can meet her current salary plus 15%.

Come on. You're wasting our time here! Not a chance! Come back later with a better offer.

Big Picture: creating a Dynamic Proxy for the PersonBean

We have a couple of problems to fix: customers shouldn't be changing their own HotOrNot rating and customers shouldn't be able to change other customers' personal information. To fix these problems we're going to create two proxies: one for accessing your own PersonBean object and one for accessing another customer's PersonBean object. That way, the proxies can control what requests can be made in each circumstance.

To create these proxies we're going to use the Java API's dynamic proxy that you saw a few pages back. Java will create two proxies for us; all we need to do is supply the handlers that know what to do when a method is invoked on the proxy.

Remember this diagram from a few pages back...

Step one:

Create two **InvocationHandlers**.

InvocationHandlers implement the behavior of the proxy. As you'll see Java will take care of creating the actual proxy class and object, we just need to supply a handler that knows what to do when a method is called on it.

Step two:

Write the code that creates the dynamic proxies.

We need to write a little bit of code to generate the proxy class and instantiate it. We'll step through this code in just a bit.

Step three:

Wrap any PersonBean object with the appropriate proxy.

When we need to use a PersonBean object, either it's the object of the customer himself (in that case, will call him the "owner"), or it's another user of the service that the customer is checking out (in that case we'll call him "non-owner").

In either case, we create the appropriate proxy for the PersonBean.

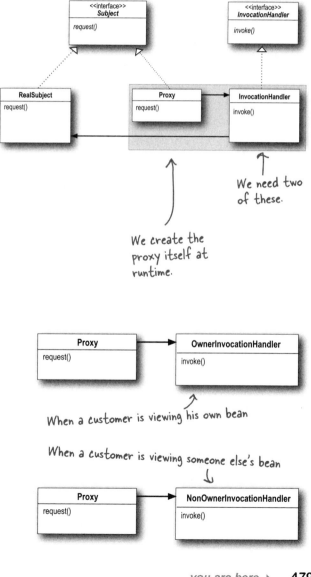

We create the proxy itself at runtime.

We need two of these.

When a customer is viewing his own bean

When a customer is viewing someone else's bean

Step one: creating Invocation Handlers

We know we need to write two invocation handlers, one for the owner and one for the non-owner. But what are invocation handlers? Here's the way to think about them: when a method call is made on the proxy, the proxy forwards that call to your invocation handler, but *not* by calling the invocation handler's corresponding method. So, what does it call? Have a look at the InvocationHandler interface:

There's only one method, invoke(), and no matter what methods get called on the proxy, the invoke() method is what gets called on the handler. Let's see how this works:

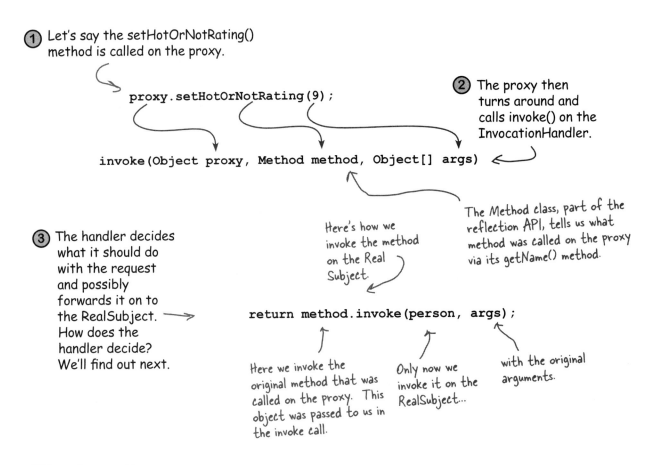

① Let's say the setHotOrNotRating() method is called on the proxy.

`proxy.setHotOrNotRating(9);`

② The proxy then turns around and calls invoke() on the InvocationHandler.

`invoke(Object proxy, Method method, Object[] args)`

The Method class, part of the reflection API, tells us what method was called on the proxy via its getName() method.

③ The handler decides what it should do with the request and possibly forwards it on to the RealSubject. How does the handler decide? We'll find out next.

Here's how we invoke the method on the Real Subject.

`return method.invoke(person, args);`

Here we invoke the original method that was called on the proxy. This object was passed to us in the invoke call.

Only now we invoke it on the RealSubject...

with the original arguments.

Creating Invocation Handlers continued...

When invoke() is called by the proxy, how do you know what to do with the call? Typically, you'll examine the method that was called on the proxy and make decisions based on the method's name and possibly its arguments. Let's implement the OwnerInvocationHandler to see how this works:

InvocationHandler is part of the java.lang.reflect package, so we need to import it.

All invocation handlers implement the InvocationHandler interface.

```java
import java.lang.reflect.*;

public class OwnerInvocationHandler implements InvocationHandler {
    PersonBean person;

    public OwnerInvocationHandler(PersonBean person) {
        this.person = person;
    }

    public Object invoke(Object proxy, Method method, Object[] args)
            throws IllegalAccessException {

        try {
            if (method.getName().startsWith("get")) {
                return method.invoke(person, args);
            } else if (method.getName().equals("setHotOrNotRating")) {
                throw new IllegalAccessException();
            } else if (method.getName().startsWith("set")) {
                return method.invoke(person, args);
            }
        } catch (InvocationTargetException e) {
            e.printStackTrace();
        }
        return null;
    }
}
```

We're passed the Real Subject in the constructor and we keep a reference to it.

Here's the invoke method that gets called every time a method is invoked on the proxy.

If the method is a getter, we go ahead and invoke it on the real subject.

Otherwise, if it is the setHotOrNotRating() method we disallow it by throwing a IllegalAccessException.

This will happen if the real subject throws an exception.

Because we are the owner any other set method is fine and we go ahead and invoke it on the real subject.

If any other method is called, we're just going to return null rather than take a chance.

Exercise

The NonOwnerInvocationHandler works just like the OwnerInvocationHandler except that it *allows* calls to setHotOrNotRating() and it *disallows* calls to any other set method. Go ahead and write this handler yourself:

Step two: creating the Proxy class and instantiating the Proxy object

Now, all we have left is to dynamically create the proxy class and instantiate the proxy object. Let's start by writing a method that takes a PersonBean and knows how to create an owner proxy for it. That is, we're going to create the kind of proxy that forwards its method calls to the OwnerInvocationHandler. Here's the code:

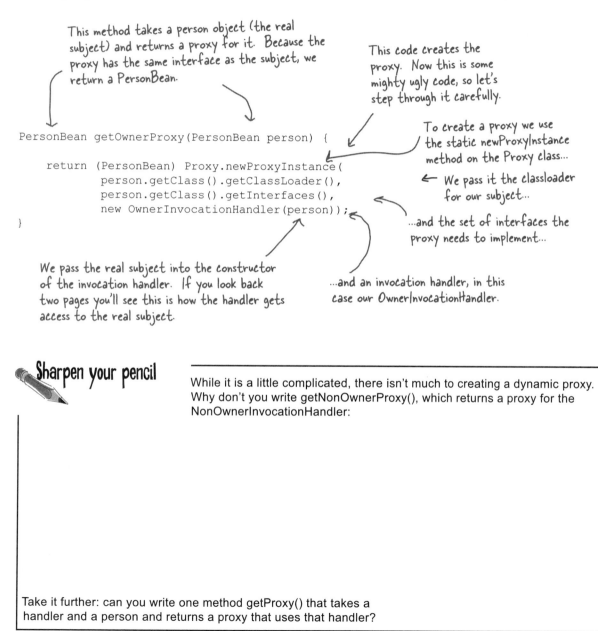

This method takes a person object (the real subject) and returns a proxy for it. Because the proxy has the same interface as the subject, we return a PersonBean.

This code creates the proxy. Now this is some mighty ugly code, so let's step through it carefully.

```
PersonBean getOwnerProxy(PersonBean person) {

    return (PersonBean) Proxy.newProxyInstance(
            person.getClass().getClassLoader(),
            person.getClass().getInterfaces(),
            new OwnerInvocationHandler(person));
}
```

To create a proxy we use the static newProxyInstance method on the Proxy class...

← We pass it the classloader for our subject...

...and the set of interfaces the proxy needs to implement...

...and an invocation handler, in this case our OwnerInvocationHandler.

We pass the real subject into the constructor of the invocation handler. If you look back two pages you'll see this is how the handler gets access to the real subject.

Sharpen your pencil

While it is a little complicated, there isn't much to creating a dynamic proxy. Why don't you write getNonOwnerProxy(), which returns a proxy for the NonOwnerInvocationHandler:

Take it further: can you write one method getProxy() that takes a handler and a person and returns a proxy that uses that handler?

Testing the matchmaking service

Let's give the matchmaking service a test run and see how it controls access to the
setter methods based on the proxy that is used.

```java
public class MatchMakingTestDrive {
    // instance variables here

    public static void main(String[] args) {
        MatchMakingTestDrive test = new MatchMakingTestDrive();
        test.drive();
    }

    public MatchMakingTestDrive() {
        initializeDatabase();
    }
    public void drive() {
        PersonBean joe = getPersonFromDatabase("Joe Javabean");
        PersonBean ownerProxy = getOwnerProxy(joe);
        System.out.println("Name is " + ownerProxy.getName());
        ownerProxy.setInterests("bowling, Go");
        System.out.println("Interests set from owner proxy");
        try {
            ownerProxy.setHotOrNotRating(10);
        } catch (Exception e) {
            System.out.println("Can't set rating from owner proxy");
        }
        System.out.println("Rating is " + ownerProxy.getHotOrNotRating());

        PersonBean nonOwnerProxy = getNonOwnerProxy(joe);
        System.out.println("Name is " + nonOwnerProxy.getName());
        try {
            nonOwnerProxy.setInterests("bowling, Go");
        } catch (Exception e) {
            System.out.println("Can't set interests from non owner proxy");
        }
        nonOwnerProxy.setHotOrNotRating(3);
        System.out.println("Rating set from non owner proxy");
        System.out.println("Rating is " + nonOwnerProxy.getHotOrNotRating());
    }

    // other methods like getOwnerProxy and getNonOwnerProxy here
}
```

Main just creates the test drive and calls its drive() method to get things going.

The constructor initializes our DB of people in the matchmaking service.

Let's retrieve a person from the DB

...and create an owner proxy.

Call a getter and then a setter

and then try to change the rating.

this shouldn't work!

Now create a non-owner proxy

...and call a getter

followed by a setter

This shouldn't work!

Then try to set the rating

This should work!

Running the code...

```
File Edit Window Help Born2BDynamic
% java MatchMakingTestDrive
Name is Joe Javabean
Interests set from owner proxy
Can't set rating from owner proxy
Rating is 7


Name is Joe Javabean
Can't set interests from non owner proxy
Rating set from non owner proxy
Rating is 5
%
```

Our Owner proxy allows getting and setting, except for the HotOrNot rating.

Our NonOwner proxy allows getting only, but also allows calls to set the HotOrNot rating.

The new rating is the average of the previous rating, 7 and the value set by the nonowner proxy, 3.

there are no Dumb Questions

Q: **So what exactly is the "dynamic" aspect of dynamic proxies? Is it that I'm instantiating the proxy and setting it to a handler at runtime?**

A: No, the proxy is dynamic because its class is created at runtime. Think about it: before your code runs there is no proxy class; it is created on demand from the set of interfaces you pass it.

Q: **My InvocationHandler seems like a very strange proxy, it doesn't implement any of the methods of the class it's proxying.**

A: That is because the InvocationHandler isn't a proxy – it is a class that the proxy dispatches to for handling method calls. The proxy itself is created dynamically at runtime by the static Proxy.newProxyInstance() method.

Q: **Is there any way to tell if a class is a Proxy class?**

A: Yes. The Proxy class has a static method called isProxyClass(). Calling this method with a class will return true if the class is a dynamic proxy class. Other than that, the proxy class will act like any other class that implements a particular set of interfaces.

Q: **Are there any restrictions on the types of interfaces I can pass into newProxyInstance()?**

A: Yes, there are a few. First, it is worth pointing out that we always pass newProxyInstance() an array of interfaces – only interfaces are allowed, no classes. The major restrictions are that all non-public interfaces need to be from the same package. You also can't have interfaces with clashing method names (that is, two interfaces with a method with the same signature). There are a few other minor nuances as well, so at some point you should take a look at the fine print on dynamic proxies in the javadoc.

Q: **Why are you using skeletons? I thought we got rid of those back in Java 1.2.**

A: You're right; we don't need to actually generate skeletons. As of Java 1.2, the RMI runtime can dispatch the client calls directly to the remote service using reflection. But we like to show the skeleton, because conceptually it helps you to understand that there is something under the covers that's making that communication between the client stub and the remote service happen.

Q: **I heard that in Java 5, I don't even need to generate stubs anymore either. Is that true?**

A: It sure is. In Java 5, RMI and Dynamic Proxy got together and now stubs are generated dynamically using Dynamic Proxy. The remote object's stub is a java.lang.reflect.Proxy instance (with an invocation handler) that is automatically generated to handle all the details of getting the local method calls by the client to the remote object. So, now you don't have to use rmic at all; everything you need to get a client talking to a remote object is handled for you behind the scenes.

WHO DOES WHAT?

Match each pattern with its description:

Pattern	Description
Decorator	Wraps another object and provides a different interface to it
Facade	Wraps another object and provides additional behavior for it
Proxy	Wraps another object to control access to it
Adapter	Wraps a bunch of objects to simplify their interface

The Proxy Zoo

Welcome to the Objectville Zoo!

You now know about the remote, virtual and protection proxies, but out in the wild you're going to see lots of mutations of this pattern. Over here in the Proxy corner of the zoo we've got a nice collection of wild proxy patterns that we've captured for your study.

Our job isn't done; we are sure you're going to see more variations of this pattern in the real world, so give us a hand in cataloging more proxies. Let's take a look at the existing collection:

Firewall Proxy controls access to a set of network resources, protecting the subject from "bad" clients.

Habitat: often seen in the location of corporate firewall systems.

Help find a habitat
_____
_____
_____
_____

Smart Reference Proxy provides additional actions whenever a subject is referenced, such as counting the number of references to an object.

Caching Proxy provides temporary storage for results of operations that are expensive. It can also allow multiple clients to share the results to reduce computation or network latency.

Habitat: often seen in web server proxies as well as content management and publishing systems.

Synchronization Proxy provides safe access to a subject from multiple threads.

Seen hanging around JavaSpaces, where it controls synchronized access to an underlying set of objects in a distributed environment.

Help find a habitat

Complexity Hiding Proxy hides the complexity of and controls access to a complex set of classes. This is sometimes called the Facade Proxy for obvious reasons.

The Complexity Hiding Proxy differs from the Facade Pattern in that the proxy controls access, while the Facade Pattern just provides an alternative interface.

Copy-On-Write Proxy controls the copying of an object by deferring the copying of an object until it is required by a client. This is a variant of the Virtual Proxy.

Habitat: seen in the vicinity of the Java 5's CopyOnWriteArrayList.

Field Notes: please add your observations of other proxies in the wild here:

It's been a LONG chapter. Why not unwind by doing a crossword puzzle before it ends?

Across

1. Group of first CD cover displayed (two words)
3. Proxy that stands in for expensive objects
4. We took one of these to learn RMI
7. Remote _____ was used to implement the gumball machine monitor (two words)
9. Software developer agent was being this kind of proxy
11. In RMI, the object that takes the network requests on the service side
14. Proxy that protects method calls from unauthorized callers
15. A _____ proxy class is created at runtime
16. Place to learn about the many proxy variants
17. Commonly used proxy for web services (two words)
18. In RMI, the proxy is called this
19. The CD viewer used this kind of proxy

Down

2. Java's dynamic proxy forwards all requests to this (two words)
5. Group that did the album MCMXC A.D.
6. This utility acts as a lookup service for RMI
8. Why Elroy couldn't get dates
10. Similar to proxy, but with a different purpose
12. Objectville Matchmaking gimmick (three words)
13. Our first mistake: the gumball machine reporting was not _____

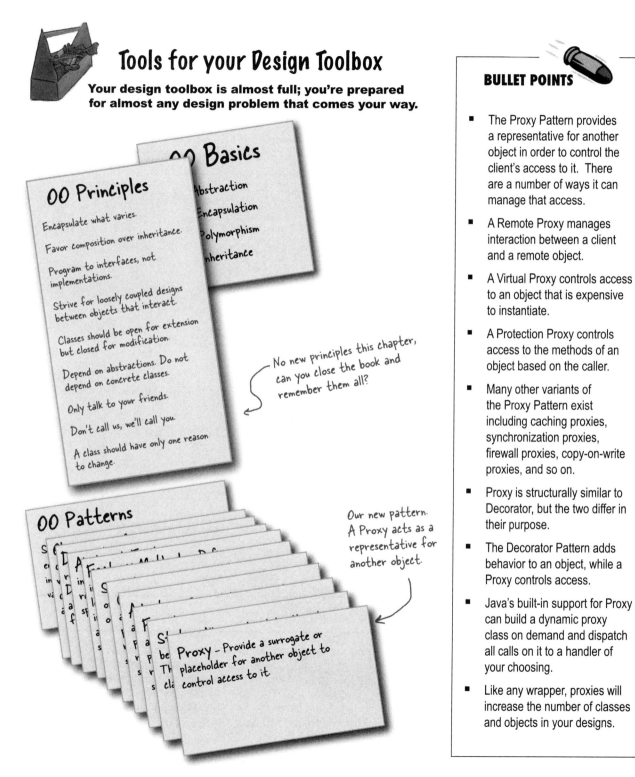

Tools for your Design Toolbox

Your design toolbox is almost full; you're prepared for almost any design problem that comes your way.

OO Basics

Abstraction

Encapsulation

Polymorphism

Inheritance

OO Principles

Encapsulate what varies.

Favor composition over inheritance.

Program to interfaces, not implementations.

Strive for loosely coupled designs between objects that interact.

Classes should be open for extension but closed for modification.

Depend on abstractions. Do not depend on concrete classes.

Only talk to your friends.

Don't call us, we'll call you.

A class should have only one reason to change.

No new principles this chapter, can you close the book and remember them all?

OO Patterns

Proxy – Provide a surrogate or placeholder for another object to control access to it.

Our new pattern. A Proxy acts as a representative for another object.

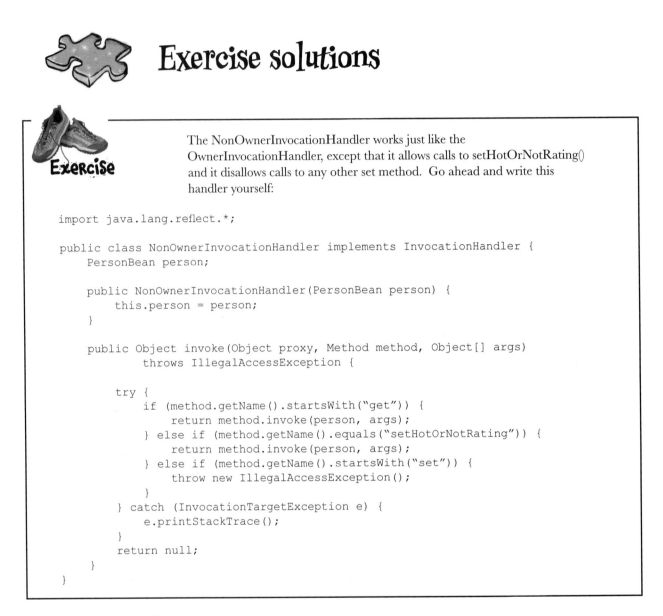

Exercise solutions

Exercise

The NonOwnerInvocationHandler works just like the OwnerInvocationHandler, except that it allows calls to setHotOrNotRating() and it disallows calls to any other set method. Go ahead and write this handler yourself:

```java
import java.lang.reflect.*;

public class NonOwnerInvocationHandler implements InvocationHandler {
    PersonBean person;

    public NonOwnerInvocationHandler(PersonBean person) {
        this.person = person;
    }

    public Object invoke(Object proxy, Method method, Object[] args)
            throws IllegalAccessException {

        try {
            if (method.getName().startsWith("get")) {
                return method.invoke(person, args);
            } else if (method.getName().equals("setHotOrNotRating")) {
                return method.invoke(person, args);
            } else if (method.getName().startsWith("set")) {
                throw new IllegalAccessException();
            }
        } catch (InvocationTargetException e) {
            e.printStackTrace();
        }
        return null;
    }
}
```

Design Class

Our ImageProxy class appears to have two states that are controlled by conditional statements. Can you think of another pattern that might clean up this code? How would you redesign ImageProxy?

Use State Pattern: implement two states, ImageLoaded and ImageNotLoaded. Then put the code from the if statements into their respective states. Start in the ImageNotLoaded state and then transition to the ImageLoaded state once the ImageIcon had been retrieved.

Exercise solutions

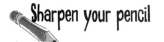
Sharpen your pencil

While it is a little complicated, there isn't much to creating a dynamic proxy. Why don't you write getNonOwnerProxy(), which returns a proxy for the NonOwnerInvocationHandler:

```java
PersonBean getNonOwnerProxy(PersonBean person) {

    return (PersonBean) Proxy.newProxyInstance(
            person.getClass().getClassLoader(),
            person.getClass().getInterfaces(),
            new NonOwnerInvocationHandler(person));
}
```

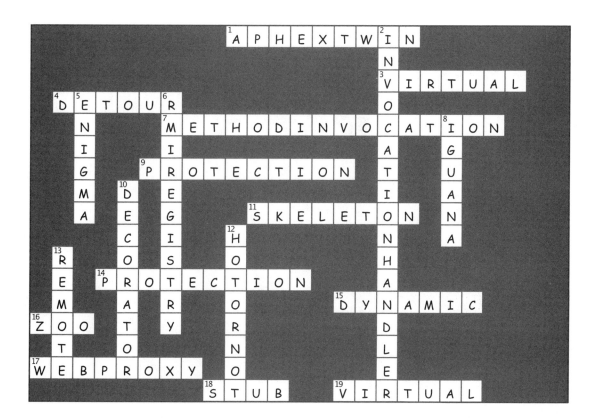

 **Ready-bake Code**

The code for the CD Cover Viewer

```java
package headfirst.proxy.virtualproxy;
import java.net.*;
import java.awt.*;
import java.awt.event.*;
import javax.swing.*;
import java.util.*;
public class ImageProxyTestDrive {
    ImageComponent imageComponent;
    JFrame frame = new JFrame("CD Cover Viewer");
    JMenuBar menuBar;
    JMenu menu;
    Hashtable cds = new Hashtable();

    public static void main (String[] args) throws Exception {
        ImageProxyTestDrive testDrive = new ImageProxyTestDrive();
    }

    public ImageProxyTestDrive() throws Exception{
        cds.put("Ambient: Music for Airports","http://images.amazon.com/images/P/
B000003S2K.01.LZZZZZZZ.jpg");
        cds.put("Buddha Bar","http://images.amazon.com/images/P/B00009XBYK.01.LZZZZZZZ.
jpg");
        cds.put("Ima","http://images.amazon.com/images/P/B000005IRM.01.LZZZZZZZ.jpg");
        cds.put("Karma","http://images.amazon.com/images/P/B000005DCB.01.LZZZZZZZ.gif");
        cds.put("MCMXC A.D.","http://images.amazon.com/images/P/B000002URV.01.LZZZZZZZ.
jpg");
        cds.put("Northern Exposure","http://images.amazon.com/images/P/B000003SFN.01.
LZZZZZZZ.jpg");
        cds.put("Selected Ambient Works, Vol. 2","http://images.amazon.com/images/P/
B000002MNZ.01.LZZZZZZZ.jpg");
        cds.put("oliver","http://www.cs.yale.edu/homes/freeman-elisabeth/2004/9/Oliver_
sm.jpg");

        URL initialURL = new URL((String)cds.get("Selected Ambient Works, Vol. 2"));
        menuBar = new JMenuBar();
        menu = new JMenu("Favorite CDs");
        menuBar.add(menu);
        frame.setJMenuBar(menuBar);
```

```
        for(Enumeration e = cds.keys(); e.hasMoreElements();) {
            String name = (String)e.nextElement();
            JMenuItem menuItem = new JMenuItem(name);
            menu.add(menuItem);
            menuItem.addActionListener(new ActionListener() {
                public void actionPerformed(ActionEvent event) {
                    imageComponent.setIcon(new ImageProxy(getCDUrl(event.getActionCom-
mand()))));
                    frame.repaint();
                }
            });
        }

        // set up frame and menus

        Icon icon = new ImageProxy(initialURL);
        imageComponent = new ImageComponent(icon);
        frame.getContentPane().add(imageComponent);
        frame.setDefaultCloseOperation(JFrame.EXIT_ON_CLOSE);
        frame.setSize(800,600);
        frame.setVisible(true);

    }
    URL getCDUrl(String name) {
        try {
            return new URL((String)cds.get(name));
        } catch (MalformedURLException e) {
            e.printStackTrace();
            return null;
        }
    }
}
```

Ready-bake Code

The code for the CD Cover Viewer, continued...

```java
package headfirst.proxy.virtualproxy;
import java.net.*;
import java.awt.*;
import java.awt.event.*;
import javax.swing.*;

class ImageProxy implements Icon {
    ImageIcon imageIcon;
    URL imageURL;
    Thread retrievalThread;
    boolean retrieving = false;

    public ImageProxy(URL url) { imageURL = url; }

    public int getIconWidth() {
        if (imageIcon != null) {
            return imageIcon.getIconWidth();
        } else {
            return 800;
        }
    }

    public int getIconHeight() {
        if (imageIcon != null) {
            return imageIcon.getIconHeight();
        } else {
            return 600;
        }
    }

    public void paintIcon(final Component c, Graphics  g, int x,  int y) {
        if (imageIcon != null) {
            imageIcon.paintIcon(c, g, x, y);
        } else {
            g.drawString("Loading CD cover, please wait...", x+300, y+190);
            if (!retrieving) {
                retrieving = true;

                retrievalThread = new Thread(new Runnable() {
                    public void run() {
                        try {
                            imageIcon = new ImageIcon(imageURL, "CD Cover");
                            c.repaint();
                        } catch (Exception e) {
```

```
                                e.printStackTrace();
                            }
                        }
                    });
                    retrievalThread.start();
                }
            }
        }
    }
}
```

```
package headfirst.proxy.virtualproxy;
import java.awt.*;
import javax.swing.*;

class ImageComponent extends JComponent {
    private Icon icon;

    public ImageComponent(Icon icon) {
        this.icon = icon;
    }

    public void setIcon(Icon icon) {
        this.icon = icon;
    }

    public void paintComponent(Graphics g) {
        super.paintComponent(g);
        int w = icon.getIconWidth();
        int h = icon.getIconHeight();
        int x = (800 - w)/2;
        int y = (600 - h)/2;
        icon.paintIcon(this, g, x, y);
    }
}
```

12 Compound Patterns

Patterns of Patterns

Who would have ever guessed that Patterns could work together?

You've already witnessed the acrimonious Fireside Chats (and you haven't even seen the Pattern Death Match pages that the editor forced us to remove from the book*), so who would have thought patterns can actually get along well together? Well, believe it or not, some of the most powerful OO designs use several patterns together. Get ready to take your pattern skills to the next level; it's time for compound patterns.

* send us email for a copy.

Working together

One of the best ways to use patterns is to get them out of the house so they can interact with other patterns. The more you use patterns the more you're going to see them showing up together in your designs. We have a special name for a set of patterns that work together in a design that can be applied over many problems: a *compound pattern*. That's right, we are now talking about patterns made of patterns!

You'll find a lot of compound patterns in use in the real world. Now that you've got patterns in your brain, you'll see that they are really just patterns working together, and that makes them easier to understand.

We're going to start this chapter by revisiting our friendly ducks in the SimUDuck duck simulator. It's only fitting that the ducks should be here when we combine patterns; after all, they've been with us throughout the entire book and they've been good sports about taking part in lots of patterns. The ducks are going to help you understand how patterns can work together in the same solution. But just because we've combined some patterns doesn't mean we have a solution that qualifies as a compound pattern. For that, it has to be a general purpose solution that can be applied to many problems. So, in the second half of the chapter we'll visit a *real* compound pattern: that's right, Mr. Model-View-Controller himself. If you haven't heard of him, you will, and you'll find this compound pattern is one of the most powerful patterns in your design toolbox.

Patterns are often used together and combined within the same design solution.

A compound pattern combines two or more patterns into a solution that solves a recurring or general problem.

Duck reunion

As you've already heard, we're going to get to work with the ducks again. This time the ducks are going to show you how patterns can coexist and even cooperate within the same solution.

We're going to rebuild our duck simulator from scratch and give it some interesting capabilities by using a bunch of patterns. Okay, let's get started...

 First, we'll create a Quackable interface.
Like we said, we're starting from scratch. This time around, the Ducks are going to implement a Quackable interface. That way we'll know what things in the simulator can quack() – like Mallard Ducks, Redhead Ducks, Duck Calls, and we might even see the Rubber Duck sneak back in.

```java
public interface Quackable {
    public void quack();
}
```
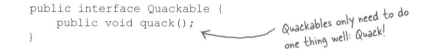
Quackables only need to do one thing well: Quack!

② **Now, some Ducks that implement Quackable**
What good is an interface without some classes to implement it? Time to create some concrete ducks (but not the "lawn art" kind, if you know what we mean).

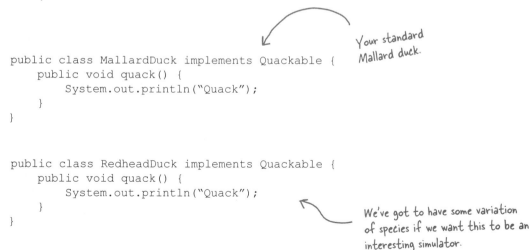

```java
public class MallardDuck implements Quackable {
    public void quack() {
        System.out.println("Quack");
    }
}
```
Your standard Mallard duck.

```java
public class RedheadDuck implements Quackable {
    public void quack() {
        System.out.println("Quack");
    }
}
```
We've got to have some variation of species if we want this to be an interesting simulator.

This wouldn't be much fun if we didn't add other kinds of Ducks too.

Remember last time? We had duck calls (those things hunters use, they are definitely quackable) and rubber ducks.

```java
public class DuckCall implements Quackable {
    public void quack() {
        System.out.println("Kwak");
    }
}
```

A DuckCall that quacks but doesn't sound quite like the real thing.

```java
public class RubberDuck implements Quackable {
    public void quack() {
        System.out.println("Squeak");
    }
}
```

A RubberDuck that makes a squeak when it quacks.

③ Okay, we've got our ducks; now all we need is a simulator.

Let's cook up a simulator that creates a few ducks and makes sure their quackers are working...

Here's our main method to get everything going.

```java
public class DuckSimulator {
    public static void main(String[] args) {
        DuckSimulator simulator = new DuckSimulator();
        simulator.simulate();
    }

    void simulate() {
        Quackable mallardDuck = new MallardDuck();
        Quackable redheadDuck = new RedheadDuck();
        Quackable duckCall = new DuckCall();
        Quackable rubberDuck = new RubberDuck();

        System.out.println("\nDuck Simulator");

        simulate(mallardDuck);
        simulate(redheadDuck);
        simulate(duckCall);
        simulate(rubberDuck);
    }

    void simulate(Quackable duck) {
        duck.quack();
    }
}
```

We create a simulator and then call its simulate() method.

We need some ducks, so here we create one of each Quackable...

... then we simulate each one.

Here we overload the simulate method to simulate just one duck.

Here we let polymorphism do its magic: no matter what kind of Quackable gets passed in, the simulate() method asks it to quack.

Not too exciting yet, but we haven't added patterns!

```
File Edit  Window  Help  ItBetterGetBetterThanThis
% java DuckSimulator

Duck Simulator
Quack
Quack
Kwak
Squeak


%
```

They all implement the same Quackable interface, but their implementations allow them to quack in their own way.

It looks like everything is working; so far, so good.

④ **When ducks are around, geese can't be far.**
Where there is one waterfowl, there are probably two. Here's a Goose class that has been hanging around the simulator.

```java
public class Goose {
    public void honk() {
        System.out.println("Honk");
    }
}
```

A Goose is a honker, not a quacker.

BRAIN POWER

Let's say we wanted to be able to use a Goose anywhere we'd want to use a Duck. After all, geese make noise; geese fly; geese swim. Why can't we have Geese in the simulator?

What pattern would allow Geese to easily intermingle with Ducks?

⑤ We need a goose adapter.

Our simulator expects to see Quackable interfaces. Since geese aren't quackers (they're honkers), we can use an adapter to adapt a goose to a duck.

```java
public class GooseAdapter implements Quackable {
    Goose goose;

    public GooseAdapter(Goose goose) {
        this.goose = goose;
    }

    public void quack() {
        goose.honk();
    }
}
```

Remember, an Adapter implements the target interface, which in this case is Quackable.

The constructor takes the goose we are going to adapt.

When quack is called, the call is delegated to the goose's honk() method.

⑥ Now geese should be able to play in the simulator, too.

All we need to do is create a Goose, wrap it in an adapter that implements Quackable, and we should be good to go.

```java
public class DuckSimulator {
    public static void main(String[] args) {
        DuckSimulator simulator = new DuckSimulator();
        simulator.simulate();
    }
    void simulate() {
        Quackable mallardDuck = new MallardDuck();
        Quackable redheadDuck = new RedheadDuck();
        Quackable duckCall = new DuckCall();
        Quackable rubberDuck = new RubberDuck();
        Quackable gooseDuck = new GooseAdapter(new Goose());

        System.out.println("\nDuck Simulator: With Goose Adapter");

        simulate(mallardDuck);
        simulate(redheadDuck);
        simulate(duckCall);
        simulate(rubberDuck);
        simulate(gooseDuck);
    }

    void simulate(Quackable duck) {
        duck.quack();
    }
}
```

We make a Goose that acts like a Duck by wrapping the Goose in the GooseAdapter.

Once the Goose is wrapped, we can treat it just like other duck Quackables.

⑦ **Now let's give this a quick run....**
This time when we run the simulator, the list of objects passed
to the simulate() method includes a Goose wrapped in a duck
adapter. The result? We should see some honking!

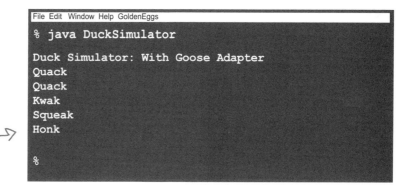

```
File Edit Window Help GoldenEggs
% java DuckSimulator

Duck Simulator: With Goose Adapter
Quack
Quack
Kwak
Squeak
Honk

%
```

There's the goose! Now the Goose can quack with the rest of the Ducks.

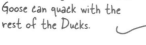 **Quackology**

Quackologists are fascinated by all aspects of Quackable behavior. One thing Quackologists have always wanted to study is the total number of quacks made by a flock of ducks.

How can we add the ability to count duck quacks without having to change the duck classes?

Can you think of a pattern that would help?

J. Brewer, Park Ranger and Quackologist

⑧ **We're going to make those Quackologists happy and give them some quack counts.**

How? Let's create a decorator that gives the ducks some new behavior (the behavior of counting) by wrapping them with a decorator object. We won't have to change the Duck code at all.

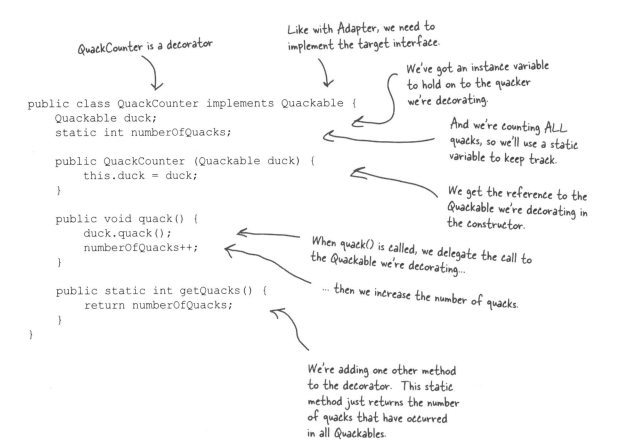

QuackCounter is a decorator

Like with Adapter, we need to implement the target interface.

We've got an instance variable to hold on to the quacker we're decorating.

And we're counting ALL quacks, so we'll use a static variable to keep track.

We get the reference to the Quackable we're decorating in the constructor.

```java
public class QuackCounter implements Quackable {
    Quackable duck;
    static int numberOfQuacks;

    public QuackCounter (Quackable duck) {
        this.duck = duck;
    }

    public void quack() {
        duck.quack();
        numberOfQuacks++;
    }

    public static int getQuacks() {
        return numberOfQuacks;
    }
}
```

When quack() is called, we delegate the call to the Quackable we're decorating...

... then we increase the number of quacks.

We're adding one other method to the decorator. This static method just returns the number of quacks that have occurred in all Quackables.

⑨ **We need to update the simulator to create decorated ducks.**

Now, we must wrap each Quackable object we instantiate in a
QuackCounter decorator. If we don't, we'll have ducks running
around making uncounted quacks.

```java
public class DuckSimulator {
    public static void main(String[] args) {
        DuckSimulator simulator = new DuckSimulator();
        simulator.simulate();
    }
    void simulate() {
        Quackable mallardDuck = new QuackCounter(new MallardDuck());
        Quackable redheadDuck = new QuackCounter(new RedheadDuck());
        Quackable duckCall = new QuackCounter(new DuckCall());
        Quackable rubberDuck = new QuackCounter(new RubberDuck());
        Quackable gooseDuck = new GooseAdapter(new Goose());

        System.out.println("\nDuck Simulator: With Decorator");

        simulate(mallardDuck);
        simulate(redheadDuck);
        simulate(duckCall);
        simulate(rubberDuck);
        simulate(gooseDuck);

        System.out.println("The ducks quacked " +
                    QuackCounter.getQuacks() + " times");
    }

    void simulate(Quackable duck) {
        duck.quack();
    }
}
```

Each time we create a Quackable, we wrap it with a new decorator.

The park ranger told us he didn't want to count geese honks, so we don't decorate it.

Here's where we gather the quacking behavior for the Quackologists.

Nothing changes here; the decorated objects are still Quackables.

```
File  Edit  Window  Help  DecoratedEggs
% java DuckSimulator
Duck Simulator: With Decorator
Quack
Quack
Kwak
Squeak
Honk
4 quacks were counted
%
```

Here's the output!

Remember, we're not counting geese.

> This quack counting is great. We're learning things we never knew about the little quackers. But we're finding that too many quacks aren't being counted. Can you help?

You have to decorate objects to get decorated behavior.

He's right, that's the problem with wrapping objects: you have to make sure they get wrapped or they don't get the decorated behavior.

Why don't we take the creation of ducks and localize it in one place; in other words, let's take the duck creation and decorating and encapsulate it.

What pattern does that sound like?

(10) We need a factory to produce ducks!

Okay, we need some quality control to make sure our ducks get wrapped. We're going to build an entire factory just to produce them. The factory should produce a family of products that consists of different types of ducks, so we're going to use the Abstract Factory Pattern.

Let's start with the definition of the AbstractDuckFactory:

We're defining an abstract factory that subclasses will implement to create different families.

```
public abstract class AbstractDuckFactory {

    public abstract Quackable createMallardDuck();
    public abstract Quackable createRedheadDuck();
    public abstract Quackable createDuckCall();
    public abstract Quackable createRubberDuck();
}
```

Each method creates one kind of duck.

Let's start by creating a factory that creates ducks without decorators, just to get the hang of the factory:

```java
public class DuckFactory extends AbstractDuckFactory {

    public Quackable createMallardDuck() {
        return new MallardDuck();
    }

    public Quackable createRedheadDuck() {
        return new RedheadDuck();
    }

    public Quackable createDuckCall() {
        return new DuckCall();
    }

    public Quackable createRubberDuck() {
        return new RubberDuck();
    }
}
```

DuckFactory extends the abstract factory.

Each method creates a product: a particular kind of Quackable. The actual product is unknown to the simulator – it just knows it's getting a Quackable.

Now let's create the factory we really want, the CountingDuckFactory:

CountingDuckFactory also extends the abstract factory.

```java
public class CountingDuckFactory extends AbstractDuckFactory {

    public Quackable createMallardDuck() {
        return new QuackCounter(new MallardDuck());
    }

    public Quackable createRedheadDuck() {
        return new QuackCounter(new RedheadDuck());
    }

    public Quackable createDuckCall() {
        return new QuackCounter(new DuckCall());
    }

    public Quackable createRubberDuck() {
        return new QuackCounter(new RubberDuck());
    }
}
```

Each method wraps the Quackable with the quack counting decorator. The simulator will never know the difference; it just gets back a Quackable. But now our rangers can be sure that all quacks are being counted.

⑪ **Let's set up the simulator to use the factory.**

Remember how Abstract Factory works? We create a polymorphic method that takes a factory and uses it to create objects. By passing in different factories, we get to use different product families in the method.

We're going to alter the simulate() method so that it takes a factory and uses it to create ducks.

First we create the factory that we're going to pass into the simulate() method.

```java
public class DuckSimulator {
    public static void main(String[] args) {
        DuckSimulator simulator = new DuckSimulator();
        AbstractDuckFactory duckFactory = new CountingDuckFactory();

        simulator.simulate(duckFactory);
    }

    void simulate(AbstractDuckFactory duckFactory) {
        Quackable mallardDuck = duckFactory.createMallardDuck();
        Quackable redheadDuck = duckFactory.createRedheadDuck();
        Quackable duckCall = duckFactory.createDuckCall();
        Quackable rubberDuck = duckFactory.createRubberDuck();
        Quackable gooseDuck = new GooseAdapter(new Goose());

        System.out.println("\nDuck Simulator: With Abstract Factory");

        simulate(mallardDuck);
        simulate(redheadDuck);
        simulate(duckCall);
        simulate(rubberDuck);
        simulate(gooseDuck);

        System.out.println("The ducks quacked " +
                            QuackCounter.getQuacks() +
                            " times");
    }

    void simulate(Quackable duck) {
        duck.quack();
    }
}
```

The simulate() method takes an AbstractDuckFactory and uses it to create ducks rather than instantiating them directly.

Nothing changes here! Same ol' code.

Here's the output using the factory...

Same as last time, but this time we're ensuring that the ducks are all decorated because we are using the CountingDuckFactory.

```
File Edit Window Help EggFactory
% java DuckSimulator
Duck Simulator: With Abstract Factory
Quack
Quack
Kwak
Squeak
Honk
4 quacks were counted
%
```

Sharpen your pencil

We're still directly instantiating Geese by relying on concrete classes. Can you write an Abstract Factory for Geese? How should it handle creating "goose ducks"?

It's getting a little difficult to manage all these different ducks separately. Is there any way you can help us manage ducks as a whole, and perhaps even allow us to manage a few duck "families" that we'd like to keep track of?

Ah, he wants to manage a flock of ducks.

Here's another good question from Ranger Brewer:
Why are we managing ducks individually?

This isn't very manageable!

```
Quackable mallardDuck = duckFactory.createMallardDuck();
Quackable redheadDuck = duckFactory.createRedheadDuck();
Quackable duckCall = duckFactory.createDuckCall();
Quackable rubberDuck = duckFactory.createRubberDuck();
Quackable gooseDuck = new GooseAdapter(new Goose());

simulate(mallardDuck);
simulate(redheadDuck);
simulate(duckCall);
simulate(rubberDuck);
simulate(gooseDuck);
```

What we need is a way to talk about collections of ducks and even sub-collections of ducks (to deal with the family request from Ranger Brewer). It would also be nice if we could apply operations across the whole set of ducks.

What pattern can help us?

(12) **Let's create a flock of ducks (well, actually a flock of Quackables).**

Remember the Composite Pattern that allows us to treat a collection of objects in the same way as individual objects? What better composite than a flock of Quackables!

Let's step through how this is going to work:

Remember, the composite needs to implement the same interface as the leaf elements. Our leaf elements are Quackables.

```java
public class Flock implements Quackable {
    ArrayList quackers = new ArrayList();

    public void add(Quackable quacker) {
        quackers.add(quacker);
    }

    public void quack() {
        Iterator iterator = quackers.iterator();
        while (iterator.hasNext()) {
            Quackable quacker = (Quackable)iterator.next();
            quacker.quack();
        }
    }
}
```

We're using an ArrayList inside each Flock to hold the Quackables that belong to the Flock.

The add() method adds a Quackable to the Flock.

Now for the quack() method — after all, the Flock is a Quackable too. The quack() method in Flock needs to work over the entire Flock. Here we iterate through the ArrayList and call quack() on each element.

 Code Up Close

Did you notice that we tried to sneak a Design Pattern by you without mentioning it?

```java
public void quack() {
    Iterator iterator = quackers.iterator();
    while (iterator.hasNext()) {
        Quackable quacker = (Quackable)iterator.next();
        quacker.quack();
    }
}
```

There it is! The Iterator Pattern at work!

(13) Now we need to alter the simulator.

Our composite is ready; we just need some code to round up the ducks into the composite structure.

```java
public class DuckSimulator {
    // main method here

    void simulate(AbstractDuckFactory duckFactory) {
        Quackable redheadDuck = duckFactory.createRedheadDuck();
        Quackable duckCall = duckFactory.createDuckCall();
        Quackable rubberDuck = duckFactory.createRubberDuck();
        Quackable gooseDuck = new GooseAdapter(new Goose());
        System.out.println("\nDuck Simulator: With Composite - Flocks");

        Flock flockOfDucks = new Flock();

        flockOfDucks.add(redheadDuck);
        flockOfDucks.add(duckCall);
        flockOfDucks.add(rubberDuck);
        flockOfDucks.add(gooseDuck);

        Flock flockOfMallards = new Flock();

        Quackable mallardOne = duckFactory.createMallardDuck();
        Quackable mallardTwo = duckFactory.createMallardDuck();
        Quackable mallardThree = duckFactory.createMallardDuck();
        Quackable mallardFour = duckFactory.createMallardDuck();

        flockOfMallards.add(mallardOne);
        flockOfMallards.add(mallardTwo);
        flockOfMallards.add(mallardThree);
        flockOfMallards.add(mallardFour);

        flockOfDucks.add(flockOfMallards);

        System.out.println("\nDuck Simulator: Whole Flock Simulation");
        simulate(flockOfDucks);

        System.out.println("\nDuck Simulator: Mallard Flock Simulation");
        simulate(flockOfMallards);

        System.out.println("\nThe ducks quacked " +
                        QuackCounter.getQuacks() +
                        " times");
    }

    void simulate(Quackable duck) {
        duck.quack();
    }
}
```

Create all the Quackables, just like before.

First we create a Flock, and load it up with Quackables.

Then we create a new Flock of Mallards.

Here we're creating a little family of mallards...

...and adding them to the Flock of mallards.

Then we add the Flock of mallards to the main flock.

Let's test out the entire Flock!

Then let's just test out the mallard's Flock.

Finally, let's give the Quackologist the data.

Nothing needs to change here, a Flock is a Quackable!

Let's give it a spin...

```
File Edit  Window  Help  FlockADuck
% java DuckSimulator
Duck Simulator: With Composite - Flocks
Duck Simulator: Whole Flock Simulation
Quack
Kwak
Squeak
Honk
Quack
Quack
Quack
Quack

Duck Simulator: Mallard Flock Simulation
Quack
Quack
Quack
Quack

The ducks quacked 11 times
```

Here's the first flock.

And now the mallards.

The data looks good (remember the goose doesn't get counted).

Safety versus transparency

You might remember that in the Composite Pattern chapter the composites (the Menus) and the leaf nodes (the MenuItems) had the *same* exact set of methods, including the add() method. Because they had the same set of methods, we could call methods on MenuItems that didn't really make sense (like trying to add something to a MenuItem by calling add()). The benefit of this was that the distinction between leaves and composites was *transparent*: the client didn't have to know whether it was dealing with a leaf or a composite; it just called the same methods on both.

Here, we've decided to keep the composite's child maintenance methods separate from the leaf nodes: that is, only Flocks have the add() method. We know it doesn't make sense to try to add something to a Duck, and in this implementation, you can't. You can only add() to a Flock. So this design is *safer* – you can't call methods that don't make sense on components – but it's less transparent. Now the client has to know that a Quackable is a Flock in order to add Quackables to it.

As always, there are trade-offs when you do OO design and you need to consider them as you create your own composites.

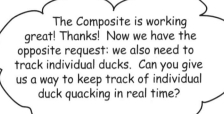

The Composite is working great! Thanks! Now we have the opposite request: we also need to track individual ducks. Can you give us a way to keep track of individual duck quacking in real time?

Can you say "observer?"

It sounds like the Quackologist would like to observe individual duck behavior. That leads us right to a pattern made for observing the behavior of objects: the Observer Pattern.

(14) First we need an Observable interface.

Remember that an Observable is the object being observed. An Observable needs methods for registering and notifying observers. We could also have a method for removing observers, but we'll keep the implementation simple here and leave that out.

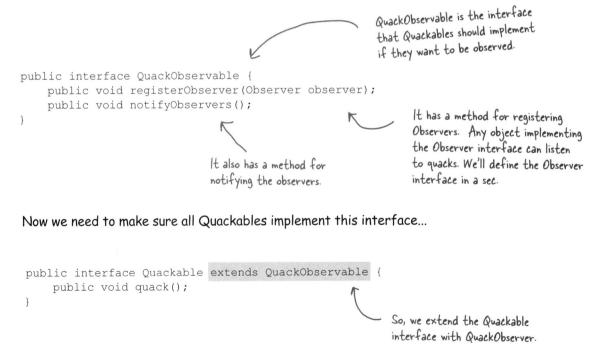

QuackObservable is the interface that Quackables should implement if they want to be observed.

```java
public interface QuackObservable {
    public void registerObserver(Observer observer);
    public void notifyObservers();
}
```

It also has a method for notifying the observers.

It has a method for registering Observers. Any object implementing the Observer interface can listen to quacks. We'll define the Observer interface in a sec.

Now we need to make sure all Quackables implement this interface...

```java
public interface Quackable extends QuackObservable {
    public void quack();
}
```

So, we extend the Quackable interface with QuackObserver.

the concrete
…le can handle

…enting registration and
…s (like we did in Chapter
… differently this time:
…istration and notification
…rvable, and compose it
…ay we only write the real
…le just needs enough
…ss Observable.

…elper class...

Stop looking at me. You're making me nervous!

QuackObserverable

Observable must implement QuackObservable because these are the same method calls that are going to be delegated to it.

In the constructor we get passed the QuackObservable that is using this object to manage its observable behavior. Check out the notify() method below; you'll see that when a notify occurs, Observable passes this object along so that the observer knows which object is quacking.

```
…ments QuackObservable {
    ArrayList();

    …servable duck) {

    …ver(Observer observer) {
    …);

    …s() {
    …servers.iterator();
    …t()) {
    = (Observer)iterator.next();
    …ck);
```

Here's the code for registering an observer.

And the code for doing the notifications.

…Quackable class uses this helper...

(16) **Integrate the helper Observable with the Quackable classes.**

This shouldn't be too bad. All we need to do is make sure the Quackable classes are composed with an Observable and that they know how to delegate to it. After that, they're ready to be Observables. Here's the implementation of MallardDuck; the other ducks are the same.

```java
public class MallardDuck implements Quackable {
    Observable observable;

    public MallardDuck() {
        observable = new Observable(this);
    }

    public void quack() {
        System.out.println("Quack");
        notifyObservers();
    }

    public void registerObserver(Observer observer) {
        observable.registerObserver(observer);
    }

    public void notifyObservers() {
        observable.notifyObservers();
    }
}
```

Each Quackable has an Observable instance variable.

In the constructor, we create an Observable and pass it a reference to the MallardDuck object.

When we quack, we need to let the observers know about it.

Here's our two QuackObservable methods. Notice that we just delegate to the helper.

Sharpen your pencil

We haven't changed the implementation of one Quackable, the QuackCounter decorator. We need to make it an Observable too. Why don't you write that one:

17 **We're almost there! We just need to work on the Observer side of the pattern.**

We've implemented everything we need for the Observables; now we need some Observers. We'll start with the Observer interface:

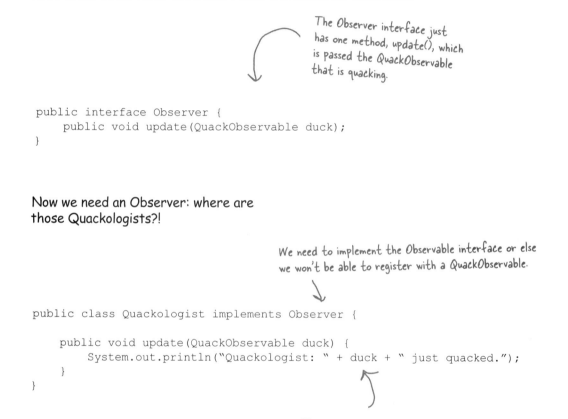

The Observer interface just has one method, update(), which is passed the QuackObservable that is quacking.

```
public interface Observer {
    public void update(QuackObservable duck);
}
```

Now we need an Observer: where are those Quackologists?!

We need to implement the Observable interface or else we won't be able to register with a QuackObservable.

```
public class Quackologist implements Observer {

    public void update(QuackObservable duck) {
        System.out.println("Quackologist: " + duck + " just quacked.");
    }
}
```

The Quackologist is simple; it just has one method, update(), which prints out the Quackable that just quacked.

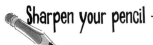

Sharpen your pencil

What if a Quackologist wants to observe an entire flock? What does that mean anyway? Think about it like this: if we observe a composite, then we're observing everything *in* the composite. So, when you register with a flock, the flock composite makes sure you get registered with all its children (sorry, all its little quackers), which may include other flocks.

Go ahead and write the Flock observer code before we go any further...

(18) **We're ready to observe. Let's update the simulator and give it try:**

```java
public class DuckSimulator {
    public static void main(String[] args) {
        DuckSimulator simulator = new DuckSimulator();
        AbstractDuckFactory duckFactory = new CountingDuckFactory();

        simulator.simulate(duckFactory);
    }

    void simulate(AbstractDuckFactory duckFactory) {

        // create duck factories and ducks here

        // create flocks here

        System.out.println("\nDuck Simulator: With Observer");
        Quackologist quackologist = new Quackologist();
        flockOfDucks.registerObserver(quackologist);

        simulate(flockOfDucks);

        System.out.println("\nThe ducks quacked " +
                            QuackCounter.getQuacks() +
                            " times");
    }

    void simulate(Quackable duck) {
        duck.quack();
    }
}
```

All we do here is create a Quackologist and set him as an observer of the flock.

This time we'll we just simulate the entire flock.

Let's give it a try and see how it works!

This is the big finale. Five, no, six patterns have come together to create this amazing Duck Simulator. Without further ado, we present the DuckSimulator!

```
File Edit Window Help DucksAreEverywhere
% java DuckSimulator
Duck Simulator: With Observer
Quack
Quackologist: Redhead Duck just quacked.
Kwak
Quackologist: Duck Call just quacked.
Squeak
Quackologist: Rubber Duck just quacked.
Honk
Quackologist: Goose pretending to be a Duck just quacked.
Quack
Quackologist: Mallard Duck just quacked.
Quack
Quackologist: Mallard Duck just quacked.
Quack
Quackologist: Mallard Duck just quacked.
Quack
Quackologist: Mallard Duck just quacked.
The Ducks quacked 7 times.

%
```

After each quack, no matter what kind of quack it was, the observer gets a notification.

And the quackologist still gets his counts.

there are no
Dumb Questions

Q: So this was a compound pattern?

A: No, this was just a set of patterns working together. A compound pattern is a set of a few patterns that are combined to solve a general problem. We're just about to take a look at the Model-View-Controller compound pattern; it's a collection of a few patterns that has been used over and over in many design solutions.

Q: So the real beauty of Design Patterns is that I can take a problem, and start applying patterns to it until I have a solution. Right?

A: Wrong. We went through this exercise with Ducks to show you how patterns *can* work together. You'd never actually want to approach a design like we just did. In fact, there may be solutions to parts of the duck simulator for which some of these patterns were big time overkill.

Sometimes just using good OO design principles can solve a problem well enough on its own.

We're going to talk more about this in the next chapter, but you only want to apply patterns when and where they make sense. You never want to start out with the intention of using patterns just for the sake of it. You should consider the design of the DuckSimulator to be forced and artificial. But hey, it was fun and gave us a good idea of how several patterns can fit into a solution.

What did we do?

We started with a bunch of Quackables...

A goose came along and wanted to act like a Quackable too. So we used the *Adapter Pattern* to adapt the goose to a Quackable. Now, you can call quack() on a goose wrapped in the adapter and it will honk!

Then, the Quackologists decided they wanted to count quacks. So we used the *Decorator Pattern* to add a QuackCounter decorator that keeps track of the number of times quack() is called, and then delegates the quack to the Quackable it's wrapping.

But the Quackologists were worried they'd forget to add the QuackCounter decorator. So we used the *Abstract Factory Pattern* to create ducks for them. Now, whenever they want a duck, they ask the factory for one, and it hands back a decorated duck. (And don't forget, they can also use another duck factory if they want an un-decorated duck!)

We had management problems keeping track of all those ducks and geese and quackables. So we used the *Composite Pattern* to group quackables into Flocks. The pattern also allows the quackologist to create sub-Flocks to manage duck families. We used the *Iterator Pattern* in our implementation by using java.util's iterator in ArrayList.

The Quackologists also wanted to be notified when any quackable quacked. So we used the *Observer Pattern* to let the Quackologists register as Quackable Observers. Now they're notified every time any Quackable quacks. We used iterator again in this implementation. The Quackologists can even use the Observer Pattern with their composites.

That was quite a Design Pattern workout. You should study the class diagram on the next page and then take a relaxing break before continuing on with the Model-View-Controller.

A ~~bird's~~ duck's eye view: the class diagram

We've packed a lot of patterns into one small duck simulator! Here's the big picture of what we did:

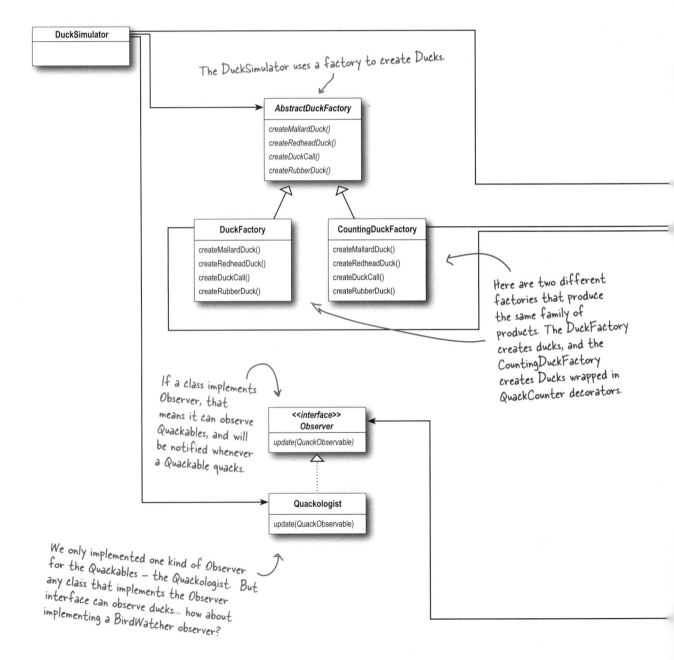

The DuckSimulator uses a factory to create Ducks.

Here are two different factories that produce the same family of products. The DuckFactory creates ducks, and the CountingDuckFactory creates Ducks wrapped in QuackCounter decorators.

If a class implements Observer, that means it can observe Quackables, and will be notified whenever a Quackable quacks.

We only implemented one kind of Observer for the Quackables – the Quackologist. But any class that implements the Observer interface can observe ducks... how about implementing a BirdWatcher observer?

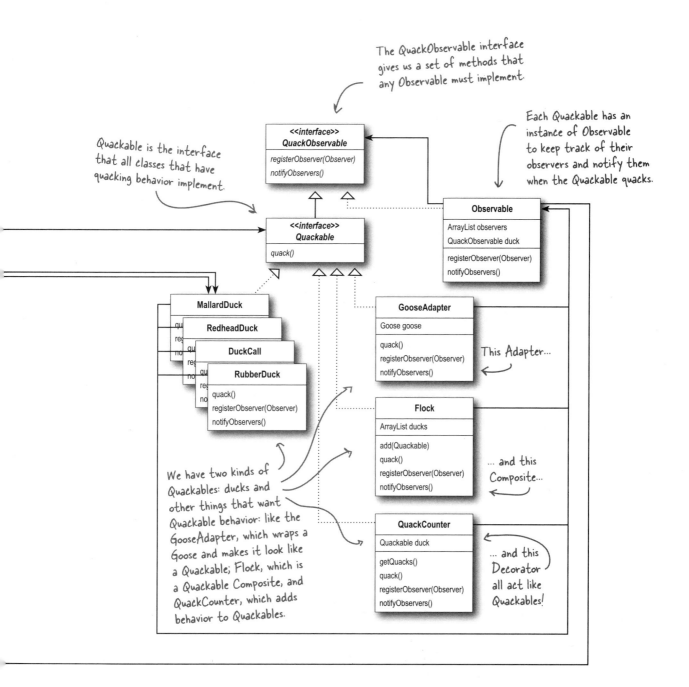

The QuackObservable interface gives us a set of methods that any Observable must implement.

Quackable is the interface that all classes that have quacking behavior implement.

Each Quackable has an instance of Observable to keep track of their observers and notify them when the Quackable quacks.

<<interface>> QuackObservable

registerObserver(Observer)
notifyObservers()

<<interface>> Quackable

quack()

Observable

ArrayList observers
QuackObservable duck

registerObserver(Observer)
notifyObservers()

MallardDuck

RedheadDuck

DuckCall

RubberDuck

quack()
registerObserver(Observer)
notifyObservers()

GooseAdapter

Goose goose

quack()
registerObserver(Observer)
notifyObservers()

This Adapter...

Flock

ArrayList ducks

add(Quackable)
quack()
registerObserver(Observer)
notifyObservers()

... and this Composite...

QuackCounter

Quackable duck

getQuacks()
quack()
registerObserver(Observer)
notifyObservers()

... and this Decorator all act like Quackables!

We have two kinds of Quackables: ducks and other things that want Quackable behavior: like the GooseAdapter, which wraps a Goose and makes it look like a Quackable; Flock, which is a Quackable Composite, and QuackCounter, which adds behavior to Quackables.

The King of Compound Patterns
If Elvis were a compound pattern, his name would be Model-View-Controller, and he'd be singing a little song like this...

Model, View, Controller
Lyrics and music by James Dempsey.

MVC's a paradigm for factoring your code
into functional segments, so your brain does not explode.
To achieve reusability, you gotta keep those boundaries clean
Model on the one side, View on the other, the Controller's in between.

View

Creamy Controller

Model

Model View, it's got three layers like Oreos do
Model View Controller
Model View, Model View, Model View Controller

Model objects represent your application's raison d'être
Custom objects that contain data, logic, and et cetera
You create custom classes, in your app's problem domain
you can choose to reuse them with all the views
but the model objects stay the same.

You can model a throttle and a manifold
Model the toddle of a two year old
Model a bottle of fine Chardonnay
Model all the glottal stops people say
Model the coddling of boiling eggs
You can model the waddle in Hexley's legs

Model View, you can model all the models that pose for GQ
Model View Controller

So does Java!

View objects tend to be controls used to display and edit
Cocoa's got a lot of those, well written to its credit.
Take an NSTextView, hand it any old Unicode string
The user can interact with it, it can hold most anything
But the view don't know about the Model
That string could be a phone number or the works of Aristotle
Keep the coupling loose
and so achieve a massive level of reuse

Model View, all rendered very nicely in Aqua blue
Model View Controller

You're probably wondering now
You're probably wondering how
Data flows between Model and View
The Controller has to mediate
Between each layer's changing state
To synchronize the data of the two

It pulls and pushes every changed value

Model View, mad props to the smalltalk crew!
Model View Controller

Model View, it's pronounced Oh Oh not Ooo Ooo
Model View Controller

There's a little left to this story
A few more miles upon this road
Nobody seems to get much glory
From writing the controller code

Well the model's mission critical
And gorgeous is the view
I might be lazy, but sometimes it's just crazy
How much code I write is just glue
And it wouldn't be so tragic
But the code ain't doing magic
It's just moving values through

And I don't mean to be vicious
But it gets repetitious
Doing all the things controllers do

And I wish I had a dime
For every single time

I sent a TextField StringValue.

Model View
How we gonna deep six all that glue
Model View Controller

Controllers know the Model and View very intimately
They often use hardcoding which can be foreboding for reusability
But now you can connect each model key that you select to any view property

And once you start binding
I think you'll be finding less code in your source tree

Yeah I know I was elated by the stuff they've automated
and the things you get for free

And I think it bears repeating
all the code you won't be needing
when you hook it up in ~~IB~~ ——— Using Swing.

Model View, even handles multiple selections too
Model View Controller

Model View, bet I ship my application before you
Model View Controller

EAR POWER

Don't just read! After all this is a Head First book... grab your iPod, hit this URL:
http://www.headfirstlabs.com/books/hfdp/media.html
Sit back and give it a listen.

Cute song, but is that really supposed to teach me what Model-View-Controller is? I've tried learning MVC before and it made my brain hurt.

No. Design Patterns are your key to the MVC.

We were just trying to whet your appetite. Tell you what, after you finish reading this chapter, go back and listen to the song again – you'll have even more fun.

It sounds like you've had a bad run in with MVC before? Most of us have. You've probably had other developers tell you it's changed their lives and could possibly create world peace. It's a powerful compound pattern, for sure, and while we can't claim it will create world peace, it will save you hours of writing code once you know it.

But first you have to learn it, right? Well, there's going to be a big difference this time around because *now you know patterns!*

That's right, patterns are the key to MVC. Learning MVC from the top down is difficult; not many developers succeed. Here's the secret to learning MVC: *it's just a few patterns put together.* When you approach learning MVC by looking at the patterns, all of the sudden it starts to make sense.

Let's get started. This time around you're going to nail MVC!

Meet the **Model-View-Controller**

Imagine you're using your favorite MP3 player, like iTunes. You can use its interface to add
new songs, manage playlists and rename tracks. The player takes care of maintaining a little
database of all your songs along with their associated names and data. It also takes care of
playing the songs and, as it does, the user interface is constantly updated with the current song
title, the running time, and so on.

Well, underneath it all sits the Model-View-Controller...

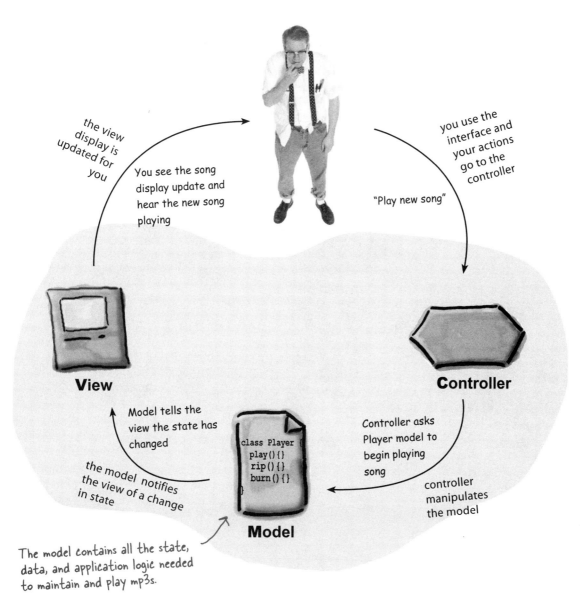

the view display is updated for you

You see the song display update and hear the new song playing

you use the interface and your actions go to the controller

"Play new song"

View

Controller

Model tells the view the state has changed

Controller asks Player model to begin playing song

```
class Player {
    play(){}
    rip(){}
    burn(){}
}
```

the model notifies the view of a change in state

controller manipulates the model

Model

The model contains all the state, data, and application logic needed to maintain and play mp3s.

A closer look...

The MP3 Player description gives us a high level view of MVC, but it really doesn't help you understand the nitty gritty of how the compound pattern works, how you'd build one yourself, or why it's such a good thing. Let's start by stepping through the relationships among the model, view and controller, and then we'll take second look from the perspective of Design Patterns.

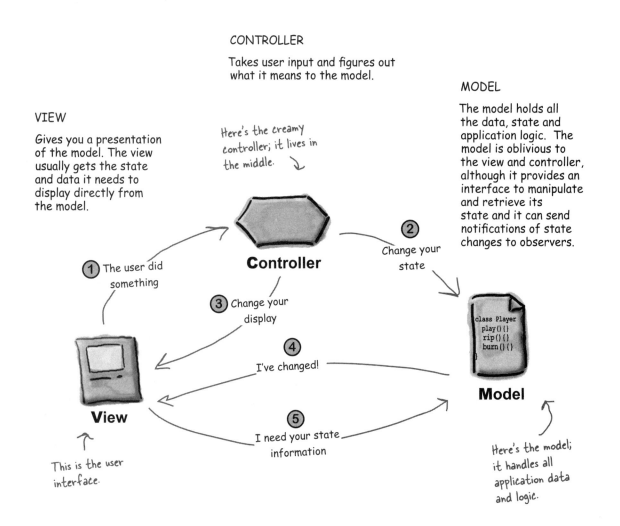

CONTROLLER

Takes user input and figures out what it means to the model.

MODEL

The model holds all the data, state and application logic. The model is oblivious to the view and controller, although it provides an interface to manipulate and retrieve its state and it can send notifications of state changes to observers.

VIEW

Gives you a presentation of the model. The view usually gets the state and data it needs to display directly from the model.

Here's the creamy controller; it lives in the middle.

Controller

1 The user did something

2 Change your state

3 Change your display

4 I've changed!

5 I need your state information

class Player {
   play() {}
   rip() {}
   burn() {}
}

Model

View

This is the user interface.

Here's the model; it handles all application data and logic.

(1) You're the user — you interact with the view.
The view is your window to the model. When you do something to the view (like click the Play button) then the view tells the controller what you did. It's the controller's job to handle that.

(2) The controller asks the model to change its state.
The controller takes your actions and interprets them. If you click on a button, it's the controller's job to figure out what that means and how the model should be manipulated based on that action.

(3) The controller may also ask the view to change.
When the controller receives an action from the view, it may need to tell the view to change as a result. For example, the controller could enable or disable certain buttons or menu items in the interface.

(4) The model notifies the view when its state has changed.
When something changes in the model, based either on some action you took (like clicking a button) or some other internal change (like the next song in the playlist has started), the model notifies the view that its state has changed.

(5) The view asks the model for state.
The view gets the state it displays directly from the model. For instance, when the model notifies the view that a new song has started playing, the view requests the song name from the model and displays it. The view might also ask the model for state as the result of the controller requesting some change in the view.

---

there are no
Dumb Questions

Q: Does the controller ever become an observer of the model?

A: Sure. In some designs the controller registers with the model and is notified of changes. This can be the case when something in the model directly affects the user interface controls. For instance, certain states in the model may dictate that some interface items be enabled or disabled. If so, it is really controller's job to ask the view to update its display accordingly.

Q: All the controller does is take user input from the view and send it to the model, correct? Why have it at all if that is all it does? Why not just have the code in the view itself? In most cases isn't the controller just calling a method on the model?

A: The controller does more than just "send it to the model", the controller is responsible for interpreting the input and manipulating the model based on that input. But your real question is probably "why can't I just do that in the view code?"

You could; however, you don't want to for two reasons: First, you'll complicate your view code because it now has two responsibilities: managing the user interface and dealing with logic of how to control the model. Second, you're tightly coupling your view to the model. If you want to reuse the view with another model, forget it. The controller separates the logic of control from the view and decouples the view from the model. By keeping the view and controller loosely coupled, you are building a more flexible and extensible design, one that can more easily accommodate change down the road.

Looking at MVC through patterns-colored glasses

We've already told you the best path to learning the MVC is to see it for what it is: a set of patterns working together in the same design.

Let's start with the model. As you might have guessed the model uses Observer to keep the views and controllers updated on the latest state changes. The view and the controller, on the other hand, implement the Strategy Pattern. The controller is the behavior of the view, and it can be easily exchanged with another controller if you want different behavior. The view itself also uses a pattern internally to manage the windows, buttons and other components of the display: the Composite Pattern.

Let's take a closer look:

Strategy

The view and controller implement the classic Strategy Pattern: the view is an object that is configured with a strategy. The controller provides the strategy. The view is concerned only with the visual aspects of the application, and delegates to the controller for any decisions about the interface behavior. Using the Strategy Pattern also keeps the view decoupled from the model because it is the controller that is responsible for interacting with the model to carry out user requests. The view knows nothing about how this gets done.

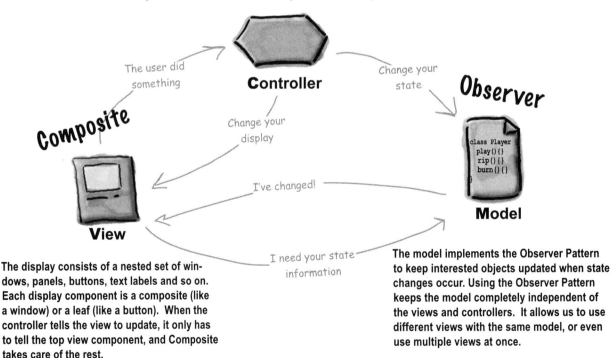

The display consists of a nested set of windows, panels, buttons, text labels and so on. Each display component is a composite (like a window) or a leaf (like a button). When the controller tells the view to update, it only has to tell the top view component, and Composite takes care of the rest.

The model implements the Observer Pattern to keep interested objects updated when state changes occur. Using the Observer Pattern keeps the model completely independent of the views and controllers. It allows us to use different views with the same model, or even use multiple views at once.

Observer

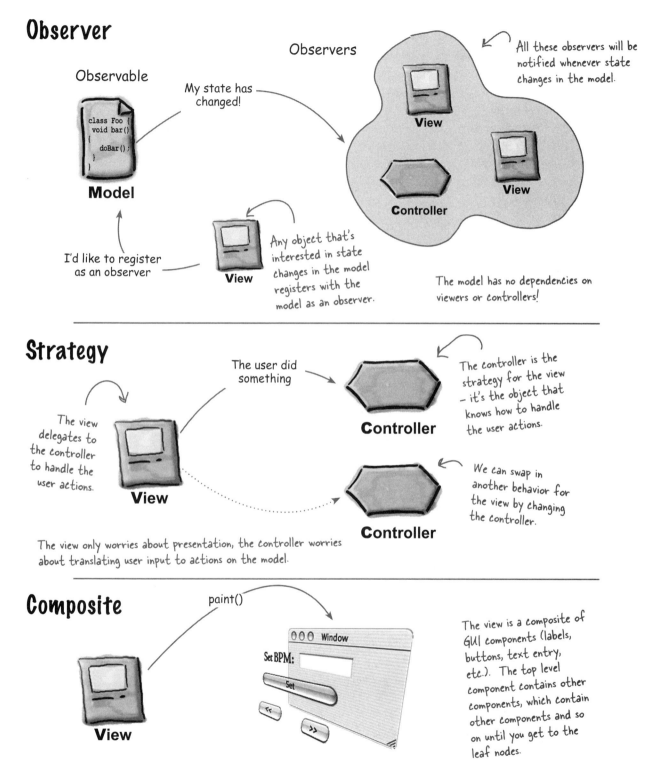

Observable

Observers

Any object that's interested in state changes in the model registers with the model as an observer.

My state has changed!

```
class Foo {
    void bar()
    {
        doBar();
    }
}
```

Model

View

All these observers will be notified whenever state changes in the model.

Controller

View

I'd like to register as an observer

View

The model has no dependencies on viewers or controllers!

Strategy

The user did something

The view delegates to the controller to handle the user actions.

View

Controller

The controller is the strategy for the view — it's the object that knows how to handle the user actions.

Controller

We can swap in another behavior for the view by changing the controller.

The view only worries about presentation, the controller worries about translating user input to actions on the model.

Composite

paint()

View

○○○ Window

Set BPM:

Set

<<

>>

The view is a composite of GUI components (labels, buttons, text entry, etc.). The top level component contains other components, which contain other components and so on until you get to the leaf nodes.

Using MVC to control the beat...

It's your time to be the DJ. When you're a DJ it's all about the beat. You might start your mix with a slowed, downtempo groove at 95 beats per minute (BPM) and then bring the crowd up to a frenzied 140 BPM of trance techno. You'll finish off your set with a mellow 80 BPM ambient mix.

How are you going to do that? You have to control the beat and you're going to build the tool to get you there.

Meet the Java DJ View

Let's start with the **view** of the tool. The view allows you to create a driving drum beat and tune its beats per minute...

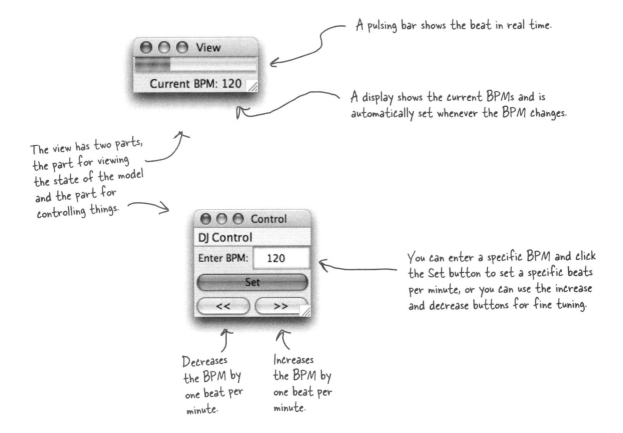

A pulsing bar shows the beat in real time.

A display shows the current BPMs and is automatically set whenever the BPM changes.

The view has two parts, the part for viewing the state of the model and the part for controlling things.

You can enter a specific BPM and click the Set button to set a specific beats per minute, or you can use the increase and decrease buttons for fine tuning.

Decreases the BPM by one beat per minute.

Increases the BPM by one beat per minute.

Here's a few more ways to control the DJ View...

You can start the beat kicking by choosing the Start menu item in the "DJ Control" menu.

You use the Stop button to shut down the beat generation.

Notice Stop is disabled until you start the beat.

Notice Start is disabled after the beat has started.

All user actions are sent to the controller.

The controller is in the middle...

The **controller** sits between the view and model. It takes your input, like selecting "Start" from the DJ Control menu, and turns it into an action on the model to start the beat generation.

The controller takes input from the user and figures out how to translate that into requests on the model.

Controller

Let's not forget about the model underneath it all...

You can't see the **model**, but you can hear it. The model sits underneath everything else, managing the beat and driving the speakers with MIDI.

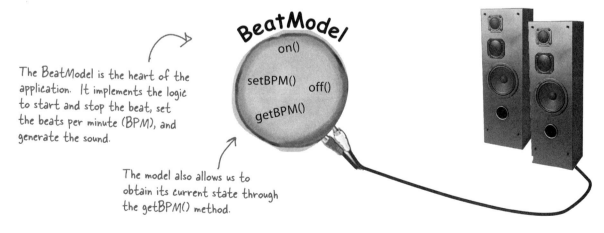

The BeatModel is the heart of the application. It implements the logic to start and stop the beat, set the beats per minute (BPM), and generate the sound.

The model also allows us to obtain its current state through the getBPM() method.

Putting the pieces together

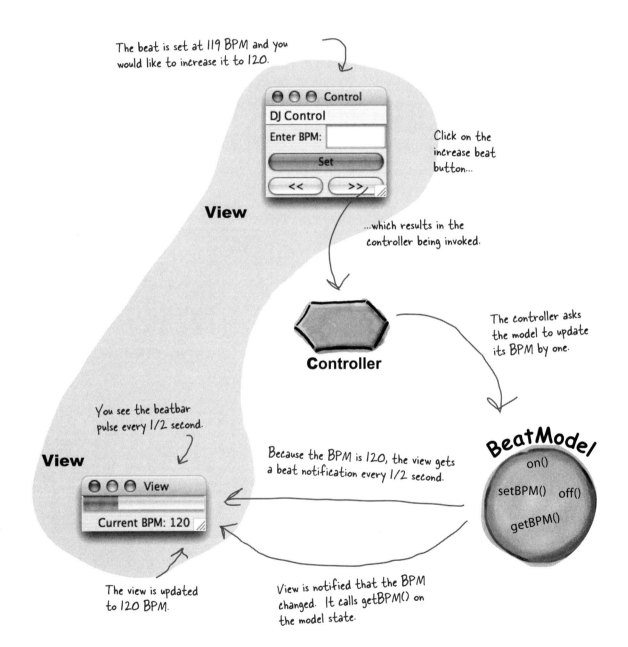

The beat is set at 119 BPM and you would like to increase it to 120.

View

Click on the increase beat button...

...which results in the controller being invoked.

Controller

The controller asks the model to update its BPM by one.

BeatModel

on()

setBPM()   off()

getBPM()

You see the beatbar pulse every 1/2 second.

View

Because the BPM is 120, the view gets a beat notification every 1/2 second.

Current BPM: 120

The view is updated to 120 BPM.

View is notified that the BPM changed. It calls getBPM() on the model state.

Building the pieces

Okay, you know the model is responsible for maintaining all the data, state and any application logic. So what's the BeatModel got in it? Its main job is managing the beat, so it has state that maintains the current beats per minute and lots of code that generates MIDI events to create the beat that we hear. It also exposes an interface that lets the controller manipulate the beat and lets the view and controller obtain the model's state. Also, don't forget that the model uses the Observer Pattern, so we also need some methods to let objects register as observers and send out notifications.

Let's check out the BeatModelInterface before looking at the implementation:

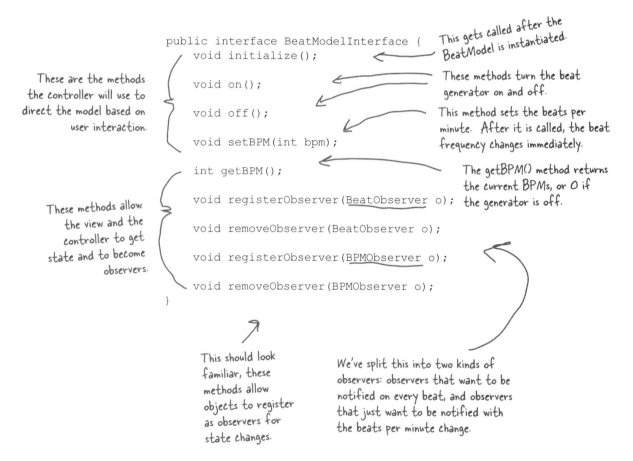

```
public interface BeatModelInterface {
    void initialize();

    void on();

    void off();

    void setBPM(int bpm);

    int getBPM();

    void registerObserver(BeatObserver o);

    void removeObserver(BeatObserver o);

    void registerObserver(BPMObserver o);

    void removeObserver(BPMObserver o);
}
```

This gets called after the BeatModel is instantiated.

These methods turn the beat generator on and off.

This method sets the beats per minute. After it is called, the beat frequency changes immediately.

The getBPM() method returns the current BPMs, or 0 if the generator is off.

These are the methods the controller will use to direct the model based on user interaction.

These methods allow the view and the controller to get state and to become observers.

This should look familiar, these methods allow objects to register as observers for state changes.

We've split this into two kinds of observers: observers that want to be notified on every beat, and observers that just want to be notified with the beats per minute change.

Now let's have a look at the concrete BeatModel class:

This is needed for the MIDI code.

We implement the BeatModelInterface.

```java
public class BeatModel implements BeatModelInterface, MetaEventListener {
    Sequencer sequencer;
    ArrayList beatObservers = new ArrayList();
    ArrayList bpmObservers = new ArrayList();
    int bpm = 90;
    // other instance variables here

    public void initialize() {
        setUpMidi();
        buildTrackAndStart();
    }

    public void on() {
        sequencer.start();
        setBPM(90);
    }

    public void off() {
        setBPM(0);
        sequencer.stop();
    }

    public void setBPM(int bpm) {
        this.bpm = bpm;
        sequencer.setTempoInBPM(getBPM());
        notifyBPMObservers();
    }

    public int getBPM() {
        return bpm;
    }

    void beatEvent() {
        notifyBeatObservers();
    }

    // Code to register and notify observers

    // Lots of MIDI code to handle the beat
}
```

The sequencer is the object that knows how to generate real beats (that you can hear!).

These ArrayLists hold the two kinds of observers (Beat and BPM observers).

The bpm instance variable holds the frequency of beats – by default, 90 BPM.

This method does setup on the sequencer and sets up the beat tracks for us.

The on() method starts the sequencer and sets the BPMs to the default: 90 BPM.

And off() shuts it down by setting BPMs to 0 and stopping the sequencer.

The setBPM() method is the way the controller manipulates the beat. It does three things:

(1) Sets the bpm instance variable

(2) Asks the sequencer to change its BPMs.

(3) Notifies all BPM Observers that the BPM has changed.

The getBPM() method just returns the bpm instance variable, which indicates the current beats per minute.

The beatEvent() method, which is not in the BeatModelInterface, is called by the MIDI code whenever a new beat starts. This method notifies all BeatObservers that a new beat has just occurred.

Ready-bake Code

This model uses Java's MIDI support to generate beats. You can check out the complete implementation of all the DJ classes in the Java source files available on the headfirstlabs.com site, or look at the code at the end of the chapter.

The View

Now the fun starts; we get to hook up a view and visualize the BeatModel!

The first thing to notice about the view is that we've implemented it so that it is displayed in two separate windows. One window contains the current BPM and the pulse; the other contains the interface controls. Why? We wanted to emphasize the difference between the interface that contains the view of the model and the rest of the interface that contains the set of user controls. Let's take a closer look at the two parts of the view:

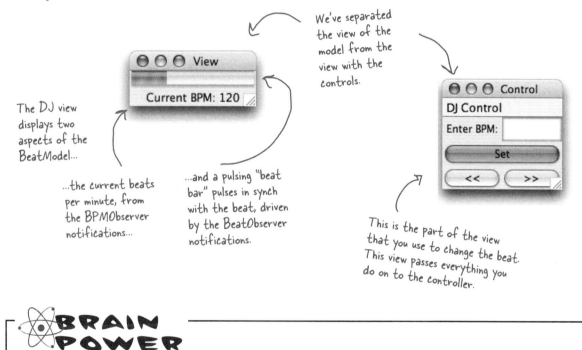

We've separated the view of the model from the view with the controls.

The DJ view displays two aspects of the BeatModel...

...the current beats per minute, from the BPMObserver notifications...

...and a pulsing "beat bar" pulses in synch with the beat, driven by the BeatObserver notifications.

This is the part of the view that you use to change the beat. This view passes everything you do on to the controller.

⚛ BRAIN POWER

Our BeatModel makes no assumptions about the view. The model is implemented using the Observer Pattern, so it just notifies any view registered as an observer when its state changes. The view uses the model's API to get access to the state. We've implemented one type of view, can you think of other views that could make use of the notifications and state in the BeatModel?

A lightshow that is based on the real-time beat.

A textual view that displays a music genre based on the BPM (ambient, downbeat, techno, etc.).

Implementing the View

The two parts of the view – the view of the model, and the view with the user interface controls – are displayed in two windows, but live together in one Java class. We'll first show you just the code that creates the view of the model, which displays the current BPM and the beat bar. Then we'll come back on the next page and show you just the code that creates the user interface controls, which displays the BPM text entry field, and the buttons.

Watch it!

> **The code on these two pages is just an outline!**
>
> *What we've done here is split ONE class into TWO, showing you one part of the view on this page, and the other part on the next page. All this code is really in ONE class - DJView.java. It's all listed at the back of the chapter.*

DJView is an observer for both real-time beats and BPM changes.

```java
public class DJView implements ActionListener, BeatObserver, BPMObserver {
    BeatModelInterface model;
    ControllerInterface controller;
    JFrame viewFrame;
    JPanel viewPanel;
    BeatBar beatBar;
    JLabel bpmOutputLabel;

    public DJView(ControllerInterface controller, BeatModelInterface model) {
        this.controller = controller;
        this.model = model;
        model.registerObserver((BeatObserver)this);
        model.registerObserver((BPMObserver)this);
    }

    public void createView() {
        // Create all Swing components here
    }

    public void updateBPM() {
        int bpm = model.getBPM();
        if (bpm == 0) {
            bpmOutputLabel.setText("offline");
        } else {
            bpmOutputLabel.setText("Current BPM: " + model.getBPM());
        }
    }

    public void updateBeat() {
        beatBar.setValue(100);
    }
}
```

The view holds a reference to both the model and the controller. The controller is only used by the control interface, which we'll go over in a sec...

Here, we create a few components for the display.

The constructor gets a reference to the controller and the model, and we store references to those in the instance variables.

We also register as a BeatObserver and a BPMObserver of the model.

The updateBPM() method is called when a state change occurs in the model. When that happens we update the display with the current BPM. We can get this value by requesting it directly from the model.

Likewise, the updateBeat() method is called when the model starts a new beat. When that happens, we need to pulse our "beat bar." We do this by setting it to its maximum value (100) and letting it handle the animation of the pulse.

Implementing the View, continued...

Now, we'll look at the code for the user interface controls part of the view. This view lets you control the model by telling the controller what to do, which in turn, tells the model what to do. Remember, this code is in the same class file as the other view code.

```java
public class DJView implements ActionListener,  BeatObserver, BPMObserver {
    BeatModelInterface model;
    ControllerInterface controller;
    JLabel bpmLabel;
    JTextField bpmTextField;
    JButton setBPMButton;
    JButton increaseBPMButton;
    JButton decreaseBPMButton;
    JMenuBar menuBar;
    JMenu menu;
    JMenuItem startMenuItem;
    JMenuItem stopMenuItem;

    public void createControls() {
        // Create all Swing components here
    }
    public void enableStopMenuItem() {
        stopMenuItem.setEnabled(true);
    }

    public void disableStopMenuItem() {
        stopMenuItem.setEnabled(false);
    }

    public void enableStartMenuItem() {
        startMenuItem.setEnabled(true);
    }

    public void disableStartMenuItem() {
        startMenuItem.setEnabled(false);
    }

    public void actionPerformed(ActionEvent event) {
        if (event.getSource() == setBPMButton) {
            int bpm = Integer.parseInt(bpmTextField.getText());
            controller.setBPM(bpm);
        } else if (event.getSource() == increaseBPMButton) {
            controller.increaseBPM();
        } else if (event.getSource() == decreaseBPMButton) {
            controller.decreaseBPM();
        }
    }
}
```

This method creates all the controls and places them in the interface. It also takes care of the menu. When the stop or start items are chosen, the corresponding methods are called on the controller.

All these methods allow the start and stop items in the menu to be enabled and disabled. We'll see that the controller uses these to change the interface.

This method is called when a button is clicked.

If the Set button is clicked then it is passed on to the controller along with the new bpm.

Likewise, if the increase or decrease buttons are clicked, this information is passed on to the controller.

Now for the Controller

It's time to write the missing piece: the controller. Remember the controller is the strategy that we plug into the view to give it some smarts.

Because we are implementing the Strategy Pattern, we need to start with an interface for any Strategy that might be plugged into the DJ View. We're going to call it ControllerInterface.

```java
public interface ControllerInterface {
    void start();
    void stop();
    void increaseBPM();
    void decreaseBPM();
    void setBPM(int bpm);
}
```

Here are all the methods the view can call on the controller.

These should look familiar after seeing the model's interface. You can stop and start the beat generation and change the BPM. This interface is "richer" than the BeatModel interface because you can adjust the BPMs with increase and decrease.

Design Puzzle

You've seen that the view and controller together make use of the Strategy Pattern. Can you draw a class diagram of the two that represents this pattern?

And here's the implementation of the controller:

The controller implements the ControllerInterface.

```java
public class BeatController implements ControllerInterface {
    BeatModelInterface model;
    DJView view;

    public BeatController(BeatModelInterface model) {
        this.model = model;
        view = new DJView(this, model);
        view.createView();
        view.createControls();
        view.disableStopMenuItem();
        view.enableStartMenuItem();
        model.initialize();
    }

    public void start() {
        model.on();
        view.disableStartMenuItem();
        view.enableStopMenuItem();
    }

    public void stop() {
        model.off();
        view.disableStopMenuItem();
        view.enableStartMenuItem();
    }

    public void increaseBPM() {
        int bpm = model.getBPM();
        model.setBPM(bpm + 1);
    }

    public void decreaseBPM() {
        int bpm = model.getBPM();
        model.setBPM(bpm - 1);
    }

    public void setBPM(int bpm) {
        model.setBPM(bpm);
    }
}
```

The controller is the creamy stuff in the middle of the MVC oreo cookie, so it is the object that gets to hold on to the view and the model and glues it all together.

The controller is passed the model in the constructor and then creates the view.

When you choose Start from the user interface menu, the controller turns the model on and then alters the user interface so that the start menu item is disabled and the stop menu item is enabled.

Likewise, when you choose Stop from the menu, the controller turns the model off and alters the user interface so that the stop menu item is disabled and the start menu item is enabled.

If the increase button is clicked, the controller gets the current BPM from the model, adds one, and then sets a new BPM.

Same thing here, only we subtract one from the current BPM.

NOTE: the controller is making the intelligent decisions for the view. The view just knows how to turn menu items on and off; it doesn't know the situations in which it should disable them.

Finally, if the user interface is used to set an arbitrary BPM, the controller instructs the model to set its BPM.

Putting it all together...

We've got everything we need: a model, a view, and a controller. Now it's time to put them all together into a MVC! We're going to see and hear how well they work together.

All we need is a little code to get things started; it won't take much:

```java
public class DJTestDrive {
    public static void main (String[] args) {
        BeatModelInterface model = new BeatModel();
        ControllerInterface controller = new BeatController(model);
    }
}
```

First create a model...

...then create a controller and pass it the model. Remember, the controller creates the view, so we don't have to do that.

And now for a test run...

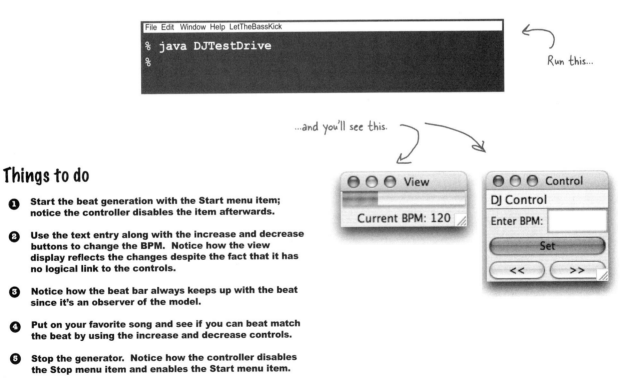

Run this...

...and you'll see this.

Things to do

❶ Start the beat generation with the Start menu item; notice the controller disables the item afterwards.

❷ Use the text entry along with the increase and decrease buttons to change the BPM. Notice how the view display reflects the changes despite the fact that it has no logical link to the controls.

❸ Notice how the beat bar always keeps up with the beat since it's an observer of the model.

❹ Put on your favorite song and see if you can beat match the beat by using the increase and decrease controls.

❺ Stop the generator. Notice how the controller disables the Stop menu item and enables the Start menu item.

Exploring Strategy

Let's take the Strategy Pattern just a little further to get a better feel for how it is used in MVC. We're going to see another friendly pattern pop up too – a pattern you'll often see hanging around the MVC trio: the Adapter Pattern.

Think for a second about what the DJ View does: it displays a beat rate and a pulse. Does that sound like something else? How about a heartbeat? It just so happens we happen to have a heart monitor class; here's the class diagram:

HeartModel
getHeartRate()
registerBeatObserver()
registerBPMObserver()
// other heart methods

We've got a method for getting the current heart rate.

And luckily, its developers knew about the Beat and BPM Observer interfaces!

BRAIN POWER

It certainly would be nice to reuse our current view with the HeartModel, but we need a controller that works with this model. Also, the interface of the HeatModel doesn't match what the view expects because it has a getHeartRate() method rather than a getBPM(). How would you design a set of classes to allow the view to be reused with the new model?

Adapting the Model

For starters, we're going to need to adapt the HeartModel to a BeatModel. If we don't, the view won't be able to work with the model, because the view only knows how to getBPM(), and the equivalent heart model method is getHeartRate(). How are we going to do this? We're going to use the Adapter Pattern, of course! It turns out that this is a common technique when working with the MVC: use an adapter to adapt a model to work with existing controllers and views.

Here's the code to adapt a HeartModel to a BeatModel:

We need to implement the target interface, in this case, BeatModelInterface.

```java
public class HeartAdapter implements BeatModelInterface {
    HeartModelInterface heart;

    public HeartAdapter(HeartModelInterface heart) {
        this.heart = heart;
    }
    public void initialize() {}

    public void on() {}

    public void off() {}

    public int getBPM() {
        return heart.getHeartRate();
    }

    public void setBPM(int bpm) {}

    public void registerObserver(BeatObserver o) {
        heart.registerObserver(o);
    }

    public void removeObserver(BeatObserver o) {
        heart.removeObserver(o);
    }

    public void registerObserver(BPMObserver o) {
        heart.registerObserver(o);
    }

    public void removeObserver(BPMObserver o) {
        heart.removeObserver(o);
    }
}
```

Here, we store a reference to the heart model.

We don't know what these would do to a heart, but it sounds scary. So we'll just leave them as "no ops."

When getBPM() is called, we'll just translate it to a getHeartRate() call on the heart model.

We don't want to do this on a heart! Again, let's leave it as a "no op".

Here are our observer methods. We just delegate them to the wrapped heart model.

Now we're ready for a HeartController

With our HeartAdapter in hand we should be ready to create a controller and get the view running with the HeartModel. Talk about reuse!

The HeartController implements the ControllerInterface, just like the BeatController did.

```java
public class HeartController implements ControllerInterface {
    HeartModelInterface model;
    DJView view;

    public HeartController(HeartModelInterface model) {
        this.model = model;
        view = new DJView(this, new HeartAdapter(model));
        view.createView();
        view.createControls();
        view.disableStopMenuItem();
        view.disableStartMenuItem();
    }

    public void start() {}

    public void stop() {}

    public void increaseBPM() {}

    public void decreaseBPM() {}

    public void setBPM(int bpm) {}
}
```

Like before, the controller creates the view and gets everything glued together.

There is one change: we are passed a HeartModel, not a BeatModel...

...and we need to wrap that model with an adapter before we hand it to the view.

Finally, the HeartController disables the menu items as they aren't needed.

There's not a lot to do here; after all, we can't really control hearts like we can beat machines.

And that's it! Now it's time for some test code...

```java
public class HeartTestDrive {
    public static void main (String[] args) {
        HeartModel heartModel = new HeartModel();
        ControllerInterface model = new HeartController(heartModel);
    }
}
```

All we need to do is create the controller and pass it a heart monitor.

And now for a test run...

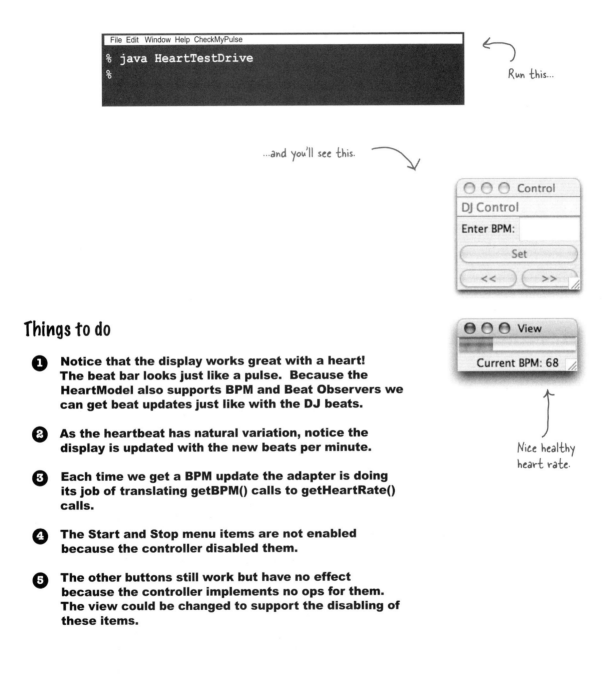

File Edit Window Help CheckMyPulse

```
% java HeartTestDrive
%
```

Run this...

...and you'll see this.

○ ○ ○ Control

DJ Control

Enter BPM:

Set

<<   >>

○ ○ ○ View

Current BPM: 68

Nice healthy heart rate.

Things to do

1 **Notice that the display works great with a heart! The beat bar looks just like a pulse. Because the HeartModel also supports BPM and Beat Observers we can get beat updates just like with the DJ beats.**

2 **As the heartbeat has natural variation, notice the display is updated with the new beats per minute.**

3 **Each time we get a BPM update the adapter is doing its job of translating getBPM() calls to getHeartRate() calls.**

4 **The Start and Stop menu items are not enabled because the controller disabled them.**

5 **The other buttons still work but have no effect because the controller implements no ops for them. The view could be changed to support the disabling of these items.**

MVC and the Web

It wasn't long after the Web was spun that developers started adapting the MVC to fit the browser/server model. The prevailing adaptation is known simply as "Model 2" and uses a combination of servlet and JSP technology to achieve the same separation of model, view and controller that we see in conventional GUIs.

Let's check out how Model 2 works:

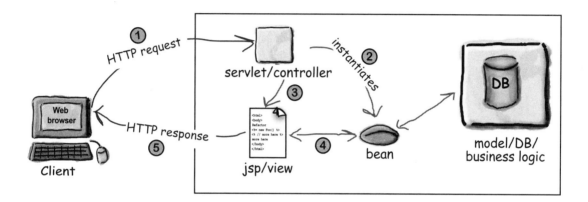

① **You make an HTTP request, which is received by a servlet.**

Using your web browser you make an HTTP request. This typically involves sending along some form data, like your username and password. A servlet receives this form data and parses it.

② **The servlet acts as the controller.**

The servlet plays the role of the controller and processes your request, most likely making requests on the model (usually a database). The result of processing the request is usually bundled up in the form of a JavaBean.

③ **The controller forwards control to the view.**

The View is represented by a JSP. The JSP's only job is to generate the page representing the view of model (④ which it obtains via the JavaBean) along with any controls needed for further actions.

⑤ **The view returns a page to the browser via HTTP.**

A page is returned to the browser, where it is displayed as the view. The user submits further requests, which are processed in the same fashion.

You don't even want to know what life was like before Model 2 came on the scene. It was ugly.

former DOT COM'er

Model 2 is more than just a clean design.

The benefits of the separation of the view, model and controller are pretty clear to you now. But you need to know the "rest of the story" with Model 2 – that it saved many web shops from sinking into chaos.

How? Well, Model 2 not only provides a separation of components in terms of design, it also provides a separation in *production responsibilities*. Let's face it, in the old days, anyone with access to your JSPs could get in and write any Java code they wanted, right? And that included a lot of people who didn't know a jar file from a jar of peanut butter. The reality is that most web producers *know about content and HTML, not software*.

Luckily Model 2 came to the rescue. With Model 2 we can leave the developer jobs to the guys & girls who know their Servlets and let the web producers loose on simple Model 2 style JSPs where all the producers have access to is HTML and simple JavaBeans.

Model 2: DJ'ing from a cell phone

You didn't think we'd try to skip out without moving that great BeatModel over to the Web did you? Just think, you can control your entire DJ session through a web page on your cellular phone. So now you can get out of that DJ booth and get down in the crowd. What are you waiting for? Let's write that code!

The plan

(1) Fix up the model.
Well, actually, we don't have to fix the model, it's fine just like it is!

(2) Create a servlet controller
We need a simple servlet that can receive our HTTP requests and perform a few operations on the model. All it needs to do is stop, start and change the beats per minute.

(3) Create a HTML view.
We'll create a simple view with a JSP. It's going to receive a JavaBean from the controller that will tell it everything it needs to display. The JSP will then generate an HTML interface.

 Geek Bits

Setting up your Servlet environment

Showing you how to set up your servlet environment is a little bit off topic for a book on Design Patterns, at least if you don't want the book to weigh more than you do!

Fire up your web browser and head straight to *http://jakarta.apache.org/tomcat/* for the Apache Jakarta Project's Tomcat Servlet Container. You'll find everything you need there to get you up and running.

You'll also want to check out *Head First Servlets & JSP* by Bryan Basham, Kathy Sierra and Bert Bates.

Step one: the model

Remember that in MVC, the model doesn't know anything about the views or controllers. In other words it is totally decoupled. All it knows is that it may have observers it needs to notify. That's the beauty of the Observer Pattern. It also provides an interface the views and controllers can use to get and set its state.

Now all we need to do is adapt it to work in the web environment, but, given that it doesn't depend on any outside classes, there is really no work to be done. We can use our BeatModel off the shelf without changes. So, let's be productive and move on to step two!

Step two: the controller servlet

Remember, the servlet is going to act as our controller; it will receive Web browser input in a HTTP request and translate it into actions that can be applied to the model.

Then, given the way the Web works, we need to return a view to the browser. To do this we'll pass control to the view, which takes the form of a JSP. We'll get to that in step three.

Here's the outline of the servlet; on the next page, we'll look at the full implementation.

We extend the HttpServlet class so that we can do servlet kinds of things, like receive HTTP requests.

```java
public class DJView extends HttpServlet {

    public void init() throws ServletException {
        BeatModel beatModel = new BeatModel();
        beatModel.initialize();
        getServletContext().setAttribute("beatModel", beatModel);
    }

    // doPost method here

    public void doGet(HttpServletRequest request,
                      HttpServletResponse response)
            throws IOException, ServletException
    {
        // implementation here
    }
}
```

Here's the init method; this is called when the servlet is first created.

We first create a BeatModel object...

...and place a reference to it in the servlet's context so that it's easily accessed.

Here's the doGet() method. This is where the real work happens. We've got its implementation on the next page.

Here's the implementation of the doGet() method from the page before:

```java
public void doGet(HttpServletRequest request,
                  HttpServletResponse response)
    throws IOException, ServletException
{
    BeatModel beatModel =
        (BeatModel)getServletContext().getAttribute("beatModel");

    String bpm = request.getParameter("bpm");
    if (bpm == null) {
        bpm = beatModel.getBPM() + "";
    }

    String set = request.getParameter("set");
    if (set != null) {
        int bpmNumber = 90;
        bpmNumber = Integer.parseInt(bpm);
        beatModel.setBPM(bpmNumber);
    }

    String decrease = request.getParameter("decrease");
    if (decrease != null) {
        beatModel.setBPM(beatModel.getBPM() - 1);
    }
    String increase = request.getParameter("increase");
    if (increase != null) {
        beatModel.setBPM(beatModel.getBPM() + 1);
    }
    String on = request.getParameter("on");
    if (on != null) {
        beatModel.start();
    }
    String off = request.getParameter("off");
    if (off != null) {
        beatModel.stop();
    }

    request.setAttribute("beatModel", beatModel);

    RequestDispatcher dispatcher =
        request.getRequestDispatcher("/jsp/DJView.jsp");
    dispatcher.forward(request, response);
}
```

First we grab the model from the servlet context. We can't manipulate the model without a reference to it.

Next we grab all the HTTP commands/parameters...

If we get a set command, then we get the value of the set, and tell the model.

To increase or decrease, we get the current BPMs from the model, and adjust up or down by one.

If we get an on or off command, we tell the model to start or stop.

Finally, our job as a controller is done. All we need to do is ask the view to take over and create an HTML view.

Following the Model 2 definition, we pass the JSP a bean with the model state in it. In this case, we pass it the actual model, since it happens to be a bean.

Now we need a view...

All we need is a view and we've got our browser-based beat generator ready to go!
In Model 2, the view is just a JSP. All the JSP knows about is the bean it receives
from the controller. In our case, that bean is just the model and the JSP is only
going to use its BPM property to extract the current beats per minute. With that
data in hand, it creates the view and also the user interface controls.

Here's our bean, which the servlet passed us.

```jsp
<jsp:useBean id="beatModel" scope="request" class="headfirst.combined.djview.BeatModel" />

<html>
<head>
<title>DJ View</title>
</head>
<body>

<h1>DJ View</h1>
Beats per minutes = <jsp:getProperty name="beatModel" property="BPM" />
<br />
<hr>
<br />

<form method="post" action="/djview/servlet/DJView">
BPM: <input type=text name="bpm"
            value="<jsp:getProperty name="beatModel"
            property="BPM" />">
 

<input type="submit" name="set" value="set"><br />
<input type="submit" name="decrease" value="<<">
<input type="submit" name="increase" value=">>"><br />
<input type="submit" name="on" value="on">
<input type="submit" name="off" value="off"><br />
</form>

</body>
</html>
```

Beginning of the HTML.

Here we use the model bean to extract the BPM property.

Now we generate the view, which prints out the current beats per minute.

And here's the control part of the view. We have a text entry for entering a BPM along with increase/decrease and on/off buttons.

And here's the end of the HTML.

NOTICE that just like MVC, in Model 2 the view doesn't alter the model (that's the controller's job); all it does is use its state!

Putting Model 2 to the test...

It's time to start your web browser, hit the DJView Servlet and give
the system a spin...

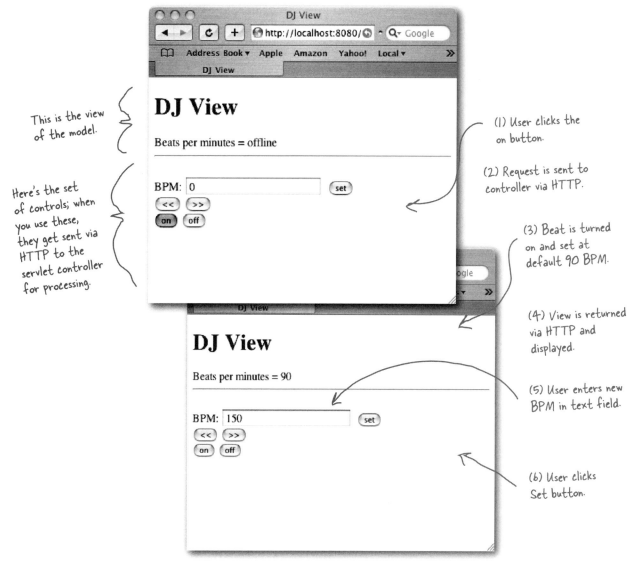

This is the view of the model.

Here's the set of controls; when you use these, they get sent via HTTP to the servlet controller for processing.

(1) User clicks the on button.

(2) Request is sent to controller via HTTP.

(3) Beat is turned on and set at default 90 BPM.

(4) View is returned via HTTP and displayed.

(5) User enters new BPM in text field.

(6) User clicks Set button.

(7) HTTP request is made.

(8) Controller changes model to 150 BPMs

(9) View returns HTML reflecting the current model.

```
○ ○ ○                          DJ View
◀  ▶   C   +   ⊙ http://localhost:8080/djvi⊙  ·  Q⁻ Google
    📖   Address Book▾  Apple  Amazon  Yahoo!  Local▾  News▾   »
            DJ View
```

DJ View

Beats per minutes = 150
_____

BPM: [   ]   (set)
(<<) (>>)
(on) (off)

Things to do

1 First, hit the web page; you'll see the beats per minute at 0. Go ahead and click the "on" button.

2 Now you should see the beats per minute at the default setting: 90 BPM. You should also hear a beat on the machine the server is running on.

3 Enter a specific beat, say, 120, and click the "set" button. The page should refresh with a beats per minute of 120 (and you should hear the beat increase).

4 Now play with the increase/decrease buttons to adjust the beat up and down.

5 Think about how each step of the system works. The HTML interface makes a request to the servlet (the controller); the servlet parses the user input and then makes requests to the model. The servlet then passes control to the JSP (the view), which creates the HTML view that is returned and displayed.

Design Patterns and Model 2

After implementing the DJ Control for the Web using Model 2, you might be wondering where the patterns went. We have a view created in HTML from a JSP but the view is no longer a listener of the model. We have a controller that's a servlet that receives HTTP requests, but are we still using the Strategy Pattern? And what about Composite? We have a view that is made from HTML and displayed in a web browser. Is that still the Composite Pattern?

Model 2 is an adaptation of MVC to the Web

Even though Model 2 doesn't look exactly like "textbook" MVC, all the parts are still there; they've just been adapted to reflect the idiosyncrasies of the web browser model. Let's take another look...

Observer

The view is no longer an observer of the model in the classic sense; that is, it doesn't register with the model to receive state change notifications.

However, the view does receive the equivalent of notifications indirectly from the controller when the model has been changed. The controller even passes the view a bean that allows the view to retrieve the model's state.

If you think about the browser model, the view only needs an update of state information when an HTTP response is returned to the browser; notifications at any other time would be pointless. Only when a page is being created and returned does it make sense to create the view and incorporate the model's state.

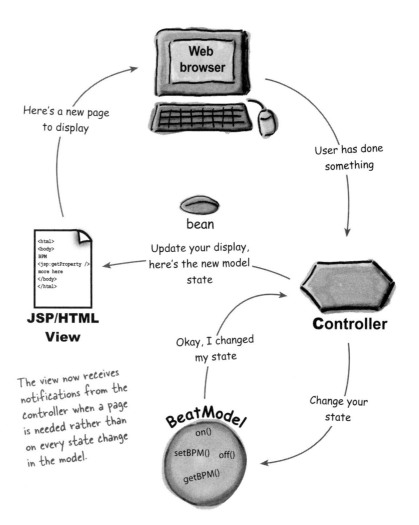

you are here ▶   557

Strategy

In Model 2, the Strategy object is still the controller servlet; however, it's not directly composed with the view in the classic manner. That said, it is an object that implements behavior for the view, and we can swap it out for another controller if we want different behavior.

Composite

Like our Swing GUI, the view is ultimately made up of a nested set of graphical components. In this case, they are rendered by a web browser from an HTML description, however underneath there is an object system that most likely forms a composite.

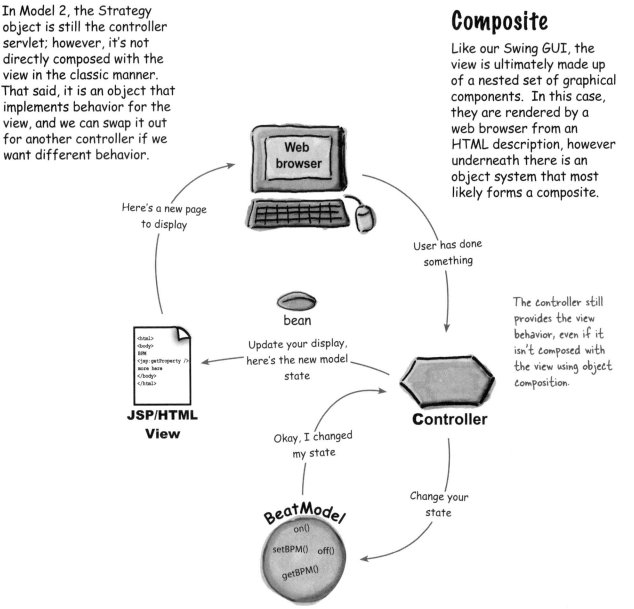

Web browser

Here's a new page to display

User has done something

bean

The controller still provides the view behavior, even if it isn't composed with the view using object composition.

```
<html>
<body>
BPM
<jsp:getProperty />
more here
</body>
</html>
```

JSP/HTML View

Update your display, here's the new model state

Controller

Okay, I changed my state

Change your state

BeatModel
on()
setBPM()   off()
getBPM()

Q: It seems like you are really hand waving the fact that the Composite Pattern is really in MVC. Is it really there?

A: Yes, Virginia, there really is a Composite Pattern in MVC. But, actually, this is a very good question. Today GUI packages, like Swing, have become so sophisticated that we hardly notice the internal structure and the use of composite in the building and update of the display. It's even harder to see when we have Web browsers that can take markup language and convert it into a user interface.

Back when MVC was first discovered, creating GUIs required a lot more manual intervention and the pattern was more obviously part of the MVC.

Q: Does the controller ever implement any application logic?

A: No, the controller implements behavior for the view. It is the smarts that translates the actions from the view to actions on the model. The model takes those actions and implements the application logic to decide what to do in response to those actions. The controller might have to do a little work to determine what method calls to make on the model, but that's not considered the "application logic." The application logic is the code that manages and manipulates your data and it lives in your model.

Q: I've always found the word "model" hard to wrap my head around. I now get that it's the guts of the application, but why was such a vague, hard-to-understand word used to describe this aspect of the MVC?

A: When MVC was named they needed a word that began with a "M" or otherwise they couldn't have called it MVC.

But seriously, we agree with you, everyone scratches their head and wonders what a model is. But then everyone comes to the realization that they can't think of a better word either.

Q: You've talked a lot about the state of the model. Does this mean it has the State Pattern in it?

A: No, we mean the general idea of state. But certainly some models do use the State Pattern to manage their internal states.

Q: I've seen descriptions of the MVC where the controller is described as a "mediator" between the view and the model. Is the controller implementing the Mediator Pattern?

A: We haven't covered the Mediator Pattern (although you'll find a summary of the pattern in the appendix), so we won't go into too much detail here, but the intent of the mediator is to encapsulate how objects interact and promote loose coupling by keeping two objects from referring to each other explicitly. So, to some degree, the controller can be seen as a mediator, since the view never sets state directly on the model, but rather always goes through the controller. Remember, however, that the view does have a reference to the model to access its state. If the controller were truly a mediator, the view would have to go through the controller to get the state of the model as well.

Q: Does the view always have to ask the model for its state? Couldn't we use the push model and send the model's state with the update notification?

A: Yes, the model could certainly send its state with the notification, and in fact, if you look again at the JSP/HTML view, that's exactly what we're doing. We're sending the entire model in a bean, which the view uses to access the state it needs using the bean properties. We could do something similar with the BeatModel by sending just the state that the view is interested in. If you remember the Observer Pattern chapter, however, you'll also remember that there's a couple of disadvantages to this. If you don't go back and have a second look.

Q: If I have more than one view, do I always need more than one controller?

A: Typically, you need one controller per view at runtime; however, the same controller class can easily manage many views.

Q: The view is not supposed to manipulate the model, however I noticed in your implementation that the view has full access to the methods that change the model's state. Is this dangerous?

A: You are correct; we gave the view full access to the model's set of methods. We did this to keep things simple, but there may be circumstances where you want to give the view access to only part of your model's API. There's a great design pattern that allows you to adapt an interface to only provide a subset. Can you think of it?

Tools for your Design Toolbox

You could impress anyone with your design toolbox. Wow, look at all those principles, patterns and now, compound patterns!

OO Principles

Encapsulate what varies.

Favor composition over inheritance.

Program to interfaces, not implementations.

Strive for loosely coupled designs between objects that interact.

Classes should be open for extension but closed for modification.

Depend on abstractions. Do not depend on concrete classes.

Only talk to your friends.

Don't call us; we'll call you.

A class should have only one reason to change.

OO Basics

Abstraction
Encapsulation
Polymorphism
Inheritance

OO Patterns

Proxy – Provide a surrogate or placeholder for another object to control access to it.

Compound Patterns

A Compound Pattern combines two or more patterns into a solution that solves a recurring or general problem.

We have a new category! MVC and Model 2 are compound patterns.

BULLET POINTS

- The Model View Controller Pattern (MVC) is a compound pattern consisting of the Observer, Strategy and Composite patterns.

- The model makes use of the Observer Pattern so that it can keep observers updated yet stay decoupled from them.

- The controller is the strategy for the view. The view can use different implementations of the controller to get different behavior.

- The view uses the Composite Pattern to implement the user interface, which usually consists of nested components like panels, frames and buttons.

- These patterns work together to decouple the three players in the MVC model, which keeps designs clear and flexible.

- The Adapter Pattern can be used to adapt a new model to an existing view and controller.

- Model 2 is an adaptation of MVC for web applications.

- In Model 2, the controller is implemented as a servlet and JSP & HTML implement the view.

Exercise solutions

Sharpen your pencil

The QuackCounter is a Quackable too. When we change Quackable to extend QuackObservable, we have to change *every* class that implements Quackable, including QuackCounter:

> QuackCounter is a Quackable, so now it's a QuackObservable too.

```java
public class QuackCounter implements Quackable {
    Quackable duck;
    static int numberOfQuacks;

    public QuackCounter(Quackable duck) {
        this.duck = duck;
    }

    public void quack() {
        duck.quack();
        numberOfQuacks++;
    }

    public static int getQuacks() {
        return numberOfQuacks;
    }

    public void registerObserver(Observer observer) {
        duck.registerObserver(observer);
    }

    public void notifyObservers() {
        duck.notifyObservers();
    }
}
```

Here's the duck that the QuackCounter is decorating. It's this duck that really needs to handle the observable methods.

All of this code is the same as the previous version of QuackCounter.

Here are the two QuackObservable methods. Notice that we just delegate both calls to the duck that we're decorating.

Sharpen your pencil

What if our Quackologist wants to observe an entire flock? What does that mean anyway? Think about it like this: if we observe a composite, then we're observing everything *in* the composite. So, when you register with a flock, the flock composite makes sure you get registered with all its children, which may include other flocks.

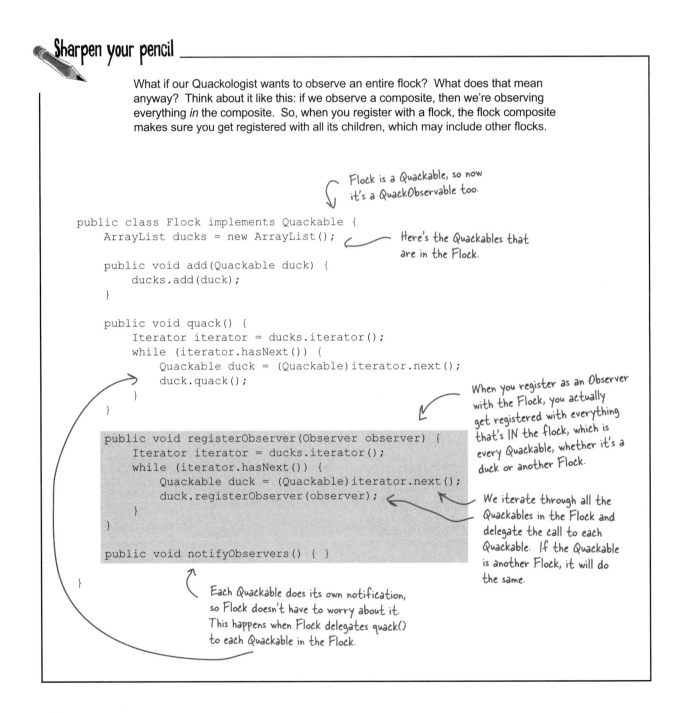

Flock is a Quackable, so now it's a QuackObservable too.

```
public class Flock implements Quackable {
    ArrayList ducks = new ArrayList();

    public void add(Quackable duck) {
        ducks.add(duck);
    }

    public void quack() {
        Iterator iterator = ducks.iterator();
        while (iterator.hasNext()) {
            Quackable duck = (Quackable)iterator.next();
            duck.quack();
        }
    }

    public void registerObserver(Observer observer) {
        Iterator iterator = ducks.iterator();
        while (iterator.hasNext()) {
            Quackable duck = (Quackable)iterator.next();
            duck.registerObserver(observer);
        }
    }

    public void notifyObservers() { }

}
```

Here's the Quackables that are in the Flock.

When you register as an Observer with the Flock, you actually get registered with everything that's IN the flock, which is every Quackable, whether it's a duck or another Flock.

We iterate through all the Quackables in the Flock and delegate the call to each Quackable. If the Quackable is another Flock, it will do the same.

Each Quackable does its own notification, so Flock doesn't have to worry about it. This happens when Flock delegates quack() to each Quackable in the Flock.

We're still directly instantiating Geese by relying on concrete classes. Can you write an Abstract Factory for Geese? How should it handle creating "goose ducks?"

You could add a createGooseDuck() method to the existing Duck Factories. Or, you could create a completely separate Factory for creating families of Geese.

Design Class

You've seen that the View and Controller together make use of the Strategy Pattern. Can you draw a class diagram of the two that shows this pattern?

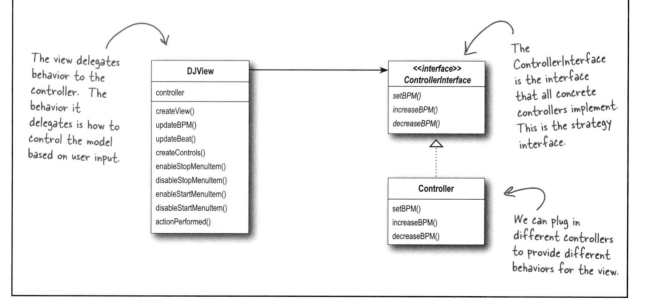

The view delegates behavior to the controller. The behavior it delegates is how to control the model based on user input.

DJView
controller
createView()
updateBPM()
updateBeat()
createControls()
enableStopMenuItem()
disableStopMenuItem()
enableStartMenuItem()
disableStartMenuItem()
actionPerformed()

<<interface>> ControllerInterface
setBPM()
increaseBPM()
decreaseBPM()

Controller
setBPM()
increaseBPM()
decreaseBPM()

The ControllerInterface is the interface that all concrete controllers implement. This is the strategy interface.

We can plug in different controllers to provide different behaviors for the view.

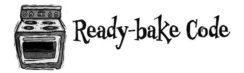 **Ready-bake Code**

Here's the complete implementation of the DJView. It shows all the MIDI code to generate the sound, and all the Swing components to create the view. You can also download this code at http://www.headfirstlabs.com. Have fun!

```java
package headfirst.combined.djview;

public class DJTestDrive {
    public static void main (String[] args) {
        BeatModelInterface model = new BeatModel();
        ControllerInterface controller = new BeatController(model);
    }
}
```

The Beat Model

```java
package headfirst.combined.djview;

public interface BeatModelInterface {
    void initialize();

    void on();

    void off();

    void setBPM(int bpm);

    int getBPM();

    void registerObserver(BeatObserver o);

    void removeObserver(BeatObserver o);

    void registerObserver(BPMObserver o);

    void removeObserver(BPMObserver o);
}
```

```
package headfirst.combined.djview;

import javax.sound.midi.*;
import java.util.*;
public class BeatModel implements BeatModelInterface, MetaEventListener {
    Sequencer sequencer;
    ArrayList beatObservers = new ArrayList();
    ArrayList bpmObservers = new ArrayList();
    int bpm = 90;
    // other instance variables here
    Sequence sequence;
    Track track;

    public void initialize() {
        setUpMidi();
        buildTrackAndStart();
    }

    public void on() {
        sequencer.start();
        setBPM(90);
    }

    public void off() {
        setBPM(0);
        sequencer.stop();
    }

    public void setBPM(int bpm) {
        this.bpm = bpm;
        sequencer.setTempoInBPM(getBPM());
        notifyBPMObservers();
    }

    public int getBPM() {
        return bpm;
    }

    void beatEvent() {
        notifyBeatObservers();
    }


    public void registerObserver(BeatObserver o) {
        beatObservers.add(o);
    }

    public void notifyBeatObservers() {
        for(int i = 0; i < beatObservers.size(); i++) {
```

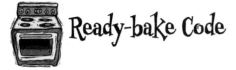
Ready-bake Code

```
            BeatObserver observer = (BeatObserver)beatObservers.get(i);
            observer.updateBeat();
        }
    }

    public void registerObserver(BPMObserver o) {
        bpmObservers.add(o);
    }

    public void notifyBPMObservers() {
        for(int i = 0; i < bpmObservers.size(); i++) {
            BPMObserver observer = (BPMObserver)bpmObservers.get(i);
            observer.updateBPM();
        }
    }


    public void removeObserver(BeatObserver o) {
        int i = beatObservers.indexOf(o);
        if (i >= 0) {
            beatObservers.remove(i);
        }
    }



    public void removeObserver(BPMObserver o) {
        int i = bpmObservers.indexOf(o);
        if (i >= 0) {
            bpmObservers.remove(i);
        }
    }



    public void meta(MetaMessage message) {
        if (message.getType() == 47) {
            beatEvent();
            sequencer.start();
            setBPM(getBPM());
        }
    }

    public void setUpMidi() {
        try {
            sequencer = MidiSystem.getSequencer();
```

```
            sequencer.open();
            sequencer.addMetaEventListener(this);
            sequence = new Sequence(Sequence.PPQ,4);
            track = sequence.createTrack();
            sequencer.setTempoInBPM(getBPM());
        } catch(Exception e) {
                e.printStackTrace();
        }
    }

    public void buildTrackAndStart() {
        int[] trackList = {35, 0, 46, 0};

        sequence.deleteTrack(null);
        track = sequence.createTrack();

        makeTracks(trackList);
        track.add(makeEvent(192,9,1,0,4));
        try {
            sequencer.setSequence(sequence);
        } catch(Exception e) {
            e.printStackTrace();
        }
    }

public void makeTracks(int[] list) {

    for (int i = 0; i < list.length; i++) {
       int key = list[i];

       if (key != 0) {
          track.add(makeEvent(144,9,key, 100, i));
          track.add(makeEvent(128,9,key, 100, i+1));
       }
    }
}

public  MidiEvent makeEvent(int comd, int chan, int one, int two, int tick) {
    MidiEvent event = null;
    try {
        ShortMessage a = new ShortMessage();
        a.setMessage(comd, chan, one, two);
        event = new MidiEvent(a, tick);

    } catch(Exception e) {
        e.printStackTrace();
    }
    return event;
}
}
```

The View

```java
package headfirst.combined.djview;

public interface BeatObserver {
    void updateBeat();
}



package headfirst.combined.djview;

public interface BPMObserver {
    void updateBPM();
}



package headfirst.combined.djview;

import java.awt.*;
import java.awt.event.*;
import javax.swing.*;
public class DJView implements ActionListener,  BeatObserver, BPMObserver {
    BeatModelInterface model;
    ControllerInterface controller;
    JFrame viewFrame;
    JPanel viewPanel;
    BeatBar beatBar;
    JLabel bpmOutputLabel;
    JFrame controlFrame;
    JPanel controlPanel;
    JLabel bpmLabel;
    JTextField bpmTextField;
    JButton setBPMButton;
    JButton increaseBPMButton;
    JButton decreaseBPMButton;
    JMenuBar menuBar;
    JMenu menu;
    JMenuItem startMenuItem;
    JMenuItem stopMenuItem;


    public DJView(ControllerInterface controller, BeatModelInterface model) {
        this.controller = controller;
        this.model = model;
        model.registerObserver((BeatObserver)this);
        model.registerObserver((BPMObserver)this);
    }

    public void createView() {
```

```
        // Create all Swing components here
        viewPanel = new JPanel(new GridLayout(1, 2));
        viewFrame = new JFrame("View");
        viewFrame.setDefaultCloseOperation(JFrame.EXIT_ON_CLOSE);
        viewFrame.setSize(new Dimension(100, 80));
        bpmOutputLabel = new JLabel("offline", SwingConstants.CENTER);
        beatBar = new BeatBar();
        beatBar.setValue(0);
        JPanel bpmPanel = new JPanel(new GridLayout(2, 1));
        bpmPanel.add(beatBar);
        bpmPanel.add(bpmOutputLabel);
        viewPanel.add(bpmPanel);
        viewFrame.getContentPane().add(viewPanel, BorderLayout.CENTER);
        viewFrame.pack();
        viewFrame.setVisible(true);
    }


    public void createControls() {
        // Create all Swing components here
        JFrame.setDefaultLookAndFeelDecorated(true);
        controlFrame = new JFrame("Control");
        controlFrame.setDefaultCloseOperation(JFrame.EXIT_ON_CLOSE);
        controlFrame.setSize(new Dimension(100, 80));

        controlPanel = new JPanel(new GridLayout(1, 2));

        menuBar = new JMenuBar();
        menu = new JMenu("DJ Control");
        startMenuItem = new JMenuItem("Start");
        menu.add(startMenuItem);
        startMenuItem.addActionListener(new ActionListener() {
            public void actionPerformed(ActionEvent event) {
                controller.start();
            }
        });
        stopMenuItem = new JMenuItem("Stop");
        menu.add(stopMenuItem);
        stopMenuItem.addActionListener(new ActionListener() {
            public void actionPerformed(ActionEvent event) {
                controller.stop();
                //bpmOutputLabel.setText("offline");
            }
        });
        JMenuItem exit = new JMenuItem("Quit");
        exit.addActionListener(new ActionListener() {
            public void actionPerformed(ActionEvent event) {
                System.exit(0);
            }
        });
```

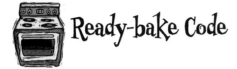 **Ready-bake Code**

```
        menu.add(exit);
        menuBar.add(menu);
        controlFrame.setJMenuBar(menuBar);

        bpmTextField = new JTextField(2);
        bpmLabel = new JLabel("Enter BPM:", SwingConstants.RIGHT);
        setBPMButton = new JButton("Set");
        setBPMButton.setSize(new Dimension(10,40));
        increaseBPMButton = new JButton(">>");
        decreaseBPMButton = new JButton("<<");
        setBPMButton.addActionListener(this);
        increaseBPMButton.addActionListener(this);
        decreaseBPMButton.addActionListener(this);

        JPanel buttonPanel = new JPanel(new GridLayout(1, 2));

        buttonPanel.add(decreaseBPMButton);
        buttonPanel.add(increaseBPMButton);

        JPanel enterPanel = new JPanel(new GridLayout(1, 2));
        enterPanel.add(bpmLabel);
        enterPanel.add(bpmTextField);
        JPanel insideControlPanel = new JPanel(new GridLayout(3, 1));
        insideControlPanel.add(enterPanel);
        insideControlPanel.add(setBPMButton);
        insideControlPanel.add(buttonPanel);
        controlPanel.add(insideControlPanel);

        bpmLabel.setBorder(BorderFactory.createEmptyBorder(5,5,5,5));
        bpmOutputLabel.setBorder(BorderFactory.createEmptyBorder(5,5,5,5));

        controlFrame.getRootPane().setDefaultButton(setBPMButton);
        controlFrame.getContentPane().add(controlPanel, BorderLayout.CENTER);

        controlFrame.pack();
        controlFrame.setVisible(true);
    }

    public void enableStopMenuItem() {
        stopMenuItem.setEnabled(true);
    }

    public void disableStopMenuItem() {
        stopMenuItem.setEnabled(false);
```

```
    }

    public void enableStartMenuItem() {
        startMenuItem.setEnabled(true);
    }

    public void disableStartMenuItem() {
        startMenuItem.setEnabled(false);
    }

    public void actionPerformed(ActionEvent event) {
        if (event.getSource() == setBPMButton) {
            int bpm = Integer.parseInt(bpmTextField.getText());
            controller.setBPM(bpm);
        } else if (event.getSource() == increaseBPMButton) {
            controller.increaseBPM();
        } else if (event.getSource() == decreaseBPMButton) {
            controller.decreaseBPM();
        }
    }

    public void updateBPM() {
        int bpm = model.getBPM();
        if (bpm == 0) {
            bpmOutputLabel.setText("offline");
        } else {
            bpmOutputLabel.setText("Current BPM: " + model.getBPM());
        }
    }

    public void updateBeat() {
        beatBar.setValue(100);
    }
}
```

The Controller

```
package headfirst.combined.djview;

public interface ControllerInterface {
    void start();
    void stop();
    void increaseBPM();
    void decreaseBPM();
    void setBPM(int bpm);
}
```

Ready-bake Code

```
package headfirst.combined.djview;

public class BeatController implements ControllerInterface {
    BeatModelInterface model;
    DJView view;

    public BeatController(BeatModelInterface model) {
        this.model = model;
        view = new DJView(this, model);
        view.createView();
        view.createControls();
        view.disableStopMenuItem();
        view.enableStartMenuItem();
        model.initialize();
    }

    public void start() {
        model.on();
        view.disableStartMenuItem();
        view.enableStopMenuItem();
    }

    public void stop() {
        model.off();
        view.disableStopMenuItem();
        view.enableStartMenuItem();
    }

    public void increaseBPM() {
        int bpm = model.getBPM();
        model.setBPM(bpm + 1);
    }

    public void decreaseBPM() {
        int bpm = model.getBPM();
        model.setBPM(bpm - 1);
    }

    public void setBPM(int bpm) {
        model.setBPM(bpm);
    }
}
```

The Heart Model

```java
package headfirst.combined.djview;

public class HeartTestDrive {
    public static void main (String[] args) {
        HeartModel heartModel = new HeartModel();
        ControllerInterface model = new HeartController(heartModel);
    }
}
```

```java
package headfirst.combined.djview;
public interface HeartModelInterface {
    int getHeartRate();
    void registerObserver(BeatObserver o);
    void removeObserver(BeatObserver o);
    void registerObserver(BPMObserver o);
    void removeObserver(BPMObserver o);
}
```

```java
package headfirst.combined.djview;
import java.util.*;

public class HeartModel implements HeartModelInterface, Runnable {
    ArrayList beatObservers = new ArrayList();
    ArrayList bpmObservers = new ArrayList();
    int time = 1000;
    int bpm = 90;
    Random random = new Random(System.currentTimeMillis());
    Thread thread;

    public HeartModel() {
        thread = new Thread(this);
        thread.start();
    }

    public void run() {
        int lastrate = -1;

        for(;;) {
            int change = random.nextInt(10);
            if (random.nextInt(2) == 0) {
                change = 0 - change;
            }
            int rate = 60000/(time + change);
            if (rate < 120 && rate > 50) {
                time += change;
```

```
                notifyBeatObservers();
                if (rate != lastrate) {
                    lastrate = rate;
                    notifyBPMObservers();
                }
            }
            try {
                Thread.sleep(time);
            } catch (Exception e) {}
        }
    }
    public int getHeartRate() {
        return 60000/time;
    }

    public void registerObserver(BeatObserver o) {
        beatObservers.add(o);
    }

    public void removeObserver(BeatObserver o) {
        int i = beatObservers.indexOf(o);
        if (i >= 0) {
            beatObservers.remove(i);
        }
    }

    public void notifyBeatObservers() {
        for(int i = 0; i < beatObservers.size(); i++) {
            BeatObserver observer = (BeatObserver)beatObservers.get(i);
            observer.updateBeat();
        }
    }

    public void registerObserver(BPMObserver o) {
        bpmObservers.add(o);
    }

    public void removeObserver(BPMObserver o) {
        int i = bpmObservers.indexOf(o);
        if (i >= 0) {
            bpmObservers.remove(i);
        }
    }

    public void notifyBPMObservers() {
        for(int i = 0; i < bpmObservers.size(); i++) {
            BPMObserver observer = (BPMObserver)bpmObservers.get(i);
            observer.updateBPM();
        }
    }
}
```

Ready-bake Code

The Heart Adapter

```
package headfirst.combined.djview;
public class HeartAdapter implements BeatModelInterface {
    HeartModelInterface heart;

    public HeartAdapter(HeartModelInterface heart) {
        this.heart = heart;
    }

    public void initialize() {}

    public void on() {}

    public void off() {}

    public int getBPM() {
        return heart.getHeartRate();
    }

    public void setBPM(int bpm) {}

    public void registerObserver(BeatObserver o) {
        heart.registerObserver(o);
    }

    public void removeObserver(BeatObserver o) {
        heart.removeObserver(o);
    }

    public void registerObserver(BPMObserver o) {
        heart.registerObserver(o);
    }

    public void removeObserver(BPMObserver o) {
        heart.removeObserver(o);
    }
}
```

The Controller

```java
package headfirst.combined.djview;

public class HeartController implements ControllerInterface {
    HeartModelInterface model;
    DJView view;

    public HeartController(HeartModelInterface model) {
        this.model = model;
        view = new DJView(this, new HeartAdapter(model));
        view.createView();
        view.createControls();
        view.disableStopMenuItem();
        view.disableStartMenuItem();
    }

    public void start() {}

    public void stop() {}

    public void increaseBPM() {}

    public void decreaseBPM() {}

    public void setBPM(int bpm) {}
}
```

13 Better Living with Patterns

Patterns in the *Real World*

Ahhhh, now you're ready for a bright new world filled with Design Patterns. But, before you go opening all those new doors of opportunity, we need to cover a few details that you'll encounter out in the real world – that's right, things get a little more complex than they are here in Objectville. Come along, we've got a nice guide to help you through the transition on the next page...

The Objectville Guide to
Better Living with Design Patterns

Please accept our handy guide with tips & tricks for living with patterns in the real world. In this guide you will:

☞ Learn the all too common misconceptions about the definition of a "Design Pattern."

☞ Discover those nifty Design Pattern Catalogs and why you just have to get one.

☞ Avoid the embarrassment of using a Design Pattern at the wrong time.

☞ Learn how to keep patterns in classifications where they belong.

☞ See that discovering patterns isn't just for the gurus; read our quick HowTo and become a patterns writer too.

☞ Be there when the true identity of the mysterious Gang of Four is revealed.

☞ Keep up with the neighbors – the coffee table books any patterns user must own.

☞ Learn to train your mind like a Zen master.

☞ Win friends and influence developers by improving your patterns vocabulary.

Design Pattern defined

We bet you've got a pretty good idea of what a pattern is after reading this book. But we've never really given a definition for a Design Pattern. Well, you might be a bit surprised by the definition that is in common use:

> **A Pattern** is a solution to a problem in a context.

That's not the most revealing definition is it? But don't worry, we're going to step through each of these parts, context, problem and solution:

The **context** is the situation in which the pattern applies. This should be a recurring situation.

Example: You have a collection of objects.

The **problem** refers to the goal you are trying to achieve in this context, but it also refers to any constraints that occur in the context.

You need to step through the objects without exposing the collection's implementation.

The **solution** is what you're after: a general design that anyone can apply which resolves the goal and set of constraints.

Encapsulate the iteration into a separate class.

This is one of those definitions that takes a while to sink in, but take it one step at a time. Here's a little mnemonic you can repeat to yourself to remember it:

"If you find yourself in a context with a problem that has a goal that is affected by a set of constraints, then you can apply a design that resolves the goal and constraints and leads to a solution."

Now, this seems like a lot of work just to figure out what a Design Pattern is. After all, you already know that a Design Pattern gives you a solution to a common recurring design problem. What is all this formality getting you? Well, you're going to see that by having a formal way of describing patterns we can create a *catalog* of patterns, which has all kinds of benefits.

> I've been thinking about the three-part definition, and I don't think it defines a pattern at all.

You might be right; let's think about this a bit... We need a *problem*, a *solution* and a *context*:

Problem: How do I get to work on time?

Context: I've locked my keys in the car.

Solution: Break the window, get in the car, start the engine and drive to work.

We have all the components of the definition: we have a problem, which includes the goal of getting to work, and the constraints of time, distance and probably some other factors. We also have a context in which the keys to the car are inaccessible. And we have a solution that gets us to the keys and resolves both the time and distance constraints. We must have a pattern now! Right?

BRAIN POWER

We followed the Design Pattern definition and defined a problem, a context, and a solution (which works!). Is this a pattern? If not, how did it fail? Could we fail the same way when defining an OO Design Pattern?

Looking more closely at the Design Pattern definition

Our example does seem to match the Design Pattern definition, but it isn't a true pattern. Why? For starters, we know that a pattern needs to apply to a recurring problem. While an absent-minded person might lock his keys in the car often, breaking the car window doesn't qualify as a solution that can be applied over and over (or at least isn't likely to if we balance the goal with another constraint: cost).

It also fails in a couple of other ways: first, it isn't easy to take this description, hand it to someone and have him apply it to his own unique problem. Second, we've violated an important but simple aspect of a pattern: we haven't even given it a name! Without a name, the pattern doesn't become part of a vocabulary that can be shared with other developers.

Luckily, patterns are not described and documented as a simple problem, context and solution; we have much better ways of describing patterns and collecting them together into *patterns catalogs*.

Next time someone tells you a pattern is a solution to a problem in a context, just nod and smile. You know what they mean, even if it isn't a definition sufficient to describe what a Design Pattern really is.

Q: Am I going to see pattern descriptions that are stated as a problem, a context and a solution?

A: Pattern descriptions, which you'll typically find in pattern catalogs, are usually a bit more revealing than that. We're going to look at pattern catalogs in detail in just a minute; they describe a lot more about a pattern's intent and motivation and where it might apply, along with the solution design and the consequences (good and bad) of using it.

Q: Is it okay to slightly alter a pattern's structure to fit my design? Or am I going to have to go by the strict definition?

A: Of course you can alter it. Like design principles, patterns are not meant to be laws or rules; they are *guidelines* that you can alter to fit your needs. As you've seen, a lot of real-world examples don't fit the classic pattern designs.

However, when you adapt patterns, it never hurts to document how your pattern differs from the classic design – that way, other developers can quickly recognize the patterns you're using and any differences between your pattern and the classic pattern.

Q: Where can I get a patterns catalog?

A: The first and most definitive patterns catalog is *Design Patterns: Elements of Reusable Object-Oriented Software*, by Gamma, Helm, Johnson & Vlissides (Addison Wesley). This catalog lays out 23 fundamental patterns. We'll talk a little more about this book in a few pages.

Many other patterns catalogs are starting to be published in various domain areas such as enterprise software, concurrent systems and business systems.

Geek Bits

May the force be with you

The Design Pattern
definition tells us that
the *problem* consists of a
goal and a *set of constraints*.
Patterns gurus have a term
for these: they call them
<u>forces</u>. Why? Well, we're sure
they have their own reasons, but if
you remember the movie, the force
"shapes and controls the Universe."
Likewise, the forces in the pattern
definition shape and control the solution.
Only when a solution balances both sides of
the force (the light side: your goal, and the dark
side: the constraints) do we have a useful pattern.

This "force" terminology can be quite confusing
when you first see it in pattern discussions, but
just remember that there are two sides of the force
(goals and constraints) and that they need to be
balanced or resolved to create a pattern solution. Don't
let the lingo get in your way and may the force be with you!

Frank: Fill us in, Jim. I've just been learning patterns by reading a few articles here and there.

Jim: Sure, each pattern catalog takes a set of patterns and describes each in detail along with its relationship to the other patterns.

Joe: Are you saying there is more than one patterns catalog?

Jim: Of course; there are catalogs for fundamental Design Patterns and there are also catalogs on domain specific patterns, like EJB patterns.

Frank: Which catalog are you looking at?

Jim: This is the classic GoF catalog; it contains 23 fundamental Design Patterns.

Frank: GoF?

Jim: Right, that stands for the Gang of Four. The Gang of Four are the guys that put together the first patterns catalog.

Joe: What's in the catalog?

Jim: There is a set of related patterns. For each pattern there is a description that follows a template and spells out a lot of details of the pattern. For instance, each pattern has a *name*.

Frank: Wow, that's earth-shattering – a name! Imagine that.

Jim: Hold on Frank; actually, the name is really important. When we have a name for a pattern, it gives us a way to talk about the pattern; you know, that whole shared vocabulary thing.

Frank: Okay, okay. I was just kidding. Go on, what else is there?

Jim: Well, like I was saying, every pattern follows a template. For each pattern we have a name and a few sections that tell us more about the pattern. For instance, there is an Intent section that describes what the pattern is, kind of like a definition. Then there are Motivation and Applicability sections that describe when and where the pattern might be used.

Joe: What about the design itself?

Jim: There are several sections that describe the class design along with all the classes that make it up and what their roles are. There is also a section that describes how to implement the pattern and often sample code to show you how.

Frank: It sounds like they've thought of everything.

Jim: There's more. There are also examples of where the pattern has been used in real systems as well as what I think is one of the most useful sections: how the pattern relates to *other* patterns.

Frank: Oh, you mean they tell you things like how *state* and *strategy* differ?

Jim: Exactly!

Joe: So Jim, how are you actually using the catalog? When you have a problem, do you go fishing in the catalog for a solution?

Jim: I try to get familiar with all the patterns and their relationships first. Then, when I need a pattern, I have some idea of what it is. I go back and look at the Motivation and Applicability sections to make sure I've got it right. There is also another really important section: Consequences. I review that to make sure there won't be some unintended effect on my design.

Frank: That makes sense. So once you know the pattern is right, how do you approach working it into your design and implementing it?

Jim: That's where the class diagram comes in. I first read over the Structure section to review the diagram and then over the Participants section to make sure I understand each classes' role. From there I work it into my design, making any alterations I need to make it fit. Then I review the Implementation and Sample code sections to make sure I know about any good implementation techniques or gotchas I might encounter.

Joe: I can see how a catalog is really going to accelerate my use of patterns!

Frank: Totally. Jim, can you walk us through a pattern description?

All patterns in a catalog start with a <u>name</u>. The name is a vital part of a pattern – without a good name, a pattern can't become part of the vocabulary that you share with other developers.

The <u>motivation</u> gives you a concrete scenario that describes the problem and how the solution solves the problem.

The <u>applicability</u> describes situations in which the pattern can be applied.

The <u>participants</u> are the classes and objects in the design. This section describes their responsibilities and roles in the pattern.

The <u>consequences</u> describe the effects that using this pattern may have: good and bad.

<u>Implementation</u> provides techniques you need to use when implementing this pattern, and issues you should watch out for.

<u>Known uses</u> describes examples of this pattern found in real systems.

SINGLETON   Object Creational

Intent

Et aliquat, velesto ent lore feuis acillao rperci tat, quat nonsequam il ea at nim nos do enim qui eratio ex ea faci tet, sequis dion utat, volore magnis.

Motivation

Et aliquat, velesto ent lore feuis acillao rperci tat, quat nonsequam il ea at nim nos do enim qui eratio ex ea faci tet, sequis dion utat, volore magnis.Rud modolore dit laoreet augiam iril el dipis dionsequis dignibh eummy nibh exequat. Duis nulputem ipsim esecte conullut wissi.

Os nisissenim et lumsandre do con el utpatuero corercipis augue doloreet luptat amet vel iuscidunt digna feugue dunt num etummy nim dui blaor sequat num vel etue magna augiat.

Aliquis nonse vel exer se minissequis do dolortis ad magnit, sim zzrillut ipsummo dolorem dignibh euguer sequam ea am quate magnim illam zzrit ad magna feu facinit delit ut

Applicability

Duis nulputem ipisim esecte conullut wissiEctem ad magna aliqui blamet, conullandre dolore magna feuis nos alit ad magnim quate modolore vent lut luptat prat. Dui blaore min ea feuipit ing enit laore magnibh eniat wisissecte et, suscilla ad mincinci blam dolorpe rcilit irit, conse dolore dolore et, verci enis enit ip elesequisl ut ad esectem ing ea con eros autem diam nonullu tpatiss ismodignibh er.

Structure

Singleton
static uniqueInstance
// Other useful Singleton data...
static getInstance()
// Other useful Singleton methods...

Participants

Duis nulputem ipisim esecte conullut wissiEctem ad magna aliqui blamet, conullandre dolore magna feuis nos alit ad magnim quate modolore vent lut luptat prat. Dui blaore min ea feuipit ing enit laore magnibh eniat wisissecte et, suscilla ad mincinci blam dolorpe rcilit irit, conse dolore dolore et, verci enis enit ip elesequisl ut ad esectem ing ea con eros autem diam nonullu tpatiss ismodignibh er

- A dolore dolore et, verci enis enit ip elesequisl ut ad esectem ing ea con eros autem diam nonullu tpatiss ismodignibh er
  - A feuis nos alit ad magnim quate modolore vent lut luptat prat. Dui blaore min ea feuipit ing enit laore magnibh eniat wisissec
  - Ad magnim quate modolore vent lut luptat prat. Dui blaore min ea feuipit ing enit

Collaborations

- Feuipit ing enit laore magnibh eniat wisissecte et, suscilla ad mincinci blam dolorpe rcilit irit, conse dolore.

Consequences

Duis nulputem ipisim esecte conullut wissiEctem ad magna aliqui blamet, conullandre:

1. Dolore dolore et, verci enis enit ip elesequisl ut ad esectem ing ea con eros autem diam nonullu tpatiss ismodignibh er.
2. Modolore vent lut luptat prat. Dui blaore min ea feuipit ing enit laore magnibh eniat wisissecte et, suscilla ad mincinci blam dolorpe rcilit irit, conse dolore dolore et, verci enis enit ip elesequisl ut ad esectem.
3. Dolore dolore et, verci enis enit ip elesequisl ut ad esectem ing ea con eros autem diam nonullu tpatiss ismodignibh er.
4. Modolore vent lut luptat prat. Dui blaore min ea feuipit ing enit laore magnibh eniat wisissecte et, suscilla ad mincinci blam dolorpe rcilit irit, conse dolore dolore et, verci enis enit ip elesequisl ut ad esectem.

Implementation/Sample Code

DuDuis nulputem ipisim esecte conullut wissiEctem ad magna aliqui blamet, conullandre dolore magna feuis nos alit ad magnim quate modolore vent lut luptat prat. Dui blaore min ea feuipit ing enit laore magnibh eniat wisissecte et, suscilla ad mincinci blam dolorpe rcilit irit, conse dolore dolore et, verci enis enit ip elesequisl ut ad esectem ing ea con eros autem diam nonullu tpatiss ismodignibh er.

```
public class Singleton {
    private static Singleton uniqueInstance;

    // other useful instance variables here

    private Singleton() {}

    public static synchronized Singleton getInstance() {
        if (uniqueInstance == null) {
            uniqueInstance = new Singleton();
        }
        return uniqueInstance;
    }

    // other useful methods here
}
```

Nos alit ad magnim quate modolore vent lut luptat prat. Dui blaore min ea feuipit ing enit laore magnibh eniat wisissecte et, suscilla ad mincinci blam dolorpe rcilit irit, conse dolore dolore et, verci enis enit ip elesequisl ut ad esectem ing ea con eros autem diam nonullu tpatiss ismodignibh er.

Known Uses

DuDuis nulputem ipisim esecte conullut wissiEctem ad magna aliqui blamet, conullandre dolore magna feuis nos alit ad magnim quate modolore vent lut luptat prat. Dui blaore min ea feuipit ing enit laore magnibh eniat wisissecte et, suscilla ad mincinci blam dolorpe rcilit irit, conse dolore dolore et, verci enis enit ip elesequisl ut ad esectem ing ea con eros autem diam nonullu tpatiss ismodignibh er.

DuDuis nulputem ipisim esecte conullut wissiEctem ad magna aliqui blamet, conullandre dolore magna feuis nos alit ad magnim quate modolore vent lut luptat prat. Dui blaore min ea feuipit ing enit laore magnibh eniat wisissecte et, suscilla ad mincinci blam dolorpe rcilit irit, conse dolore dolore et, verci enis enit ip elesequisl ut ad esectem ing ea con eros autem diam nonullu tpatiss ismodignibh er. alit ad magnim quate modolore vent lut luptat prat. Dui blaore min ea feuipit ing enit laore magnibh eniat wisissecte et, suscilla ad mincinci blam dolorpe rcilit irit, conse dolore dolore et, verci enis enit ip elesequisl ut ad esectem ing ea con eros autem diam nonullu tpatiss ismodignibh er.

Related Patterns

Elesequisl ut ad esectem ing ea con eros autem diam nonullu tpatiss ismodignibh er. alit ad magnim quate modolore vent lut luptat prat. Dui blaore min ea feuipit ing enit laore magnibh eniat wisissecte et, suscilla ad mincinci blam dolorpe rcilit irit, conse dolore dolore et, verci enis enit ip elesequisl ut ad esectem ing ea con eros autem diam nonullu tpatiss ismodignibh er.

This is the pattern's <u>classification</u> or category. We'll talk about these in a few pages.

The <u>intent</u> describes what the pattern does in a short statement. You can also think of this as the pattern's definition (just like we've been using in this book).

The <u>structure</u> provides a diagram illustrating the relationships among the classes that participate in the pattern.

Collaborations tells us how the participants work together in the pattern.

<u>Sample code</u> provides code fragments that might help with your implementation.

<u>Related patterns</u> describes the relationship between this pattern and others.

there are no
Dumb Questions

Q: Is it possible to create your own Design Patterns? Or is that something you have to be a "patterns guru" to do?

A: First, remember that patterns are *discovered*, not created. So, anyone can discover a Design Pattern and then author its description; however, it's not easy and doesn't happen quickly, nor often. Being a "patterns writer" takes commitment.

You should first think about why you'd want to – the majority of people don't *author* patterns; they just *use* them. However, you might work in a specialized domain for which you think new patterns would be helpful, or you might have come across a solution to what you think is a recurring problem, or you may just want to get involved in the patterns community and contribute to the growing body of work.

Q: I'm game; how do I get started?

A: Like any discipline, the more you know the better. Studying existing patterns, what they do and how they relate to other patterns is crucial. Not only does it make you familiar with how patterns are crafted, it prevents you from reinventing the wheel. From there you'll want to start writing your patterns on paper, so you can communicate them to other developers; we're going to talk more about how to communicate your patterns in a bit. If you're really interested, you'll want to read the section that follows these Q&As.

Q: How do I know when I really have a pattern?

A: That's a very good question: you don't have a pattern until others have used it and found it to work. In general, you don't have a pattern until it passes the "Rule of Three." This rule states that a pattern can be called a pattern only if it has been applied in a real-world solution at least three times.

So you wanna be a design patterns star?

Well listen now to what I tell.

Get yourself a patterns catalog,

Then take some time and learn it well.

And when you've got your description right,

And three developers agree without a fight,

Then you'll know it's a pattern alright.

To the tune of "So you wanna be a Rock'n Roll Star."

So you wanna be a Design Patterns writer

Do your homework. You need to be well versed in the existing patterns before you can create a new one. Most patterns that appear to be new, are, in fact, just variants of existing patterns. By studying patterns, you become better at recognizing them, and you learn to relate them to other patterns.

Take time to reflect, evaluate. Your experience – the problems you've encountered, and the solutions you've used – are where ideas for patterns are born. So take some time to reflect on your experiences and comb them for novel designs that recur. Remember that most designs are variations on existing patterns and not new patterns. And when you do find what looks like a new pattern, its applicability may be too narrow to qualify as a real pattern.

Get your ideas down on paper in a way others can understand. Locating new patterns isn't of much use if others can't make use of your find; you need to document your pattern candidates so that others can read, understand, and apply them to their own solution and then supply you with feedback. Luckily, you don't need to invent your own method of documenting your patterns. As you've already seen with the GoF template, a lot of thought has already gone into how to describe patterns and their characteristics.

Have others try your patterns; then refine and refine some more. Don't expect to get your pattern right the first time. Think of your pattern as a work in progress that will improve over time. Have other developers review your candidate pattern, try it out, and give you feedback. Incorporate that feedback into your description and try again. Your description will never be perfect, but at some point it should be solid enough that other developers can read and understand it.

Don't forget the rule of three. Remember, unless your pattern has been successfully applied in three real-world solutions, it can't qualify as a pattern. That's another good reason to get your pattern into the hands of others so they can try it, give feedback, and allow you to converge on a working pattern.

Use one of the existing pattern templates to define your pattern. A lot of thought has gone into these templates and other pattern users will recognize the format.

Name
Intent
Motivation
Applicability
Structure
Participants
Collaborations
...

Match each pattern with its description:

Pattern	Description
Decorator	Wraps an object and provides a different interface to it.
State	Subclasses decide how to implement steps in an algorithm.
Iterator	Subclasses decide which concrete classes to create.
Facade	Ensures one and only object is created.
Strategy	Encapsulates interchangeable behaviors and uses delegation to decide which one to use.
Proxy	Clients treat collections of objects and individual objects uniformly.
Factory Method	Encapsulates state-based behaviors and uses delegation to switch between behaviors.
Adapter	Provides a way to traverse a collection of objects without exposing its implementation.
Observer	Simplifies the interface of a set of classes.
Template Method	Wraps an object to provide new behavior.
Composite	Allows a client to create families of objects without specifying their concrete classes.
Singleton	Allows objects to be notified when state changes.
Abstract Factory	Wraps an object to control access to it.
Command	Encapsulates a request as an object.

Organizing Design Patterns

As the number of discovered Design Patterns grows, it makes sense to partition them into classifications so that we can organize them, narrow our searches to a subset of all Design Patterns, and make comparisons within a group of patterns.

In most catalogs you'll find patterns grouped into one of a few classification schemes. The most well-known scheme was used by the first pattern catalog and partitions patterns into three distinct categories based on their purposes: Creational, Behavioral and Structural.

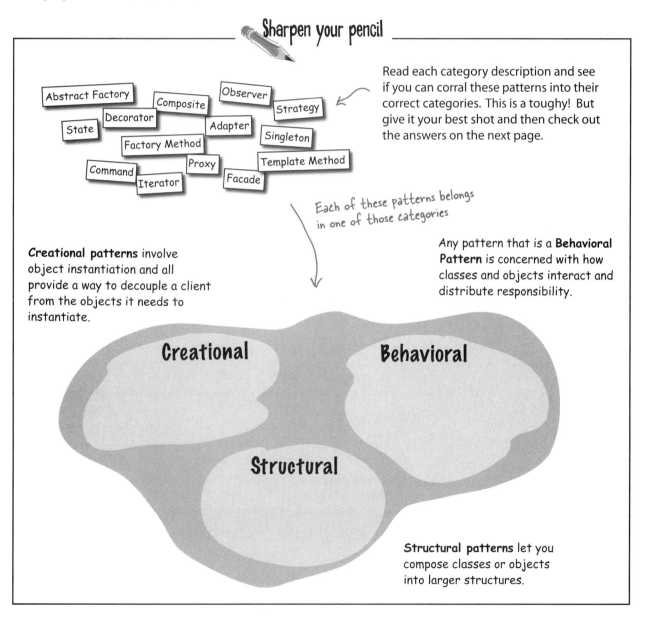

Sharpen your pencil

Abstract Factory · Composite · Observer · Strategy · State · Decorator · Adapter · Singleton · Factory Method · Command · Proxy · Template Method · Iterator · Facade

Read each category description and see if you can corral these patterns into their correct categories. This is a toughy! But give it your best shot and then check out the answers on the next page.

Each of these patterns belongs in one of those categories

Creational patterns involve object instantiation and all provide a way to decouple a client from the objects it needs to instantiate.

Any pattern that is a **Behavioral Pattern** is concerned with how classes and objects interact and distribute responsibility.

Creational

Behavioral

Structural

Structural patterns let you compose classes or objects into larger structures.

Solution: Pattern Categories

Here's the grouping of patterns into categories. You probably found the exercise difficult, because many of the patterns seem like they could fit into more than one category. Don't worry, everyone has trouble figuring out the right categories for the patterns.

Creational patterns involve object instantiation and all provide a way to decouple a client from the objects it needs to instantiate.

Any pattern that is a **Behavioral Pattern** is concerned with how classes and objects interact and distribute responsibility.

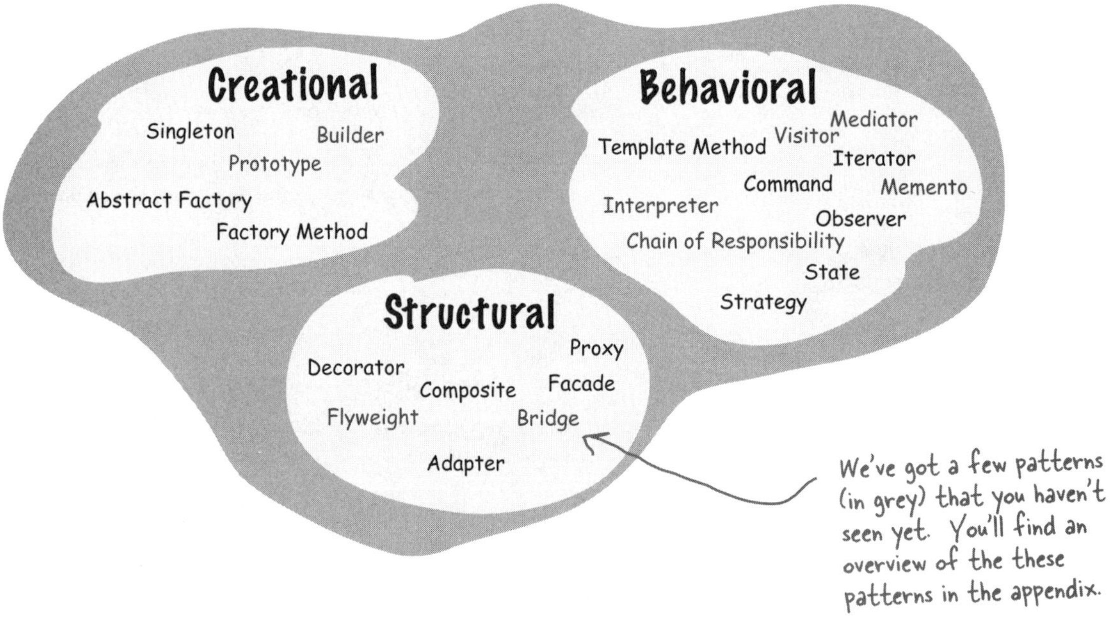

Creational

Singleton   Builder
Prototype
Abstract Factory
Factory Method

Behavioral

Mediator
Template Method   Visitor
Iterator
Command   Memento
Interpreter
Observer
Chain of Responsibility
State
Strategy

Structural

Proxy
Decorator
Composite   Facade
Flyweight   Bridge
Adapter

We've got a few patterns (in grey) that you haven't seen yet. You'll find an overview of the these patterns in the appendix.

Structural patterns let you compose classes or objects into larger structures.

Patterns are often classified by a second attribute: whether or not the pattern deals with classes or objects:

Class patterns describe how relationships between classes are defined via inheritance. Relationships in class patterns are established at compile time.

Object patterns describe relationships between objects and are primarily defined by composition. Relationships in object patterns are typically created at runtime and are more dynamic and flexible.

Class

Template Method

Factory Method   Adapter

Interpreter

Object

Composite   Visitor Iterator
Decorator   Command Memento
Proxy   Facade
Strategy   Observer
    Chain of Responsibility
Bridge   Mediator
Flyweight   Prototype   State
Abstract Factory   Builder
Singleton

Notice there's a lot more object patterns than class patterns!

Q: Are these the only classification schemes?

A: No, other schemes have been proposed. Some other schemes start with the three categories and then add subcategories, like "Decoupling Patterns." You'll want to be familiar with the most common schemes for organizing patterns, but also feel free to create your own, if it helps you to understand the patterns better.

Q: Does organizing patterns into categories really help you remember them?

there are no
Dumb Questions

A: It certainly gives you a framework for the sake of comparison. But many people are confused by the creational, structural and behavioral categories; often a pattern seems to fit into more than one category. The most important thing is to know the patterns and the relationships among them. When categories help, use them!

Q: Why is the Decorator Pattern in the structural category? I would have thought of that as a behavioral pattern; after all it adds behavior!

A: Yes, lots of developers say that! Here's the thinking behind the Gang of Four classification: structural patterns describe how classes and objects are composed to create new structures or new functionality. The Decorator Pattern allows you to compose objects by wrapping one object with another to provide new functionality. So the focus is on how you compose the objects dynamically to gain functionality, rather than on the communication and interconnection between objects, which is the purpose of behavioral patterns. But remember, the intent of these patterns is different, and that's often the key to understanding which category a pattern belongs to.

Master and Student...

Master: *Grasshopper, you look troubled.*

Student: *Yes, I've just learned about pattern classification and I'm confused.*

Master: *Grasshopper, continue...*

Student: *After learning much about patterns, I've just been told that each pattern fits into one of three classifications: structural, behavioral or creational. Why do we need these classifications?*

Master: *Grasshopper, whenever we have a large collection of anything, we naturally find categories to fit those things into. It helps us to think of the items at a more abstract level.*

Student: *Master; can you give me an example?*

Master: *Of course. Take automobiles; there are many different models of automobiles and we naturally put them into categories like economy cars, sports cars, SUVs, trucks and luxury car categories.*

Master: *Grasshopper, you look shocked, does this not make sense?*

Student: *Master, it makes a lot of sense, but I am shocked you know so much about cars!*

Master: *Grasshopper, I can't relate **everything** to lotus flowers or rice bowls. Now, may I continue?*

Student: *Yes, yes, I'm sorry, please continue.*

Master: *Once you have classifications or categories you can easily talk about the different groupings: "If you're doing the mountain drive from Silicon Valley to Santa Cruz, a sports car with good handling is the best option." Or, "With the worsening oil situation you really want to buy a economy car, they're more fuel-efficient."*

Student: *So by having categories we can talk about a set of patterns as a group. We might know we need a creational pattern, without knowing exactly which one, but we can still talk about creational patterns.*

Master: *Yes, and it also gives us a way to compare a member to the rest of the category, for example, "the Mini really is the most stylish compact car around", or to narrow our search, "I need a fuel efficient car."*

Student: *I see, so I might say that the Adapter pattern is the best structural pattern for changing an object's interface.*

Master: *Yes. We also can use categories for one more purpose: to launch into new territory; for instance, "we really want to deliver a sports car with ferrari performance at miata prices."*

Student: *That sounds like a death trap.*

Master: *I'm sorry, I did not hear you Grasshopper.*

Student: *Uh, I said "I see that."*

Student: *So categories give us a way to think about the way groups of patterns relate and how patterns within a group relate to one another. They also give us a way to extrapolate to new patterns. But why are there three categories and not four, or five?*

Master: *Ah, like stars in the night sky, there are as many categories as you want to see. Three is a convenient number and a number that many people have decided makes for a nice grouping of patterns. But others have suggested four, five or more.*

Thinking in Patterns

Contexts, constraints, forces, catalogs, classifications... boy, this is starting to sound mighty academic. Okay, all that stuff is important and knowledge *is* power. But, let's face it, if you understand the academic stuff and don't have the *experience* and practice using patterns, then it's not going to make much difference in your life.

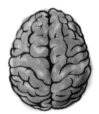

Your Brain on Patterns

Here's a quick guide to help you start to *think in patterns*. What do we mean by that? We mean being able to look at a design and see where patterns naturally fit and where they don't.

Keep it simple (KISS)

First of all, when you design, solve things in the simplest way possible. Your goal should be simplicity, not "how can I apply a pattern to this problem." Don't feel like you aren't a sophisticated developer if you don't use a pattern to solve a problem. Other developers will appreciate and admire the simplicity of your design. That said, sometimes the best way to keep your design simple and flexible is to use a pattern.

Design Patterns aren't a magic bullet; in fact they're not even a bullet!

Patterns, as you know, are general solutions to recurring problems. Patterns also have the benefit of being well tested by lots of developers. So, when you see a need for one, you can sleep well knowing many developers have been there before and solved the problem using similar techniques.

However, patterns aren't a magic bullet. You can't plug one in, compile and then take an early lunch. To use patterns, you also need to think through the consequences on the rest of your design.

You know you need a pattern when...

Ah... the most important question: when do you use a pattern? As you approach your design, introduce a pattern when you're sure it addresses a problem in your design. If a simpler solution might work, give that consideration before you commit to using a pattern.

Knowing when a pattern applies is where your experience and knowledge come in. Once you're sure a simple solution will not meet your needs, you should consider the problem along with the set of constraints under which the solution will need to operate — these will help you match your problem to a pattern. If you've got a good knowledge of patterns, you may know of a pattern that is a good match. Otherwise, survey patterns that look like they might solve the problem. The intent and applicability sections of the patterns catalogs are particularly useful for this. Once you've found a pattern that appears to be a good match, make sure it has a set of consequences you can live with and study its effect on the rest of your design. If everything looks good, go for it!

There is one situation in which you'll want to use a pattern even if a simpler solution would work: when you expect aspects of your system to vary. As we've seen, identifying areas of change in your design is usually a good sign that a pattern is needed. Just make sure you are adding patterns to deal with *practical change* that is likely to happen, not *hypothetical change* that may happen.

Design time isn't the only time you want to consider introducing patterns, you'll also want to do so at refactoring time.

Refactoring time is Patterns time!

Refactoring is the process of making changes to your code to improve the way it is organized. The goal is to improve its structure, not change its behavior. This is a great time to reexamine your design to see if it might be better structured with patterns. For instance, code that is full of conditional statements might signal the need for the State pattern. Or, it may be time to clean up concrete dependencies with a Factory. Entire books have been written on the topic of refactoring with patterns, and as your skills grow, you'll want to study this area more.

Take out what you don't really need. Don't be afraid to remove a Design Pattern from your design.

No one ever talks about when to remove a pattern. You'd think it was blasphemy! Nah, we're all adults here; we can take it.

So when do you remove a pattern? When your system has become complex and the flexibility you planned for isn't needed. In other words, when a simpler solution without the pattern would be better.

If you don't need it now, don't do it now.

Design Patterns are powerful, and it's easy to see all kinds of ways they can be used in your current designs. Developers naturally love to create beautiful architectures that are ready to take on change from any direction.

Resist the temptation. If you have a practical need to support change in a design today, go ahead and employ a pattern to handle that change. However, if the reason is only hypothetical, don't add the pattern, it is only going to add complexity to your system, and you might never need it!

Center your thinking on design, not on patterns. Use patterns when there is a natural need for them. If something simpler will work, then use it.

Master and Student...

> **Master:** Grasshopper, your initial training is almost complete. What are your plans?
>
> **Student:** I'm going to Disneyland! And, then I'm going to start creating lots of code with patterns!

Master: Whoa, hold on. Never use your big guns unless you have to.

Student: What do you mean, Master? Now that I've learned design patterns shouldn't I be using them in all my designs to achieve maximum power, flexibility and manageability?

Master: No; patterns are a tool, and a tool that should only be used when needed. You've also spent a lot of time learning design principles. Always start from your principles and create the simplest code you can that does the job. However, if you see the need for a pattern emerge, then use it.

Student: So I shouldn't build my designs from patterns?

Master: That should not be your goal when beginning a design. Let patterns emerge naturally as your design progresses.

Student: If patterns are so great, why should I be so careful about using them?

Master: Patterns can introduce complexity, and we never want complexity where it is not needed. But patterns are powerful when used where they are needed. As you already know, patterns are proven design experience that can be used to avoid common mistakes. They're also a shared vocabulary for communicating our design to others.

Student: Well, when do we know it's okay to introduce design patterns?

Master: Introduce a pattern when you are sure it's necessary to solve a problem in your design, or when you are quite sure that it is needed to deal with a future change in the requirements of your application.

Student: I guess my learning is going to continue even though I already understand a lot of patterns.

Master: Yes, grasshopper; learning to manage the complexity and change in software is a life long pursuit. But now that you know a good set of patterns, the time has come to apply them where needed in your design and to continue learning more patterns.

Student: Wait a minute, you mean I don't know them ALL?

Master: Grasshopper, you've learned the fundamental patterns; you're going to find there are many more, including patterns that just apply to particular domains such as concurrent systems and enterprise systems. But now that you know the basics, you're in good shape to learn them!

Your Mind on Patterns

BEGINNER MIND

"I need a pattern for Hello World."

The Beginner uses patterns everywhere. This is good: the beginner gets lots of experience with and practice using patterns. The beginner also thinks, "The more patterns I use, the better the design." The beginner will learn this is not so, that all designs should be as simple as possible. Complexity and patterns should only be used where they are needed for practical extensibility.

As learning progresses, the Intermediate mind starts to see where patterns are needed and where they aren't. The intermediate mind still tries to fit too many square patterns into round holes, but also begins to see that patterns can be adapted to fit situations where the canonical pattern doesn't fit.

INTERMEDIATE MIND

"Maybe I need a Singleton here."

ZEN MIND

"This is a natural place for Decorator."

The Zen mind is able to see patterns where they fit naturally. The Zen mind is not obsessed with using patterns; rather it looks for simple solutions that best solve the problem. The Zen mind thinks in terms of the object principles and their trade-offs. When a need for a pattern naturally arises, the Zen mind applies it knowing well that it may require adaptation. The Zen mind also sees relationships to similar patterns and understands the subtleties of differences in the intent of related patterns. *The Zen mind is also a Beginner mind* — it doesn't let all that pattern knowledge overly influence design decisions.

WARNING: Overuse of design patterns can lead to code that is downright over-engineered. Always go with the simplest solution that does the job and introduce patterns where the need emerges.

Wait a minute; I've read this entire book and now you're telling me NOT to use patterns?

Of course we want you to use Design Patterns!

But we want you to be a good OO designer even more.

When a design solution calls for a pattern, you get the benefits of using a solution that has been time tested by lots of developers. You're also using a solution that is well documented and that other developers are going to recognize (you know, that whole shared vocabulary thing).

However, when you use Design Patterns, there can also be a downside. Design Patterns often introduce additional classes and objects, and so they can increase the complexity of your designs. Design Patterns can also add more layers to your design, which adds not only complexity, but also inefficiency.

Also, using a Design Pattern can sometimes be outright overkill. Many times you can fall back on your design principles and find a much simpler solution to solve the same problem. If that happens, don't fight it. Use the simpler solution.

Don't let us discourage you, though. When a Design Pattern is the right tool for the job, the advantages are many.

Don't forget the power of the shared vocabulary

We've spent so much time in this book discussing OO nuts and bolts that it's easy to forget the human side of Design Patterns – they don't just help load your brain with solutions, they also give you a shared vocabulary with other developers. Don't underestimate the power of a shared vocabulary, it's one of the *biggest benefits* of Design Patterns.

Just think, something has changed since the last time we talked about shared vocabularies; you've now started to build up quite a vocabulary of your own! Not to mention, you have also learned a full set of OO design principles from which you can easily understand the motivation and workings of any new patterns you encounter.

Now that you've got the Design Pattern basics down, it's time for you to go out and spread the word to others. Why? Because when your fellow developers know patterns and use a shared vocabulary as well, it leads to better designs, better communication and, best of all, it'll save you a lot of time that you can spend on cooler things.

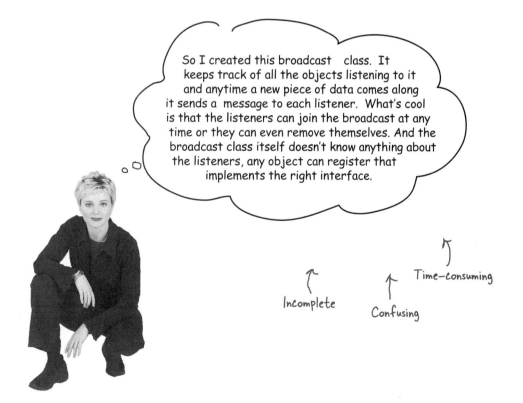

Top five ways to share your vocabulary

1 In design meetings: When you meet with your team to discuss a software design, use design patterns to help stay "in the design" longer. Discussing designs from the perspective of Design Patterns and OO principles keeps your team from getting bogged down in implementation details and prevent many misunderstandings.

2 With other developers: Use patterns in your discussions with other developers. This helps other developers learn about new patterns and builds a community. The best part about sharing what you've learned is that great feeling when someone else "gets it!"

3 In architecture documentation: When you write architectural documentation, using patterns will reduce the amount of documentation you need to write and gives the reader a clearer picture of the design.

4 In code comments and naming conventions: When you're writing code, clearly identify the patterns you're using in comments. Also, choose class and methods names that reveal any patterns underneath. Other developers who have to read your code will thank you for allowing them to quickly understand your implementation.

5 To groups of interested developers: Share your knowledge. Many developers have heard about patterns but don't have a good understanding of what they are. Volunteer to give a brown-bag lunch on patterns or a talk at your local user group.

Succinct

Precise

Complete

Observer

Cruisin' Objectville with the Gang of Four

You won't find the Jets or Sharks hanging around Objectville, but you will find the Gang of Four. As you've probably noticed, you can't get far in the World of Patterns without running into them. So, who is this mysterious gang?

Put simply, "the GoF," which includes Erich Gamma, Richard Helm, Ralph Johnson and John Vlissides, is the group of guys who put together the first patterns catalog and in the process, started an entire movement in the software field!

How did they get that name? No one knows for sure; it's just a name that stuck. But think about it: if you're going to have a "gang element" running around Objectville, could you think of a nicer bunch of guys? In fact, they've even agreed to pay us a visit...

The GoF launched the software patterns movement, but many others have made significant contributions, including Ward Cunningham, Kent Beck, Jim Coplien, Grady Booch, Bruce Anderson, Richard Gabriel, Doug Lea, Peter Coad, and Doug Schmidt, to name just a few.

Your journey has just begun...

Now that you're on top of Design Patterns and ready to dig deeper, we've got three definitive texts that you need to add to your bookshelf...

The definitive Design Patterns text

This is the book that kicked off the entire field of Design Patterns when it was released in 1995. You'll find all the fundamental patterns here. In fact, this book is the basis for the set of patterns we used in *Head First Design Patterns*.

You won't find this book to be the last word on Design Patterns – the field has grown substantially since its publication – but it is the first and most definitive.

Picking up a copy of *Design Patterns* is a great way to start exploring patterns after Head First.

The authors of Design Patterns are affectionately known as the "Gang of Four" or GoF for short.

Christopher Alexander invented patterns, which inspired applying similar solutions to software.

The definitive Patterns texts

Patterns didn't start with the GoF; they started with Christopher Alexander, a Professor of Architecture at Berkeley – that's right, Alexander is an *architect*, not a computer scientist. Alexander invented patterns for building living architectures (like houses, towns and cities).

The next time you're in the mood for some deep, engaging reading, pick up *The Timeless Way of Building* and *A Pattern Language*. You'll see the true beginnings of Design Patterns and recognize the direct analogies between creating "living architecture" and flexible, extensible software.

So grab a cup of Starbuzz Coffee, sit back, and enjoy...

Other Design Pattern resources

You're going to find there is a vibrant, friendly community of patterns users and writers out there and they're glad to have you join them. Here's a few resources to get you started...

Websites

The Portland Patterns Repository, run by Ward Cunningham, is a WIKI devoted to all things related to patterns. Anyone can participate. You'll find threads of discussion on every topic you can think of related to patterns and OO systems.

`http://c2.com/cgi/wiki?WelcomeVisitors`

The **Hillside Group** fosters common programming and design practices and provides a central resource for patterns work. The site includes information on many patterns-related resources such as articles, books, mailing lists and tools.

`http://hillside.net/`

Conferences and Workshops

And if you'd like to get some face-to-face time with the patterns community, be sure to check out the many patterns related conferences and workshops. The Hillside site maintains a complete list. At the least you'll want to check out OOPSLA, the ACM Conference on Object-Oriented Systems, Languages and Applications.

The Patterns Zoo

As you've just seen, patterns didn't start with software; they started with the architecture of buildings and towns. In fact, the patterns concept can be applied in many different domains. Take a walk around the Patterns Zoo to see a few...

Architectural Patterns are used to create the living, vibrant architecture of buildings, towns, and cities. This is where patterns got their start.

Habitat: found in buildings you like to live in, look at and visit.

Habitat: seen hanging around 3-tier architectures, client-server systems and the web.

Application Patterns are patterns for creating system level architecture. Many multi-tier architectures fall into this category.

Field note: MVC has been known to pass for an application pattern.

Domain-Specific Patterns are patterns that concern problems in specific domains, like concurrent systems or real-time systems.

Help find a habitat

J2EE

Business Process Patterns describe the interaction between businesses, customers and data, and can be applied to problems such as how to effectively make and communicate decisions.

Seen hanging around corporate boardrooms and project management meetings.

Help find a habitat

Development team

Customer support team

Organizational Patterns describe the structures and practices of human organizations. Most efforts to date have focused on organizations that produce and/or support software.

User Interface Design Patterns address the problems of how to design interactive software programs.

Habitat: seen in the vicinity of video game designers, GUI builders, and producers.

Field notes: please add your observations of pattern domains here:

_____

_____

_____

_____

Annihilating evil with Anti-Patterns

The Universe just wouldn't be complete if we had patterns and no anti-patterns, now would it?

If a Design Pattern gives you a general solution to a recurring problem in a particular context, then what does an anti-pattern give you?

> An **Anti-Pattern** tells you how to go from a problem to a BAD solution.

You're probably asking yourself, "Why on earth would anyone waste their time documenting bad solutions?"

Think about it like this: if there is a recurring bad solution to a common problem, then by documenting it we can prevent other developers from making the same mistake. After all, avoiding bad solutions can be just as valuable as finding good ones!

Let's look at the elements of an anti-pattern:

An anti-pattern tells you why a bad solution is attractive. Let's face it, no one would choose a bad solution if there wasn't something about it that seemed attractive up front. One of the biggest jobs of the anti-pattern is to alert you to the seductive aspect of the solution.

An anti-pattern tells you why that solution in the long term is bad. In order to understand why it's an anti-pattern, you've got to understand how it's going to have a negative effect down the road. The anti-pattern describes where you'll get into trouble using the solution.

An anti-pattern suggests other patterns that are applicable which may provide good solutions. To be truly helpful an anti-pattern needs to point you in the right direction; it should suggest other possibilities that may lead to good solutions.

Let's have a look at an anti-pattern.

An anti-pattern always looks like a good solution, but then turns out to be a bad solution when it is applied.

By documenting anti-patterns we help others to recognize bad solutions before they implement them.

Like patterns, there are many types of anti-patterns including development, OO, organizational, and domain specific anti-patterns.

Here's an example of a software development anti-pattern.

Just like a Design Pattern, an anti-pattern has a name so we can create a shared vocabulary.

The problem and context, just like a Design Pattern description.

Tells you why the solution is attractive.

The bad, yet attractive solution.

How to get to a good solution.

Example of where this anti-pattern has been observed.

Adapted from the Portland Pattern Repository's WIKI at http://c2.com/ where you'll find many anti patterns and discussions.

Anti-Pattern

Name: Golden Hammer

Problem: You need to choose technologies for your development and you believe that exactly one technology must dominate the architecture.

Context: You need to develop some new system or piece of software that doesn't fit well with the technology that the development team is familiar with.

Forces:

- The development team is committed to the technology they know.

- The development team is not familiar with other technologies.

- Unfamiliar technologies are seen as risky.

- It is easy to plan and estimate for development using the familiar technology.

Supposed Solution: Use the familiar technology anyway. The technology is applied obsessively to many problems, including places where it is clearly inappropriate.

Refactored Solution: Expanding the knowledge of developers through education, training, and book study groups that expose developers to new solutions.

Examples:

Web companies keep using and maintaining their internal homegrown caching systems when open source alternatives are in use.

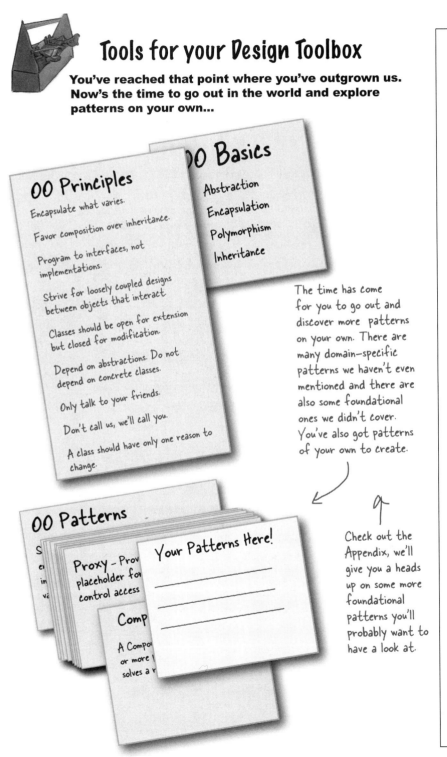

Tools for your Design Toolbox

You've reached that point where you've outgrown us. Now's the time to go out in the world and explore patterns on your own...

OO Basics

Abstraction

Encapsulation

Polymorphism

Inheritance

OO Principles

Encapsulate what varies.

Favor composition over inheritance.

Program to interfaces, not implementations.

Strive for loosely coupled designs between objects that interact.

Classes should be open for extension but closed for modification.

Depend on abstractions. Do not depend on concrete classes.

Only talk to your friends.

Don't call us, we'll call you.

A class should have only one reason to change.

The time has come for you to go out and discover more patterns on your own. There are many domain-specific patterns we haven't even mentioned and there are also some foundational ones we didn't cover. You've also got patterns of your own to create.

OO Patterns

S...

Proxy - Prov...
placeholder for...
control access...

Your Patterns Here!

_____

_____

_____

Comp...

A Compo...
or more...
solves a...

Check out the Appendix, we'll give you a heads up on some more foundational patterns you'll probably want to have a look at.

BULLET POINTS

- Let Design Patterns emerge in your designs, don't force them in just for the sake of using a pattern.

- Design Patterns aren't set in stone; adapt and tweak them to meet your needs.

- Always use the simplest solution that meets your needs, even if it doesn't include a pattern.

- Study Design Pattern catalogs to familiarize yourself with patterns and the relationships among them.

- Pattern classifications (or categories) provide groupings for patterns. When they help, use them.

- You need to be committed to be a patterns writer: it takes time and patience, and you have to be willing to do lots of refinement.

- Remember, most patterns you encounter will be adaptations of existing patterns, not new patterns.

- Build your team's shared vocabulary. This is one of the most powerful benefits of using patterns.

- Like any community, the patterns community has its own lingo. Don't let that hold you back. Having read this book, you now know most of it.

Leaving Objectville...

Boy, it's been great having you in Objectville.

We're going to miss you, for sure. But don't worry – before you know it, the next Head First book will be out and you can visit again. What's the next book, you ask? Hmmm, good question! Why don't you help us decide? Send email to booksuggestions@wickedlysmart.com.

Match each pattern with its description:

Pattern	Description

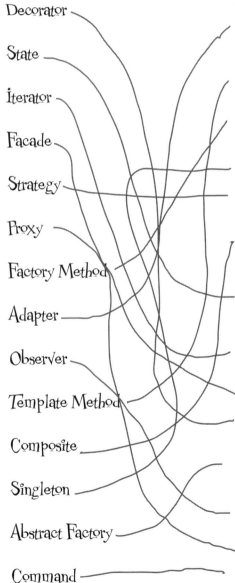

Pattern

Decorator

State

Iterator

Facade

Strategy

Proxy

Factory Method

Adapter

Observer

Template Method

Composite

Singleton

Abstract Factory

Command

Description

Wraps an object and provides a different interface to it.

Subclasses decide how to implement steps in an algorithm.

Subclasses decide which concrete classes to create.

Ensures one and only object is created.

Encapsulates interchangeable behaviors and uses delegation to decide which one to use.

Clients treat collections of objects and individual objects uniformly.

Encapsulates state-based behaviors and uses delegation to switch between behaviors.

Provides a way to traverse a collection of objects without exposing its implementation.

Simplifies the interface of a set of classes.

Wraps an object to provide new behavior.

Allows a client to create families of objects without specifying their concrete classes.

Allows objects to be notified when state changes.

Wraps an object to control access to it.

Encapsulates a request as an object.

14 Appendix

Appendix: Leftover Patterns

Not everyone can be the most popular. A lot has changed in the last 10 years. Since *Design Patterns: Elements of Reusable Object-Oriented Software* first came out, developers have applied these patterns thousands of times. The patterns we summarize in this appendix are full-fledged, card-carrying, official GoF patterns, but aren't always used as often as the patterns we've explored so far. But these patterns are awesome in their own right, and if your situation calls for them, you should apply them with your head held high. Our goal in this appendix is to give you a high level idea of what these patterns are all about.

Bridge

Use the Bridge Pattern to vary not only your implementations, but also your abstractions.

A scenario

Imagine you're going to revolutionize "extreme lounging." You're writing the code for a new ergonomic and user-friendly remote control for TVs. You already know that you've got to use good OO techniques because while the remote is based on the same *abstraction*, there will be lots of *implementations* – one for each model of TV.

This is an abstraction. It could be an interface or an abstract class.

Every remote has the same abstraction.

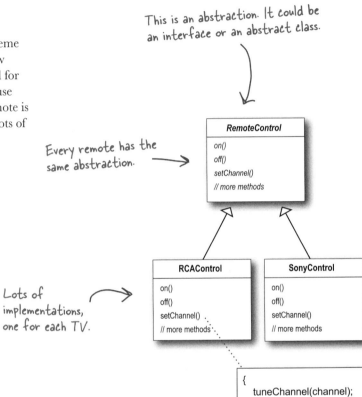

Lots of implementations, one for each TV.

Your dilemma

You know that the remote's user interface won't be right the first time. In fact, you expect that the product will be refined many times as usability data is collected on the remote control.

So your dilemma is that the remotes are going to change and the TVs are going to change. You've already *abstracted* the user interface so that you can vary the *implementation* over the many TVs your customers will own. But you are also going to need to *vary the abstraction* because it is going to change over time as the remote is improved based on the user feedback.

So how are you going to create an OO design that allows you to vary the implementation *and* the abstraction?

Using this design we can vary <u>only</u> the TV implementation, not the user interface.

Why use the Bridge Pattern?

The Bridge Pattern allows you to vary the implementation *and* the abstraction by placing the two in separate class hierarchies.

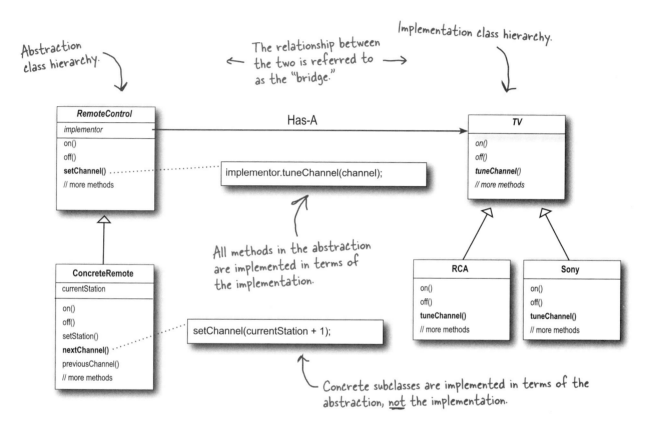

Abstraction class hierarchy.

The relationship between ← the two is referred to → as the "bridge."

Implementation class hierarchy.

All methods in the abstraction are implemented in terms of the implementation.

Concrete subclasses are implemented in terms of the abstraction, <u>not</u> the implementation.

Now you have two hierarchies, one for the remotes and a separate one for platform specific TV implementations. The bridge allows you to vary either side of the two hierarchies independently.

Bridge Benefits

- Decouples an implementation so that it is not bound permanently to an interface.
- Abstraction and implementation can be extended independently.
- Changes to the concrete abstraction classes don't affect the client.

Bridge Uses and Drawbacks

- Useful in graphic and windowing systems that need to run over multiple platforms.
- Useful any time you need to vary an interface and an implementation in different ways.
- Increases complexity.

Builder

Use the Builder Pattern to encapsulate the construction of a product and allow it to be constructed in steps.

A scenario

You've just been asked to build a vacation planner for Patternsland, a new theme park just outside of Objectville. Park guests can choose a hotel and various types of admission tickets, make restaurant reservations, and even book special events. To create a vacation planner, you need to be able to create structures like this:

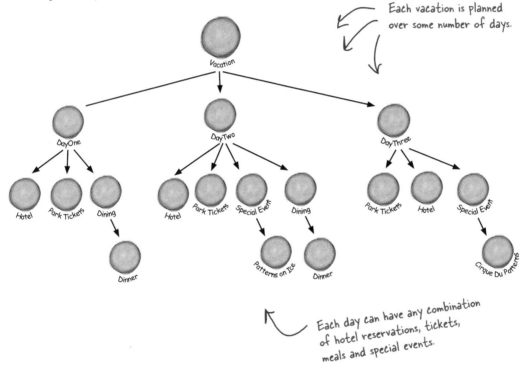

Each vacation is planned over some number of days.

Each day can have any combination of hotel reservations, tickets, meals and special events.

You need a flexible design

Each guest's planner can vary in the number of days and types of activities it includes. For instance, a local resident might not need a hotel, but wants to make dinner and special event reservations. Another guest might be flying into Objectville and needs a hotel, dinner reservations, and admission tickets.

So, you need a flexible data structure that can represent guest planners and all their variations; you also need to follow a sequence of potentially complex steps to create the planner. How can you provide a way to create the complex structure without mixing it with the steps for creating it?

Why use the Builder Pattern?

Remember Iterator? We encapsulated the iteration into a separate object and hid the internal representation of the collection from the client. It's the same idea here: we encapsulate the creation of the trip planner in an object (let's call it a builder), and have our client ask the builder to construct the trip planner structure for it.

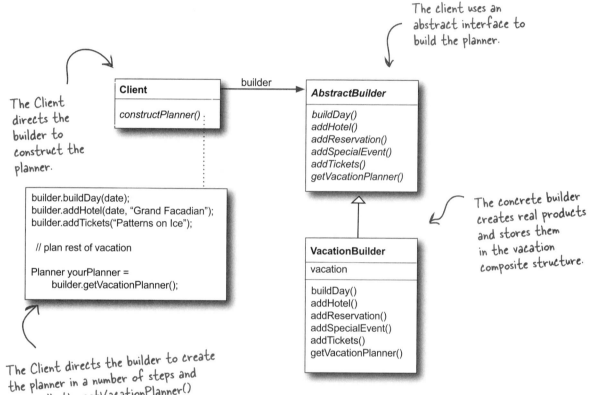

The client uses an abstract interface to build the planner.

The Client directs the builder to construct the planner.

```
builder.buildDay(date);
builder.addHotel(date, "Grand Facadian");
builder.addTickets("Patterns on Ice");

// plan rest of vacation

Planner yourPlanner =
    builder.getVacationPlanner();
```

The concrete builder creates real products and stores them in the vacation composite structure.

The Client directs the builder to create the planner in a number of steps and then calls the getVacationPlanner() method to retrieve the complete object.

Builder Benefits

- Encapsulates the way a complex object is constructed.
- Allows objects to be constructed in a multistep and varying process (as opposed to one step factories).
- Hides the internal representation of the product from the client.
- Product implementations can be swapped in and out because the client only sees an abstract interface.

Builder Uses and Drawbacks

- Often used for building composite structures.
- Constructing objects requires more domain knowledge of the client than when using a Factory.

Chain of Responsibility

Use the Chain of Responsibility Pattern when you want to give more than one object a chance to handle a request.

A scenario

Mighty Gumball has been getting more email than they can handle since the release of the Java-powered Gumball Machine. From their own analysis they get four kinds of email: fan mail from customers that love the new 1 in 10 game, complaints from parents whose kids are addicted to the game and requests to put machines in new locations. They also get a fair amount of spam.

All fan mail needs to go straight to the CEO, all complaints go to the legal department and all requests for new machines go to business development. Spam needs to be deleted.

Your task

Mighty Gumball has already written some AI detectors that can tell if an email is spam, fan mail, a complaint, or a request, but they need you to create a design that can use the detectors to handle incoming email.

You've got to help us deal with the flood of email we're getting since the release of the Java Gumball Machine.

How to use the Chain of Responsibility Pattern

With the Chain of Responsibility Pattern, you create a chain of objects that examine a request. Each object in turn examines the request and handles it, or passes it on to the next object in the chain.

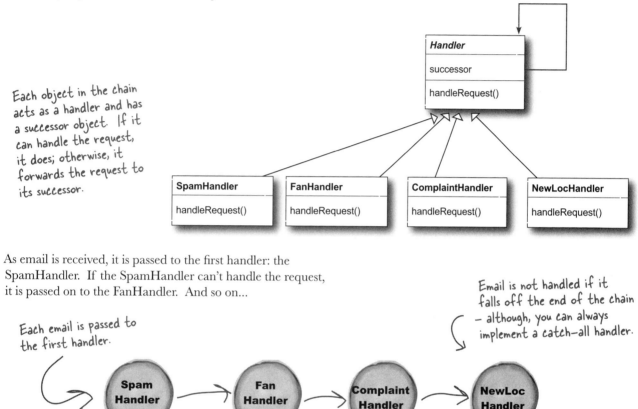

Each object in the chain acts as a handler and has a successor object. If it can handle the request, it does; otherwise, it forwards the request to its successor.

As email is received, it is passed to the first handler: the SpamHandler. If the SpamHandler can't handle the request, it is passed on to the FanHandler. And so on...

Each email is passed to the first handler.

Email is not handled if it falls off the end of the chain — although, you can always implement a catch–all handler.

Chain of Responsibility Benefits

- Decouples the sender of the request and its receivers.
- Simplifies your object because it doesn't have to know the chain's structure and keep direct references to its members.
- Allows you to add or remove responsibilities dynamically by changing the members or order of the chain.

Chain of Responsibility Uses and Drawbacks

- Commonly used in windows systems to handle events like mouse clicks and keyboard events.
- Execution of the request isn't guaranteed; it may fall off the end of the chain if no object handles it (this can be an advantage or a disadvantage).
- Can be hard to observe the runtime characteristics and debug.

Flyweight

Use the Flyweight Pattern when one instance of a class can be used to provide many "virtual instances."

A scenario

You want to add trees as objects in your hot new landscape design application. In your application, trees don't really do very much; they have an X-Y location, and they can draw themselves dynamically, depending on how old they are. The thing is, a user might want to have lots and lots of trees in one of their home landscape designs. It might look something like this:

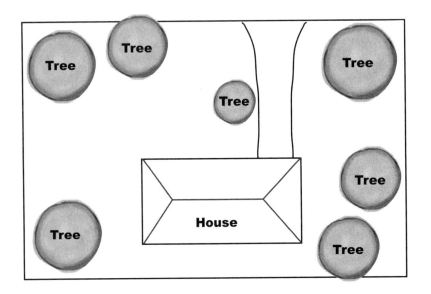

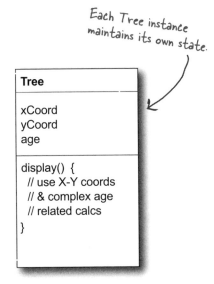

Each Tree instance maintains its own state.

```
Tree
─────────────
xCoord
yCoord
age
─────────────
display() {
  // use X-Y coords
  // & complex age
  // related calcs
}
```

Your big client's dilemma

You've just landed your "reference account." That key client you've been pitching for months. They're going to buy 1,000 seats of your application, and they're using your software to do the landscape design for huge planned communities. After using your software for a week, your client is complaining that when they create large groves of trees, the app starts getting sluggish...

Why use the Flyweight Pattern?

What if, instead of having thousands of Tree objects, you could redesign your system so that you've got only one instance of Tree, and a client object that maintains the state of ALL your trees? That's the Flyweight!

All the state, for ALL of your virtual Tree objects, is stored in this 2D-array.

One, single, state-free Tree object.

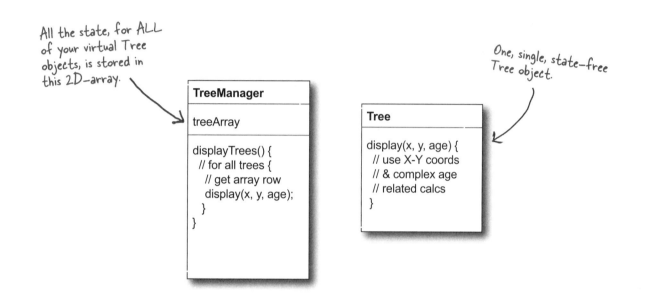

```
TreeManager

treeArray

displayTrees() {
  // for all trees {
    // get array row
    display(x, y, age);
  }
}
```

```
Tree

display(x, y, age) {
  // use X-Y coords
  // & complex age
  // related calcs
}
```

Flyweight Benefits

- Reduces the number of object instances at runtime, saving memory.
- Centralizes state for many "virtual" objects into a single location.

Flyweight Uses and Drawbacks

- The Flyweight is used when a class has many instances, and they can all be controlled identically.
- A drawback of the Flyweight pattern is that once you've implemented it, single, logical instances of the class will not be able to behave independently from the other instances.

Interpreter

Use the Interpreter Pattern to build an interpreter for a language.

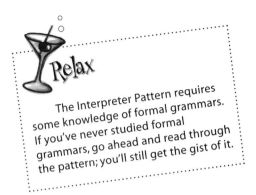

A scenario

Remember the Duck Pond Simulator? You have a hunch it would also make a great educational tool for children to learn programming. Using the simulator, each child gets to control one duck with a simple language. Here's an example of the language:

```
right;
while (daylight) fly;
quack;
```

Turn the duck right.

Fly all day...

...and then quack.

Now, remembering how to create grammars from one of your old introductory programming classes, you write out the grammar:

A program is an expression consisting of sequences of commands and repetitions ("while" statements).

```
expression ::=  <command> | <sequence> | <repetition>
sequence ::= <expression> ';' <expression>
command ::= right | quack | fly
repetition ::= while '(' <variable> ')'<expresion>
variable ::= [A-Z,a-z]+
```

A sequence is a set of expressions separated by semicolons.

We have three commands: right, quack, and fly.

A while statement is just a conditional variable and an expression.

Now what?

You've got a grammar; now all you need is a way to represent and interpret sentences in the grammar so that the students can see the effects of their programming on the simulated ducks.

How to implement an interpreter

When you need to implement a simple language, the
Interpreter Pattern defines a class-based representation for its
grammar along with an interpreter to interpret its sentences.
To represent the language, you use a class to represent each
rule in the language. Here's the duck language translated
into classes. Notice the direct mapping to the grammar.

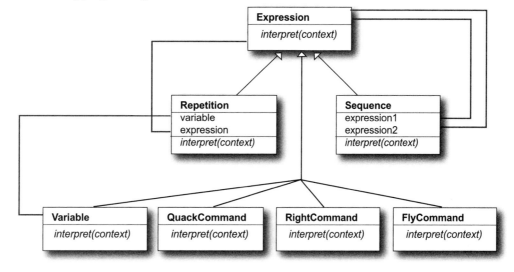

To interpret the language, call the interpret() method on each
expression type. This method is passed a context – which
contains the input stream of the program we're parsing – and
matches the input and evaluates it.

Interpreter Benefits

- Representing each grammar rule in a class makes
  the language easy to implement.
- Because the grammar is represented by classes, you
  can easily change or extend the language.
- By adding additional methods to the class structure,
  you can add new behaviors beyond interpretation,
  like pretty printing and more sophisticated program
  validation.

Interpreter Uses and Drawbacks

- Use interpreter when you need to implement a
  simple language.
- Appropriate when you have a simple grammar and
  simplicity is more important than efficiency.
- Used for scripting and programming languages.
- This pattern can become cumbersome when the
  number of grammar rules is large. In these cases a
  parser/compiler generator may be more appropriate.

Mediator
Use the Mediator Pattern to centralize complex communications and control between related objects.

A scenario

Bob has a Java-enabled auto-house, thanks to the good folks at HouseOfTheFuture. All of his appliances are designed to make his life easier. When Bob stops hitting the snooze button, his alarm clock tells the coffee maker to start brewing. Even though life is good for Bob, he and other clients are always asking for lots of new features: No coffee on the weekends... Turn off the sprinkler 15 minutes before a shower is scheduled... Set the alarm early on trash days...

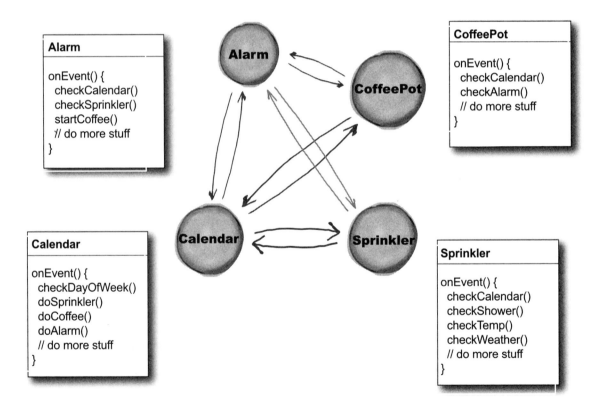

```
Alarm

onEvent() {
  checkCalendar()
  checkSprinkler()
  startCoffee()
  // do more stuff
}
```

```
CoffeePot

onEvent() {
  checkCalendar()
  checkAlarm()
  // do more stuff
}
```

```
Calendar

onEvent() {
  checkDayOfWeek()
  doSprinkler()
  doCoffee()
  doAlarm()
  // do more stuff
}
```

```
Sprinkler

onEvent() {
  checkCalendar()
  checkShower()
  checkTemp()
  checkWeather()
  // do more stuff
}
```

HouseOfTheFuture's dilemma

It's getting really hard to keep track of which rules reside in which objects, and how the various objects should relate to each other.

Mediator in action...

With a Mediator added to the system, all of the appliance objects can be greatly simplified:

- They tell the Mediator when their state changes.
- They respond to requests from the Mediator.

Before adding the Mediator, all of the appliance objects needed to know about each other... they were all tightly coupled. With the Mediator in place, the appliance objects are all *completely decoupled* from each other.

The Mediator contains all of the control logic for the entire system. When an existing appliance needs a new rule, or a new appliance is added to the system, you'll know that all of the necessary logic will be added to the Mediator.

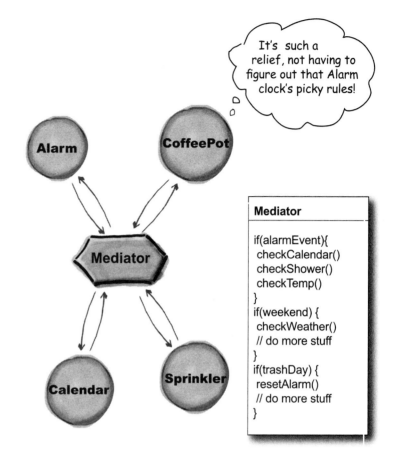

> It's such a relief, not having to figure out that Alarm clock's picky rules!

Mediator

```
if(alarmEvent){
  checkCalendar()
  checkShower()
  checkTemp()
}
if(weekend) {
  checkWeather()
  // do more stuff
}
if(trashDay) {
  resetAlarm()
  // do more stuff
}
```

Mediator Benefits

- Increases the reusability of the objects supported by the Mediator by decoupling them from the system.
- Simplifies maintenance of the system by centralizing control logic.
- Simplifies and reduces the variety of messages sent between objects in the system.

Mediator Uses and Drawbacks

- The Mediator is commonly used to coordinate related GUI components.
- A drawback of the Mediator pattern is that without proper design, the Mediator object itself can become overly complex.

Memento

Use the Memento Pattern when you need to be able to return an object to one of its previous states; for instance, if your user requests an "undo."

A scenario

Your interactive role playing game is hugely successful, and has created a legion of addicts, all trying to get to the fabled "level 13." As users progress to more challenging game levels, the odds of encountering a game-ending situation increase. Fans who have spent days progressing to an advanced level are understandably miffed when their character gets snuffed, and they have to start all over. The cry goes out for a "save progress" command, so that players can store their game progress and at least recover most of their efforts when their character is unfairly extinguished. The "save progress" function needs to be designed to return a resurrected player to the last level she completed successfully.

> Just be careful how you go about saving the game state. It's pretty complicated, and I don't want anyone else with access to it mucking it up and breaking my code.

The Memento at work

The Memento has two goals:

- Saving the important state of a system's key object.
- Maintaining the key object's encapsulation.

Keeping the single responsibility principle in mind, it's also a good idea to keep the state that you're saving separate from the key object. This separate object that holds the state is known as the Memento object.

GameMemento

savedGameState

Client

```
// when new level is reached
Object saved =
    (Object) mgo.getCurrentState();

// when a restore is required
mgo.restoreState(saved);
```

While this isn't a terribly fancy implementation, notice that the Client has no access to the Memento's data.

MasterGameObject

gameState

```
Object getCurrentState() {
  // gather state
  return(gameState);
}

restoreState(Object savedState) {
  // restore state
}

// do other game stuff
```

Memento Benefits

- Keeping the saved state external from the key object helps to maintain cohesion.
- Keeps the key object's data encapsulated.
- Provides easy-to-implement recovery capability.

Memento Uses and Drawbacks

- The Memento is used to save state.
- A drawback to using Memento is that saving and restoring state can be time consuming.
- In Java systems, consider using Serialization to save a system's state.

Prototype

Use the Prototype Pattern when creating an instance of a given class is either expensive or complicated.

A scenario

Your interactive role playing game has an insatiable appetite for monsters. As your heros make their journey through a dynamically created landscape, they encounter an endless chain of foes that must be subdued. You'd like the monster's characteristics to evolve with the changing landscape. It doesn't make a lot of sense for bird-like monsters to follow your characters into underseas realms. Finally, you'd like to allow advanced players to create their own custom monsters.

It would be a lot cleaner if we could decouple the code that handles the **details** of creating the monsters from the code that actually needs to create the instances on the fly.

Yikes! Just the act of **creating** all of these different kinds of monster instances is getting tricky... Putting all sorts of state detail in the constructors doesn't seem to be very cohesive. It would be great if there was a single place where all of the instantiation details could be encapsulated...

Prototype to the rescue

The Prototype Pattern allows you to make new instances by copying existing instances. (In Java this typically means using the clone() method, or de-serialization when you need deep copies.) A key aspect of this pattern is that the client code can make new instances without knowing which specific class is being instantiated.

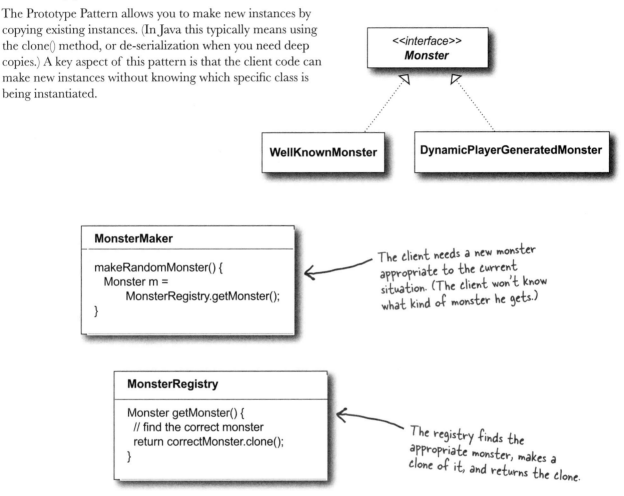

MonsterMaker

```
makeRandomMonster() {
    Monster m =
        MonsterRegistry.getMonster();
}
```

The client needs a new monster appropriate to the current situation. (The client won't know what kind of monster he gets.)

MonsterRegistry

```
Monster getMonster() {
    // find the correct monster
    return correctMonster.clone();
}
```

The registry finds the appropriate monster, makes a clone of it, and returns the clone.

Prototype Benefits

- Hides the complexities of making new instances from the client.
- Provides the option for the client to generate objects whose type is not known.
- In some circumstances, copying an object can be more efficient than creating a new object.

Prototype Uses and Drawbacks

- Prototype should be considered when a system must create new objects of many types in a complex class hierarchy.
- A drawback to using the Prototype is that making a copy of an object can sometimes be complicated.

Visitor

**Use the Visitor Pattern when you want to
add capabilities to a composite of objects
and encapsulation is not important.**

A scenario

Customers who frequent the Objectville Diner and Objectville
Pancake House have recently become more health conscious. They
are asking for nutritional information before ordering their meals.
Because both establishments are so willing to create special orders,
some customers are even asking for nutritional information on a
per ingredient basis.

Lou's proposed solution:

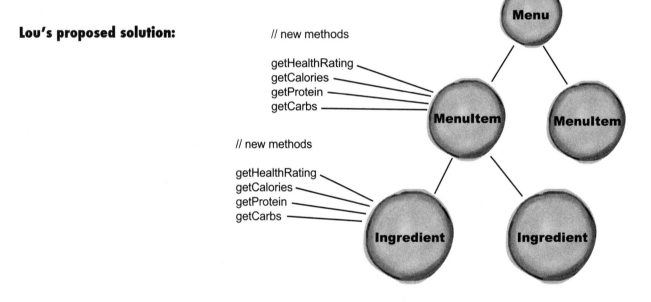

```
// new methods

getHealthRating
getCalories
getProtein
getCarbs
```

```
// new methods

getHealthRating
getCalories
getProtein
getCarbs
```

Mel's concerns...

"Boy, it seems like we're opening Pandora's box. Who knows what
new method we're going to have to add next, and every time we
add a new method we have to do it in two places. Plus, what if
we want to enhance the base application with, say, a recipes class?
Then we'll have to make these changes in three different places..."

The Visitor drops by

The Visitor must visit each element of the Composite; that functionality is in a Traverser object. The Visitor is guided by the Traverser to gather state from all of the objects in the Composite. Once state has been gathered, the Client can have the Visitor perform various operations on the state. When new functionality is required, only the Visitor must be enhanced.

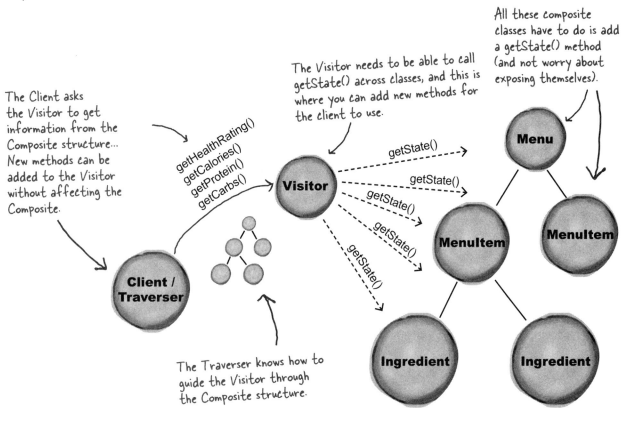

The Client asks the Visitor to get information from the Composite structure... New methods can be added to the Visitor without affecting the Composite.

The Visitor needs to be able to call getState() across classes, and this is where you can add new methods for the client to use.

All these composite classes have to do is add a getState() method (and not worry about exposing themselves).

The Traverser knows how to guide the Visitor through the Composite structure.

Visitor Benefits

- Allows you to add operations to a Composite structure without changing the structure itself.
- Adding new operations is relatively easy.
- The code for operations performed by the Visitor is centralized.

Visitor Drawbacks

- The Composite classes' encapsulation is broken when the Visitor is used.
- Because the traversal function is involved, changes to the Composite structure are more difficult.

Index

A

Abstract Factory Pattern 156. *See also* Factory Pattern

Adapter Pattern

  advantages 242

  class adapters 244

  class diagram 243

  combining patterns 504

  defined 243

  duck magnets 245

  Enumeration Iterator Adapter 248

  exercise 251

  explained 241

  fireside chat 247, 252–253

  introduction 237

  object adapters 244

Alexander, Christopher 602

annihilating evil 606

Anti-Patterns 606–607

  Golden Hammer 607

application patterns 604

architectural patterns 604

B

Bridge Pattern 612–613

Builder Pattern 614–615

bullet points 32, 74, 105, 162, 186, 230, 270, 311, 380, 423, 491, 560, 608

C

business process patterns 605

CD Cover Viewer 463

Chain of Responsibility Pattern 616–617

change 339

  anticipating 14

  constant in software development 8

  identifying 53

Choc-O-Holic, Inc. 175

class explosion 81

code magnets 69, 179, 245, 350

cohesion 339–340

Combining Patterns 500

  Abstract Factory Pattern 508

  Adapter Pattern 504

  class diagram 524

  Composite Pattern 513

  Decorator Pattern 506

  Observer Pattern 516

Command Pattern

  class diagram 207

  command object 203

  defined 206–207

  introduction 196

  loading the Invoker 201

Colophon

All interior layouts were designed by Eric Freeman, Elisabeth Freeman, Kathy Sierra and Bert Bates. Kathy and Bert created the look & feel of the Head First series. The book was produced using Adobe InDesign CS (an unbelievably cool design tool that we can't get enough of) and Adobe Photoshop CS. The book was typeset using Uncle Stinky, Mister Frisky (you think we're kidding), Ann Satellite, Baskerville, Comic Sans, Myriad Pro, Skippy Sharp, Savoye LET, Jokerman LET, Courier New and Woodrow typefaces.

Interior design and production all happened exclusively on Apple Macintoshes—at Head First we're all about "Think Different" (even if it isn't grammatical). All Java code was created using James Gosling's favorite IDE, *vi*, although we really should try Erich Gamma's Eclipse.

Long days of writing were powered by the caffeine fuel of Honest Tea and Tejava, the clean Santa Fe air, and the grooving sounds of Banco de Gaia, Cocteau Twins, Buddha Bar I-VI, Delerium, Enigma, Mike Oldfield, Olive, Orb, Orbital, LTJ Bukem, Massive Attack, Steve Roach, Sasha and Digweed, Thievery Corporation, Zero 7 and Neil Finn (in all his incarnations) along with a heck of a lot of acid trance and more 80s music that you'd care to know about.

And now, a final word from Head First Labs...

Our world class researchers are working day and night in a mad race to uncover the mysteries of Life, the Universe and Everything—before it's too late. Never before has a research team with such noble and daunting goals been assembled. Currently, we are focusing our collective energy and brain power on creating the ultimate learning machine. Once perfected, you and others will join us in our quest!

You're fortunate to be holding one of our first protoypes in your hands. But only through constant refinement can our goal be achieved. We ask you, a pioneer user of the technology, to send us periodic field reports of your progress, at fieldreports@headfirstlabs.com

And next time you're in Objectville, drop by and take one of our behind the scenes laboratory tours.

Now that you've applied the Head First approach to Design Patterns, why not apply it to the rest of your life?

Come join us at the Head First Labs Web site, our virtual hangout where you'll find Head First resources including podcasts, forums, code and more.

But you won't just be a spectator; we also encourage you to join the fun by participating in discussions and brainstorming.

What's in it for you?

- Get the latest news about what's happening in the Head First World.

- Participate in our upcoming books and technologies.

- Learn how to tackle those tough technical topics (say that three times fast) in as little time as possible.

- Look behind the scenes at how Head First books are created.

- Meet the Head First authors and the support team who keep everything running smoothly.

- Why not audition to be a Head First author yourself?

http://www.headfirstlabs.com

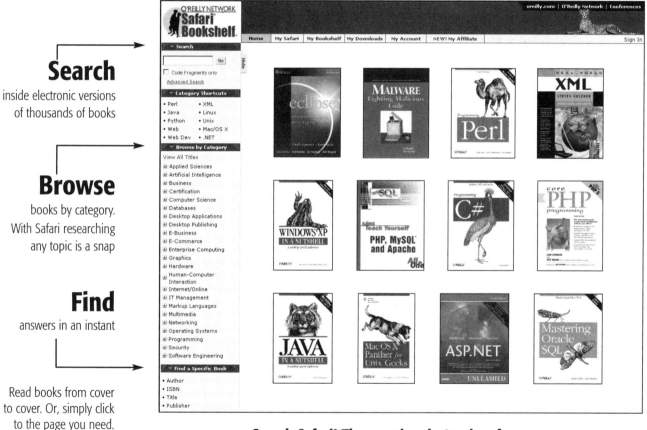

Related Titles Available from O'Reilly

Java

Ant: The Definitive Guide

Better, Faster, Lighter Java

Eclipse

Eclipse Cookbook

Enterprise JavaBeans,
4th Edition

Hardcore Java

Head First Java

Head First Servlets & JSP

Head First EJB

Hibernate:
A Developer's Notebook

J2EE Design Patterns

Java 1.5 Tiger:
A Developer's Notebook

Java & XML Data Binding

Java & XML

Java Cookbook, *2nd Edition*

Java Data Objects

Java Database Best Practices

Java Enterprise Best Practices

Java Enterprise in a Nutshell,
2nd Edition

Java Examples in a Nutshell,
3rd Edition

Java Extreme Programming
Cookbook

Java in a Nutshell, *4th Edition*

Java Management Extensions

Java Message Service

Java Network Programming,
2nd Edition

Java NIO

Java Performance Tuning,
2nd Edition

Java RMI

Java Security, *2nd Edition*

JavaServer Faces

Java ServerPages, *2nd Edition*

Java Servlet & JSP Cookbook

Java Servlet Programming,
2nd Edition

Java Swing, *2nd Edition*

Java Web Services in a Nutshell

Learning Java, *2nd Edition*

Mac OS X for Java Geeks

Programming Jakarta Struts
2nd Edition

Tomcat: The Definitive Guide

WebLogic:
The Definitive Guide

O'REILLY®

Our books are available at most retail and online bookstores.
To order direct: 1-800-998-9938 • *order@oreilly.com* • *www.oreilly.com*
Online editions of most O'Reilly titles are available by subscription at *safari.oreilly.com*

Keep in touch with O'Reilly

1. Download examples from our books

To find example files for a book, go to:

www.oreilly.com/catalog

select the book, and follow the "Examples" link.

2. Register your O'Reilly books

Register your book at *register.oreilly.com*

Why register your books?
Once you've registered your O'Reilly books you can:

- Win O'Reilly books, T-shirts or discount coupons in our monthly drawing.
- Get special offers available only to registered O'Reilly customers.
- Get catalogs announcing new books (US and UK only).
- Get email notification of new editions of the O'Reilly books you own.

3. Join our email lists

Sign up to get topic-specific email announcements of new books and conferences, special offers, and O'Reilly Network technology newsletters at:

elists.oreilly.com

It's easy to customize your free elists subscription so you'll get exactly the O'Reilly news you want.

4. Get the latest news, tips, and tools

www.oreilly.com

- "Top 100 Sites on the Web"—PC Magazine
- CIO Magazine's Web Business 50 Awards

Our web site contains a library of comprehensive product information (including book excerpts and tables of contents), downloadable software, background articles, interviews with technology leaders, links to relevant sites, book cover art, and more.

5. Work for O'Reilly

Check out our web site for current employment opportunities:

jobs.oreilly.com

6. Contact us

O'Reilly & Associates
1005 Gravenstein Hwy North
Sebastopol, CA 95472 USA

TEL: 707-827-7000 or 800-998-9938
       (6am to 5pm PST)

FAX: 707-829-0104

order@oreilly.com
For answers to problems regarding your order or our products. To place a book order online, visit:

www.oreilly.com/order_new

catalog@oreilly.com
To request a copy of our latest catalog.

booktech@oreilly.com
For book content technical questions or corrections.

corporate@oreilly.com
For educational, library, government, and corporate sales.

proposals@oreilly.com
To submit new book proposals to our editors and product managers.

international@oreilly.com
For information about our international distributors or translation queries. For a list of our distributors outside of North America check out:

international.oreilly.com/distributors.html

adoption@oreilly.com
For information about academic use of O'Reilly books, visit:

academic.oreilly.com

O'REILLY®

Our books are available at most retail and online bookstores.
To order direct: 1-800-998-9938 • *order@oreilly.com* • *www.oreilly.com*
Online editions of most O'Reilly titles are available by subscription at *safari.oreilly.com*